United States Division of Entomology

Insect Life

Volume 4

United States Division of Entomology

Insect Life
Volume 4

ISBN/EAN: 9783337826338

Printed in Europe, USA, Canada, Australia, Japan

Cover: Foto ©Andreas Hilbeck / pixelio.de

More available books at **www.hansebooks.com**

U. S. DEPARTMENT OF AGRICULTURE.

DIVISION OF ENTOMOLOGY.

PERIODICAL BULLETIN.

October, 1891.   to   August, 1892.

INSECT LIFE

Vol. IV.

DEVOTED TO THE ECONOMY AND LIFE-HABITS OF INSECTS, ESPECIALLY IN THEIR RELATIONS TO AGRICULTURE.

EDITED BY

C. V. RILEY, Entomologist,

AND

L. O. HOWARD, First Assistant,

WITH THE ASSISTANCE OF OTHER MEMBERS OF THE DIVISIONAL FORCE.

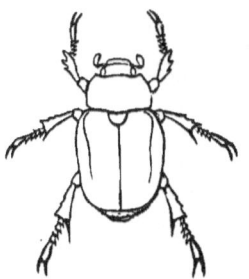

[PUBLISHED BY AUTHORITY OF THE SECRETARY OF AGRICULTURE.]

WASHINGTON:
GOVERNMENT PRINTING OFFICE.
1892.

TABLE OF CONTENTS.

CONTENTS OF NOS. 1 AND 2.

	Page.
SPECIAL NOTES	1
THIRD ANNUAL MEETING, ASSOCIATION ECONOMIC ENTOMOLOGISTS	4
PRESIDENT'S INAUGURAL ADDRESS......*James Fletcher*..	4
DESTRUCTIVE LOCUSTS OF NORTH AMERICA, TOGETHER WITH NOTES ON THE OCCURRENCES IN 1891......*Lawrence Bruner*..	18
CHILO SACCHARALIS IN NEW MEXICO......*C. H. Tyler Townsend*..	24
A NOTE ON THE WHITE GRUB OF ALLORHINA......*C. H. Tyler Townsend*..	25
NOTES OF INTEREST......*C. H. Tyler Townsend*..	26
NOTES ON BLACKBERRY BORERS AND GALL MAKERS......*John B. Smith*..	27
THE SQUASH BORER, MELITTIA CUCURBITÆ, AND REMEDIES THEREFOR......*John B. Smith*..	30
NOTE ON A COTTON CUT-WORM......*G. F. Atkinson*..	31
NOTE ON A NEMATODE LEAF DISEASE......*G. F. Atkinson*..	31
KEROSENE EMULSION AND PYRETHRUM......*C. V. Riley*..	32
WORK OF THE SEASON IN MISSISSIPPI......*H. E. Weed*..	34
NOTE ON THE HORN FLY IN OHIO......*D. S. Kellicott*..	35
NOTES OF THE SEASON......*Eleanor A. Ormerod*..	36
NOTES ON THE RECENT OUTBREAK OF DISSOSTEIRA LONGIPENNIS......*E. A. Popenoe*..	41
NOTES ON A CORN CRAMBID......*M. H. Beckwith*..	42
NOTES OF THE YEAR IN NEW JERSEY......*John B. Smith*..	43
GOVERNMENT WORK AND THE PATENT OFFICE......*C. V. Riley*..	46
A NOTE ON PARASITES......*L. O. Howard*..	48
REPORT OF A TRIP TO KANSAS TO INVESTIGATE REPORTED DAMAGES FROM GRASSHOPPERS......*Herbert Osborn*..	49
THE CLOVER-SEED CATERPILLAR (*Grapholitha interstinctana* Clem.)......*H. Osborn* and *H. A. Gossard*..	56
STANDARD FITTINGS FOR SPRAY MACHINERY......*William B. Alwood*..	58
ENTOMOLOGICAL WORK IN CENTRAL PARK......*E. B. Southwick*..	59
SOME HISTORIC NOTES......*A. J. Cook*..	62
AN EXPERIMENT WITH KEROSENE EMULSIONS......*Herbert Osborn*..	63
A NOTE ON SILK CULTURE......*Paul Wallace*..	64
NOTES ON A FEW BORERS......*G. C. Davis*..	64
THE POPLAR GONIOCTENA......*A. J. Cook*..	67
NOTES OF THE SEASON FROM SOUTH DAKOTA......*J. M. Aldrich*..	67
A NOTE ON REMEDIES FOR THE HORN FLY......*William B. Alwood*..	68
THE CHINCH BUG DISEASE AND OTHER NOTES......*F. H. Snow*..	69
REVISED LIST OF MEMBERS OF THE ASSOCIATION OF ECONOMIC ENTOMOLOGISTS	73

	Page
EXTRACTS FROM CORRESPONDENCE	74

Fertilization of Yucca in Australia—A new Saw-fly Enemy to Sweet Potatoes—Injurious Insects of Utah—Reappearance of the Wheat Strawworm in Kansas—Allorhina injuring Oaks—Ducks and the Colorado Potato Beetle; Additional Note—Kerosene Emulsion Treatment for the Rose-chafer—the Strawberry Weevil on Blackberries—Predaceous Habit of Histeridæ—Imbricated Snout-beetle injuring Apple Trees—A Longicorn Pine-borer injuring Shoes—Blister Beetles on Cabbage—The European Leopard Moth injuring Maples—A Phycitid Moth attacking Pecan Buds—A Corn Crambus in Delaware—Treatment for the Horn Fly—A new Enemy to Currants—A California Thrips on the Potato—Rocky Mountain Locust in North Dakota—Habits of Mantispa—A Correction.

GENERAL NOTES	81

Lead-boring Insects—Damage to Turnip and Swede Crops in Eastern Britain—Locusts in the Vilayet of Aleppo, Syria—Another Government Entomologist Appointed—A Curious Bit of Entomological Classification—A Criticism of Circular No. 1 of this Division—The Host Plants of North American Aphididæ—A new Radish Enemy in California—North American Species of Trypoxylon—Destroying the Rose-chafer—Quassia for the Hop Aphis—Silk Nests of Mexican Social Larvæ—A Strange Story—Was he Crazed by Mosquitoes or by Heat?—The true Male of Pocota grandis.

CONTENTS OF NOS. 3 AND 4.

SPECIAL NOTES	87
THE LARGER CORN STALK-BORER (illustrated) .... L. O. Howard..	95
LIFE HISTORY OF THE 12-SPOTTED DIABROTICA (illustrated)..... C. V. Riley...	104
A NEW HERBARIUM PEST (illustrated) .... C. V. Riley..	108
UGIMYIA SERICARIÆ ROND., THE PARASITE OF THE JAPANESE SILKWORM ....Joseph Mik..	113
FURTHER NOTES ON PANCHLORA (illustrated)................C. V. Riley..	119
SOME STUDIES OF THE CLOVER HAY WORM, ASOPIA COSTALIS. F. M. Webster..	121
SOME OF THE BRED PARASITIC HYMENOPTERA IN THE NATIONAL COLLECTION—Continued..	122
THE THREE PEAR PSYLLAS...	127
THE FIRST INTRODUCTION OF BLASTOPHAGA IN CALIFORNIA.... Gustav Eisen..	128
COMMENTS ON THE FIFTH REPORT OF THE U. S. ENTOMOLOGICAL COMMISSION...John Hamilton..	129
EXTRACTS FROM CORRESPONDENCE	132

Injurious Insects of Nebraska—Fall Web-worm Parasites in Indian Territory—Notes on California Insects; the Vedalia and other Ladybirds—An injurious Flee-beetle in Utah—A new Enemy to Pear Leaves—A Grapevine Flea-beetle of New Mexico—Notes on the Palm Weevil—*Rhynchites bicolor* injuring cultivated Roses—The Coleoptera in the National Museum—A good Collection of Agrilus in the National Museum—A Leaf-miner infesting Sour Gum—Disappearance of the Gypsy Moth in England—Remedies for Squash Borer—Forest Injury by the Oak Edema—On the Treatment of Tent Caterpillars—The Catalpa Sphinx—Peach Trees injured by *Gortyna nitela*—Hair Worm Parasite of the Codling Moth—False Chinch-bug in Wyoming—Kerosene Emulsion successful against the Chinch-bug—Old Broods of the Seventeen-year Locust—Note on a Leaf-hopper—Destructiveness of the Corn-root Plant-louse in Nebraska—A parasite of the Cottony Maple Scale—The

EXTRACTS FROM CORRESPONDENCE—Continued.
Purple Scale of the Orange in Montserrat—Notes on Buffalo Gnats—The Horn Fly in Kentucky—Non-migratory Locust Devastations in Nevada—The Grasshopper Plague in Michigan—Grasshopper Notes in Idaho—A Flight of White Ants—The Malodorous Lace-wing—A Ground Squirrel Parasite—Poisonous Qualities of a northern Centipede.

GENERAL NOTES 148
Chrysomelid Larvæ in Ants' Nests—A Compendium of Economic Zoölogy—A Generic synopsis of the Coccidæ—Work in Algeria with a Fungus Disease of the Locust—A novel Mode of using Disease Germs—Mortality among Flies in the District—A favorable View of the English Sparrow—Occasional Development of Wings in normally apterous Hemiptera—An Argument against spraying for Scale Insects—New Means against Orange Pests—Late Entomological Publications of the National Museum—Tiger Beetle Larvæ vs. *Colias philodice*—The Reported Death of M. Künckel d'Herculais—A new Hæmatobia; the Moose Fly—Miss Ormerod's Resignation—The Bumble Bee in New Zealand—Some of our Insects in Jamaica—Living Insect Larvæ in the Intestines of a Child—New Bee Flies—A Bark-louse from Ants' Nests—*Oebalus pugnax* an Enemy to Grasses—New Food-plant of *Rhodobænus 13-punctatus*—Living Larvæ in the Ear—Bad Work by Yellow Jackets—Death from a Bee Sting—A predaceous Capsus—Water Beetles found in an old Gasometer—Hickory Horned Devil injuring Cotton—A new Food-plant of Icerya—The Ladybird of the Egyptian Icerya—Reappearance of *Icerya purchasi*—The Pear Midge in New York—A possible new Insecticide—Bitten by a Katipo—Entomological Society of Washington.

CONTENTS OF NOS. 5 AND 6.

SPECIAL NOTES 163
WHEAT AND GRASS SAW-FLIES (illustrated).... *C. V. Riley and C. L. Marlatt*.. 168
THE IMPORTATION OF A HESSIAN FLY PARASITE FROM EUROPE.. *S. A. Forbes*.. 179
THE ORIGIN AND DEVELOPMENT OF PARASITISM AMONG THE SARCOPTIDÆ.
.... *H. Garman*.. 182
ORIGIN AND DEVELOPMENT OF THE PARASITIC HABIT IN MALLOPHAGA AND PEDICULIDÆ..*Herbert Osborn*.. 187
THE USE OF GRAPE BAGS BY A PAPER-MAKING WASP..... *Mary E. Murtfeldt*.. 192
THE METHODS OF PUPATION AMONG THE CHALCIDIDÆ (illustrated).
.... *L. O. Howard*.. 193
NOTES ON GRASS INSECTS IN WASHINGTON, D. C ....*Herbert Osborn*.. 197
AN INTERESTING AQUATIC BUG (illustrated) 198
HOMINIVOROUS HABITS OF THE SCREW WORM IN ST. LOUIS.
.... *Mary E. Murtfeldt*.. 200
ANOTHER SPIDER-EGG PARASITE ....*L. O. Howard*.. 202
EXTRACTS FROM CORRESPONDENCE 202
Another Lead-boring Insect (illustrated)—Red Ants in California—Gall on a common Weed—A Clerid Beetle found in Plush—A Twig-girdler of Fig Trees—An old Enemy of the Colorado Potato Beetle—Do Ground Beetles destroy Peach-tree Borers?—Good Results from Spraying for Codling Moth—The Tin Can Remedy for Cut-worms—A Sphinx Larva feeding on Mints—The Clover-hay Worm—A California Twig-borer: Is it Anarsia?—The Red-humped Caterpillar killed by Parasites—Treatment of Grain infested with Angoumois Moths—Treatment of the Boll Worm—The Strawberry Leaf-roller—The Electric-light Bug—Woolly Root-louse of the Apple—The Grape Phylloxera in the

EXTRACTS FROM CORRESPONDENCE—Continued.
United States—Mites on a Maple Aphid—Scales from Tahiti—Plant-louse on Celery—The Rose Diaspis—Scale-insects from Trinidad—A Vegetarian Mosquito—Gregarious "Snake-worms"—Abundance of the Clover Mite in Michigan—Urine recommended for Eel-worms.

GENERAL NOTES 215
Vedalia and Icerya in New Zealand—The Chinese Insect-fungus Drug (illustrated)—The Difficulty of disinfecting imported Plants—Fumigating at Night not necessary—Hemlock Damage by the Larch Sawfly—A Clematis Root-borer (illustrated)—The Spread of the Gypsy Moth—Micropteryx: A remarkable Lepidopterous Larva—Damage to Apple Trees near London—An Enemy of the Tussock Moth—The Black Vine-weevil: A Hot-house Pest—Hemp as a Protection against Weevils—Cave Glow-worms of Tasmania—The best Mosquito Remedy—The True Bugs or Heteroptera of Tennessee—The Phylloxera in France and the American Vine—Remedies for the Phylloxera at the Cape of Good Hope—Abundance of the Pear-tree Psylla in New York—The Evolution of a Newspaper Statement—A Note on Physiological Chemistry—Annual Meeting of the Entomological Society of Ontario—A Japanese Parasite of the Gypsy Moth—Prof. Smith's European Trip—A useful Beetle Mite—Change of Location—Entomological Society of Washington.

CONTENTS OF NOS. 7 AND 8.

SPECIAL NOTES 231
THE POTATO-TUBER MOTH (*Lita solanella* Boisd.) (illustrated) 239
A GENUS OF MANTIS EGG-PARASITES (illustrated) 242
NOTES ON THE GRAIN TOXOPTERA (*Toxoptera graminum* Rond.). *F. M. Webster* .. 245
THE LARGER DIGGER-WASP (illustrated) .... *C. V. Riley* .. 248
THE HABITS OF ELASMUS (illustrated) .... *L. O. Howard* .. 253
BEES OF GREAT VALUE TO FRUIT AND SEED GROWERS ...... *Frank Benton* .. 254
SOME BRED WEST VIRGINIA BRACONIDÆ .... *A. D. Hopkins* .. 356
NOTES ON THE HABITS OF SOME CALIFORNIA COLEOPTERA. *D. W. Coquillett* .. 260
EARLY PUBLISHED REFERENCES TO SOME OF OUR INJURIOUS INSECTS ....
.... *F. M. Webster* .. 262
THE COLOR OF A HOST AND ITS RELATION TO PARASITISM ....
.... *C. W. Stiles and A. Hassall* .. 265
EXTRACTS FROM CORRESPONDENCE 266
The Effects of a Spider Bite on a Child—Insect Pests in Bermuda—Insect Injury to Cocoanut Palms—Biological Notes on Micracis, Chramesus, and Coscinoptera—Remedies for Wireworms—Coleopterous Larvæ in a Cistern—A Longicorn Borer in Apple Roots—Was it Diabrotica 12-punctata?—The Clover-leaf Beetle in western Pennsylvania—The Rice Weevil in dry Hop Yeast—How to Kill Tree-borers—Note on the Carphoxera Herbarium Pest—Treatment of the Squash Borer—Where are the Eggs of the Clover Hay-worm laid?—The Box-elder Bug attacking Fruit in Washington State—Notes on the "Blood-sucking Cone-nose"—The Orange-leaf Aleyrodes—Orange Chionaspis in Florida—On the Treatment of Human Patients affected with Screw Worm—Bot-fly Larvæ burrowing under the Skin of Man—The Horn Fly in Mississippi—A southern Cricket destructive to the Strawberry—Insanity caused by Mosquito Bites; Hibernation of Mosquitoes—Death of an Infant from a Spider Bite—On the poisonous Bite of the Spider, *Latrodectus mactans*—Death due to the Whip Scorpion and Tarantula—Tame Birds as Insect Destroyers.

	Page.
GENERAL NOTES	279

More International Exchanges of Vedalia—Harmless Spider Bites—Insect Embryology—A European White Grub Fungus—Paris Green and the Honey Bee—East India Beetles—The Colorado Potato-beetle in Nova Scotia—A remarkable Butterfly Enemy—A Note on the Angoumois Grain-moth—Injury to Foliage by Arsenites; A cheap Arsenite; Combination of Arsenites and Fungicides—The Corn Root Aphis—Mosquito Larvæ as supposed internal Parasites—The Henry Edwards Collection—Locusts in Egypt—Lepidoptera whose Females are wingless—Tobacco Insects in Florida—Insect Diseases of the Mediterranean Orange—Spraying for the Codling Moth—A new Locality for *Icerya purchasi*—The use of Vaseline with Carbon Bisulphide—Mr. Koebele's recent Sendings—A Leaf-miner in Wheat—Entomological Society of Washington.

CONTENTS OF NOS. 9 AND 10.

SPECIAL NOTES	293
THE PEA AND BEAN WEEVILS (illustrated)	297
THE OX BOT IN THE UNITED STATES: HABITS AND NATURAL HISTORY OF *Hypoderma lineata* (illustrated) .... *C. V. Riley*..	302
THE RAVAGES OF THE LEOPARD MOTH IN BROOKLYN (illustrated), *Nicolas Pike*..	317
HOW FAR DO BEES FLY? .... *Frank Benton*..	319
NOTE ON THE WATER-BUG FOUND BY Rev. J. L. Zabriskie, *E. Bergroth, M. D.*..	321
THE LOCUST OR GRASSHOPPER OUTLOOK	321
EARLY PUBLISHED REFERENCES TO SOME OF OUR INJURIOUS INSECTS, II, *F. M. Webster*	323
STRANGE DEVELOPMENTS OF STOMATA ON *Carya alba* caused by Phylloxera, *D. A. Owen*	327
EXTRACTS FROM CORRESPONDENCE	327

Destruction of Plant-lice in the Egg State—Remedies for Leaf-cutting Ants—A new Fumigator for Scale-insects—Life-history of and Remedies against the Mosquito; the House Fly—Is the Ground-beetle, *Scarites subterraneus*, herbivorous?—The so-called California "Wine Bee"—Grasshopper Outlook in California for 1892—Loss from Grain Weevils in Texas: the Bisulphide of Carbon Remedy—Addition of Lime to the Arsenical Spray—Physianthus *vs.* the Codling Moth: a Disclaimer—A Sesiid Pest of the Persimmon—A Cayenne Pepper Feeder—An early Use of Kerosene—List of Coccidæ observed in Jamaica—The Broken-tail Snail in Bermuda—Bumble-bees and the Production of Clover Seed.

GENERAL NOTES	335

Insects on the Surface of Snow—Vedalia in South Africa—Legislation against Insects in California—Raphidia in New Zealand—The Strawberry Leaf-Roller in Kentucky—*Icerya rosæ* in Jamaica—The Phylloxera at the Cape of Good Hope—A new Tree Band—A true Bug damaging Peanuts in China—Sarcophaga in the Human Ear—The Japanese Peach Moth—A new West Indian Sugar-cane Enemy—The Hop Louse in the extreme Northwest—More California notes—A Honey Bee Enemy in California—The Angoumois Grain-Moth in Pennsylvania—The South African Ladybird Enemy of Icerya—On the Date of the Introduction of the European Wheat Saw-fly—An Important Publication on Spiders—An Aleyrodes on the Strawberry—Abundance of *Attagenus piceus* in Illinois—Quassia *vs.* Petroleum for the Hop Louse—A western Enemy of the White-marked Tussock Moth—A new Cotton-stainer in Jamaica—

GENERAL NOTES—Continued.
Additions to the Insect Collection of the American Museum—The Use of Electricity against Migratory Locusts—Another Imported Scale-insect—A new Plant-louse Enemy—The Twin-screw Mosquito—Economic Entomology in New South Wales—Living Vedalias at last reach Egypt—Self-mutilation in Orthoptera—North American Tachinidæ—New Species of Coleoptera—Fourth Annual Meeting of the Association of Economic Entomologists—Entomological Society of Washington.

CONTENTS OF NOS. 11 AND 12.

	Page.
SPECIAL NOTES	353
SOME INTERRELATIONS OF PLANTS AND INSECTS (illustrated) C. V. Riley, Ph. D.	358
A NEW ICERYA PARASITE...........L. O. Howard..	378
THE WEST INDIAN RUFOUS SCALE (Aspidiotus articulatus Morgan) .... T. D. A. Cockerell..	380
LIFE-HISTORY OF Calothysanis amaturaria Walk., A GEOMETRID MOTH (illustrated) ....A. S. Packard, M.D...	382
STEPS TOWARDS A REVISION OF CHAMBERS'S INDEX, WITH NOTES AND DESCRIPTIONS OF NEW SPECIES...........Lord Walsingham..	384
SUGAR-CANE INSECTS IN NEW SOUTH WALES...........Albert Koebele..	385
NOTES ON LACHNOSTERNA...........G. H. Perkins..	389
THE FIRST LARVAL STAGE OF THE PEA WEEVIL	392
EXTRACTS FROM CORRESPONDENCE	393

On some of the insects described by Walsh—A Chalcid Fly in a new Role: Is it parasitic on the Clothes Moth?—On Figs grown without Caprification—On the Beaver Parasite—Blister Beetles in Texas—The Twelve-spotted Asparagus Beetle—A Wood-borer mistaken for a Household Pest—A new Fruit Pest: *Syneta albida* Lec—On the date of introduction of the Potato Tuber-moth—The East Indian Sugar-cane Borer—Florida Wax Scale on LeConte Pear—The Horn Fly in the South—The Horn Fly in Florida—A new Owl Parasite—Notes on Spiders—Grasshopper Depredations in Ohio in 1891—Tin-can Remedy and Paper Wrappers for Cut-worms ....

NOTES FROM CORRESPONDENCE............	399
GENERAL NOTES	402

Additional Note on the Sugar-cane Pin-borer—The Blood Tissue of Insects—Damage to Boots and Shoes by *Sitodrepa panicea*—The Weevils of the Tertiary—New Application of the Term "Wire-worm"—Feather Felting—Damage to Carnations by the Variegated Cut-worm—A Larch Enemy—Hessian Fly in New Zealand—Increase of the Wheat Straw-worm—Great Damage by Buffalo Gnats—The Hop Louse in Oregon—Food-plant and new Habitat of the Montserrat Icerya—A Disease caused by Parasites in the ears of Carnivora—The Itch caused among Cats and Rabbits by *Sarcoptes minor*—Fungus Disease of the Migratory Locust—The Saltbush Scale of Australia—A proposed Insecticide for Tea Bushes—Another Instance of the Value of Spraying Fruit Trees—A new Insecticide—The Ibis as a Locust Destroyer—A Scale-eating Mouse—Spiders of the District of Columbia—Annual Meeting of the Entomological Club of the American Association for the Advancement of Science for 1892—Entomological Society of Washington.

SPECIAL NOTES.

The Association of Economic Entomologists.—The bulk of this number is occupied with the official proceedings of the Association of Economic Entomologists, which we publish at the request of the Association. The meeting this year was held in Washington, August 17 and 18, and was an unqualified success. The average attendance at the meetings was 33, and of the American members 27 were present. The increase in membership and in interest which this meeting exemplified is very encouraging.

Miss Murtfeldt's Outlines of Entomology.*—Miss Murtfeldt has prepared in popular shape a pamphlet of 130 pages, with a view of introducing farmers and horticulturists to the science of entomology. The ordinary text books seem intended for advanced students, and the object of the author of this paper has been to produce a perfectly elementary work. She goes carefully over the subject of the general structure of insects, defining the terms commonly in use, treats of the transformations and the classifications and names, and in short chapters discusses the main forms of each of the orders. The work is unfortunately marred by many misprints, particularly in the technical names, from the fact that the author was unable to read the proofs of a portion of the paper. These, however, will undoubtedly be corrected in another edition, and at most do not seriously detract from the value of the paper. Some 50 figures of typical insects are given and duly acknowledged.

Handbook of Australian Insects.†—In a handy volume of 150 pages, illustrated by 14 colored plates of insects and 13 in black and white of insecticide apparatus, Mr. French, the Victorian entomologist, has pre-

---

* Outlines of Entomology, prepared for the use of farmers and horticulturists at the request of the Secretary of the State Board of Agriculture and the State Horticultural Society of Missouri. By Mary E. Murtfeldt, Jefferson City, Mo., 1891.

† A Handbook of the Destructive Insects of Victoria, with notes on the methods to be adopted to check and extirpate them. Prepared by order of the Victorian Department of Agriculture by C. French, F. L. S., F. R. H. S., Government Entomologist. Part I. Melbourne, 1891.

sented a great deal of information which will be of value to the agriculturists of Australia. This is only the first part of a work which bids fair to be extensive. As an introductory number this contains an introduction to entomology taken from Miss Ormerod's Manual and a brief account of the classification of insects taken from Westwood's Introduction. This matter is followed by an account of the noxious insects of Victoria which attack the Apple, Pear, Apricot, and Cherry. Some fourteen species are mentioned, of which six occur in this country, namely, the Woolly Aphis, the Codling Moth, the Oyster-shell Bark Louse of the Apple, the Red Spider, the Pear Slug, and the Pear-leaf Blister-mite. The matter concerning insecticides and spraying apparatus is brought together at the close of the volume.

Dr. Weed's last Ohio Bulletin.*—We have received the last bulletin prepared by Dr. C. M. Weed as entomologist of the Ohio Station. It includes three articles: (1) Miscellaneous Experiments in the Control of Injurious Insects; (2) Some Common Cabbage Insects; (3) Three Imported Clover Insects. Under the head of miscellaneous experiments are given the details of trials of the arsenites and the Bordeaux mixture, carbonate of copper, and Paris green, the arsenites and lime spraying for the Plum Curculio, whitewashing for the Rose Bug, experiments with remedies for the Striped Cucumber Beetle, and tobacco as an insecticide. The experiments are all interesting, but no new results have been obtained. The second article treats of the Imported Cabbage Worm, the Cabbage Plusia, the Zebra Caterpillar, the Wavy-striped Flea-beetle, and Cabbage Cut-worms, while the three imported clover insects are the Root Borer, the Seed Midge, and the Hay Worm. Our figures of all these insects are reprinted, and their treatment includes nothing new.

Swedish Injurious Insects.—We have received from Prof. Sven Lampa, the State entomologist of Sweden, a report on the injurious insects which were prominent in Sweden during 1890. The Onion Fly (*Anthomyia ceparum*), the Wheat Fly (*Chlorops tæniopus*), the Wheat Midge (*Diplosis tritici*), Wire Worms, the Frit Fly, one of the Saw Flies (*Lophyrus rufus*), a Cut Worm (*Hadena basilinea*), the Red-footed Bean-weevil (*Bruchus rufimanus*), and the Winter Moth (*Cheimatobia brumata*), are the principal species treated.

New Jersey Bulletin on the Rose Chafer.†—An excellent summary of all the known facts concerning this insect is given by Professor Smith in this bulletin. The extraordinary abundance of the insect in the State

---

* Bulletin of the Ohio Agricultural Experiment Station, second series, vol. I, No. 2. Columbus, Ohio, February, 1891.

† Bulletins of the New Jersey Agricultural College Experiment Station. Bulletin 82, The Rose-chafer or Rose Bug, by John B. Smith, Entomologist. New Brunswick, July, 1891.

of New Jersey is said to date back some four to six years, and resembles an "irruption" of some 20 years ago. The eggs in New Jersey are said to be laid from the 10th to the 20th of January, and the facts already recorded are confirmed, that the larva feeds on the roots of plants, preferably grass, in light soil, descending below the frost line in winter and ascending in spring, transforming to pupa in April or early in May, the beetles appearing from May 19 to 27. The length of the larval state is not yet ascertained.

The main portion of the bulletin is occupied by an account of experiments with different remedies. The arsenites were found to be useless because of their slow action. The copper mixtures were also found to be useless. Pyrethrum was found to be ineffective as a killing agent, while it is thought to be too expensive to use as a stupefier. The author has accepted Colonel Pearson's statement that no chafers were killed by the application of kerosene emulsion, and has conducted no experiments himself, which is much to be regretted. Kerosene extract of pyrethrum was ineffective. Lime was found not to be a reliable remedy or preventive. The favorable experiences which we have quoted from correspondents in different parts of the country are explained by Professor Smith in the statement that "Ohio Rose Bugs must lack the robust constitution of their New Jersey *confrères*, or, what is more likely, they were not so abundant and had an ample chance at more palatable food." He found that tobacco was "eaten with immense relish, both in the form of X. O. Dust and finely ground stems." Acetic acid, quassia and digitaline proved failures. Corrosive sublimate acted as a preventive, but was found to be too destructive to plant life to enable its practical use. The same resulted from the use of muriate of ammonia and cyanide of potassium. The odorless insecticides, sludge, kainit, and alum were also failures. His experiments with hot water, however, seemed satisfactory. Heated to 125° or higher the beetles were instantly killed, but great difficulty was found in reaching the insects with a sufficiently high temperature. Several forms of an apparatus for collecting the beetles are figured, and the bagging of grapes is highly recommended. The author suggests in conclusion that the farmer should, *first*, prevent the breeding of the insects on his own land by using the heaviest land only for grass and keeping as little light land as possible in sod, while thorough cultivation in May will destroy many of the pupæ; *second*, plant a few rows of blackberries around the vineyards to attract the first hordes; a few rose bushes or spiræas will answer the same purpose; *third*, use early or late blooming varieties of grapes and stimulate the vines by fertilizers to force the blossoms, and by inducing a heavy bloom get a surplus which will stand some thinning by insects. Keep a man with a collector constantly at work at least once a day for three weeks. The bulletin is written for the practical man and in the most popular style, but it will prove most valuable to the fruit growers of the State, and Professor Smith has shown his usual energy in his treatment of the subject.

THIRD ANNUAL MEETING ASSOCIATION OF ECONOMIC ENTOMOLOGISTS.

AUGUST 17, MORNING SESSION.

The third annual meeting was held in the Columbian University building, Washington, D. C. The meeting was called to order at 9:45 a. m., President Fletcher in the chair. Thirty-eight persons were present, among whom were the following members:

W. B. Alwood, Virginia; W. H. Ashmead, District of Columbia; G. F. Atkinson, Alabama; M. H. Beckwith, Delaware; Lawrence Bruner, Nebraska; A. J. Cook, Michigan; E. W. Doran, Maryland; James Fletcher, Canada; L. O. Howard, District of Columbia; D. S. Kellicott, Ohio; J. A. Lintner, New York; C. L. Marlatt, District of Columbia; Herbert Osborn, Iowa; Theodore Pergande, District of Columbia; G. H. Perkins, Vermont; E. A. Popenoe, Kansas; C. V. Riley, District of Columbia; J. B. Smith, New Jersey; E. B. Southwick, New York; J. M. Stedman, North Carolina; F. M. Webster, Ohio; H. E. Weed, Mississippi; F. H. Chittenden, District of Columbia; A. B. Cordley, District of Columbia; G. H. Hudson, New York; B. P. Mann, District of Columbia; M. E. Murtfeldt, Missouri.

The President then delivered his annual address:

PRESIDENT'S INAUGURAL ADDRESS.

By JAMES FLETCHER, *Dominion Entomologist, of Canada.*

GENTLEMEN: It is not my intention to delay you upon this occasion either with a lengthened or an elaborate address, but I shall endeavor for a short time to direct your attention to some subjects for discussion which I trust may be found of interest and benefit to all present. These subjects are all of a nature which it seems to me may more appropriately be brought before this association than before any of the other entomological organizations.

I am of the opinion that our meetings, to be of the greatest use to economic entomologists, should be largely of an informal nature; in fact, they should be meetings where workers can meet students in the same line of research and exchange experiences. We must all, to a large measure, go over the same ground and learn for ourselves the general principles of the structure and habits of insects which affect so closely the choice and application of the proper remedies to avert or mitigate their attacks upon crops. This training, however, is essentially necessary in the same way that learning the alphabet is necessary for one who wishes to read or speak accurately; but it is beyond this point that the advantages of our association may be recognized. There is not, perhaps, any single line of practical science, certainly not one approaching it in the importance of the results attained, in which students have to work so much alone and cut off from companions of congenial tastes. Marvel at it as we may, we, who know the exquisite beauty and sustaining charms of the insect world, cannot but acknowledge that entomology is not a popular study, and although in this respect there is a gradual change taking place for the better, still all the same it is with feelings akin to amusement and patronage that the ordinary farmer of the country allows himself to listen to arguments that there is after all *some* use in studying the habits of insects.

Probably most of us present have occasionally had the opportunity of addressing farmers' institute meetings, and know well that although, after the meeting is over, there are invariably more inquiries about common insect crop pests than any other subject which may have been discussed, and when the meeting breaks up it is always the entomologist who is detained to answer the questions of those who did not like to stand up and speak before the others; yet for all this, probably most of you will recognize the extreme similarity which exists between the expectant smile which meets you from every part of the audience when you are introduced to speak on insects in a new locality and that which greets the announcement of the high-class comic songs which are usually dispensed on those occasions. You also know the necessity, and have probably been often asked by the chairman at these meetings in so many words, to begin with some joke "to catch the attention of the audience." An appeal must then be made to their pockets, and you must remind them of the crops destroyed and dollars lost by depredations of pests which levy tribute every year, as the turnip flea-beetle, cutworms, potato-beetles, etc.

You explain the simplicity of many remedies and the great saving that will follow their application. They had not thought of these things; gradually the smiles die out and the other extreme of seriousness is reached. They awaken now; with bodies leaning forward and heads raised they drink in every word; their eyes brighten and their mouths gradually open with wonder at the losses they have suffered and might have prevented had they but known of these simple things before. It touches them to the quick to be told that 10 cents' worth of Paris green would have saved their crop of gooseberries or currants; have done away with the necessity of sowing their turnips two or three times at a hundred times the cost; that 10 cents expended in spraying an apple or plum tree would have given them a return of three or four dollars' worth of good fruit; that by simply wrapping a piece of newspaper around their young cabbages or tomatoes at the time of setting them out they might have saved a loss of perhaps 75 per cent of their crop from the ravages of cutworms. In short, that by following the advice of entomologists, those who study the habits of what they had always called indiscriminately "bugs," they might have saved much that had disappeared from under their very eyes.

But I need not now pursue this thought further. Encouraged by the apparent interest taken in the subject by the audience, one is sometimes tempted to speak too long; but we must be discreet. Farmers, as a rule, prefer a few new thoughts at a time and to have these plainly put. Having finished, we perhaps sit down amidst applause and requests to go on, and perhaps hear such complimentary remarks exchanged as "I tell you what it is, there *is* something in what he says," or, in a tone of surprise, "that bug man was pretty good." No. Farmers and ordinary individuals throughout the country who are dependent upon them for food do not know, nor as a class appreciate, what they do now, might, and will in the future, owe to the labors of the entomologist. The consequence is that those who do take up the study are few and isolated from each other. Moreover, I maintain that there is no branch of natural science or practical agriculture to which it is second in importance. The amounts lost and the value of produce which might be saved every year in our staple crops alone, by following the advice of a competent entomologist, are so enormous and of late years have been so often proved, that before long the value of these studies must certainly be recognized. The chief hindrance is the widespread and incomprehensible ignorance on the part of both growers and consumers of agricultural produce of the present generation. This ignorance is rapidly being dissipated by means of the various agricultural colleges and experiment stations all over the world, where the rising generation is being trained.

It will soon be seen that the scientific or accurate study of the habits of insects, by which we are enabled to prevent the injury or loss of existing crops, of which we have already learned the use or necessity, confers far greater benefits on the community at large than the discovery or introduction of new products of which we have not as yet felt the need. But there is no natural study which presents so many different aspects, or which provides so many subjects concerning which its students, although they must know something, find it quite impossible to inform themselves thoroughly, which, in short, demands that its different branches must be taken up by several specialists bound together by some bond, so that the knowledge gradually accumulated by one may, at need, be available for all. Such a bond I believe we have in the Association of Economic Entomologists, where members have an opportunity of meeting once a year a large number of colleagues working in the same field, but upon different lines, with whom they can compare experiences and particularly can discuss any difficulties which may have arisen in the prosecution of their work during the year.

It is for this special reason that I set so much value upon an informal style of meeting, where the association can, as it were, go into committee and a member can not only bring specimens for exhibition or identification, but can ask as many short questions as he likes and receive answers at once, together with opinions and comments, if necessary, from all present. Methods of applying and the most advantageous materials and proportions to be used in the manufacture of insecticides, the discussion of new discoveries either of materials or apparatus which may have come prominently before the public during the year, the most convenient modes of collecting, mounting, and preserving material for study—all these seem to me to be subjects particularly appropriate for discussion before our association, concerning which, too, information is so badly needed now that the very progress of the science is seriously impeded by the want of it and which I think can not so well be brought up before any other existing body. Now these matters, although small in themselves, when neglected become of great importance, from the negative results which come out of them. I therefore took the liberty of addressing a circular to each member of the association as well as to all economic entomologists of whom I could find the postal addresses, requesting them to come to this meeting prepared to derive the greatest possible advantage from intercourse with the eminent entomologists resident at Washington and those others who would surely be gathered together here; also at the same time to try to make the meeting enjoyable to others by favoring us with short notes of their operations during the year.

I am pleased to announce that one of our foreign members, Miss Ormerod, has sent us an interesting account of her work during the past year which will be read during the meeting.

Thanks to the kindness of Professor Riley and the trouble taken by our secretary, Mr. Howard, arrangements have been made that the visiting entomologists may take the greatest advantage of the opportunities afforded by the meeting being held at Washington, and I would suggest that all should improve this opportunity by examining and above all by taking copious notes of the various entomological machines, so many of which have originated in the Division of Entomology, under Professor Riley. To-morrow a certain time will be devoted to the discussion of insecticides and the machinery for their application. I am convinced, after many failures, that success in treating insects just as much depends upon having the proper apparatus as upon the insecticide used, and I draw your attention now to this subject because of the exceptional advantages offered here, not only from having the machines to examine, but also the able members of the staff to explain their uses; for my own part I have found it quite impossible to judge of and compare the merits of these, in many cases, expensive machines, by simply reading the available descriptions, and I think we should make the most of this opportunity. My only regret is that every economic entomologist in the country is not present. You will see by the printed program which has been submitted to you that there are papers upon many important subjects, and arrangements have been made by which our meetings shall not clash with those of either of the other bodies before which entomological papers are to be read, so that there is nothing to prevent members wishing to do so from being present at the reading of all these papers during this week. By a mutual arrangement with the president of the Entomological Club of the A. A. A. S. authors have been requested to submit papers of economic interest to this association whilst those of scientific or systematic nature will come before the club or the section of biology.

I trust, gentlemen, I may not be considered presumptuous if I make use of the opportunity, which you forced upon me when you elected me to this honorable position at the last annual meeting, to lay before you some ideas which have occurred to me by which we can make our work more useful and also secure better facilities for making it popular throughout the country. Why is it that the botanist, the chemist, and the geologist do not elicit the amusement only, from the ignorant, which is called forth by the entomologist in prosecuting his investigations? While not for one moment wishing to belittle their work I maintain stoutly that not one of these or all combined can compare with entomology in its possibilities when tested by the rule of *Cui bono?* The silent respect accorded these sciences is no doubt largely due to supposed, not to call them fictitious, virtues.

The botanist has from ancient times been inseparably associated with medicine and the discovery of a panacea for all the ills to which mortal man is heir. Even in the wilderness, with a handful of herbs he is exempt from molestation by either Indian or white man run wild. The chemist again deals with things unintelligible to the masses, illustrated with loud noises and nasty smells, and there has come down with him from the middle ages a sort of twin-brotherhood with the alchemist and the practicers of other dark arts—the possibility of his discovering in his laboratory an easy means of creating, without hard work, gold, that which is by most men most coveted and for which many will commit crime or be induced to acts mean and contemptible. Too true even today are Virgil's words: "*Quid non mortalia pectora coges, Auri sacra fames!*" What will you not compel mortal breasts to do, cursed lust for gold! The geologist, with his pick, or his humble but sordid, vulture-like follower, the "prospector," means to the uneducated eye a public benefactor, who may find that purest but most degrading metal, the search for which is the mainspring and motor of so many lives. Who that has traveled in the far West has not seen the magic effect in removing difficulties of the words "I am working for the Geological Survey?" And yet—I say it not as a wail—there is no such respect for the "bug sharp" or "grasshopper tenderfoot," who has saved them there, in that very country, the very means of subsistence, and he is only treated to shakes of the head and sinister looks, as though he were some dangerous character, when in answer to their questions "What are they for?" "What do you do with them?" he can not assure his interrogators that he either eats or, that which last of all he would do, sells his specimens.

But I have said that the change for the better in this respect has even now set in. Already the most highly civilized nations of the world nobly headed by the Government of the most practical and energetic people on the face of the globe, the inhabitants of the United States of America, have seen the advantage of appointing specialists who can devise means for the prevention of the enormous losses of revenue due to the attacks of injurious insects. Germany, England and her colonies, notably Canada and particularly the province of Ontario, France, Italy, and other nations, all have followed the lead, and our favorite science has now changed from a study and amusement of the few to one of the most important branches of practical agriculture, the elements of which must be known by all engaged in tilling the soil or they will surely suffer. Already it finds a place upon the curricula of many of our schools and colleges and before long will force itself upon the notice of others. There has been a rapid development in this line, not only in this country, but everywhere, during the last two or three years, and many new men have come to the front. My presumption does not carry me so far as to criticise these or other workers; but perhaps I may be permitted to refer to some of the dangers which beset a newly appointed entomologist, and particularly a young one. In such a task one must necessarily (for safety's sake) refer to what has occurred to himself in his own experience. The first consideration must of course always be to succeed in the work which you have undertaken, and I can not help thinking that some err considerably when they think that they will be expected to know everything and must answer every question offhand. On this point I am speaking particularly of our relations with farmers, who are as a rule very practical men, made so by the exigencies of their lives, but who are frequently those who have not had the advantages of a liberal education, and consequently have not the consideration and moderation which that alone gives. Moreover, as there is no policy so poor, because it is invariably seen through, as that which prompts an entomologist, when seeking information from one whom he knows is better posted than himself, to try and hide his lack of knowledge by making excuses why he does not recognize that exact specimen, or by asking indefinite questions in the hope of getting what he requires, without in so many words acknowledging his ignorance, so in the same way does he expose himself to the contempt and want of confidence from those in whom he most desires to inspire respect, by trying to put them off with an indefinite answer. It has been my experience that a modest and honest acknowledgment of ignorance is no disgrace and brings no degradation with it, whilst an assumption of knowledge which we do not possess is a constant menace, which, if once detected, is never forgotten. It is the old tale, "honesty is the best policy;" but this must not end the matter; we must be honest with ourselves, and having once detected our lack of knowledge upon any subject which comes under our notice, we must use every means in our power of supplying the deficiency, and if we make a systematic study of every investigation which we undertake, taking all the time careful records of what we see, even with regard to the commonest insects, we shall frequently have the satisfaction of finding that not only have we observed all that others have, but many other things besides which will raise our simple investigation from a mere study into a scientific record. No man can possibly know everything even about his favorite study, and the sooner he knows it the better for his work.

A subject frequently referred to, but which can not too often be repeated, is the necessity, or even, if we put it in another way, policy, of making the fullest acknowledgment of all assistance received from others, whether it be from their writings or otherwise. I know of nothing which so belittles a man's work as to find that it is derived without acknowledgment from some one else. It is not at all infrequent, I am sorry to say, to find whole sentences and clauses inserted in published writings without even quotation marks. An evidence of this is found in the innumerable mistakes which are perpetuated and handed down from author to author before they are detected as errors. Again, too great stress can not, I think, be laid upon the propriety of invariably acknowledging the source of all illustrations used. These are of the greatest assistance, and yet they are frequently used without a word of acknowledgment.

Now, all of this is essentially unwise from the base standpoint of policy alone; for although nothing may be said about the matter, be sure that every instance is noticed and stands forth as a black blot on the face of good work.

A defect which is occasionally discernible in some writings upon economic entomology is the want of a thorough grounding in the first elements of the science. This is easily detected; there is an uncertainty and indefiniteness about the work. It is like that of an artist who begins to paint pictures before he has learned to draw well. A far greater blemish, however, which has, I think, seriously impeded progress and effective work, is the fact that entomologists as a rule do not know enough about the collateral subjects which affect their studies. Their efforts are for the most part directed towards the protection of farm crops, and yet how few make a study or have much knowledge even of the elements of farming and horticulture, the growth and management of the various kinds of crops, the effects of different fertilizers, early and late planting, the rotation of crops, and the pruning and cultivation of trees and shrubs.

All of these are of paramount importance. The knowledge is necessary, and therefore must be acquired. A certain knowledge of botany is most important and will be constantly giving advantages to the one who possesses it over those who do not.

With regard to the presentation of the results of our labors for the use of others, one thing which should be avoided as much as possible is the recommendation of remedies which we have not actually tested ourselves. There are so many useless and untrustworthy remedies now published, particularly through newspapers, that great caution is necessary. Different conditions sometimes require differing remedies, according to circumstances; but I think that the best and fewest possible remedies should be given for any insect treated of, so as to simplify the application as much as can be done. There is no doubt that the most valuable remedies are those which are simplest. As the late Mr. Frazer Crawford, of South Australia, has well said, a remedy must be (1) *effective*, so as to attain the object aimed at; (2) *inexpensive*, so as to be practical—worth the trouble and expense of application; (3) *simple*, so as to avoid as far as possible all chance of mistakes in applying it.

At the last meeting of the association, in Champaign, Ill., I had the honor of a conversation with Assistant Secretary, the Hon. Edwin Willits, and he mentioned that he was frequently asked for information as to the advisability of large expenditures for entomological purposes, and that although entomologists frequently spoke of the large losses from insects, we did not provide politicians—and particularly himself—with data by which they could explain and justify these expenditures, which those who understood them knew to be of such enormous importance, and when we wished to point out the great injuries done by insects we had to go back continuously to old published records which we had all been quoting for upwards of 10 or 20 years. Now we find upon investigation that accurate estimates of damage done by insects are exceedingly difficult to arrive at, and the figures are so large that we are rather afraid to quote them ourselves lest we should prevent rather than encourage investigation, and it has been the custom of entomologists to minimize the estimates for fear they should not be believed. Now the necessity has arisen, I think, and I lay it before the association for action, in the direction of gathering together some reliable recent statistics in a short form which may be printed for distribution, and which will cover the more important injuries to date, and the part the work of the entomologist has played in reducing injury or preventing loss, so that we may overcome this difficulty and provide legislators and ourselves with data with which to meet this argument. After a careful examination and great effort to obtain data I have found that there are certain of these large estimates which appear to be reliable. I think better results will follow the publication of a few quite reliable statistics, which may be taken as typical instances, than by accumulating a large number of items which would increase the chance of error and might not be read so carefully. By way of example I will refer to the chinch bug. I have examined carefully the estimates which have been published concerning that particular insect, and the following are probably quite reliable and appear to have been made with due regard to all collateral considerations, as the increased value of the saved crop, the cost of remedial measures, and similar subjects.

In 1864 Dr. Shimer's estimate, which I find was drawn up with very great care, put the loss in the one State of Illinois to the corn and grain crops at $73,000,000. In Dr. Riley's Reports on the Injurious Insects of Missouri, we find in 1874 there was a reliable estimate of the loss to that State by the same insect of $19,000,000. In 1887 Professor Osborn's estimate, founded upon the reports of the correspondents of the State Agricultural Society of Iowa, put the loss in that State on corn and grain at $25,000,000 ; and lastly, Mr. Howard's estimate, as given in the entomologist's report for 1887, for the nine States infested by the chinch bug in that year, was $60,000,000.

Now, gentlemen, I think that these statistics of the injuries to crops by one insect alone are probably as reliable as any we can get, and they give a good argument which we may use as showing the depredations of insects; but it is not sufficient that we can convince people that great injury is going on; we must show that we are doing something to mitigate this injury. In Professor Comstock's Report for 1879 the estimate of the possible loss in years of general prevalence of the cotton Aletia is placed at $30,000,000 through the cotton States. The injuries by grasshoppers in the different States of the Union and also occasionally through the British North American provinces have been so enormous that figures hardly give an idea of the injury they do, but they are known by all to be enormous.

As an instance, however, of what may be done to mitigate their attacks I would merely mention those for this year, which seem to have been very considerable. In the States of North Dakota and Minnesota it is probable that at least $400,000 have been saved on account of work done by direct advice of entomologists—work they have in some instances forced upon the farmers. Two hundred thousand dollars is a probable estimate of the amount saved by plowing the land last autumn. Another equal amount has been saved by the use of "hopperdozers." Professor Bruner tells me that a sufficient number of grasshoppers have been actually taken this year, which if left alone and allowed to lay their eggs might next year have devastated the whole crops of those two States and the adjoining parts of Manitoba. These successful operations have been carried on by the State entomologist of Minnesota, Professor Lugger, and by Professor Waldron, of North Dakota, ably aided by the advice and assistance of the agent of the Department of Agriculture, Professor Bruner, under Professor Riley's instructions; and I think it is no exaggeration to say that at least $400,000 have been actually saved in hard cash on this year's crop, not to speak of the enormous loss which would most probably have followed next year had they been left alone, and had climatic conditions been favorable for their increase.

The amount of damage done to crops every year is so vast that the figures excite incredulity from those who do not study crop statistics. The agricultural products of the United States are estimated at about $3,800,000,000. Of this it is thought that about one-tenth is lost by the ravages of insects. This is in many cases unnecessary. In short a sum of $380,000,000 is given up without a murmur and almost without a struggle by the people of the United States.

Crops of all kinds are injured, and simple remedies are known for many of the attacks and are more or less adopted. Some have already come into general use. Paris green is now applied to potato fields almost as much as a matter of course, as manure is to fertilize the soil. As an instance of how a saving may be made even in well-established methods, I give the following: Through the work of Mr. W. B. Alwood, of the Virginia experiment station, improved machinery and the water mixtures of poisons have come into general use amongst the farmers and potato-growers in the Norfolk region, and some of the largest growers now claim that they at present do for from $40 to $60 what used to cost them from $500 to $600. To-day in California and Florida orange trees are universally treated with kerosene and resin emulsions or poisonous gas for scale insects.

In the treatment of cabbage caterpillars, pyrethrum diluted with four times its weight of common flour, and then kept tightly closed for 24 hours, leaves nothing to be desired, and thousands of dollars are yearly saved to small growers who most need the assistance.

Many excellent remedies have been devised by a mere modification of existing agricultural methods. Instances of these are found in the early and late sowing or harvesting of some crops, as sowing turnips between the broods of the turnip flea-beetle, the late planting of cabbage for the root maggot, the late sowing of wheat for the Hessian fly, etc. In the 1879 report of the U. S. Department of Agriculture was first detailed the only successful method of treating the clover-seed midge by cutting or feeding off the first crop before the young larvæ are sufficiently matured to leave the heads and go into the ground to pupate. This was simply a change of one week, by which not only is the insect destroyed, but the clover is saved in better condition than under the old method.

During the present summer Professor Osborn has discovered that a serious pest of the clover plant, *Grapholitha interstinctana*, a small moth, may be destroyed in all its stages by simply stacking the hay soon after it is cut.

In the Southern States Mr. Howard Evarts Weed writes to me with regard to the cotton worm: "The loss would indeed be great were it not for the fact that the planters keep it in check by the prompt application of Paris green in a dry form. The only method now used is to apply it by means of two sacks attached to a pole and borne through the plantations by a negro mounted on a mule who rides down the rows of plants. This gives perfect satisfaction, and the farmers of the State tell me that they want no better remedy for this insect."

Mr. F. W. Mally writes on the same subject: "The benefit which the public generally derives from the researches of economic entomologists is well illustrated by the result of the cotton-worm investigation published in the Fourth Report of the U. S. Entomological Commission. In that report estimates of damage, etc., are given, and I will only allude to the benefit which the planters have derived from the report. Formerly, planters waited until the August brood of the Aletia issued and depredated on their cotton. This brood may be called the migratory one, since it spreads over vast areas of cotton fields. At that time, too, the planters used Paris green just as they purchased it from the dealers. They have now been educated to know that the Aletia propagates in certain quite well defined centers earlier in the season, and that if taken in July (or about five weeks earlier than they had been accustomed to), they can prevent their spreading to larger areas. Now, too, they dilute the Paris green with flour and finely-sifted wood ashes, greatly reducing the cost of the poison per acre. At the same time the acreage or area to which poison is now applied has been reduced tenfold, at least. For example, here in the Red River Valley, for 30 miles up and 50 miles down the river in July there were only two plantations (together about 2,000 acres) upon which Aletia was found. In August this brood would have spread over almost the entire section mentioned. Paris green was applied to this limited infested area, and the larger areas saved from injury. The saving is hardly to be estimated. The above appears to me to be one of the greatest triumphs of economic entomology, and, I may truthfully say, also of my most estimable chief, Dr. C. V. Riley."

With regard to another injurious insect, the following facts well illustrate what may be done by following the advice of an experienced entomologist.

During the year 1885 the Hon. Moses Fowler, a wealthy banker and landowner of Lafayette, Ind., applied to Prof. F. M. Webster, an agent of the U. S. Department of Agriculture, then located at that place, for relief from very serious depredations by an unknown enemy to his corn, which was damaging some of his fields from 5 to 75 per cent, he having this year 10,000 acres of land devoted to this crop. Upon examination the depredator proved to be the well-known corn-root worm, the larva of *Diabrotica longicornis*. Mr. Fowler estimated the loss in his fields by reason of this insect at $10,000, with a probability of still greater injury the following year. On the advice of Mr. Webster, the next season he sowed 5,000 acres of the worst infested lands to oats, and the following year the other 5,000 acres was treated in the same manner, the first 5,000 acres being this year again devoted to corn.

As a result of a continuation of this rotation the pest has been practically exterminated, thereby, according to Mr. Fowler's estimate, saving him $10,000 per annum.

Professor Osborn has shown that grass insects destroy much produce. He estimates that the small leaf-hoppers (*Jassidæ*) destroy as much food from two acres of pasture as would feed one head of stock. From recent experiments he has found that it is possible by the use of hopperdozers to reduce the numbers of these insects so materially that, upon two plots chosen for their similarity of the conditions of the growth, the amount of hay produced upon a plot which was once treated with the hopperdozer was 34 per cent greater than upon the corresponding untreated plot.

I have said that the study of economic entomology is many sided and requires many workers. It is equally true that all who would keep up with the rapid development which is going on all the time must work day and night, early and late. The various habits of so many different objects of study, many of them nocturnal, require constant attention.

In conclusion, I would urge on every one the great importance of keeping the most careful notes of everything which affects their work, not only of what is seen in one's own investigations, but of whatever is found in the literature of the different subjects studied. There is perhaps no detail of our work which so well repays the slight extra trouble which it involves as making all notes carefully, completely, and neatly, and then putting them away systematically, so that they can be found when required suddenly on some future occasion. Our "private notes," as we call them, should, I think, be made with the greatest possible care, not only for our own sakes, but to insure that they may be of use to others after we are gone. Who has not felt the disappointment on looking through the collection of some great worker suddenly called away from this life, of finding rare and interesting specimens, without a single note of locality, date, or other information, and how comparatively useless such specimens, and even the labor by which they were bred or procured, are thus rendered. We all know this, and yet how, too often, do we put aside material without labels, thinking that we know and shall remember all about them. After many years of much wasted labor I have come to the conclusion that a few specimens well preserved, properly mounted, and with full notes, are far more valuable than a large number of specimens without these characters. When a collector once gets the habit of accumulating a large number of specimens of everything he sees, he very soon gets careless about putting them away while they are in good condition, and has not time to make the proper notes.

Not only should notes be taken of what we ourselves have seen, but much time will be saved if an index book be kept of all literature which passes through our hands. Even in this we must protect our ourselves. The time of an enthusiastic entomologist is necessarily short, and he has not time to "look through" books on his work to see if they are good, with the idea that he will remember where to get the contained information at some future time. All reading must be done earnestly and keenly as though we should never again have an opportunity of seeing the book in question. Let all our labor be work, not play. I think it is John Ruskin who defines work as systematic effort with a definite end in view, while unsystematic effort, no matter how severe the labor may be, if it have no definite end, is merely play. In the index book should be entered a reference to the page where any facts which strike us as useful are to be found. Some restraint will be necessary, when this work is once taken in hand systematically, not to index what is not useful, as well as that which is. It is very easy to get a mania for indexing, and then the gems we are picking out may soon be lost amongst less valuable matter. Whatever we have to read or whatever we have to see, let us give it our fullest possible attention with the idea that at some future time the information may be useful. A tale that is told about Henry Ward Beecher illustrates this very well, and is probably known to many of you. Upon one occasion he was driving in the country and his horse cast a shoe. He had always made it a rule of his life that whenever he had to see anything done he gave it his fullest attention, with the idea that at some time he might require the knowledge so obtained. He had frequently stood by whilst his horse was being shod, and, consequently, when, after a time, he reached a country village and found that the smith was away from home, the tale goes, he felt so confident of the knowledge he had acquired from watching carefully other horseshoes made that he lighted the fire, fashioned and finished a shoe, and shod his horse. He drove on about 10 miles and reached another village. Upon passing the forge of the village blacksmith he thought it wise to have his work examined, so went in and explained the circumstances and asked the man to see if all were well. The smith looked critically at the shoe, examined it from every point of view, looked at the nails and the way in which they were clinched, and then raising himself up, said: "Look here, mister, if you made that shoe yourself and put it on, as you say, you had better give up preaching and take to smithing."

Gentlemen, I thank you for the kind hearing you have given me, and I trust we may have a pleasant and useful meeting.

Mr. Osborn, in discussing the address, thought that the subject suggested by the President, of the great importance of careful statistics, could hardly be overestimated. He moved the appointment of a committee of three to operate with Mr. Fletcher to prepare, if possible, some careful statistics as to the amount of insect damage, and as to the benefit resulting from the work of economic entomologists.

Mr. Riley indorsed the suggestion. He had been greatly gratified with the address and with the many valuable ideas which the President had put forward. Most entomologists who had treated of the losses occasioned by insects to agriculture have followed in the wake of Walsh, who had stated a quarter of a century ago, upon general estimates, that the annual loss from injurious insects in America was $300,000,000. Since his time the values in crops have greatly increased and the proportionate injury should have also increased; but we must take into consideration the advance in economic entomological knowledge, which has greatly reduced the proportionate loss. The loss is at most a relative thing, and we must always remember that with a decrease in the amount of the crop its money value is correspondingly increased. The present year is an exception, and we have abundant crops in this country with high prices as a result of failure in other parts of the world. He hoped that Mr. Osborn's motion, which he seconded, would be adopted, and he felt sure that such a committee would accomplish good results.

Mr. Smith spoke of the unreliability of the testimony of farmers on the question of insect damage, and adduced as an instance the fact that this year the Melon Plant-louse is very abundant in New Jersey, and that all melon injury is attributed to this insect, but upon careful examination the main trouble is found to be a bacterial disease.

Mr. Weed spoke in the same line, and stated that in Mississippi great damage was attributed to the Boll Worm of Cotton, which was not done by this insect, a number of species uniting in producing it.

Mr. Popenoe had found a similar misapprehension with regard to affairs in Colorado, and damage to the potato crop by the Colorado Beetle was laid at the door of the locust so abundant there, *Dissosteira longipennis*.

Mr. Fletcher was of the opinion that the statistics should be gotten up by the entomologists themselves by the most careful personal examination and without reliance upon the statements of farmers.

Mr. Smith called particular attention, not to the confusion of the damage done by different insects, but to the confusion of insect damage with that brought about by fungus or bacterial disease.

The motion was put and carried, and the President appointed Messrs. Riley, Osborn, and Smith as the committee.

On motion of Mr. Howard it was resolved that the committee be authorized to publish their results in case sufficient data for publication should be collected before the next annual meeting.

The Secretary reported that the minutes of the last meeting had been published in No. 5, vol. III, INSECT LIFE; that the past Secretary had transferred the treasury to him with a deficit of 38 cents, and that he had been at some expense for circulars, postage, and posters.

On motion of Mr. Cook, a tax of $1 was levied on each member present.

By vote of the Association, Dr. James Stimson, of Watsonville, Cal., was elected a member. The credentials of Mr. H. E. Weed, of Mississippi, were presented by Mr. Fletcher; those of Mr. F. L. Washburn, of Oregon, by Mr. J. B. Smith; those of Mr. J. W. Toumey, of Arizona, by Mr. Weed; those of Mr. F. H. Chittenden, of the Department of Agriculture, Mr. A. B. Cordley, of the Department of Agriculture, and Mr. F. J. Niswander, of Wyoming, by Mr. Howard. All were inscribed as members of the Association. Mr. A. S. Olliff, of Sydney, New South Wales, was inscribed as a foreign member. A communication was read from Mr. Forbes concerning the desirability of holding the meeting of 1893 with the Columbian Exposition at Chicago. Action upon this communication was deferred.

On motion of Mr. Smith, it was resolved that all insecticide papers should be brought together on the programme for Tuesday afternoon.

Mr. Bruner presented the following paper:

DESTRUCTIVE LOCUSTS OF NORTH AMERICA, TOGETHER WITH NOTES ON THE OCCURRENCES IN 1891.

By LAWRENCE BRUNER, *Lincoln, Nebr.*

In introducing this subject it is my intention to speak shortly upon the various species of locusts which have appeared in injurious numbers within the limits to be designated with each species. Some of these species have covered a vast area of territory and have caused extensive injury from time to time, while others have appeared over limited areas and have caused but slight injuries; yet these injuries have been sufficient to necessitate their mention among the destructive species of the country. Taking them all together we have exactly twelve destructive locusts within the territory designated.

Selecting the species as they occur to me, I will mention first the Long-winged Locust, *Dissosteira longipennis*. During the early part of July reports came from the eastern and southeastern portions of Colorado of locust depredations. The first of these was that trains had been stopped by grasshoppers getting on the rails of the Santa Fé Railroad 100 miles or thereabouts east of Denver. Shortly after this reports appeared in the newspapers of serious damage being done around the point where they were first mentioned as stopping trains. About this time other reports of depredations came in from North Dakota and Minnesota and other portions of the West and Northwest. On the strength of these reports Professor Riley instructed me to visit the localities for the purpose of ascertaining the extent of country overrun, the actual and possible future injury which might result, and the exact identity of the species concerned. Being a Nebraska man and looking out for first interests, I naturally went to Colorado, the nearest locality to my home from which reports had been received. I first visited Akron, Colorado, the nearest point on the Burlington and Missouri line to the region infested. There securing a team and driving to the south only about 6 miles, the advance guard of the enemy was encountered. Imagine my surprise at finding here an entirely new insect as far as destructive locusts are concerned. Here in Colorado, and in immense numbers, was the *Dissosteira longipennis*, an insect usually considered rare in collections and one heretofore only known to occur over the higher portions of the plains lying to the eastward of the Rocky Mountains, in the States of Wyoming, Colorado, and New Mexico. This insect, as ascertained from inquiry, covered an area of about 400 square miles of territory in sufficient numbers to materially injure the grasses growing on the ranges of the entire region, and amongst these grasses the species of *Bouteloua* or Gramma grasses, and the Buffalo grass, *Buchloë dactyloides*. Grains and other cultivated plants did not appear to be especially attractive to it. In fact very little or no injury was done by it to the cultivated crops growing within the region infested. About the same time that I was investigating this insect upon its northern line of injury Professors Snow and Popenoe were studying it upon the southern border of its range, and they found practically the same food habits there that I had noted in the north, and by inquiry found that the insects had come into that country from the south last fall and had laid their eggs over a large area. This year when the eggs hatched the young began to move from their breeding centers in all directions, seeking open places and the edges of plowed fields and following roadways. This trait of seeking open spots this season is probably due to the habit of the insect of naturally living on open ground, where grasses are short and scattering. The present year was very wet in this particular region and caused an undergrowth of grasses; hence the desire to find the natural conditions under which the insect lives. The young began moving, and, finding these open places, congregated there. Having thus congregated, they must naturally feed, and they swept the grasses clean around these spots. So noticeable was this that, in certain spots where they had gathered about the hills of a species of ant which raises mounds of small gravel and cuts away the vegetation for some distance around them, they had enlarged these areas in some places for fully half an acre. This year Messrs. Snow and Popenoe observed them flying southward with such ease, by reason of their long wings, that they resembled birds.

Dissosteira obliterata, Thomas.—Closely related to the above, and very similar in appearance to it, is a second species of these large, long-winged locusts, which was found in injurious numbers along with *Camnula pellucida* in Idaho last year. It was quite common in the Wood River country lying north of Shoshone and in the vicinity of Boisé City, Idaho. One form of this species was described by Saussure as *Dissosteira spurcata* in his *Prodromus Œdipodorum*. This is not the *Œdipoda obliterata* of Stoll.

Camnula pellucida.—This is the insect which has occasionally been very destructive in parts of California and Nevada. It has since spread eastward into Idaho, where it is very destructive the present season, covering an area of at least 1,300 square miles of territory. It also appears in great numbers, with several other species, in the Red River

Valley of Minnesota, North Dakota, and Manitoba. I also observed it abundantly in the Prickly Pear and Gallatin Valleys of Montana, near the mouth of the Yellowstone, in North Dakota, in portions of Wyoming, Colorado, and the extreme western part of Nebraska. It also occurs in the New England States and British America. This is a species which readily adapts itself to any new locality, being the most easily acclimated of any of our injurious locusts. When once domiciled, it is there to stay, and will require our earnest attention from time to time in the future. In fact I consider this locust, though not migratory, fully as destructive as the Rocky Mountain or true migratory locust, from the fact that it so soon becomes acclimated.

Acridium americanum, Drury.—This large handsome locust is the species which occasionally devastates Yucatan, Central America, and Mexico, and even reaches the United States in injurious numbers along our southern coasts. It has also been known in dangerous numbers as far northward as the Ohio River, and occurs sparingly as far north as the northern States, but I imagine never reaches British America.

Dendrotettix longipennis, the Post Oak Locust of Texas.—During the spring of 1887, while visiting Washington County, Tex., to investigate a local outbreak of an injurious locust, I heard of a species that was attacking the oaks of that particular region, and in some places entirely defoliating them. On my way from the region where I had been working to the city of Brenham, we passed through the infested locality, and I obtained some of the insects in question, which were then in the larval stage. A careful examination proved the insect to be new and congeneric with a species heretofore collected only in the vicinity of St. Louis, Mo., and which also occurred only on oak. About a year later this species was described by Professor Riley under the above name. The insect occurs in two forms, long-winged and short-winged. The former flies with great ease and often leaves the trees in midday and alights in fields and other clearings; with the least disturbance it flies to the tops of the adjoining trees. The larvæ and pupæ are also exceedingly active and run over the branches and trunks of trees with great rapidity. The eggs are laid in the ground around the bases of the trees. An area of at least 50 square miles of forests was completely defoliated by these insects during that and the previous year.

Melanoplus spretus, Thomas, the Rocky Mountain or Migratory Locust.—This is the insect which is generally referred to as *the* destructive locust of North America and has caused more injury during the past 20 years than any dozen of the other species combined. It is this species which we most fear on account of its migratory habits; so marked is this trait that swarms hatching on the Saskatchewan have been traced to the Gulf of Mexico in one season. Its habits have been so frequently described that further mention is unnecessary. Suffice it to say that at the present time it is again decidedly on the increase along our northern boundary. During the present year reports of its injury were received from Minnesota, North Dakota, and Manitoba by the Department of Agriculture, and upon investigation I found these reports to be only too true. In Minnesota and Dakota the authorities, ably assisted by the efforts of settlers, have been carrying on a vigorous warfare with marked results, which will doubtless save their crops from devastation next season.

Melanoplus atlanis, Riley, the Lesser Migratory Locust.—This locust, which very frequently becomes very injurious on account of its excessive increase, is somewhat smaller than the Rocky Mountain species. It is also migratory in its habits, but to a much less degree than is *spretus*. In its distribution this insect is much more widely spread than the preceding, being common in almost all parts of our country from the Mexican boundary to the fifty-third degree of north latitude, and even beyond in some parts of the country. It is the species which most frequently does the locust injury in the New England States, much of that in our Northern States, and some in the extreme Northwest. It has also been known to become injurious even in the Middle and Southern States. In its distribution *atlanis* appears to be more partial to hilly or mountainous country, and especially is this noticeable in reference to its appearance in destructive numbers. It also seems to prefer wooded or mixed country to the open prairie or plains.

As would naturally be expected from its wide distribution, this particular locust presents some variation in its size, color, and, to some extent also, its structure. At any rate there appear to be three well-marked forms of the species to be met with within the confines of North America.

Melanoplus devastator, Scudd.—A third species of the genus Melanoplus is the one that occasionally appears in destructive numbers in portions of California and the adjoining States. It is about the same size as the *atlanis* just mentioned, and often does considerable injury to the crops of the regions where it occurs. Although this locust is known to inhabit almost the entire region lying to the west of the main divide of the Rocky Mountains and to reach even beyond in Montana and Colorado, it has never, to my knowledge, been injurious except in Nevada, California, Arizona, and Oregon. This species also occurs in two forms, viz, small and large, being the spring and fall broods as nearly as I have been able to decide from specimens in collections.

Melanoplus bivittatus, Say, the Two-striped Locust.—This is our common species of native grasshopper all over the country, and the one that so frequently becomes injurious in our gardens and about the edges of fields. It occurs from the Atlantic to the Pacific, and from the Gulf of Mexico to the Saskatchewan. Its increase in destructive numbers appears, however, to be confined chiefly to the regions lying between the Rocky Mountains and the Atlantic. This locust also appears to vary considerably in its size and color. There are, however, two well defined forms, the one receiving the name *birittatus* and the other going by that of *femoratus*, the latter occurring only northward.

Melanoplus differentialis, Thomas, the Differential Locust.—Next to the species just mentioned we frequently find a second species of our large native locusts appearing in destructive numbers. This latter species occurs in the Western and Middle States only, and is here very often known to become unduly numerous and destructive to both the field and the garden crops. It has been reported at different times to have been present in such numbers in portions of Illinois, Indiana, Missouri, Kansas, Iowa, and Nebraska. A melanic or black form is quite frequent in portions of Nebraska and Kansas; but otherwise it is quite permanent in its character.

Melanoplus ponderosus, Scudd., the Ponderous Locust.—An insect very closely related to the preceding is that known to the entomologist by the above name. It is a native of several of our Southern States, and has on several occasions been a depredator of crops in portions of central Texas. As the name would imply, it is of robust form, and has a somewhat similar appearance to *differentialis*.

Melanoplus femur-rubrum, De G., the Red-thighed Locust.—Last on the list of destructive locusts for North America north of Mexico, is herewith presented the one that perhaps enjoys the greatest geographical range of all of our species. It is the common locust in all parts of the country from the Atlantic to the Pacific and from the Arctic circle to Central America. Its devastations, while perhaps not as vast as some of the preceding, have been more frequent and have occurred at more localities than those of any other one. Like the *birittatus*, *differentialis*, and several of our non-destructive species, *femur-rubrum* is a frequenter of rather low places and rank vegetation.

After giving these brief notes on the various species of locusts that have been known in the past to have been connected with the injuries from this class of insects within the country, it will not come amiss for me to say a few words about the subject for the present year, and to give my opinion as to the probable outlook for the coming year. Briefly, then, let me say that there have been received reports of locust injury from the following States: Alabama, Mississippi, Texas, New Mexico, Arizona, California, Idaho, Colorado, Kansas, Nebraska, North Dakota, Minnesota, Iowa, Indiana, Ohio, Michigan, and New York. In fact, there have been more separate reports received the present year than ever heretofore from this cause.

Now a word or two as to the different species of these destructive locusts that are responsible for the injuries of the present year. In California the *devastator* is present; the *Camnula pellucida* is known to be unduly common in Idaho, Minnesota, North Dakota, and parts of the Rocky Mountain region; the Rocky Mountain or Migratory locust is the one that is responsible for much of the injury that has been reported from the Red River Valley of Minnesota and North Dakota as well as in Manitoba to the north of the international boundary; *Melanoplus differentialis* is the one that must receive much of the blame for Kansas and Nebraska injury, while in the States of Indiana and Ohio *femur-rubrum* and *bivittatus* are the guilty parties. *Melanoplus atlanis* is present in injurious numbers in the Red River Valley along with *bivittatus*, *spretus*, and the *Camnula pellucida*. In Colorado and New Mexico for the first time *Dissosteira longipennis* has appeared as one of the injurious species of the country.

While all of these locusts, along with most every other species of the group which are native to North America, are to be counted as injurious, the particular one that has been the dread of the whole country, and especially of the region lying between the Mississippi River and the Rocky Mountains, is the Migratory species—*Melanoplus spretus*. This insect is now on the increase in a limited area on our northern boundary and across the line in the province of Manitoba. By continuing the prompt and energetic efforts that are being carried out by the populace and State authorities of the States of Minnesota and North Dakota we can be assured of success only provided the Canadian government will also see the advantage of coöperation at this time. This, let me state, is all the more necessary at this particular time, as all reports seem to indicate that at present this locust is not present in abnormal numbers in any other part of the entire country. A stamping out of the pest in this region might, therefore, forever give immunity from their further injury.

Finally, let me urge on the inhabitants of all infested regions that "a stitch in time saves nine." In other words, we do not know what the climatic conditions may be a year hence—whether they will be such as to favor the hoppers or not—so we should do the wise thing and stamp out the pest. This has been done time and again in the past, and the recent work in the North shows how very profitable is the warfare when carried on persistently. By the plowing under of the eggs laid last fall, and the use of the kerosene pans or hopper dozers in the destruction of the young locusts that did hatch, the twelve counties in the two States of Minnesota and North Dakota saved, by actual computation, on wheat alone, the sum of $400,000. This, mind you, was in a year not considered a locust year, and does not take into consideration what was saved to the region in other crops and the injury that might have resulted next year had the hoppers not been destroyed. With every favoring circumstance, the comparatively few locusts of this one species that have thus far been destroyed the present year, in this region would have been sufficient to overrun, at least calculation, the entire area of the State of Minnesota, the two Dakotas and Nebraska, along with portions of Iowa and Kansas. True, these favoring circumstances might never occur, but it is always best to be on the safe side. This we should know from our past experiences with this same insect.

"Native" locusts, while perhaps not to be dreaded equally as much as the species just spoken of, certainly can commit an equal amount of injury when size and numbers of the insects are taken into consideration. They can not, it is true, get up and fly away to regions new, but they are equally rapid breeders, with favoring conditions. They can be destroyed equally as well, if not better, than can the Rocky Mountain species, on account of their local restriction, even in the regions where found.

Mr. Southwick had noticed *Melanoplus femur-rubrum* flying to the tops of grasses towards sunset in the fields near New York City.

Mr. Osborn had noticed the same habit. He spoke of the great difficulty of estimating the damage done by grasshoppers. Some discussion followed upon this point by Messrs. Southwick and Atkinson.

Mr. Cook stated that *M. femur-rubrum* had been very abundant in Michigan for three or four years back, but that he had had no difficulty in estimating the damage to oats. He thought that the outlook in Michigan was not at all serious, and considered that perhaps Mr. Bruner's prediction was too doleful.

Mr. Bruner stated that we can not take any chances. The black picture is justifiable if it will make people work to destroy the insects and the local species have it in their power to become serious pests.

Mr. Webster stated that *femur-rubrum* is the species which is doing the damage in Ohio. He had noticed a fungus parasite working to a considerable extent near Columbus.

Mr. Smith thought that Mr. Bruner's point that it is unsafe to predict comparative immunity on account of a tendency of farmers to shirk work was a very good one.

Mr. Cook stated that there was another side to be considered, for if the entomologists predicted danger and the farmers did no work and the plague did not come, the entomologists would be forever discredited.

Mr. Weed spoke of the Cotton Worm, and stated that where the planters were always ready with their stock of Paris green they were in condition to fight the worm whenever it appeared in numbers.

Mr. Webster thought it was always best to tell the truth and to frankly admit all inability to give valid predictions.

Mr. Fletcher was of the opinion that in all probability predictions can be made more confidently in the Western country worked over by Mr. Bruner than in Canada and the region spoken of by Professor Cook.

Mr. Marlatt read the following paper by Mr. Townsend:

CHILO SACCHARALIS IN NEW MEXICO.

By C. H. Tyler Townsend, *Las Cruces, N. Mex.*

On July 8, 1891. I found a considerable number of stalks of young corn on the college farm infested with a borer. The borer enters by a hole in the stalk a short distance above the ground, and bores down into the root. It makes its burrow exactly down through the center of the stalk, and some go upward a considerable distance also. The infested stalks are easily known by the tassel, and most of the top being entirely withered and white or yellow. Some stalks showed the work of more than one borer evidently, unless the same one had eaten out and then eaten in in other places. In several stalks the live chrysalids of the borer were found near the bottom of their burrows, in the root, about even with the surface of the ground. From these pupæ two of the moths were bred, issuing July 12. Sorghum grown near the infested corn on the college grounds could not be found infested by the borer. The same borers were sent to the college from Eddy, New Mexico, with report of much damage to corn. In many cases on the college farm the chrysalids were found dead and decaying in the burrows in the stalks. A dead larva was also found some distance above ground in a stalk. More dead pupæ than live ones were found, and probably this is the result of irrigation which makes it too damp for the pupæ lodged in the roots and engenders disease.

In discussing the paper Mr. Weed said that this insect damaged corn to some slight extent in Mississippi and considerably more so in Louisiana.

Mr. Howard said that this species is spreading northward rapidly through the Southern States and has reached the southern border of Maryland, but that it is not a pest to be feared with the methods of careful cultivation in vogue at the north.

Another paper by Mr. Townsend was read by Mr. Marlatt:

A NOTE ON THE WHITE GRUB OF ALLORHINA.

By C. H. Tyler Townsend, *Las Cruces, N. Mex.*

On the 30th of April, 1891, I had a spot of ground on Judge Wood's place, near Mesilla, dug into for white grubs. The particular spot dug into was selected because white grubs had been found in it before, although I was assured by Judge Wood that not a particle of vegetation, not even a weed, had grown on it for at least three years, and probably four. It was a bare spot in the back yard, and by digging over a square foot or two of ground 16 grubs were secured, at from 6 to 10 inches below the surface. These grubs were all about the same size, and apparently nearly full grown. The ground contained no roots of any kind, but their food habits in this barren soil were explained in this manner: They were left over night in a tin can in earth in which was also placed an elongate white larva about an inch and a half long that had been found in the earth at the same time with the grubs. The next morning nothing but the caudal extremity of this larva could be found; the white grubs had devoured it. If this carnivorous habit is known of *Allorhina* I am not aware of it. I know that some other Scarabaeid larva have been found occasionally carnivorous. But *Allorhina* I had supposed lived only on roots of grass or other plants.

There is no complaint in this country of injury to roots of alfalfa or grasses by white grubs, yet the adults swarm in the summer and destroy much fruit, and the ground is full of their grubs.

Ten of the above grubs were placed in a jar of earth to breed. On July 24, 1891, two imagos of *A. nitida* were found in the jar on the surface of the earth.

Mr. Alwood stated that he had bred a dipterous parasite from the adult of *Allorhina nitida*.

Mr. Marlatt thought that this instance of Mr. Townsend's was interesting, but that it proved no general habit. He considered that the ground was probably rich in vegetable matter so as to afford food for the white grubs.

Mr. Smith thought that it would be interesting to know what the other larva fed on.

Mr. Popenoe expressed himself as surprised at the extreme southwestern distribution of the species.

Mr. Marlatt then read a third paper by Mr. Townsend:

NOTES OF INTEREST.

By C. H. Tyler Townsend, *Las Cruces, N. Mex.*

A specimen of the Colorado Potato-beetle (*Doryphora 10-lineata*) was taken July 12, 1891, on our common wild purple-flowered *Solanum* here. It is the only specimen I have seen here.

The Bean Epilachna is in full force on the college farm. All stages, from eggs to adults, found last of July. Some experiments in spraying with Paris green were tried. The results up to August 1 were negative, neither the insects nor the plants being killed. The solutions were purposely made very weak.

The latter part of July, 1891, the Bollworm (*Heliothis armigera*) was found in nearly every ear of corn in a patch on the college farm. They were of all sizes and colors, and were accompanied almost invariably by large numbers of Coleopterous (Elaterid?) larvæ, which seemed to work entirely independently of the worms, and bored all through the ripening kernels, doing much destruction.

A leaf-miner was found on the vine during June, 1891, but was not bred. It mines the substance from between the two skins of the leaf, and its gallery may be seen plainly, with its small grub at the terminus of it.

On the 15th of June, 1891, I found a rather large number of adults of a Rose Chafer (*Macrodactylus* sp.) on the leaves of the vine in a vineyard about a mile from this place. They had eaten the leaves very badly and were nearly all *in coitu*, but were found on only two or three vines. They soon afterward all disappeared.

A leaf-miner on the cottonwoods here (*Populus fremontii*) annually destroys the whole first crop of leaves on nearly every tree in the valley. April 30, 1891, nearly every cottonwood presented a thoroughly blistered appearance, caused by the inside of almost every leaf on the tree having been entirely eaten out, leaving the blistered-like skins of the leaves alone on the trees. This appearance continued for a couple of weeks until the trees gradually put forth a whole new crop of leaves. The second crop of leaves was but little infested this year, though I am told that in some years they also are nearly destroyed. I was unable to breed this miner.

The vine-leaf hopper has been studied. Eggs deposited singly, last of April, beneath skin of leaf, marked by a minute globule of exuded sap. Hatched last of May or first of June. Kerosene emulsion on the young hoppers, diluted fifteen times, proved effective; I. X. L. compound only partially so.

Owing to a misunderstanding of one of the names in this paper a slight discussion on the habits of *Aleochara* followed.

Mr. Schwarz considered the larva of these beetles not to be true parasites, but simply predatory.

Mr. Fletcher had bred larvæ of this genus from puparia of the cabbage maggot, in which no holes of egress or ingress could be discovered, and considered them to be true parasites.

Mr. Schwarz said that Mr. Coquillett had noticed the larva of *Aleochara* enter the puparia of *Anthomyia*, and stated, moreover, that the beetle larva has no approach to the parasitic habitus.

Mr. Southwick mentioned the occurrence of mites upon *Scarites subterraneus*.

Mr. Webster mentioned the abundance of *Uropoda americana* at Columbus, on *Diabrotica* and a large number of other insects.

Mr. Alwood and Mr. Atkinson spoke of the abundance of beetle mites in their localities.

Mr. Smith read the following paper:

NOTES ON BLACKBERRY BORERS AND GALL MAKERS.

By JOHN B. SMITH, *New Brunswick, N. J.*

Blackberries are raised in New Jersey on a very large scale, and near Hammonton, in Atlantic County, several hundreds of acres are devoted to this fruit. After many trials, the "Early Wilson" was selected by growers as the most satisfactory variety for size, flavor, date, and shipping qualities, and it forms the bulk of the crop. A few other varieties are raised to extend the season; but the "Wilson" is the staple. Unfortunately it adds to its many excellent qualities that of extreme susceptibility to insect attack, and of all the varieties grown in New Jersey this only is killed down in a few years unless carefully looked after.

I began my studies on the insect pests of the blackberry in the early part of the present year, before yet the canes had begun to leaf out, and found that all the pests infested cane or root.

One of the chief pests is the well-known *Agrilus ruficollis*, or red-necked blackberry cane-borer. Its life history has been worked out by others, and I have nothing of any importance to add. The well-known galls usually indicate the position of the borer, and how to get rid of it is the question. I say the galls *usually* indicate the position of the borer, because, though there can be no gall without a borer, we can have a borer without a gall. If a gall be split the length of the cane it will be seen that the wood is not involved in the gall growth, but only the bark. The insects emerge from the canes in early summer, May 25 to July 10, the month of June being the time of greatest abundance. The egg is laid by the female at the base of a leaf stalk, and I believe it is not thrust into the tissue, but is simply laid at the base of the stalk or in the bud there starting. It was not until late in July that any larvæ were found. The first sign of their presence was a dead bud at the leaf axil, and where the stem was carefully examined almost every dead bud showed traces of having been eaten into, the minute and very slender young larva being found under the bark near by.

Usually they run up the main shoot; but where laterals have become well developed, they often go into these, especially where more than one egg was laid in the same place. In neglected fields, often as many as three eggs may be found at a single point, and five leaf axils may be infested on a single stalk. The young larva bores upward in a corkscrew channel in the sap wood, as much in the bark as in the wood, until early August. Some are at that period only one-fourth of an inch long and almost nothing in diameter, while others are half an inch in length and reasonably stout. Sometimes a larva will make only two or three long circles around the cane and then, while yet minute, will pierce the cane and get into the pith. Where this is done, no visible gall forms. Others, however, and usually those in large, stout canes, will circle the stalk half a dozen times or more in succession, the girdles not more than one-eighth of an inch apart. The first trace of a gall I found in early August, when a slight ridge appears over every larval gallery, so that the course of the borer is perfectly traceable on a smooth stem. As the cane grows the sawdust and excrement in the galleries seem to swell and enlarge and also to destroy the vitality of the tissues around it, until, instead of the girdlings becoming smaller, they really become more prominent, and the abnormal growth of tissue continues. In some cases, as stated, no galls appear; but this is somewhat exceptional. In raspberry I have not found the galls, while borers have been found not rarely. This indicates that some of the exempt varieties of blackberries may simply form no galls. I am the more inclined to believe this, because I have seen beetles in no small numbers in "exempt" fields. I believe, too, that killing the cane is due, not to the injury in the pith, but to the injury done under the bark. Beyond this, the history of the insect is well known; but I am not aware that the gall formation has been as fully observed. Of course the remedy is obvious. Cutting the galls out thoroughly in early spring and burning the cuttings is certain. This is already practiced by our best fruit growers, and they are not much troubled. Unfortunately there are many who seem unable to understand their own interests, and will delay cutting or refuse to burn. Some fields, too, belong to men of other occupations, and as they become unprofitable, they allow them to go to ruin and to become breeding places for all sorts of pests, fungous and insect.

Next in order, and indeed sometimes even worse, is the larva of a Sesiid, probably *Bembecia marginata*, Harr. The eggs of this insect, which I have not yet seen, are laid late in August or in September. The young larva hatches that same fall, and in the following spring is found in canes of the previous year's growth, boring only a short distance up from the roots. It is then less than half an inch long and of a faint reddish tint, which it loses as the summer advances. In July it leaves the cane on which usually no fruit has set, and attacks a new shoot, eating around the base and burrowing up between bark and wood. The shoot wilts, but the larva seems not to travel more until the following spring. It is then an inch long, white in color, and with a brown head. It eats at the crown until the new shoots are large and vigorous, and early in July the wilting shoot in infested fields indicate the whereabouts of the larvæ. They pupate in August, one pupa newly formed being found on the 10th, and a number on the 23d, but at these dates no imago was yet noticed. One pupa had wriggled out through the stem at the latter date, apparently ready to transform. The insect is important because it cuts two years' growth of infested hills. The remedy is also mechanical. It consists in cutting the shoots as they wilt close to the crown, and destroying the contained larva.

Sometimes in June a hill will suddenly wilt and die as if burnt. Search will in all cases reveal an enormous longicorn larva, which I make out to be that of *Prionus laticollis*. In some old fields it is very mischievous, boring huge channels in the main root. I am not aware that this has been heretofore noted as infesting blackberries, and simply record the habit.

Another insect infesting growing canes escaped me during the present season because unexpected and unnoticed. In cutting some new shoots I found them marked, through the pith from base nearly to tip, a distance of three or four feet, by a larval channel. The new canes had been already topped a first time and I missed the culprit. In some fields not yet topped I found that the borer had emerged or had been parasitized, fragments only remaining, which seemed to prove it Lepidopterous. No apparent damage was done by the insect and none of the bored stems died.

A little gall on young shoots, found very locally only, is formed by a *Cecidomyiid* very near to *Lasioptera farinosa*, if not identical with it. The young shoots are always trimmed out before the imago emerges in spring, and no damage is done. The larva is also parasitized quite frequently, and only a few imagos were obtained. The relations of the parasites to each other is still somewhat obscure, and one of the species may be secondary.

AFTERNOON SESSION.

Meeting called to order at 4 p. m. by President Fletcher; 29 persons were present.

Mr. Smith read the following:

THE SQUASH BORER, MELITTIA CUCURBITÆ, AND REMEDIES THEREFOR.

By JOHN B. SMITH, *New Brunswick, N. J.*

The most dangerous enemy to squash culture in New Jersey is undoubtedly this borer. Its life history is already fairly well known, and the question of remedies is the vital one. Those usually recommended have not proved eminently satisfactory in practice, and cutting out is still most generally relied upon. Summer squashes are badly infested, but have a large stout stem and usually mature a crop before the borers can kill the vine. Of the later varieties the Hubbard is the favorite, not only of the grower, but of the borer. The missing links in the life history seemed to be in the egg stage, and these were carefully observed by me during the present season. I found in every case one or more eggs at the base of the plant, as near to the root as possible, and usually on the underside of the stem, *i. e.*, that portion of it resting on the ground. The moth evidently gets as near to the base of the plant as possible, and deposits her eggs as far towards the root as her ovipositor will extend. Rarely the egg will be found at the axil of the first or second leaf stalk; but it is at such points that the insects rest at night. The egg itself is chestnut brown in color, in form a flattened disk and of quite large size. The shell is quite hard and chitinous, but brittle. It is not readily pervious to the kerosene emulsion diluted 12 times, but is readily crushed. This stage is quite a protracted one, lasting at least 12 and probably often 15 days. The young larva when it leaves the egg moves off less than an inch and immediately enters the stem. This habit accounts for the ill success of the arsenical mixtures applied to the stem. The difficulty of getting all around it is great in the first place, and the larva eats so little that it has at least an even chance for escape. The kerosene emulsion might be more satisfactory but for the difficulty of getting the application on the under side of the stem. When the egg-laying habits were observed the experiment patch was examined, all the spare vines pulled up so as to verify the universal presence of eggs, and then with the fingers the base of the vines were rubbed thoroughly. This was intended to crush the eggs, and it was effective. The process was twice repeated, and two or three larvæ only escaped. The other vines continued healthy and free to date. Where planting can be deferred to July the vines will be free from borers, and this is the plan adopted by some large growers. In small or garden patches, rubbing the stems of the vines near base will prove effective and is a simple and cheap remedy. Planting summer squashes as traps and destroying the vines before the insects mature would also be a good way to avoid injury.

Mr. Riley asked whether Mr. Smith had tried the ordinary method of mounding the vines with ashes.

Mr. Smith said that he had not, and that he thought that this practice would simply oblige the moths to lay their eggs higher up the stalk.

Mr. Alwood said that he had found all cucurbitaceous plants quite resistant against the injurious effects of kerosene, and inasmuch as he had been successful against *Diabrotica* with kerosene emulsion, he thought that this substance would be available against the borer.

Mr. George F. Atkinson presented the following:

NOTE ON A COTTON CUT-WORM.

By G. F. ATKINSON, *Auburn, Ala.*

[Secretary's abstract.]

During the early part of July the author visited Greensboro, Ala., at the request of a cotton planter who complained that great damage was being done to the young cotton by worms. He found that an acre had been entirely stripped and had been plowed under and replanted. He found Noctuid larvæ at the roots of 20 or 30 of the plants, which he subsequently reared to the adult stage and proved to be *Agrotis annexa*. Experiments with Paris green seemed to show that this insect could be treated with this substance. He also found the larvæ feeding on *Amarantus*.

NOTE ON A NEMATODE LEAF DISEASE.

By G. F. ATKINSON, *Auburn, Ala.*

[Secretary's abstract.]

This worm had been found by Dr. Byron D. Halstead affecting the leaves of *Chrysanthemum* and *Coleus* in New Jersey. It makes no swelling or deformity as do many other Anguillulids, but causes a brown patch upon leaves. Mr. Atkinson has determined this as a species of the genus *Aphelenchus*. He entered into some details as to the distinguishing characteristics between Aphelenchus and Tylenchus, and showed that this species is somewhat aberrant in the genus in which he has placed it.

Mr. Smith asked whether the characters of the genitalia are constant.
Mr. Atkinson replied that they are within generic limits, but that they do not differ with species except as regards the distance from the anal end of the body to the genitalia. Mr. Atkinson further stated that he thinks that these Nematodes reach the leaves by being borne up in the axils of the leaves as the plants grow.

Mr. Riley asked whether it was not possible that the young might work their way up the plants to the leaves during rain.

Mr. Atkinson agreed as to the possibility of this method, and further stated that he had received what he supposed to be the *Tylenchus tritici* or *scandens* of Europe, from grass in Colorado.

Mr. Riley read the following paper:

KEROSENE EMULSION AND PYRETHRUM.

By C. V. RILEY, *Washington, D. C.*

In the *Rural New Yorker* of June 20, 1891, Dr. Albert E. Menke, director of the Arkansas Experiment Station, criticises a review of Bulletin No. 15 of his station, published in INSECT LIFE. The principal point raised by Dr. Menke is that kerosene extract of pyrethrum, made intoan emulsion with soap and water, is entirely different from an aqueous extract of pyrethrum made into an emulsion with soap and kerosene, as recommended by Professor Gillette. He also disputes the statement that the idea of combining kerosene and pyrethrum was given him by Prof. Jerome McNeill.* Professor McNeill has experimented with both the Gillette and the Menke combinations, and in a recent communication he confirms the statement that he first suggested the combination of these two substances to Dr. Menke and gives the results of his experience as follows:

In preparing, in accordance with your directions, Dr. Menke's mixture, I used the proportions given in Bulletin No. 15 of the Arkansas Station. The extract of pyrethrum was made by simply digesting the powder in kerosene for three or four hours. The resulting emulsion is good, and it is about as effective on the Cabbage Worm as he claimed it to be on the Cotton Worm. Mr. Gillette's mixture I made with the same proportion of soap, kerosene, and pyrethrum as the first mixture contained. * * * The emulsion was made in the usual manner, and then it was diluted with the kerosene tea. When Dr. Menke's mixture was diluted equally, there was no difference between the two in appearance or odor. In using dilutions of the same strength fewer worms survived the application of Mr. Gillette's solution, but the difference was immaterial, as, when I applied the mixture without knowing which I was using, I could not always tell which of the two I had employed. Such in brief are the conclusions I have reached after a considerable number of experiments with the two. I shall not be satisfied, however, without further trial of these mixtures upon different worms. One thing that has disturbed my satisfaction with these ex-

---

* An error was made in the proportions of veratrin given in INSECT LIFE, in that one-fourth pound was written instead of one-fourth ounce. Three lines above this error, however, the correct proportions are mentioned, which is sufficient evidence that the error was a clerical one.

periments is, that in many cases where I had applied a dilution of a given strength to larvæ of different age, the younger larvæ seemed less affected than the older. Concerning the difference between an aqueous extract of pyrethrum made into an emulsion with kerosene and soap, and a kerosene extract of pyrethrum made into an emulsion with soap and water, there is no practical difference. It may be of some slight interest to scientific people to know that the aqueous extract and the kerosene extract are technically different. As far as their use is concerned these two are absolutely one. If there is any practical difference between them, the aqueous extract emulsion is preferable. I have never made any public claim to having originated the idea that kerosene would dissolve the insecticide principle of pyrethrum. What I wanted to announce the discovery of was, that the two insecticides, kerosene and pyrethrum, could be combined in an emulsion which would be more effective than either. When I was assured by Mr. Mally (an agent of the Division) that he had made such a mixture while working with Mr. Gillette, my personal interest in the matter ceased. Dr. Menke claims to have discovered an "entirely new" insecticide which is remarkable for its cheapness. I think I have shown that it is composed of the same materials which may be used in the same proportions so that the difference between his emulsion and Mr. Gillette's is in method of preparation, and in this respect his method is decidedly the inferior. The chief difficulty in the use of pyrethrum in kerosene emulsion is the cost when compared with the cost of the arsenites in the form of powder or in solution.

* * * * * *

Mr. Smith had tried the kerosene-pyrethrum combination according to Menke's formula, but had found it of no use against the Rose Chafer.

In response to a question by Mr. Smith, Mr. Alwood stated that he buys imported powder for from 38 to 40 cents per pound at wholesale in New York. For buhach he has to pay 75 cents per pound and considers that one is as good as the other. He finds that he can keep the powder in bulk for two or three years, with care.

Mr. Webster stated that he could buy it by the 10 or 20 pounds in La Fayette, Ind., at 30 cents per pound.

Mr. Alwood stated that in his opinion this powder must be adulterated on account of the cost of production in Dalmatia.

Mr. Smith buys in Philadelphia for 25 cents per pound.

Mr. Weed had found kerosene combined with pyrethrum perfectly useless against the Harlequin Cabbage Bug. Kerosene emulsion is also ineffective against the same insect.

Mr. Alwood, however, had found it effective for this insect.

Mr. Weed stated that he had killed the plants, but not the bugs. He has found the eggs of this insect to hatch in three days in Mississippi (first brood), those of the second brood hatching in two days, and those of the later brood in four days. These periods, however, are not definite, and considerable variation occurs.

Mr. Smith finds this species in southern New Jersey, but never upon cabbages.

Mr. Doran stated that the bugs can be caught upon Mustard before the cabbages are set out.

Mr. Weed said that he had experimented in that direction and recommended the application of pure kerosene upon the first brood of bugs upon Mustard.

Mr. Bronk had traced an attack of this Cabbage Bug from Kale to Cabbage, the Kale having been destroyed and but three plants accidentally left.

Mr. Osborn said that Mr. Gillette conducted his kerosene-pyrethrum experiments nearly a year before his results were published, awaiting confirmative evidence.

Mr. Riley said that the great efficacy claimed for these combinations of Mr. Menke and Mr. Gillette will not be borne out by further experiment. Against the Boll Worm his agents have not found them thorough antidotes.

The Association then adjourned.

AUGUST 18, MORNING SESSION.

The Association was called to order by President Fletcher at 9:30 a.m. Thirty-four persons were present. The minutes of Monday meeting were read and approved. On motion, a nominating committee, consisting of Messrs. Howard, Weed, and Bruner, was appointed.

Mr. Weed presented the following notes:

WORK OF THE SEASON IN MISSISSIPPI.

By H. E. WEED, *Agricultural College, Mississippi.*

[Secretary's abstract.]

There has been no one great outbreak the present season. Last year stock was injured by the Screw Worm quite extensively, but the planters are now treating with carbolic-acid washes and are lessening the damage. The Cotton Leaf-worm and the Boll Worm are the principal insect enemies of the State. The former is only just appearing and will not be destructive. The Boll Worm was injurious last fall owing to wet weather. *Ægeria pyri* occurs abundantly in apple trees, but not in pear. *Hippodamia convergens* he has proven to be an injurious insect, as he has seen it feeding upon the leaves of cabbage. Moreover he has poisoned with Paris green and killed the beetles. The Chinch Bug occurs in the western part of the State on corn. The cabbage crop is almost invariably destroyed by the Harlequin Bug and other insects. The Plum Curculio is very abundant upon peaches. Cattle Ticks (*Ixodes bovis*) are very abundant in the Southern part of the State. The remedy in use is to feed the cattle equal parts of sulphur and salt continously.

The question of the action of the sulphur was brought up by Mr. Fletcher and Mr. Marlatt, and Dr. Marx stated that the sulphur was eliminated by the sudoriferous glands, thus bringing it into contact with the ticks.

Mr. Smith considered Mr. Weed's experiments with Paris green against *Hippodamia convergens* not conclusive as indicating their phytophagic habit, as the beetles might have been feeding upon plant lice and thus have been poisoned by the Paris green.

Mr. Popenoe stated that he had found *Hippodamia* feeding upon rust spores.

Mr. Weed described the treatment of Cotton for the Cotton Worm by means of a long pole carried across a mule's back with a bag of Paris green hanging to each end of the pole. In this way four rows of Cotton can be treated at once with undiluted Paris green.

Mr. Webster stated that in Louisiana four sacks were thus strung upon a single pole.

Mr. Kellicott presented the following note:

NOTE ON THE HORN FLY IN OHIO.

By D. S. KELLICOTT, *Columbus, Ohio.*

Since the full accounts of the Horn Fly given in INSECT LIFE and elsewhere, I, as many others doubtless, have sought for it wherever I had an opportunity. I remember no reports of its occurring west of the Atlantic border, but it certainly has a foothold in central Ohio. During the first week of July last I found it in great numbers on the farm of Mr. A. Freed, Pleasant Township, Fairfield County. Large patches were seen on the backs and about the horns. The animals referred to had been dehorned, but the fly, true to its instincts, congregated about the stumps. At Sugar Grove, 8 miles south, a few were found, whilst at Rockbridge, 4 miles farther down the Hocking Valley, none were to be found. There appears to be none north of the first-mentioned station, as I had a fair opportunity to examine cattle at Lakeside (Licking reservoir). They have not been seen at Columbus. It seems from the limited observations I have been able to make that it is spreading southward from near Lancaster. The Baltimore and Ohio Railway passes but a short distance north of this place, and it is easy to see that it is possible, or indeed probable, that it was introduced by transportation in cattle cars from the East.

Mr. Smith stated that the Horn Fly was not injurious in any part of New Jersey last year, stockmen adopting the plan of spraying with fish-oil compound. He also stated that the plastering of the dung was practiced in his State in small stock yards.

Mr. Howard said that even in large grazing fields this latter plan is often practicable in spite of the objections which stock-growers urge. At the time when the flies are ovipositing the cattle are generally congregated in some one spot for shade.

Mr. Lintner said that he heard of the fly in the southeastern portion of New York State.

Mr. Osborn said that there had been an unverified report of its occurrence in Iowa. He believes that the plaster treatment of the dung will be practicable in his State.

Mr. Fletcher said that many remedies which are considered impracticable by farmers prove eventually to be very practicable, and he instanced the poisoned ball system for cutworms, and said that standing grain can be sprayed with knapsack pumps.

The Secretary then read the following, which was addressed to the President, Mr. Fletcher:

NOTES OF THE SEASON.

By ELEANOR A. ORMEROD, *St. Albans, England.*

You pay me the compliment of suggesting that I should send a short report of my entomological work of this year up to present date. But though it would indeed be a gratification to me if anything I could mention should be thought of interest, yet I feel such a hesitation in submitting anything I can say to such a supremely well skilled tribunal as that of the meeting of the Association of Economic Entomolgists at Washington, that I will rather endeavor to give, in letter form to yourself, some notes of what we have been doing, from which, if you judge fit, you could lay some points, with my best respects, before the meeting.

Paris green.—I think that I may now report the use of Paris green in fluid state (as a remedy for attacks of orchard caterpillars) as having thoroughly taken root in this country. It is not yet as widely spread as could be wished, but the very large amount of inquiry sent me during the spring and summer months as to the nature and method of application of the remedy gives me good hope that its use is extending.

We have nearly, if not entirely, overcome the clamor as to the use of a "deadly poison," and now I have rather to attend to the other side of the question and warn as to the necessities of care.

My correspondents are not without a sort of dry jocoseness in the matter, for having cautioned one inquirer that if he sprayed his gooseberries he had better have a large gooseberry pie made and *consumed* by himself and household as a proof that all was right, I presently received a donation of as fine green gooseberries as could be desired. Did he wish to transfer the experiment, I wonder? About effect of Paris green on leafage, one of my correspondents reports to me that in his plum gardens (32 acres) he syringed twice with Paris green at a strength of 1 ounce to 10 gallons, using the "Gelair" sprayer. He did not begin until the plum blossoms fell, and had to syringe twice because of the badness of the attack, also because rain came. The syringing was very carefully done so that there was no observable dropping from the leaves, and on the 10th instant he wrote me: " I have an extraordinary crop of plums in consequence."

With regard to foliage of the sprayed trees, he says:

I find that the Pershore Egg Plum, Victoria, and Damsons, have their foliage quite uninjured and looking very healthy; but Czar and Rivers Early Prolific are decidedly injured, and New Orleans in a lesser degree. These are all the varieties I grow. Evidently some varieties of plums are much more easily injured than others by Paris green. (I. R).

I hope, before preparing my next annual report, to obtain detailed information on this subject from various quarters, but I think the further observation of my correspondent (M. J. Riley, of Putley Court, W. Ledbury) well worth attention *here* until *we* are more experienced.

I syringed 60 acres of apple trees which were badly attacked by caterpillars, 1 ounce to 20 gallons, which seemed to kill the caterpillars, so that one naturally asks, why make it any stronger for plums? (I. R).

But I find difficulty in persuading people to be moderate, as they desire a strong spraying to do all the work at once.

M. J. Riley further notes, relatively to effect of method of spraying, that last year (before we could procure proper sprayers) he had only common garden syringes; that he syringed " Damascenes," badly infested, with the same strength of Paris green now used with success on several kinds of plums, namely, 1 ounce to 10 gallons, and too much being put on so that the trees dripped, the lower branches were killed.

After our real difficulties, and the boundless and fathomless amount of damage and trouble predicted last year, it is a very great satisfaction to me to have trustworthy reports of the excellent state of foliage of trees properly sprayed last year, and also to find the greatly lessened amount of caterpillar presence which occurs compared to previous appearances where Paris green applications or banding have been *properly* attended to.

But I should be ungrateful and fail in proper thankfulness if I did not acknowledge that, for this benefit to British fruit-growers from the use of Paris green, we are indebted, I believe, primarily, to the exertions of our respected friend, now holding the distinguished office of Entomologist of the Department of Agriculture of the United States of America, and likewise to the careful working forward of the subject both in the United States of America and Canada, and for myself I am bound to say (and I hope you will permit me to acknowledge) that but for the efficient and kind help you were good enough to give myself and our Gresham committee, I greatly doubt if we could have pushed the subject to its present well-based standing.

Our Gresham fruit committee is doing good work by the investigation of the members being extended to all other noticeably injurious fruit attacks which they discover to be present. These are entered on at their meetings. Where the insect pest is unknown to them they forward it to me and I identify (or procure its identification) for them, and with the addition of their practical observations of life history, and means of prevention and remedy, added to what we find recorded, we make serviceable advance.

It would be very advantageous if we had more such committees, for the work is so very *real*. No make believe or fanciful remedies gain the stated formal approval of a body of experienced fruit-growers whose returns depend on the treatment of their crops.

This year we have been working up for one thing, the Raspberry Beetle, *Byturus tomentosus*, Fab., which Mr. C. D. Wise finds at the Toddington fruit grounds, may be best got rid of by shaking down into bags moistened or sprinkled with paraffin.

The Raspberry Bud Caterpillar of the *Lampronia rubiella*, Bjerk., has also been greatly troubling raspberry growers by its injury to the young buds and sometimes in the canes. We hope by gathering the infested buds or neighboring bunches of leaves in which the larva has pupated, and destroying these, to have forestalled much recurrence of next year's attack.

Plum Sawfly has also made a slight, and Apple Saw-fly a very decidedly injurious appearance. I conjecture that the similarity (to general inspection) of the attack of the latter to that of the Codling Moth Caterpillar has caused it not to be generally noticed before, and I hope to be able to add some notes on the changes in appearance of the larvæ. In all respects of habits and appearance preceding pupation this Sawfly larva agrees with such descriptions as I have access to of that of the *Tenthredo testudinea* Klug (= *Hoplocampa testudinea* Klug), but *previously* I find that instead of the head being tawny or pale chestnut, and little trace of color above the caudal extremity, that the head is pitchy black, and there is also a pitchy black plate above the tail preceded by a cross band and a few small markings also pitchy or black.

We have traced this change by the observer (Mr. Wm. Coleman, of Cranfield, Beds.) watching specimens for me in natural conditions through their transformations. I think that if this change has not been noted it will be of serviceable interest to record it, as on first glance the variously marked larvæ appear to be of different species.

For prevention of recurrence of this attack I am suggesting lightly shaking infested trees over cloths sprinkled with some mineral oil, so that the caterpillars which are very fairly active should not escape. Plum Sawfly has been only reported from one locality.

The bud-galls on Black Currant caused by the *Phytoptus ribis* or Black Currant Gall Mite have been present to a seriously destructive extent. We know of no remedy for this attack excepting use of soft soap and sulphur wash, or, as a preventive of spread, breaking off the bud-galls. We, however, have found this year that parasites are at work in the persons of Chalcids, which we have not yet identified specifically, and from some small amount of further observation I venture to hope that we may find a dipterous larva is also aiding us in preventive service.

I fear these simple matters may not be worth your attention, but I just mention them as a part of the work to which our fruit growers are giving careful attention.

The field crop insect pests have been very prevalent this year, and at this time we have just begun a heavy visitation at three places in the east of England of the larvæ of the *Plutella cruciferarum* Zell (Diamond-back Moth as we call it). But I ought not to venture to intrude on your time more than with just two observations more.

One, that I find the distorted growth of heads of Tares (*Vicia sativa*) which I drew attention to in my fourteenth report is originated by the presence of Cecidomyiid larvæ. I found them present in large numbers, and have carefully figured the head and caudal extremity and likewise the anchor process, which agrees so minutely with that of *Cecidomyia leguminicola* Lintner that I am looking forward with impatience to the development of the imago. My special colleague in observation of this attack (Mr. A. Hamlin, of Chellowes Park, Lingfield) has planned an arrangement in the open field by which the imagos when they rise from the soil will (according to all ordinary habits of insect procedure) be safely trapped conveniently for examination. I am sparing no pains also myself to develop the imagos, though I have not the opportunity to attempt to rear the larvæ in absolutely natural and undisturbed circumstances.

My other observation is regarding the *Hypoderma bovis*, the Warble Fly. We are still fighting ignorance and idleness and downright knavery, which are the supports of continuance of this attack; but I had the great satisfaction this summer of hearing from Mr. Bailey, the head master of the Aldersey Grammar School, Bunbury, Tarporly, Cheshire, that it was not worth while to give me a detailed report again this year, as for all practical purposes the attack was now stamped out in the district.

This gratifies me exceedingly. Some six or eight years ago Warbles were described "as plentiful as blackberries" in the district, and, under the teaching of their admirably intelligent master, the boys, who are mainly sons of farmers and agricultural laborers, set themselves yearly to clear all the cattle they had access to of the maggots. I had yearly detailed reports of quantity killed, and now I can point to the district and to the satisfaction of the cattle owners as a proof of what can be done by the simplest hands where head and heart go to the work.

But now I ought not to add another word, and if there is anything in the foregoing pages which you think worthy of bringing before the distinguished Entomological meeting at Washington it will be a great gratification to me. I should like much to be present myself, with the double pleasure of seeing many whom I know by their letters are kind friends to myself, and also learning much that would be of enormous benefit to me. (Torrington House, St. Albans, England, July 20, 1891.)

Mr. Southwick moved a vote of thanks to Miss Ormerod for her excellent paper. Adopted.

Mr. Osborn spoke of the great value of Miss Ormerod's work against the Warble Fly as showing how combination among workers can bring about almost entire immunity from this pest. Miss Ormerod's plan should be adopted in this country.

Mr. Fletcher also spoke highly of Miss Ormerod's work in this investigation.

Mr. Marlatt, however, stated that the plan of gathering the bots from the backs of cattle can only be practiced in the East, where the cattle are domestic, and will not pay for the trouble in the West, where the cattle are wild and would have to be roped and thrown.

Mr. Fletcher thought, however, that the saving of hide value alone would pay for this trouble.

Mr. Southwick thought that it would be a very easy matter to rope and throw the cattle in the West, and considered that it would pay.

Mr. Osborn called attention to the fact that the majority of Western cattle are sent East and slaughtered so that the bots have no chance of maturing. He insisted upon the ease of stamping this pest out in restricted localities in this manner, since the flies do not migrate to any extent.

Mr. Kellicott stated that he had known the Warble Fly to be very bad in Oswego County, New York.

Mr. Lintner stated that it is not a general pest in New York State, but occasionally a local one. Mr. Lintner further stated that Miss Ormerod has proven the Plum to be less susceptible to the arsenites in England than the Apple—a remarkable fact and not at all in accordance with our experience in this country. This difference probably depends upon climate and upon difference in varieties.

Mr. Southwick suggested the reference of this question to the botanists.

Mr. Fletcher stated that different varieties of plums show with him great difference in susceptibility to this treatment. He spoke of the great variation in the texture of the leaf and in other particulars in the varieties of Plums. Much work must be done in this direction. He also mentioned the great susceptibility of the Peach.

Mr. Alwood mentioned the fact that the addition of lime water to the arsenical mixture absolutely prevents the burning of the foliage.

Mr. Cook had found the Bot-fly attack much less in cleared farms than in wooded farms. In regard to the arsenites, he said that an abundance of Aphids and consequent weakening of the vitality of the tree might make it more susceptible.

Mr. Smith suggested that the water referred to by Miss Ormerod might contain lime salts so as to make the application more innocuous. He stated that the chemical reasons for the prevention of injury to foliage by the addition of lime water are given in the appendix to his annual report of the present year.

Mr. Popenoe presented the following:

NOTES ON THE RECENT OUTBREAK OF DISSOSTEIRA LONGIPENNIS.

By E. A. POPENOE, *Manhattan, Kans.*

[Secretary's abstract.]

July 10 to 19 the author visited the northern part of Lincoln County, Colo., on account of newspaper reports of the stopping of trains by grasshoppers. He found a strip of country 16 by 25 or 30 miles in extent fairly covered with locusts, which proved to be *Dissosteira longipennis*, a western isotype of the eastern *D. carolina*. They were congregated especially in the boundaries of this area. The country is poor and planted here and there to Corn and Sorghum, and there are occasional patches of garden vegetation. The season has been favorable and cool. The locusts are said to have come in swarms from the South last fall and to have settled along the Big Sandy Creek in a patch two or three miles in circumference, in which they layed their eggs in great numbers. Upon hatching this spring the young spread outwards. At the time of his visit in the northern part of the strip the insects were in the last larval and pupal stages, with very few imagos. At the south line, however, the winged individuals were very abundant and flew like birds. The young hoppers had the habit of crawling up the side of buildings for a few feet, presumably for warmth. They were not strictly confined to roads, but traveled over bluffs and rounded hills, eating the buffalo and gramma grass. The winged individuals flew always to the south, but the others spread regularly outwards in all directions. The line of march was quite visible at some distance on the hillsides, and sheep-growers had to change the localities of their flocks. In marching, as a general thing, they preferred to follow the roads, moving quite rapidly, about 1 mile in 6 hours for 6 or 8 hours in a day only. They are credited with all the destruction which has been done by all kinds of insects, and he thinks that they did but very little damage to potatoes and corn, although marching through the fields in great numbers. At the time of his visit they were marching through wheat fields in the same way, but since he left they have done some damage to this crop. Many dead ones were noticed in one locality, but no signs of parasitism were found. It is supposed that they were destroyed by hail. In his opinion the insect occurs generally upon low ground rather than upon high ground.

Mr. Bruner said that this species is very seldom found below 3,000 feet or above 5,500 feet elevation. It occurs in Nebraska, Kansas, Colorado, Wyoming, and northeastern New Mexico. It preferably locates itself on the side of hills or the upper portion of slopes where the vegetation is scattered. Its near ally, *D. carolina*, is found throughout North America following civilization in cattle yards, roads, and streets. He had also seen the dead locusts in one locality in eastern Colorado and considered that they had been killed by hail.

Mr. Popenoe said that he had really found that they had stopped trains, but upon steep grades only and by greasing the rails.

Mr. Osborn has found this species in southwestern Kansas in the higher portions of river valleys and feeding upon the grass along the roads.

Mr. Beckwith presented the following:

NOTES ON A CORN CRAMBID.

By M. H. BECKWITH, *Newark, Del.*

[Secretary's abstract.]

For three years the author had heard complaints in the southern counties of Delaware of an insect called by the people a "Cutworm." This year at the experiment farm at Dover many hills were destroyed by this insect which he had had an opportunity to study. The land was in Timothy last year and planted to Corn the present season. Large numbers of the larvæ were found, sometimes 30 in a hill, working around the outside of the stalk below the surface of the ground in silken galleries, but not boring into the heart of the stalk. He had sent specimens of the moth which he reared to the Department of Agriculture and it had been determined for him as *Crambus caliginosellus*. He had tried Paris green, but does not know with what effect·

Mr. Smith had heard of a similar attack on Corn in New Jersey. He advised the farmers to put on a heavy dose of kainit just after plowing and had heard no more complaints.

Mr. Osborn suggested that if the insect works like *Crambus exsiccatus* plowing at the right time will prove effective.

Mr. Howard said that the insect was abundant in 1886 at Bennings, Md., and that the only remedy which he was able to suggest at that time was plowing immediately after harvest.

Mr. Alwood doubted whether kainit would act as well as the refuse salt from meat-packing establishments, which he had found to be a good cut-worm remedy if sowed before planting.

Mr. Smith recommended kainit because it is a fertilizer as well as an insecticide.

Mr. Alwood stated that kainit is a bad form of potash for tomatoes and potatoes.

Mr. Southwick said that his grandfather used to drop a salt herring into each corn hill as a preventive against Cutworms.

Mr. Beckwith said that he had applied a fertilizer and salt in Delaware for Cabbage and thus prevented Cutworms, as he proved by a check experiment.

Mr. Alwood uses tobacco also in fertilizers as insecticides.

Mr. Smith presented the following paper:

NOTES OF THE YEAR IN NEW JERSEY.

By John B. Smith.

During the spring of 1890 the larvæ of the Clover-leaf Beetle, *Phytonomus punctatus*, appeared in great numbers and threatened to become seriously destructive. A fungoid disease opportunely attacking them, the vast majority were killed off before they were more than half grown. Some few escaped, however, and the threat of injury was repeated during the spring of 1891. The numbers were not so great, however, and the fungus disease stepped in as before, destroying the larvæ before they had done serious injury.

Complaints of twig blight in apple were made early in the season, and on investigation two coleopterous insects were found to be concerned in it. One of these, the larva of *Eupogonius tomentosus*, bored through the center of the new wood, or rather that made during the previous year, and killed the twig. The beetles appeared in June. The other was a small Scolytid, probably *Hypothenemus*, which made short galleries in the extreme tip of the twigs infested by the Longicorn larva. It is probable that this attack is secondary, and not made while the wood was sound.

Some discussion was had at our last meeting concerning the points of the tree attacked by the larva of *Saperda candida*. This led me to observe carefully during the present season, and I find that while in quince the attack is almost exclusively at the base of the tree, in apple and pear, any part of the trunk and even the larger branches may be attacked. The larvæ are more numerous at the base, as a rule, but the other localities are not by any means exceptional. I know that no other larvæ were concerned, because I cut out pupæ and imagines as well, and am certain of my facts.

Peach borers, the larvæ of *Sannina exitiosa*, are now largely treated by mechanical coatings to the trunk. The favorite means is the one recommended by me in the bulletins of the station and at farmers' meetings. It is simply a thick whitewash with Paris green and glue added. I have never discouraged the use of other mechanical coatings, but have taken great pains to explain that no remedial results must be expected; that the measure was protective merely. The use of paint, as suggested by Mr. Alwood, does not find favor, owing to a fear that injury may result to the tree.

Blackberry insects have been particularly observed; but as I have already described these, a mere mention here is all that is needed.

The Rose-chafer, *Macrodactylus subspinosus*, has been less destructive than usual. My studies on this insect have appeared in bulletin form, and I need only emphasize here that all my tests of remedial measures were made in the field under ordinary field conditions, and that the results are such as would likely be obtained by a farmer employing them.

The Grape Flea-beetle made its appearance very early in the year, before even the leaves had made their appearance, and began eating the buds. I recommended collecting in kerosene pans early in the day, and this proved effective. About a pint of the beetles were sent me in grateful acknowledgment.

Root maggots have been very abundant, and onions have been most severely attacked. In some places the young sets have been completely destroyed. This pest is now pretty well distributed in the trucking districts around Philadelphia.

Aphides on orchard fruits, and particularly on apple, became very abundant during a three weeks' drought near New Brunswick, and blackened tips everywhere caused serious alarm. A cold storm lasting two days broke the drought, and apparently checked the multiplication of the species. There was no further increase of injury, at any rate, and no other complaints reached me.

The melon vines have suffered greatly from attacks of Aphides, but still more from a bacterial disease. The damage done by the latter is quite usually attributed to the Aphides.

I have made some study of squash insects, more particularly of the "Borer" *Melittia ceto*, of which I have previously spoken. The Striped Beetle, *Diabrotica vittata*, does not bother our large growers very much. When they seem abundant, they use lime or plaster on a day when there is a gentle wind, sowing it on broadcast. The beetles fly before it and are driven off the field. The next man takes up the work on his field, and so the beetles are driven off until they reach some unguarded field which is then usually injured quite seriously. *Epilachna borealis* has been very abundant, and has eaten characteristic patches at the edges of the leaves. The insects made their appearance as soon as the squashes were well up, but did not begin mating or ovipositing until the middle of July. Larvæ were not found until August. This gives quite a long period for the mature insect. It is easily kept in check by the use of the arsenites.

The Corn Bill-bug, *Sphenophorus sculptilis*, appeared in large numbers in Burlington, Salem, and Gloucester Counties, and perhaps in other surrounding regions. The beetle drilled the characteristic holes in the young plants at or near the surface and thus destroyed many acres of corn. I advised replanting after a short delay, and the second crop of plants was undisturbed. The insect was a new one to growers, and its appearance in such numbers caused consternation. They were most numerous on old sod, but by no means confined to such land.

Diplosis pyrivora has been complained of as an injurious species for the first time. It has reached Newark, Montclair, Elizabeth, and Paterson, so far as my information extends, and has probably been in some orchards for at least three years. Where it first made its start in this State I have been unable to ascertain. The Lawrence pear is the one most generally attacked, in one orchard over 90 per cent of the fruit being infested. From an examination of the infested fruit I believe the egg is laid in the ovary, or if not that, the young larva does not pierce the fruit, but follows the pistil into the ovary or seed chamber, the opening in this variety of pear being quite wide. In many cases also this same passage is used by the larva to leave the fruit where it remains sound and does not crack. This promises to be one of the most dangerous of the fruit pests.

Spraying fruit trees with London purple has been very generally practiced in New Jersey and always with most gratifying results An unexpected result has been the destruction of the fungus on the pear which so generally disfigures varieties like the Bartlett. Fruit on sprayed trees is fine and clean, that on the others is spotted and clouded and of an inferior grade.

The Plum curculio has made a plum crop almost impossible in New Jersey. I made only one experiment myself during the season, spraying one tree with the kerosene emulsion, 1 to 12, once a week for six weeks. At the end of that period nearly every plum on the tree had from one to six larvæ, and I called the experiment a failure. Several growers who had a few trees only report a favorable result in spraying with the arsenites, and there seems little doubt but that a certain percentage of fruit can be saved in this way. For small trees of choice varieties I suggested cutting out the egg. This was done in a few cases with absolute success. It leaves only a trifling scar, no more than that of the original puncture, and is certain in effect. Of course this would not answer on a commercial scale, but for choice fruit in the garden it is not impractical, and might be used to supplement spraying with arsenites.

I have followed out my inquiries into the actions of certain fertilizers as insecticides, and am more than ever convinced that in kainit we have a powerful agent for the destruction of forms infesting sod-land. Where this material is used before planting corn even on old sod, cutworms and wireworms will do no injury. In addition I always advise fall plowing to give the winter a chance. Direct experiments in the laboratory show that Elater larvæ will die in soil that contains kainit, though it acts slowly and two weeks are required to produce a complete result. The experiments will be given in detail elsewhere.

Mr. Alwood, in discussing, said that he had recommended London purple against *Fuscicladium* for some years.

Mr. Riley presented the following paper:

GOVERNMENT WORK AND THE PATENT OFFICE.

By C. V. RILEY, *Washington, D. C.*

[Author's abstract.]

The paper was based on a patent recently obtained by three parties in California for the treatment of trees by hydrocyanic acid gas for the destruction of scale-insects and other insects that injuriously affect trees. It reviewed at length the efforts of the Department in this line of investigation and showed conclusively that this gas treatment had originated and been perfected by one of the agents of the Division of Entomology, who had, in fact, for the past five years, been carrying on a series of experiments in this particular line under the author's direction; that so soon as the treatment came to be recognized as of the greatest utility and perfected so that it was cheap and available to all needing to use it, application for a patent was made by the parties in question, and in spite of an official protest from the Department of Agriculture pending the application, a patent was finally granted, as, under the law, the Commissioner of Patents has no right to consider *ex parte* testimony pending examination, even though offered by an officer of the Government in the interest of the public. The fact that the process had been fully described and recorded in official reports from the Department of Agriculture did not prevent the issuing of the patent. So valuable is this treatment considered that an effort has been made in southern California to subscribe the sum of $10,000 to buy the right from the patentees. The author remarked that he personally had no hesitation in advising the orange-growers to pay no heed to the claims of the patentees, and that it would be wiser to combine to oppose them if suit were brought than to subscribe to give them an undeserved and valuable royalty.

His own conviction was that the patent was invalid and the certificate but a piece of paper carrying no absolute evidence of priority of invention; and it is greatly to be regretted that, through legal technicality or otherwise, it should ever have been granted.

The author mentioned other cases of this kind where, after years of labor and large expenditures on the part of the Department of Agriculture, valuable results had been obtained. In some cases they took the form of mechanisms, which were described and figured in the official reports; in other cases of mere discoveries. He said:

There is nothing more discouraging to an officer of the Government engaged in original investigations, with a view to benefiting the public, than the efforts of various private individuals to appropriate the results, of which the foregoing case is an example. I have been engaged now for nearly a quarter of a century either as a State or Government officer in investigations, having for their object in the main the protection of plants and domestic animals from the attacks of injurious insects. Either directly or with the aid of assistants these investigations have resulted in some important discoveries of universal application, and I can say with pride that, though often urged to take personal advantage of such discoveries, I have in no single instance accepted a fee for information given, or received a dollar from any application of these discoveries, even where others have reaped fortunes. As a salaried officer my duty was plain, and I make the statement, without boastfulness and simply to emphasize the discouraging fact, that in every instance where the benefit to the public has been great, either the honor has been contested by private parties or else means have been taken by private individuals to control, through patent or otherwise, the discoveries for their personal ends.

It would seem that on this account the Patent Office should endeavor, in considering applications for patents for objects which the Government is already endeavoring to accomplish, to ascertain fully what the Government has done, as any other course will tend to pervert, discourage, and neutralize all honest efforts made by other Departments of the Government for the public good. It would seem, also, that there is need of some modification of the law in so far as Government evidence is concerned.

Mr. B. P. Mann said that no patent can be held valid unless held by the inventor. The Government ought to get out a patent on the broad invention, and it could then prevent the present holders of the patent from using it.

Mr. Riley and Mr. Mann further discussed the subject.

The president announced that a reception, to which all were invited, would be held at Mr. Riley's residence, Sunbury, Wyoming avenue, at 7 o'clock this evening.

The meeting then adjourned.

AFTERNOON SESSION.

The meeting was called to order at 2:30 p. m. by President Fletcher. Twenty-eight persons were present. The minutes of the preceding session were read and approved. The committee on nominations reported the following nominations for the ensuing year:

For president, J. A. Lintner, of New York.
For first vice-president, S. A. Forbes, of Illinois.
For second vice-president, J. H. Comstock, of New York.
For secretary, F. M. Webster, of Ohio.

On motion, the report of the committee was adopted, the committee was discharged, and the officers named were declared elected. The name of George H. Hudson, of Plattsburg, New York, was presented by Mr. Lintner; that of H. A. Morgan, of Louisiana, by Mr. Weed; that of B. P. Mann, of the District of Columbia, by Mr. Bruner, and that of Miss M. E. Murtfeldt, of Missouri, by Mr. Riley. All of these names were ordered inscribed upon the roll of members.

On motion of Mr. Howard, seconded by Mr. Smith, it was resolved that the next meeting of the society be held at the place of, and two days preceding, the next meeting of the American Association for the Advancement of Science.

Mr. Riley read a paper entitled "*Dermestes vulpinus* and Tobacco," which is held for publication elsewhere.

Mr. Southwick stated that he had found *Dermestes* under the bark of a mahogany log in New York, and that it had entered this crevice for pupation after having originally fed upon some animal matter.

Mr. Howard read the following note :

A NOTE ON PARASITES.

By L. O. HOWARD, *Washington, D. C.*

The object of this brief note is to impress upon the members of this association the fact that one can not be too careful in statements for publication concerning the relation between a given parasite and its host.

The possibilities of error are very great, as a few instances will show.

In 1882, while studying the Army Worm at Huntsville, Ala., I noticed an Ichneumonid walking about a fence-rail over which the worms were swarming in countless numbers. The parasite was apparently excited, walked and flew from one part to another, occasionally alighted upon a caterpillar and brought her ovipositor into position. I captured her, and in my notes wrote " Found ovipositing upon the larva of *Leucania unipuncta.*" Now it transpires that this Ichneumonid was *Bassus scutellatus*, and, as the concensus of rearing experiments shows, the species of this genus are parasites of Diptera, and my inference was in all probability entirely mistaken. If the original observation had been published it would have been absolutely necessary for perfect safety to have detailed the circumstances in order that future students should not be misled.

Recently a well-known entomologist sent to Professor Riley specimens of the common *Pteromalus puparum* with the record " Reared from the cells of a mud-wasp." From what we know of the habits of this parasite we may take it for granted that had the entomologist in question examined the cells of his mud-wasp he would have found specimens of some lepidopterous larva or pupa stored up as food for the young of the wasp and that from these stored-up insects the parasite had emerged.

Within the last few weeks specimens of a Chalcidid were received from a most careful observer and excellent collector, with the statement that they were reared from the eggs of a saw-fly deposited in a willow leaf. While I am not in the habit of discrediting any statement which this gentleman makes, and while I have learned by experience that his accuracy is something astonishing in this world of error, the fact remains that this parasite is plainly from the known habits of its near relatives an enemy of some lepidopterous or dipterous leaf miner, and that never under any circumstances could it have been an egg parasite. He had probably put his willow leaf in a pill box and had later found the parasites in the box. He did not examine the leaf carefully for traces of a leaf miner or he would never have sent in the record.

Where the parasite is reared from a gall or from a twig burrowed by some other insect it often happens that it is assumed to be parasitic upon the gall maker or upon the most abundant twig borer. Such an assumption should never be made without a complete statement of the facts and without the most careful examination of gall and twig, to see whether they were not inhabited by other insects either as inquilines or parasites, or in the case of twigs as perhaps unnoticed borers.

Instances like these might be multiplied, but this will suffice to indicate the absolute necessity, first, of extreme care in forming conclusions, second, of detailing all circumstances which may possibly have led to error. It is only by such careful work as this that we can ever arrive at proper conclusions concerning the group habits of parasites. Our present published records are full of error and require a most careful sifting of evidence, which in many instances can no longer be obtained. The most heterogeneous and unlikely errors in many genera are published, and the discriminating work is of extremely slow accomplishment.

Mr. Fletcher stated that he had seen an Ichneumon ovipositing upon a glume of wheat upon which there was no insect.

Mr. Doran stated that he had reared a parasite from *Bruchus scutellaris*.

Mr. Howard stated that this parasite was probably an undescribed species of Mr. Ashmead's genus *Bruchophagus*.

Mr. Osborn presented the following paper:

REPORT OF A TRIP TO KANSAS TO INVESTIGATE REPORTED DAMAGES FROM GRASSHOPPERS.

By HERBERT OSBORN, *Ames, Iowa*.

In accordance with instructions received July 24, to visit and report on grasshopper injury in western Kansas, I started the following morning for Kansas and improved every opportunity on the way to learn of grasshopper injury. The following account is in advance of a report prepared for Dr. Riley. At Des Moines, where I waited a few hours for the Kansas City train, I went through a large number of Kansas papers, kindly placed at my service in the office of the State Register and Iowa Homestead, without, however, getting any information except assertions in some places that there were no hoppers in Kansas.

From a gentleman lately through Arizona I learned of the appearance of considerable numbers in that Territory, and the expectation that these might be travelling eastward. At Kansas City I was equally unsuccessful, the only information received there being the statement of railroad men as to the occurrence of hoppers on the railroad in Colorado (the case investigated by Professors Snow and Popenoe), and of some in Arizona, along the line of the Atchison, Topeka and Santa Fé Railroad.

At Topeka I went first to the office of the State Board of Agriculture. The Secretary, Mr. Mohler, was absent, but the gentlemen present, Messrs. Longshore and Nyswander, kindly gave me a full statement as to the information the office contained.

They receive reports from over 600 correspondents who are scattered over the entire State, the western portion being well represented. They assured me that not a single report had been received by them which mentioned injury from grasshoppers, and they were positive that no damage was being done.

At the newspaper offices I received similar replies, except that in the office of the *Kansas Democrat* I learned of a report that some damage had been done in Kearney County. As this report, however, was somewhat indefinite, I hesitated to make it the basis of a special trip to the extreme southwest part of the State, and Lawrence being so near at hand, I concluded to go there to see if Professor Snow had any recent information.

Professor Snow was absent, but his assistant, Mr. V. L. Kellogg, kindly gave me all the information he could. He said that they had heard nothing from the region that had been examined by Professors Snow and Popenoe in Colorado, except that the winged insects were moving south, and he was sure that none of these had entered Kansas.

He also informed me that they had received information of injuries at Garden City, and showed me specimens of *Caloptenus differentialis* and *bivittatus* received from there.

This information tending to substantiate the report of damage in Kearney County, I decided to visit Garden City, and took the first train for that place. On the way I kept careful outlook for any signs of damage, and improved the opportunity of occasional stops to collect specimens and inquire of residents as to the prevalence of grasshoppers. All answers agreed in denial of any unusual numbers of grasshoppers or of injury from them, and it was not till I reached Garden City that I learned of any damage. Here I was told that the alfalfa fields were being ruined, and it was only a short time after my arrival that I was in a field a mile from town where the conditions showed at once the state of affairs to be serious.

The alfalfa was badly stripped, the blossoms and seed entirely eaten up, and in many patches the stems were stripped bare of leaves, looking brown and dead.

The grasshoppers, mostly *differentialis*, with a considerable number of *bivittatus*, when rising in front of me as I walked through the field, formed a cloud eight or ten feet high and so dense as to hide objects beyond them. Here I noticed a number of grasshoppers dead from the attacks of parasitic *Tachina*.

From this field I went to another, owned by the same man, which was also well filled with grasshoppers, but the injury here was less, especially around the buildings, where a large number of turkeys were doing excellent service in killing the hoppers and at the same time adding rapidly to their own weight.

In a field of sorghum directly adjoining there was also considerable injury, but *differentialis* seemed scarce, while a bright green species, *Acridium frontalis* Thos., was abundant and apparently the principal agent of destruction. This species was also noticed here and in other places occurring in great abundance on the wild sunflower so common on these plains, and the question arose whether this was not its natural food plant and its attacks on sorghum incidental.

The day following I spent the forenoon with Dr. Sabin, who kindly furnished a horse and cart and accompanied me in examining a number of farms within five miles of Garden City, where alfalfa fields and orchards were injured. I met and talked with a number of farmers who had suffered from grasshopper depredations, and the information received from them with what I gained by personal observation satisfied me that losses could be avoided by proper measures.

I learned that the same injuries extended farther west along the river where alfalfa was grown, and I proceeded from Garden City to Lakin, observing on the way that all alfalfa fields showed presence of grasshoppers, but that in some cases the bloom was still free from serious injury or destroyed only in patches. At Lakin I learned that injury had been serious, especially on the place of Mr. Longstreth, some two miles from town. Some fields near the river and occupying low land were noticed in full bloom and showing little damage, but still grasshoppers could be found in abundance by closer inspection of the fields.

Mr. Longstreth's son, being in town, drove me out to his father's farm, and accompanied me on a tour through his extensive orchard of ten acres, his oat fields and alfalfa fields, in all of which the damage had been serious. Many of the trees in the orchard were entirely stripped of leaves, and in some cases the bark had been eaten from the limbs. The alfalfa presented the same appearance as observed in other fields. I found here a great many dead grasshoppers, whose empty shells attested the activity of *Tachinæ*.

I was told by Mr. Longstreth that skunks were amongst the most active enemies of the grasshoppers, and he believed played an important part in reducing them. He had even seen one up in an apple tree catching hoppers on the limbs.

I learned at Lakin that alfalfa was also grown in the next county west, at Syracuse, and that damage was also reported there, but on reaching the place found the injury slight as compared with the other places visited. In fact, aside from one farm on which some damage to alfalfa and orchard had occurred I could learn of no loss. *Caloptenus differentialis* I found in some numbers, and there is little doubt that unless some effort is made this fall and next spring to destroy eggs and young they will multiply as in other localities, and probably by next season prove as destructive as in them.

As this point carried me into the westernmost row of counties in the State, and there was no report of damage farther on, I determined to cross northward to the Missouri Pacific Road, in order to follow up some rumors regarding damage from grasshoppers at some points intervening, and which, from the descriptions given, seemed possibly to be due to *Dissosteira longipennis*. No point where serious loss occurred was found, however, and this species occurred but sparingly at points between Syracuse and Tribune, and occurred at Horace only in small numbers, too few to cause any apprehension for the immediate future at least. Taking the Missouri Pacific, I passed through to Kansas City without finding any evidence of damage from grasshoppers, and as I could learn of no other localities in the State than in the three counties examined where such damage was reported, I returned to Ames, and will now proceed to a detailed account of the territory examined, the species observed, and the special measures needed to meet the outbreak in this section.

THE TERRITORY AFFECTED.

The damaged territory is quite easily defined and might very properly be said to coincide with the irrigated portion of the Arkansas Valley lying in Finney, Kearney, and Hamilton Counties in southwest Kansas. The entire irrigated district, however, is not equally injured and there are some fields much less damaged than others. The whole area covered extends with occasional breaks a distance of about fifty miles along the river and forms a strip from one to five miles wide but limited entirely to areas where irrigation has been practiced, and within this limit is dependent upon the kind of crops raised.

The greater damage was observed at Garden City, though nearly as bad was seen at Lakin, and but little was found at Syracuse, corresponding as near as I could learn pretty closely with the length of time since alfalfa has been made a principal crop on the irrigated lands.

THE CROPS AFFECTED.

Alfalfa is the crop in which there is the most loss, but orchards are suffering badly, and were they extensive throughout the district would very probably present the heavier loss.

The alfalfa crop is a very profitable one and easily grown with irrigation and has been very extensively planted, the fields devoted to it covering many thousands of acres.

The injury to this crop is of such a nature that I believe practical remedies may be adopted, and, as will be stated later, active measures should be adopted this fall and next spring.

THE AMOUNT OF INJURY.

The great loss this year has resulted from the destruction of the seed crop. In many fields this has been a total failure, and the loss may be considered as covering thousands of acres and involving many thousands of dollars. One man who had something over 100 acres in alfalfa considered that his loss amounted to about $2,000. While he expected to cut and use the crop for hay, the damage had been such that the hay would be little better than after the seed crop had been secured, and he reckoned the full loss of the seed crop for the season. In some cases farmers were cutting for hay when they had intended to allow the crop to go to seed, and in this way were reducing the amount of their loss by the value of the crop of hay cut early over what the hay would be worth after maturing seed, the latter, of course, being much less valuable than the hay cut before seed matures. In many cases the farmers had been depending largely upon the crop of seed to help them out of debt, and the loss from the grasshopper injury falls heavily upon them.

THE SPECIES DOING THE DAMAGE.

The Differential Locust is, I think, chargeable with fully nine-tenths of the destruction, both in alfalfa and orchards, and the reasons for its increase in this section seem to me quite evident. The irrigated fields of alfalfa furnish it with favorite food in abundance throughout the year, and have given it an opportunity to multiply rapidly without exhausting its food supply.

The ditches which traverse the fields and possibly parts of the fields themselves furnish a most excellent location for the deposition of eggs, the ground being compact and for the most part undisturbed throughout the year. That the eggs are deposited in or alongside the ditches is indicated by several facts, though at the time of my visit the locusts, while pairing, were none of them ovipositing. In the first place, the greatest damage has occurred in strips on either side of the ditches, and only in the worst fields extends over the entire field; second, at the time of my visit the pairing individuals were quite evidently collecting more particularly in these locations; third, the testimony of those who seemed to have observed most closely agreed in placing the greatest number of young hoppers in spring along the borders of the ditches, a point which is clearly supported by the injured strips so plainly to be seen. No one whom I questioned had seen the locusts in the act of ovipositing.

The ditches contain no water during a large part of the year, and in fall the compact bottom, which doubtless affords more moisture than the fields in general, would seem an excellent place for the deposition of eggs, as well as the banks on either side. Judging by the habits of these and allied species in other locations it would be hard to conceive a more favorable place for the deposition of eggs, and it seems to me very probable that this, as well as the suitability and abundance of the food, may be considered an important factor in the rapid increase of the species in the last three or four years, an increase that has taken place directly with the cultivation of alfalfa by irrigation.

It would seem also that this habit renders the insect especially open to attack, and I see no reason why concentrated effort may not entirely prevent a repetition of the damage another year.

MEASURES RECOMMENDED.

The situation, it seems to me, is one deserving serious attention, but one which offers every hope for successful work, if the residents of the affected localities can but be induced to make a little effort at the proper time.

The injury for the present season is mainly past, as the grasshoppers are in large part mature, many already pairing, and the loss of the seed crop, the heaviest part of the loss, beyond repair. The effort, therefore, must be toward preventing the damage another year, and it seems to me very desirable that the Division should distribute to the people of this section a careful set of directions for their guidance this fall and next spring in working against the grasshoppers.

The means which appear to me from inspection of the ground to promise most successful results would be as follows:

(1) To thoroughly break up the surface of the ground in and along the ditches before winter by harrowing thoroughly, cultivating or shallow plowing, thus exposing the eggs to winter weather and natural enemies.

(2) Wherever practicable, to flood the ground for a day or two at the time young locusts are hatching. I was told that the young hoppers were entirely unaffected by water, as they would crawl up the alfalfa stems and escape, and it is probable that sufficient flooding to accomplish much good in this region is out of the question. My only hope in this line would be in watching carefully for the time of hatching, and using the water before the hoppers had obtained any growth, and if abundant along the ditches, putting a little kerosene on the water.

(3) A use of the hopperdozer as early in the season as possible, when I believe the treatment of a strip eight or ten feet wide on each side of the ditches would destroy so large a part of their numbers as to prevent any serious damage. As I learned from a number of parties the hoppers are scarcely half grown when the first crop is cut, it would seem that immediately after cutting the first crop would be the best time to use the hopperdozer. The hoppers would be large enough to jump readily and the dozers could be run very easily. It would be difficult to use them at any other time than directly after a crop was cut, as the dense growth of alfalfa would obstruct their movement.

My strongest recommendation would be the urging of effort in breaking up egg masses before winter, and then in case locusts still appear in any number in spring to resort to the dozers at first opportunity. I believe active use of these measures will be effectual, with a cost but trifling compared with the value of the crop to be saved.

The information as to the species and the measures needed are covered very fully in your Bulletin on Destructive Locusts, and with some specific instruction regarding the treatment of ditches in this special locality would, I think, give the people of the district affected all the information necessary to protect themselves, and it would seem advisable to send a number of copies of that bulletin to the postmasters at Garden City, Lakin, and Syracuse to distribute to farmers, who would make use of them, as well as to those whose names I will furnish for this purpose.

OTHER SPECIES OBSERVED.

The species next to *differentialis* that I should call most abundant in the injured fields was *bivittatus;* but taken alone its damage would have been insignificant. Its habits are so nearly like those of *differentialis* that I see no occasion to give it further mention, and I have little doubt that any measures adopted against *differentialis* will prove as effective against this species.

Still other species occurred, but seemed generally distributed, and so far as injury in the devastated fields is concerned need no mention.

THE LONG-WINGED LOCUST.

Dissosteira longipennis was taken in some numbers at all points visited in Finney, Kearney, Hamilton, and Greeley Counties, and as this species has caused so much injury in eastern Colorado this season, I took rather special pains to note its abundance and inquire as to any destruction resulting from it. At no point did it occur in destructive numbers, and I should not look for any injury from it in these localities in the near future at least.

Most of those noticed were winged, some still fresh from the pupa stage. In general all the winged ones, when disturbed, moved southward, but nothing like a general migration was seen. At Lakin I was told by a Mr. Logan that a large black-winged grasshopper had been common near that place, and when winged had traveled uniformly southward.

PARASITES AND DISEASE.

The many parasitized grasshoppers noted indicated a multiplication of such forms and these will undoubtedly accomplish much in reducing the numbers that can deposit eggs this fall, but I should deem it unwise to depend on them and to omit the active measures already urged.

The most general parasite was apparently the Tachina flies, as the great majority of dead hoppers were found to be completely devoured within, and in most cases the opening through which the maggot had issued was to be seen. Adult *Tachinæ* were also observed in the infested fields.

Some of the dead grasshoppers had the appearance of having been affected with *Entomophthora*, and I gathered a number in order to make an effort to cultivate the disease, but as yet have nothing to report in this line. The dead hoppers will be kept with living ones, and if the latter take the disease we may hope to still further multiply the disease by inoculating still others, and then an effort can be made to distribute the disease in the fields. Its spread, however, is evidently slow, and I do not think other measures should be neglected this season for a plan which is still uncertain.

Among the natural enemies observed, toads were perhaps the most common, some of the fields containing great numbers of them, especially of half-grown individuals, and these would seem capable of greatly reducing the numbers of hoppers. A dead one, which saved me the necessity of making a dissection to get positive proof, showed in the partly decomposed stomach the legs and other parts of grasshoppers, proving that, as would be inferred from presence of toads in the fields, their mission was to feed upon the grasshoppers.

The attacks of skunks upon grasshoppers, as stated by Mr. Longstreth, have already been mentioned.

As the tendency is for natural enemies to multiply with the increase of any species of insect, we may look for increased assistance from this source by another year, and in connection with the measures already urged, these ought by another year to keep the insect entirely within the limits of destructiveness.

Mr. Osborn then read the following paper:

THE CLOVER-SEED CATERPILLAR.

(*Grapholitha interstinctana* Clem.)

By H. Osborn and H. A. Gossard, *Ames, Iowa*.

On the evening of the 23d of May many small dark brown moths were noticed flying about a clover field upon the College Farm. They were resting upon the blossoms and among the leaves, and upon being disturbed would fly a few paces and then settle again. These moths proved upon examination to be *Grapholitha interstinctana* Clemens, the parent forms of the Clover-seed caterpillar mentioned in the Entomologist's Report to the Commissioner of Agriculture in 1880. We had during the past winter received specimens of clover seed which we suspected of being damaged by this pest, which has been reported as injurious in some of the states east of us in the last year or two. The moths are also remembered as occurring at Ames in numbers some eight or ten years ago. They were not, however, at that time connected with any damage observed in clover fields.

The moths increased in number from the time they were first observed until, by the 3d of June, in the early evening, when the field lay between the observer and the sun, a perfect cloud of them could be seen hovering over the blossoms as far as the eye could reach. They would spring up from under the foot like grasshoppers in a meadow on a sunshiny day. It was also noticed that they were pairing freely at this time.

On the 24th of June an examination of 177 heads of clover taken from the field before mentioned showed 91 heads infested with the caterpillar of the moth as against 86 not infested. Many of the larvæ were full grown and some were spinning their cocoons. The hay was cut at this date. An examination the next day, June 25, of 48 clover heads taken from scattered bunches on the college campus showed 8, or 16⅔ per cent., of the whole infested. Examining 42 heads from a different field, cut on the 23d and 24th of June, only 3, or 7 per cent., were found infested.

The damage was done by eating into the young florets and later into the seed vessels, causing the heads to dry up and the flowers to shell from the receptacles like chaff.

The larva is a small, greenish white caterpillar, with a dark brown head, about .25 to .30 of an inch long when full grown, many of them becoming tinged with red toward the hinder extremity as they approach the time of pupation. About the 24th of June the adults had nearly all disappeared, a few stragglers only being found by diligent search. Of a number of larvæ preserved in a breeding cage the first pupa was found July 14, but a visit the same day to the field before mentioned proved the second brood of the adults to have already appeared. An examination of dried bunches of hay left on the field disclosed some larvæ in the heads, which had spun their cocoons to pupate, from which it is concluded that the caterpillars can live in the cut hay for a considerable time if not hampered in their movements. An examination of the hay from the same field stored in the barn showed all the larvæ to be dead. A dead pupa was also found, but nothing living. There were no empty pupa cases found to indicate that any moths had escaped from the hay thus stored. It seems certain, therefore, that everything that was subjected to the pressure and heat incident to storage was killed. The remedy, then, for this pest, which has caused the destruction of probably 50 per cent of the clover seed in the field observed, is to cut the hay soon after the first brood of larvæ appears, or in early June. The hay should be carefully cleaned from the field, so that no larvæ will find harbor in stray bunches which have not been gathered up. Scattered clover growing by the roadsides and in the fence corners should also be carefully mown at this time, and the heads at least disposed of in some manner to insure the destruction of the larvæ they may contain. This method can not but prove effective in reducing the second brood of the moths, and will also operate against the clover-seed midge *Cecidomyia leguminicola*.

The track of the larva is very uniformly from the base of the head upward, and the younger larvæ are almost invariably found near the base and beginning their work on the florets there. It would seem, therefore, that the eggs are deposited at the base of the receptacle, and the larvæ upon hatching may begin at once upon the older florets. In working upward, roughly speaking, they usually form an irregular spiral track around the receptacle.

The delicate, white, silken cocoons of this insect are spun in the head among the dried florets, frass and bits of eroded but undevoured flowers so covering them with brown as to make them difficult of detection. The pupæ work their way entirely out of their cocoons and drop to the ground before bursting their pupa cases, which may be found in abundance on the ground from which a brood has just issued.

The second brood was observed pairing during the last week of July, and August 5 the larvæ were found in great numbers, one having at that time spun its cocoon preparatory to pupating. The rate of growth would seem to establish that there are three broods per year at Ames, and possibly, though not probably, four. [In advance from a forthcoming Bulletin, No. 14, of the Iowa Experiment Station.]

Mr. Alwood presented a communication, of which he has furnished the following abstract:

STANDARD FITTINGS FOR SPRAY MACHINERY.

By WILLIAM B. ALWOOD, *Blacksburgh, Va.*

[Abstract by author.]

It is my desire to briefly present to this Association a matter with which doubtless many of your members are already familiar, and which I feel confident will meet the hearty approval of all the economic workers. At the Champaign meeting of the Association of Agricultural Colleges and Experiment Stations, held in November, 1890, I presented a paper before the botanical section, dealing with some of the newer forms of machinery used in fungicidal work, and pointed out the great inconveniences under which we labored from the diversity of styles and sizes of fittings and thread connections used in the various machines now offered by manufacturers. The subject was considered of such importance that a motion was carried to ask the sections of entomology and horticulture to unite with the botanists in appointing a conjoint committee, which should be charged with recommending to manufacturers such styles and sizes of connections and fittings as were thought to be most convenient in the practical work of treating injurious insects and the fungus diseases of plants. This committee, as finally organized, was composed of the writer, as chairman, Mr. D. G. Fairchild, assistant mycologist of the Department of Agriculture, and Prof. James Troop, horticulturist of the Indiana Experiment Station.

This committee issued a circular letter to manufacturers which met with a very general and cordial response from them. Nearly every one fully indorsed the ideas set forth by the committee, and most of the prominent parties agreed to carry out the committee's suggestions so far as practicable with the state of their business. By the time standard styles of fittings could be circulated among the makers of spray machinery the season of '91 was so far advanced that we could not hope to affect much change during the current year. However, now that interest and sympathy with this effort have been awakened, we believe that it is possible through united effort to secure all we ask in this line. While we are all aware that the members of this Association are in large part station entomologists, it is also true that some very prominent members are not connected with station work; hence my reasons for bringing this subject before you for discussion. To any one who has had actual experience in field work the importance of better, and, I will say, uniformly standard sizes of fittings, can not be doubted, and to aid in securing this desideratum is the chief purpose of my paper.

I shall at an early date publish an illustrated circular dealing with the question of styles and sizes of fittings, which will give detailed information, both for the use of manufacturers and the special workers.

On motion of Mr. Smith, seconded by Mr. Lintner, it was—

Resolved, That the Association of Economic Entomologists heartily indorses the work of the committee from the Association of Agricultural Colleges and Experiment Stations, appointed for the purpose of consulting the manufacturers of spray machinery, with the end in view of securing the adoption of standard sizes of connections and attachments on such machinery.

Further, the Association of Economic Entomologists urges upon the manufacturers of this machinery the importance of acceding to the request of this committee. The association requests the committee to publish its recommendations, with drawings and descriptions, for the information of manufacturers and special workers, and to include in this publication a list of all manufacturers who have agreed to conform to the standard sizes.

Mr. Kellicott stated that in his opinion firms which will not comply with the request to manufacture standard fittings should be requested to furnish an adapter to their machines which will enable their use with the standard fittings.

Mr. Southwick presented the following:

ENTOMOLOGICAL WORK IN CENTRAL PARK.

By E. B. SOUTHWICK, *New York, N. Y.*

[Author's abstract.]

The work of the entomologists of the department of public parks is in the care of trees, shrubs, and plants, under the directions issued by the president of the board of commissioners.

The work of removing the egg masses of *Orgyia leucostigma* was the first done in this department, when 12 men were employed to clean the trees, benches, walls, and stonework in the parks. The first autumn of our work we collected 13 bushels of these cocoons and egg masses, leaving those cocoons that were apparently parasitized until the final cleaning. The large elms on the Mall were thoroughly cleaned with steel brushes made for the work, and each tree received a wash to destroy any insects that might be in the crevices of the bark. This work of collecting (and burning in the furnace) has been carried on each year as the force would allow, in this way keeping them in subjection. We now treat them in four different ways:

(1st) By hand-picking, of which bushels are each year taken from the trees with tools especially adapted for this work.

(2d) By jarring the larvæ down with a pole, so arranged that a blow from a mallet on a projection placed at the large end of the pole will jar any down that may be on the branches. With a sudden blow most of them will fall to the ground, when they can be crushed.

(3d) By poisoning the foliage with London purple, which is quite effective and used especially on very large trees that can not be treated otherwise.

(4th) By poisoning or spraying the trunks of large trees with an emulsion of petroleum and carbolic acid. This penetrates most of the cocoons sufficiently to kill the inmates, the disadvantage being that it kills the parasites too. This method is only resorted to when the egg masses are very numerous and we are short of help, and as a means of reducing the next brood. Large numbers of trees were so treated this season to arrest the late summer hatchings.

The next insect in abundance and destructive working was the Bag Worm, *Thyridopteryx ephemeræformis*. Whole portions of the parks were literally stripped of their foliage; many of the trees on the drives were nearly as bare as in winter. So abundant were they that the branches were strung with their cases, and with one push of the instrument prepared for collecting them, a handful of these cases would be taken. Four kinds of tools were made for this work, and the cases were collected and destroyed. In this way nearly 22 bushels have been collected and destroyed.

The *Datanas* have always been abundant in the parks, and as many as 15 pounds of caterpillers have been taken from a single tree. These are collected while massed, as is their habit, and then destroyed.

Hyphantria cunea is very abundant in our parks and has been destroyed by cutting down the webs as far as was possible. If the tree was too valuable, they have been twisted out with poles made especially for this work. In some cases spraying has been resorted to, but as this does not remove the unsightly web, the most practical thing to do is to remove the whole colony.

Clisiocampa americana has this year appeared in our parks for the first time, and in great abundance. The webs that appear on the trees before they are in full leaf can be easily removed, and in this way the finer trees can be protected. The eggs are also removed in the late autumn and winter, as they are very conspicuous.

Vanessa and *Grapta* sp. are sometimes very abundant, and are collected and destroyed as soon as discovered. *Cecropia* and *Eacles* are always abundant and on many of the smaller trees do much damage. These are hand-picked and destroyed.

Alypia octomaculata is one of our most troublesome caterpillars, the great abundance of *Ampelopsis* vines in the parks, and especially around it, covering "squatter sovereignty" houses, affords congenial food for its rapid propagation. In the parks the vines are twice annually treated with a solution of London purple, applied with a spraying machine. This is found most effective and the vines do not seem to be injured as easily as most plants by the arsenites.

The Elm Beetle, *Galeruca xanthomelæna*, has given us an immense amount of trouble, and many thousand trees have been sprayed each year for their destruction, and with good effect. The means we have adopted during the past three years is rather more in the preventive line. As soon as the first eggs are found that part of the tree is at once sprayed. I am inclined to think the Elm Beetle is double-brooded with us.

The Elm Borer, *Zeuzera pyrina*, is getting to be very destructive with us, already twelve species of trees and shrubs are affected by it, and during the past year two men were kept during May at collecting the larvæ from broken branches. All branches as soon as detected in a weak or broken state are removed and the larvæ extracted. In very choice trees the limbs are carefully examined and where holes can be found bisulphuret of carbon is put in with an oil can and putty put over the hole. This is only resorted to in the case of rare trees and shrubs.

For scale insects the trees are washed with preparations and then cleaned with steel brushes, leaving all in fine condition. Many thousand trees and shrubs have in this way been put in fair condition.

A large number of poisons have been experimented with for *Aphis* and other insects, due notice of which will be given in reports soon to be published.

The spraying machine used by the department of public parks is a two-barrel machine manufactured by the Nixon Nozzle Company, Nixon, Illinois. This machine, to better adapt it for city work, has been entirely remodeled. A set of strong cab wheels, with a strong axle, was first made, then a pair of strong easy springs, so as to make the tank less liable to jars. The tank was lined with zinc entire, and on top of the tank was placed a well about a foot high to keep the liquid from flushing over. On the rear of the tank was placed a box for poisons, hose, etc., and on the front a box for coats, lunches, and collecting cases and bottles. On one side of the machine and running nearly to the horse's breast was placed the bamboo pole used to elevate the hose, and on the other side long-handled pruning shears. Thus equipped the men drive all over the city and are at any time or place ready for work at short notice.

Our parks comprehend nearly 4,000 acres and are from one extreme to the other 16 miles apart. The work with the present force and appliances is chiefly centered in the island parks and places.

Mr. Cook read a paper entitled :

SOME HISTORIC NOTES.

By A. J. COOK, *Agricultural College, Michigan.*

Upon special request, I am very pleased to state the following facts regarding the early use of the kerosene emulsion and of the arsenites.

I used kerosene and soap mixture, as I then called it, successfully in 1877. I used very nearly the same proportions that I prefer now, heated it to dissolve the soap, and I think made a permanent mixture. Dr. C. V. Riley argues that I only made a temporary mixture, which he says was made years before, although I have been unable to find the record. Whether it were an emulsion or not, it was very successfully used, as successfully as in later years. That I appreciated the importance of the *emulsion*, or even recognized it or produced it except as an accident, is not true. Messrs. Barnard, Hubbard, and Riley did this as the result of extended experimentation, and heralded the facts forth to the world, and I gladly accord to them the chief credit.

As to Paris green, I believe my friend Hon. J. S. Woodward, of Lockport, N. Y., was the first to announce it as a specific against the Codling Moth, which he did in the autumn of 1878. He relates to me that he advised a neighbor to use it to destroy the canker worms. The neighbor observed that the trees treated were very free from Codling Moth larvæ, and Mr. Woodward divined the cause. I had a very similar experience the same year. Mr. J. W. Tafft, of Plymouth, Mich., came to me in 1878 with specimens of canker worms, which he said were destroying his orchard. I advised Paris green, which he used with the same results that greeted Mr. Woodward's neighbor. Mr. David Allen reported the facts to me. I said, can it be possible that the poison has worked this double benefit ? I will test the matter. Mr. Woodward had already announced his belief in the matter. In 1879 I made the first careful test and proved by a most crucial test that Paris green was not only a specific against the insect but safe to use. The results of these experiments were given at the Boston meeting of the American Association for the Advancement of Science, August, 1879. The results which I then secured were remarkable beyond what may usually be expected or hoped for. This was because I treated a small tree and took special pains that every fruit should receive the poison. As great care to-day will meet with the same success. Thus while Mr. Woodward was the first to suggest and announce this remedy, I was the first to prove and announce positively that it is both safe and effective. So far as I know I was also the first to determine the best proportion—1 pound to 200 gallons of water—and to show that it is safe to pasture in an orchard at once after the poison is applied if the application is properly made.

Mr. Osborn read the following paper:

AN EXPERIMENT WITH KEROSENE EMULSIONS.

By HERBERT OSBORN, *Ames, Iowa.*

The most satisfactory method of preparing the valuable kerosene emulsion is desired by all and a comparative test made this season may be of interest.

The first was a preparation in which the formula advocated by Professor Cook was carefully followed, using the hard soap and not the soft soap formula, the materials while still hot being thoroughly mixed with an egg beater.

The result was that we had what appeared to be an excellent emulsion, but in a glass jar we could soon see a separation taking place, the white emulsified part rising to the top and the water or soapsuds gradually increasing at the bottom. This continued until there was about two-thirds or a little more of soapsuds and one-third or less of emulsion above it.

While this at first could be readily mixed again a day later, the soapsuds in the bottom had hardened into a jelly that when mixed with additional water would but incompletely dissolve and the clots included caused great inconvenience by clogging the nozzle.

The other preparation made according to the usual formula for soap emulsion (the Riley-Hubbard formula) emulsified and remained fixed with but a very few drops of soapsuds gathering at the bottom, even after days of standing, showing that the proportions were such that the soap water and kerosene balanced each other. This thickened to a buttery consistence, but dissolved perfectly in water, and only a trace of oil arose to the surface when thus mixed.

A microscopical examination of the substance prepared by Professor Cook's formula showed the buttery mass above to be apparently a good emulsion and the jelly-like mass below to contain scarcely any traces of oil globules. A similar examination of the second preparation showed in different samples as usual a uniform emulsion.

I conclude that in the first case I formed an emulsion, that is the oil was broken into minute globules and these coated with a film of soapsuds so that they did not coalesce, but that there was such an excess of soapsuds that the emulsion separated therefrom and rose to the top.

It is evident, I think, at sight that the preferable preparation is the one which combines the proportions so that no excess of either ingredient results, for, as indicated, the hardening of the thick soapsuds results in clots and these interfere with spraying, while to skim off the emulsion and leave the mass below is a useless labor and loss of material.

In the Riley-Hubbard formula we have evidently the exact proportions carefully determined, and I feel obliged to recommend this formula when giving advice to those wishing instructions as to preparation of kerosene emulsion.

Mr. Wallace read a note of which the following is an abstract:

A NOTE ON SILK CULTURE.

By PAUL WALLACE, *Los Angeles, Cal.*

[Secretary's abstract.]

The author reviewed the attempts which have been made to raise Silkworms in this country, and stated that they had proven the entire adaptability of the United States to this industry. He stated that all that was needed to make it a success was either a bounty paid by the Government or an import duty upon raw silk, but to his own personal knowledge attempts in this direction were thwarted by the work of large silk manufacturers who were bitterly opposed to the establishment of silk culture in America. He urged that the Association should use its best efforts to foster a popular sentiment antagonistic to such efforts on the part of the manufacturers of silk.

Mr. Lintner, in discussing this paper, contended that there is no question as to our ability to raise good silk, but that it will not pay. He spoke particularly of the work of the division of entomology in experimenting in this direction.

Mr. Cook read the following article by Mr. G. C. Davis:

NOTES ON A FEW BORERS.

By G. C. DAVIS, *Agricultural College, Michigan.*

If we go on the principle that "every little helps," even though it be slight and incomplete, then perhaps a few notes incidentally picked up on our forest borers may be of some utility at this time. Dr. Packard's work on forest insects, so recently issued, is of inestimable value to the working entomologist, but by the reporting of the few observations we happen to make while at our other work we can make the volume still more complete and helpful. Perhaps the habits of some of these species may already be known, but as they have not been specially reported in this work, reference is here made to them.

From the maple was reared the Cerambycid borer *Acanthoderes decipiens*. It was found as a pupa in the rude chip case just under the bark. The cylindrical burrow made in its exit extended well in toward the heart of the tree and through quite sound wood.

Another Cerambycid, *Leptura proxima*, was found quite numerous in blocks of hard maple sawed from the tree the winter previous. The grubs were quite large, and it was thought that they would pass through the transformations that season, but it was not until a year from the following May that the first beetle issued. From the data given it seems that the borer must require two or more years to reach maturity.

In "Forest Insects" Dr. Packard mentions *Lyctus striatus* under the list headed "Found in rotten oak wood; not known to be injurious." We have quite recently found them issuing from a red oak floor in one of our college halls. The floor was laid two years previous to the time of this appearance, and the lumber was seasoned at that time. The beetles issued from the sap wood only, and probably were feeding there when the tree was sawed into lumber.

In order to learn more of their habits quite a number were placed in a glass jar containing a branch of green oak, one of dead oak, and a seasoned stick from the shop. The beetles preferred the latter when first introduced, and made themselves at home by boring a hole entirely through it diagonally the first night. Mating took place in a few hours after issuing and eight days later ovipositing was first noticed. Mating again took place before each egg was deposited. This seems essential, as a female was placed by herself immediately after mating the first time, and, although watched for several weeks after the others had died, no sign of ovipositing was noticed. The branch of green oak was preferred in depositing the eggs, and none were placed on the stick from the shop. Ovipositing occurred about once in half an hour and lasted but one day. One week after oviposition young larvæ were found. We are in hopes to get the complete life history from them.

From the oak posts of one of our summer houses were taken quite a number of *Phymatodes dimidiatus* along with *P. varius*. Four different kinds of wood—elm, maple, hickory, and ironwood—besides the oak, enter into the construction of the chalet, but none of the others showed signs of borers, while the oak was well perforated. The species seem to work mostly just beneath the bark.

Two specimens of *Alaus oculatus* were taken in the trunk of a white oak near the partially decayed heart. A full-grown larva of this was also found in the trunk of a "sappy" aspen.

On the 10th of June a piece of bark was torn from an aspen (*Populus tremuloides*) that had but recently died, and under it signs of insect depredations were quite evident. Upon further investigation the bark and wood were found to be almost entirely separated. Underneath, the wood was yet sound and quite green. Here were found galleries penetrating almost to the heart, and in them were found *Enchodes sericea* in the imago stage, although some of them were yet in the pupa case and nearly as soft and white as a pupa.

These beetles belong to the family Melandryidæ, which contains a number of quite diversified genera that in general live on fungi or under bark. As far as their habits are known those living under bark do not seem to be injurious as borers, and whether we can consider this species as merely working in decayed wood or as a borer in green wood can hardly be decided by this one instance. It is certain that the larvæ are *capable* of penetrating sound wood.

The beautiful little Buprestid, *Pœcilonota cyanipes* was reared from the aspen. When found, June 9, it was in the pupa state in the axil between the body of the tree and quite a large branch. So much had been eaten around the base that the branch was already dead. Mr. Harrington reports capturing the species on a dead willow stump, and Mr. Fletcher a specimen on a dead aspen stump in Ontario.

Galls made on branches of the willow, *Salix discolor* by *Agrilus torpidus* have been found quite common in certain districts near here, and in other districts was found *Saperda concolor* in galls equally as numerous. In no case yet noticed have the two been found in close proximity. The galls made by the Buprestid are an oval swelling of the live branch very similar to the one made by the Saperda. Inside there is a difference in the architecture of the home. While the Saperda remains mostly within the swelling and makes its exit through it, the Agrilus bores an oval gallery downward from the gall, sometimes in the pith, but oftener indiscriminately through the wood, and makes its exit often an inch and a half below. The imago issued about a month later than the Saperda.

From the Saperda galls were reared two species of parasites. One of these is *Pimpla pedalis* and the other belongs to the genus Bracon, which we have yet been unable to get named.

Galls on the willow also yielded us a few specimens of the handsome Sesiid, *Sciapteron tricincta*, as named by Professor Fernald. The galls did not differ in appearance externally from the others. Inside the gall a tunnel was made downward along the center for an inch. The whole cavity was lined with a soft, delicate, though very strong, buff cocoon, and undisturbed in this silken bed the larva passed through its transformations to the moth.

From *Hylesinus aculeatus*, the Ash Scolytid, was reared a species of Bracon, pronounced by Mr. Ashmead as probably a new species.

From a species of trefoil, *Ptelea trifoliata*, was reared a species of the Tineid genus *Hyponomeuta*. Wherever the shrub was found the thin white web was quite common early in the spring before the leaves were out. These webs were always at the terminal portions of the green shoots. The caterpillars, entering the stalk usually at the terminal bud, would bore down through the pith some three to six inches in the shoots connected by the web. The larvæ seem to remain in the stalk only part of the time, but spend the remainder of the time above in the web. The twigs, of course, are killed down as far as the larvæ go, which greatly mars the symmetry and beauty of the bush. This habit of boring is probably a generic characteristic, as several European species are mentioned as having similar habits.

Mr. Cook read the following note:

THE POPLAR GONIOCTENA.

By A. J. COOK, *Agricultural College, Michigan.*

The past spring the poplars about the Michigan Agricultural College were seriously and extensively defoliated by a Chrysomelid beetle, *Gonioctena pallida* Linn. The larvæ were first found in early June, so that we did not have the eggs. The larva is much like the Elm-leaf Beetle in form and color. The beetles appeared June 21. They are yellowish brown, except the eyes, epicranium, two horn-like spots, and a central oval spot on the posterior portion of the prothorax, the scutellum, two large spots, one on each elytron near the scutellum, two nearly as large rounded spots near the suture, and just posterior to the center, three small spots along the lateral margins, and the entire underside of the body except a narrow margin, which are black.

The beetles came forth late in June, but we found no larvæ or eggs.

The Secretary then read the following notes:

NOTES OF THE SEASON FROM SOUTH DAKOTA.

By J. M. ALDRICH, *Brookings, S. Dak.*

Cutworms have been more injurious than ever before. From limited data, I judge that the loss in the State reaches several millions of dollars. Corn, flax, gardens, and other crops suffered about in the order mentioned.

At our station the large Willow Sawfly (*Cimbex americana*) is much less injurious than for several years. I have reared six or seven species of parasites from it, four of them being numerous.

The Cottonwood Leaf Beetle is with us in large numbers, as usual. Our experiments in spraying with arsenites for this insect are more successful than heretofore, and I now feel confident that it can be controlled (though not exterminated) by this method. Our new Russian poplars, so desirable in other respects, are chosen by the beetle in preference to cottonwood.

Gooseberries have suffered from a combined attack of the Spanworm (*Eufitchea ribearia*) and the Sawfly. I have not observed the latter in our State till this year,

The Ash Borer (*Trochilium fraxini* Lugger) is still increasing rapidly, and will probably destroy most of the ash trees in the neighborhood of the station in two or three seasons more. The Ash Sawfly and the Sphinxes (Ceratomias) are assisting to a noticeable extent. The ash is a bad investment in our locality.

In May the station procured five colonies of bees, aiming merely to see what they would do, with ordinary care, in a region devoid of natural timber with its accompanying honey plants (the nearest is five miles away). We have now increased to ten strong colonies. I have taken off 35 pounds of fine honey, and shall probably get 100 pounds or so of fall honey. Considering that the original swarms were weak, I think the record good so far. Of course the winter will try them.

A building 16 by 32 was erected this year for our department. It has a wing 12 feet square for bees. In the main part we have an office and a small breeding room. We moved into the new quarters July 1.

Mr. Alwood read the following paper by title:

A NOTE ON REMEDIES FOR THE HORN FLY.

By WM. B. ALWOOD, *Blacksburgh, Va.*

This plague to cattle, which has now become so common throughout several of the Atlantic coast States, demands attention from workers in economic entomology. Doubtless some very good recommendations have been made by Dr. Riley, Professor Smith, and others, but as conditions vary we are bound to treat such questions from the standpoint of local practicability. The recommendation to lime the droppings when practical may prove a very good way of dealing with this pest, but with me it is quite impractical from the fact that lime is neither cheap nor easy to procure, and this is the case in many parts of Virginia.

Some two years since, from a suggestion of mine in a lecture at Charlottesville, Va., the late Henry M. Magruder began the use of kerosene emulsion on his dairy cattle. The application was made with a Japy knapsack pump, and though it had to be repeated with frequency, proved a considerable success. During the year 1890 I frequently recommended this remedy, stating that the standard emulsion (Hubbard formula) should be diluted ten to fifteen times.

The Horn Fly did not become troublesome at our place, which is in the upper mountains of southwest portion of the State, until late in 1890, and I did not, as a consequence, have opportunity to treat this insect myself. However, the present year they showed themselves in abundance in July, and I concluded to try my own recommendations.

The experiments were made upon ten dairy cows, beginning with plain emulsion diluted ten times. I found that this killed a majority of the flies actually wetted with it, and produced considerable immunity from attack for the space of one to two days. Desiring to make the treatment more effective, I used as diluent a water extract of tobacco waste, made by thoroughly boiling one pound of tobacco in each gallon of water. This used with emulsion, 1 to 10 parts, gave almost perfect immunity for a period of three days.

My work shows that two treatments with this preparation per week almost entirely relieve the cattle from annoyance. I make the application with a knapsack pump fitted with a cyclone nozzle. The work is most conveniently done just after milking in the morning. Two men treat the cows rapidly, requiring about one minute per cow, and using from one to two pints of liquid. The preparation as given above causes no particularly unpleasant odor, and thus far the milkers have made no complaint whatever concerning its use on the cows.

The President announced that he had received letters of regret from Mr. J. H. Comstock, Mr. C. W. Hargitt, Mr. H. Garman, Mr. C. P. Gillette, and Mr. C. H. Tyler Townsend.

On motion of Mr. Alwood, seconded by Mr. Smith, it was resolved that Mr. Riley be requested to publish the proceedings of this meeting in INSECT LIFE, and on motion of Mr. Smith, seconded by Mr. Bruner, the Secretary was instructed to send an abstract of the proceedings to the *Canadian Entomologist*.

On motion of Mr. Southwick, the Association passed a vote of thanks to Mr. Riley and the members of his office force for the courtesies to members during the meeting of the Association.

On motion of Mr. Osborn, a vote of thanks was extended to the President for his able efforts to make the meeting a success.

The Association then adjourned.

L. O. HOWARD,
Secretary.

Just after the adjournment of the meeting the following communication was received from Mr. Snow, one of the vice-presidents of the Association, which, although it can not properly be incorporated in the minutes, may be properly appended here:

THE CHINCH BUG DISEASE AND OTHER NOTES.

By F. H. SNOW, *Lawrence, Kans.*

In response to your circular letter asking for notes of work done in economic entomology during the past year I beg to submit the following brief and incomplete account of the work done in Kansas this year under my direction in the matter of the artificial dissemination of a contagious disease or diseases among chinch bugs:

The legislature of the State of Kansas at its last session in the winter of 1890–'91 made an appropriation of $3,500, available during the years 1891–'92, for the purpose of carrying on these experiments. With this money I have been enabled to largely increase the facilities of my laboratory and to conduct on a rather extended scale practical experiments in the field. According to a provision in the act of appropriation, I am required to make a monthly report to be printed in the official State paper of Kansas, the *Topeka Daily Capital*. From my last report, made on July 15, I quote as follows:

Since making the last report, June 15, the wheat has ripened and mostly been harvested. The chinch bugs at harvest time left the wheat fields and invaded the fields of young corn. The experiments of 1889 and 1890 were carried on among bugs in the corn fields, and the experiments of this year in wheat fields are thus new features in the work. The results have been gratifying, but the reports from this year's corn fields and the investigations of my field assistant, Mr. Hickey, show that the massing of the bugs in the hills of corn offers more favorable conditions for the successful workings of the disease than the usual conditions incident to the presence of bugs in wheat.

The hatching and appearance of the young bugs is a feature in the work added since the last report. It is with satisfaction that I note the evident communicability of the disease from old to young bugs by contact. The young bugs are as susceptible to the infection as the old ones.

The part of the State reporting bugs in the corn fields lies between 96° 30' and 98° 30' west longitude; or between a line drawn through Marshall, Pottawatomie, along the eastern boundary of Geary, Morris, Chase, and along the eastern boundary of Greenwood, Elk and Chautauqua Counties, and a line drawn along the eastern boundary of Jewell, Mitchell, Lincoln, Ellsworth, Rice, Reno, Kingman, and Harper Counties. This bug-infested belt extends clear across the State from north to south. Scattering reports of the presence of the bugs are in from various eastern counties, and from a few west of the 98° 30' line.

Up to date (11 a. m., July 15) infected bugs have been sent out from my laboratory to 1,700 applicants. To several of these applicants second lots of infected bugs have been sent, owing to failure to use the first lot for various reasons, and occasionally because of failure to get good results from the first experiment. But as many, if not more, persons have got dead bugs from fields wherein the bugs are dying because of infection sent out from my laboratory as have received bugs directly from me. Each successful field experiment has been the means of establishing a secondary distributing center. It is evident that the experiment of killing chinch bugs by infection with fungoid and bacterial disease is being given a trial on a large scale. The reports for the past month (June 15 to July 15) have been gratifying, in that they show a good percentage of success. However, reports are not made out as carefully as they should be, and worse, many experimenters make no reports. I desire to have a report on every lot of infected bugs sent out.

Because of the difficulty of getting careful reports from the field, I sent out Mr. E. C. Hickey, an intelligent university student doing special work in natural history, as a field agent. Mr. Hickey's last trip was through Chautauqua, Harvey, Sumner, Cowley, Butler, Greenwood, and Elk Counties, lasting from June 12 to July 6. He visited seventy-two persons who had experimented with infected bugs, and found over 80 per cent of the seventy-two experiments successful. Mr. Hickey personally visited the corn fields, and verified by careful observations the statements of the farmers.

The laboratory facilities for sending out infected bugs have been largely increased, and all demands can be promptly met. Application for infected bugs received in the morning's mail are answered with bugs and directions on the noon outgoing trains. The work of scientific investigation in the laboratory is going on steadily and carefully. Inoculation experiments from pure cultures of Sporotrichum will be reported on next month. A feature of the work unnoticed previously in this report is the prevalence of Empusa, the fungus with which the first successful experiments were conducted. Empusa and Sporotrichum develop side by side in the infecting cages, and dead bugs sent in from fields where the bugs are dying show both fungi. At the close of the season I hope to present a full report of the laboratory investigations, which the brief monthly reports offer no space for. Prof. S. A. Forbes, the eminent State entomologist of Illinois, who has experimented in his laboratory on the development of parasitic fungi in insects, and who early noted the bacterial disease of the chinch bugs, visited my laboratory last week. He expressed the hope that a series of field experiments such as are now being carried on in Kansas could be conducted in Illinois.

In closing, I may say that the outcome of the work so far this year is highly encouraging.

Since making this report the requests for infected bugs have grown much less numerous. The laboratory experiments have been carried on with more attention paid to bacteria. So far I have been unable to successfully infect bugs in the laboratory from pure cultures of Sporotrichum. The Sporotrichum grows readily on a medium composed of beef broth and Irish moss, and pure cultures are easily obtained. Other experiments with these cultures are necessary, however, to make this statement positive. Empusa will not fruit on the plates. It behaves very peculiarly. Long erect filaments are sent out strikingly different from the customary hyphæ, but no spores are produced. As regards the bacteria, I am assured that the forms in my cultures are identical with Burrill's *Micrococcus insectorum*, two slides of which have been furnished me by Professor Forbes. This Micrococcus is found almost without exception in bugs which have died in the field and been sent in for examination. Another Micrococcus, larger and almost perfectly circular in optical plane, is often present in dead and dying bugs. Spraying experiments with fluids containing this Micrococcus give no successful results in infection.

I am not in position at present to make a full report of the season's work in the field and laboratory. This report I shall make in the late fall.

* * * * * * *

Other injurious insects besides the chinch bug in Kansas especially noticeable this year were the Hessian Fly, in about the same abundance as usual. Much damage is annually done by this pest. The Wheat Straw Worm (*Isosoma tritici*) was reported from a dozen or more counties of the state in June. It occasioned considerable alarm and really did some damage to the wheat in central and western Kansas. I received reports of the presence of the worm from twenty-seven correspondents. It appeared in wheat which had been planted on stubble ground, though the state of affairs shown in one or two reports contradicted this general condition. One correspondent reports the worm in wheat planted on sod; another in a field of 40 acres new ground, only grown to wheat once before, plowed last fall and after the wheat had come up fed off so close that the field looked quite bare. The Wheat Head Army Worm (*Leucania albilinea*) was reported in June from a few fields. However, little damage was done.

An attempted grasshopper scare was put down by a little investigation. Grasshoppers were reported to be in immense numbers in eastern Colorado and overflowing into Kansas. I made a trip to the infested region and found the grasshoppers to be a local species (*Dissosteira longipennis*), which was in great abundance over about 300 square miles of country near Arriba, Colo. Of course, no danger to Kansas was to be feared from these locusts. Arriba is 70 miles west of the Kansas line. The limits of the infested area extended approximately from Limon 16 miles east, 9 miles north, 7 miles west, and diagonally southeast to Hugo, 15 miles. Within this area the two favored grasses of the range, buffalo and gramma grass, were eaten to the ground. The swarms when visited (July 17) were almost entirely composed of pupæ. Reports agree that the eggs from which these swarms were hatched were deposited last fall by the locusts which flew into this area in August and September from the south. And by observations during my trip and by regular reports received since then I discovered that the locusts as fast as their wings were acquired were flying south. Whenever there was a favoring wind from the north the winged individuals would rise high in the air and fly directly southward, having massed in great numbers along the southern boundary of the infested area. When the wind was from the south, however, no flying would be indulged in.

The rate of progress of the army of immature locusts was northward at the rate of 9 miles in about two weeks; eastward at the rate of $2\frac{1}{2}$ miles in 12 days. Over the face of the country traversed by the hosts the ground looked bare and brown, owing to the almost complete destruction of the grass leaves. When the devouring multitudes were at work upon the grass the noise of the grinding of their jaws was distinctly audible as a well-defined crackling sound. About the station of Limon the hogs of the town were fattening upon the locusts, which also furnished food for turkeys, chickens, and hawks.

REVISED LIST OF MEMBERS OF THE ASSOCIATION OF ECONOMIC ENTOMOLOGISTS.

AMERICAN MEMBERS.

William B. Alwood, Blacksburgh, Va.
J. M. Aldrich, Brookings, S. Dak.
William H. Ashmead, Department Agriculture, Washington, D. C.
George F. Atkinson, Auburn, Ala.
M. H. Beckwith, Newark, Del.
Charles J. S. Bethune, Port Hope, Ontario, Canada.
Lawrence Bruner, West Point, Nebr.
John P. Campbell, Athens, Ga.
F. H. Chittenden, Department Agriculture, Washington, D. C.
J. H. Comstock, Ithaca, N. Y.
A. J. Cook, Agricultural College, Mich.
D. W. Coquillett, Los Angeles, Cal.
A. B. Cordley, Department Agriculture, Washington, D. C.
E. W. Doran, Agricultural College, Md.
C. H. Fernald, Amherst, Mass.
James Fletcher, Ottawa, Ontario, Can.
S. A. Forbes, Champaign, Ill.
H. Garman, Lexington, Ky.
C. P. Gillette, Fort Collins, Colo.
F. W. Goding, Rutland, Ill.
C. W. Hargitt, Oxford, Ohio.
Charles A. Hart, Champaign, Ill.
F. L. Harvey, Orono, Me.
F. H. Hillman, Reno, Nev.
A. D. Hopkins, Kanawha Station, W. Va.
George H. Hudson, Plattsburgh, N. Y.
George D. Hulst, 15 Himrod street, Brooklyn, N. Y.
L. O. Howard, Department Agriculture, Washington, D. C.
D. S. Kellicott, Columbus, Ohio.

J. A. Lintner, State House, Albany, N. Y.
Otto Lugger, St. Anthony Park, Minn.
B. Pickman Mann, Patent Office, Washington, D. C.
C. L. Marlatt, Department Agriculture, Washington, D. C.
John Marten, Champaign, Ill.
H. A. Morgan, Baton Rouge, La.
Mary E. Murtfeldt, Kirkwood, Mo.
F. J. Niswander, Laramie, Wyo.
Herbert Osborn, Ames, Iowa.
A. S. Packard, Providence, R. I.
Theo. Pergande, Department Agriculture, Washington, D. C.
C. H. Perkins, Burlington, Vt.
E. A. Popenoe, Manhattan, Kans.
E. Baynes Reed, Esquimault, B. C.
C. V. Riley, Department Agriculture, Washington, D. C.
John B. Smith, New Brunswick, N. J.
F. H. Snow, Lawrence, Kans.
E. B. Southwick, Arsenal Building, Central Park, New York.
J. M. Stedman, Durham, N. C.
Jas. Stimson, M. D., Watsonville, Cal.
H. E. Summers, Knoxville, Tenn.
Roland Thaxter, New Haven, Conn.
J. W. Toumey, Tucson, Ariz.
C. H. T. Townsend, Las Cruces, N. Mex.
F. L. Washburn, Corvallis, Oregon.
F. M. Webster, Columbus, Ohio.
Clarence M. Weed, Hanover, N. H.
H. E. Weed, Agricultural College, Miss.
E. V. Wilcox, Columbus, Ohio.
C. W. Woodworth, Berkeley, Cal.

FOREIGN MEMBERS.

T. D. A. Cockerell, Kingston, Jamaica.
Eleanor A. Ormerod, Torrington House, St. Albans, England.

A. S. Olliff, Sydney, Australia.
Arthur E. Shipley, Cambridge, England.

EXTRACTS FROM CORRESPONDENCE.

Fertilization of Yucca in Australia.

Having read several of your letters relating to the pollinization of Yucca by *Pronuba* species exclusively, I understand why the plants have no fruit here where else they grow extremely well. However, either some of the Pronubas have been introduced here, of which I have no information, or else some native moth has adapted itself to the function, for on November 11, 1889, while on a visit to our Agricultural College at Roseworthy with the Field Naturalist Section of the Royal Society of South Australia, I noticed fruits in abundance on a tree in the garden of the director, Professor Lowrie, to which I drew the attention of several of the party at the time and also afterwards mentioned the fact in the Royal Society. As my office duties prevented my making observations personally at a distant locality, nothing further has been learned about the subject since. As I thought the matter might interest you, I inclose the only fruit secured at the time. * * *—[J. G. O. Tepper, Curator of Insects, Somerset Place, Norwood, South Australia, May 11, 1890.

REPLY.—I am very much obliged to you for your kindness in sending me the Yucca pod accompanying your favor of the 11th ultimo. * * * The Yucca pod showed no trace of *Pronuba* and the fertilization of the plant must be explained on the same exceptional grounds on which I have already explained similar pollinization of Yucca in other countries where *Pronuba* can scarcely occur. The pod, though very much shriveled, shows it to belong to the *aloifolia* section of the genus, but without a knowledge of the leaf and flower it would be risky to decide specifically. I shall be very much obliged to you if you can at some future time send a larger supply, since it frequently happens, even where *Pronuba* occurs, that the pods are free from its larva.—[June 16, 1890.]

A New Sawfly Enemy to Sweet Potatoes.

I have sent you by to-day's mail a box containing some flies and their eggs on some sweet potato leaves. Last year was the first time they made their appearance in my potato patch. They came the 1st of July and deposited their eggs on the leaves; when the eggs hatched these worms would eat the leaves to a comb. This continued for about 4 weeks. The potatoes, wherever the fly was, did not make any yield at all. This year the fly made its appearance at the same time they did last year. Will you please tell me what kind of a fly they are, and whether they will do any serious damage?—[George W. Stockley, Keller, Virginia, July 2, 1891.

REPLY.—The insect which you send is entirely new as an enemy of the Sweet Potato. It is a sawfly known scientifically as *Schizocerus privatus*. Some 5 years ago another species of the same genus was discovered feeding upon Sweet Potato at Ocean Springs, Mississippi. You will find it described on page 44 of no. 2, vol. I, of INSECT LIFE. Should this insect become very abundant it can be readily killed by the application of Paris green in the proportion of one-fourth of a pound of the poison to forty gallons of water. It is hardly likely, however, that it will prove to be much of a pest.—[July 8, 1891.]

Injurious Insects of Utah.

Utah is certainly a most unfavorable place to make observations in economic entomology, for there are neither grasshoppers nor crickets here this year. There is only one important insect enemy visible at the present season, viz, that Tent-caterpillar which has been sent to you on several occasions from this Territory. I failed to see it in Salt Lake City, as well as near Mill Creek, which is in the center of the lower cultivated (*i. e.*, irrigated) area of Utah. I saw it first at Park City at an altitude of about 9,500 feet, near the snow line, feeding on a species of wild *Cratægus*. Of course there is no horticulture carried on at this altitude, but since we are in the upper part of the cultivated district (east of Utah Lake) we find this Clisiocampa about as numerous and destructive as *Hyphantria cunea* is in the worst years at Washington. It is confined to the apple trees, and only when these are utterly defoliated does it attack the plum trees which are in the immediate vicinity, and then only such as have their branches interlocking with the apple. The caterpillars are now fullgrown and develop a marked migratory instinct; *i. e.*, very few web-up on the apple trees, but they descend and wander about, webbing up in fence corners, and more especially between the leaves of other bushes and trees, and by this habit they become injurious also to the gooseberries, currants, etc., because the webbed-up leaves of these are drying up. The species will no doubt have parasites, but I fail to find any insect enemies, since there are neither Calosomas nor large Heteroptera to be seen in the gardens. But there is a bacterial disease raging among the caterpillars, and thousands may be seen clinging, dead, to the fences or tree trunks. The pear and cherry trees are absolutely free from this pest, nor did I succeed in finding here a single specimen on the few wild-growing bushes (there are no trees here).

Not a single other orchard or field-crop pest seems to exist here, but in the gardens of Salt Lake City the Woolly Aphis, *Schizoneura lanigera*, has fairly established itself, doing great damage there, but apparently not yet distributed over the open country. The Cottony Maple Scale, *Pulvinaria innumerabilis*, is also at Salt Lake City on the box elder, *Negundo aceroides*, but not very abundant.—[E. A. Schwarz, American Fork, Utah, June 22, 1891.

Reappearance of the Wheat Straw-worm in Kansas.

I beg to inform you of the reappearance in damaging numbers of the "Wheat Straw-worm," your *Isosoma tritici*. It is quite prevalent throughout central and northwestern Kansas and the damage in some counties will be very severe. In this (McPherson) county, I do not estimate the damage to exceed 5 per cent. They occur usually above the joint near the head, showing that the eggs were deposited late in the season. As a result, but little damage is done, owing to the practical ripening of the head at this time and before the larva has had time to develop.—[W. Knaus, McPherson, Kans., June 18, 1891.

REPLY.—Thorough thrashing ought to reduce the numbers of this insect considerably; but if it does any great damage, we also have a remedy in our hands by sacrificing the straw and burning it, as so few of the insects will be found in the stubble that this source of reinfection is very slight.—[June 22, 1891.]

Allorhina Injuring Oaks.

It would be difficult at present to estimate the extent of injury done by the insects of which a specimen was sent you. They seem to increase in numbers, and their size and the hardness of their wing cases prevent the insectivorous birds from doing them much harm, though the jay birds appear to eat a few of them. The mocking birds, catbirds, etc., do not molest them.

They bore into and extract the sap from the tender branches of the trees, and the leaves soon wither, the branch becomes dry, and either of its own weight or from the force of the wind, breaks and hangs down. The natural growth about the town consists principally of black and scrub or post oaks, and the insects seem to prefer the juices of the black oak, almost entirely neglecting the other variety.

In feeding the insect confines itself, so far as I have been able to observe, to the tops of the trees, presumably because it finds there the new and consequently tender growth.—[Frank Triplett, Springfield, Mo., July 22, 1891.

NOTE.—The beetle referred to is *Allorhina nitida*.—Eds.

Ducks and the Colorado Potato Beetle: Additional Note.

In INSECT LIFE, vol. III, No. 9-10, page 390, I find an article on Ducks and the Colorado Potato Beetle. I wish to add a little experience of last year in my garden, where I had a small patch of potatoes. In this patch my two ducks and one drake were very partial and not one of the Philistines (bugs) could be found. We thought they had left for better clover feed, but on reading the article in INSECT LIFE I think it is another proof of the duck's usefulness in that field of labor or direction.—[John Taylor, New Sharon, Me., July 14, 1891.

Kerosene Emulsion Treatment for the Rose Chafer.

Having another year's experience with the Rose Chafer, I will relate it for the benefit of others. Last year, as I wrote you, I found shaking on stretchers saturated with crude petroleum the only effective remedy. This year I experimented with a preparation called sludgite, a combination of petroleum and soap. Found it of no avail. Then I prepared a lot of kerosene emulsion, 2 gallons of oil, 1 gallon of water, one-half pound common soap. First to test it I caught a number of the bugs, dipped them in the emulsion and found that every one died in a few minutes. I tried dipping in the sludgite solution and found that it did not kill them. Then I diluted the emulsion, one part of emulsion to eight parts of water. Found by dipping it was just as effective in killing the bugs as the standard emulsion. I sprayed my vines and found it killed some and disturbed all. Thinking this might not be effective, I discontinued on grape vines, but found a lot of cherry trees and peach trees infested with them. I sprayed about twenty cherry trees from which hundreds of bugs could have been picked, and was so successful that after two sprayings not a bug could be found; neither did they trouble the trees, either peach or cherry, again. I am inclined to think we may have an effective remedy in the emulsion, and I think it will be more effective when warmed.—[E. H. Wynkoop, Catskill, N. Y., July 31, 1891.

The Strawberry Weevil on Blackberries.

I inclose a few Curculionids that are proving quite destructive to the buds of blackberries (especially of the Wachusett variety) about here. I find nothing about any such pest in the literature of my own library. Can you give me the name or any references?—[George Dimmock, Canobie Lake, N. H., June 15, 1891.

REPLY.—This is a species commonly known in collections as *Anthonomus musculus* and which I have treated in my report for 1885 under the caption of "Strawberry Weevil." You will find a somewhat elaborate article in this report on pages 276 to 282, while the species is illustrated on Plate 7 at Figs. 5 and 6.—[June 18, 1891.]

Predaceous Habit of Histeridæ.

All of the authors which I have been able to consult upon the habits of Histeridæ (Packard, Harris, Le Baron, and Horn) state that these insects live in excrements, in decayed animal or vegetable matter, beneath the bark of trees, in ants' nests, and so on, but none of them even so much as hint at their predaceous habits. A few weeks ago I saw an adult *Hister sexstriatus* Lec. attack a nearly full-grown larva of *Agrotis ypsilon* Rott., seizing it with its jaws as a cat would a rat and holding on despite the attempts of the cut-worm to escape. This was late in the afternoon of a cloudy day, and as my time was limited, I placed both specimens in my cyanide bottle, where the unequal combat soon terminated.—[D. W. Coquillett, Los Angeles, Cal., June 8, 1891.

Imbricated Snout-beetle injuring Apple Trees.

I mail you a little box of bugs which I found in young apple trees ; the largest ones ate the young growth all off.—[H. J. Lamb, Stillwater, Payne County, Oklahoma, June 5, 1891.

REPLY.— * * * The beetle which is injuring the young growth of your apple trees is the so-called Imbricated Snout-beetle (*Epicærus imbricatus*). The breeding habits of this insect are not known, but your apple trees can probably be protected if the beetles are very numerous by spraying with Paris green or London purple in the proportion of 1 pound of the poison to 200 gallons of water.—[June 13, 1891.]

A Longicorn Pine-borer injuring Shoes.

We send a carton containing a bug and shoes which in our thirty years' experience we "never saw the like." You will see the tissue paper and hole in the box was evidently eaten by the bug. You will also notice the destruction to the shoes it has done. Please let us know what it is.—[Winch Bros., 150-156 Federal street, Boston, Mass., May 17, 1891.

REPLY.—The specimen is the common Longicorn Pine-borer (*Monohammus confusor* Kirby). It has probably hatched out from the pine wood of the shoebox and finding its way obstructed, it has tried to eat its way through, but has only succeeded in getting inside the box, neither pasteboard nor kid-skin being especially suited to its masticating powers.—[May 20, 1891.]

Blister Beetles on Cabbage.

An army of which these are specimens has possession of a large mature bed of cabbages, which they have riddled, and a footstep is enough to make them hurriedly drop to the soil, which, from their numbers, then resembles a vast colony on the move.—[Note made at Jacksonville, Florida, May 25, 1891. C. B. Bagster, Vineland, N. J.

REPLY.—The specimens are the Three-striped Blister-beetle (*Epicauta lemniscata* Fab.), previously known to occur in potato fields. Cabbage is a new food-plant for this species.

The European Leopard Moth injuring Maples.

FIRST LETTER.—On the 25th of June, 1890, I wrote you for information concerning a borer which has been damaging my young maple trees. I send you herewith the shell of the pupa and the moth itself. I refer you to vol. III, No. 4 of INSECT LIFE, page 161, which gives my letter and your views on the subject in the absence of the specimen I sent. This insect is doing great damage in my neighborhood.—[Thomas R. Clark, Riverside Park, New York, N. Y., July 6, 1891.

REPLY.—The insect is the so-called Leopard Moth (*Zeuzera pyrina*) introduced from Europe. It has now become firmly established in this country. In Europe it attacks the Linden, Soap tree, Walnut, Elm, Apple, Pear, Mountain Ash, Chestnut, Birch, Alder, and a few other trees. The moths usually issue in June, and there is probably one generation annually. This insect will be a difficult one to fight if, as is so often the case, it increases in numbers more rapidly in America than in its native home. With your young maples you are advised to spray with London purple or Paris green in the proportion of one-fourth pound of the poison to 50 gallons of water, just at this time of the year, in order to poison such larvæ as may be about hatching from the eggs and entering the twigs or trunks. Later in the season every branch which is observed to wilt should be pruned and burned with the contained larvæ.—[July 8, 1891.]

SECOND LETTER.—Since writing you I find that nearly all the maple trees in the streets of Astoria, Long Island, a suburb of this city, are filled on the under side of the branches with what look like little spots of white cotton wool about a quarter of an inch apart. They are so thickly lined with these that the branches on the under side look white. I find upon examination that these are the eggs of the moth, which, judging from one I have in my possession, must lay a mass of them in 24 hours. This being the first time I have noticed what I describe above and the first year that they have made their appearance in that section, I fear we are doomed to a great deal of trouble unless something can be used, not too costly, to destroy them.—[Thomas R. Clark, Riverside Park, New York City, July 13, 1891.

THIRD LETTER.—This year I have noticed a great number of the European Leopard Moth, the larvæ of which attack the Maple of every variety, except the Rock Maple, in the upper part of the city. The larvæ generally enter the trunks of young trees about two inches from the ground, although the height varies in some instances. They seem to bore upward very rapidly, attacking the heart of the tree, and rendering it so weak that a strong breeze will break it off.

This spring I have found in at least sixteen instances, within an area of 35 feet, the shell abandoned by the larvæ on its transformation into the moth state. The moths are large, and those confined lay large quantities of eggs in coils or ribbons, immediately upon emerging from the shell; they seem to exist without any sustenance for a week or more in confinement.

As this species is very new to this country I am watching the developments with interest, and will report later. The moths seem very tenacious of life, although sluggish. This insect, unless some effective plan of extermination is found, is going to prove very destructive to shade trees in this vicinity. Already I notice that the larvæ have developed to half the size of the moth, in the crotches of trees, covered by a very thin gauze or webbing only, so that the elements do not seem to affect them very much.—[Frederic F. Culver, 80 Broadway, New York City, July 17, 1891.

A Phycitid Moth attacking Pecan Buds.

I have mailed you to-day a box containing some of the chrysalides from the worms that attacked the pecan bud in the early spring, which may help to determine the kind. I would suggest that it may be what we call the "Careless Weed worm." Please let me hear from you as to what remedies to apply in early spring so that I could eradicate same.—[F. A. Swinden, Brownwood, Tex., June 17, 1891.

REPLY.—I have bred the moth, and find that it is probably new to science. I have reared the same thing here in the District of Columbia from the twigs of hickory It is entirely different from the insect which is the parent of what you call " Careless Weed worm," and is probably a specific enemy of the hickory. Knowing the habits of this early generation only it will be impossible to suggest an efficacious remedy.— [June 26, 1891.]

A Corn Crambus in Delaware.

I send you by this mail two specimens of the insects reared from the larvæ that were working on corn. These are the first that have appeared in my breeding cages. The larvæ can seldom be found at this date in the corn fields. I have made a thorough search and have been able to obtain a very few specimens of the larvæ.—[M. H. Beckwith, Newark, Del., July 17, 1891.

REPLY.—The specimens which you send show that the species damaging corn is *Crambus caliginosellus*, an insect which does precisely the same damage at Benning, Maryland, a few miles from Washington. We wrote up this insect in 1886, and had figures made, but the account has never been published.—[July 22, 1891.]

Treatment for the Horn Fly.

* * * In reply to your question "What is being done by the people in your neighborhood in regard to the Horn Fly?" I have to say, hardly anything. There is a spasmodic attempt being made to fight this pest, but nothing systematic. On our place we have several times thoroughly annointed our fattening cattle with a mixture of axle grease, tar, and carbolic acid. This keeps the fly from worrying them for several days. This week I had a mixture of fish oil, tar, and carbolic acid thoroughly rubbed over our milk stock. The flow of milk has not been very much increased as yet. Heretofore their time has been taken up in fighting the flies, which made them so restless it was hard to milk them at all. Now they stand much better and, in fact, this mixture has been of great benefit. I shall have it renewed in a few days, and shall advise our people through our county papers to use this or some similar remedy. If you find out any other remedies for this pest, keep me posted. * * *
—[J. S. Strayer, Port Republic, Va., June 26, 1891.

A New Enemy to Currants

I send you a bug which I find feeding on white and red currants. I have not been able to find it on any of the forest growth here and in 6 years have not seen one like it. I presume it is not an abundant insect.—[H. Stewart, Highlands, Macon County, North Carolina, June 10, 1891.

REPLY.—* * * The insect is the so-called Leaf-footed Plant-bug (*Leptoglossus phyllopus*). It is found commonly throughout the South and, although its habits are normally predaceous, it has occasionally been noticed to pierce cotton bolls and the buds of different plants. It has not before been noticed, so far as I am aware, as an enemy of currants. If it is sufficiently abundant to do much damage I would advise you to spray with a dilute kerosene emulsion made according to the formula given on page 3 of Circular No. 1, second series.—[June 22, 1891.]

A California Thrips on the Potato.

I mail you to-day specimens of a Thrips that is very injurious to the leaves of potato plants in various portions of Los Angeles County. I find them only on the under side of the leaves, and when numerous they cause the part of the leaf which they attack to wither and finally to die. I saw one field of about 100 acres of potatoes of which a large percentage of the plants had been seriously injured by these pests. I also found them in large numbers on Onion, and this species may prove to be the same as the one I sent you specimens of from onions last year. Besides potatoes and onions I also found them in large numbers on a plant commonly known as "Tumbleweed;" on this they were even more numerous than on the Potato. I would be glad to receive the name of this Thrips and to learn whether or not it is an introduced species. I am now carrying on a series of experiments against it with Paris green and whale-oil soap and will report results.—[D. W. Coquillett, Los Angeles, Cal., June 8, 1891.

REPLY.— * * * This is the same species which you sent last year upon onion, and is a new species of the true genus *Thrips*.—[June 17, 1891.]

Rocky Mountain Locust in North Dakota.

FIRST LETTER.—I send you by mail a few specimens of an insect that has made its appearance here in some spots in great numbers. We believe it to be the Rocky Mountain Locust. It was first noticed a week ago. They seem to have been hatched on stubble land that was not plowed. Their ravages have so far been confined to grain bordering on such land. At night they leave the grain and roost on the ends of prairie grass near by. Whenever they walk or jump it is towards the south,

They are reported from three neighborhoods.—[J. Dexter Peirce, Larimore, N. Dak., June 20, 1891.

REPLY.— * * * The insect is undoubtedly the Rocky Mountain Locust, *Caloptenus spretus*. Please send full particulars concerning the extent of country over which the insect occurs at present, and as to its numbers. Strenuous efforts should be made to stamp it out, and the best means to accomplish this are given in Bulletin No. 25 of this division. * * * [June 27, 1891.]

SECOND LETTER.—The locust, *Caloptenus spretus*, has made its appearance upon a strip of country about 10 or 15 miles wide, extending from Larimore, Grand Forks County, to the boundary line, and, I hear, north of the line. They appear almost entirely on unplowed stubble. Where they are thickest (judging by the pans) there are about two bushels on each acre, ranging from one-third grown to little ones. They do not cover all the country, but are in patches here and there.

There has been a feeble effort to fight them with pans containing tar or kerosene and water. The latter works best. The State is about to give up the fight, as there are no funds available. Funds and men are needed to fight them. People are very apathetic, especially outside the district already invaded. * * * Can the Government do anything for us? The States to the south are liable to be invaded if they are not stopped here. There are no funds available here, and the farmers are too poor to fight them themselves unless material is furnished them.—[J. Dexter Peirce, Larimore, N. Dak., July 3, 1891.]

[NOTE.—Owing to the fact that no appropriation was available to the authorities of the Department of Agriculture out of which materials for fighting the pest could be supplied, Mr. Peirce's request could not be granted. It was clearly a case for the State to take hold of, and two years ago Minnesota met similar conditions by a special appropriation, and by hard work and the expenditure of $3,500 the invasion of this insect was completely stamped out.]

Habits of Mantispa.

I send by to-day's mail a specimen for identification. I showed it to Prof. G. W. Dunn, of Oakland, Cal., and to Dr. Lorenzo Yates and Prof. H. C. Ford, both of this city, neither of whom could classify it. I shall feel greatly obliged if you will give me its class and name.—[T. N. Snow, Santa Barbara, Cal., June 12, 1891.

REPLY.— * * * It is a species of the Neuropterous genus Mantispa, a remarkable genus of which only three or four species are known in this country. So far as I know this one has not been specifically described. These insects are remarkable not only for their curious figure, which somewhat resembles that of the "Rear-Horse" or "Praying Mantis" of the order Orthoptera, but also from their habits, as their larvæ are parasitic in the egg-sacs of spiders. The eggs of the only species which has been carefully studied (a European form) are rose-red in color and are fastened upon stalks. They are laid in July and the larvæ issue 21 days later. They pass the winter without food and the following spring find their way into the nests of certain spiders, where they feed upon the young. The Mantispa larva undergoes two changes of form and in about a month changes to pupa, the adult issuing in time to lay the eggs the following July.—[June 23, 1891.]

A Correction.

In INSECT LIFE, vol. II, page 260, there is a note entitled "North European Dragon Flies," dealing with Dr. Trybom's paper "Odonater insamlade under Svenska expeditionen till Jenisej, 1876," and stating that these species were collected in "North Sweden." But the Yenisey River is in Siberia, and Siberia is not in Sweden nor in Europe at all. It is desirable that this curious mistake should be corrected. [E. Bergroth, Tammerfors, Finland.]

GENERAL NOTES.

LEAD-BORING INSECTS.

We notice in the *Scientific American* of June 13, 1891, an item quoted from the *Gesundheit's Ingenieur* of January 15, 1891, in which K. Hartmann relates a case of a lead pipe " cut through by an insect that was actually found with its head in the hole pierced by it. A workman was called to repair a defective pipe which had been injured on a previous occasion, as was reported, by a 'nail hole' occurring in a soldered joint. This time the worm (a 'wood wasp') causing the mischief was found *in situ*. The hole on the exterior of the pipe was of a rounded form, about one-quarter of an inch long by one-eighth inch wide, and the penetration was through the entire thickness of the metal."

FIG. 1.—Minié ball gnawed by wood-boring larva, nat. size (after C. R. Dodge).

A similar instance of an insect boring through metal was reported by Mr. Charles R. Dodge in *Field and Forest* for June, 1877, p. 217. He says:

We recently received a singular specimen of insect injury in the shape of a "minié" ball which had been gnawed through by a wood-boring larva. The ball had been fired into a red oak tree, probably during the war, and when split out of the log, a few days ago, was found in the track of a full grown larva, probably of an Orthosoma, the burrow leading directly through the bullet. This the grub had evidently struck at its concave end, boring two-thirds its length and coming out at one side, somewhat below the apex. The larva was found in the burrow, alive, only a short distance above the bullet, the latter nearly retaining its normal shape, the end only having been slightly flattened. The specimen was found by Dr. W. O. Eversfield near the Agricultural College, Maryland, and both bullet and larva are preserved together.

We publish an illustration of the minié ball described above, now preserved in the National Museum, showing the burrow of the larva from the concave end of the bullet upward and outward.

DAMAGE TO TURNIP AND SWEDE CROPS IN EASTERN BRITAIN.

Bell's Messenger of July 27 contains an account of the damage which is being done the present season on the east coast of Britain to the turnip and swede crops by the caterpillar of the Diamond-back Moth (*Plutella cruciferarum*), known in this country as the Cabbage Plutella. Miss Ormerod is said to have issued a leaflet on the subject and to have distributed it widely through the affected region. The principal districts affected are about Lowestoft, in Norfolk; Holbeach, in Lincolnshire, and several localities in Yorkshire and Northumberland, Berwick, the Lothians, Fife, and Forfar.

7911—No. 1——6

LOCUSTS IN THE VILAYET OF ALEPPO, SYRIA.

The following consular dispatch from Mr. E. Bissinger, United States consul at Beirut, transmitted by the Department of State to the Secretary of Agriculture, possesses considerable interest as indicating still further the prevalence of locusts all over the locust areas of the world during 1890 and 1891:

The province of Aleppo has not only been infested with the cholera, but invaded by locusts as well, as will be observed from the following brief report, based upon information from United States Consular Agent F. Poche, in Aleppo, which, in the abstract, is as follows:

The spring rains failed us this year in the vilayet of Aleppo, and in the mutessarrifiate of "Deir-el-Zor," and as the locusts did not find sufficient nourishment they invaded wheat, barley, cotton and sesame fields, sparing neither; nor did meadows, trees, or vegetable gardens escape these voracious creatures. In one word, there is desolation everywhere. Cotton and sesame fields are almost entirely destroyed, while wheat will barely yield one-half, and barley scarcely a third of the average yearly crops.

The evil could, in all probability, have been prevented, to a certain extent at least, had the measures usually adopted, been employed in time. These consist of—

I. The plowing of the ground about the middle of July in those localities where the locusts are known to have deposited their eggs.

II. The buying up, beginning of this period to the time of their hatching, of all the eggs deposited.

II. Collecting and burying the locusts; this to be done from the time of hatching until able to fly.

By honestly and intelligently employing the funds designated for this purpose, the gravity of the situation might have been greatly diminished, even if the evil could not have been entirely abated; as it is, the £2,000, voted by the State, and the £3,000, collected from the people, have been lost to the Treasury and to the people, as no efforts were made until after the locusts were able to fly and had ravaged the country.

ANOTHER GOVERNMENT ENTOMOLOGIST APPOINTED.

Information has reached us of the appointment of our valued correspondent, Mr. A. Sidney Olliff, late assistant in the museum at Sydney, to the newly instituted office of entomologist in the Department of Agriculture of New South Wales. His duties will consist largely in the investigation of insects affecting fruits and crops, and in publishing, for the benefit of the agriculturist, the results of his studies.

A CURIOUS BIT OF ENTOMOLOGICAL CLASSIFICATION.

The time-honored joke of the verdict of the English railway guard concerning the classification of the "'edge-'og as a hinsect" is paralleled by an item from *Bell's Messenger*, (London, July 27, 1891), in which it is stated that a collection of butterflies, consigned to a high legal official in Duisburg, Germany, was detained at the custom-house. Upon inquiry the fact was elicited that the customs officials had come to the conclusion that, as butterflies have wings, they must be classed as poultry, and so be subjected to the same duty. It was only after much time and patience had been expended on the part of the entomologist that the officials concluded that the butterflies came under the domain of science and art and were not subject to duty.

A CRITICISM OF CIRCULAR NO. 1 OF THIS DIVISION.

In the *Scientific American* of July 25, Mr. N. W. Motheral, of Hanford, Cal., criticises the resin, caustic soda, and fish-oil wash given upon page 4 of circular No. 1 of this division as a remedy against the San José scale (*Aspidiotus perniciosus*), stating that it is not only comparatively worthless but harmful to the tree. In recommending this wash we distinctly stated that it should only be applied in winter or during the dormant period, and that during the growing period it will cause the loss of foliage and fruit. As a substitute, Mr. Motheral recommends a mixture of lime and sulphur diluted with water. This mixture, while it will probably destroy the young lice during their hatching period, will, in our estimation, have no effect upon the insects after the scale is formed, while the resin wash absolutely prevents hatching.

THE HOST PLANTS OF NORTH AMERICAN APHIDIDÆ.

Another new worker comes forward in the person of Mr. T. A. Williams, of South Dakota, who has just published, as special bulletin No. 1 from the Department of Entomology of the University of Nebraska, a tolerably complete list of the food-plants of the Aphididæ of North America. The list seems full and will undoubtedly be of considerable value. We greatly regret, however, that the author has not made it bibliographical, at least to the extent of indicating the original descriptions of the species mentioned, for to use it in its present shape requires a thorough knowledge of the literature of the group.

A NEW RADISH ENEMY IN CALIFORNIA.

We have received from Dr. James H. Lowe, Knight's Ferry, Cal., the eggs and newly hatched young of a bug which he found upon the leaves of Radish, and which is quite probably *Murgantia munda*.

NORTH AMERICAN SPECIES OF TRYPOXYLON.

We have received a valuable paper on the North American species of the Digger Wasps of the genus Trypoxylon, by Mr. William J. Fox, of Philadelphia. He finds twenty species in this genus, and carefully tabulates them, following his table with full descriptions of each species. The work is evidently done with such care that it encourages us in the hope that we have here a student who will eventually bring the fossorial Hymenoptera into such a condition that these interesting insects can be readily determined by collectors.

DESTROYING THE ROSE CHAFER.

Mrs. George Chrisman, of Rockingham County, Va., in a letter to the *Country Gentleman* of July 2, 1891, proposes a novel course to be followed under certain circumstances in fighting this noted pest. She has observed that during the first day of their appearance they follow a stream or damp ground of some sort, never flying high, and can be tracked to the hatching ground in that way. She drains the hatching grounds and applies salt heavily as a fertilizer. On the second day, according to her observations, they seem to be stronger, and leave the water course, flying higher, when it is difficult to track them. The circumstances in her locality seem to be peculiar, but where similar surroundings are found her plan is a good one.

QUASSIA FOR THE HOP APHIS.

Washington and Oregon hop-growers are again trying some of the old remedies against the Hop Aphis. Among these a strong decoction of quassia chips, diluted at the rate of one hundred gallons of water to "a few gallons" of the decoction, was recently recommended through the columns of a California journal. Careful experiments made in the New York hop yards some years ago (see Report of the Entomologist, 1888) showed that while a similar wash kills the lice when they are reached, it will not spread like an oily mixture, and it is therefore greatly inferior to a well prepared kerosene emulsion.

SILK NESTS OF MEXICAN SOCIAL LARVÆ.

In reference to the note on pages 482–483 of vol. III, with the above heading, Mr. S. H. Scudder has kindly referred us to his remarks on page 1,038 of his "Butterflies of New England," in which, in discussing the general characteristics of the sub-family Pierinæ, he refers to species in the subfamily which are social, including *Aporia cratægi*, a European caterpillar, which lives in company "beneath a web spread over the hawthorn bushes." He refers to the Mexican species as *Eucheira socialis*, which is found at an elevation of 3,200 metres above the sea, "where the nest, as described by Humboldt and Westwood, is 8 inches long, and made of tough layers of parchment-like silk, which Humboldt says can be used as writing paper, and indeed was used as such by the early Spanish fathers. It is suspended from a tree, and has a hole in the bottom for the entrance and exit of the caterpillars. Within this sac they undergo their transformations, and, being thus protected, the chrysalids are attached to the inner walls by their hinder extremity only, having no need of the supporting girth that is otherwise invariably used throughout this family."

In reference to the same item, our esteemed correspondent, Dr. Alfred Dugés, of Guanajuato, Mexico, has sent us the following:

In INSECT LIFE, vol. III, Nos. 11 and 12, p. 483, I find the description of a large cocoon found on the *Madroño* (*Arbutus* sp.?), and I notice that it is not known to what

Lepidopteron to attribute it. We have at Guanajuato (Santa Rosa mountains) exactly similar cocoons on the *Madrono*. These are the nests of *Eucheira socialis* Westw., as I have been able to assure myself. I have only one specimen of this butterfly, of which I have been able to breed neither larva nor pupa; but in the month of December many of these cocoons are brought to Guanajuato as curiosities only, for they serve no useful purpose, though it is possible to write perfectly well on their surface. I have felt impelled to give you these details, in order to clear up the obscure point of the question.

A STRANGE STORY.

Under the caption "Millions of Fire-flies," the *Philadelphia Times* publishes a strange story, which we reproduce herewith in its entirety. Equally startling accounts are of constant occurrence in our daily papers, some of them true and many otherwise. Of the former, several have received mention in INSECT LIFE, notably in vol. III (p. 477), where several cases are cited of insects occurring in such swarms as to cause temporary stoppage of whole railway trains.

The so-called "fire-flies" are not true flies, but beetles of the family Lampyridæ. They are not known to migrate, and such a swarm as here reported and the consequent illumination seem hardly credible. To cause such an illumination not millions but billions of the beetles would be required. Yet the congregation of these insects in such exceptional numbers is not impossible, and we would be glad of any verification of this report from any of the readers of INSECT LIFE:

DUNBAR, *August* 12.

This town was a night or two ago treated to a most remarkable and beautiful spectacle. Shortly after dusk the people were surprised and puzzled to behold what appeared to be a cloud of light come sweeping up from the woods lying back of the town, but on reaching the streets it was seen that the light was occasioned by an immense swarm of fire-flies. This swarm, numbering millions, dispersed itself through the village, illuminating everything with a light more golden than that of day, and warmer than the moon's cold beams.

People recognized each other without difficulty, and the print of a newspaper was to be read with ease. The houses were filled with the darting, flashing insects, which seemed to be panic-stricken from some mysterious cause. Lamps were extinguished by the swarms, and carpets ruined by them as they were crushed by the foot, while delicate plants and flower beds were destroyed by the weight of the clustering flies.

It took several hours for the swarm to pass through the town, but it slowly disappeared in the direction of the river, lighting the fields as it went, alarming the country people as it approached and arousing the cattle and poultry, which seemed to mistake it for dawn. Nothing being seen of it next day, and no report of its being seen elsewhere having been received, it is believed that it gradually dispersed itself over the marshes. Where the insects came from is also a matter of conjecture, as well as the reason of the sudden invasion. On the morning after their visit they were found in drifts under the hedges and fences, and against the sides of the houses, while quantities of provisions left exposed were destroyed by their presence.

WAS HE CRAZED BY MOSQUITOES OR BY HEAT?

In the last issue of INSECT LIFE (vol. III, p. 487) a case was cited of a boy having become insane from destroying caterpillars. The *North*

American, of Philadelphia, of August 13, 1891, instances the following similar case, insanity occurring, it was believed, from the poisonous bites of mosquitoes:

ELIZABETH, N. J., *August* 13.

Alexander Gordon, a fancy goods dealer here, became a raving maniac to-day from loss of sleep caused by the torture he endured from mosquito bites, combined with the intense heat. He ran through the streets with nothing on but his drawers, and when finally captured by the police, he tore off the only garment he had on, and it was necessary to wrap a rubber blanket around him to get him to the county jail, where he had to be put in a strait-jacket. It is said his blood had been poisoned by New Jersey's venomous pests.

THE TRUE MALE OF POCOTA GRANDIS.

In his synopsis of the North American Syrphidæ Dr. Williston describes this large and handsome Syrphid fly from a single specimen from the State of Washington which is now in the collection of the U. S. National Museum. By a clerical or proof-reader's error, the sex of the type is stated in the synopsis to be male. Prof. O. S. Westcott, however, last May, sent us the true male, which he collected on Vancouver Island the summer before. The male has the contiguous eyes found in allied species and genera, but the most remarkable thing about it is a long curved spine at the base of the middle femora, and which is one-third the length of the femur itself; otherwise this sex does not differ from the female. Professor Westcott captured the specimens on an enormous elder bush.

SPECIAL NOTES.

Entomological Work at the Iowa Experiment Station.*—This Bulletin contains, as its fifth article, reports of the entomological work of Herbert Osborn and H. A. Gossard. The subtitles are: The Clover-seed Caterpillar (*Grapholitha interstinctana* Clem.), Experiments with the Hopperdozer for Grass Leaf-hoppers, Kerosene emulsion for Plant-lice, Note on Grasshoppers, The Flavescent Clover-weevil (*Sitones flavescens* All.), and the Wheat Bulb-worm (*Meromyza americana*). As the first of these articles appeared in the last number of INSECT LIFE in the Proceedings of the Association of Economic Entomologists, it will not require further mention. The second describes a home-made hopperdozer and the results of its use on the campus of the Iowa Agricultural College. Many grass leaf-hoppers were captured, and multitudes of the Clover Mite (*Bryobia pratensis*) were also caught. The hay crop from the treated portion of the campus was compared with that taken from an untreated portion of the same size, with a result of 34 per cent in favor of the treated plat. The authors conclude that the yield of hay or pasture land may be increased from one-fourth to one-third at a cost not exceeding 10 cents per acre, by the use of the hopper-dozer. The conclusion arrived at from experiments with kerosene emulsion for plant lice is, that this substance is a perfect remedy against these insects, if the application is thoroughly made, and that it need not be repeated to give certain results. The note on grasshoppers comprehends a brief summary of the outbreaks of the season and a few paragraphs upon the ordinary remedies. The most interesting note in the bulletin is that announcing the appearance of *Sitones flavescens* in injurious numbers upon clover in Iowa. This weevil is imported from Europe, and while it has been found to be abundant in clover fields in the Eastern States during the past few years, its occurrence as far west as Iowa is unwelcome news. The Wheat Bulb-worm has been found at Ames in moderate numbers, but it is preyed upon abundantly by *Coelinius*, its Braconid parasite, and injurious multiplication is not feared.

---
* Iowa Agricultural Experiment Station, Bulletin No. 14, Des Moines, August, 1891.

Annual Report of the Entomologist of the New Jersey Experiment Station.—Prof. J. B. Smith's Annual Report as Entomologist of the Agricultural Experiment Station of New Jersey has just been published as an author's extra from the Annual Report of the Station for 1890. The report includes a reconsideration of the different topics which have been treated in the bulletins published from time to time during the year, together with a few additional notes on insects of less importance than those treated in the bulletins. A most interesting appendix to this report is a series of chemical tests, mainly with London purple, Paris green, and white arsenic, made by the chemist of the New Jersey Station. These tests were undertaken with a view of indicating the exact proportions of lime and water to be added to the arsenical mixtures to prevent the burning of the foliage of the plants treated, and were suggested by certain statements made by Mr. Gillette, of the Colorado Station. It was found that the object of adding the lime water was to take up the soluble arsenic and unite with it in the form of normal calcium arsenite, which is insoluble in water. The amount of arsenious oxide in London purple varies considerably in different samples, but for ordinary use it is recommended that a mixture of one pound of London purple to three-fourths of a pound of fresh lime be thoroughly mixed in one gallon of hot water and allowed to digest about two hours. If the water can be conveniently kept hot during the entire time, it will be advisable to do so. Water can then be added in sufficient quantities to bring it to the desired strength, and it will be found that, with the average sample of the purple, the soluble arsenic has been taken up by the lime. In Paris green there is a very small amount of soluble arsenic—in one sample only 0.4 per cent was found. This small quantity can be readily rendered insoluble by the addition of a small quantity of lime when mixing. With white arsenic, a substance which we have only been able to use with cold water, without injury to the trees, experiments show that, by the addition of lime in the proportion of 1.5 parts by weight to 1 part of the arsenious oxide, all of the soluble arsenic will be made insoluble.

Bacterial Disease of the Chinch Bug.—We have just received from Prof. S. A. Forbes, State entomologist of Illinois, a copy of his paper entitled, "On a Bacterial Insect Disease," reprinted from the September number of the *North American Practitioner*. The disease, *Micrococcus insectorum* Burrill, is confined to a single portion of the digestive tract, which is fully described. The closing remarks, particularly the paragraph bearing upon the economic value of the disease, are specially interesting and conform so closely to our own views in the matter, and have such an important bearing on Prof. Snow's work, that we quote them entire:

Concerning the utilization of artificial cultures of Micrococcus for a propagation of this disease among insects not affected, I am at present able to say but little, as I have not yet succeeded, in either season when it was common, in finding lots of chinch bugs sufficiently free from it to make them suitable subjects for experimental attempts at its transfer. It will be readily understood by any one that it is useless to test the utility of artificial cultures of the disease germs by applying them to insects which are already affected by the disease in question. The first step of any really scientific investigation of the economics of this matter is to determine positively the absence of the disease in the lots of insects to be used in the experiments. Every lot of chinch bugs thus far obtained by me from central, south central, and northern Illinois during the months of July and August of this year gave evidence, under critical study, of the presence of this microbe in the cœca of a larger or smaller percentage of pupæ and imagos. My previous observations—less carefully made, however, than my recent ones—have been to the general effect that hibernating chinch bugs and young preceding the so-called pupa state are little liable to the spontaneous occurrence of the intestinal trouble, and I consequently do not despair of finding, before the present season is over, opportunity for experiments which will determine beyond question the economic value of this chinch bug cholera.

In comparing this with similar human diseases we must take account of the poverty of the circulatory fluid of the chinch bug and the simplicity of its circulatory apparatus, which forbid the marked development of any of their phenomena of fever or inflammation. Indeed, it seems to me that insect diseases generally are characterized by the absence of a vigorous physiological reaction which their relatively low structure, nervous and circulatory, makes impossible. The features of this disease, for example, I think may be wholly accounted for, consistently with the physiology of the insect, as results of the simple destruction of the epithelium of the cœca and the consequent suppression of the functions of those organs, combined with the toxic effects of the products of bacterial action.

Is it not quite possible that the student of pathology may find in the study of the diseases of those lower forms of life, experiments prepared for him by Nature which it would be quite impossible for him to imitate on animals of more complicated sensitive and sympathetic organization; and that he may thus sometimes simplify a problem whose complexity must otherwise prevent its solution?

Injurious Insects of New South Wales.—Since we last referred to the entomological matter in the *Agricultural Gazette of New South Wales*, we have received parts 4, 5, and 6 of volume II. Mr. Olliff has, in part 4, an interesting article on the Fig Leaf Beetle (*Galerucella semipullata*), a species which feeds in all stages on the young shoots and foliage of wild and cultivated figs. Figures of all stages are given, as well as a detailed account of the life history. Spraying with Paris green is recommended as a remedy. In part 5 the same author treats of a Tachinid parasite of the Plague Locust, figuring it in all stages, and giving a technical description by Mr. F. A. Skuse under the name *Masicera pachytili*. This parasite has appeared in great numbers, and in one locality from 60 to 70 per cent of the grasshoppers were affected by it. He also makes some mention in the same number of a species of Chermes on Pine, the Oyster-shell Bark-louse of the Apple, and the Orange Rust-mite. In part 6, Mr. Olliff publishes an account of the Pine Case-moth, *Oiketicus huebneri*, with a full-page plate illustrating its transformations. It is closely related to the Bag Worm of the United States, and has proved a serious pest to the Pine in New South Wales. He also mentions the fact that one of the walking-stick insects, known as *Podacanthus wilkinsoni*, has been damaging Eucalyptus trees in the vicinity of Walcha, New England, New South Wales. The same number contains a description of *Dactylopius herbicola*, a new scale insect infesting the stems of grass near Penrith, New South Wales, by Mr. W. M. Maskell.

Economic Entomology in Mississippi.*—In Bulletin No. 14, of the Mississippi Station, received September 24, Mr. H. E. Weed treats of the Screw Worm, the Pea and Bean Weevils, the Striped Cucumber-beetle, the Peach-tree Borer, the Ox Warble Fly, the Plum Curculio, the Codling Moth, insecticides, and spraying machinery. The Screw Worm article is a thorough and careful summary of the habits of the insect, drawn up from personal observation. The best remedy is said to depend upon the condition of the wound. Preference is given to chloroform in a fresh case, and to carbolic acid in older cases. In treating of remedies for the Pea and Bean weevils we notice that Mr. Weed adopts the plan suggested by Prof. A. J. Cook, of inserting a gas pipe to the bottom of the quarantine bin in order to send the carbon bisulphide to the bottom of the mass of peas. This, as we have elsewhere stated, involves an erroneous principle, and we have recommended that the bisulphide be placed in shallow vessels on the *top* of the weevil-infested mass, as the vapor is heavier than air and falls rather than rises. The peas, beans, or grain will be more thoroughly permeated in this way. The other articles are mainly compiled.

A Bulletin on Plant-lice, from Wyoming.†—Mr. F. J. Niswander, the recently appointed entomologist of the Wyoming Experiment Station, has published a short bulletin on the subject of Plant-lice, which we notice as the first entomological publication from this State. The bulletin gives the habits of Plant-lice in a general summary, but mentions particularly the species occurring upon Cottonwood, *Pemphigus populimonilis*, and *Chaitophorus riminalis*. A number of the natural enemies are mentioned, and the kerosene emulsion (Cook formula) is recommended as a remedy, whether or not from the author's experience does not appear.

---

* Mississippi Agricultural Experiment Station, Bulletin No. 14, Injurious Insects. Howard Evarts Weed, Entomologist, Agricultural College, Mississippi, March, 1891.
† Wyoming Experiment Station, Bulletin No. 2. Plant-lice. Laramie, August, 1891.

The Wheat Midge in Ohio.*—In a recent bulletin of the Ohio Agricultural Experiment Station our agent, Mr. F. M. Webster, treats of the Wheat Midge, and brings together all of the earlier references to the appearance, spread, and depredations of this species within the State of Ohio. He republishes Fitch's figures of the insect and summarizes the life history, recommending as the only thoroughly practical preventive the deep plowing of the wheat stubble in the fall, thereby covering the insects so deep in the earth that they are unable to reach the surface in the spring. This should be done as soon as possible after harvest. The burning of the stubble before plowing is also recommended, and a rotation of crops is said to add to the efficacy of the plowing. The author has found larvæ, which he thinks belong to this species, under the sheaths of young plants. He has also reared the adults from the heads of rye in July and from volunteer wheat from September 1 to November 3.

Injurious Insects in Queensland.—We have just received Bulletin No. 10 of the Department of Agriculture of Queensland, which is a report of several agricultural conferences held in Queensland during 1891. One of the papers published in this bulletin is an abstract of an address given by Prof. E. M. Shelton, who recently went out from this country to take a position in Queensland. His address dealt with the subject of insect pests, and was an admirable summary of some of the general facts connected with economic entomology. He spoke particularly of the arsenical sprays and the use of kerosene emulsion, and exhibited a spray pump and cyclone nozzle, showing the character of the spray. He recommended the bisulphide of carbon for grain weevils, and announced the fact that he was experimenting with kainit as a fertilizer and as a remedy for underground insects. His remarks were received with much interest, and the agriculturists of Queensland are evidently very much alive to the necessity for work against injurious insects.

A Bulletin from New Mexico.†—Mr. Townsend treats, in his first bulletin as entomologist of the New Mexico Agricultural College Experiment Station, of some of the insects injurious to fruits in that Territory. The insects treated are the Grape Leaf-hopper, the Grapevine Flea-beetle, The Codling Moth, the Oyster-shell Bark-louse, the Woolly Root Aphis of the Apple, the Scurfy Bark-louse, the Apple-tree Tent-cater-

---
* Bulletin of the Ohio Agricultural Experiment Station, Second Series, vol. IV, No. 5, September 1, 1891. Article VIII, The Wheat Midge, *Diplosis tritici*, by F. M. Webster, Consulting Entomologist.

† New Mexico Agricultural College Experiment Station. Bulletin No. 3. A preliminary account of some insects injurious to fruits, by C. H. Tyler Townsend, Las Cruces, January, 1891.

pillar, the Peach-tree Borer, the Peach Aphis, the Green June-bug *(Allorhina nitida)* the Plum Aphis, and the Twelve-spotted Diabrotica. The bulletin is a summary of the known habits of these species, with indications of the best methods of treatment, the article on the Vine Leaf-hopper being perhaps the most important.

Corrections to Packard's Report on Forest Tree Insects.—We call attention to a valuable article, in another part of this number, by Dr. John Hamilton, regarding certain corrections and additions to Dr. Packard's report on forest insects.

The changes which Dr. Hamilton proposes in the nomenclature of various species of Coleoptera are justified by the law of priority, and nearly all of his other corrections and suggestions are fully justified. Similar synonymical or critical notes could be made in nearly all the other orders of insects, and no one will be more thankful to receive them than Dr. Packard himself, as he has particularly requested such corrections and additions, and is fully aware of the imperfections of the report in this respect. It is further due to ourselves to state in this connection that while aiding Dr. Packard so far as time would permit in the getting out of the report, it was utterly impossible and would have been entirely inappropriate to include all the facts and information at our command, and that for want of time the unpublished notes which were furnished to Dr. Packard were limited to certain trees and were neither revised nor amplified. In connection with Dr. Hamilton's coleopterological comments it may be well to add a few further facts and suggestions, referring, as he has done, to the pages of Packard's report which evoke them.

In cases where economic articles are quoted from the older American authors, the names employed by said authors should, in our judgment, be used in note or brackets, where they are superseded by some prior name. If, for instance, *Hylurgops glabratus* Zett. is used to supersede the name of *Hylastes pinifex* Fitch, without reference to the latter's name, it would be difficult for anyone not especially familiar with the synonymy of Coleoptera to refer, for the sake of identification, to Fitch's original article.

In reference to the misapplication of popular names which Dr. Hamilton calls attention to, in the case of *Magdalis olyra* Hb., the same may be said of a large number of other names. When the names are based on the food-habit, they have become misnomers chiefly through subsequent experience and investigation having multiplied the food-plants. A striking case in point is that of the Clover Stem-borer (*Languria mozardi*), which is now known to bore in the stems of a number of common weeds.

(Page 215.) *Balaninus rectus* Say.—Our article quoted by Dr. Packard was published in the *Canadian Entomologist* just 20 years ago (vol.

III, 1871, pp. 137, 138), or before the appearance of the synopsis of *Balaninus* by Dr. Horn, and long before that by Mr. Blanchard. After the appearance of the former paper we had ascertained by further rearing and comparison that the specimens formerly considered by us as *B. rectus* were all referable to *B. uniformis* Lec.

We take this opportunity to place on record an abstract of our notes on the breeding habits of this genus.

Balaninus proboscideus Fabr.—Bred in August, 1881, from Chinquapin nuts collected at Washington, D. C., in September, 1880. The larvæ were noticed to leave the nuts on September 30, 1880.

One beetle found by Mr. L. O. Howard, October 3, 1879, with its beak imbedded in a Chinquapin nut near Washington, D. C.

One beetle received from Massachusetts with the note "from Chestnut."

Balaninus caryæ Horn.—One specimen bred from Hickory nuts, August 3, 1871, at St. Louis, Mo.

Specimens bred July 13, 1877, from Hickory nuts collected at St. Louis, Mo., October 8, 1876.

One specimen is marked "Bred from acorn September 17, 1873," but no further notes are preserved.

Several specimens received November 21, 1885, from Mr. J. T. Richardson, Clarksville, Montgomery County, Tenn., with the statement that they puncture the stalks of tobacco plants.

Balaninus rectus Say.—Two specimens bred from Chinquapin nuts collected at Washington, D. C., September, 1880.* One specimen issued from the ground on August 16, 1881, and the other on February 15, 1882.

Several specimens bred July 30, 1886, from larvæ infesting Chestnuts received November 2, 1885, from Mr. Fred H. Card, Sylvania, Bradford County, Pa.

Balaninus uniformis Lec.—Several specimens marked "bred from acorns September 17, 1873" without further notes. Others bred April 26, 1875, from acorns collected near St. Louis, Mo., October 17, 1874. On September 21, 1875, one of these larvæ was still alive.

One specimen found on leaves of Hazel, Cadet, Mo., Mr. J. G. Barlow, Oct. 1, 1886.

Balaninus quercus Horn.—Specimens bred from acorns by Mr. J. Pettit, of Grimsby, Ontario, were received October, 1871.

Balaninus nasicus.—One specimen bred April 26, 1875, from the same lot of acorns from which *B. uniformis* was obtained (see above).

Many specimens bred in April and May, 1883, from acorns of *Quercus grisea* received July 26, 1882, from Mr. H. K. Morrison, Fort Grant, Ariz. (This is published in Dr. Packard's report.)

(Page 470.) *Chrysomela pallida* Say.—This article has many errors. The description of the larva is credited to Mr. French instead of to Mr. Coquillett (*Canad. Entom.* XV, 1883, p. 21). The description itself would apply to many Chrysomelid larvæ but can not be referred to any species

---

*This is the same lot of Chinquapin nuts from which *B. proboscideus* had been bred as mentioned above.

of *Chrysomela* or *Doryphora*. The description of the imago is a copy of Say's description of *Colaspis pallida*, now known as *Metachroma pallidum*,* and the reason why Dr. Packard considered this as being identical with Coquillett's species is not clear unless he was misled by Mr. Coquillett's incorrect reference to Say as the author of his species, and the fact that Dr. Packard gives 15 millimetres as the length of the beetle instead of $\tfrac{15}{100}$ of an inch adds to the confusion. In the absence of typical specimens it is difficult to determine positively Mr. Coquillett's species, though it is probably *Chrysomela pallida* of Linnæus, now known as *Gonioctena pallida* Linn., which Prof. A. J. Cook reports as injurious to *Populus tremuloides* in Michigan.

(Page 529.) *Galeruca sanguinea*.—Packard's description of the beetle, according to Mr. Schwarz, can only be referred to *Galeruca (Adimonia) caricollis* Lec., which is a common northern species.

(Page 660.) *Micracis suturalis* Lec.—Dr. Hamilton's statement that this species, as well as *M. aculeata*, requires two years for its development is of great interest and in contradistinction to previous experience regarding the life duration of Scolytidæ.

(Page 367.) *Apion rostrum*.—Mr. Schwarz has already pointed out (Proc. Entom. Soc. Washington, II, No. 1, 1891, p. 76) that this species should no longer be referred to among the Black Locust insects and that the *Apion* so common on this tree is *A. nigrum* Hbst.

(Page 372.) *Spermophagus robiniæ*.—The impossibility of this species breeding in the seeds of *Robinia pseudacacia* has also already been pointed out by Mr. Schwarz (l. c.). Eichhoff asserts that there are two annual generations; while Judeich and Nitsche, the latest authorities, state that the development is not as regular as described by former authors, and that, in some species at least, three generations are distributed over two years. At any rate, no species is said to have a biennial generation, and before accepting the corrections of Dr. Hamilton's statement we would suggest the retardation in development caused by indoor breeding.

The first introduction of Blastophaga psenes into California.—On page 408, volume III, we published some correspondence relative to the desirability of importing the European Blastophaga into California for the Smyrna fig. We have recently seen numerous newspaper statements to the effect that such an importation has already been accomplished the present summer, but these accounts have been conflicting in some important points and lacking in essential details. We, therefore, take pleasure in giving in this number an authoritative account of the successful experiment from the pen of Mr. Gustav Eisen, of San Francisco, a well-known authority on grape and fig culture, with whom we have corresponded for some time upon this subject.

---

* The larvæ of the species of *Metachroma* still remain unknown, but there is every reason to believe that they are root-feeders and not leaf-feeders.

THE LARGER CORN STALK-BORER.*

(*Diatræa saccharalis* F.)

By L. O. Howard.

The attention of English-speaking people was first called, in a scientific way, to the ravages of a lepidopterous borer in sugar-cane by the Rev. Lansdown Guilding in his account of the insects infesting the sugar-cane, in the Transactions of the Society of Arts, 1828, vol. XLVI, pp. 143–153. He described the insect as *Diatræa sacchari*, and for his paper, which comprehended also an account of the sugar-cane and palm weevils, he was awarded the gold Ceres medal of the society. His studies were made in the island of St. Vincent in the West Indies, and from its occurrence there at this early date, and from Guilding's statement that it had been long known, there is reason to suppose that the insect may be an indigene of South America or of the West Indies, where the cultivation of sugar-cane was first begun in America.

In 1856 a select committee, appointed to investigate the damage caused by the cane borer in Mauritius, reported through W. Bojer, and the insect, which is called in the report *Proceras sacchariphagus*, was treated at some length, and an account was given of its introduction into the island. In the same year Westwood reviewed this report at length in the *Gardeners' Chronicle* of July 5, gave a woodcut of the insect, and pointed out that it was probably identical with the species described by Guilding at St. Vincent. He also called attention to the fact that the species named many years previously by Fabricius as *Phalæna saccharalis* is probably the same thing.

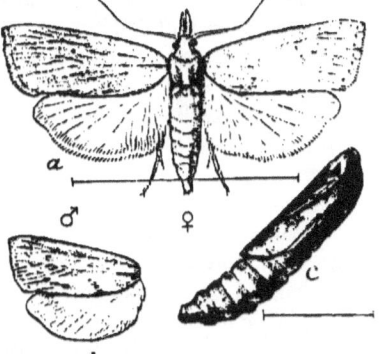

Fig. 2.—*Diatræa saccharalis*: *a*, female; *b*, wings of male; *c*, pupa—enlarged (original).

This insect was described by Fabricius (*Entomologia systematica*, vol. III, part 2, p. 238), from South America, no more definite locality being given. The probabilities are, however, that he refers to Dutch Guiana on account of the early settlement of that country and from the fact that he refers to a figure of the larva by Myhlenfels. He makes the statement that it feeds in sugar-cane, perforating and destroying the stalks and becoming a pest in plantations. He describes the larva as six-footed, of a pale hyaline color, and with the head and eight spots brown. The larval description, however, is drawn up from a figure by Myhlenfels, which may have

---

* Read before the Society for the Promotion of Agricultural Science, Washington, Aug. 17, 1891.

been inaccurate. As Fabricius's work was published in 1793, further evidence is thus afforded that the insect is indigenous to the western hemisphere. This insect still does similar damage in the vicinity of the original source of our information, as is indicated by two articles by Miss Ormerod in the Proceedings of the Entomological Society of London, 1879, xxxiii–xxxvi and xxxvi–xl, and by the reports of Mr. Im-Thurm, curator of the British Guiana Museum at Georgetown, published some time previously, but which we have not seen.

In an added note to his *Gardener's Chronicle* article Westwood states that according to information given him by "an intelligent Jamaica cane-grower" the borer was very destructive in Jamaica some 15 years previously [1842], but that its ravages had been greatly checked by allowing the refuse to accumulate on the ground and then firing the whole plantation, the old roots subsequently throwing up more vigorous shoots.

Mr. H. Ling Roth has studied what he believes to be the same species in Queensland (Parasites of the Sugar-cane, reprinted from the *Sugar Cane*, March and April, 1885. London, 1885). And in the same year M. A. Delteil (La Canne à sucre, Paris, 1885) treats of the Mauritius borer and considers it to have been imported from Java, whereas the 1856 commission had considered that it was derived from Ceylon. In 1890 Dr. W. Kruger published in the Berichte der Versuchsstation für Zuckerrohr in West Java, Heft I, Dresden, 1890, an account of the Javan sugar-cane borers, and figures and describes a species determined as *Diatræa striatalis* Snell., which almost precisely resembles our species, and which he says occurs not only in Java, but also in Borneo, Sumatra, and Singapore. In this same report another similar borer is described by Snellen as *Chilo infuscatellus*.

The West Indian cane borer made its appearance in the sugar-cane plantations of Louisiana at an early date. J. B. Avequin, writing in the *Journal de Pharmacie* for 1857 (vol. xxxii, pp. 335–337), upon the enemies of the sugar-cane in the Antilles and Louisiana, stated that during the two or three preceding years this insect had spread over some of the cane fields of Louisiana, but without having caused up to that time any great damage. He thought that the early frosts towards the end of October or November destroyed great numbers. It appears to have been first noticed in the parish of St. John Baptist in the year 1855.

Since this time the insect must have been constantly present in the Louisiana cane fields, and has probably been reintroduced from time to time with fresh shipments of seed cane from the West Indies. In the fall of 1878 a few specimens were sent to Dr. Riley by a correspondent in Assumption Parish, Louisiana, and in the spring of 1879 Mr. E. A. Schwarz sent in a bit of cane containing larvæ from the Bahamas. In the spring of 1881, I was sent to Louisiana by Professor Comstock, then entomologist of the Department of Agriculture, to study the sugar-cane beetle (*Ligyrus rugiceps*), and had the opportunity of studying this borer upon the plantation of Dr. J. B. Wilkinson, some 40 miles south of New Orleans on the Mississippi River. Dr. Wilkinson informed me that in 1857 they were very abundant in the Lower Mississippi, and that the crop upon one plantation was utterly destroyed, the cane breaking to pieces as they attempted to cut it. A summary of the observations which I made at that time was published in Special Report No. 11 of the Department of Agriculture, and in the Annual Report for 1880, pp. 240–242.

The life history as then ascertained is briefly as follows: In early spring the parent moth lays her eggs upon the leaves of the young cane near the axles and the young borer penetrates the stalk at or near the joint and commences to tunnel, usually upwards, through the soft pith. The larval growth is rapid and the borer is active, and frequently leaves the stalk at one place and enters at another, making several holes in the course of its growth. When ready to transform, it burrows to the surface, making a hole for the exit of the future moth, and transforms to the pupa state. There are several generations in the course of a season and the insect hibernates in the larval state within the stalks.

It must be a number of years since what is apparently this same insect first transferred its attentions in part from sugar-cane to corn, as it is figured upon one of Glover's unpublished plates as "injuring maize in South Carolina." In July of 1881 specimens of the insect were received from Abbeville County, S. C., and were studied at the Division of Entomology. The considerable damage which was done in that locality was treated in the Annual Report of the Department of Agriculture for 1880, pp. 243–245. It was also received about the same time from Lincoln County, Ga., where the damage to the corn crop was estimated by a correspondent of the Department at from 10 to 25 per cent.

Late in the summer of 1881 I was sent by Professor Riley on a trip through South Carolina and Georgia, principally to study rice insects, but also to give some attention to the smaller corn stalk-borer (*Pempelia lignosella*). I then incidentally found the work of this larger borer in an extensive field near Atlanta, Ga., and very abundantly near Columbia, S. C., upon the plantation of Mr. James Sims. It was there the exception to find a stalk which had not one or more holes in it. The work of the late broods had not apparently injured the "make" very much, and frequently a stalk which had contained several larvæ bore its full and hard ears of corn. The *early* weakening of the stalk was what had proved destructive. The worm seemed never to deform the stalk, and the larva was almost invariably found above ground in the first three sections. I found one stalk, for instance, which in these three sections was riddled by no less than thirty holes and the center of which was completely eaten out. According to my observations in that locality, the insect was confined to high ground, and no trace of it was found in the cornfields along the Congaree River, where I studied Bill-bug damage to the corn crop.

For nine years nothing was heard at the Department about damage done by this insect to corn, save that in his report on Insects Injurious to Garden Crops in Florida (Bulletin No. 14, Division of Entomology), Mr. Ashmead mentioned the fact that this species damages corn near Jacksonville. In 1889 Mr. W. J. Thompson, of Louisiana, wrote concerning damage to sorghum, which he had begun to grow upon his large plantation in St. Marys Parish, and in an article in the *Louisiana Sugar Planter*, of November 2, 1889 (reprinted in INSECT LIFE, vol. II, pp. 389, 390), Mr. Thompson recommended, as the outcome of his particular experience, the remedies which I had suggested in 1881, viz, the burning of the tops, the avoiding of flat or round mats for seed cane, and the planting of canes in the autumn, selecting such as are least affected.

There can be no doubt, however, but that the insect has been gradually on the increase in more northern cornfields for a number of years, occurring usually in such small numbers as to be unnoticed. The only serious outbreaks seem to have been those in Lincoln County, Ga., and Abbeville County, S. C., in 1881. That the worms may have been quite abundant in many fields without being noticed by planters, or at least without attracting sufficient attention to cause a report to State or Government authorities, is shown by my observations near Columbia, just mentioned.

Through favorable seasons and through gradual increase the species has now, however, become a somewhat serious pest as far north as the Maryland border line, as we have recently ascertained. In July, 1890, Mr. W. J. Morton, of Fredericksburg, Va., sent in a few specimens to the Division with the statement that the corn crop was suffering severely in his neighborhood (INSECT LIFE, vol. III, p. 64). The third week in July, 1891, Mr. Fielding Lewis, an employé of the Department of Agriculture, brought to the Division from his place in King George County, some 40 miles south of Washington, some sections of cornstalk completely riddled by this larva.

On July 24, Mr. Cordley, of the Division of Entomology, was sent to Chatterton Landing, Potomac River, King George County, and he brought home considerable material and reported that examination of twenty-seven fields showed about 25 per cent of the stalks to be infested. Early planted corn was found to be worst infested. Of corn planted during the first and second weeks in April, 25 per cent was affected; of that planted in the third and fourth weeks in April, 20 per cent was affected; of that planted May 1 to 15, 15 per cent was affected; of that planted from the 15th to the 31st of May, 12 per cent was attacked; while of that planted from the 1st to the 15th of June, about 8 per cent was affected. Corn planted after the 1st of June was not infested to any extent. The average injury to crops planted upon stalk land or land in corn last year was 25 per cent, while the average injury to corn planted on sod land was 10 per cent. One sod field, with stalk land on three sides, was found to have been injured 20 per cent. Corn on high or low land seemed to be affected in about the same proportion. On Mr. Lewis's place, one field was found in which over 50 per cent of the stalks were damaged, and upon the farm of a Mr. Taylor nearly every stalk in one field contained borers, and his yield was estimated to have been reduced to from 6 to 8 barrels per acre to 2 barrels.

Most of the larvæ were found below the second joint. In one stalk, from which Mr. Cordley took 12 larvæ, they were arranged as follows: Seven below first joint, 1 between first and second, 3 between second and third, and 1 between third and fourth. In another stalk from which 8 larvæ were taken, 1 was found in the tap root, 5 between first and second joints, 1 between fifth and sixth joints, and 1 between eighth and ninth joints.

Dr. J. S. Massey, of Comorn, King George County, Va., an intelligent gentleman who has paid considerable attention to this insect the present season, informed Mr. Cordley that in his opinion the territory embraced between the Rappahannock and Potomac rivers and extending from Fredericksburg to the Chesapeake Bay was pretty well infested by the borer, which first made its appearance in this section during the season of 1890 on the farm of Senator Newton, of Comorn. Subsequent to Mr. Cordley's visit I made some effort to ascertain by correspondence and otherwise whether the insect occurred in a more accessible locality than Chatterton Landing, but was unable to hear of it in the vicinity of Colonial Beach, a summer resort some 20 miles farther down the river, to which Washington steamers run daily.

FIG. 3.—Work of larger corn stalk-borer: a, general appearance of stalk infested by first brood; b, same cut open to show pupa and larval burrow (original).

August 8, however, I visited this latter locality, and although individuals about the resort were unable to give me any information, I was fortunate in finding the borer in the first cornfield which I visited. Large well-grown stalks of corn were infested only to a slight extent and then evidently only by large larvæ which had migrated from smaller stalks which had been killed some time previously. On the farm of Mr. J. S. Newton, of Maple Grove, Westmoreland County, some 6 miles from Colonial Beach, considerable damage had been done to young corn planted about the 1st of May in a very large field which was grown to corn the previous year. The damage was first noticed by Mr. Newton about July 1, although the worms had undoubtedly been at work for several weeks at that time. At the time of my visit (August 9, 1891) at least 98 per cent of the worms had transformed to pupæ and the moths had issued. I found some pupæ, however, and a few larvæ which had not yet changed. This corn by July 1, when the damage was first noticed, had reached a height of from a foot to 18 inches, and every infested stalk on August 9 remained at this height, stunted and deformed, the only visible sections of the stalk averaging not more than $1\frac{1}{2}$ inches in length. The larval burrow was invariably in the first section and usually extended down into the tap root, and in no case were more than two burrows found in the same stalk.

From these observations we may conclude that the insect is normally two-brooded in Virginia, the moths laying the eggs for the first brood during May, the larvæ arriving at maturity from the middle of July on, transforming to pupæ and issuing as moths in from ten days to two weeks later. The eggs for the second brood must be laid soon afterwards on the well-grown stalks and the larvæ must be full-grown by harvest time. Judging from our experience with the specimens from South Carolina in 1881 and with the individuals in sugar-cane in the spring of the same year the insect will hibernate in the larval state in the stalk and in this fact we have our simple means of cure.

With the more careful and thorough methods of cultivation in the North this insect will have no chance for its life. It will reach its maximum in localities like parts of South Carolina where corn is simply stripped for fodder in early August and the bare stalk with the ear attached stands until after the cotton is picked, ginned, and shipped, and where even after the ears are harvested the stalks are seldom burned. In Virginia, however, the conditions are nearly as favorable for the continuous development of the insect. Where it is not intended to follow corn with winter grain the corn is cut in October and the butts stand in the ground until the following spring, affording the larvæ safe places of hibernation. Even in plowing for another crop of corn in the spring many of the old stalks are not destroyed but still remain standing through winter. Under these conditions there is no check whatsoever to the increase of the pest. Where winter grain follows corn the stalks are not thoroughly dragged off (they seem never to be systematically pulled as in some parts of Maryland and other localities) and even when dragged off and collected they are not burned.

Where, however, the old stalks are systematically removed from the field and burned after harvest or during winter, or where a constant rotation of crops is practiced, the corn stalk-borer will never become a serious pest, and the Virginia and South Carolina farmers have it in their hands to check it at any time by pursuing these methods.

THERE ARE SEVERAL DISTINCT SUGAR-CANE BORERS.

Ever since Guilding described his *Diatræa sacchari*, nearly all crambid borers in sugar-cane have been assumed to be identical with this species. I assume that Guilding's insect may be identical with our Louisiana borer since it is West Indian, and is likely to have been introduced into Louisiana with seed cane. I can not, however, consult the descriptions of Guilding as his work is inaccessible. There are no salient points which would readily distinguish the moth or the pupa in a brief or a popular description; but the larva is rather peculiar among the Crambidæ. The ordinary form in corn (Fig. 4, *a*) when full-grown is about 25 millimeters long, stout, 5 millimetres in diameter, and of the ordinary subcylindrical form. It is dirty white in color and is profusely spotted with black or brown, the ordinary piliferous spots being large and dark colored. They are arranged about as in the larva of *Heliothis armigera*. The anterior dorsal spots of the last two thoracic and first seven abdominal joints are large and round, those on the eighth and ninth abdominal joints being confluent (Fig. 4, *e*). The posterior dorsal spots are more widely separated, are transversely elongated, and become confluent, forming a band on the second and third thoracic joints (Fig. 4, *d*). The head and thoracic plate are honey yellow. There is considerable variation in the size of these

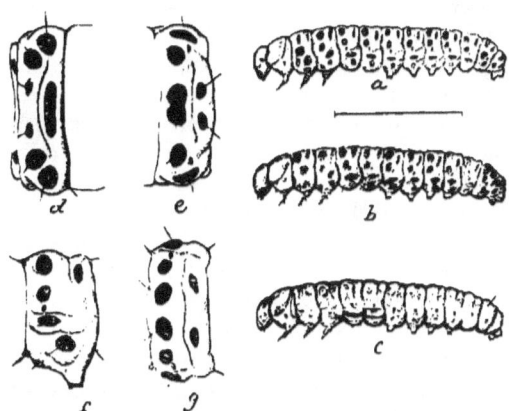

FIG. 4.—*Diatræa saccharalis*: *a, b, c*, varieties of larva enlarged; *d*. third thoracic segment; *e*, eighth abdominal segment; *f*. abdominal segment from side; *g*, same from above—still more enlarged (original).

spots, and in some individuals they are comparatively small, while in others (alcoholic) they are so large as to give the whole larva a brownish effect. There are frequently in the alcoholic specimens two subdorsal purplish longitudinal lines, and the head and prothoracic plate vary from bright honey-yellow to brown.

The Mauritius larva is described by Westwood as follows:

> The caterpillar has the head covered with a black plate, and the neck is also covered with a paler colored plate, and the body is furnished with a number of short black hairs arising from small black points connected laterally by a pink band.

This description shows the Mauritius species to be different from ours, and presumably from the West Indian form.

Fabricius's description of the larva of the South American species is as follows:

Larva hexapoda, pallide hyalina: capite punctisque utrinque octo brunneis.

This also differs from our species, but the description was drawn up from a figure only which may have been more or less inaccurate.

The Queensland borer is described by H. Ling Roth as "a white caterpillar with a purple speckled back, one and a quarter inches in length." This is more like our species.

The British Guiana borers received in 1879 by Miss Ormerod from Mr. D'Urban, of Exeter, resemble our own from the few brief words of description which she gives:

* * * and the larvæ also have larger spots than those figured and accompanying the excellent paper given by Professor Westwood. * * *

Dr. Kruger describes four distinct lepidopterous borers from Java: *Scirpophaga intacta* Snell., *Grapholitha schistaceana* Snell., *Chilo infuscatellus* Snell., and *Diatraea striatalis* Snell. Of these the latter, as elsewhere stated, is extremely similar to our species in corn.

All of the larvæ which we had seen from sugar-cane up to the present year were entirely white, with yellow head and thoracic shield, but these were all full-grown individuals ready for hibernation, or which had hibernated (Fig. 4, c). In Prof. Comstock's article (Annual Report of the Department of Agriculture for 1880) it is shown that all hibernating larvæ found in corn by his correspondent, Dr. Anderson, of Abbeville County, S. C., were pure white without a trace of brown spots. Therefore the brown spots on the midsummer individuals in corn in South Carolina and Virginia afford no argument for the nonidentity of the sugar-cane and corn borers. Moreover specimens from sugar-cane from Florida collected in October of the present year show the brown spots and variation of the color of head and prothoracic shield noticed in corn specimens and are in fact indistinguishable from these. In addition to this, from my observations in Westmoreland County, Va., the past August, it seems probable that the loss of the spots is characteristic of the perfectly full-grown larva, as at this late date the few delayed individuals of the first brood are all white.

There may be, however, still some doubt as to the identity of the sugar-cane borer of Louisiana and the corn stalk-borer of more northern States, but it is thought worth while to place these facts concerning the corn stalk-borer on record at the present time and to await an absolute decision as to identity until a large series of moths from both food plants can be reared and carefully examined by one more competent in the study of the Crambidæ.* The larvæ collected by Schwarz in the

---

*Prof. Riley, who has examined the moths, both from corn and sugar-cane, since the above was written, finds that they all belong to one species. Of over fifty specimens reared there is great variation both as to the distinctness of the transverse lines and of the terminal series of dots, and as to the general ground color. It is also noticeable that the later-bred specimens from the South are, on the whole, darker. The males are generally much darker than the females. The material leaves no question that *obliteratellus* Zeller and *crambidoides* Grote, are, as they have been made by Prof. Fernald, merely synonyms.

Bahamas show the identity of the West Indian borer, which we can not but suppose is Guilding's *Diatræa sacchari*, with the Louisiana cane borer.

Concerning the South American species and those of Mauritius, Java, and Queensland there is doubt, and it seems altogether likely that in different parts of the world we have several distinct species of Crambidæ uniting in the sugar-cane-boring habit, although those of South America and Java may be identical with our own.

ANOTHER FOOD PLANT.

Mr. Pergande, of the Division of Entomology, discovered, June 25, a small larva boring in the stalks of Gama grass or Sesame grass (*Tripsacum dactyloides*) at the southern end of the Long Bridge crossing the Potomac River at Washington. Other larvæ were found from time to time, and full-grown specimens were found July 14. These precisely resembled the larvæ found in corn farther south in Virginia, and August 13 the first moth issued, setting at rest any doubt as to the identity of this species with the corn stalk-borer. The Gama grass has a large stem and grows to a height of 6 or more feet, and its leaves are almost as large as those of Indian corn, to which it is closely allied. It grows wild in moist soils from Connecticut southwards, and has been used for fodder. The borer in this food plant introduces a variation in habit, and it feeds mainly in the upper joints, some larvæ even having been found by Mr. Pergande feeding upon the seed head. At my suggestion he examined, on August 12, the corn fields adjoining this patch of Gama grass, and found that, while the grass was quite extensively infested, but one stalk of corn had been bored by this larva.

We have then as the food plants of this insect the four closely related species, *Sorghum vulgare*, *Saccharum officinarum*, *Tripsacum dactyloides*, and *Zea mays*.

Where the Gama grass grows in any quantity in the vicinity of cornfields it will, therefore, be very necessary to burn it over every winter, an act of easy accomplishment and one which will probably materially reduce the numbers of the hibernated individuals which would otherwise fly out over the cornfields in spring.

ADDITIONAL NOTE.

Since this article was written a note by Mr. C. H. Tyler Townsend was read before the Association of Economic Entomologists at Washington, August 17, in which he stated that he had found the larva of the sugar-cane borer infesting corn in two localities in New Mexico, and, in discussion, Mr. H. E. Weed stated that the same insect was occasionally found in corn in Mississippi. It may also be mentioned that Prof. H. A. Morgan has treated of the damage to sugar-cane in Louisiana in Bulletin No. 9, Second Series of the Louisiana Experiment Station.

ON THE HABITS AND LIFE HISTORY OF DIABROTICA 12-PUNCTATA OLIV.

By C. V. RILEY.

In *Psyche* for February and March, 1891, Prof. H. Garman, of the Kentucky Agricultural Experiment Station, gives a detailed and lengthy summary of the literature on the subject of the habits of this well-known enemy of cucurbitaceous plants, and follows with a careful account of his observations upon its early states, showing that during 1889–'90 the damage of the larvæ to corn attracted attention over a wide area of country, including the States of Virginia, Alabama, Mississippi, Louisiana, Arkansas, Kentucky, Illinois, and Ohio. His own observations began July 15, 1889, and in brief may be summarized as follows:

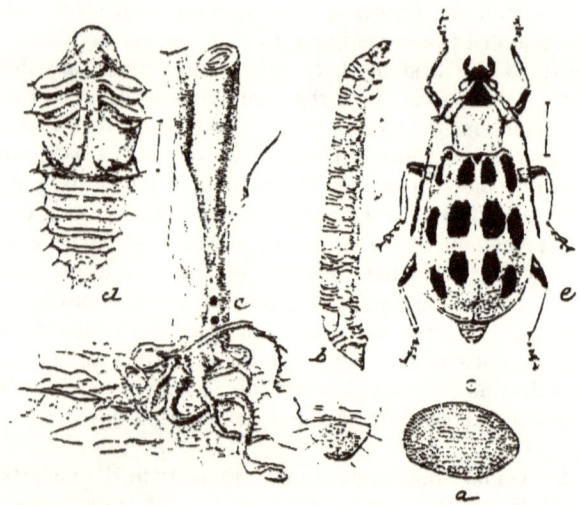

FIG. 5.—*Diabrotica 12-punctata*: a, egg—greatly enlarged; b, larva; c, corn-stalk showing punctures, d, pupa; e, adult—b, d, and c enlarged (original).

The young larvæ were noted upon July 15, 1889, and became full grown by the 29th of the same month, they having pupated in small cells in the earth at the latter date. Adult beetles dissected at this time contained eggs of a relatively large size. August 3 most of the larvæ had pupated. No very young worms were seen, and one adult was found. A second brood was expected, but towards the end of August the females had disappeared and none were observed with developed eggs during the remainder of the season. Larvæ and pupæ were rare from this time on until the first of November, when, in a field of late-planted corn, numerous larvæ, pupæ, and recently transformed adults were found. Observations made by Mr. Lugger showed that the insect breeds upon the roots of Rudbeckia, and Professor Garman surmises that the majority of the second brood will be found to breed upon this food-plant, as corn planted sufficiently late to enable root-breeding is rare. The adult beetle was found at all times from July 10, 1889, to December, 1890, while during the winter it was found among rubbish in strawberry beds, and in gardens and meadows. During the fall and winter those taken and dissected contained no developed eggs, but in the latter part of May, 1890, when the corn was a few inches high, the females collected contained eggs in an advanced stage of development. No eggs were found after oviposition, but the author concludes that they are placed like those of *D. longicornis* in the ground at the roots of the corn.

In the course of his treatment of previous writings, Professor Garman justly calls in question a statement made in INSECT LIFE, vol. I, p. 59, where, by a typographical oversight, this insect is said to have "bred" upon instead of "fed" upon melons. The error is self-evident from the language and from the tenor of the article, which does not treat of larval habits but of the food-habits of the beetle. We would bring together here our record of observation, communicated to Mr. Garman, and an abstract of which he has published in *Psyche* for May last.

Our knowledge of the corn-feeding habit of the larvæ of this insect dates from April 30, 1883, when Judge Lawrence Johnson forwarded from Allenton, Wilcox County, Ala., a number of larvæ, of which he wrote as follows:

I sent you last week from Allenton specimens of the same destructive "bud worm" that I once mentioned as heard of but not seen. This is about the right time, for they are now going into the pupa stage, and in the sand you will find one of the pupæ. The worm leaves the corn after doing its mischief, and the pupa referred to was found immediately under the stalk among the roots. I have never met with this worm except on the prairie regions of southern Alabama, but have heard of it in Mississippi.

The larvæ sent by Judge Johnson transformed to pupæ May 8, and the beetles were obtained May 21, 1883. The injury done is to young corn immediately or soon after germination, the larvæ burrowing into and eating the stalk just above the root. The common name of "bud worm," by which the larva is known in the South, is derived from this habit.

October 3, 1884, Judge Johnson again forwarded alcoholic specimens of the larvæ and beetles, obtained from Maj. M. F. Berry, of Pachuta, Miss. Judge Johnson wrote that—

From March to the middle of May they so abounded in the southern belt of the Mississippi prairie as to destroy the corn crop. We have no corn except a little of the early planting (before the middle of March), and the late corn planted after the 15th of May. This last was a second or third planting of the same fields and might have done well but for the unusual drouth of the period, this year unusually persistent. If you can suggest a certain remedy you will immortalize yourself in southern Mississippi.

On June 18, 1886, Mr. Lukens, of Mount Vernon, Va., complained that his young corn was being ruined by some small worms, a field of sweet corn being chiefly affected. Examination showed the damage to be caused by this insect, and we had some extended observations made on its habits by Mr. Pergande, from whose notes the following facts are summarized:

The general aspect of the field was as though it had been attacked by *Crambus*, the central leaf wilting and drooping and the whole plant exhibiting a withered appearance. In a great many of the rows not a single plant was left, every one having been attacked and destroyed as soon as it made its appearance above the ground, and in many cases the plant was killed almost as soon as sprouted. The corn still standing was about six inches high and the greater portion of it had been recently infested, as was plainly indicated by the withering of the central blades. Examination of these plants almost invariably disclosed the larva, sometimes buried for two-thirds of its length, actively at work in the heart of the plant immediately above the roots, working in precisely the manner of *Crambus*, of which, however, no specimens could be found.

Two or three of the Diabrotica larvæ, which are here also known as the "bud worm," were occasionally found in a single hill of corn.

Larvæ collected June 18 changed to pupæ June 22, and the beetles appeared July 6. A number of the beetles were at once placed in a jar with earth and corn plants to ascertain the facts regarding their oviposition. On the day following, July 7, large numbers of eggs had been placed below the surface of the soil near the plants, in cracks, or immediately about the base of the plants. They were placed either singly or in groups of two or twelve, or even more.

From these eggs larvæ were subsequently obtained. These, when first noted on July 15, were already of considerable size, but were not carried to full growth on account of the difficulty of obtaining the plants of corn.

The above indicates that this insect is at least double-brooded, in which respect it differs from the closely allied *D. longicornis*, which is single-brooded and winters usually in the egg, though occasionally in the adult state.

The second brood of *Diabrotica 12-punctata* doubtless winters over, and deposits eggs about the young corn or other plants in the spring. Eggs of the last brood are also perhaps deposited in the fall, and winter over, as is usually the case with *longicornis*.

Mr. Webster's experience with this insect in Tensas Parish, La., during April, 1887, published in our Annual Report for 1887, is, we believe, the first published record of the corn-feeding habit of this insect.

No pupæ, as stated, were found, but the larvæ and beetles were collected and forwarded to the Department in quantity, and the connection between the two was unequivocally shown by comparison with the complete material already in our possession. In addition to these records, we have received the larvæ from Mr. J. M. Thomas of Abbeville, S. C., with the report of their boring into young corn; and on May 31 Mr. William H. Ashmead found the larvæ in numbers in young corn in Somerset County, Md., where they occurred in company with one of the wire-worms (*Drasterius elegans* Fabr.). Mr. Ashmead in his report (INSECT LIFE, III, p. 54) erroneously referred the larva to *Diabrotica vittata*, and the mistake was not discovered until the article was in print. Early in October, 1890, Mr. Webster forwarded a larva, without much doubt of this insect, which he had just taken in the act of eating into the stem of Wheat in early sown fields. The larva sent was identified by comparison with specimens in our possession. This discovery adds a very interesting fact to our knowledge of the food-plants of the larva of this insect.

The adult is known to be a very general feeder, and our unpublished notes show that it has been found feeding on the blades of Corn, eating long slender holes, as observed, and Mr. Pergande has observed them feeding on mold and on the leaves of *Solanum carolinense*. They have also been found in the vicinity of Washington, feeding on the ears of green Corn, and Mr. Webster reports that he has found them eating the partly matured kernels of wheat. In Bulletin 22 of this Division, p. 52, Mr. Webster also reports their feeding on Wheat, Cabbage, Cauliflower, and Beans in April, and on volunteer Oats in December. This autumn we have found it for the first time a grievous nuisance in our garden, as it has destroyed the choicest roses just as they were about to open.

Its seriously defoliating young apple trees, reported in INSECT LIFE, I, p. 58, is recorded on the authority of Mr. William B. Alwood, but from the investigation of similar injury the year following by Mr. Marlatt (INSECT LIFE, I, p. 365) it appears that Mr. Alwood had overestimated the damage occasioned by this insect—the injury in great part being chargeable to *Lachnosterna*.

The early stages of *Diabrotica 12-punctata* are scarcely different from those of *D. longicornis*, which have been so admirably described by Professor Forbes in his first report as State entomologist of Illinois. The *egg* (Fig. *a*) is larger, being 0.03 by 0.02 of an inch as against 0.025 by 0.015 in the case of *longicornis*. In color, instead of being dirty white, it is dull yellowish. The hexagonal pits are exactly like those on the eggs of *longicornis* but are perhaps smaller, as there are 30 to 35 in its entire length as against 20 only in the smaller egg of *longicornis*. The minute depressions which occur in the bottom of the pits of the latter species are also found in the eggs of *12-punctata*. (See fig 5 *a*.)

The *larva* differs from that of *longicornis* only in being somewhat larger. Before changing to the pupa it attains a length of 0.5 inch as against 0.4 in the case of *longicornis*. In some specimens there are two minute tubercles near the apex of the anal plate above, but these are not constant and are sometimes entirely wanting, as is always the case in *longicornis*.

Briefly, the larva is linear in shape, the first two segments tapering to the head, and is yellowish-white in color, with the head, thoracic legs, and anal plate brownish. Beneath the last segment is a prominent false leg or pro-leg, which is not shown in the drawing. A few scattering hairs occur on the body and a number of longer ones on the border of the anal plate. (See Fig. 5 b.)

Before transforming the larva contracts very considerably and the posterior portion becomes greatly enlarged. This contraction was already begun in the specimen figured.

The *pupa* affords few, if any, characters except that of size to separate it from the pupa of *longicornis*. The illustration (Fig. 5 d) indicates the characters sufficiently well. The wing-pads are, however, too much abbreviated.

The *beetle* is too well known to need further description. It is well represented in the accompanying illustration (Fig. 5 e). The colors are black and yellow, or yellowish-green—the latter being the prevailing shade of the wings.

We have reared two Dipterous parasites from this insect—one from the larva and pupa, and a Tachinid from the beetle. The larva of the latter escapes from the beetle through the suture between the pro-and meso-sternum. The puparium is covered with spines.

A NEW HERBARIUM PEST.

By C. V. RILEY.

(*Carphoxera* nov. gen., *ptelearia* n. sp.)

In September, 1890, a number of small Geometrid larvæ, recalling somewhat in appearance those of the genus Aplodes, were found by the botanists of the Department of Agriculture infesting certain dried plants in the Department herbarium, and especially those which had been received from Mexico and Lower California from Dr. Edward Palmer. Dr. J. N. Rose first observed it in January, 1890, on plants from La Paz, but it was still more abundant in a collection from the State of Columa, Mexico, made in the beginning of the present year. The first moth emerged October 22, 1890, and others were subsequently reared from material received from time to time from the Department herbarium. While the larva was first discovered, as stated, on Mexican plants, it has not confined its work to such plants, but has spread to others, and is by far the most destructive herbarium pest which the botanists in charge have to deal with. Plants of the genus Coulterella, for example, which were sent by Dr. Rose to Dr. O. Hoffman in Berlin, have been reported as so injured that but one perfect flower remained; yet, according to the observations of Mr. L. H. Dewey, in overhauling the herbarium, the insect's work is still mostly confined to southwestern plants; after those from Mexico, chiefly those from California. In some cases eastern plants have not been attacked, even when associated with western, but in one case at least, viz, *Rhus toxicodendron*, eastern plants have been extensively infested.

The larvæ feed on the flowers and also to some extent on the leaves. More rarely they feed on the hard fruits and seeds. The following list of the plants upon which the larva had been found prior to its work on *Rhus* will be of interest in this connection. It has been kindly prepared for me by Mr. Dewey, who read a short note on the subject at the late meeting of the Botanical Club A. A. A. S.:

Species.	Order.	Locality.
Ptelea aptera	Rutaceæ	Southern California.
Ceanothus sorediatus	Rhamnaceæ	Southern California.
Dalea seemannii	Leguminosæ	Southern California.
Lupinus coccineus	Leguminosæ	Arizona.
Purshia tridentata	Rosaceæ	Arizona.
Prunus demissa	Rosaceæ	Southern California.
Ribes viburnifolia	Saxifragaceæ	Southern California.
Epilobium angustifolium*	Onagraceæ	Eastern Massachusetts.
Arctostaphylos oppositifolius	Ericaceæ	Southern California.
Eriodictyon glutinosum	Hydrophyllaceæ	Southern California.
Gilia rusbyi	Polemoniaceæ	Arizona.
Pentstemon secundiflorus	Scrophulariaceæ	Arizona.
Audibertia clevelandii	Labiatæ	Southern California
Dracocephalum parviflorum	Labiatæ	Arizona.
Salvia ballotæflora	Labiatæ	Arizona.

* E. angustifolium grows in the west but mostly in northern California and Oregon.

The eggs are laid upon the plants or on any surrounding object. They are but slightly attached, bluntly ovoid, 0.3 millimetres wide and 0.4 millimetres long. They are steel-gray in color, the shell white, with

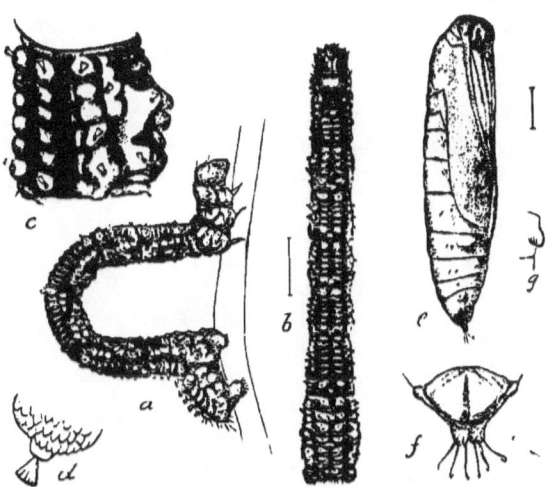

FIG. 6. *Carphoxera ptelearia*: *a*, larva from side; *b*, do. from above; *c*, side view of abdominal joint of same; *d*, tubercle of same; *e*, pupa; *f*, do. cremaster; *g*, do. abdominal projection—*a, b, d*, enlarged about 6 times; *c, d, f*, still more enlarged (original).

faint iridescence when empty, and faintly and irregularly reticulate. The duration of the larval period has not been determined. Growth, however, is very slow and the period from the egg to the full larval growth is variable. The larval life extends in some cases certainly over a period of three months. When full grown the larvæ attain a length, extended, of 8 millimetres; contracted, when disturbed or at rest, of 5 to 6 millimetres. Whenever disturbed they contract considerably, and become rigid and motionless. The larva is shown in characteristic positions in the accompanying illustration (Fig. 6, *a*, *b*). It is dull grayish in color, varying considerably in different specimens. On reaching full growth, the larva constructs a cocoon of loose white silk, forming an irregular open network, as shown in Fig. 7, *b*. The cocoon is usually placed in a fold of the leaf or is otherwise protected by the plant, and is occasionally partly covered with bits of anthers or fragments of leaves. In shape it is irregularly ovoid and is about 6 by 3.5 millimetres. The change to pupa takes place about three days after the cocoon is completed, and the moth usually appears 18 to 20 days after pupation. The pupa is 5 millimetres in length, somewhat robust, and is slightly yellowish in color, with sutures and tip brownish, the latter being quite dark. A peculiar pad or flap-like projection occurs on the side of the fifth abdominal joint (Fig. 6, *e*, *g*). The cremaster is produced, notched at the tip, and armed with six long hooked hairs or spines (Fig. 6, *f*). The adult insect is about 5 millimetres long, and expands from 12 to 14 millimetres. The general color is grayish yellow, inclining to saffron, the primaries being somewhat darker. The wings are marked (Fig. 7) with transverse bands of dusky shade and each wing has a discal spot. The head is dark brown, with the antennæ, including a large spot on the vertex, yellowish. The under surface is nearly concolorous, the dark bands being less distinct and the discal spots more intensified. The fringes are concolorous with the ground-color and with black dots beyond the veins.

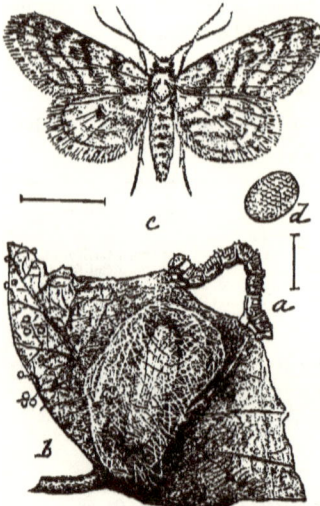

FIG. 7. *Carphoxera ptelearia:* *a*, larva; *b*, cocoon; *c*, moth; *d*, egg—all enlarged (original).

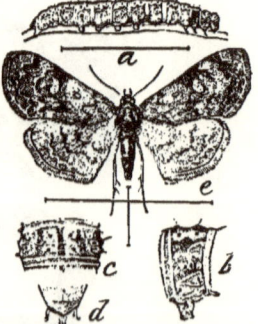

FIG. 8. *Helia æmula:* *a*, larva enlarged; *b*, joints of same, lateral view; *c*, do. dorsal view; *d*, tip of body—still more enlarged; *e*, adult (original).

This insect has become a source of positive alarm in the Department herbarium, on account of its rapid increase and the harm it occasions. It behooves botanists to be on the lookout for it and to adopt such measures as will insure immunity from it if dry specimens are being received from Mexico and the Southwest, or from herbaria in which it is known to occur. The custom of botanists of poisoning their plants with corrosive sublimate to protect them from various enemies, such as book mites, Psoci, etc., should give immunity from the attacks of this insect if the poison has been thoroughly applied. If to the corrosive sublimate a quantity of arsenic is added the protection will be more effectual. I would also recommend as very useful in disinfecting herbaria of this and other pests an air-tight quarantine box of zinc or galvanized iron, in which plants may be temporarily placed and submitted to the fumes of bisulphide of carbon, which are very sure to destroy all insect life.

The fact that this insect has appeared on dry plants from the comparatively arid western regions may furnish a clue to its original habit. It would seem possible, if not probable, that it normally feeds on the dead or dry plants of Mexico and adjacent arid regions, and that it has simply adapted itself to the somewhat similar conditions prevailing in herbaria.

This is the first true Geometrid, so far as I know, recorded as feeding on dry and dead vegetation. In the Pyralidina a number of species are known to be not only truly carnivorous, feeding on other insects, but also to feed upon grass and rejectimenta as well as dead leaves. Some Tineina are also known to have similar habits, while in the Deltoid group of the Noctuids several genera are known to me as feeding on dead leaves. Thus *Helia* (*Epizeuxis*) *æmula* Hübn. (Fig. 8) has been found in the autumn feeding on dead leaves of Hickory in Virginia, the larva hibernating and the imago issuing the following spring. *Palthis asopialis* Guen. and *Zanclognatha minivalis* Grote (Fig. 9) have also been found feeding on

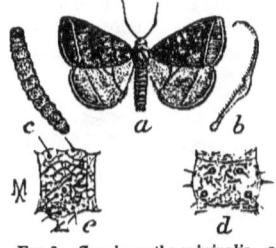

Fig. 9.—*Zanclognatha minivalis:* a, adult; b, ♂ antenna; c, larva; d, e, joints of same; a, and c, natural size; b, d, and e, enlarged (original).

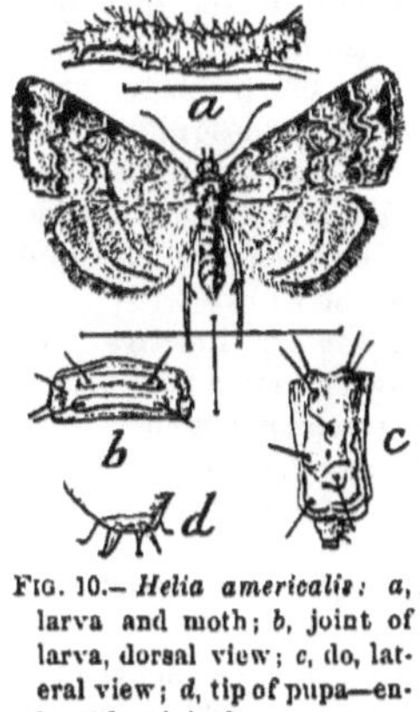

the dead leaves of Oak. These facts are recorded in Packard's Report on Forest Insects (Fifth Report U. S. Entomological Commission) from my notes, but it is worthy of remark that Packard also bred *H. æmula* from larvæ beaten from spruce trees, though whether they were feeding on the dead leaves or on the living was not ascertained. So *Helia americalis* Guen. (Fig. 10), as recorded by me in the *American Naturalist*, October, 1883, has been found in the nests of *Formica integra* Nylander (which, according to Mr. Pergande, is a race of *rufa*). It was originally found in such nests by Messrs. Pergande and Schwarz and has since been ascertained to be very common in such situations. Yet Guenée records this species, but without authority, as living on leguminous

Fig. 10.— *Helia americalis: a*, larva and moth; *b*, joint of larva, dorsal view; *c*, do, lateral view; *d*, tip of pupa—enlarged (original).

plants. *Myrmicocela ochracella*, a European lepidopteron allied to the Tineina, is also known to occur in ants' nests. In most of these cases it is probable that the species preferred the dead vegetation to the living, and such we know to be the case with the Pyralid, *Asopia costalis*, the Clover Hay-worm.

As might have been supposed, from the region of country whence it comes, the insect under consideration has been somewhat difficult to place. It is without question a new species, and though having the general aspect of Eupithecia, nevertheless, upon close study of its structure, has affinities nearer to Acidalia; but it can not be placed in either of these genera nor in any other of the Phalænid genera characterized in Packard's Monograph or known to occur in America. In fact it hardly fits into any of the subfamily definitions, and will, perhaps, some day be included in a separate subfamily, but for the present it may be placed in the Acidalinæ. It is characterized below:

CARPHOXERA gen. nov.

Having most of the characters of the subfamily Acidalinæ, as defined by Packard, except in the primaries being subfalcate, and the first subcostal venule (vein 11) short and not originating at the subcostal cell, but some distance beyond it. Agrees with Acidalia in having the head short, the front being somewhat sunken between the large globose eyes, the antennæ being simple or nearly so in both sexes, the pectinations being but slight, and in the short, slender palpi barely projecting beyond the front. Differs from Acidalia in the longer, narrower primaries; in the subcostal cell being elongate or rhomboidal; in the first subcostal venule (vein 11) being short, not much longer than the second and originating beyond the apex of the subcostal cell. The fifth subcostal venule (vein 7) branches from vein 8 at a point between the first and second subcostal venules. Legs slender and elongate, the hind tibiæ not thickened, spurred; tarsi as long as or longer than the tibiæ.

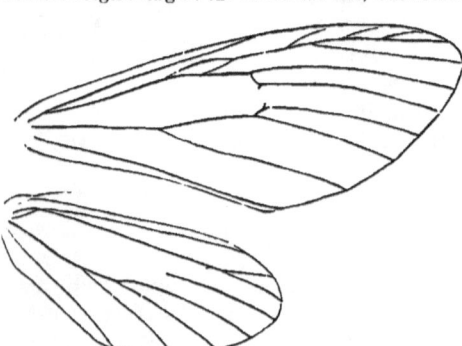

FIG. 11.—*Carphoxera ptelearia;* outline of wings, showing venation. Enlarged. (Original.)

CARPHOXERA PTELEARIA n. sp. *Imago.*— ♀ ; average length, 4 to 5 millimetres; alar expanse, 12 to 14 millimetres. *Head*, including eyes, dark brown except a large transverse oval spot on the vertex, including the base of the antennæ, which is pale luteous; palpi, dark brown; antennæ, luteous above and behind, darker beneath; where they are faintly serrate. *Thorax* and *abdomen* pale luteous, flecked with brown; legs slightly more dusky; wings sparsely scaled.

Primaries grayish-yellow inclining to saffron, with the ordinary discal patch and five more or less distinct obliquely-transverse bands, as follows: one rather broad, and across basal one-fourth of the wings, arched posteriorly near costa, and thence obliquing basally to inner border, along which it extends to inner angle; a second of same width, obliquing more directly from middle of costa to middle of inner border, and often coalescing with the discal spot; a third, narrower, but more coincident with the basal, starting from outer third of costa and reaching outer fourth of inner border; a fourth, subterminal, more pale and diffused, anteriorly parallel with and close to third, more irregular and jagged posteriorly, and the fifth, terminal and also faint, narrowing toward anal angle and broadening toward costa; all, especially 1, 2, and 3, are broadened and intensified on costal and inner borders; fringe broad, concolorous, with nine more or less distinct dark spots along base in a line with the veins.

Secondaries.—Slightly paler in color, with four less distinct transverse dark bands; the first across basal fourth, the second across middle and involving discal spot, the third more diffuse and between it and the terminal and the fourth terminal; the basal two darker and narrower than the others; all somewhat intensified and broadened on the inner border. Fringe marked with dark spots near base and in line with the veins.

Under surface of the wings somewhat darker than upper surface, more uniform in shade, with the pattern of the upper surface more faintly discernible except the discal spot, which is more intense.

No especial sexual colorational differences, the males being somewhat smaller and having rather darker front legs.

There is some variation, not only in the general color but also in the distinctness of the transverse lines. In some of the specimens there are a number of dusky scales on the light background between the bands, making these more diffuse; in others the bands are very abruptly and distinctly separated from the ground color.

Egg.—Bluntly ovoid, 0.04 millimetres in length, pale grayish and usually quite delicate, but firm enough to retain its shape after hatching, and irregularly reticulate.

Full-grown larva.—Seven millimetres in length, normal, and possessing but one pair of abdominal prolegs, pale olive gray, with medial dorsal and subdorsal darker lines; head honey-yellow inclining to brownish; antennae paler and with a few pale short fleshy bristles; the whole body is transversely wrinkled on the longer and middle segments, showing from six to seven or more of these transverse folds. In the dorsal region on each of the anterior and posterior folds are two spatulate processes arising from rounded tubercles, while subdorsally and laterally there are a series of about four to each segment and subventrally two of these same spatulate processes. On the anal segment these spatulate processes are more numerous and close together.

Pupa.—The pupa is characterized chiefly by a lateral projection on the fifth abdominal joint and by a somewhat brief cremaster with six rather long hooked bristles.

Described from numerous specimens.

UGIMYIA SERICARIÆ ROND., THE PARASITE OF THE JAPANESE SILKWORM.

By Prof. JOSEPH MIK, *Vienna, Austria.*[*]

Through the kind intercession of Prof. C. V. Riley, of Washington, I received the larva, puparium and one pair of the imago of the Tachinid fly which Rondani, without having any knowledge of the imago, had named (Boll. Soc. Entom. Ital., T. II, 1870, p. 137) *Ugimyia sericariæ*.

---

[*] Translated from the German in the Weiner entomologische Zeitung, vol. IX, No. 10, December, 1890, pp. 309-316, and published in INSECT LIFE at the suggestion of the author.

From the notes received regarding the parasitic mode of life of the larva as well as from a study of the larva and the puparium which had been communicated to him, Rondani recognized the parasite as a Tachinid and undertook to erect for the same a new genus, *Ugimyia* (from the popular name of the parasite "*Uji*").[*]

Soon afterward, Professor Cornalia received the fly of which he furnished a description—but an unsatisfactory one—introducing the species under the name of *Ugimyia sericariæ* Rond. (l. c., p. 223).[†]

In spite of the insufficient character of his description of the fly, Cornalia will have to be cited as the author of the species; for in the previously published note by Guérin Méneville (Comptes Rendus de l'Ac. d. Sciences, Paris, April 18, 1870, p. 844) there is a new name for the parasite, viz, *Tachina oudji*, but certainly no description whatever.[‡]

Several other articles by different authors have been published on this parasite,[§] which is called Uji in its native home, but a correct inter-

---

[*] The larvae of the Tachinidae are by no means so fully known that upon this stage alone a new genus could be established.

[†] To give an example of the character of this description I quote the following: "Le ali sono due. Il margine anteriore o costa e grosso, con delle dentellature. Questo margine e lungheggiato da una nervatura sottomarginale. Dall' angolo poi partono 6 altre radiate che vanno assottigliandosi al margine libero posteriore. Questo in vicinanza all' inserzione presenta la smarginatura e il lobo, notto sotto il nome di cucchiaio. Al di dietro di esso havvi una traccia di bilanciere." The figures of the imago given by Professor Cornalia also prove the want of correct observation (l. c., tav. III, Figs. 14–22); they are all quite poor and incorrect. In Fig. 14 (dorsal view of the fly) the general form is well represented, but the legs are altogether too thin, the wings show a venation running in arbitrary directions, and, also, there is nothing of a correct pubescence to be seen in the figure. The head from above (Fig. 15) is a very queer figure; the frontal bristles are arbitrarily drawn and resemble a wooden set net. Fig. 16 (head from the side) is entirely wrong—no bristles whatever. Fig. 14 represents the male, judging from the long claws, still the front is in the drawing broader than the eye. Professor Meinert, likewise, finds fault with the illustrations (cf. Entom. Meddelels, Kopenhagen, 1890, II, p. 162, line 5 from bottom).

[‡] Since the Comptes Rendus are not readily accessible I quote the above note verbatim: "M. Guérin Méneville adresse des observations sur la nature de l'uji ou oudji, insecte parasite qui a fait éprouver recemment une diminution notable a la production des graines de vers à soie au Japon. Les observations faites recemment par M. Adams, Sécret. d. 1. legation d'Angleterre au Japon, qui a pu voir à la fois le ver, la chrysalide et la mouche a l'état parfait, et qui a publié des figures de l'insecte à ces trois états font voir que l'oudji est un diptère, comme la mouche chinoise signalée par M. Castellani et comme la mouche française qui a si facilement adopté le ver à soie de l'ailante. Il propose de lui donner le nom de *Tachina oudji*."

[§] The bibliographical references are found in the following articles by Dr. Meinert: "How does the Ugimyia larva imbed itself in the Silkworm?" (Ann. and Mag. Nat. Hist., London, 1890, pp. 103–104), and "Ugimyia Larven og dens Leie i Silkeormen" (Entom. Meddel., 1890, II Bd., pp. 162–163). For the sake of completeness I cite here the note by Guérin, mentioned in Cornalia's article (l. c.) in Révue Universelle de sériculture, No. 3, April 1870; also the notes by Bigot (Bul. Soc. Entom. France, 1888, p. xxxix; by Riley [and Howard] (Insect Life, 1888, vol. I, p. 62) and by myself (Verh. Zool. Bot. Ges., Wien, 1889, Sitz. Ber. 51).

pretation of the species regarding its systematic position has, so far as known to me, not yet been given by any one. Those who have expressed an opinion on this subject either possessed an insufficient knowledge in dipterology, or they were in doubt or made erroneous statements, since they drew their conclusions solely from the insufficient descriptions and illustrations of the imago of this parasite.

Aside from those determinations, according to which the Uji belongs to the Tachinidæ, we find in the literature three opinions regarding the genus to which this fly should be referred.

The first statement is made by Cornalia, who, in the above-cited article, while discussing Guérin's note* on *Tachina oudji*, says that this fly probably belongs to the subgenus *Phorocera*.

During the years 1883–'85 Prof. C. Sasaki, of Tokyo, Japan, carefully investigated this parasite and published the results in the Journal of the College of Science, Imperial University, Tokyo, 1886, vol. I, part 1, without discussing, however, the question of the systematic position of the fly.

In my review of this interesting paper in Wien. Ent. Zeit. (1888, p. 45) I indicated that judging from the figure given by Sasaki the fly appeared to resemble Nemoræa. But nothing that was certain could be said, since neither from the description nor from the figure could the characters necessary to the determination of the genus be made out. Sasaki's description of the fly is, however, the best which we have so far. He calls the parasite erroneously *Ugimyia sericaria* Rond. instead of *sericariæ* Rond.

Mons. Bigot, of Paris, arrived at a different result. His conclusion, drawn from Sasaki's figure, is that *Ugimyia sericariæ* should be referred to the genus *Leskia* R. Desv. (cf. Bull. Soc. Ent. France, 1888, p. lxxxix). However, a glance at Sasaki's tab. I, Fig. 3, where the wings are repre-

---

*As already stated there is in this note nothing regarding the systematic position of the Uji, but it is possible that Guérin expressed an opinion on this point in an article in *Révue et Magaz. Zoöl.*, ser. 2, tom. 22, pp. 178-181, cited after Meinert, which is unknown to me. It is possible that Cornalia only thought of *Phorocera*, because Guérin had bred a species of this genus from the Ailanthus silkworm. It would seem to be of interest to reproduce here Cornalia's words (*Boll. Soc. Entom. Ital.*, 1870, p. 219): "Il Guérin infatti pote osservare nell baco dell' Ailanthus, da lui introdotto in Europa, una mosca parasitta la cui larva vive nel bruco e nella crisalide di quello; e la *Phorocera pumicata* Meig. La *Saturnia cynthia* dunque originaria della China, ha qui pure fra noi la sua malattia del moscone." I also quote here what Cornalia says in connection with these remarks: "E qui opportuno il dire che il conte Castellani, il quale fu in China in cerca di buon seme del bombice del gelso, nel suo libretto sul' Educazione del baco da seta in China (*Firenze*, 1860, pp. 139-148), accenna come anche nell'impero chinese il baco del gelso sia soggetto ad asser vittima di una mosca, che ne fa strage, mosca che il Guérin chiamo *Tachina castellanii*. Dalla descrizione che il viaggiatore italiano fa del parasitto non si potrebbe ritenere differente la specie giapponese dalla chinese; ma cio solo potranno decidere ulteriori e precise osservazioni. Secondo l'Adams l'Ugi attaca al Giappone anche la *Saturnia* (della quercia) *Yama-mai*, diffuse pure in Europa per opera del Guérin." I believe that *Tachina castellanii* Guér. is only a manuscript name.

sented, contradicts at once Mons. Bigot's assertion; this is not the venation of *Leskia*. Moreover, the figures of the imago show a very stout form of the body, so that it can not possibly be united with *Leskia*.*

This is all that is known to me from the literature regarding the attempts to fix the systematic position of *Ugimyia*. Having subsequently seen the imago I was enabled to properly interpret this parasite of the silkworm (cf. Verh. Zoöl. Bot. Ges., Wien. 1889. Sitz. Ber., p. 51) and arrived at the following conclusion:

Ugimyia sericariæ has all the essential characters of the genus *Sturmia* Rob. Desv.† and could very well be referred to this genus. It differs, however, from *Sturmia* by the pubescence of the abdomen. *Sturmia* having on the dorsum of the first and second abdominal segments marginal macrochetæ which are entirely wanting in *Ugimyia sericariæ*. At the present state of the classification of *Tachinidæ*, this difference may be sufficient to consider *Ugimyia sericariæ* as the type of a new genus for which I propose the name *Crossocosmia* mihi. The characters of this genus are as follows:

Crossocosmia n. g.—First and second abdominal segments on the dorsum without marginal and discal macrochetæ, the first two joints of the antennal seta very short and almost absent. Everything else as in the genus *Sturmia* R. Desv.

The synonymy of the species is as follows:

Sturmia (Crossocosmia) sericariæ Corn.
Ugimyia sericariæ Cornalia. 1870 (*Ugimyia serricariæ* Rond. 1870).
Tachina oudji Guérin. 1870. (?) *Tachina castellanii* Guér. (i. litt?).

In order to distinguish *Crossocosmia* from other allied genera it suffices to point out the following characters which, at the same time, plainly show the close relationship with *Sturmia*. Front in the ♂ wide, still wider in the ♀; in the former the frontal orbits are hairy and furnished with erect bristles which, arranged in a row, descend to the base of the third antennal joint, where they are more approached to the internal margin of the eyes than to the frontal stripe. Besides these there are in the female two anteriorly curved and stronger external bristles (orbital bristles). The antennæ are inserted above the middle of the eyes, joint 3 being at least twice as long as joint 2. The eyes are naked,‡ the palpi well developed, facial ridges nearly parallel,

---

Leskia aurea in the caterpillars of Sesiids (cf. Wachtl., Wien. Ent. Zeit., 1882, p. 278; and Brischke, Schrift. d. Naturf. Ges., Danzig. 1884, Sep., p. 2).

† The name *Sturmia* R. Desv. was changed by Rondani to *Blepharipa* (Prodrom., 1856, I. p. 71); by Kowarz to *Ctenocnemis* (Verh. Zoöl. Bot. Ges., 1875. p. 460); and by Brauer to *Blepharipoda* (Denkschr. Akad. Wiss., Wien. 1889. p. 96). All these changes are superfluous) cf. Wien. Ent. Zeit., 1890. p. 155). In his *Fauna*, Schiner united the genus *Sturmia* with *Masicera*, but this is no longer admissible in the light of our recent knowledge of the family Tachinidæ.

‡ Under strong magnifying power the eyes in *Crossocosmia* appear to be beset with extremely scattered, short, rod-like, but fine, yellowish hairs, but even under a good lens they appear to be naked, so that the genus can well be placed among those with naked eyes.

wide, cushion-like, elevated, and with several rows of bristles, which, however, ascend only to the tip of the third antennal joint. The genæ are densely covered with erect hairs; on the lower margin of the same are longer setæ. The bristles of the head are more dense in the female than in the male, but in the latter the bristles are somewhat longer. The scutellum has, besides the marginal bristles, on the disk two very pronounced macrochetæ amidst the shorter pubescence. The abdomen shows along the entire hind margin of the third segment one row of macrochetæ; the fourth segment is, on its upper surface, beset with long hairs and bristles, the latter being denser in the male than in the female. Aside from these there are no macrochetæ. The wings have no distinct marginal thorn; the posterior transverse vein is nearer to the curvature of the fourth longitudinal vein, which has no appendicular branch, than to the small transverse vein. The posterior tibiæ are furnished on the upper side with a row of equally long, very stout and dense setæ, which sometimes are closely applied to each other so that the tibia has the appearance of being unistriately ciliate. The pulvilli and the claws are longer in the ♂ than in the ♀ ; the front tarsi of the latter are hardly flattened.

I must remark here that in his Hist. Naturelle des Dip. des Environs de Paris (1863, I, p. 893), Robineau Desvoidy has established a genus, *Verreauxia*, on a Tachinid from Tasmania, which appears to be very closely allied to *Crossocosmia* m. It agrees with the latter in the arrangement of the bristles of the abdomen as well as in the shortness of the two basal joints of the arista, but the frontal pubescence is quite different, and is described as follows: "Front n'ayant que de cils raids, petits et peu prononcés."

Regarding the specific determination as given by Sasaki, in his above cited paper, the following points could be added: The fly resembles in general appearance *Nemoræa pellucida*, Meig.* The antennæ are shorter in the male than in the female; the first and second joints, as well as the blackish pubescent palpi, the suctorial flaps of the proboscis, and the distinctly separated oval margin are rust colored; the arista is long, moderately thick at basal half, thence gradually narrowing. The frontal stripe is velvety black, the frontal orbits are black inferiorly, with whitish pruinescence, which extends more densely over the whole face and over the genæ, and which has a more yellowish tinge in the ♂ . The bluish-black thorax is sparsely grayish-white pruinose, especially in front, and has four narrow, equidistant, black longitudinal stripes, of which the two inner ones do not extend much beyond the transverse suture, and show between them, anteriorly, a trace of a median stripe.†
The scutellum is rust-brown with a slight whitish tinge; the bluish-

---

*There is no need of changing this to *Nemoræa conjuncta* Rond.

†The four rows of dorso-central bristles consist in front of the transverse suture, of three bristles in each row, behind the transverse suture the two inner rows have three bristles each, the outer ones each four.

black abdomen shows likewise at the anterior margins of the segment a whitish (in the ♂ more yellowish) tinge of wide extent, which, at the median line, is interrupted by a black, narrow longitudinal stripe. The yellowish-red maculation of the ♂ occupies the sides of the first three segments. The third segment has on the dorsum about six macrochetæ. The genitalia are not visible. The tibiæ are dark piceous, nearly black, but rust-brown in transparent light; knees rust-brown. The posterior tibiæ have on their upper side very densely placed cilia, not mentioned by Sasaki, who also incorrectly figures the bristles on thorax and abdomen. The claws of the ♂ are rusty-yellow, black at tip; the black portion of the anterior claws appears to break off easily, since it is wanting in my specimen. The female has the claws black and more persistent. The pulvilli are rusty yellow. The wings are fuscous, and along the longitudinal veins rusty brown, the curvature of the apical transverse vein [Spitzenquerader] is nearly rectangular, the posterior transverse vein is only above the fifth longitudinal vein a little curved; there are from two to three bristles at the base of the third longitudinal vein. The tegulæ are large, pure white, the small halteres yellow.

NOTE.—In regard to the puparium, Mr. Sasaki has made a quite important error to which Professor Brauer had previously called my attention. By an examination of the puparium itself I have now been able to ascertain the following: The operculum of the puparium divides in the process of opening into two halves, a lower and an upper one. A longitudinal furrow, running over the anterior terminal point of the puparium and extending on each side as far as the anterior margin of the metathoracic segment (the fifth segment, according to Sasaki), shows the mode of the future splitting of the operculum. This furrow runs along the sides of the puparium, and Sasaki, while (on Pl. VI, Figs. 12 and 13) correctly representing two puparia from the ventral side, has figured the operculum turned around 90 degrees. In Fig. 12 the suture, $c, d.$, appears therefore erroneously on the ventral side of the puparium, whereas in reality it runs along the sides of the puparium, and can for this reason not be seen in a ventral illustration. In the same way the opened operculum in Fig. 13 is turned around 90 degrees. The two small circles on the ventral side of the fifth segment in both of the figures just cited are not stigmata, as stated by Sasaki in his descriptions, but small warts which originate in the puparium.

Finally, I desire to call attention to Sasaki's remarkable observation, according to which the eggs are deposited by the fly on the under side of the mulberry leaves; that they are eaten by the silkworm with the latter, and that they develop afterward to young larvæ in the intestinal canal of the caterpillar. Although Sasaki has established the identity of the eggs on the leaves with those in the vagina of the fly; although experiments have been made in Japan with caterpillars in well closed breeding cages; further, although Meinert is likewise of the opinion that the caterpillar introduces into itself the eggs of the parasite with the food, and that the same could well be the case with many other caterpillars infested with Tachinids, yet I can not suppress some doubt regarding this mode of involuntary introduction of the parasite. Professor Riley has also expressed his doubt on this point (INSECT LIFE, 1888, vol. I, p. 62.) The peculiar provisions in female Tachinids for the deposition of the eggs, their hasty behavior while in search of the hosts, and further, the fact that many eggs of the parasites must be crushed by the caterpillar in feeding; finally, the observation (cf. Rob. Desv. Ann. Soc. Ent., France, 1850, p. 162) that in Tachinids oviposition on the host actually takes place—all this renders the unusual introduction said to take place in the Uji hardly probable.

FURTHER NOTES ON PANCHLORA.

By C. V. RILEY.

Since publishing the article on the viviparous cockroach in the last number of INSECT LIFE, I have ascertained some further interesting facts relative to the viviparity of the insect. In conversation with Mr. Gustave Guttenberg, teacher of biology in the Pittsburg High School, at the recent meeting of the A. A. A. S., and also by a letter received from him August 27, transmitting specimens, he informed me that he had found a green cockroach which, while being examined by one of his scholars, had given birth to about thirty living young, besides some individuals still in their "pupa cases" [egg sacs] and a cluster of about twelve "pupæ" [eggs] arranged side by side. The adult insect was said to have been yellowish-green, while the young were about the same color. These were active and began to scatter at once. The specimens in question proved, as I suspected, to be an adult female with young, of *Panchlora viridis*. The eggs were arranged in a double row side by side, with no visible enveloping membrane. A number of them had hatched, and others still contained embryonic larvæ. The young larvæ that were born viviparously were much darker in general color than the adult, but were lighter colored than the specimens previously obtained by me. The arrangement of the eggs was not perfect, and indicated that the cluster, as it originally existed, had been broken up, and also that a number of the eggs were separated, so that the exact shape of the mass could not be determined.

Very fortunately, however, another specimen of the insect was recently forwarded to me by Dr. Carl F. Gissler, of Brooklyn, N. Y., with the report that he had captured it on his window sill, and that it was alive. The insect in question, which was a large pregnant female, died in transit. Dissection, however, resulted in obtaining a perfect egg-cluster. This was arranged in a semicircle, and consisted of a double row of closely packed eggs, as shown in the accompanying illustration (Fig. 12), the cluster comprising about forty-four eggs. No enveloping membrane again was apparent. The individual eggs were considerably narrowed by lateral compression of the abdominal joints toward the inner and smaller circumference of the semicircle, and all of them plainly showed the segmentation of the future insect, the more developed being just ready to burst from the enveloping shell. The individual eggs are a trifle over 2 millimetres long, and the egg-cluster, in longest diameter from tip to tip, is about 8 millimetres. The eggs were not all of the same color, the more mature being darker than the rest.

These two specimens, with the additional facts obtained on the reproductive habits of the insect, confirm the viviparity of this insect.

In the case of the specimen collected by Mr. Guttenberg the only living young had been deposited by the female, and there is very little question that some of the eggs afterwards extruded were defective and would not have produced living young. All the evidence seems to point to the fact that the young hatch within the abdomen of the female. The shell of the egg is a very delicate affair and after the hatching of the young becomes a mere shred, and in the first specimen examined no trace of a case could be found after hatching. Yet a more careful examination of the mass contained in the second specimen sent by Dr. Gissler shows that there is a partial case or covering of the mass. The genital pouch, which is formed by the folding back of the external integument far into the interior of the abdomen, is rather larger in this species than in other cockroaches so far as known, and the invagination extends back through rather more than two segments. The young hatch within this vaginal chamber, which is large enough to afford space for their movement and post-natal development. The eggs developed in the twin ovaries are matured in couples and passed out into the vaginal space. The typical egg capsule or oötheca of other roaches is, according to Miall and Denny, formed about the eggs within the vaginal pouch from a fluid secreted by the many-branched colleterial glands which open into the under side of the uterus near the extremity of the latter. This egg-capsule is practically wanting in *Panchlora viridis* and can be detected only by very carefully dissecting the egg cluster, when a thin membranous sheath is found to inclose the inner or basal half of the mass or about one-half the length of the eggs. Judging from this rudimentary nature of the egg capsule, if this partially inclosing membrane may be so styled, the colleterial glands must be much reduced or almost wanting in *Panchlora*.

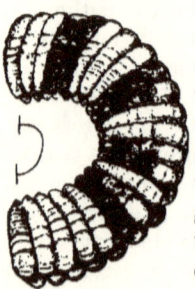

Fig. 12. *Panchlora viridis*: egg mass — enlarged (original).

SOME STUDIES OF THE CLOVER HAY-WORM, ASOPIA COSTALIS.

By F. M. WEBSTER, *Special Agent.*

Although much has been written of this insect, yet, so far as the writer has been able to gather from the literature to which we have had access, little if anything has been learned of its habits since it was studied by Dr. Riley, as portrayed in his Sixth Report on Insects of Missouri, p. 102.

Late in April of the present year we received a number of these larvæ from Prof. W. I. Chamberlain, of Hudson, Summit County, Ohio, with the statement that they were destroying hay in that neighborhood. In accordance with instructions from Professor Riley we visited the farm of Mr. Chamberlain on April 27, in order to investigate the matter and see if some means could be devised whereby the pest could be destroyed.

On arriving at our destination we found that a stack of about 20 tons, standing in the open field, had been damaged fully 50 per cent, although the hay was fully three-quarters timothy. About 5 tons of this hay was handled over and re-stacked beside the old site, in the mean time being thoroughly dusted with a mixture of 10 pounds of powdered pyrethrum thoroughly mixed in 50 pounds of flour. This was done with the understanding that the whole stack was to be removed in a short time, when the results of the application could be ascertained. A small quantity of hay thus treated and piled up to one side was examined next day, and a majority of the larvæ were found to have been destroyed. The stack, however, contrary to our expectations, was allowed to stand for nearly six months, when of course all hope of learning anything of the effect of the experiment had long before vanished. The result, though admitted a failure in this case, demonstrated the practicability of the measure, and the smaller experiment gave evidence of its efficiency. Other farmers in the vicinity reported serious losses through the same insect, and in some cases the hay had been so badly injured that it had been burned on the ground, and this, too, as early as late September or early in October of the previous year.

A great number of larvæ were taken from Mr. Chamberlain's hay, and placed in breeding cages. These continued to feed on the dry hay for a considerable time, pupæ being first observed on May 25. Growing clover plants were now transplanted to the breeding cage. Moths issued from cocoons on June 12, and also on later dates. . To all appearances the eggs were placed in the heads of the clover, which, with the rest of the plant, was kept alive and growing. On July 1, young larvæ, some very small, others half-grown, were found in the heads now turning brown but not dead, and the leaves being green. August 6, pupæ and larvæ, both partly and quite full-grown, were taken from the cage, and two days later adults also began to emerge. These adults were placed in a breeding cage, with fresh growing clover plants which had been carefully transplanted and kept in growing condition. In the heads of this last planting larvæ were found on August 15.

From these experiments it may be concluded, so far as conclusions can be drawn from a single series of experiments, that the eggs may be deposited on the plants in the field, and thus the larvæ be drawn to the stack or mow; and, also, the eggs may be deposited in the stacks in the field early in August. The prospect of protecting the hay from attack certainly does not look very encouraging, nor is the outlook for assistance of parasites much more favorable, as I have not reared a single species that was clearly parasitic on the hay worm.

Mr. W. B. Hall, writing from Wakeman, Huron County, Ohio, states that these worms have been very troublesome, especially in his barn. A straw tick left on old hay in one of his mows was thickly covered with cocoons during May and June. Under date of June 29, he mentions observing the moths, at that time in considerable numbers, especially about straw stacks and straw sheds. The fondness of this insect for old, compact masses of hay is well known, but it seems very doubtful about this being their exclusive habitat during summer, or that a careful burning of all old stack bottoms, etc., would secure immunity from the fall and winter attacks of the pest.

SOME OF THE BRED PARASITIC HYMENOPTERA IN THE NATIONAL COLLECTION.

(Continued from p. 464 of vol. III.)

Family **PROCTOTRYPIDÆ**.

Subfamily **Bethylinæ**.

Parasites. *Hosts.*

Goniozus cellaris (Say) .... Geometrid larva from wheat stubble. Lafayette, Ind., Sept. 17, 1884.
Goniozus foveolatus Ashm .... Tineid larva in dry fungus. Georgiana, Fla., April 14, 1882.
Perisemus prolongatus Prov .... *Crambus caliginosellus*, Aug. 28, 1888. Lafayette, Ind.
Laelius trogodermatis Ashm., MS .... *Trogoderma* larva. Washington, D. C., Nov. 1, 1884.

Subfamily **Dryininæ**.

Labeo typhlocybæ Ashm., MS .... *Typhlocyba* sp. on *Celtis* and Elm. Washington, D. C., July 23, 1883.

Subfamily **Spalangiinæ**.

Cerocephala scolytivora Ashm., MS ...... Scolytid, new genus and species, on *Ficus pedunculata*. Key West, Fla., April 14, 1887.

Parasites. *Hosts.*

Cerocephala pityophthori Ashm., MS .... *Pityophthorus consimilis* Lec. Haw Creek, Fla., April, 1887.
Spalangia hæmatobiæ Ashm., MS .... *Hæmatobia serrata*. Collected in Virginia, Sept. 13, 1887.
Spalangia drosophilæ Ashm., MS .... Dipterous puparium in Rice, Savannah, Ga., Aug. 29, 1881; also reared by Ashmead, at Jacksonville, Fla., from *Drosophila* sp. in Orange.

Subfamily **Ceraphroninæ**.

Lygocerus triticum Taylor .... *Siphonophora arenæ*. New Brunswick, N. J., July 17, 1890.
Lygocerus 6-dentatus Ashm., MS .... *Sarrothripa rawayana*. Washington, D. C., July 22, 1886 (?).
Lygocerus californicus Ashm., MS .... Cecidomyiid gall on *Larra mexicana*. Los Angeles, Cal. (?).
Ceraphon salicicola Ashm., MS .... Bred from old willow wood, which was partly covered with fungus, and infested with Coleopterous larvæ. Los Angeles, Cal. (?).
Aphanogmus floridanus Ashm.,MS .... Cecidomyiid larva feeding on Red Spider, Los Angeles, Cal. (?); also from a lot of twigs, containing eggs of *Cicada septendecim*, Arlington, Va., Aug. 11, 1885.

Subfamily **Scelioninæ**.

Phanurus ovivorus Ashm., MS .... Heteropterous eggs, Washington, D. C., Sept. 10, 1885; also from Curculionid on catkins of Black Birch, June 19, 1889.
Telenomus ichthyuræ Ashm., MS .... Eggs *Ichthyura inclusa*. Washington, D. C.
Telenomus podisi Ashm., MS............. Eggs *Podisus modestus* Stal. St. Louis, Mo., June 9, 1879; Kirkwood, Mo.
Telenomus graptæ How .... Eggs *Grapta interrogationis*. Washington, D. C., Sept. 19, 1886.
Telenomus gnophæliæ Ashm., MS .... Eggs *Gnophælia hopferi* Grote. Sisson, Cal., Aug. 14, 1890.
Telenomus spilosomatis Ashm., MS ...... Eggs *Spilosoma virginica*. Washington, D. C.
Telenomus cœlodasidis Ashm., MS ...... Eggs *Cœlodasys leptinoides*. Washington, D. C., Aug. 31, 1882.
Telenomus arzamæ Riley., MS .... Eggs *Arzama obliquata*. Washington, D. C., June 4, 20, and June 24, 1884.
Telenomus heliothidis Ashm., MS .... Eggs *Heliothis armigera*. Shreveport, La., in June, 1891.
Telenomus hubbardi Ashm., MS .... Eggs Reduviid sp. Centreville, Fla., Sept. 4, 1880.
Telenomus lavernæ Ashm., MS .... Eggs *Laverna luciferella*. Washington, D. C., June 21, 1884.
Telenomus rileyi How .... Eggs *Apatura clyton*. Fairbury, Ill., March 22, 1884.
Telenomus clisiocampæ Riley., MS ...... Eggs *Clisiocampa americana*, Westerville, Nebr., March 23, 1889; also eggs *Clisiocampa* sp., Placer County, Cal.

| Parasites. | Hosts. |

Telenomus bifidus Riley .... Eggs *Hyphantria textor.* Washington, D. C., July 27, 1886.
Telenomus koebelei Ashm., MS .... Unknown eggs on Solidago. Alameda, Cal., Dec. 12, 1887.
Telenomus gossypiicola Ashm., MS ...... Eggs of Lepidopteron on Cotton. Bougere P. O., Concordia Parish, La., Aug. 16, 1880.
Telenomus chrysopæ Ashm., MS .... Eggs *Chrysopa* sp. Washington. D. C., July.
Telenomus geometræ Ashm., MS .... Eggs unknown Geometrid moth on Wild Cherry. No date or locality.
Telenomus californicus Ashm., MS .... Eggs *Orgyia* sp. Los Angeles, Cal.
Trisholcus podisi Ashm., MS .... Eggs *Podisus spinosus.* Philadelphia, Pa.
Trisholcus thyantæ Ashm., MS .... Eggs *Thyanta custator.* Selma, Ala.
Trisholcus euschistus Ashm .... Eggs *Euschistus servus* Say. Ithaca, N. Y.
Prosacantha caraborum Riley, MS .... Eggs *Scarites subterraneus.* Washington, D. C., June 14, 1883, and June 26, 1884.
Acoloides saitidis How .... Eggs Araneid *Saitis pulex.* Lincoln, Nebr.
Cacus œcanthi Riley, MS .... Eggs *Oecanthus niveus,* Fredonia, Kans., March 23, 1881; Lafayette, Ind.; also from eggs *Oecanthus latipennis,* Cadet, Mo., June 3, 1884.
Baryconus œcanthi Riley, MS .... Eggs *Oecanthus niveus.* Lincoln, Nebr.; no date.
Macroteleia floridana Ashm .... From stems of Timothy infested with larvæ of *Languria.* Lafayette, Ind.
Hadronotus leptocorisæ How .... Eggs *Zelus bilobus* Say. Crescent City, Fla.
Hadronotus largi Ashm., MS............ Eggs *Largus succinctus.* Los Angeles, Cal.
Hadronotus rugosus How................ Extracted from the supposed eggs of *Dysdercus suturellus.* Eggs *Anasa tristis.* Fort George Island, Fla., May 20, 1880; Kirkwood, Mo., Aug. 2, 1882.
Hadronotus anasæ Ashm................ Eggs *Anasa tristis.* Fort George Island, Fla., May 20, 1880; Kirkwood, Mo., Aug. 2, 1882.
Hadronotus floridanus Ashm............. Eggs *Metapodius femoratus.* Cocoanut Grove, Fla., May 16, 1886.
Scelio ovivora Riley..................... Eggs *Dissosteira carolina.* Mass. No date.
Scelio calopteni Riley, MS .... Eggs *Caloptenus atlanis.* Boscawen, N. H., June 27, 1883.
Scelio luggeri Riley, MS................. Eggs *Caloptenus* sp. St. Anthony Park, Minn., July, 1889.
Scelio ernsti Riley, MS .... Eggs *Acridium melanocera.* Caracas, Venezuela, Jan. 22, 1885.

Subfamily **Platygasterinæ.**

Inostemma horni Ashm .... Cecidomyiid gall in blossoms of *Vernonia noveboracensis,* Washington, D. C., June 5, 1886.
Inostemma californica Ashm., MS........ Cecidomyiid gall on *Telypodium integrifolium.* Los Angeles County, Cal. No date of rearing.
Amblyaspis minutus Ashm., MS.......... *Cecidomyia* sp., in squash. St. Louis, Mo., July 10, 1870.

Parasites.	Hosts.
Isorhombus arizonensis Ashm., MS	Cecidomyiid gall on unknown plant. Fort Huachuca, Ariz., May 8, 1883.
Polymecus lupinicola Ashm., MS	Cecidomyiid gall on *Lupinus athoreu*. San Francisco, Cal., Nov., 1885.
Polymecus alnicola Ashm., MS	*Cecidomyia serrulata* O. S., on Alder. Washington, D. C., April 30 and May 1, 1884.
Synopeas cornicola Ashm., MS	Cecidomyiid gall on *Cornus paniculata*. Kirkwood, Mo., April 3.
Synopeas antennariae Ashm., MS	*Cecidomyia antennariæ* Wheeler. Milwaukee, Wis., May 31, 1888.
Anopedias error (Fitch)	*Diplosis tritici*. Lafayette, Ind., June 14, 1884.
Amitus aleurodinis Hald	*Aleurodes* sp. on *Acer dasycarpum*. Arlington, Va., March 29, 1882.
Trichacis rufipes Ashm., MS	From acorns infested with *Balaninus nasicus* and *Blastobasis glandulella*. St. Louis, Mo. Prob. from cecid. inquiline.
Trichacis rubicola Ashm., MS	Cecidomyiid stem gall on Blackberry, Cadet, Mo., June 16, 1883; also Cecidomyiid gall on *Vernonia noveboracensis*, Washington, D. C., June 9, 1886.
Platygaster herrickii Pack	*Cecidomyia destructor* Say. Lafayette, Ind., April 4, 1889.
Platygaster caryæ Ashm	Cecidomyiid gall on Hickory. Washington, D. C., May 5, 1884.
Platygaster aphidis Ashm., MS	*Aphis* sp. on *Chenopodium album*. Richfield Springs, N. Y., Feb. 9, 1887.
Platygaster philanna Walker	*Diplosis nigra* Meigen. Hornsea, Yorks, England.
Ceroplatymerus caryæ Ashm	Cecidomyiid gall on Hickory. St. Louis, Mo., April 4, 1885.
Polygnotus striaticeps Ashm	Cecidomyiid gall on Bigelovia or Artemisia, Newhall, Los Angeles County, Cal., July, 1886; also from *Aspidiotus* sp., San Diego, Cal.
Polygnotus salicicola Ashm., MS	Cecidomyiid gall on midrib of leaves of Willow. Los Angeles, Cal., 1887.
Polygnotus proximus Ashm., MS	*Cecidomyia ananassæ* Riley on Cypress. No date given.
Polygnotus eurotiæ Ashm., MS	Cecidomyiid gall on *Eurotia canata*. San Bernardino County, Cal., April 17, 1887.
Polygnotus solidaginis Ashm	Cecidomyiid gall on *Solidago*, Bushberg, Mo., Sept. 21, 1876; also from same gall, Kirkwood, Mo., Sept. 13, 1885.
Polygnotus viticola Ashm., MS	Cecidomyiid gall on petiole of Grapevine. Washington, D. C., March 31, 1882.
Polygnotus artemisiæ Ashm., MS	Cecidomyiid gall on *Artemisia*. Lancaster, Los Angeles County, Cal., Dec. 6, 1887.
Polygnotus cynipscicola Ashm	*Neuroterus batatus* Fitch. Arlington, Va., July 3, 1883.
Polygnotus coloradensis Ashm	Cecidomyiid gall on Sage Bush. Fort Garland, Col., June 25, 1883.
Polygnotus utahensis Ashm., MS	Cecidomyiid gall on *Artemisia tridentata*. Pariah, Utah, July, 1881.

Parasites.   *Hosts.*

Polygnotus rubi Ashm., MS..............*Cecidomyia farinosa* O. S. on Blackberry.
 Arlington, Va., March 30, 1886.
Polygnotus vernoniae Ashm., MS........Trypeta gall on *Vernonia noveboracensis*.
 Arlington, Va., June 15 and 16, 1886; also
 from Cecidomyiid gall on *Vernonia fasciculata*, St. Louis, Mo., June 8, 1886.
Polygnotus tumidus Ashm., MS..........*Cecidomyia symmetrica* O. S., on Oak.
 Washington, D. C., Feb. 25, 1881.
Polygnotus alnicola Ashm., MS ....Cecidomyiid gall from flower bud of Alder.
 Washington, D. C., July 31, 1886.
Polygnotus pinicola Ashm., MS..........*Cecidomyia pini-inopis* O. S. on *Pinus inops*.
 Washington, D. C., May 14, 1879.
Polygnotus euurae Ashm., MS............*Euura s.-nodus* Walsh. St. Louis, Mo.,
 Feb. 24, 2879.
Polygnotus atriplecis Ashm., MS.........Cecidomyiid gall on *Atriplex canescens*.
 Barstow, San Bernardino County, Cal.,
 April and May, 1887. (?)
Polygnotus huachucae Ashm., MS.......Cecidomyiid pod-like gall on unknown
 plant, Fort Huachuca, Arizona. June 6,
 1883; Cecidomyiid stem-gall on Sunflower, Fort Grant, Arizona, June 5, 1882,
 and from a Cecidomyiid gall on Sensitive
 Plant, Fort Huachuaca, Arizona.
Polygnotus diplosidis Ashm., MS ....*Diplosis* sp. on Pine. New Brunswick, N.
 J., Feb. 12, 1891.
Polygnotus actinomeridis Ashm., MS ....Cecidomyiid gall on *Actinomeris*. Washington, D. C., April 23, 1884.
Polygnotus californicus Ashm., MS......Cecidomyiid gall on *Baccharis pilularis*.
 San Francisco, Cal., June 10 and 23, 1883;
 Alameda, Cal., Dec. 17 and 19, 1885.
Polygnotus astericola Ashm., MS ....Cecidomyiid gall on Aster. Holderness,
 N. H., May 21, 1884.
Polygnotus asynaptae Ashm., MS........Cecidomyiid gall on *Asynapta* sp. Maywood, Ill.
Polygnotus hiemalis Forbes..............*Cecidomyia destructor* Say. La Porte, Ind.,
 May 14, 1889; Blair. Nebr., Aug. 16, 1876.

Subfamily **Proctotrypinæ**.

Proctotrypes obsoletus Say..............*Stelidota strigosa*. Washington, D. C., Dec.
 9, 1879.

Subfamily **Diapriinæ**.

Diapria conica Fabr....................*Eristalis tenax*. Albany, N. Y., Oct. 10, 1890
 (Dr. J. A. Lintner).
Diapria muscæ Ashm., MS..............From dipterous puparia found in the
 ground, Sacramento County, Cal., Sept.,
 1890.
Phænopria hæmatobiæ Ashm., MS.......*Hæmatobia serrata*. Virginia, Sept. 12,
 1889.

THE THREE PEAR TREE PSYLLAS.

We had occasion some time since to abstract Dr. F. Loew's remarks on the Psyllas which inhabit the Pear, from his Neue Beiträge zur Kenntniss der Psylliden, and as the subject is of interest in this country we reproduce it here.

The Pear (*Pyrus communis* L.) is known to be the food plant of three species of *Psylla*, viz, *Psylla pyrisuga* Foerst., *P. pyri* L., and *P. pyricola* Foerst., the last of which also occurs occasionally on the Apple (*Pyrus mali*). The imagoes of these species appear from June to August, depending on the climate, and when first matured are light in color, but gradually assume a darker coloration as the season advances. They hibernate over winter in the crevices of bark and other protected situations, and deposit eggs in the fall and spring upon the buds and leaves of the pear trees. The young larvæ of *Psylla pyrisuga* infest the leaves and the young succulent shoots, but after the second molt they migrate first to the older twigs, but still of the same year's growth, and later go gradually to the older and more woody parts of the previous year's growth and cover it in larger or smaller closely-packed clusters. The larvæ of *Psylla pyri* and *P. pyricola*, on the contrary, always appear on the stunted or fruit-bearing twigs, where they inhabit the buds and the angles between the petioles and twigs, and sometimes also the underside of the leaves.

Psylla pyrisuga is found throughout central Europe, appearing almost every year in large numbers, and is quite a serious pest. *Psylla pyri* is a comparatively rare species, appearing always in small restricted colonies, but is widely distributed. *Psylla pyricola* occurs in some localities in large numbers, and particularly infests dwarf Pears and the varieties which are trained on trellises, and often occasions considerable damage. The following characters will serve to separate the three species mentioned:

(1) The entire length to the tip of the closed wings of the male at least 3.7 millimetres; of the female at least 4 millimetres. Front and hind wings colorless, transparent, and without spots, except that occasionally the pterostigma may be somewhat reddish or brownish; the forceps of the male viewed from the side is straight and of uniform width to near the tip, where it tapers suddenly to a point, and is about three-fourths the length of and as broad or a little broader than the genital plate. *Psylla pyrisuga* Foerst.

(2) Entire length to the tip of the closed wings in the male not exceeding 3.5 millimetres; in the female 3.7 millimetres. General color of the front wings either pale wine yellow or hyaline and marked about the middle of the cells with yellowish, brownish, or blackish shades, particularly in the region of the apical margin. Apex of the clavus black, with a small black spot or shade behind it in the posterior basal cell. The apex of the clavus of the hind wing is also black, or sometimes the entire clavus.

(*a*) Frontal cones or protuberances of pale specimens yellowish or greenish white or with a brownish ring at the apex in front. In dark-colored specimens the frontal cones are reddish brown or dark brown, with a large yellow or reddish yellow spot on the center above, with a white or yellowish dot at the extreme tip. The front wings, in pale specimens, with yellowish reflections in the cells, particularly toward the apical margin, and with the veins yellow or pale brown; in darker specimens, with a brownish, grayish, or black shade in the cells and with the veins pale brown or black. Forceps of the male, viewed from the side, always as long as the genital plate, narrow, acutely pointed, sickle shaped, the apex recurved and having a tooth-like projection at the base. *Psylla pyri* L.

(*b*) Basal two-thirds of the frontal cones or protuberances red or reddish brown; the apical one-third white or yellowish. The front wings, including the veins, even in dark specimens, of a pale wine yellow, somewhat lighter colored at the base than at the apex, and without any markings whatever. The forceps of the male, viewed from the side, two-thirds the length but distinctly narrower than the genital plate, straight, and of almost uniform width to the middle, from which point it gradually narrows to the pointed apex. *Psylla pyricola* Foerst.

J. Scott mentions *Psylla simulans* Foerst., on pear trees but Loew only found this species upon apple in connection with *P. pyricola*. *P. simulans* is distinguished from *P. pyri*, with which it is nearest allied, by the front wings being transparent even in the youngest individuals with brownish or blackish shades in the cells. The tip of the clavus is larger with more black and in the hind basal cell there is a brownish or blackish stripe along the whole fold of the clavus in the male just as in *P. pyricola*, but a little brighter. In other respects it agrees with *P. pyri*.

THE FIRST INTRODUCTION OF BLASTOPHÁGA PSENES INTO CALIFORNIA.

By GUSTAV EISEN, *San Francisco, Cal.*

The *Blastophaga psenes* or Capri Fig Wasp was introduced into California last August for the first time. The history of the introduction of this insect is in short as follows:

In the fall of 1890 I visited the orchard and nursery of Mr. James Shinn, of Niles, Alameda County, Cal., for the purpose of comparing the various Smyrna fig varieties growing on his place. These figs had been introduced here some ten years previously by the San Francisco Bulletin Company direct from Smyrna. They consist of three distinct varieties of edible figs and of one tree of the Capri Fig or Wild Fig. These Smyrna varieties have never borne any perfect figs, the crop dropping off before the figs begin to mature. During my visit I called Mr. Shinn's attention to the necessity of introducing the *Blastophaga psenes*, and as the Capri Fig growing on his place was the only large tree of the kind in California, it would only be necessary to have the first colony of insects placed there. Mr. Shinn then mentioned that he had a friend in Smyrna, a certain missionary, Mr. J. Bliss, who could possibly be made to interest himself in our case. I gave some advice as to how the importation should be made and left the correspondence to Mr. Shinn.

One day, in the latter part of August of this year, Mr. J. Shinn, jr., called on me in San Francisco, informing me that the box with Capri figs and Blastophagæ had just arrived and that many of the insects were alive, apparently just hatching out. I at once went to Mr. Shinn's place to help distribute the colony. On my arrival I found that the box had been placed under the Capri Fig tree and that many of the Blastophagæ had already escaped. The box contained about one dozen figs nearly as large as small walnuts, all being quite dry, one or two having decayed. I noticed that from the pressure in the box many of the figs were closed and the Blastophagæ unable to escape. I therefore cut all the figs open and thus released probably several thousand Blastophagæ.* The box was suspended in the fig tree and the small insects soon made their way to the surrounding fig trees. Upon opening some Smyrna figs a few hours later, for the purpose of pollinating them artificially, I found that several Blastophagæ had already entered them. As to the Capri Fig tree I found on it no figs which I thought of proper size to receive the Blastophagæ, some being too small, others again too large. It is, however, possible that some figs escaped my notice as the fig tree is a large one, probably reaching twelve feet in height; and only a coming year will show the final success of this, the first importation.

The Capri Figs were collected at Lokia, near Smyrna, Asia Minor, the last days of June. The 2d day of July the box reached Smyrna and the 18th of the same month it arrived at New York. On the 23d it reached Mr. Shinn at Niles, in California. Thus it required only about twenty-five days to reach us, a time short enough to insure full success to any similar importation. The best way to forward Capri Figs is not to wrap them in cotton or paper, but simply to place them in layers in a small paper box; each fig as well as each layer should be separated by a small wad of paper, sufficiently firm to prevent the figs from shaking and rolling. If each separate fig is wrapped up too tight in paper it is liable to decay.

COMMENTS ON THE FIFTH REPORT OF THE U. S. ENTOMOLOGICAL COMMISSION.

By JOHN HAMILTON, M. D., *Allegheny, Pa.*

In looking over the Fifth Report of the U. S. Entomological Commission, Department of Agriculture, recently published, several inadvertences have been observed in the nomenclature of various species of Coleoptera. As the editor, A. S. Packard, M. D., PH. D., in the introduction invites corrections, etc., the following are submitted, as well as a few remarks to render some of the statements clearer.

---

*The majority of Blastophagæ were winged females; a few were wingless males. I noticed no parasites.

(Page 69.) *Chrysobothris chlorocephala* is *scitula* Gory (Horn.)

(Page 80.) The Oak-bark Weevil. *Magdalis olyra* Herbst. This would seem to be a misnomer. from the fact that this beetle. as is well known. breeds more abundantly in deadened and diseased hickory than it does in oak. *Scolytus 4-spinosus* Say. is no doubt often credited with its work.

(Page 81.) *Hylecœtus americanus* Harris is *H. lugubris* Say.

(Page 91.) *Leptura zebra* Oliv. is *L. nitens* Forst. (Horn).

(Page 215.) The Acorn Worm. *Balaninus rectus* Say. This is. with our present knowledge. rather a misnomer; for while *rectus* may infest acorns occasionally. it is usually bred from chestnuts and chinquapins. According to the records of breeding from nuts and acorns. the following names would be appropriate. if any are requisite:

The great Chestnut Weevil-worm. *Balaninus* (*caryatrypes*) *proboscideus* Fabr.

The smaller Chestnut Weevil-worm *B. rectus* Say. (This has also been bred once from acorns from Arizona.)

The Hazel-nut Weevil. *B. obtusus* Blanch.

The Hickory-nut Weevil. *B. caryæ* Horn.

The Acorn Weevils. *B. quercus* Horn; *B. uniformis* Lec.; *B. nasicus* Say.

Owing to the difficulty of separating the species. the statements of observers till recently are of doubtful value when at variance with the preceding. Breeding frequently in different parts of the country and ascertaining exactly what is bred may give more diversified food habits than the foregoing.

(Page 223.) *Dendroides canadensis* Latr. is now *bicolor*. Newm.

(Page 237.) *Galeruca calmariensis* Linn. The beetle mentioned by Fitch under this name is the preceding. *G. xanthhomelæna* Schr., and Smith has delineated a variety. probably *G. gelatinariæ* Fab. *G. calmariensis* Linn. is not known to occur in North America, and. moreover. feeds on aquatic plants.

(Page 288.) *Stenosphenus notatus* Oliv. This beetle breeds in dead hickory limbs. requiring two years for its transformation. The larva changes to a beetle in the fall. but does not emerge till the spring.

(Page 293.) *Dorcaschema nigrum* Say. Breeds abundantly in dead hickory limbs and requires two years for its development. The description is misplaced by the printer. and follows *Thysanœs fimbricornis*.

(Page 296.) 33. *Sinoxylon basilare* Say is correctly recorded. 34. Red-shouldered Apate. *Apate basilaris* Say; this is the same as the preceding. *S. basilare*.

(Page 327.) The Hickory-nut Weevil. *Balaninus nasicus* Say. This is a misnomer. as a correctly determined *B. nasicus* has never been recorded as bred from the nuts of the hickory. The species which depredates on hazel-nuts is *B. obtusus* Blanch., not described at the time Mr. Harrington published the article cited.

(Page 350.) *Balaninus caryatrypes* now *proboscideus* Fab. More recent observation is that all the larvæ enter the ground in the fall and that none of them remain in the nuts till spring, which is stated to be probable.

(Page 367.) *Apion rostrum* Say. Whether this species depends on the locust is uncertain. *A. nigrum* Hbst. does so certainly. There is one or more species found on it here in great abundance, which is neither of the two named. Several species will probably be found to infest this tree when an expert skillful enough to accurately separate them shall appear.

(Page 372.) *Spermophagus robiniæ* Fab. This beetle can not breed in the seeds of Robinia as it is many times too large; it is known, however, to inhabit the seeds of *Gleditschia triacanthus*, Honey Locust; hence the error has probably arisen.

(Page 470.) *Chrysomela pallida*. I can not find that Say has described any species corresponding with the description here, *i. e.*, larvæ 8 millimetres long, beetle 15 millimetres long. The only Chrysomelians I can find described by Say under the name *pallida* are *Metachroma* (Colaspis) *pallida*, which is only 3.5 to 4 millimetres long, and *Hispa pallida*, supposed to be *Odontota rosea* Weber, which is similar in size.

(Page 529.) *Galeruca sanguinea*. This is a European beetle not yet known to occur in America. The insect intended is not very clear, as its description is inadequate.

(Page 532.) *Galeruca vittata* is a *Diabrotica*.

(Page 543.) *Neoclytus capræa*. The larvæ of this beetle bore into felled ash timber, which, if not used till the second year, is often found to be worthless. Healthy growing trees seem to be free from attack. The beetle emerges from the wood near the end of two years, the pupa becoming an imago late in the fall which hibernates till early spring in the larval burrow.

Tylonotus bimaculatus Hald. This species breeds abundantly in deadened hickory, requiring two years for its transformations.

(Page 591.) *Phyllodecta vittellinæ* Linn. The beetle meant is probably *P. vulgatissima* Linn., which is occasionally found in abundance on *Salix longifolia*. The older authors, it is true, mention *P. vittellinæ* as occurring about Lake Superior and in British America, but another comparison of specimens seems necessary to confirm this.

(Page 630.) *Haltica alni* is *H. bimarginata* Say, the older name.

(Page 641.) *Balaninus nasicus* Say. Harris only supposed the beetles found paired on hazel to be *nasicus*, but in view of present knowledge it can scarcely be doubted the species was *obtusus*.

(Page 660.) *Micracis suturalis* Lec. This species, as well as *M. aculeata* Lec., breeds abundantly in dead hickory limbs, requiring two years for its transformation.

(Page 696.) *Eupogonius pinivora* Fitch (Rep. IV, p. 712). This appears from the description to be a valid species, but has not been catalogued.

(Page 700.) *Ædilis nodosus* Fab., *A. obsoletus* Oliv. American systematists place these in *Acanthocinus*.

(Page 700.) *Euderces pini* Oliv. All on page 701 following "regarding the confusion" to the bottom belongs to this species, having been dislocated by the printer in making up the form.

(Page 720.) 47. *Pityophthorus sparsus* LeConte; 48. *Xyleborus sparsus* LeConte. These two are the same thing, the former being the correct name.

(Page 726.) *Hypomolyx pinicola* (Couper) is *H. piceus* DeGeer, which is likewise native in Europe and in northern Asia.

(Page 727.) *Crypturgus atomus* Lec. is *C. pusillus* Gyll., a species which also is an inhabitant of Europe. *C. atomus* is mentioned in several places, as on pp. 825, 861, 872.

(Page 802.) *Anomala pinicola* Mels. is *A. lucicola* Fabr.

(Page 810.) *Hylobius stupidus* Bohm. is *Pachylobius picivora* Germ.

(Page 826.) *Hylurgops pinifex* Fitch is *Hylastes glabratus* Zett., a species likewise native in northern Asia and in Europe.

(Page 913.) *Metachroma 6-notata* Say is now *Paria canella* Oliv. (Horn).

(Page 913.) *Liopus facetus* Say is a *Lepturges*.

EXTRACTS FROM CORRESPONDENCE.

Injurious Insects of Nebraska.*

FIRST LETTER.—May Beetles (*Lachnosterna* spp.). The larvæ of these beetles were very numerous during the early part of the season, when young corn was first up. I heard many reports about damage done to the plants by cutworms, and upon investigation I found that the greater part of the damage was done by these larvæ. They coiled themselves at the root of the plant where the sprout left the seed and ate it off so as to kill the plant, and I am sure that a great portion of damage laid to cutworms was done by these insects. I do not know that the beetles do any damage to speak of.

Willow Saw-fly (*Cimbex americana*).—The larvæ of this insect were present in large numbers, doing great damage to the willows of this vicinity. The writer has in view a willow hedge in the vicinity that has for three consecutive years been completely defoliated and at present writing it is again covered with the worms. During the time of oviposition this peculiar hedge was completely alive with the saw-flies. The following observances may be of some use as to the habits. The writer noticed that trees on high ground were more liable to be attacked than those growing in damp places along stream beds, and also that young trees were more damaged than older ones, and that they do not eat the common wild or slough willow growing naturally along water courses. The effect of the insect on the hedge mentioned was to give the trees a peculiarly stunted look where repeatedly defoliated.

The Smeared Acronycta (*Acronycta oblinita*).—These are present during the fall months and are mostly found feeding upon the Smartweed and very seldom upon other plants, so they can hardly in their present numbers be called injurious.

---

*The names of insects are for the most part taken from and the work based upon Bulletins Nos. 5 and 14 of the Nebraska State Experiment Station by Lawrence Bruner, entomologist.

The Walnut-Caterpillar (*Datana angusii*).—This caterpillar is frequently very injurious to small walnut trees and often defoliates large ones that are situated away from natural timber, but does not seem to bother the trees growing wild in natural forests or along creek banks. On August 10, 1889, the writer observed at the foot of some walnut trees bunches of these worms congregated, fully as large as a peck measure.

Yellow-necked Apple-tree Caterpillar (*Datana ministra*).—This caterpillar does great damage to young apple trees, and also at times to larger ones. It has been observed to completely defoliate trees three years from the nursery. It has not made its appearance this season at this date.

Fall Web-worm (*Hyphantria cunea*, Drury).—Present in quite numerous colonies some seasons, but seems to favor dry seasons; does not do as much damage as the preceding.

Corn Ear-worm or Boll Worm.—This was very numerous last year; hardly a perfect ear of corn could be found, and the excrement of the worm was so thick that, in husking, large quantities accumulated among the corn in wagons and crib; it does great damage from the fact that it makes it very hard to get perfect corn for seed.

Codling Moth.—Very numerous; nearly half of the apple crop was infested by this moth; such apples as Ben Davis, Jonathan, etc., were more affected than such as Wine-sap, Romanite, and apples of like quality. It has already made its appearance in green Ben Davis apples on the writer's premises, its effects being easily seen by the apples falling to the ground.

Among other insects I may mention will be found the Plum Curculio, not very numerous; the white scale which was on willow and cottonwood trees at the writer's premises for three years past has not made any appearance so far this season.—[William N. Hunter, Nebraska, July 23, 1891.

SECOND LETTER.—The Corn Root-worm (*Diabrotica longicornis*). July 31: The effects of this worm are commencing to make themselves shown after heavy rain (that is, what was planted to corn last year and again this year). Last year they were not present, at least I did not see or hear of any, but possibly the lack of rainfall to soften the ground may have had the effect of leaving the corn standing instead of its blowing down. August 17: Its effects were more plain to be seen after the heavy rain of the 14th and 15th; the mature beetles are plentifully present (August 22); noticed complaints in local papers from the western end of the county that this worm has been doing great damage. Since heavy rains accompanied by wind its effects have been already shown. September 15: The mature insects are very numerous. I noticed them feeding extensively upon the flowers of the wild sunflower growing alongside of the cornfields. They seem to favor this weed above all other vegetation except corn.

The Apple-tree Tent-caterpillar and the Codling Moth are fully up to the average years. The former is much worse than for a number of years past.

The Green-striped Maple Worm made its first appearance in this vicinity September 10, and in comparatively few numbers.

Chinch Bug (*Blissus leucopterus*). I noticed the first appearance of this bug in small numbers on August 5; the pink larvæ of the second age were most abundant. Also noticed some of the short-winged variety at a later date, though it has not done any damage to crops worth mentioning.

August 2. I noticed the first appearance of the Walnut Caterpillar (*Datana angusii*) on some large walnut trees, but not in very extensive numbers. September 15. This worm has proved very numerous and quite destructive to the foliage.—[William N. Hunter, Nebraska, September 15, 1891.

Fall Web-worm Parasites in Indian Territory.

Since reading your article on the parasites of *Hyphantria cunea*, in Bulletin No. 19, I have reared several species. I inclose for identification a few of these bred species, both primary and secondary. No. 1 I take to be *Meteorus hyphantriæ* and cocoons.

No. 2 I hardly can tell what to call, unless it is a coarctate cocoon or pupa, for this is within the dried larval skin. The imago of this is a long-antennæd parasite with yellow legs and the size of *Meteorus hyphantriæ*. This is not surely the Ichneumon spoken of in Bulletin No. 10 as *Limneria pallipes*. I found those in the webs. No. 3, the greenish secondary, was bred from this cocoon or pupa. Besides this green secondary I have bred large numbers of small black parasites No. 4, from both *Meteorus hyphantriæ* and these coarctate pupæ. Inclosed will also be found some pupal shells of a fly taken from Mud-dauber cells. Though very numerous, I can not rear the perfect fly on account of the little black secondaries found inclosed with them. How do these flies gain access to the cells of the Mud-dauber, or do they deposit ovæ in spiders that the cells are filled with? Are the cocoons inclosed (No. 5) those of *Apanteles hyphantriæ*? If so, I have bred the same species from the Fall Webworm, from a large green larva, probably that of *Sphinx 5-maculata*, and a species of fall larvæ with tufts of yellow hair. I find the cocoons in the webs of *Hyphantria cunea*.—[A. N. Caudell, Indian Territory, September 23, 1891.

REPLY.—No. 1 is *Meteorus hyphantriæ*. (No. 2) is a *Hyphantria* larva parasitized by *Limneria*. The greenish secondary parasite (No. 3) is one of the species of *Pteromalus* and the small black secondary (No. 4) is *Elasmus atratus*. The parasite from the fly puparia from the Mud-dauber's cell is extremely interesting. It is *Melittobia pelopæi*. The great interest attaching to this rearing arises from the fact that the species of *Melittobia* have heretofore been reared only from hymenopterous insects. The eggs may be laid before the cells are closed by the wasp, or the adult female may gnaw through the cell. The cocoons (No. 5) are those of *Apanteles hyphantriæ*. The species which you reared from the Sphinx larva is undoubtedly different, although belonging to the same genus. It was probably *Apanteles congregatus*. * * *—[October 8, 1891.

Notes on California Insects; the Vedalia and other Ladybirds.

I inclose a box containing insect work and specimens. On the grounds of one of our citizens I noticed on a small tree of California Laurel (*Umbellularia californica*), a peculiar folding of the points of many leaves, so as to form a triangular-shaped little house for some insect. I opened a few of them and found a little brown or black beetle about one-sixteenth of an inch long. Then I found another Ladybug, much larger, ocher color; then another, I think, six-stabbed.

My impression is that some spider had folded the leaves, spun a web-like cocoon, and the Ladybugs have cut into it to get the spider or the eggs.—[L. D. Morse, M. D., California, September 10, 1891.

P. S.—The place from which these specimens were taken is one of the finest in this vicinity. Two years ago it was completely covered with the Icerya. When Mr. Koebele came down here we planted the Vedalia there. The result has been wonderful—the place is now almost clear of the pest.

The owner of the place says I ought to have a pension for the good I had done, but I told her that it was the Entomologist of the U. S. Department of Agriculture that deserved the credit. I was only a helper to carry out what had been started by others.

REPLY.— * * * I am unable to decide whether the peculiar folding of the leaves of the Laurel is the work of the spiders, the webs of which some of them contain, or the tent-houses or protections constructed by Tortricid or Pyralid larvæ in which to spin up and pupate.

Both spiders and Lepidopterous larvæ construct retreats of this kind, and if the latter are the architects of the ones sent, the spiders and ladybirds were doubtless present to prey upon the larvæ or pupæ of the Lepidoptera.

You can probably tell by an examination of the fresh leaves whether a lepidopterous larva has any connection with the work or not, and if you find anything of interest I shall be glad to have you furnish us with specimens.

The small brown ladybird is *Scymnus collaris* Melsh., and the larger spotted one is *Hippodamia convergens* Guer.
Nothing but the skins and webs of the spiders were received, and from these the species can not be determined.—[September 18, 1891.]

An injurious Flea-beetle in Utah.

FIRST LETTER.—I inclose some insects which are doing considerable damage to young tomato plants and young beans. They feed chiefly on the under side of the leaves, but feed on both sides during the middle of the day. At night they shelter themselves under clods, especially where the plants are coming up. They crawl under the uplifted crust and not only shelter themselves but feed on the young plant before it gets above ground. Will you be so kind as to tell me what it is, and whether or not its life history is known?

I first tried spraying with Paris green, but the plants were so small that I could not wet the under side of the leaves. Am now using arsenic mixed with flour and applying with bellows, but have not yet had time to note its effect.—[E. S. Richman, Utah, June 9, 1891.

SECOND LETTER.—When I wrote you before I said I should try Paris green mixed with flour, but as I could not get the article in town I used white arsenic, and the application was followed almost immediately by a rain which killed over half the plants. I have since used kerosene emulsion with good results. Plants should be sprayed during the middle of the day while the insects are active. During the cooler portions of the day they have sheltered under clods and whatever rubbish may be available.—[E. S. Richman, Utah, July 3, 1891.

REPLY.—The specimens came safely and proved to be a species known as *Epitrix subcrinita* Lec. Your account of your experience is very interesting and the results are quite what I should have anticipated.—[July 11, 1891.]

A new Enemy to Pear Leaves.

In going through our pear trees, we noticed a little black-winged insect that was eating the soft leaves and doing considerable damage, considering their numbers. We inclose samples of both the insects and the leaves. Possibly you can tell us what they are and whether there is any way in which we can get rid of them, for evidently if they are undisturbed they will become quite a nuisance.—[Smiths and Powell, New York, August 11, 1891.

REPLY.— * * * The insect which you send has no common name, but is known scientifically as *Systena frontalis* Fabr. It is comparatively new in the rôle of an enemy to pear leaves, and the best remedy will be to spray with Paris green or London purple in the proportion of one-fourth pound of the poison to 50 gallons of water.—[August 26, 1891.]

Abundance of Colorado Potato Beetle in Georgia.

* * * The Colorado Potato Beetle was very numerous in this part this season. It is the first time I have seen them in any great numbers. I first observed them about twelve or thirteen years ago; just a few straggling specimens every year until this one. I do not believe any one took the trouble to kill them, as but very few know them when they see them.—[George Noble, Georgia, July 31, 1891.

A Grapevine Flea-beetle of New Mexico.

Inclosed find box of bugs that appeared here on the evening of the 24th of this month. They came out of the ground from small holes, similar to those of ants, but came by the millions. They are devouring the grapevines. They strip a vine in about two hours. So far they have not attacked any other class of vegetation. What are they and what will rid us of them? I have killed millions of them by spraying them with coal oil, but don't know yet whether the coal oil will kill the vines or not. They have infested about twenty vineyards, and all on the same day.—[J. J. Leeson, New Mexico, June 26, 1891.

REPLY.—The insect is one of the steel-blue Flea-beetles known as *Haltica foliacea* Lec. Your remedy of spraying with kerosene is a good one, but if you use pure kerosene you will probably injure the foliage of your plants quite as much as the beetles would have done had they been unmolested. It will be better for you to prepare an emulsion of kerosene and soap according to the formula on page 5 of Circular No. 1 of this Division. I will esteem it a favor if you will notify me as to the success of your spraying applications and as to the future spread of the insect.—[July 3, 1891.]

Notes on the Palm Weevil.

I mail you to-day three cocoanut beetles which lay the eggs of the borers in the cocoanut trees. Also inclosed find a published article by myself clipped from *Home and Farm* of Louisville, Ky.; they find no remedy. I am in hopes that you will be kind enough to inform me of some remedy or protection.—[John B. Hickey, Honduras, Central America, September 14, 1891.

* * * About one month ago I cut down a small cohoon tree, very much resembling the cocoanut palm, cutting it through the tender portion—the bud. In two or three days it began to sour, and for a few evenings, between sunset and dark, I noticed several of these beetles fly to it and bury themselves an inch or more in the soft pulp, some of them remaining there all day. In about 10 days they were all gone. A month later I cut the stump off about 3 feet lower down and found it full of holes, and some ten or twelve worms about the size of a man's thumb, 1¼ inches long, with a short, hard head, resembling very much the common grub worm. Now, it is my opinion that the beetle lays the eggs of these boring worms in blooms, which, when dead, fall between the stalks, and from them come the worms which bore in the body of the tree and soon kill it. They do not make much of a hole at first, but under favorable conditions soon become large enough to do permanent damage.

The cocoanut tree is especially adapted to soil near the salt water, and during a rainy spell of a few days I have noticed a golden-colored glue or sap running out of some of the trees, but failed to find any borers in them. Burning the top of the tree with fire when the first symptoms are noted will save the tree from total destruction, but it dwarfs it so much that it is of but little good afterwards. These beetles are found in southern Florida as well as here. When a cabbage palm is cut down the stump is attacked much like the cohoon stump I have described. There are, however, old cocoanut groves in Florida which have had no experience with these borers and know nothing of them. I am in hopes that I can find some remedy or protection.

REPLY.—The cocoanut beetle which you send, and to which you refer in your printed communication to the Louisville (Ky.) *Home and Farm*, is the well-known Palm Weevil, *Rhynchophorus palmarum* Linn., which is abundant throughout Central America and a large portion of South America, extending also into the extreme southern portion of California. The Palm Weevil of Florida which develops in the Cabbage Palmetto is a different, though congeneric species, *Rhynchophorus zimmermanni* Schoenh. (*cruentatus* Fab.). There is no way of saving a cocoanut tree once badly infested by the larvæ of the weevil, and since such trees will surely die, they should be promptly felled and the infested portion burned to prevent a further multiplication of the beetles. There is, however, a preventive method, and this consists in cutting down or wounding several young trees of any wild species of palm growing in the vicinity of the cocoanut trees. The fermenting sap of the trunks of such trees, as you have yourself seen, attracts the beetles strongly, and a multitude of them can thus easily be captured and killed before they have oviposited. The trunks of the felled trees will soon be filled with the larvæ, and the infested portion should be sawed off and burned before the larvæ have matured. If concerted action on the part of owners of cocoanut trees could be obtained, this method would no doubt materially contribute toward a diminution in the number of the beetles and a consequent lessening of the damage to the cocoanut trees.—[September 25, 1891.]

Rhynchites bicolor injuring Cultivated Roses.

I forward specimens of Coleoptera which are proving very injurious to our roses. I have not known this insect as a rose pest before. The beetle can be frequently caught with its long proboscis buried deep in the rosebud, and it also seems to cut the stem, or otherwise injure the bud just at the thin part of the stalk below the calyx, and afterwards the bud droops, hangs its head, and dries up. I send you a quantity of the injured buds of three kinds of rose for examination, and I shall feel obliged for any information regarding this enemy of our beautiful flowers. I have not seen the insect upon anything but roses.—[Arthur Boyle, New Mexico, June 22, 1891.

REPLY.—The insect which is damaging your roses is a weevil known as *Rhynchites bicolor*. An insect of this same genus is found upon roses in England, and this may be the species which you have seen. It will be difficult to suggest a remedy without knowing the breeding habits of the insect. At this distance it will be impossible to advise you on this point. The early habits of the species are not known to entomologists. If you can find where the female lays her eggs and where the larvæ develop you may be able to find a remedy.—[July 3, 1891.]

The Coleoptera in the National Museum.

With this I mail you a box containing 27 species and 57 specimens, mostly Coleoptera that I noticed were lacking or but poorly represented in your collection. I will contribute more if you wish (in all orders). * * * I will be glad to contribute more material and try to make your collection a "Mecca" for students. During my visit to Washington the collection afforded me real satisfaction, enabling me to correct some errors in my own series. There are larger collections than yours, but if they are so perfect and in such order and so carefully guarded that it is dangerous to touch them for fear of breaking something, and so crowded that one can not get a specimen out to examine, then a student must hunt another place, which your collection bids fair to supply. Your North American Coleoptera seem to be very accurately named, which is a refreshing rarity as compared with other public collections, and I hope you will get all the types, as you seem to have the best place for them in the United States.—[Charles Dury, Ohio, June 6, 1891.

A good Collection of Agrilus at the National Museum.

I have this day sent to the National Museum the *Agrilus*, every specimen as it me all carefully scrutinized and correctly named after careful comparison with the Le Conte types.

The collection is a very good one—really better than the Le Conte collection, and in numbers quite equal to that of Ulke and therefore second only to mine.--[George H. Horn, Pennsylvania, August 13, 1891.

A Leaf-miner infesting Sour Gum.

Inclosed herewith I send you some leaves of Nyssa or Sour Gum. Every leaf on the tree was infested by this "Leaf-miner." I saw the tree August 6 for the first time in Glens Falls, N. Y., and then observed that *all* the leaves on the tree (there is but one in Glens Falls), were infested by this insect. I once found in *Apios tuberosa* a larva that looked like this. I had the good fortune to see the oval holes made by the insect. The cut was made by a swinging of the head from side to side, depressed and then elevated; then the convex edges of the cut were brought

together; then the insect turned and in the same way cut the other side. I did not see the final movements, as my attention was called off for a few moments, and when I again looked the pieces were cut off and lay on the bottom of the tumbler, in which a cluster of leaves were, and the edges had been drawn together. I see that some of the insects do not leave the leaf—are possibly dead from fungus.
* * *—[George F. Waters, Massachusetts, September 10, 1891.

REPLY.— * * * The Leaf-miner which infests Nyssa or Sour Gum is *Antispila nyssœfoliella* Clem. A description of the larva and cocoon, with an account of its habits, was given by Clemens in the Proc. Academy Nat. Sci., Philadelphia, Pa., in 1860. Chambers has since written on the same insect in Psyche, vol. III, p. 363.
* * * —[September 14. 1891.]

Disappearance of the Gypsy Moth in England.

* * * I observe you have had a discussion on the probability of ridding yourselves of the Gypsy Moth *Ocneria dispar*. The difficulty would be to bring about united action, the *vis inertiæ* of the ordinary man is so hard to overcome; but I suppose you know that we have unintentionally exterminated it in this country. It used to be found in our fen districts in plenty. I have some old specimens so obtained; but I think it must be forty years at least since one has been taken wild. All the modern British specimens have been bred for many generations in captivity and have become small.

It is singular that our two *dispars* have disappeared, the species in question, and also *Chrysophanus dispar*, both fen insects.

I think the Gypsy Moth must have been destroyed simply by collectors, but the *C. dispar* was destroyed by drainage indirectly; for in consequence of the rapidity with which the water accumulated during one wet season, all the larvæ were at one fell swoop drowned while feeding—alas! a well defined local form of *C. hippothœ* lost to the world. They now fetch from £ 4 to £ 5 a pair.—[J. Jenner Weir, England, August 6, 1891.

Remedies for Squash Borer.

I corresponded with you lately in regard to the Striped Cucumber Beetle. I was able to overcome, apparently, that pest, and my squash vines grew and looked vigorous, and had on large squashes, and then began to die. While the false blossoms were on, the beetle would enter them, and they would fall to the ground while the stems were green. Then I noticed that the leaves in places would turn yellow, then the leaf stem, and finally the vine. I took a wire and dug into the vine at the joint of the leaf and found a white grub, with a black head, fully an inch long. A number were in each vine. Can you tell me what makes the grub, and a preventive?—[George W. Van Eps, New York, August 31, 1891.

REPLY.—The larva found mining your squash vines is the common Squash Borer, *Melittia cucurbitæ* Harris. The parent of this larva is rarely seen, and belongs to the family of clear-winged, wasp-like moths known as Sesiidæ. The moth appears in the Middle and Northern States from the middle to the last of June, the female depositing her eggs in the morning and afternoon on the stocks of the plant just about or at the surface of the ground. Spraying with Paris green or London purple will destroy the young larvæ as they eat into the stem. but is not as successful as it might be, owing to the fact that it is difficult to get the mixture to wet the vine on the underside where the egg is deposited and where the larvæ enter the plant. Professor Smith, of the New Jersey Station, has found a more satisfactory remedy to consist in lifting the vines and rubbing the underside of the leaf with the finger, thus crushing the eggs. This should be done twice or three times during the egg-laying season, say from the middle to the last of June, at intervals of about a week. In Mr. Smith's experience this process was eminently successful. Where planting can be deferred until July the moths will have disappeared and no injury need be feared. The old remedy consisted in cutting out the larvæ, and this should still be practiced in the case of any that escape the treatment indicated above. The larvæ are of slow growth, and are found in the vines up to the end of September or even into October. When fully mature they leave the vines and burrow into the soil, changing to pupæ, and pass the winter in this stage, transforming to moths the following spring.—[September 4, 1891.

Forest Injury of the Oak Edema.

The Oak Edema, *E. albifrons*, is very bad in Michigan. Whole forests of Oak, Elm, and Maple are being entirely stripped of foliage. Of course, it is not likely that such serious devastation will occur next year, and the defoliation so late is not so serious as when it occurs earlier, yet such extensive raids are worthy of record, so I send it for INSECT LIFE.—[A. J. Cook, Michigan, September 12, 1891.

On the Treatment of Tent Caterpillars.

I would like to know if you can give me any light on the subject of getting rid of the Tent Caterpillar; they are ruining my business in this State, as bee-keepers are getting but little, and in many places, no honey, hence you see they do not want supplies. This year I have not obtained a pound of honey from 123 colonies from Basswood, and as we expect nine-tenths of our honey from that source we will either have to quit the business or get rid of the worms in some way. After they stripped the Basswood trees last summer they then went on the Oak and Elm until our heavy forests in these parts looked as naked as winter. I wrote to the Department of Agriculture three or four years ago about the matter and was told that there was little danger of their appearing in the same districts more than one or two years, but they have been increasing ever since. I have read a few articles concerning the experiments for killing Chinch Bugs by spreading a disease among them with infested bugs and wondered if something could not be done in the same line with the Tent Caterpillar.—[F. C. Erkel, Minnesota, October 3, 1891.

REPLY.—There is nothing to be hoped for in the way of contagious disease which can be artificially controlled, and if the Tent Caterpillars are growing worse in your neighborhood your only release will be by the most energetic measures. It is an open question whether it will pay you to go through the woods in your neighborhood and destroy the webs wherever they are seen, either by spraying a Paris green or London purple solution into them, or by burning them off with torches, but no other remedy can be suggested. It should be done early in the season, as soon as the webs appear, and before the Basswood begins to bloom.—[October 8, 1891.]

The Catalpa Sphinx.

I have a splendid Catalpa tree which has been so infested with a large, rapacious worm, that I had made up my mind to have it cut down, when I thought perhaps you could suggest some remedy for this pest. When the leaves were fully grown, and the bloom putting out in June, a great number of worms appeared on the leaves, about half grown when noticed, and eating *ravenously*. In a few days they were fully grown, and in a few more days every leaf was eaten up, and those that had not been shaken off the tree fell off, or crawled down and disappeared.

The tree put out fresh leaves, and when they were *half grown* I looked closely and found myriads of the young inch-long worms hard at work, eating away for life. This last crop did not make so long a stay, seeming to be full grown in a few days, and left before the leaves all disappeared. When grown it is three inches long, a bright green color underneath, with a black stripe down the back and a white stripe on either side of the black one. It is the handsomest worm I know, with no horns or repulsive looking stings about it. What can I do to save the tree? It is twelve years old, and I never noticed any worms on it till four years ago, when we shook them down and killed them.—[Mrs. R. E. Peyton, Virginia, September 30, 1891.

REPLY.— * * * The caterpillar which is damaging your Catalpa tree is the larva of the common Catalpa Hawk-moth, *Sphinx catalpæ*. This insect, until within a year or so, has been considered rather rare by entomologists, but for some reason has become very numerous in this section of the country. * * * The best remedy will be to spray the tree with London purple or Paris green in the proportion of one-fourth of a pound of the poison to 50 gallons of water. This, however, will be a difficult thing to do unless you have on your place a strong double-acting force pump fitted with a long hose which can be elevated into the tree, yet it is the only remedy which can be suggested beyond destroying the caterpillars as they descend the tree to transform to chrysalides in the soil.—[October 3, 1891.]

Peach Trees injured by Gortyna nitela.

I have some peach twigs, or rather tops, showing work of an insect entirely new to me and to this locality. They have already destroyed twenty of my peach buds, and are at work as vigorously as ever. We cut off and destroy by fire the tops as soon as we find them withering. By splitting you will find a worm in the stock with a black belt around it. In the box is a moth and caterpillar that I found on the little trees.—[W. N. Irvin, Ohio, June 30, 1891.

REPLY.—The insect which is injuring the tops of your Peach trees by boring into them is the so-called Stalk-borer, *Gortyna nitela*. This insect seldom damages perennial plants, but is found commonly boring into potato and tomato plants, corn, rag-weed, and various other annuals. It is therefore not a specific pest of your crop, and its occurrence may be held to be more or less accidental. They will doubtless soon leave your peaches; indeed, there is no remedy possible beyond pruning and burning the infested twigs before the bud-worms leave them.—[July 3, 1891.]

Hair Worm Parasite of the Codling Moth.

Inclosed herewith you will find a "what is it," found in the core of an apple by Mrs. A. M. Chapin of this place. When found it was nicely coiled. It assumed its present distorted position when exposed to the light and air.—[I. J. Jamison, Pennsylvania, September 5, 1891.

REPLY.— * * * The specimen sent is one of the so-called hair-worms of a species which has several times before been found in apples in this country. It is parasitic on the larva of the apple worm or Codling Moth, and sometimes leaves its host before the latter has escaped from the fruit, and remains coiled in the hollow at the core of the apple. The scientific name of this worm is *Mermis acuminata*, and it has been taken directly from the larva of the Codling Moth found under bands placed about the tree, so that there is no doubt whatever about its being parasitic on the larva of this insect. A closely related species is parasitic on grasshoppers, crickets, and allied insects.—[September 8, 1891.]

False Chinch Bug in Wyoming.

By request of the farmers of this vicinity I have sent you a bottle containing what is supposed to be Chinch Bugs. They were found by a farmer living about twenty miles from this town, who states that he shook this number from a grease-wood bush, and that the ground and shrubbery in that vicinity were covered with the insect. He found by marking the place where they were first discovered that they traveled at the rate of one mile in three days, and were at that time working toward his wheat and alfalfa field. It is supposed that the insect was brought into this country from Colorado or Nebraska, as grain from these two States has of late been shipped in here, and the insect was first discovered on the roads leading into the town. * * *—[R. M. Crawford, Wyoming, August 31, 1891.

REPLY.— * * * The specimens prove to be chiefly pupæ of an insect having the common name of the False Chinch Bug, on account of its close resemblance to the

141

true Chinch Bug, for which it is frequently mistaken. Its scientific name is *Nysius angustatus* Uhler, and it is somewhat closely allied to the true Chinch Bug both in systematic position and in habit. An account of it is given in the report of the Entomologist contained in the Annual Report of this Department for 1884, pp. 315-317. It is a very general feeder, and in fact there are but few plants that it will not attack. It frequently occurs in injurious numbers, particularly in the Mississippi Valley and westward. It mostly affects garden crops, such as potatoes, turnips, cabbages, etc., and small fruits, such as the strawberry, but is not often a serious pest of cereals * * *.—[September 8, 1891.]

Kerosene Emulsion successful against the Chinch Bug.

The kerosene emulsion has been satisfactory to us in preventing chinch bugs from injuring the corn. We are trying the remedy at a farm 4 miles out of town. The bugs were very numerous in an 8-acre field of winter wheat. When this was cut most of them moved to an oat field adjoining, but a good many to a cornfield which corners on the wheat field. The owner had tried to kill them with Paris green, applied as for the Colorado potato beetle. The Paris green mixture injured the corn somewhat, but had not killed a bug as far as I could see. Four rows back we cut out the corn. A deep furrow was plowed along this vacant space in which green corn was placed. The bugs traveled from the grain field and attacked the corn outside the furrow as well as that lying in it. We used the kerosene emulsion, diluting it one to ten, applying it with a sprinkling pot, washing them off the standing corn and sprinkling the stalks in the furrow, applying every second or third day. We have followed this plan now for about ten days, and must keep it up a few days longer since most of the bugs are in the oats, which are nearly ready to cut. As soon as the oats are cut, of course they will move on to the corn. This will bring on the last contest. There is no question of winning if we persist. I hear of the remedy being successfully used in several parts of the State. I inclose a copy of the circular which was most hastily prepared and sent out over the State from this station. I also inclose a letter from Dr. E. Fred Russell, of Poynette, Wis. It was at Dr. Russell's place that I saw the emulsion first used. He was following closely the directions given by you on page 81 of the report of the Department of Agriculture for 1887. It gives me great pleasure to have this opportunity of bearing testimony to the good results to our agriculture from your Division.—[W. A. Henry, Wisconsin, August 3, 1891.

Old Broods of the Periodical Cicada.

The writer has witnessed every periodical advent of the "Seventeen-year Locust" (*Cicada septendecim*) in this present century—1817, 1834, 1851, 1868, 1885—and in course its next appearance will be in June, 1902. Although a schoolboy in 1817, I remember how it delighted me as I passed along the woody school path to give the drooping limbs of the forest, bending with these winged insects, a sudden jerk and see them hunt other resting places. They were more numerous that year than we have seen them since. The gray squirrel, in 1834 especially, fattened on them, as both were far more plentiful in those primitive days.

The belt of country in which these insects make their appearance in the years given above runs through Illinois, Indiana, Ohio, Pennsylvania, Maryland, eastward; in localities north and south of this they have other years of maturity. The Thirteen-year Locust is unknown to the writer.

We have noticed that in all these years the seasons were always favorable for their appearance, an early opening of spring and fine favorable weather following, their advent commencing the 1st of June and lasting through that month. Although three weeks are given as the period of their winged state in sunshine, yet all do not leave the ground in one day and cast their mundane coats, so their day seems longer.—[Luke Smith Motte, Ohio.

Note on a Leaf-hopper.

Inclosed find specimens of insects which I find feeding on the California Hedge Plant. They are new in this city, this year being their first appearance. Their ravages are apparent, though not yet serious.—[Henry Allison, Texas, July 2, 1889.

REPLY.—The insect which feeds upon your "California Hedge Plant" is one of the leaf-hoppers known as *Ormenis pruinosa*. The best remedy for this insect will be the application of a dilute kerosene emulsion made according to the formula given upon page 3 of Circular No. 1, new series.—[July 8, 1891.]

Destructiveness of the Corn-root Plant-louse in Nebraska.

I write these few lines to mention the destructiveness of these lice on our corn crop of the last season. Some signs of their destructiveness were noticed last year, when they were so small that only a good eye could see them. They were light green in color. As they grew in size for two or three weeks, their color changed to a light yellow, and then they disappeared. I do not know where. As the corn became an inch or two high we noticed it began to turn in color from a healthy green to a sickly yellow. This was only in places. On close examination the roots of the corn plants were found to be infested by scores of these little green lice. They continued their destructive work for a month or more, thus killing or spoiling each plant upon which they fed. They did not eat the plant, but only sapped it through the thin portions of the epidermis. They worked in spots of from one-half to 10 acres in a place, all through the corn fields of this section of the country. Where they worked the corn is a failure. Some farmers have lost as high as one-third of their crop, while others have lost but a trifle. In all, the amount destroyed by these lice would amount to a greater quantity than would be believed.

So far no effectual remedy is known, but a new mode of planting corn is looked to as being the only way of getting rid of these pests. I have noticed that when corn was planted on ground that had raised a crop of small grain the previous year, no lice were to be seen, while on ground where corn had been grown for previous years the lice were sure to be found.

From my observations of the past season, I would suggest that the following measures be adopted: Plant corn one year alternately with small grain, as, while the small grain is growing, the lice eggs that were deposited in that ground the previous year will hatch, and the young finding no corn upon which to feed, will starve. Of course many will emigrate to neighboring fields, but by repeating this method for several successive years, these lice will surely be thinned out.—[James Pearson, Nebraska, August 25, 1891.

A Parasite of the Cottony Maple Scale.

I inclose herewith a small Hymenopteron which I take to be a parasite on the Cottony Maple Scale. In examining the foliage of maples to-day I found them running up and down the twigs. When they would reach a scale they would run over it once or twice and then turn round and apply the tip of the abdomen to the edge of the scale, remaining in this position a short time, depositing eggs probably. I will, as soon as possible, take other specimens and endeavor to breed some of them later on.—[Warren Knans, Kansas, July 3, 1891.

REPLY.—I am very much obliged to you for the parasite which you found apparently ovipositing upon *Pulvinaria*. It is *Comys fusca* Howard, described in the Annual Report of this Department for 1880, and bred from a species of *Lecanium* on Oak from Mobile, Ala. It has never been bred from *Pulvinaria*, and your observation is therefore an interesting one. You ought to be able to find still other parasites, and I hope you will send in any you may be able to breed.—[July 8, 1891.]

The Purple Scale of the Orange in Montserrat.

The Icerya insect has not reappeared in our lime orchards which is the reason why Mr. Hamilton has not written to you for the ladybirds. We are, however, overrun with the Purple Scale (*Mytilaspis citricola*) and our emulsions do not seem to penetrate the egg covers. It is impossible to keep up a continuous succession of striving to kill each brood of insects as it hatches out, and the spraying does not therefore seem to meet the difficulty. My object in writing to you is to ask whether you know of any parasite which we could introduce to prey upon the Purple Scale as the ladybird does upon the Icerya. These natural antidotes seem to be the best, if only one can get hold of them.—[Joseph Sturge, England, July 4, 1891.

REPLY.—No satisfactory enemy of the Purple Scale is known to this country. Very few insects seem to attack it, and it will not be worth while to attempt to import any of these into Montserrat. I do not know how the climate of Montserrat differs from that of the orange growing regions of Florida, but in the latter State the kerosene emulsion spray is only to be applied during the time of year when the young lice are hatching. The periods are rather irregular, and hatching is more or less continuous throughout the year. As a rule, however, in Florida, new generations begin in March, June, and September, and at the end of each of these months the application of insecticides meets with the greatest success. A similar state of affairs will, probably, upon close examination, be found in Montserrat.—[July 17, 1891.]

Notes on Buffalo Gnats.

During the winter of 1890 we had the water in Red River and its swamps higher than ever known before in its history, just the condition most favorable for the breeding of the Buffalo Gnat, yet we had very few of them as compared with preceding springs. I account for this apparent paradox by stating that the winter of 1890 was such a mild one that the gnats kept on hatching out during the months of December, January, February, and March. They made their appearance so gradually as not to give much trouble at the regular time, which is the latter part of February and during March.

We also had comparatively few of them last spring, although the water conditions were favorable during the winter and spring months. I account for this from the fact that during last fall the water in our bayous became so low as almost to cease flowing. No current at all could be noticed in the vicinity of the raft, which is the home of their larvæ. I think that all the larvæ in these regions must have died, owing to the stagnant water, and that the gnats that we did have came from larvæ that were brought down from upper Red River when that stream rose during the winter. If this is a fact, then we can predict that we will not be troubled with many of them the coming spring, because Red River is at present about as low as it was at this time last year. No current can be noted now about on rafts, and I hope that the larvæ are all dead.

I took a trip along the region of rafts a few days ago, and found that owing to the very low stage of water quite a number of fish were dying, and millions of shrimps were putrefying on the banks of the streams, causing a great stench for miles. I think that every shrimp in this part of Bayou Pierre must be dead. These shrimp are dead by the barrelful in a bayou where there is still some current.

The water in Bayou Pierre where they have died in such numbers is from 10 to 20 feet deep. Now, if the lack of current can cause the death of shrimps in such vast numbers, why should the larvæ of the Buffalo Gnat not perish from the same cause? Can you tell me why the shrimp die in this way? They do not need the current to bring them their food as do the Buffalo-gnat larvæ.—[G. A. Frierson, Louisiana, September 27, 1891.

REPLY.— * * * We are very much obliged to you for this information regarding Buffalo Gnat matters in your vicinity. We are pleased that you have been so fortunate the past two seasons and are of the opinion that your explanations are correct. We hope that you will keep us informed as to further developments. We regret that you have been unable to have the rafts removed.

The crustacean which you call a shrimp is probably the freshwater prawn of the Mississippi River, *Palæmon ohionis*. I can not surmise the cause of its mortality.—[October 3, 1891.]

The Horn-fly in Kentucky.

I wish to report the presence with us this season, for the first time in injurious numbers, of the Horn-fly. All cattle feeders in my vicinity have noticed the unusual numbers of small flies on their cattle during the summer and our attention was more particularly directed to them when our cattle on delivery weighed from 100 to 150 pounds less per head than they should. In fact, in three months' grazing our cattle have not gained over 50 pounds per head, whereas they should have gained that much each month. In your 1889 report you do not seem to speak very favorably of kerosene emulsion. Why is this? Do you doubt its effects being sufficiently lasting or would you anticipate any ill effects upon the animals from its use? If it would answer the purpose I think it could be more readily applied from a knapsack sprayer than other preparations, and then, too, the ingredients could be readily obtained by every handler of cattle. I still have some cattle and the flies are as bad as ever.—[P. T. Henshaw, Oldham County, Ky., August 20, 1891.

REPLY.—You are mistaken in supposing that I do not believe that the kerosene emulsion will be a good substance to apply to cattle. I am quite of the opinion that where they can be treated by means of a knapsack sprayer with this substance, about twice a week, the flies will be kept from the cattle and the resulting loss of flesh and diminution in milk will be to a large extent avoided. * * *—[August 24, 1891.]

Non-migratory Locust Devastations in Nevada.

I take the liberty of sending specimens of the grasshoppers which have been very destructive over a certain region of desert country where the few fertile margins of streams are cultivated for grain, hay, and fruit. Grain growing during the winter months and ripening early in May escapes the hoppers, who do not hatch out till May. They then destroy the summer crops, consisting chiefly of alfalfa (here called lucerne) and fruits—grapes, pomegranates, figs, pears, and almonds, being the chief fruits.

It would long ago have been a region of importance for exporting these fruits if the hoppers had not devastated it continually for a long term of years. I send these specimens and this description in the hope that your entomologist may be able to suggest some practicable chemical means of destruction. Any substance that could be conveyed on the irrigating streams so as to reach every portion of the crop, and would not injure vegetation, such as the hydrocarbon compounds, might be made the vehicle of conveying the destructive agent, if such can be found. Purely mechanical means are scarcely practicable on a large field. I have tried the California remedy of arsenic with flour and sugar in a paste, and can not say what it would do if genuine. The 10 pounds of arsenic I tried did not kill any hoppers; I think it was simply a swindle, the merchant sending flour and lime instead of arsenic. These grasshoppers are everyway local and never migrate; they will be many years spreading over a few miles of country, as for instance, the neighboring valley of the Muddy, the lowest settlement, has had them now 22 years without intermission. Some years they were not quite so thick, other years thick enough to eat off the grapevines three times during the summer and the leaves off all the cottonwoods, so that big trees would dry up. They ate the alfalfa clear to the ground, while the other towns in the valley, from 7 to 30 miles off, had none of the hoppers, or so few that they did no harm. This season they have spread over all the valley. I had a vineyard of 10 acres—10,000 vines—at St. Thomas. If the hoppers had been absent it would have yielded annually 5,000 to 8,000 gallons of wine; as it was it has yielded less than the amount of State taxes paid on the land, and I could only find tenants by reason of a dwelling-house being on the place.

At this place, Rioville, I have succeeded in killing off the hoppers so that they have not been able to do much damage yet. This season I have had a vast quantity of them, beginning to show with the second cut of hay in May in alarming numbers; I then had 3 or 4 men follow the mower with shovels, striking the hoppers down and crushing them, and, early each morning, I followed along the ditches where they would collect on any grass or brush higher than the rest like roosting chickens, and I got large numbers in that way, probably 500 to 1,000 each morning. By this means a very formidable swarm, whose increase in a season would have amounted to an overwhelming and all-destructive mass, has been reduced so that it is now difficult to find specimens. All attempts to drive these hoppers into rivers or to any safe distance are wholly futile; no way remains but to kill them, and to make sure that they are dead; for they will often bear a full stroke with a shovel, especially if any grass is under them, and still live and prosper, and it is no inconvenience to them to go without a head for a day or two at least.

It is quite common to talk of them as "millions," and they look formidable enough, but if a man kills 500 a day the swarm looks less in a few days; those that are gone are not seen fifty times a day looking like 10,000, and shortly they are perceptibly decreased and become wary and shy, needing extra diligence to catch. If mornings are cool they become numb and are easily got, though unfortunately only about daylight, when unluckily many men are "numb" too. This process has, however, succeeded with me on 40 acres of alfalfa, and it is simply a question of putting on effort enough; will probably fail with hired "help" only, as it requires an unyielding determination to win. Probably a roller of 800 to 1,000 pounds' weight and about 5 feet long, so as to just cover the swath of the mower, and to follow directly after it, would crush the bulk of them, and one man following up could dispatch such as escaped the roller. As each female hopper lays from 75 to 100 eggs, and they breed two or three times in a season, it is of the utmost importance that the first appearance in spring should be followed by instant action.

No. 1, large green, and the smaller one of half growth are, I think, the Arabian locust. The No. 2, reddish-brown above and yellow underneath, is the toughest. The No. 3 is a kind generated, it seems, in the middle patch and chiefly found there.

A small, crimson-colored, round insect sometimes attacks and kills them, but not usually before the hoppers have leveled the field and left a brown desert behind and deposited the eggs of a coming generation.

Some chemical substance of practicable application would be a boon to this region; the mechanical means I have indicated are too tiresome for general use, as many farmers are too busy to apply them.—[Daniel Bonelli. Lincoln County, Nev., August 2, 1891.

REPLY.—The green locust is *Acridium shoshone*, while the yellow one is *Caloptenus differentialis* and the slender one is *Caloptenus bivittatus*. All are comparatively local non-migratory species. The mechanical means mentioned in Bulletin No. 25 of the Division of Entomology will be the most satisfactory method of destroying them. No thoroughly easy way is known. You are advised to get some genuine arsenic and to try the bran-arsenic treatment, which you seem to have tried with a spurious substance. * * * —[August 24, 1891.]

The Grasshopper Plague in Michigan.

I take the liberty to write to you in regard to a grasshopper plague. In some parts of this country they are destroying everything in the line of grass, oats, corn, wheat, rye, and vegetables, even potatoes. At present writing they have infested about one-fourth of the cultivated area, but they are on the wing and spreading rapidly. Our stock will have to go. We have no pasture now and can not raise anything to winter it. I have read of Professor Snow's method of disposing of chinch bugs and have thought the grasshoppers might be reached in the same way.—[James Dodd, Manistee County, Mich., June 27, 1891.

REPLY.—Your letter of June 27 has been received and referred to the entomologist, who reports that he has sent you by accompanying mail a copy of Bulletin No. 25 of his division, which treats of destructive locusts or "grasshoppers" and the best remedies to be used against them. He will be obliged if you will kindly send in specimens of the insect of which you complain, and for this purpose a frank and return envelope are inclosed.—[July 2, 1891.]

Grasshopper Notes from Idaho.

I returned from my Idaho trip on the evening of the 14th, and will send you a detailed report of it at a later date. Found that the region devastated last year was greatly increased the present year, and that in addition to the *Camnula pellucida*, which has been the chief depredator in this region, three species of *Melanoplus* and the Western Cricket (*Anabrus simplex*) are also present in damaging numbers.

The other locusts that I deem of sufficient importance to demand the attention of the settlers are the following: *Melanoplus bivittatus*, *M. atlanis*, *M. fœdus*, this last-named insect being the one referred to as very numerous in the vicinity of Boisé City last year.

The large crickets entered the valley from the southwest and passed over the greater portion of the Camas Prairie in a northeasterly direction, leaving eggs in many places. Most of the crickets had left the region before I visited it. While but few eggs were left in the valley by the *Camnula pellucida*, I am fearful that, everything being favorable, the other three species of locusts named above are present in sufficient numbers to warrant some exertions being made on the part of the authorities toward fighting the pest.

In my collecting during this trip I found specimens of at least three species that I believe are new hoppers. These were all taken at about 9,000 feet elevation.—[Lawrence Bruner, Nebraska, September 16, 1891.

A Flight of White Ants.

We have had dry weather until to-day, when, after a good shower, my little boys, who are observant of natural phenomena, exclaimed, "See the insects!" The air was full of them. They came up suddenly from the east. They flew from 2 to 20 feet high. They lasted for about twenty minutes; then another wonder awaited us. They fell along the ground and their wings began to drop off. They paired, one following another closely. Numerous red ants picked them up rapidly and carried them off. I send you some of them and should be glad to hear what they are.—[L. F. Bickford, Texas. July 16, 1891.]

REPLY.—This is one of the so-called White Ants, *Termes morio*. As you are doubtless aware, these insects, although called "White Ants," belong to the Neuroptera, an entirely different order from the true ants. They live, however, in colonies in much the same way, and feed preferably upon dead and decaying wood. You will find their nests in the timbers of old houses and in old logs and wood. In tropical countries they build enormous nests. You are, perhaps, familiar with the accounts of the nests of the African Termites. The males and females acquire wings at certain times of the year and swarm in great numbers. The flights of such forms in the open air have been seldom observed, but if you will notice page 146 of the second volume of the Standard Natural History you will see an account of the immense swarm of *Termes flavipes* at Cambridge, Mass., on the morning of May 19, 1878. Some of the old houses in this city are badly infested with this latter species, and the winged individuals swarm very early in the season.—[July 22, 1891.]

The Malodorous Lace-wing.

Inclosed I send you a curious insect, captured last night in my family room. The remarkable thing about this fly is that, when alive, it emits a most offensive and disagreeable odor, filling the room. I thought some of the family had stepped into something very offensive and brought it into the room. My wife, however, said it was one of these flies, and soon found this specimen near the lamp, it having come in through the open window, as I suppose. Several different persons examined this fly while it was alive and can testify to its most remarkable and abominable smell. Fortunately, this insect is by no means numerous here, this being only the third specimen I have seen. * * *—[E. Scott Brown, Allen County, Ky., September 1, 1891.

REPLY.—* * * The insect in question is one of the lace-winged flies, a species of Chrysopa. Some of these insects emit a very disagreeable odor, as you describe, especially when handled. The lace-winged flies are strictly beneficial insects, the larvæ, called Aphis lions, being especially voracious and feeding upon other soft-bodied insects, and particularly Aphides or plant lice. One peculiarity of the insect consists in the method of the parent in depositing its eggs. These are placed in groups on long pedestals and present a very peculiar appearance. The young larva, when hatched, climbs down the pedestal and wanders around in search of prey. When full-fed it spins a circular cocoon attached to a leaf or twig, and the adult insect ultimately escapes by cutting a circular lid in one side of the cocoon.—[September 7, 1891.

A Ground Squirrel Parasite.

I send you by mail to-day three grubs taken from the body of a half-grown ground squirrel (*Spermophilus 13-lineatus*) killed July 7. They were in the skin between the posterior extremities. There were four, but one was lost. Are they a common parasite of this animal, and could they be used in any way to exterminate the squirrel? They are such a pest to the farmers, digging up many acres of corn before it sprouts.—[B. B. Gillett, Kansas, July 10, 1891.

REPLY.—The specimens which you send are very interesting and do not agree with the larvæ of the Emasculating Bot-fly which commonly infests squirrels and gophers in the East, and an account of which you will find upon page 214 of INSECT LIFE, volume I. Your larvæ are entirely new to the national collection, and I trust that you will make an effort, if you have the opportunity, to breed the adult fly by allowing the larvæ to enter the earth in a covered box or jar. Perhaps, if you will send them to us alive in tightly packed earth, we may be able to take better care of them.—[July 17, 1891.]

Poisonous Qualities of a Northern Centipede.

I send for identification what appears to be a relative of the Centipedes. They are known here as "Earwigs." They are not generally thought to be poisonous, but I am sure this is an error, as my experience with this one goes to prove. It made itself known at night by a very vigorous bite which immediately awoke me and continued painful for some time afterward, and from the swelling as well as pain attending the bite I am convinced that it can be classed as a poisonous insect.—[J. T. Park, Tennessee, October 5, 1891.

REPLY.—The Centipede which you send is a species known as *Scolopendra woodii*. This is a more or less northern representative of the well-known poisonous Centipede of the West Indies and other warmer localities, and there is no doubt about the possession of poison fangs by all the members of the genus Scolopendra. The effect of the bite in a warm climate is very variable, being at some times excessively virulent and painful and at others causing little inconvenience. It is doubtful, however, whether the bite of *S. woodii* could ever be dangerous, and as a matter of fact your personal experience of the bite of this species is the first with which I have ever met. It is therefore of considerable interest.—[October 9, 1891.]

GENERAL NOTES.

CHRYSOMELID LARVÆ IN ANTS' NESTS.

Mr. T. D. A. Cockerell has, in the July (1891) number of the *Entomologist's Monthly Magazine*, an article on two case-bearing Chrysomelid larvæ from Colorado, one of them being found in the nests of an ant, "apparently *Formica fusca*," the other occuring under rocks. Dr. Hamilton, to whom specimens of the former larva were submitted by Mr. Cockerell, declares them as "very probably the larva of *Coscinoptera vittigera*," and is inclined to think that their occurrence among ants is merely accidental. It seems that both Dr. Hamilton and Mr. Cockerell have overlooked a note which we published in the *American Naturalist* for 1882, p. 508, where we first called attention to the myrmecophilous habit of the larva of *C. dominicana*. We had then received numerous specimens of the cases found in Wisconsin in a large ants' nest. Subsequently the same cases were found by Mr. Pergande, at Washington, D. C., among the colonies of *Camponotus melleus*, and last year we received from Mr. H. G. Hubbard another large lot of the same cases, found at Helena, Mont., in the hills of *Formica obscuripes*. In all these instances we succeeded in breeding the imago, which proved to be *C. dominicana*, and from our experience it seems safe to say that the occurrence among ants of this Chrysomelid larva is not accidental, but rather normal. This does not imply, however, that larvæ do not feed on old leaves remote from ants' nests, since in our account of the transformations of the species (Sixth Rep. Ins. Mo., p. 127) we have shown that it does. Whether or not Mr. Cockerell's species from Colorado is *C. vittigera* it is not possible to tell without having bred the imago. His short description of the case and the larva agrees very well with *C. dominicana* as described and figured in our Sixth Missouri Report. Still it is possible that the cases and larvæ of the two species resemble each other so closely that they can be distinguished only upon careful comparison.

The larvæ of two European species of Clythra are known to live with ants, and some years ago we received from Mr. H. K. Morrison cases of a Chrysomelid found in an ant's nest in Arizona. These evidently belong to the Clythrini, but are specifically if not generically different from *Coscinoptera dominicana*. From these records, few as they are in comparison with the large number of species the habits of which are still unknown, it is safe to say that at least some species of the tribe Clythrini must be considered as myrmecophilous in the larva state.

That in the case-bearing Chrysomelid larvæ the case serves as a protection from enemies there can be do doubt; but if Mr. Cockerell says that the case-making habit in Coscinoptera may have been acquired as a protection against the bite of the ants, he forgets that many other soft-bodied and quite unprotected insects live peacefully in company with the most ferocious ants, and further, that we have a multitude of case-bearing Chrysomelidæ (Cryptocephalus and allied genera) which do not live with ants. There is little or nothing known regarding the relationship of the myrmecophilous Chrysomelids to their hosts, but it is safe to say that the presence of these inquilines is not in any way injurious or annoying to the ants, and that the behavior of the latter toward the former is friendly, or at least indifferent.

A COMPENDIUM OF ECONOMIC ZOÖLOGY.*

The European literature is rich in more or less useful manuals of injurious or beneficial animals of one class or another, but we do not remember having seen a recent work which covers the whole domain of economic zoölogy in so complete a manner as that which has just been published by Dr. J. Ritzema Bos, professor in the Agricultural College at Wageningen, and upon a perusal of this well-illustrated popular work we are convinced that it will be extremely useful not only to the farmer, gardener, and forester of Germany, for whom it is primarily intended, but also to all interested in the economy of animals. The nearest approach to this volume which has been published of late is Raillet's Zoologie Médicale et Agricole (Paris, 1886), but this deals more with the medical side of the subject.

The importance of entomology to agriculture in its widest sense becomes very apparent from this work, for the insects alone (although only those of central Europe are treated) occupy more than one-half of the 827 pages of the volume. Some families toward the end of the entomological portions are treated very inadequately, e. g., the Coccidæ get only two pages; the Pediculi and Mallophaga combined occupy but little more than one page; and the Arachnida are not alluded to at all among the beneficial animals. The Insecta are generally treated in the customary sequence of the orders and families, each of them having a short introduction on general characteristics and development. In Lepidoptera, however, the vast number of injurious caterpillars of all families are divided primarily according to the food-plants and other objects they attack. The clothes-moths are strangely enough omitted. In the large divisions "deciduous trees" and "coniferous trees" further subdivisions are made: first, according to the mode of attack (buds, trunk, leaves, etc.), and secondarily, according to structural characters of the caterpillars. This renders the whole arrangement somewhat awkward and confusing to the untrained reader in spite of the references and cross-references given in numbers. The Scolytidæ, Tenthredinidæ, and Aphididæ are treated in the alphabetical sequence of food-plants, and here the arrangement is quite perspicuous.

The condensation of the life-histories is admirably done, and the author has not only used the literature but has added largely from his

* Thierische Schädlinge und Nützlinge für Ackerbau, Viehzucht, Wald- und Gartenbau, von Dr. J. Ritzema Bos, Berlin (Paul Parey,)1891.

own rich experience. The descriptions are given as briefly and concisely as possible and are free from technical terms.

The introduction to the work is largely devoted to entomology, and the chapters on influence of food, influence of climatic conditions, and more especially that on the influence of natural enemies, are worth reading.

There is also in the introduction a general consideration of preventive measures and direct remedies, while in the body of the book itself special remedies or preventives are given with each species, or at least with each group of species. The American reader will often be amazed at the direct remedies recommended by Dr. Bos. On account of the cheapness of labor in Europe, the most primitive remedy, viz, hand-picking, can be successfully practiced against many insects where in America it is practically out of the question. Many of our modern American remedies, however, are overlooked; for instance, the use of arsenical poisons is nowhere recommended. London purple is not mentioned at all, and Paris green only once (by name), in the introduction and incidentally in reference to its use in America against the Colorado Potato-beetle. The kerosene emulsion is not mentioned. Equally strange is the absence of any allusion to the improved spraying nozzles and pumps; in fact, no spraying apparatus at all is mentioned except (p. 559) a "little syringe"—probably an old-fashioned gardener's syringe—and a "thick brush" with which the fluid is scattered over the plants. If the progress of American economic entomology had not been ignored thus entirely, Dr. Bos would have been able in many instances to suggest safe and effective remedies. The omission of hellebore as a well-established remedy for various insects is also noticeable, and finally, we are surprised that no mention is made of the improved insect lime which dispenses with the costly paper or tin bands (pp. 28, 29.)

A useful index in which the animals are arranged according to the alphabetical sequence of the host plants or host animals and a general index of popular and scientific names (here we chance to note the omission of *Ephestia* and *Hepialus*) conclude the work.

A GENERIC SYNOPSIS OF THE COCCIDÆ.

Mr. W. H. Ashmead has published in the current volume of the Transactions of the American Entomological Society a generic synopsis of the subfamilies, tribes, and genera of the bark lice of the world, based on the writings of Signoret, Targioni, Löw, Maskell, Comstock, Atkinson, and others. He has divided the subfamily Coccinæ into four tribes, viz: Acanthococcini, Dactylopiini, Coccini, and Kermesini. The Lecaniinæ he divides into the following tribes: Signorettini, Pulvinariini, Lecaniini, and Lecaniodiaspini. In this subfamily he adds a new genus, Bernardia, but with no description beyond a brief entry in his tables, and also with no indication of the type. We may state, however, that he informs us that the genus was founded upon *Lecanium oleæ* Bernard, the common Black Scale of California. It is separated from Lecanium proper by an additional joint in the antenna of the adult ♀, and by the loss of two of the eight hairs on the anal genital ring. The subfamily Diaspinæ is divided into two tribes, Aspidiotini and Leucaspini. Altogether 65 genera are tabulated.

Synopses to be of most service should be made as a result of serious previous work in the family. As an illustration: in *Lepidosaphes* Shimer, which is here substituted for the better known and more generally accepted *Mytilaspis* Targioni, the chief distinguishing feature between the male and female scales, viz, the lack of the medial scale (or second molt) in the former is not given.

WORK IN ALGERIA WITH A FUNGUS DISEASE OF THE LOCUST.

The results of the investigations of MM. Künckel and Langlois of a cryptogamic disease which sometimes attacks the Migratory Locust (*Schistocerca peregrina* Oliv.) of Africa, as reported in the Bulletin of the Société Entomologique de France, Séance de 24 Juin, are not encouraging. The disease appeared among some specimens collected by M. Künckel, but the mortality was insignificant, the contamination of one by another appearing to be very difficult. He isolated a couple, the male of which died with signs of infection, and the female was thereupon mated with a second male, which died in turn, but without any signs of infection. Special conditions appear to be necessary for the development of the parasite, as the author was only able to establish its presence upon those individuals which were captured in damp situations, and in captivity it was only possible to produce the disease upon a certain number of individuals by the use of damp cloths. The eggs were completely resistant, and in fact the disease attacked only those individuals which had reached the full term of their evolution, and even with these was transmitted from one to the other with great difficulty. The authors conclude as follows:

Knowing, therefore, the conditions of existence and development of locusts in Africa, it does not seem possible to base any hopes on a mode of destruction which depends upon the artificial development of the fungus parasite observed on the Migratory Locusts.

The disease experimented with by MM. Künckel and Langlois has been determined by M. A. Giard as *Lachnidium acridiorum*, n. sp. In the discussion which followed the reading of this paper M. J. Gazagnaire urged upon the Algerian Locust service the importance of confining themselves to practical work by means of the same methods which have been used for the past three years against the local cricket, *Stauronotus maroccanus*, namely, by the use of the Cypriote apparatus, liquid insecticides, and the collection of the egg cases by a numerous force well organized and directed. In his opinion the total destruction of the locust in Algeria is a dream the fulfillment of which is, if possible at all, very remote. There will still occur many invasions, and all that can be done is to diminish as much as possible their disastrous effects and render their injury supportable to the colonists. He considered that there could be no profit in sending out from the moist jars of the laboratory the spores which, in the hope of some individuals, would deliver Algeria from the scourge of the locusts.

A NOVEL MODE OF USING DISEASE GERMS.

In many directions the commercial enterprise of the French people is making itself felt. We have elsewhere referred to the striking advances which have been made in France in the making of insecticide machinery and the object of the present writing is to call the attention of our readers to a new branch of entomological commerce just instituted by a French firm. We have received a circular from Fribourg & Hesse, 26 Rue des Écoles, Paris, offering for sale culture tubes for the destruction of the White Grub. The circular gives an introductory statement to the effect that the recent researches of Prillieux, Delacroix, and Giard have established the fact that there exists a specific vegetable parasite of the White Grub which destroys it. Following the learned methods of Pasteur, Messrs. Fribourg & Hesse have undertaken the artificial production of this parasite—*Botrytis tenella*—upon a vast scale and offer to agriculturists tubes containing the spores, by the aid of which they will be able to utilize the discovery. They guarantee their cultures to be capable of communicating the disease to several hundred worms. Trial tubes are advertised at 50 centimes, while the commercial article costs 6 francs.

The following methods of employment are recommended:

(1) Take about a hundred White Grubs and put them in an earthenware vessel of sufficiently large size, the bottom of which should be covered with a bed of earth or sand about a centimetre in depth and slightly moist. Sink the vessel in the ground in a cool shady place.

(2) Pulverize very finely between the fingers the contents of the tube and scatter them over the grubs in the vessel. The fragments which will not crush between the fingers should be mixed with a little moist earth and scattered over the grubs. Every grub should be touched by the powder.

(3) Cover the vessel with pieces of board on which wet cloths should be placed, or, better, wet moss.

(4) At the end of six hours the grubs are attacked by the disease. They should be taken one by one and placed in different parts of the field, at a depth of about 20 centimetres in the ground, taking care not to injure them. Put them gently in the soil and cover them with earth. Choose preferably the worst infested places in which to put the diseased grubs.

It is a good plan to keep some of the diseased grubs from the vessel; with this in view put them in a flower pot with moist earth. At the end of fifteen days the grubs should be dead, swollen, and of a clear rosy tint.

MORTALITY AMONG FLIES IN THE DISTRICT.

The comparative scarcity of flies of all sorts this summer in the District has been a matter of comment, whereas in neighboring towns flies have been unusually troublesome. This anomaly may find its explanation in the remarkable destruction of certain flies by a common *Empusa* disease. In a recent stroll through the grounds of the Agricultural Department the under side of the leaves of various trees was found to be quite thickly covered with dead flies, attached by a fungous growth. The abundance of the flies can be surmised from the fact that a single leaf not infrequently contained as many as eight or ten specimens. The flies, for the most part, belong to a common species, *Pollenia rudis* Fabr., which occurs abundantly in the late summer and fall on out-door vegetation, but include various smaller forms, some of which are probably referable to the House Fly, and among others, the common species *Lucilia cæsar*. I do not know that the occurrence of flies in such numbers, destroyed by this disease on outdoor vegetation, has hitherto been recorded. Mr. W. T. Swingle has kindly examined the flies for me, and reports that the disease is not the common fungous disease of the House Fly (*Empusa muscæ*), isolated cases of which are not uncommon in houses during the late summer and early fall, but is one of R. Thaxter's new species, viz, *E. americana*, which occurs as far as known always outdoors on vegetation, etc.

The discovery of this great mortality among flies is interesting, in view of the economic importance which the subject of the diseases of insects bids fair to assume in the near future, and would seem to indicate that the season has been especially favorable for the propagation of such diseases.—C. L. MARLATT.

A FAVORABLE VIEW OF THE ENGLISH SPARROW.

We have received from the author, Mons. P. Pélicot, honorary member of the Protective Societies of Paris and Brussels, a very interesting brochure entitled "Un Passerean a Protéger," which is an attempt to rehabilitate the sparrow in public estimation. The work is popular in style, and while we do not agree with the author's conclusions, we can recommend the book as a most interesting contribution to a vexed question. In support of his argument that the sparrow is beneficial rather than harmful, he gives a table of the estimates made by several authors of the numbers of insects devoured by a sparrow in a given time. These approximations vary from that of Blatin, who gives "approximate estimates" that two sparrows will destroy 1,200 insects (*Hannetons*—chafers) in 12 days, to the estimate of Tschudi, who thinks that a single sparrow will destroy 1,500 larvæ in 24 hours. The author deprecates the slaughter of the sparrows by gun or poison, and gives as a sure protection for fruit trees and garden crops the stringing of threads of red wool, or of any other striking color, on the branches of the trees, or on small stakes close by the crop to be protected. This very simple device he claims to have tested himself and found it a perfect protection from the sparrows. It may be worth trying by those who believe that the sparrows do more harm than good. The style of the book is attractive, but the statements, many of them, will not bear the test of scientific inquiry.

OCCASIONAL DEVELOPMENT OF WINGS IN NORMALLY APTEROUS HEMIPTERA.

Mr. J. W. Douglas, in a review of Mr. F. B. Pascoe's recent work on the Darwinian theory of the origin of species (*The Entomologists' Monthly Magazine*, April, 1891, p. 109), calls attention to the statement that "Some of our Hemiptera, *Nabis*, *Pithanus*, *Pyrrhocoris*, etc., ordinarily wingless, are sometimes found in hot summers to have well-developed wings." As Mr. Douglas remarks, all these species normally have rudiments of elytra, but there are other species quite apterous in which at times macropterous individuals appear, in which case the respective forms are so divergent as to be considered distinct. But he does not believe that such dimorphism occurs only in hot summers, and mentions having observed it in cold seasons also, when there was nothing exceptional in the weather to favor such development. He believes that at present no satisfactory explanation can be given. May it not be that the development of wings is dependent somewhat on the food supply of the insects, and they are produced to enable a more extended migration, rendered necessary by a diminution of the food supply or the overdevelopment of the species? The abnormal appearance, locally, of winged specimens of a wingless species can not be satisfactorily explained by the theory of a reversion to a winged ancestral type, since this would account for isolated cases, but would hardly explain the general appearance of winged individuals.

AN ARGUMENT AGAINST SPRAYING FOR SCALE-INSECTS.

In the *California Fruit Grower* of January 31 we notice a communication from Mr. F. Righter, who states that at the last meeting of the Campbell Horticultural Society the subject of the best materials to destroy the brown apricot scale was discussed, and that it was generally concluded that it was better not to spray at all, as those orchards which had not been sprayed were found upon examination to be freer from scale than those which had been sprayed annually. Orchards which had not been sprayed and which were at one time badly infested with this scale were said to be now entirely free from the pest. If these facts are correct the deduction is also correct, but it is evident that some important natural enemy of this bark louse has been at work. It was the supposition of the members of the society that the Vedalia had killed off the scale, but this is entirely contrary to the experience of our agents and correspondents. It seems certain that Vedalia will prey upon nothing in this country but *Icerya purchasi*. The item in its present shape, however, is calculated to do considerable harm, and no horticulturist should neglect spraying in consequence of this exceptional experience.

NEW MEANS AGAINST ORANGE PESTS.

The effectiveness of the kerosene emulsion against fruit scale insects, and of the kerosene emulsion combined with sulphur against the Red Spider, has been pretty conclusively shown by experimentation in Florida. The *Florida Agriculturist*, quoted in the *American Garden* for July, 1891, states that in this connection the Rev. Lyman Phelps, who has given much talented research to the subject, uses bisulphate of soda, 10 pounds to 50 gallons of water, and finds this a safe and efficacious remedy. A stronger solution than that named is liable to injure the foliage. He also expresses the opinion that the insect pest will prove a friend to the careful cultivator, as a careful and industrious man will adopt vigorous and effective treatment and thus keep his grove in a healthy condition, while his indolent neighbor will neglect his trees until the damage is so great as to put him out of the race. The sentiment, which is not a new one, is also not a bad one, and the progressive fruit grower will have to realize it and recognize the necessity of adopting improved methods or he will certainly fail of success in his business.

LATE ENTOMOLOGICAL PUBLICATIONS OF THE NATIONAL MUSEUM.

We have not yet mentioned the fact that the Proceedings of the U. S. National Museum have recently contained three entomological articles which have been issued under special covers as Nos. 837, 838, and 839. These are: Notes on North American Myriopoda of the family Geophilidæ, with descriptions of three genera, by O. F. Cook and G. N. Collins; Contributions towards a Monograph of the Noctuidæ of Temperate North America, a revision of Homohadena, Grote, by John B. Smith; and Contributions towards a Monograph of the Noctuidæ of Temperate North America, a revision of the species of Hadena referable to Xylophasia and Luperina, by John B. Smith.

TIGER-BEETLE LARVÆ VS. COLIAS PHILODICE.

Mr. R. R. Rowley, of Curryville, Mo., describes (*Canadian Entomologist*, XXIII, April, 1891, p. 92) a very curious case of the destruction of butterflies, *Colias* and *Pieris*, chiefly *C. philodice*, by the larvæ of some Tiger Beetle. During a drought in August, in 1886, he noticed a great bunch of Coliads about one of the few moist clay slopes or banks of a nearly dry brook. Some of them while fluttering violently seemed unable to rise and upon taking one of the struggling butterflies by the wing he found that they were firmly held to the ground by having their abdomens drawn into the burrows of Tiger-beetle larvæ, these voracious grubs actually eating them alive.

The bank was found to be strewn with mutilated specimens of *philodice*, and upon his retiring a few yards the thirsty butterflies returned and those which alighted over burrows were quickly seized by their enemies. This is certainly a very unusual occurrence.

THE REPORTED DEATH OF M. KÜNCKEL D'HERCULAIS.

Entomologists in this country were greatly shocked last May by a dispatch which appeared in many of our newspapers, purporting to come from Algiers May 18, announcing the death under remarkable circumstances of M. Jules Künckel d'Herculais, ex-president of the Entomological Society of France, and French commissioner to Algiers to study the Migratory Locust. It was stated that this well-known entomologist was overcome by a swarm of locusts and almost completely devoured by them. We were loath to believe this statement, and in consequence waited for its verification before publishing M. Künckel's obituary in INSECT LIFE, though we based on the report some notes of his work in a communication to the *Scientific American*. It now appears that he is still alive, and will doubtless take great pleasure in seeing for himself the great esteem in which he is held in the entomological world, by reading a variety of obituary notices in several languages. The *Bulletin Entomologique* of the Société Entomologique de France, dated the 24th of June, quotes from a paper read by M. Künckel before the Agricultural Society of Algiers on May 30, 12 days after the date of his reported death.

A NEW HÆMATOBIA: THE MOOSE FLY.

Mr. William A. Snow, University of Kansas, Lawrence, has given a very interesting account (*Canadian Entomologist*, XXIII, April, 1891, pp. 87–89) of a near relative of the Horn-fly (*Hæmatobia serrata*) which attacks the moose in the great cranberry swamps of northern Minnesota. The insect was studied and collected by Prof. L. L. Dyche, the enthusiastic naturalist-hunter of the University of Kansas.

The flies were originally discovered on skinning the first moose shot. A number of the flies were found 2 or 3 inches within the creature's rectum, where they were supposed to have crawled to oviposit.

Afterwards, in 19 moose killed, Professor Dyche found the flies about them, not leaving the carcasses as long as they lay unskinned, which was frequently from 24 to 36 hours.

The flies are said to prefer the region of the head, rump, and legs, where the hair is shortest, and are supposed to be similar in habit to the Horn-fly, although no observations could, of course, be made on living animals.

Mr. Snow finds the species to be distinct from *serrata*, and described the male and female as *Hæmatobia alcis*.

MISS ORMEROD'S RESIGNATION.

Miss Ormerod has just issued to her friends and correspondents a little slip announcing her resignation of the office of consulting entomologist of the Royal Agricultural Society of England, partly, as she states, on account of her health. With the advent of cold weather she finds she can not attend committee meetings without risk. Moreover, some misapprehension has recently arisen as to the amount of claim which the council might exercise in directing her services, and as to the claim which the council might have on information in her hands. In spite of the fact that this trouble seems to have blown over, Miss Ormerod feels that she can work with more comfort if free of all claims whatever. She proposes to carry on her extremely valuable work as a private individual. We are very glad to learn that the publication of her reports will not be interrupted. For 14 years she has worked untiringly and unselfishly, and has occupied almost alone the field of economic entomology in England. Any change in her plans which would interrupt her entomological work would be a distinct loss to agriculture.

THE BUMBLE BEE IN NEW ZEALAND.

The introduction of the Bumble Bee into New Zealand a few years ago to secure the fertilization of the red clover, and the remarkable success of this venture, are matters of record. In a recent paper in the *New Zealand Journal of Science*, noticed in *The Entomologist's Monthly Magazine* for May, 1891, Mr. George M. Thomson, F. L. S., presents an interesting article on the introduced Bombi in New Zealand, giving also a list of the plants and flowers which are visited by these bees. He makes the interesting statement that, with a few exceptions, he has never heard of these bees visiting the flowers of indigenous plants, but states that they have become so extraordinarily abundant that the question has even arisen in his mind as to whether they would not become as serious a pest to the apiarist as the rabbits have proved to the farmer and cultivator, on account of their absorbing so much of the nectar of the flowers. He also points out the remarkable fact in connection with the life of the Bumblebee in New Zealand, that in many parts of the colony it does not seem to hibernate at all, but is to be seen daily on flowers all the year round.

SOME OF OUR INSECTS IN JAMAICA.

Mr. T. D. A. Cockerell, curator of the Institute of Jamaica, has sent us recently several insects which he finds in Jamaica and which are at the same time well known in this country. He finds among scale insects the common Round Scale (*Lecanium hemisphæricum*), the Purple Scale (*Mytilaspis citricola*), and the Florida Red Scale (*Aspidiotus ficus*). He also sends the moth of the common Melon Worm (*Eudioptis hyalinata*) and the abundant *Anomis erosa* of Florida, and, what is more interesting, informs us that he has captured the Army Worm moth (*Leucania unipuncta*, of the form *asticta*). This is the first record of this last species from the West Indies, although from its occurrence in South America and Florida this locality was quite to be expected. He also sends a specimen of what seems to be *Synchlora rubivoraria*. This is the common Raspberry Geometer of this country.

LIVING BEETLE LARVÆ IN THE INTESTINES OF A CHILD.

Dr. G. Sandberg gives an account in the *Entomol. Tidskrift*, 1890, (pp. 77–80) of the occurrence of living coleopterous larvæ in the intestines of his 10-year old son. After the boy had been complaining for more than two years of colic, pain in his breast, headache, and nausea, more serious symptoms manifested themselves, especially at night. He would start from his sleep shrieking and delirious, with subsequent headache, prostration, and exhaustion. The use of vermifuges and the consequent excretion of small "pin worms" brought about no improvement in his condition, and this was not accomplished until recourse was had to stronger purgatives and the subsequent expulsion of two full-grown Elaterid larvæ, about 2 centimetres in length, of the species *Agrypnus murinus*.

NEW BEE-FLIES.

In the *West American Scientist* for September, 1891, Mr. D. W. Coquillett publishes descriptions of two new genera and three new species of Bombyliidæ of the group Paracosmus. All are described from captured specimens taken in California. They are *Amphicosmus* n. gen.; *elegans* n. sp.; *Metacosmus* n. gen.; *exilis* n. sp.; *Paracosmus insolens* n. s.

In the August number of the same journal he describes two additional species of the genus Lordotus and gives a synoptical table of the eight species known to inhabit the United States. He also adds a description of *Toxophora casta* and gives a revised table of the species of this genus.

A BARK-LOUSE FROM ANTS' NESTS.

Mr. J. W. Douglas publishes in No. 21 of his *Notes on some British and Exotic Coccidæ* (*Entomolgist's Monthly Magazine*, second series, vol. II) a description of *Orthesia occidentalis* n. sp., from specimens collected by Mr. T. D. A. Cockerell at West Cliff, Colo., at an altitude of 7,700 feet, in the nests of an ant of the genus Myrmica. This occurrence is of decided interest, as no species of Orthesia has heretofore been found in such a location, nor does any species feed upon the roots of plants.

ŒBALUS PUGNAX AN ENEMY OF GRASSES.

Under the above title Mr. H. Garman, of Lexington, Ky., gives (*Psyche*, April, 1891, p. 61), a statement of his observation of the habits of *Œbalus pugnax*, which shows that this insect, hitherto considered as predaceous, is also, and perhaps generally, a vegetable feeder, affecting particularly the grasses of the genus *Setaria* and *Panicum*. He describes the eggs and habits of the insect and refers to the statement in the fourth report of the U. S. Entomological Commission, p. 97, that the species has been observed attacking the Cotton Worm. The facts brought out by Mr. Garman indicate for this species what is already known for allied Pentatomids, as for instance *Nezara hilaris* Say, namely, that they are both carnivorous and herbivorous.

NEW FOOD-PLANT OF RHODOBÆNUS 13-PUNCTATUS.

This insect, which we mentioned in our Third Missouri Report as burrowing into the stalks of the common Cockle-burr (*Xanthium strumarium*), and in our general index to the Missouri reports as having been reared from Helianthus in Texas, and afterward noted in the first volume of INSECT LIFE as infesting the stems of various weeds, including Ambrosia and the Thistle, has been found by Mr. C. M. Weed to breed in the stems of the Cupweed, *Silphium perfoliatum*. Mr. Weed published this note in the *American Naturalist* for December, 1890, and although this notice is late, the matter is of too much interest to be overlooked.

LIVING LARVÆ IN THE EAR.

Popular Science News for September 9, 1891, quotes from an otological journal to the effect that a case has recently been recorded in which a farmer removed a fly which had crawled into his ear and two days later was seized with an intense pain, accompanied by bleeding. Two days later he sought medical advice, and on syringing 15 living larvæ were removed. The meatus was found to be much reddened, swollen, and bleeding, but the drum was intact. The insect was probably the Screw Worm, *Lucilia macellaria*.

BAD WORK BY YELLOW JACKETS.

An Associated Press dispatch from Indianapolis, Ind., dated September 25, states that Mr. Riley Smart, a prominent young man of Monroe Township, of that State, had just died from the effects of being stung in forty-two different places by Yellow Jackets. On the same day the Washington papers contained an account of a serious accident to Prof. A. K. Spence, dean of the faculty of Fiske University, and his wife, from a Yellow Jacket stinging their horse as they were driving in the suburbs of this city. The frightened animal plunged over a bridge and crushed the professor and his wife beneath the vehicle. Their injuries, while very serious, have not as yet resulted fatally.

DEATH FROM A BEE STING.

Well-authenticated accounts of death from the sting of the honey bee are sufficiently rare to render any positive instance of interest. The *Evening Star*, of this city, contained on August 25 a circumstantial account of the death of Mr. William H. Danley, a strong man of vigorous constitution, who carried the mail from Tivoli, a village of Pennsylvania, to the Williamsport and North Branch Railway station, from the sting of an ordinary honey bee upon one of his fingers. The hand at once commenced swelling, and in 10 minutes after being stung the man fell into a comatose condition and died before aid could be summoned, only 15 minutes having elapsed from the time he was stung.

A PREDACEOUS CAPSUS.

An interesting note is published in the *Entomologische Nachrichten*, Jahrgang XVII. heft 2. by C. Verhoeff. to the effect that he has observed *Capsus capillaris* feeding upon *Aphis rosae*. An individual was observed to insert its proboscis in the abdomen of the plant-louse between the honey tubes.

WATER BEETLES FOUND IN AN OLD GASOMETER.

An interesting note is published in the *Entomologist's Monthly Magazine* for March. 1890. which indicates that *Dytiscus marginalis* may live under extraordinary conditions. A number of specimens were found living in rusty water at the bottom of a hole left when the iron casing of a gasometer had been removed. both water and mud being strongly impregnated with gas. Mr. T. H. Hall. the writer of the note. who secured the specimens. states that they carried a strong odor of gas even after they had had two or three baths of fresh water. The old gas-holder must have been their home for a long period of beetle life. judging from the time of year when they were found and from the number of both sexes seen. The water was partly inclosed and was quite stagnant. being unconnected with any other water. They could have migrated had they desired to do so. They were quite active. and seem undoubtedly to have remained entirely from choice.

HICKORY HORNED DEVIL INJURING COTTON.

Through Dr. Tate Powell. of Starke. Fla.. we learn that the larva of *Citheronia regalis* has been doing considerable damage to sea-island cotton in Bradford County the present season.

A NEW FOOD-PLANT OF THE FLUTED SCALE.

Mr. C. R. Orcutt. of San Diego. Cal.. has recently sent us specimens of *Icerya purchasi* from the Mission Valley. which he found upon *Hymenoplea salsola*. This plant has not previously been mentioned as a food-plant of the Fluted Scale.

TEMPERATURE OF WEEVIL-INFESTED PEAS.

On page 59. volume I. Mr. Howard published a short note concerning some observations by Judge Lawrence Johnson. upon a remarkable increase of temperature of a mass of cow peas infested by *Bruchus scutellaris*. The same observation has recently been made again by Mr. William D. Richardson. of Fredericksburg. Va. We quote from a letter from Mr. Richardson addressed to Mr. Schwarz. dated November 1. 1891:

August 13 I had occasion to move a bag of peas which had been in the corner of my room (in our farm house) for a month or more. and from which thousands of *Bruchus scutellaris* had been emerging. On touching the bag I was surprised at the temperature, and observed as follows:

Time, 8:40 a. m.; thermometer on northwest side of house 70° F.; in my room, 70°. When placed in the bag it rose 10° in one minute, and in six minutes more registered 88°. This temperature continued for two weeks, when it commenced to fall, the beetles soon after ceasing to emerge.

REAPPEARANCE OF ICERYA PURCHASI.

We learn from a recent California journal that the Fluted Scale has made its appearance in considerable numbers at St. Helena, Napa County. This is quite in accordance with our predictions, for we have by no means believed that the pest was fully exterminated by the Vedalia.

THE PEAR MIDGE IN NEW YORK.

We have not yet noted the fact that Dr. Lintner has discovered the Pear Midge (*Diplosis pyrivora*), which we treated in our Annual Report for 1885, along the Hudson River. Up to the past year it was known only in the single locality near Meriden, Conn., where we studied it.

A POSSIBLE NEW INSECTICIDE.

O. Loew, in the Berichte der Deutschen Chemischen Gesellschaft, XXIII, page 3203, announces that hydrazine sulphate in the proportion of one-fifth of a gramme to 1 litre of water kills immediately algæ, fission organisms, molds, schizomycetes, and other low types of water organisms. It is also poisonous upon dogs and Guinea-pigs, and unfortunately is also injurious to young shoots and buds of plants. The *Gardener's Chronicle* for August 15 recommends its trial under the head of "A New Insecticide," but its deleterious effect upon both plant life and the life of mammalia would apparently restrict its use to the comparatively small group of household pests.

BITTEN BY A KATIPO.

We are indebted to Mr. R. Allan Wight, of Auckland, New Zealand, for the following clipping from a New Zealand paper:

AUCKLAND, *May* 11.

A few days ago the well-known waterman of this port, Harry Keane, received a bite from what he states was a Katipo, while down on the island of Motutapu rabbit shooting. The bite resulted in great pain and considerable swelling of the leg on which he was bitten. He has been in the hospital ever since, and it is not yet certain whether he will not lose his leg.

ENTOMOLOGICAL SOCIETY OF WASHINGTON,

THURSDAY, OCTOBER 1, 1891.

The following persons were elected members of the Society: E. W. Doran, A. G. Masius, F. C. Test, W. T. Swingle, active members; H. E. Weed, W. H. Harrington, E. A. Popenoe, corresponding members.

Mr. Heidemann exhibited some interesting new species of Capsidæ taken the past season on Red Cedar, Willow, and Linden.

Mr. Ulke exhibited and remarked on the habits of a number of rare or new aquatic Coleoptera found by him the past summer in the Blue Ridge Mountains, near Monterey, Md.

Mr. Ulke also exhibited a pale larviform female of a species of *Phengodes* which he found abundantly in the Blue Ridge Mountains, no males, however, being discovered. The species was thought by Professor Riley to be *Ph. laticollis*, and the relative abundance of the males and females of *Phengodes* was discussed by Riley and others.

Mr. Schwarz exhibited specimens of *Emphylus americanus* taken by H. G. Hubbard and himself in a colony of *Formica sanguinea* near Alto, Utah, at an elevation of about 9,000 feet.

Mr. Ashmead read a paper on the peculiar Chalcid genus *Melitobia* Westw., in which he discussed (1) its synonymy with *Anthophorabia* Newport, concluding that *Melitobia* should take precedence; (2) its structure and position in the classificatory system, deciding that it belongs to the subfamily *Tetrastichinæ* and not with the *Elachistinæ* where it is now placed; and (3) its habits, recording the rearing of *M. megachilis* Pack. from *Megachile centuncularis* Linn.; *M. pelopœi* Ashm. from *Pelopœus cementaria* in Kansas by Professor Popenoe and in Florida by himself; and a new species which he described as *M. chalybii*, bred from the cells of *Chalybion cœruleum* taken in Maryland.

Discussed by Messrs. Howard, Theo. Gill, Riley, Schwarz, and others.

Dr. Marx presented a paper entitled "Preliminary Notes on the Classification of the Ixodidæ," in which he discussed the views of previous authors on the classification of these parasites and concluded to accept with some modification the scheme of Koch, as follows: Order, Acari; Suborder, Cynorhastes; Tribe I, Cetocari with families, Argasidæ and Eschatorephalidæ; Tribe II, Antiocari with families Hæmelastaridæ, Ixodidæ, and Rhipistomidæ.

The paper also included generic synopses of the genera of the several families. The scheme differs from Koch's in adding one new family, and suppressing one genus and adding three new ones. The paper was discussed by Professor Gill and others.

Mr. Howard read a note on the "Appearance of Mealy Bugs parasitized by *Leptomastix*," in which he referred to the habits of the species of this Encyrtid genus of Chalcid parasites and said that his attention had been recently called by Miss Sullivan to the curious fact that Mealy Bugs parasitized by *L. dactylopii* almost entirely lose their waxy secretion and swell up into yellow objects closely resembling Dipterous puparia, which resemblance is heightened by the fact that the parasite in issuing cuts free a cap at the end of the scale just as the Dipterous insect forces off the end of its puparium. Discussed by Messrs. Riley, Ashmead, and Howard.

Professor Fernow gave a report on the results in Europe of the use of the new insect lime against *Psilura monacha*, the use of which he stated had been a perfect success. He described the process of quarantining infested areas by surrounding them with poles which are then smeared with the lime, and also various machines used to apply the lime to trees. Discussed by Professor Riley and others.

Professor Riley made remarks on "A New Herbarium Pest," an article upon which is published in this number. Professor Riley gave some additional notes on *Panchlora viridis*, which are also published in this number.

C. L. MARLATT,
Recording Secretary.

SPECIAL NOTES.

Mr. Koebele's second Trip to Australia.—We have not yet mentioned in these pages the fact that Mr. Koebele has been sent out to Australia and New Zealand a second time on a search for beneficial insects. The California State Legislature last winter appropriated $5,000 for sending some one to Australia for this purpose, and this sum was placed at the disposal of the State Board of Horticulture. The board soon afterward made application to the Secretary of Agriculture to have Mr. Koebele sent, placing the entire appropriation at the Secretary's disposal. To this proposition the Secretary assented on condition that Mr. Koebele should go under instructions from the Department, his salary as an agent of the Division of Entomology being continued (his expenses only to be paid by the State Board of Horticulture), and that his report should be made to the Department of Agriculture, the desire being to coöperate as far as possible with the Board. Accordingly, such instructions were given as seemed best to promote the object in view, cautioning Mr. Koebele particularly to run no risk, in his sendings from Australia, of importing with the beneficial insects any injurious species not now existing in the United States which it might prove disastrous to introduce, and taking advantage of the occasion also to have him make every effort to collect in California certain beneficial species to take with him to Australasia, indicating such species as prey upon cosmopolitan insects or species which the colonies mentioned have derived from America. Mr. Koebele sailed on the August steamer, stopping at Honolulu and Auckland, and arriving at Sydney the latter part of October. At Honolulu he left a number of living specimens of *Chilocorus bivulnerus* in the hands of our correspondent, Mr. A. Jaeger, and secured while there four species of Lady-birds of which he sent small numbers to California by steamer. These were sent for use against the Black Scale (*Lecanium oleœ*). He also found a few parasitic Chalcididæ on an undetermined Lecanium, and of these he also sent a few specimens. Upon his arrival in New Zealand some of the Lady-birds which he had taken with him were alive and began to feed at once upon Woolly Aphis. Some Syrphus Flies and Lacewing Flies were also in good condition, as were also the larvæ of the Rhaphidia which feeds upon the Codling Moth. These were left in competent charge. Specimens of *Scymnus acceptus, S. consor, S. villosus,*

S. flavihirtus, and *S. fagus* were collected and sent to California. These all prey upon various species of scale-insects, but it is hardly to be supposed that they will accomplish any better results in California than do our native species of this genus, all of which have a similar habit.

The most encouraging information comes to us under date of November 1 from Sydney. He there finds that *Orcus chalybeus*, a steel-blue Lady-bird, is a most important enemy of the Red Scale. He has found them by the hundreds, and has observed the mature insects eating the scales. All of the trees were "full of eggs," and the larvæ were swarming upon all the orange and lemon trees infested with the Red Scale. He secured and sent a large lot of the eggs and many of the adult beetles. He also sent the allied *Orcus australasiæ*, also found feeding upon the Red Scale, and a number of Scymnids, one of which was very numerous, feeding upon the same scale-insect. Another species was found feeding mainly upon the Flat Scale (*Lecanium hesperidum*) and the Black Scale (*Lecanium oleæ*). He also forwarded a number of *Leis conformis*, which, as stated in Bulletin No. 21 of this Division, is the commonest enemy of the Woolly Root-louse of the Apple. Unfortunately Mr. Koebele does not state whether the three insects mentioned as feeding upon the Red Scale were successful in holding that destructive insect in check, and upon this point naturally depends much of their value to California. Our agent at Los Angeles, Mr. D. W. Coquillett, has been instructed to spare no pains to properly care for and colonize whatever may be received from Mr. Koebele, and is fully prepared to do so. This large sending arrived at Los Angeles, we are sorry to state, in rather bad condition. Twenty-eight beetles, however, were alive, including nine of *O. chalybeus*, and no effort will be spared to keep them in good condition and to induce them to propagate.

Vedalia in Demand.—During November we had a pleasant visit from Mr. Thomas A. J. Louw, a member of the legislative assembly of the Cape of Good Hope, who was visiting this country with instructions from the Government of the Cape to look into certain matters connected with the cultivation, canning and packing of fruit, and the working of agricultural societies in this country. Among the objects of his visit there was, however, mentioned specifically that of obtaining a supply of *Vedalia cardinalis*, and he was authorized to incur any expenditure necessary to procure specimens and carry them alive to Cape Town. Mr. Louw, of course, waited upon the Secretary, who cordially commended him to the chiefs of his several divisions with instructions to afford him every facility in furthering the objects of his visit. Accordingly the Entomologist at once wrote to Mr. Coquillett to make every effort to have a good supply of living beetles on hand against Mr. Louw's arrival in California, and to use his best endeavors to make a success of the sending. We advised Mr. Louw to carry his material in two ways:

first, to prepare a galvanized-iron receptacle of convenient size, with an apartment for ice and another for the insects, so that the temperature could constantly and certainly be kept at a low point. This we conceived to be a much better plan than to rely upon the refrigerators of vessels and trains. We also urged that a duplicate lot be kept at a normal temperature, active and constantly at work and breeding throughout the journey. This method required that they should be carried in such a way that they could be examined from day to day, and that a good supply of food in the shape of living Icerya should be taken if possible on living plants in pots. We advised Mr. Louw to call upon Mr. Alexander Craw, the chief quarantine officer, on his way to Los Angeles, and we anticipate the most profitable results from his mission to this country.

In addition to Mr. Louw's effort Mr. Koebele has, in accordance with instructions, carried very large numbers of Vedalia in the egg and larva state from New Zealand to Australia, with the intention of shipping them from there to Cape Town. He found on his arrival at Sydney that no steamer would sail within a reasonable time, but he is waiting an opportunity to start his sending over. While he is in Australia we have every hope that the shipment can be made.

A Monograph of the Insects and other Animals injuring Tobacco.*—Prof. Ad. Targioni Tozzetti has just published an elaborate work on the subject of the animals and insects of growing tobacco and of the dried product, under the auspices of the Royal Excise Department, and with the assistance of the Government agencies for the manufacture and cultivation of tobacco. He has gone over the entire ground of tobacco enemies in all countries, devoting 270 of his 300 pages of text to the subject of insects proper, six pages to vertebrates, seven to snails, ten to arachnids, and one to earthworms. In all, 144 species of insects are treated, nearly all of them being delineated by means of very fair wood cuts, and their work being shown by several full-page plates. The insects are considered in their systematic order, and the matter of remedies is discussed under each insect. Where several species of a given group occur upon tobacco, synoptical tables to enable their separation are published. The work is prefaced by a bibliography and concludes with a very full index. The tobacco insect, of which there is the most complaint in this country, viz. the Cigarette Beetle (*Lasioderma serricorne*), is treated at some length. The author concludes that on account of the special abundance of this insect in tobacco brought from this country to Europe its origin may be accorded to America. As a remedy for this pest he recommends a thorough use of chloroform, bisulphide of carbon, and hydrocyanic acid gas in disinfecting warehouses and manufactories, and he also advises, where possible, the submersion of the tobacco in

---

*Animali ed Insetti del Tabacco in Erba e del Tabacco Secco. By Ad. Targioni Tozzetti. Firenze-Roma, 1891.

99 parts water for forty-eight hours, advice evidently not based on experience and not appreciative of the ease with which tobacco is spoiled for the trade.

Popular Entomology.*—We have just received from the author, Mr. William Hamilton Gibson, the well-known magazine artist, a popular work on natural history, which for abundance, elegance, and delicacy of illustrations and careful presswork has seldom been surpassed in publications of its character.

The work consists of short, chatty chapters, wonderfully varied and changing in topic, dealing with the curious or striking in various fields of natural history, but particularly with entomological and botanical subjects. No general plan or order of subjects is followed. The book is divided into four parts, viz, Spring, Summer, Autumn, and Winter, and the various topics are grouped in each as they would be suggested to one sauntering daily out of doors with no other thought than to explain any strange or curious object or phenomena connected with animate nature.

The studies are for the most part, as he says, from his own observations and experience of early years, and are written in popular style. The accuracy of the illustrations, together with the diversity of observations of curious and striking facts, original with the author, but for the most part common and well known to students, sustain the author's claim to "sharp eyes" indicated in the title.

This, together with his fertility in explanation of the phenomena observed, makes the work especially valuable for the hands of children and young people, for whom it was more particularly designed.

The author is evidently most at home and does his best work in the entomological field, and his popularization of the marvels of insect parasitism, as illustrated in the chapter on "The Bewitched Cocoon of Polyphemus" and "Those Puzzling Cocoon Clusters" (*Microgaster*), are particularly good in matter and illustrations. Of almost equal interest are many other chapters, as, for instance, "The Brownie-jugs and the Brownie" (*Eumenes fraterna*). "A Butterfly Serenade" (the voice of *Antiopa*), and many others.

Chapters on the curious in plant life are scattered through the work, and also chapter on birds, etc.

The illustrations, of which there are over 300, are, with one or two exceptions, executed by the author, are original and pleasing in design, remarkably accurate in delineation of habits and form, and give the work much of the value it possesses, the figure of Thalessa ovipositing being an apparent adaptation of the studies on this insect recorded in Vol. 1 of INSECT LIFE.

---

*Sharp Eyes: A rambler's calendar of fifty-two weeks among *Insects*, *Birds*, and *Flowers*. By William Hamilton Gibson. Illustrated by the author. New York: Harper & Bros., Franklin Square. 1892. [*Sic!*]

Spraying for the Codling Moth.—We wish to call particular attention to the letter of Mr. John S. Lupton published in "Extracts from Correspondence," as affording a marked illustration of the value of spraying apple trees with the arsenical mixtures for the Codling Moth. Few prominent apple-growers at the present day in more northern and western States doubt the advisability of this remedy. Further south it has not come so extensively into use. Mr. Lupton's experience has made him enthusiastically in favor of the remedy, and no doubt will prove to others who have been skeptical up to the present time that many hundreds of dollars can be saved by careful and proper use of London purple or Paris green.

---

*Mr. Craw on the destructive Insects of California.—Mr. Alexander Craw, Quarantine Officer and Entomologist of the California State Board of Horticulture, has just published a little fifty page pamphlet with the title given in our footnote. He divides his matter into six heads, viz: scale-insects, miscellaneous insects, beneficial insects, internal parasites, remedies, and spraying apparatus. The work upon scale-insects is very well done, and includes a compiled account of twelve of the most injurious scale-insects of California, with photographic reproductions of several, and a very good colored plate of eight species. The lithographers have made the enlarged figure of the Red Scale too light colored, and that of the San José Scale too bluish.

Under the head of "Miscellaneous Insects" the Grape Leaf-beetle (*Adoxus vitis*) is treated with a figure of its work and of the beetle itself. The Hop Aphis and the Black Aphis of the Peach, Canker-worms and the Forest Tent Caterpillar are the other insects treated. We suspect that the *Siphonophora* reported as so abundant upon Hop is not *arenæ*, but one of the other species of *Siphonophora* which we have had from this plant. We are also, in the absence of definite information, inclined to doubt the finding of the Fall Canker-worm (*Anisopteryx pometaria* Harris=*autumnata* Pack.) in California. The species which we have received from the Pacific coast is different and it is difficult to decide from the larva alone, which Mr. Craw has apparently done. In the same way the Forest Tent Caterpillar is mentioned as our old *Clisiocampa sylvatica*, whereas it is much more likely to be *C. californica* or one of the undetermined species of this genus which we have received from California. Mr. Craw gives a very good summary of remedies and spraying apparatus and avoids the difficulty of recommending any one spraying machine to the detriment of others by giving a list of sixty-four dealers in the State of California alone. This well illustrates the spread of this new manufacturing industry. We may state in regard to the

---

*California State Board of Horticulture. Division of Entomology. Destructive Insects; their natural enemies; remedies and recommendations. By Alexander Craw, Quarantine Officer and Entomologist, Sacramento, 1891.

Yellow Scale parasite, *Coccophagus citrinus* Craw, that it unquestionably belongs to the genus *Encarsia* rather than to *Coccophagus* and that the drawing is misleading, especially in the details of the thorax.

American Spiders.—We are greatly pleased to learn that Count Keyserling's magnificent work "Die Spinnen Amerikas" has not been interrupted by the lamented death of the author. The publishers, Messrs. Bauer & Raspe, of Nurnberg, after Count Keyserling's death in April, 1889, turned over his manuscripts to Dr. Marx, of this Department, whose name appears as editor of Part III. This part includes a consideration of Brazilian spiders, and treats of 240 species of 70 genera and 14 families. Vol. IV is now in course of preparation by Dr. Marx. It will take up the Epeiridæ of North, Central, and South America. For this volume Keyserling left descriptions and illustrations of over 200 species. Vol. I of the work was published in 1880, and treated of the Laterigradæ, and Vol. II upon the Theridiidæ appeared in two parts in 1884 and 1885.

WHEAT AND GRASS SAW-FLIES.

By C. V. RILEY and C. L. MARLATT.

For a number of years past notes on certain Saw-flies, the larvæ of which feed on wheat and various meadow grasses have been accumulating in the Division. A short note on a Saw-fly larva, which attacked wheat, was published in Bulletin No. 4 of this Division. The adult, however, of this species was not obtained and little was discovered of its habits and life-history except the fact mentioned of its feeding on wheat. A further reference to wheat Saw-flies occurs in the Report of the Entomologist for 1884, in which an account is given of the habits of certain Tenthredinid larvæ which were found to infest wheat near Bloomington, Ill., and afterwards at Oxford, Ind. The descriptions of two forms of larvæ are there given, but no adults were reared and the species were not determined. Since that time the habits and life-history of a number of species have been somewhat fully traced, while some additional larvæ, of which no adults have yet been obtained have been studied. In view of the fact that little, if anything, is known of the work of these insects and that they are liable at any time to assume importance, we deem it advisable to put on record the facts already obtained.

The European Corn Saw-fly (*Cephus pygmæus*) has lately been found in injurious numbers in several localities, and is treated of at length by Prof. Comstock in Bulletin No. 11, of the Cornell Experiment Station, and an article is published upon it in Vol. II of INSECT LIFE, page 286. The larva of a *Cephus* sp. has been found by Mr. Koebele, at Alameda, Cal., working in grass, and is referred to in INSECT LIFE, Vol. III, p. 71. These are the only published records of Saw-flies affecting small grains or grasses in this country.

The European Corn Saw-fly is, properly speaking, not a Saw-fly, but may be classed with the family Uroceridæ, or Horn-tails, the larvæ of which are wood-borers. The larva of Cephus resembles them in this habit in that it does not feed exteriorly on the grain, but burrows in the stalk. The genus *Cephus* with allied genera has also been separated as a distinct family, Cephidæ, connecting the Tenthredinidæ with the Uroceridæ.

The Saw-fly larvæ, which attack cereals and grasses, belong mostly to the genus *Dolerus*, the exceptions being the *Cephus* spp. just mentioned, and *Nematus marylandicus* Norton.

DOLERUS SPP.

The Saw-flies of the genus *Dolerus* are comparatively large, robust insects, of a dull black or bluish color, varied with yellow or reddish, and are represented in the United States by some seventeen species, of which the early stages of none have been recorded. They are among the earliest of the Saw-flies to appear in the spring, and are frequently found about willows feeding on the pollen of the catkins. They are also, and very commonly, taken on grass, particularly in moist and swampy localities.

In Europe there are nearly 60 described species, but here again the habits of but few of them are known, and the larvæ, on the authority of André, have been carefully described only in the case of a single species—*D. hæmatodes* Schk. This is the more remarkable because the species of this genus are abundant and widely distributed. The adults of a number of European species, however, have been reared from the larvæ, and of these larvæ brief descriptions have been made and the food-habits recorded. These records show that the larvæ of this genus feed on grasses (*Festuca*, etc.,) or on Juncus and certain other low monocotyledonous plants.

Cameron gives the food-habits of the following species: *

D. fulviventris on *Equisetum?*
D. palustris on *Equisetum palustre.*
D. gonagra on meadow grass, particularly *Festuca pratensis.*
D. hæmatodes on *Juncus* sp.
D. niger on *Festuca?*

The egg of a Dolerus has never been described or seen. The larvæ of the *Dolerus* spp. are quite uniform in color and general characteristics, and do not differ essentially from the larvæ of other Tenthredininæ. They have 22 legs, are cylindrical, and generally of a uniform grayish or slaty color dorsally and laterally, but nearly white ventrally and subventrally.

---

*A Monograph of the British Phytophagous Hymenoptera, Vol. I.

None of them are known to spin cocoons, but so far as studied they form cells of earth in which to pass the winter or undergo transformation.

The larvæ of *Dolerus* spp., found on Gramineæ in this country, represent at least five well-marked forms and may belong to as many distinct species. The adults of but two species, *D. arvensis* Say and *D. collaris* Say, have been bred.

The following general description will apply to all the forms studied:

Head large and prominent, almost as wide as first segment, more or less flattened in front, yellowish or greenish and variously marked with white or brown; eyes inclosed with a narrow dark brown or black ring.

Body elongate, tapering uniformly and gradually towards the tip, with numerous transverse wrinkles, and finely rugose or punctured; head and sides of body especially near lower edge and at tip, armed with minute whitish hairs. Color, greenish, darker or slate color on dorsum and sides; a light band covering stigmatal area.

Thoracic feet light brownish at tip, and with light colored hairs, which are longer and more numerous than on body.

The larva studied may be distinguished as follows:

(1) Length of largest specimen, 24 mm. Head, viewed from the front, hexagonal, with the angles round; face, including antennæ and mouth-parts and long oval spot on cheek, whitish; a brown band starting near the base of the mandibles and including the eyes, passes over the head in front; back of this band on the vertex the color is light yellowish brown, in some specimens scarcely darker than the oval spots on the cheeks; the genal suture separating the cheek from the vertex is usually stained with brown. Punctation of head and body rather coarse and noticeable.

(2) (*D. arvensis?*) Length of largest specimen about 20 mm. General shape of the head as in (1), except that it is less flattened or is fuller in front, especially in partly-grown specimens. The pattern of the markings is similar to (1), but the dark brown is replaced by a light yellowish brown throughout. The eyes with encircling ring are, on account of the surrounding light color, especially prominent. The head, particularly, and the body are smoother and the punctation is finer.

(3) Size of larva and shape of head as in (2); frontal brown band as in (1), except that it rarely includes the eyes; the dorsal area of the head is as in (1), or some specimens dark brown and unicolorous with frontal band; the genal suture is more distinctly marked with brown. This form is particularly distinguished by the well-defined subdorsal brownish band, which is rather sharply limited below by the light stigmatal area, and passes into the general slate color of the dorsum above.

(4) Shorter and more robust than (1). Head as wide or wider than first segment, and with very faint markings, which are somewhat irregular, but similar in general pattern to foregoing. This form is easily separated from the others by the presence on the lateral white stripe of a row of black spots, one on each segment, just above the stigmata; a similar spot occurs at the base of each of the thoracic and abdominal legs.

(5) Length, 18-20 mm. Shape of head and body as in (1). Markings of head similar to (1), except that the whitish area on the cheek, including the genal suture, is entirely covered by a branch of the brown frontal band. The dorsal area is as with (1), light yellowish brown. The occurrence of this distinct and prominent posterior branch of the frontal brown band seems to be a safe indication of a distinct species, in view of the fact that it shows no tendency to vary, and that in the case of all the other forms studied there is no indication whatever of this mark.

Dolerus sp. No. 1.—Full-grown larvæ of form (1) were found by Mr. Lugger June 18, 1886, near Baltimore cutting off the heads of wheat. Larvæ apparently identical with these, but too badly decomposed for positive identification, were received May 31, 1887, from Mr. H. A. Newland, of Middletown, Del., with the report that they were very injurious to wheat in that locality. Additional specimens in good condition and apparently full-fed were received from the same party June 4, 1887, and on June 10 still others were forwarded by C. F. Kreider, of Lebanon, Pa., who reported their doing considerable damage to wheat.

Mr. Newland writes of them that they are seldom so damaging to wheat as this year (1887) and last. He says that they cut off the stalk about four inches below the head. They do not work very rapidly, but take about fifteen minutes to cut off a single head. Last year they destroyed in many fields from three to probably five bushels to the acre. No adults were obtained.

Dolerus arvensis Say. No. 2.—The larvæ (form 2) which have been referred to this species are only so placed provisionally. The difficulty of properly separating the larvæ into lots, referable to distinct species before any material for comparison has been obtained, will be readily apparent. Larvæ evidently of different species were very commonly associated on the wheat or grasses and were placed together in breeding cages, so that the reference of particular larvæ to adults can not be made with certainty.

Larvæ (form 2) taken on timothy were received from Mr. Webster, June 14, 1884. These specimens were full grown, and an unsuccessful attempt was made to breed one of them. Again on May 28 and 29 of the year following additional larvæ in various stages of growth were sent by Mr. Webster. A quantity of these were saved in alcohol and the others were placed on growing wheat. March 22 of the following year a specimen of *D. arvensis* was obtained from this material. The only doubt as to the correctness of the reference of these larvæ to *arvensis* comes from the fact that one of the larvæ is recorded to have possessed the characteristic markings of form 4, and it may have been from this specimen that the adult came.

A single larva (form 2) was received June 18, 1886, from G. H. Cook, New Brunswick, N. J., who found it feeding on a wheat stalk, the ear of which it had cut off.

Larvæ received in 1883 from Mr. J. C. Hostetter, Minerva, Ohio, and mentioned in Bulletin No. 4 of the Division of Entomology, are in poor condition, but probably belong to this form. The attempt to rear these larvæ failed. The same larvæ were reported at about the same time by W. S. Chamberlain, secretary of the State Board of Agriculture, as occurring on wheat at Columbus, Ohio. Mr. Hostetter's letters are interesting in this connection and may be quoted in full:

> I have as fine a field of wheat as I have seen this season. This morning, in looking over it, I find upon the heads quite a number of such worms as are here inclosed.

They take a portion of the grains out of the heads they attack. They are not very numerous, perhaps three or four in a rod square. I am at a loss to know what they are or whether they will materially injure our wheat. My neighbors also have them.—June 16, 1883.

* * * I have just returned from a walk around a 20-acre field of wheat. My object was to pick off a dozen more of those worms to send you. To my utter surprise, though making diligent search, I found but three, one of which I lost on my way to the house. Only a week ago I could have found any number of them in heads of wheat, the same inclosed. You are evidently clearly right in saying we need not apprehend much damage from them. Their time is of short duration and seems to be confined to the period soon after the wheat is in head. I don't think they affect the kernels when fully formed.—June 25, 1883.

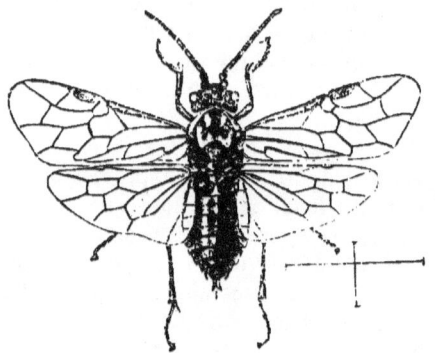

FIG. 13.—*Dolerus arvensis* Say, female (original).

D. arvensis is easily distinguished from other species of the genus by its general blue-black or violaceous color. The female, Fig. 13, is considerably larger than the male, and is further distinguished by having the prothorax and mesothorax more or less rufous. The male is uniformly blue-black, and was described and still appears in the lists as *D. unicolor*.

East of the Rocky Mountains the species is generally distributed and abundant. The National Collection contains twenty-five specimens of this species as against four each of *D. collaris* and *D. sericeus*. These were received from Connecticut, New York, New Jersey, Indiana, Missouri, Illinois, and Ohio, those from Ohio being received from H. Keenan, Quaker City, who took them on pear buds which he said they were injuring.

That they do no injury whatever to the buds or bloom of the Pear, but frequent them merely to lap up nectar or grains of pollen from the petals, has been shown by Prof. S. A. Forbes, in his Third Report on the Insects of Illinois, pp. 100–102. Prof. Forbes and other writers refer to this insect as breeding on the Willow, the only authority for which seems to come from the occurrences of the adults abundantly about the bloom of the Willow in the spring, where they are attracted by the bloom merely, as they are also to the bloom of Pear and other trees.

Dolerus sp. *No. 3.*—Larvæ of form 3 have been received from various sources, as follows: June 14, 1884, and May 28, 1885, through F. M. Webster, from Indiana, found on timothy; July 25, 1884, from L. Bruner, Nebraska, found on grass; and July 5, 1882, from J. C. Rockwood, Hammonton, N. J., who reported that they were seriously affecting the Cranberry. Mr. Schwarz visited Hammonton in August of the same year and found that the Saw-fly larvæ had been confounded with the Army Worm, which fed on the Cranberry and also on Juncus. The Sawfly larvæ feed on nothing but the *Juncus* (*J. canadensis?*). At the time of his visit, August 4, Mr. Schwarz was able to find but two larvæ.

What is evidently the same larva was found during the latter half of May, 1876, feeding on Juncus in Ofallon Park, St. Louis, Mo. These larvæ were numerous and in confinement would not feed on Blue Grass, but fed readily on the Juncus. They reached full growth June 1-13, and entered the ground. Afterwards one earthen cocoon was found in the cage, but no adults were reared.

Dolerus sp. *No. 4.*—Larvæ of form 4 were found at Oxford, Ind., by Mr. Webster, on timothy. Additional material was received June 27, 1884, and May 29 and June 13, 1885. Euplectrus larvæ were attached to the first segment of one of these. Larvæ of the same species were found June 6, 1886, feeding on Juncus in Schuetzen Park, District of Columbia. No adults were reared.

Dolerus sp. *No. 5.*—Larvæ of form 5 were received from Ch. F. Kreider, North Lebanon, Pa., June 4, 1886, with the report that they injured wheat, cutting off the heads. Three larvæ of this form were with the lot brought from near Baltimore by Mr. Lugger, June 18, 1886, and found cutting off the heads of wheat. The majority of the lot from Mr. Newland, Middletown, Del., May and June, 1887, also belong here.

Dolerus collaris, Say.—Larvæ, some of which belonged to this species, were received from Mr. Webster, May 31 and June 6 and 14, 1884, found on timothy. From these an adult was obtained April 18, 1885. Which of the several forms of larvæ belongs to this species can not be positively determined, as no material was saved.

The cocoon is 10 by 5 mm. The outer layer consists of particles of earth loosely cemented together, and is quite intimately connected with the inner layer, which consists of a brownish parchment-like material.

The adults of this species are somewhat smaller than *D. arvensis,* which they greatly resemble. They may be easily separated from *arvensis* by the shining *black* body and yellowish-red fore thorax, the latter including the prothorax and more or less of the mesothorax.

This species occurs throughout the United States and Canada. There are specimens in the National Collection from Central Missouri, Colorado, and Indiana.

Dolerus sericeus Say.—There is little question but that one form or other of the larvæ above described belong to this species, a large female of which was taken by Mr. Webster, at Lafayette, Ind., on wheat.

This species may be recognized by its being entirely black in both sexes, which easily separates it from both *D. arvensis* and *D. collaris.*

NEMATUS (MESSA?) MARYLANDICUS NORTON.

(Syn. *Nematus aureopectus* Norton.)

Of all the Saw-flies found to breed on wheat, etc., perhaps the most interesting species, both on account of its numbers and of the interesting question of generic relationship which it presents, is the one named above. This Saw-fly has been carried through two successive generations in confinement, which experience, together with notes and observations made in the field, affords a pretty full knowledge of its life-round and habits.

Larvæ evidently of this species collected on wheat were received June 6, 1884, from Mr. Webster, from Normal, Ill. Additional larvæ found feeding on timothy were sent by him from Oxford, June 23, of the same year, and still another lot found on grass was received from the same place May 28, 1885. No adults were obtained from these specimens, and larvæ of the first lot only were saved.

July 25, 1884, Mr. Lawrence Bruner forwarded us two larvæ collected July 7 in Holt County, Nebr. These are closely allied, if not identical, with the Webster material.

Mr. Webster had had better success in rearing the adults from the larvæ collected in 1884, and forwarded us eggs May 4, 1885, deposited in a blade of wheat by reared specimens. Additional eggs, in a living wheat plant, were received from Mr. Webster a little later, and from these two perfect insects were eventually obtained. Mr. Webster also successfully reared adults from eggs deposited in confinement by reared specimens.

The habits of this insect may be summarized as follows:

The adult insects (Fig. 14, *e*, male; *f*, female) appear during the latter part of April and first of May, the males antedating the females several days, as is the rule generally with Tenthredinidæ. In nature the flies do not emerge much before the last week of April, as shown by the fact that repeated sweepings of wheat fields in the middle and latter half of April failed to secure any adults. In the breeding cage specimens appeared somewhat earlier, or from April 15 to May 1.

The eggs, when first laid, are four-fifths by one-fifth millimeter, and of a light green color. They are inserted to the number of two to five or more together along the edge of the wheat blades and just beneath the epidermis (Fig. 14, *a a*). Some fifteen or sixteen days elapse before hatching, during which period the eggs increase very considerably in size

The newly hatched larva (Fig. 14, b) is from 3 to 4 mm. long, rather slender and elongate and tapering gradually from the head to the last segment; head yellowish, eyes black. Full growth is attained in about five weeks. The mature larva (Fig. 14, c) has a length of from 17 to 20 mm. and has the general form of the newly hatched larva. The head is considerably less in diameter than the first thoracic segment and is of a pale clay yellow with a greenish tinge and with the surface slightly reticulated; the eyes are black and surrounded by a narrow dark brown ring. The mandibles are tipped with brown. The color of the body is green or yellowish green, with the alimentary canal showing through the semitransparent dorsum as a line of darker green. A whitish line

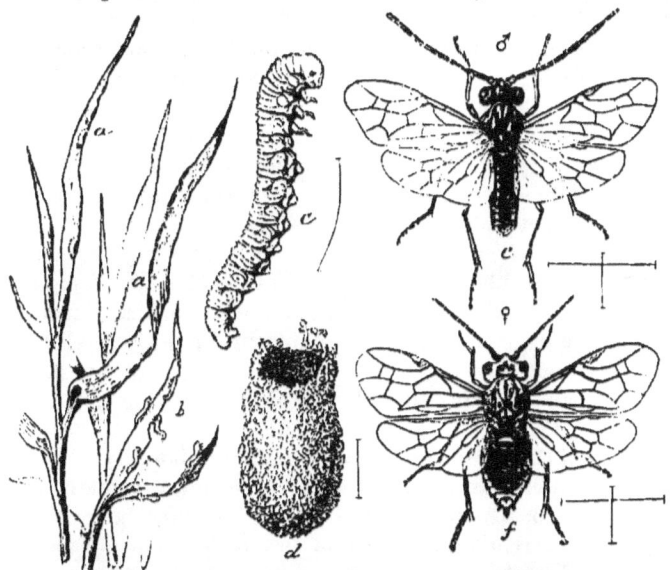

FIG. 14.—*Nematus marylandicus* Norton: *a a*, eggs in wheat blades; *b*, young larvæ; *c*, full-grown larva; *d*, cocoon from which an adult has emerged; *e* and *f*, adult insects—*e*, male; *f*, female; *a* and *b*, natural size; *c* to *f*, enlarged (original).

crosses the stigmata, which are very small and light brown in color. The head and body below the stigmata are armed with minute hairs, which are light colored except on the last segment, where they are prominent and brownish.

The larva of this insect is at once separated from the Dolerus larva by the possession of but seven pairs of abdominal feet, in which respect it agrees with a large group of Tenthredinid larvæ (Nematinæ), including the genus Nematus and its allies.

The larvæ at first feed together as shown in the illustration, but separate and are practically solitary later. They feed on the wheat blades and have not been observed to cut off the wheat heads, though there is little doubt that they will do so, since the stalk just beneath the head remains green longest.

When full-fed the larvæ enter the ground and construct long cocoons of brownish silk with which particles of earth are incorporated. The construction of the cocoon is hardly of distinct threads, but seems to be rather of a glutinous nature resembling silk. The cocoons of the male are 7.5 by 3.5 mm., and of the female 9 to 10 by 5 mm. (Fig. 14, *d*). There is but one yearly generation.

Although no observations were made on this point, our knowledge of allied species renders it almost certain that the contracted larvæ remain unchanged during the balance of the summer and over winter and do not pupate until shortly before the appearance of the winged insects in the spring.

The adult insect is about one-third of an inch long and has an expanse of wing of about two-thirds of an inch. The males and females differ markedly in shape and coloration. The female (Fig.14, *f*) is stout and in general light yellowish or ochraceous in color. A black spot on the head includes the ocelli, and the thorax is marked with two longitudinal black stripes. The abdomen is for the most part dark brown or black dorsally except the posterior lateral margin and the extreme tip. The hind feet and antennæ are also dark.

The male (Fig. 14, *e*) is much more slender and elongate than the female, and is almost black in color, the tip of the abdomen being reddish and part of the legs whitish. The antennæ of the male are much longer than in the female, equaling the body in length; they are also stouter and strongly pilose or hairy. The wings in both sexes are large and transparent, and the main or costal veins of the fore-wing and the stigma are pale.

The wings of this species possess with great uniformity a peculiarity of venation which has been employed to separate a distinct genus (*Messa*). This consists in that the second submarginal cell receives but a single recurrent vein, instead of two, as is commonly the case in the species of *Nematus*. This character can not be relied upon, although measurably constant in this species, since in other species with the normal venation of *Nematus* this peculiarity sometimes occurs, and not unfrequently a single specimen will display the venation of *Messa* on one side and of *Namatus* on the other.

This species was first described by Mr. Edward Norton from a single specimen of the male taken in Maryland (Proc. Entom. Soc. Phila., Vol. III, p. 7, 1864). The female was described as a distinct species (*Nematus aureopectus*) by Mr. Norton several years later, from specimens received from Massachusetts, New York, and Pennsylvania. (Trans. Am. Ent. Soc. Vol. I, 1867, p. 219.) The male having been first described, gives the name to the species—*N. aureopectus* becoming a synonym.

The natural food-plants of this insect are undoubtedly certain of our native grasses from which it very naturally spreads to cultivated grasses and small grains.

A single specimen of the hymenopterous parasite *Lampronota frigida* Cr. was reared from a cocoon of this Saw-fly and also an undetermined species (not found).

CEPHUS OCCIDENTALIS N. SP.

The *Cephus* sp. referred to in the opening of this article as being reared from grass in California by Mr. Koebele proves to be undescribed.

The habits of this insect are exactly similar to the European Corn Saw-fly *Cephus pygmæus*, the larvæ boring in grass working from the top towards the root and spinning in the base of the grass stem a silken tube in which it hibernates.

Before spinning up the grass stem is partly cut through (Fig. 15, *c*) to facilitate the emergence of the adult insect which takes place in May.

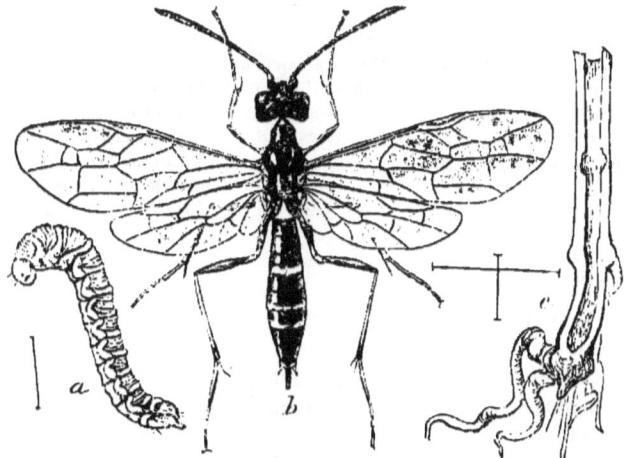

FIG. 15.—*Cephus occidentalis* n. sp: *a*, larva; *b*, adult insect, female; *c*.base of grass stalk showing excavation of larva, all inclosed (original).

The larva (Fig. 15, *a*) is about one-half inch long, cylindrical, whitish in color and with a resinous brown head. The general characteristics of shape and structure are shown in the figure. It does not differ from the larva of *Cephus pygmæus* except in being smaller and less robust.

The adult insect (Fig. 15 *b*) agrees almost exactly with *Cephus pygmæus* in coloration, coming much closer to it in this respect than to any other American species, but is in every way more slender and graceful and would never be mistaken for the European species. The head is narrower in proportion to the body and is more globular when viewed from the side. Viewed from above it narrows more posteriorly from the eyes than *pygmæus*. The grass in which this insect breeds was not determined, but is a hollow-stemmed marsh grass, probably a species of *Elymus*.

The species may be characterized as follows :

♀ Black; basal joints of the maxillary palpi, large spot on mandibles, two spots beneath anterior wings, membranous regions of thorax, small spot on lower posterior edge of dorsum of first segment, larger one on second segment, band, dentate on basal margin, on apical half of dorsum of third, fifth, and sixth segments, and more or less of the lower and apical margin of the remaining segments, lemon yellow.

Legs black, slender; spot on posterior coxæ above, upper side and tip of femora, yellow; tibiæ and tarsi reddish yellow except tips of posterior tibiæ and their tarsi, which are brownish; last joint and claws of middle and anterior tarsi also brownish.

Antennæ 20-21 jointed, longer than head and thorax, slender to joints 7, beyond which the articles are shorter and thickened.

Wings slightly smoky; veins brown except costal and margin of stigma, which are yellowish; a small infuscated spot at base of discoidal vein; second recurrent vein joins the third submarginal cell near the base of the cell; cross veins of lanceolate cell slightly curved and oblique.

Abdomen not much longer than head and thorax, strongly compressed laterally.
Length, 9-11 mm.
Exp. al., 16-19 mm.

♂ Smaller and more slender than the ♀ ; abdomen less compressed; antennæ 18-21 jointed. Coloration as in ♀ except a large spot on the clypeus, one just below the eyes in front, the entire pectal region of the thorax, and the posterior margin of the third, fifth, and remaining ventral segments, which are lemon-yellow.

The under side of the coxæ, trochanters, and femora, including the apex of the latter above, are lemon-yellow; the tibiæ and tarsi are as in the case of the ♀.

In some specimens the femora are entirely yellow or with a narrow black line on the anterior pair above, and the yellow band on the third ventral segment is occasionally obsolete.

Length, 8-9 mm.
Exp. al., 15-17 mm.

Habitat: Santa Clara County and Santa Cruz Mountains, California, Nevada, and Montana.

Described from 24 females and 14 males, of which 25 specimens from California were bred by Mr. Koebele, and 13 from Nevada and Montana were collected.

The economic importance of this insect arises from the fact that it may be expected at any time to abandon its natural food-plant in favor of the small grains, on which it can doubtless successfully develop. Such changes in the food-habits of our native insects are constantly occurring, to the great detriment of our Agriculture, as is illustrated by the attacks of the *Nematus* and *Dolerus* species on wheat, already described—these insects unquestionably normally affecting wild grass.

PARASITES AND REMEDIES.

Parasites.—A number of parasites have been found to attack the Sawfly larvæ studied. Of these two were reared from *Nematus*, *Lampronota frigida* Cr., and an undetermined form (not found), and an undetermined Ichneumonid (not found) from the *Dolerus* larvæ, described as form three.

On one of the larvæ of *Dolerus* sp. (form 4) occurred three parasitic larvæ (*Euplectrus?* sp.) attached externally to the dorsum of the first thoracic segment; and on a number of larvæ referred to form 2 received from J. C. Hostetter in 1883 occurred a number of larvæ apparently identical with the last, all fastened to the under side of the body close to the head of the host larva.

In the article in the Annual Report for 1884, already cited, Mr. Webster mentions having observed one of these larvæ (*Nematus*) with what appeared to be a species of *Ophion* that had just punctured it with its ovipositor and remained still attached to it. In the attempt to capture them the parasites escaped and the larva fell to the ground and was not found. A larva was found also with the eggs of a dipterous parasite fastened to the thoracic segments.

Remedies.—The fact that these Saw-fly larvæ pass the winter in the soil near their food-plants or in the base of the stalks will insure, in the case of wheat and other small grains, the destruction of most of them by fall or spring plowing. In the case of timothy and other grasses there is opportunity for multiplication of these insects from year to year, and it is entirely within the bounds of possibility that they may become abundant enough to effect considerable damage or to spread in injurious numbers to adjacent grain fields. In this event plowing and rotation of crops will be the remedy.

THE IMPORTATION OF A HESSIAN FLY PARASITE FROM EUROPE.

By S. A. FORBES, *Champaign, Ill.*

SIR: According to my promise I submit the following account of a recent experiment, begun at your instance and with material furnished by you, for the transfer of a European parasite of the Hessian Fly to the United States.

In accordance with arrangements made by telegraph, I received from you May 6 a package of Hessian Fly puparia, said to have been parasitized by the European species *Semiotellus nigripes*, and with this package a letter from you asking me to take charge of and liberate the parasites in an inclosure of infested wheat with an idea of introducing the species. A second package came two days later accompanied by a letter of advice from your assistant, Mr. Howard.

I had growing at the time under gauze, but otherwise in the open air, a small plot of badly infested wheat 2½ by 3 feet, in very fortunate condition for the experiment. This wheat had been transplanted March 26 from a field near Roodhouse, in Morgan County, for use in making observations on the life-history of the Hessian Fly, and contained when transferred large numbers of the insect in the hibernating puparium. Male and female adults had begun to appear in the inclosure by April 1, and these transformations continued to May 13, the greater number of them occurring about April 20, when, for a few days, more than twenty adults could be counted in the cage at a time, not to mention others doubtless concealed in the wheat.

The first lot of foreign parasites was exposed in this cage May 7, and the second lot May 11, both packages containing living adults when opened.

At the time of the first introduction eighteen of the wheat stalks were examined, and fifteen young larvæ of the Hessian fly were found upon them, and all the conditions were thus favorable to the success of the experiment. Four days after the introduction of the parasitized foreign material five freshly emerged specimens of *Semiotellus nigripes* were noticed in the cage, and others appeared May 13, June 29 and 30, and July 1, 3, 9, and 14. On the date last mentioned the wheat in the cage was overhauled, and the puparia were removed and divided into three lots; one to be kept at the office for regular observation of the transformations; one to be taken into southern Illinois and distributed through fields of stubble containing Hessian Fly puparia, and a third to be sent, in accordance with your letter of July 7, to Mr. James Fletcher, Dominion Entomologist, Ottawa, Canada.

The parasitized puparia received from Washington were all spent by this time, or perhaps some time before. Removed from the cage July 18, they were kept until October 7 without the appearance of another parasitic insect. Parasites of the new generation continued to emerge from the lot kept for observation until August 29, the exact dates being July 16, 18, 21, 23, 24, 27, 31, and August 1, 6, 10, 12, 16, 20, 23, 25, and 29.

Most of these were released in a field of moderately infested wheat stubble on the experimental farm of the Agricultural Experiment Station at Champaign, beginning with 4 specimens July 22, and adding 13 August 1, 18 August 6, 23 August 10, 15 August 12, and 4 August 20—77 adults in all being thus released at this place.

In the meantime measures had been taken to introduce the parasites on a larger scale in southern Illinois. Taking with me about two-thirds of the material obtained from our breeding-cage experiment—the parasitized puparia still in the straws—I traversed several counties from Centralia south to Union County, and thence to St. Louis and Jacksonville, stopping at intervals, but finding no satisfactory situation until I reached Scott County, July 17. On the farm of Messrs. Edward and Frederick Vantyle a field was found three miles northeast of Roodhouse the yield of which had been reduced by the Hessian Fly from about 30 to 35 bushels to the acre to 15. It was the only field in the immediate neighborhood which had been so damaged, and in this one the fly had not been noticed the year before. There was consequently little probability of excessive native parasitism of the succeeding brood, and it seemed likely that the fly would occur there this fall in volunteer grain and later in the regular sowing.

The owners agreed to leave unplowed a piece of stubble on which my specimens were scattered, while the remainder of the field was to be plowed for wheat within a few days. The fact that specimens of the *Semiotellus* continued to emerge from the check lot retained at Champaign for some weeks after this distribution is evidence that a considerable number of the parasites must have gone abroad in Scott County. Indeed, forty or fifty of them, which had completed their transformations en route, escaped from the box when it was opened in the field.

It will be seen from the foregoing narrative that we succeeded completely in breeding a generation of the foreign parasite in our plots of wheat infested by the Hessian Fly, and that these bred insects were successfully distributed to fields infested by the fly at two places in Illinois—in Champaign and Scott counties, respectively.

It should be said in conclusion that the latter part of the summer was exceedingly dry throughout central Illinois, and that as a consequence but little volunteer grain grew in either of the above localities, and that neither in this nor in the early sown wheat was there any considerable amount of Hessian Fly attack—circumstances which are to some extent unfavorable to rapid success of the experiment for the introduction of this parasite. The Vantyle farm was visited by my assistant, Mr. Marten, September 24, at which time the plowed portion of the field was being drilled to wheat. Along the margins of this plowed ground, near the plot which had been left in stubble, was a scanty growth of volunteer wheat in which, after considerable search, four nearly full grown larvæ of the Hessian Fly and one fresh puparium were found. Little other volunteer wheat was seen in the neighborhood. A brief search of the stubble remaining showed only parasitized puparia from which parasites had already escaped.

The Champaign County plot was examined September 30, when one hundred and twenty plants of volunteer wheat grown in the experimental stubble field were overhauled. In these plants two larvæ and seven puparia of the Hessian Fly were found. October 5 from forty-three plants eight puparia and two nearly full-grown larvæ were taken. As the period of the emergence of the imported *Semiotellus* was substantially the same as that of the native *S. destructor*, the two coming out side by side in our breeding cages, it seems practically certain that the imported parasite must have had as fair a chance for propagation in the field as its native congener.

We will of course keep careful watch of these localities next year, and will notify you of any observations then made bearing on the reappearance and the spread of this imported enemy of the Hessian Fly.

To C. V. RILEY,
    U. S. Entomologist.

THE ORIGIN AND DEVELOPMENT OF PARASITISM AMONG THE SARCOPTIDÆ.*

By H. GARMAN. *Lexington, Ky.*

Assuming the evolution of species through the action of natural selection as established, we are at once met, in considering the origin and development of the parasitic habit in Sarcoptidæ, with the questions, what were the originals of the family and did it diverge from the non-parasitic mites before or after the order Acarina became established? In other words, were the originals of the Sarcoptidæ mites or were they something else? A more intimate knowledge of the forms we are considering will doubtless give us better ground than we now have for conclusions on the subject. In the light of present knowledge it seems altogether probable that the immediate ancestors of the Sarcoptidæ were not only mites, but that they differed little, if at all, from species now in existence.

In deciding the position of an animal among its fellows we are prone to be influenced by the idea of our own supremacy, and to rate it by its complexity of structure or by its intelligence as shown by habit. Systematists sometimes lose sight of the fact that evolution does not always mean an increase of structural perfection, but often of the reverse process, a simplification and reduction. The simplicity due to degeneration from one cause or another is liable to be mistaken for the simplicity of lack of differentiation; and parasitic and other animals whose parts have been reduced from disuse have sometimes been placed at the beginning of a series, when their proper place, it may be, is at the end.

The Acarina seem to me a group of these degraded animals, and their place, if this is true, is not at the beginning of the line of Arachnidan descent. I subscribe to Gegenbaur's remark (Comparative Anatomy, English translation, 230, 1878):

There seems to be no doubt that degeneration is present in these, and is indicated by the parasitism which obtains in most of the families.

Reasons for considering the Acarina degraded Arachnids apply with the same force to the Sarcoptidæ among Acarina. The fact that they are parasitic and at the same time diverge but little from the free-living mites is good evidence that they are not the stem upon which the order has developed. The further fact that they are parasitic only upon mammals and birds speaks for their being a family of recent appearance. The geological history speaks to the same purpose of the order.

This view of the position of the Acarina among Arachnida, and of the Sarcoptidæ among Acarina, calls for some notice of several aberrant animals which are commonly placed with the Acarina, and frequently in or near the Sarcoptidæ, because of a supposed relationship between the Sarcoptidæ and the Vermes.

---

* Read before Section F, A. A. A. S., at the Washington meeting, August, 1891.

It is scarcely necessary to deal here with the Tardigrada and Pycnogonida, as it is evident to any one who has given the matter attention that the relations of these groups with the Acarina, and even with the Arachnida, are doubtful.

Several other forms can not be disposed of summarily. Prominent among these is the worm-like Pentastomum. As you know, its early stages are passed in the lungs and livers of vegetable-feeding mammals, and of reptiles, and in its adult state it occurs in the nasal cavities of Carnivora—an alternation very much like that of Cestodes among parasitic worms. It was placed by early naturalists among the Vermes, and its relations with the Arthropoda were first demonstrated by Van Beneden in 1848. Later, Leuckart's investigations confirmed and established this view of its affinities. Recently it has been placed with the Acarina, which group it has been supposed to connect with the Vermes through such forms as Demodex and Phytoptus.

The hypothesis is an enticing one and has facts which appear to support it; but an aberrant form, imperfectly understood, should not, it seems to me, be allowed to blind us to numerous facts furnished by geology and morphology, indicating the derivation of Arachnida from Crustacea; and we can not for a moment admit that the group Arachnida as known to us had two independent origins, one through the Crustacea the other through the Vermes. Moreover, Pentastomum shows in its embryology affinities with the Crustacea, and its post-embryonic development indicates that if it is an Acarid it is a degraded one, its larva being more nearly typical of the Acarina than the adult.

Demodex is unquestionably a mite, but has every appearance of a degraded form whose simplicity of structure is to be attributed to disuse consequent on its peculiar habits. It appears to be related with the Sarcoptidæ, and might without violence to current ideas on classification be placed in the family.

Phytoptus, while bearing a general resemblance to Demodex and Pentastomum, is more closely related with the spinning mites than with the Sarcoptidæ, and its slenderness of body and the forward position of its legs are evidently developments to favor it in its active life between the scales of buds and in the galls which its attacks induce.

In brief, I can not see in the general resemblance between Pentastomum, Demodex, and Phytoptus anything more than a chance approximation, having no philogenic significance specially pertinent to the subject in hand.

If I am right, therefore, in holding these forms to be simply extremes of degeneration, then such forms as Sarcoptes are in a sense the lowest in rank, and are probably the source from which Demodex, and perhaps also Pentastomum, sprang. In this case we must look elsewhere than to Demodex and Pentastomum for the originals of the typical Sarcoptidæ. A closely related group of mites, the Tyroglyphidæ, seems to answer most of the requirements; but before giving it further attention I wish to consider briefly the causes which probably led to the assumption of the parasitic habit.

There are three advantages in a parasitic life such as is led by the Sarcoptidæ over the independent life of their nearest allies. First, it is an escape from competition with forms better endowed for maintaining themselves as free-living organisms. Second, it is an escape from the host of predaceous insect enemies to whose attacks the roaming mites are subject. Third, it is an advantage of a food-supply not subject to the accidents that must often affect the supply available to the free-living mites.

With an advantage ever so slight in favor of a parasitic life, the stress of competition is such that individuals will be compelled to assume it, or will voluntarily do so. It is as if organic nature were plastic, and were constantly subjected to a tremendous pressure which forced it into all available unoccupied space. The necessity which leads to the struggle for existence is such pressure: the plasticity consists in the inherent tendency to vary.

Take for illustration a species the food of which is dead vegetable matter. There will come at times to individuals a scarcity of this kind of food, and hunger may force them to devour animal refuse, or through some circumstance such animal products may constantly occur among the normal food of the species, and certain individuals through physiological or morphological peculiarities may gradually acquire a fondness for such food; then if a period of scarcity of vegetable food comes these mixed feeders have the advantage and increase over their fellows. The taste for animal food becomes fixed by natural selection, and eventually we may have a variety or a species which feeds exclusively on animal food.

Supposing such species of mite to occur among dead leaves, and that the source of the animal food is refuse from the prey of some carnivorous mammal, as a wolf or fox. The accumulation of fragments of fowls and small mammals about the haunts of such carnivores would furnish an abundant supply of animal food. Among the waste from the food would be considerable waste also from the body of the wolf or fox, such as worn hair, fragments of the epidermis, and the like. If a pressure for food came to mites dependent on this supply it is easy to imagine them resorting to the bodies of the sleeping mammals themselves to browse upon the loosened epidermis, as certain mites are known to do, instead of collecting it as formerly from the ground.

This habit of resorting to the skins of living mammals would be only temporary at first, and the species would still pass most of its life among refuse or in the ground. But in time forms would arise better fitted for clinging to the skin of mammals, better able to make their way among the pelage, perhaps able to remain there at all times, displacing the less favored mites, and by selection becoming adapted to a life on the bodies of mammalia, though still feeding on the dead tissues and benefiting instead of injuring their hosts. But supposing *this* food supply became inadequate. Hunger would under such circumstances lead to the removal of all dead matter down to the quick, and might easily force mites to work into the living skin; and we should have circumstances leading to the development of a truly parasitic species.

The course of development as thus marked out is not entirely imaginary. We have in the families Tyroglyphidæ and Sarcoptidæ examples illustrating all the stages which have been indicated—vegetable feeders, mixed feeders, scavengers, commensals, and parasites—and I believe something like this was the course taken by these mites in assuming the parasitic mode of life.

As illustrating the stages mentioned I would call attention again to the Tyroglyphidæ. Its members are active mites, allied in structure to the Sarcoptidæ. Cheyletus, a predaceous genus of the family, often taken among animal refuse, as hairs, feathers, and even occasionally on the body of man, may fairly be considered an intermediate form, having the striated body of the Sarcoptidæ, but being in certain other respects one of the Tyroglyphidæ. It has been put first in one then in another group, and its place is not yet definitely fixed.

Glyciphagus spinipes, another of the family, occurs among Cantharides.

G. hippopodos has been found to produce severe sores about the hoofs of horses.

G. cursor occurs among Cantharides, feathers, and so forth.

G. prunorum was found, it is said, by Hering among dried plums, where it appears to feed on the sugar used in preserving the fruit. It is known to produce a transitory inflammation by attacking the hands of shopmen. Here we have a species which might readily assume the parasitic habit.

There are others of the family which take vegetable and animal food indifferently, and still others of the genus Rhizoglyphus, the lowest of the family, which devour only vegetable matter.

Now, when we turn to the Sarcoptidæ, and find examples infesting birds, the lowest and oldest of the two host groups, which appear to feed only on the waste of the skin, the series seems quite complete.

A few words may be added concerning those peculiarities of form and structure among Sarcoptidæ, which have special relation to a life in and on the skins of mammals and birds—though I must premise that I have nothing new to present on this part of my topic.

The characters are of two kinds, namely, (1), those which subserve a useful purpose in the economy of the species, such as the highly developed tarsal claspers of Myobia, the tarsal suckers and forcipate mandibles of Sarcoptes, and the striated and otherwise roughened skins of all the species; and (2) the degradational characters, such as the absence of ocelli and of functional limbs.

The former may all be accounted for by reference to the action of natural selection. Given a parasite with an inherent tendency to variation in all directions, some characters will appear that give their possessors some slight advantage over their fellows. Natural selection seizes upon them at once, intensifies them by the elimination of the less well-endowed individuals, until what was perhaps at first only a slightly longer or more strongly curved claw becomes eventually the elaborate apparatus for clinging to hairs which, some mites possess. The roughened skin and forcipate palpi can be accounted for in much the same way.

It is when we come to characters of the second group, those we are accustomed to consider the result of disuse, that the difficulty begins. If, as Weismann and his disciples claim, the direct results of disuse which appear in the individual are not transmitted, how is it that mites come to have no eyes and in some cases possess greatly reduced limbs? As has been admitted by Weismann, it is not clearly apparent how the presence of eyes is a disadvantage to a parasitic or a cave animal; and if it is not, why should they disappear?

If we accept Weismann's views on the transmission of somatogenic characters, we must hold that in some roundabout way these effects of disuse become blastogenic. But if disuse may affect the germ and its effects be transmitted, why may not use also be felt and its effects become hereditary? Weismann would account for the reduction of parts by supposing that when an organ ceases to come under the influence of natural selection those individuals with the organ least developed have the same chances, other things equal, as those with it most developed, and that consequently by intercrossing the organ is reduced from its highest state of perfection.

It seems plain that when selection ceased to act the organ would be reduced (and elevated) to the average of development for the species, but without selection it could not be reduced below this average—would not consequently disappear. Its variation would be in all directions, and the chances for an increase in complexity and functional activity the same as for a decrease.

We know, however, that organs which from some cause have become useless do tend to disappear, and the reason for their disappearance, if we can find it, will throw light on some of the peculiarities of the Sarcoptidæ.

We can see a disadvantage in one way in the possession of a complex but useless structure. It costs material and energy for its development which could be profitably expended in other directions. An association made up of organs, every one of which is useful, has an advantage, though it may be slight, over an association a part of whose energy goes to the support of useless members. The struggle for existence is keen. Individuals whose energy is all utilized grow faster, are more prolific, more energetic, better able to take care of themselves, and in the long run, it may be supposed, displace the ones retarded by a persistence of useless structures.

In this way I believe we may account, consistently with the best founded views on the action of natural selection, for the origin and development of the parasitic habit in Sarcoptidæ, and for those peculiarities of structure which make it a family.

In its ensemble of characters it is simply one of many illustrations of the effect of the struggle for existence and the action of natural selection. It has come into existence because its members obtained some advantage over certain other mites by taking on the parasitic habit.

This is a scant treatment of the subject, but I take it that I am not expected to present at this time an extended and detailed argument. I could have dwelt on the evidence for the degeneration of mites; could have given evidence for crustacean affinities of Pentastomum, not perhaps open to objections which can be made to relations with the Vermes; could have given evidence for the relations of Phytoptus with the spinning mites and against relations with Demodex. I have not neglected these matters with a purpose to obstruct a view of the truth. The book lies open; he who will can examine the record for himself. But it is my opinion that an examination of the subject along the lines here pointed out will satisfy the candid mind that mites are degraded Arachnida; that Sarcoptidæ are degraded mites, and are not the lowest in rank of the order; that their parasitic habit has been recently assumed, and that their immediate ancestors were free-living mites.

ORIGIN AND DEVELOPMENT OF THE PARASITIC HABIT IN MALLOPHAGA AND PEDICULIDÆ.*

By HERBERT OSBORN, *Ames, Iowa.*

Inasmuch as the Mallophaga and Pediculidæ are limited to the warm-blooded vertebrates in their host relations, it is not to be wondered at that they present many points of correspondence, and that notwithstanding the great difference in their fundamental structure there should be a number of very strong cases of parallelism in the modification of structure resulting from the similar conditions under which they live. On this account it is convenient to discuss them jointly and to compare those organs which have been most responsive to this environment.

The group Mallophaga contains an assemblage of insects very clearly defined and distinctly separated from any of the related insects, so isolated, in fact, that their position has been the subject of no little discussion. A review of this discussion is not contemplated here, and would be out of place, except so far as it might bring out the structural modifications to be met with. So far as the affinities of the group are

* Read before Section F., A. A. A. S., at the Washington meeting, August, 1891.

concerned it is now unnecessary, since the position now generally accorded to them with the Psocidæ and Termitidæ is generally accepted and its foundation on morphologic and embryologic data apparently so well established that further effort may be devoted to details of comparison and the tracing of the development of special parts.

The review of the subject by Dr. A. S. Packard,* in which he sums up carefully the work of Melnikow and Grosse and compares their results with Burgess's work on the head and mouth-parts of the Psocidæ, may be considered as final as far as regards the separation of the Mallophaga from the Hemiptera or their having any relationship with the Pediculidæ. While the Bird-lice present decided differences from the Psocidæ it does not require much effort to conceive of the transition of a herbivorous or omnivorous insect like Atropos or Clothilla to a parasite such as Menopon or Lipeurus. Both Atropos and Clothilla occur commonly in locations from which they may readily at times travel upon the bodies of either birds or mammals, and it would not require a great change in food habit for them to feed upon the epidermal scales, hairs, feathers, or tegumentary excretions of birds or mammals. With this in mind, there is no difficulty in tracing the probable evolution of this habit in the Mallophaga. We need not go far beyond any typical Menopon to find a form approaching Atropos that fed either upon animal or plant products, and which found suitable harbor and food either on the bodies of animals or in the nests or burrows which they occupied. Such species as *Menopon pallidum* even now point to this habit, in that they occur not only on the bodies of birds, but infest their perches and travel readily from these to the birds or to such animals as opportunity permits. From such species as these there are examples in abundance showing every gradation of tenacity in adherence to the host, many species even clinging to the feathers or hairs long after the death of the host, and often themselves dying there without any apparent ability to escape, except under particularly favorable opportunities.

In the Pediculidæ it is hardly possible to find at present such undoubted evidence as to close affinity, though their Hemipterous nature seems very apparent. It seems very probable that the group is one of considerable antiquity, possibly having branched from the Hemiptera proper well back toward the time of the origin of the Mammalia, and springing from a more generalized Hemipteron than any now known.

Comparing a Hæmatopinus with a typical Heteropteron and the essential differences are the absence of wings, the reduction of the joints of the rostrum, the modifications of the tarsi, and the reduction of the eyes. In these respects there is to be noted considerable agreement with Acanthia; this latter, however, still possessing the jointed rostrum and the usual form of tarsi. The correspondence is less striking than that of a Mallophagan with a Psocid, but still I think we can by such

---

* Trans. Philos. Soc. for 1887, pp. 264–272.

comparison imagine the development of a Hæmatopinus from a form similar to that of Acanthia, and since in Acanthia, as well as a number of other Hemiptera, the blood-sucking habit is already present, there is no difficulty in understanding the transition of a non-parasitic or a semi-parasitic form to the parasitic one. It must consist simply in the more and more constant attachment to the host.

In both groups the evidence seems clear that evolution has been from non-parasitic forms by way of semi-parasitic ones quite directly to the condition of constant parasitism, and taking the groups at large and comparing them with the nearest non-parasitic forms we may infer that the Mallophaga are a comparatively modern group, while the Pediculidæ give evidence of greater antiquity.

Leaving this matter, which must of necessity be somewhat speculative, we may now pass to a consideration of those structural changes which have been entailed by assumption of the parasitic habit.

Abortion of wings is one of the most common results of parasitism, and in these groups the reduction has been complete, no trace of these organs appearing, but since the wings are rudimental in Atropos and Clothilla, neither of which are parasitic, we can readily conceive that the immediate non-parasitic progenitors of Mallophaga were wingless also, and we are hardly warranted in accrediting the wing atrophy to the assumption of the parasitic habit. In fact we must look for wing structure for all these forms to some winged Psocid. This is true in part of the Pediculidæ, for we have too many instances of wing abortion without parasitic habit to affirm that this form of degradation results from parasitism. It would be more proper to say that the wing abortion is a result of disuse and that in these groups wings are absent not because the insects are parasites, but because their habits under present conditions and probably under the conditions of their non-parasitic ancestors rendered wings of little use and they became non-functional and then atrophied.

In the general form of body these groups have become adapted to their peculiar environment, and flattened bodies, sometimes greatly elongated and slender almost invariably smooth, permit of great freedom of movement within the feathers or hairy covering of their hosts.

The eyes are in many cases quite rudimental, never composed of more than a few facets, and show, as compared with free forms, constant tendency to reduction in number and but little to increase in size.

The antennæ present some interesting modifications, and in respect of number of joints there is a quite remarkable constancy in number (five) in both Mallophaga and Pediculidæ, the exceptions to this being very few, and in such cases almost all are three, but in one genus four.

Many present striking structures of sensory or clasping function. Sensory pits are prominent usually in the terminal joint and while the reduction for Mallophaga may be looked upon as from fifteen in Atropos to five (three in Trichodectes), the more perfect sensory apparatus is to be considered a specialization to meet the peculiar environment they have adopted.

The specialized structure often seen in the enlarged third joint in the males of Lipeurus and some others, and which in some cases seems well adapted to clasping, has very certainly arisen by a gradual increase in size of the terminal rim at one point, while their development in the males only indicates that they may be connected in function with the copulatory process.

A peculiarly toothed process on the nasal joint in the female *Hæmatopinus antennatus* Osborn* is also a case of special structure, the organ being apparently connected in some way with a clasping function.

In the mouth-parts we would naturally expect considerable modification, but for the Mallophaga it is remarkable how closely the Psocid structure is retained. The mandibles show no remarkable variation, being, perhaps as a rule, somewhat stouter, and the terminal part bidentate or tri-dentate. The maxillæ are modified in both Psocidæ and Mallophaga, and in the Philopteridæ have a further loss of the palpi.

The labium, which forms usually a quite conspicuous object in Mallophaga, is remarkably similar to that in Atropos, in some cases even the rudimental palpi being present. In the Pediculidæ, however, the correspondence of the oral organs with Hemiptera is obscured, the reduction of the rostrum to a one-jointed tubular structure being, if it is homologous with the labium of Hemiptera, an extreme of modification.

Some of the most interesting structures occur in the tarsi, and can be unquestionably ascribed to adaptive evolution. In Mallophaga, the tarsi present well marked types which form ready means of separating the two families Liotheidæ and Philopteridæ (excepting the aberrant Gyropus), these in Liotheidæ being composed of a short basal joint and a larger second joint with usually two articulated claws. In the Philopteridæ the tarsi are short, the basal joint thick, and the second joint small, bearing as a rule one claw, which opposes as a rule a more or less distinct tibial spur, thus forming a good clasping organ. The latter form is evidently the more specialized and while much better for the insect in its usual location renders it practically helpless when removed from its host. This difference is so great that with other structural differences it suggests the possibility of these two families having originated from independent non-parasitic ancestors. The reduction of the tarsi, however, in Gyropus is such that it is not impossible that the Philopterid form could be derived from the Liotheidæ, although I do not wish to be understood as suggesting Gyropus as a connecting link between the two families. This genus is a peculiar one, presenting some highly specialized characters, and in some respects appears to me further removed from a generalized Mallophagan than any Philopterid.

The difference in habit accompanying this difference in structure is

*Bull. 7, Div. Entomology, U. S. Dept. Agriculture, p. 25.

also marked, the Liotheidæ being much less dependent upon their hosts than the Philopteridæ. Most of them travel freely and live for some time away from their hosts, while the Philopteridæ cling fast to the host even after its death. In both groups, however, we have special structures resulting from their environment, such as the palettes upon the basal joint in Læmobothrium and allied genera, and ridged or serrated surfaces, to add to the rigidity of hold.

In Pediculidæ the tarsal structure presents some remarkable resemblances to that of Philopteridæ in the large basal joint and more slender claw-bearing joint. Special roughened, serrated, or ridged surfaces are also common on the second joint, and the claw is often serrated or roughened on the inner face. A peculiar structure which I have described in *Hæmatopinus suis** consists of an extensible pad at the end of the tibia, which is so located as by its extension to press upon the hair surrounded by the claw, and would seem a most useful organ in strengthening the hold upon the hair and adapting the clasping structure to variations in the diameter of the hair at different points. In some species the claw becomes flattened into a nail-like organ, and a certain amount of rotation of tibial parts is observed.

Reviewing now hastily the characters which have been sketched and, I think, that for the Mallophaga, with the exception of wings, the loss of which has been stated as occurring before the assumption of the parasitic habit, we must admit that parasitism has resulted in specialization and progressive evolution, not retrogression or degradation. The short antennæ of five or three joints present certainly as high a degree of development as the fifteen-jointed but simple antennæ of their free relations. The tarsi and claws present in every case specialization, and in some cases development of highly organized modifications of the simple feet. The mouth parts show specialization of mandibles and reduction, it is true, in labial and maxillar structure, but very little reduction from the Psocid type, and a reduction that need not be looked upon as rendering them inferior in any way in the use of these parts or the purposes to which they may be put.

It seems to me, therefore, that while in many cases parasitism undoubtedly results in degradation, the results, excepting for wings, in these insects have been specialization without degradation. It would seem more proper to consider that we have specialization of those organs the use of which is retained, and degradation in organs that fall into disuse, while the quite common expression that parasitism entails degradation appears to me to be in this respect somewhat inexact.

---

* Bull. 7, Div. Entomology U. S. Dept. Agriculture, p. 20.

THE USE OF GRAPE BAGS BY A PAPER-MAKING WASP.*

By MARY E. MURTFELDT.

As a premise to the observation here recorded, I may say that for a number of years the practice of inclosing the clusters of grapes in paper bags, to exclude the spores of black rot, has been very generally followed throughout St. Louis County, and especially in the vineyards of Kirkwood and vicinity.

Last summer a peculiar shredding and perforation of the exposed sides of many of these bags attracted my attention, but was attributed to the poor quality of the paper. The present season a different and better quality of bags was procured for our vineyard, but early in July I again noticed and was puzzled by the same appearance of wear.

A few days after the matter was spoken of, my sister announced that she believed she had discovered the author of the mischief in the Rust-red Social Wasp (*Polistes rubiginosus*). While standing near a grape-vine she had been attracted by the faint sound of the tearing of paper. Supposing it to be a bird, attempting to peck the fruit, she made a motion to drive it away and was surprised to find that instead of a bird it was the insect above named. In a few moments, however, it returned, and alighting upon the same bag began again, with the utmost energy, stripping off, with its jaws, fibers and layers of the paper. These were rapidly gathered, by the aid of the front tarsi, into a compact packet and finally borne away.

These observations were in the course of the next two weeks repeatedly verified. A critical examination of the fruit at that time, still hard and green, revealed not the slightest puncture even when exposed through the holes gnawed in the bags. The unavoidable conclusion, therefore, was that this wasp had made the important discovery that working over ready-made paper into nest-building material was easier than to manufacture it *de novo* from wood fiber.

It may be added that as the paper used in the construction of the bags was probably made from wood pulp, the original material was the same, but the insect in appropriating it reaped the benefit of the initial processes of manufacture.

I have had opportunity to examine but one nest of the species showing this adaptiveness since the above observations were made, but in this there seemed to me there were traces of the bag paper in the lighter and more yellowish color in portions of the walls of many of the larval cells.

No other species of Polistes or Vespa have as yet been observed to

---

*Read before the Section of Biology A. A. A. S., Washington, D. C., Aug. 22, 1891.

make use of the bag paper, nor have all individuals of *rubiginosus* learned the labor-saving trick, as I repeatedly saw them during the summer still gathering fibers of wood from fence posts and boards after their time-honored fashion.

THE METHODS OF PUPATION AMONG THE CHALCIDIDÆ.

By L. O. HOWARD.

As a rule Chalcidid larvæ which are internal feeders on their hosts transform internally into naked, more or less coarctate pupæ.

With certain Encyrtinæ, for one of which Dr. Riley has proposed the excellent descriptive name of the "inflating chalcis-fly," particularly of the genus Copidosoma, but also of Bothriothorax, Homalotylus, and perhaps others, the larvæ inhabiting the host insect in great numbers, when about to pupate, cause a marked inflation in the host larva by the formation of oval cells around the parasite. This inflation and the pupal cells which cause it are very noticeable in thin-skinned host larvæ.

FIG. 16.—Larva of Lithocolletis, which has been infested by Copidosoma, enlarged (original).

With a small larva like that of Lithocolletis the appearance of a string of dipterous puparia is produced, as shown in Fig. 16. The nature of this cocoonlike cell and the method by which it is produced are unknown. Its structure shows it not to be silk, nor yet the last larval skin of the parasite, and whether it is an adventitious tissue of the host larva or a secretion of the parasite or is explicable upon other grounds I can not say. It is a point for some expert histologist to decide with fresh material, which is not at hand at present.

FIG. 17.—Coccinellid larva infested by *Homalotylus obscurus*, enlarged (original).

An example of one of the inflating parasites in a thick-skinned host larva is shown in Fig. 17. It is a Coccinellid larva infested with *Homalotylus obscurus* m. The outlines of the parasitic cells are not so evident as in the previous figure, but the host larva is very distorted and evidently contains these cells.

Species parasitic upon endophytous larvæ, and therefore feeding externally, transform to pupæ close to the remains of the host in the burrow or leaf mine, usually attached at the anal end by the præpupal excrement. I have observed a curious variation in the case of *Chrysocharis singularis* in the mine of *Lithocolletis hamadryadella* on oak leaves which I have described in the *American Naturalist* for January, 1881. In this case the Chalcidid pupa is surrounded by small excremental pillars arranged in an ellipse and connecting the roof and floor of the mine (Fig. 18). It can not be stated whether these pillars are formed of regurgitated matter or of anal excrement, although the former hypothesis seems the more propable. It is likely that such arrangements as this will be found frequently when the parasites of the leaf-miners are carefully studied.

The internal parasites ot externally feeding larvæ also transform to outside pupæ in a few instances, as with the Eulophine genera Cratotechus and Sympiezus, and probably with other genera of this subfamily. These forms are common parasites of several large lepidopterous larvæ which feed on the leaves of oak and sycamore in the United States. The host larva affords food for a number of the parasitic larvæ and is almost entirely consumed by them. When ready to transform, the parasitic larvæ crawl out upon the leaf, void their excrement, and change to shapeless, dark-colored pupæ, nearly erect in position, the anal portion of the body being attached to the leaf by means of a small mass of light-colored excremental pellets. They seem preferably to station themselves in the form of an irregular ellipse about the remains of the host larva, each group consisting of from 15 to 40 individuals. Scudder, in his " Butterflies of New England " (p. 455), gives a happy picture of the appearance of the pupæ of an undescribed species parasitic on the larva of *Vanessa atalanta*, in the following words:

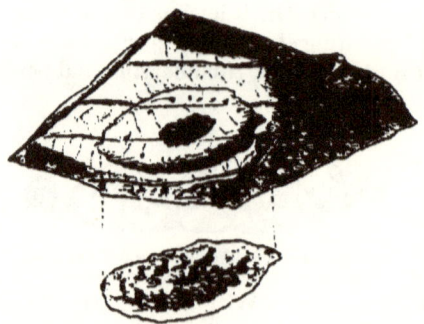

FIG. 18.—Leaf mine of *Lithocolletis hamadryadella* with top removed showing pupa of *Chrysocharis singularis* and supporting pillars, slightly enlarged (original).

And still another parasite [a species of Eulophus], the coal-black chrysalides of which one may sometimes find to the number of twenty or more, standing erect on their hinder ends around the corpse they have destroyed, like tombstones in a cemetery, a most melancholy spectacle on opening a nest to get a young caterpillar.

In correspondence with me Mr. Scudder has always referred to these as " my tombstone pupæ," and the term is an admirably descriptive one. The appearance of these larvæ is well illustrated in Fig. 19, which Dr. Riley had prepared several years ago with the intention of publishing it in connection with an account of some observations of his own upon one of these Eulophines. He has kindly allowed me to use it in this connection.

The Chalcidid larvæ which feed externally on outside feeding larvæ (and we know only one genus—Euplectrus—in which this habit prevails), spin a coarse, rough silk, attaching the depleted skin of the host insect to the leaf on which it had been feeding, and transform to pupæ side by side in a regular transverse row in the silky mass. Frequently the host larva has supported so many parasitic larvæ that their web attaches the entire shriveled skin from end to end, but again they do not occur in sufficient number to accomplish this result, and only half of the larva skin

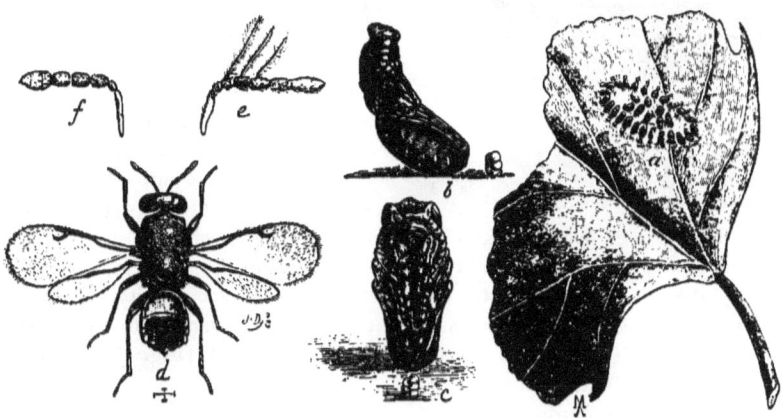

FIG. 19.—*Cratotechus sp.* a, a, groups of pupæ on sycamore leaf, natural size; b, pupa from side; c, same, from ventral side; d, adult female; e, male antenna; f, female antenna, enlarged (original).

is thus fastened (Schwarz states that with the Cotton Worm and Comstock's Euplectrus it is usually the anterior portion) and the remaining portion hangs down, is doubled back, or breaks off.

The larvæ of the closely allied genus Elachistus pupate externally, but do not spin the loose silk characteristic of Euplectrus. I have seen the naked pupæ of *Elachistus cacœciæ* attached by their anal end to the silk spun in its leaf-roll by the larva of *Cacœcia rosaceana*, while the pupæ of *E. spilosomatis* MS. are found attached in a group among the long hairs on the dorsum of the abdomen of the larva of *Spilosoma virginica* (Fig. 20). In the allied genus Miotropis, *M. platynotæ* transforms without its host in the leaf-rolls of *Platynota rostrana*, as observed by Hubbard (Orange Insects, p. 153).

Euplectrus, although it spins silk, can by no means be said to form a cocoon, and, therefore, does not form a true exception to the rule that the pupæ are naked with the Chalcididæ.

The oft-repeated and hitherto accepted observation of Haliday to the effect that *Coryna clavata* does spin a true cocoon would, however, form a distinct and unexplained exception were it not for the fact that I fully believe the statement to have been unfounded. Haliday, in speaking of plant-louse parasites (Entom. Mag. II, 99), writes:

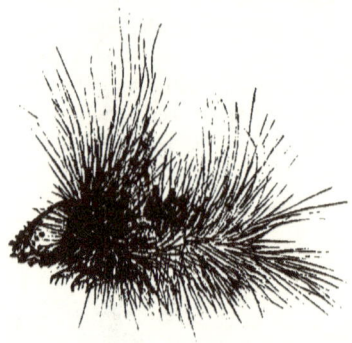

Some of these last [parasites of Aphidius] (*Coruna clavata* Walk., Ent. Mag, I, p. 386), not content with the covering which protects the Aphidius to its final change, when they are full fed leave the cavity and spin a white silky web between the belly of the Puceron and the leaf, and in this undergo their transformation.

FIG. 20.—Pupæ of *Elachistus spilosomatis* attached to shrunken larva of *Spilosoma virginica*, enlarged twice (original).

This statement has been quoted by Westwood in his Introduction and by subsequent writers, and Buckton in Volume II of his Monograph of the British Aphides gives a somewhat elaborate, illustrated account of the cocoon-spinning of a species which he calls *C. dubia*. He figures one cocoon broken open and showing several shining black pupæ which he considers to be parasites of the Coryna. Coryna, it may be stated, is identical with the pteromaline genus Pachycrepis of Foerster. Now cocoons precisely similar to those described by Foerster and figured by Buckton are found in this country (Fig. 21). Miss Murtfeldt has found them under a rose Aphidid in Missouri, and Dr. Riley tells me that he has seen them abundant under dead Aphidids upon his rose bushes in Washington. We breed from these cocoons here, not Pachycrepis, but the Aphidiid genus Praon, and, as it is quite out of the question that Praon should be hyperparasitic upon Pachycrepis, we may safely con-

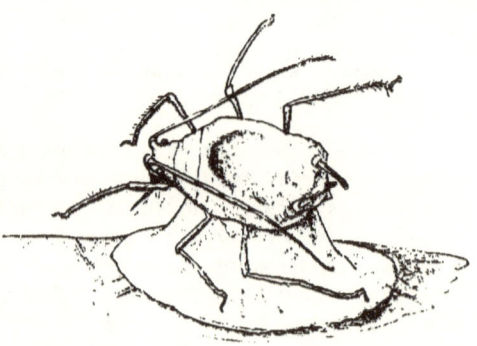

FIG. 21.—Cocoon of Praon, supposed formerly to be that of Coryna, under the body of a dead plant louse—enlarged (original).

clude that Praon makes the cocoon and that Pachycrepis (or Coryna) is a hyperparasite. It is more than likely that the several pupæ of the unknown secondary parasite figured by Buckton are those of Coryna itself, while the larva which he watched so carefully under glass, and figured in the act of making its cocoon, was undoubtedly Braconid and not Chalcidid. We know then as yet no cases in which a Chalcidid larva transforms to pupa within a true cocoon.

NOTES ON GRASS INSECTS IN WASHINGTON, D. C.

By HERBERT OSBORN, *Ames, Iowa.*

While in Washington in August, 1890, I had the opportunity of examining, by Prof. Riley's kind invitation, the lawn at his residence on Washington Heights, where various grass pests had been at work to such an extent as to cause a decided damage to the lawn. The following species were noted:

Aulacizes irrorata Fab.—One larva not quite grown, and which may have been feeding on some other plant than the grass.

Diedrocephala mollipes Say.—But few specimens of this usually common species were taken, and the majority had probably migrated to situations furnishing fresher vegetation.

Deltocephalus inimicus Say.—Quite plenty, but not so abundant as *Cicadula 4-lineata*, as shown by the results of sweeping.

Deltocephalus sayi Fitch.—Not common, and apparently occupying about the same position as regards numbers as in Iowa.

Deltocephalus retrorsus Uhl.—Two specimens only were secured, which would indicate about the same rarity as in Iowa.

Allygus (*Phlepsius irroratus*) Say.—But one specimen of this species, which is often common, was taken in the sweepings.

Athysanus exitiosa Uhl.—Not very abundant.

Athysanus? sp.—Two specimens of a small green species similar to or identical with a common species in Iowa.

Cicadula quadrilineata Forbes.—This species occurred in immense numbers, being the most abundant of all species taken in the sweep net. Prof. Forbes described this as a pest in oat fields, but it is evident from its numbers in grass that it can be a very serious pest in meadows and lawns as well. It may be mentioned that there was a small patch of oats not far from the lawn swept, but this species was swarming also to lights in the city during the evenings, which would indicate some very common food-plant near, and I think there can be no question that it breeds extensively in grass. Adults and larvæ of various sizes were taken.

Cicadula nigrifrons Forbes.—This species, also described by Prof. Forbes and from specimens associated with the preceding species, was taken in considerable numbers, but was by no means so abundant as *C. 4-lineata*. It seems very closely allied to the species described by Fitch as *Jassus 4-punctatus* and *6-punctatus*, and these last two as represented by series of specimens in the Division Collection are separated with difficulty. *C. nigrifrons* has the front much darker, but in other respects I find no constant difference. The spots on the front vertex are somewhat variable in size and distinctness, but seem to agree in position and number on all three species.

Grypotes unicolor Fitch.—But one specimen of this rather common species was taken, and as there were occasional weeds in the grass it may be considered doubtful whether it is to be included as a grass feeder.

Agallia sanguineolenta Prov.—Several specimens of a species agreeing in most respects with this common form were secured.

Of Fulgoridæ there was a species closely resembling *Delphax ornata* and a species of Liburnia that occurred in considerable numbers, and besides these there were of the Homoptera a few Aphides, the species of which were not determined, as they probably all occurred on the weeds growing with the grass.

Among the Heteroptera, *Episcopus ornatus* was fairly common, and a few specimens of *Leptoterna amoena* and a species of Geocoris were taken, as also a few examples of the carnivorous *Coriscus ferus*.

Coleoptera were represented in considerable abundance, especially the little Flea-beetle, *Chætocnema pulicaria*, which appeared to rival the *Cicadula 4-lineata* in numbers. Several specimens of *Systena tæniata* Say and *Dibolia ærea* were secured, and one specimen each of *Haltica ignita*, *Diabrotica 12-punctata*, *Paria 6-notata*, *Coccinella 9-notata*, and *Centrinus scutellum-album*, though of some of these, as for instance the *Diabrotica 12-punctata*, more specimens could have been secured if an effort had been made.

Meromyza americana occurred in imago, and of course numerous other species of Diptera were present, as well as a number of species of Ichneumonidæ and other Hymenoptera and some Thripidæ, but as special attention was not given to these no attempt will be made to present a full list here.

The determinations of the Coleoptera were made by Mr. E. A. Schwarz.

AN INTERESTING AQUATIC BUG.

In October we received from the Rev. J. L. Zabriskie, of Flatbush, L. I., a sketch of an aquatic insect which puzzled us, for while it was evidently hexapodous, it was so unlike anything we had seen before that we could not very well place it. At our solicitation Mr. Zabriskie sent us the slide from which the drawing was made, when its true nature was at once apparent, the sketch having been misleading in lacking both the head and thoracic constrictions and in various minor details. Mr. Zabriskie has published a figure and description in the October number of the *Journal of the New York Microscopical Society*, but to put needed corrections on record we have had a more detailed figure made, and publish it herewith.

The insect is plainly a member of the family Hydrobatidæ, and comes closest to Metrobates, with many of the genera of which we are familiar. It is impossible to say whether it is an immature or an adult form; but if adult, it will undoubtedly form a new genus in the family. We hope Mr. Zabriskie will be able to obtain more material. The specimen was captured in July, 1890, in the stream of the waterworks at Flatbush.

The color is blackish with sundry whitish spots visible from above; one covering the middle of the prothorax extending on to the hind margin of the head; two on the mesothorax; a lateral row on each of the first seven abdominal joints, at the base of the middle coxæ, posterior coxæ, base of the trochanters and base of the first joint of the antennæ. The antennæ (not palpi, as Mr. Zabriskie describes) are the most striking peculiarity of the insect. They are four-jointed and are evidently prehensile or raptatorial. The basal joint is stout, nearly as long as the third and

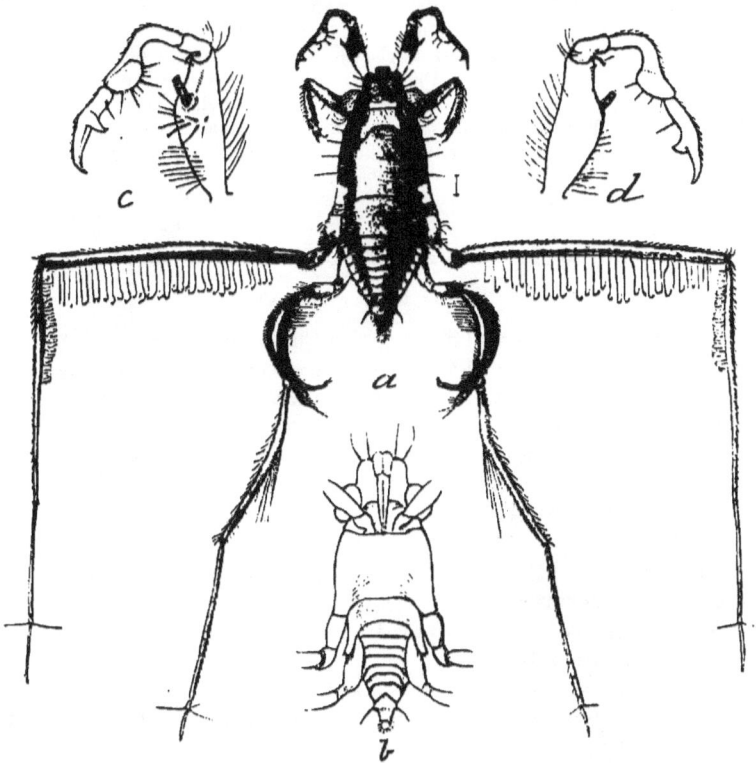

FIG. 22.—Undetermined Hydrobatid Water-bug: *a*, dorsal view; *b*, ventral view—greatly enlarged; *c*, antenna from above; *d*, same from below—still more enlarged (original).

fourth together, bulging near the middle, and furnished with a tuft of hairs or bristles abruptly cut off, and a few straggling bristles and longer and finer hairs at the sides. Joint 2 is small, with a curved spine near the nether base; joint 3 elbowed, dilated distally and beneath, with a pale hyaline disk or cushion surrounded by a few stiff hairs; terminal joint ending in a hook with a stout prong about the middle.

The beak is short and stout, reaching to the base of the prosternum. The eyes are large and globular, and there are two minute ocelli. The front legs are short and robust, the tarsi two-jointed, the basal joint almost hidden, and the terminal joint prolonged into a hook and having a claw attached at its base. Middle legs much the longest, nearly twice the length of the body; the femora furnished with a series of prominent hairs, each hooked at the tip: tibia furnished at its basal half with a denser row of shorter hairs more curved and more prominently hooked; tarsi three-jointed, the basal joint twice as long as the other two together; the second joint extremely small and with two long straight hairs at its tip; the terminal joint simple and not quite one-half as long as the basal. The hind legs have the femora so curved that when opposing each other they form nearly a complete circle, furnished inside with stout hairs and ending in an obliquely truncated point with a few hairs at the tip, and having at the truncated base a finger or process also slightly tipped with hairs; the hind tibiæ are articulated some distance back of the tip of the femora, are slightly curved in the opposite direction, fringed with hairs, and having quite a tuft of longer ones arising from the lower middle; the hind tarsi are also three-jointed, the basal joint nearly as long as the tibiæ; the second joint small, with three long straight hairs at the tip; the terminal joint simple and about one-fifth the length of the basal. Abdominal joints 8-9 and subjoint but slightly sutured dorsally, the eighth more bulging, with a stout, slightly curved spine each side. Length of body, about one-eighth inch; length from the elbow of the antennæ to the tip of the straightened legs, more than three-eighths of an inch.

HOMINIVOROUS HABITS OF THE SCREW WORM IN ST. LOUIS.

By MARY E. MURTFELDT.

A remarkable instance of illness from the attack of Screw Worm fly was brought to my notice this summer by a friend, a distinguished and successful physician in St. Louis, who, at my request, very kindly gave me a detailed account of the case. The subject was a lady who was spending the summer on a farm about ten miles from the city. Opposite this farm, as the Doctor was particular to mention, was a large sheep pasture which had been in use for that purpose for many years. One day this lady, whom for convenience we will call Mrs. A., was seized with sneezing which continued with such constancy and violence, accompanied by such peculiar sensations in the anterior nasal passages, that my friend, Dr. B., was called to attend her. He could not, however, distinguish the symptoms from those of severe influenza, and prescribed accordingly. On the second and third days he found the patient in greater distress, with face, nose, and throat much swollen and intense pain between the eyes.

On the morning of the fourth day Mrs. A.'s husband appeared early at the doctor's office, and related with horror that his wife had in sneezing expelled from her nose two or three white worms. Upon this Dr. B. summoned for consultation and assistance one of the leading surgeons of the city and by the aid of mirrors and other instruments discovered a large number of white larvae attached by their mouth hooks to the mucous membrane of all the cavities of which the physicians could obtain a view. Forceps and tweezers were brought into requisition and, with much difficulty, 25 or 30 of the larvae were extracted. Spraying with chloroform and carbolized fluids had no effect to make them loosen their hold. Indeed, upon disturbance they would contract so as to almost bury themselves in the inflamed and bleeding tissues. If I remember rightly (the account was given to me orally, not in writing, and possibly I may not get all minor particulars in proper sequence), it was not considered advisable to anæsthetize the patient, and her sufferings from the parasite and the surgical operations can be better imagined than described.

Twice or three times in as many days the physicians worked as long as they were able at the removal of the larvæ, until they had over two hundred in alcohol. Some of these were taken from behind the tonsils, entirely out of sight, by means of peculiarly curved forceps directed with the most accurate knowledge of the anatomy of the parts. In the meantime, suicidal mania had developed and the sufferer entreated her attendants to be allowed to end her life, even arguing with the doctor on the advantages which would accrue to her family, to say nothing of the relief to herself, if she were dead. Dr. B. said that he had since learned that all patients affected with Screw Worms required careful watching to prevent suicide, which, under the circumstances, is not at all surprising.

On the eighth day no more larvæ could be discovered and the patient seemed greatly relieved. Under the prescribed treatment the inflammation rapidly subsided, and in the course of a few weeks recovery was complete without any permanent injury to any part.

The specimens of larvæ shown me were nearly all full grown, but, excepting the expulsion of those which first betrayed the nature of the trouble, none were ejected by sneezing or came away naturally, although they undoubtedly would have done so in the course of another day. I inquired if any of the extracted larvæ had been placed in earth to develop, but the doctor said, "No; not being an entomologist, the subject was too revolting for him to care to pursue it further." As to the origin of the attack, the lady had an indistinct recollection of some disturbance while taking a day time nap, perhaps in a hammock or near an open window, but could not recall the fact of any insect attempting to enter her nose. In this case there was no catarrh or other cause of offensive breath so far as the doctor was aware. This case led Dr. B. to make inquiries as to the frequency of such attacks, and he learned that, with patients treated at the City Hospital, many of whom probably often slept in the daytime in the open air, the trouble was not unusual. As a favor to me he recently obtained the following statistics, which I copy from his note:

The Assistant Superintendent of the City Hospital tells me that he remembers about six cases of Screw Worm invasion in the summer of 1888; four in 1889; three in 1890, and one, so far, during the present summer. One of these cases (1890) died from the exhaustion of the attack, and one died from another disease while affected with the worm. Others recovered, but with great mutilation. Several cases, especially those of 1888, came from Texas, but some were generated in this vicinity.

Two cases of human attack by this insect were reported in the papers this summer from as far north as Wisconsin.

The practical lesson from this account is *not to sleep out of doors in the daytime with the face uncovered.*

ANOTHER SPIDER-EGG PARASITE.

By L. O. Howard.

On p. 269 of vol. II. INSECT LIFE. I erected the new Proctotrypid genus Acoloides for a species which was named *saitidis* from specimens reared from the eggs of *Saitis pulex*, a not uncommon spider, by Mr. Lawrence Bruner, of Lincoln, Nebr. I find another distinct species in this interesting genus among some spider parasites sent me by Mr. J. H. Emerton, and submit the following characterization. Mr. Ashmead, in monographing the Proctotrypidæ, has found several other species which fit into this genus and which he will describe in his forthcoming work. None of these, however, have been reared, but it is quite likely that they will also prove to be parasites upon spider-eggs.

ACOLOIDES EMERTONII, n. sp., *Female.*—Length, 1.4 mm.; expanse, 1.5 mm.; black, shining, but closely microscopically punctulate; antennæ brown-black, the scape pale at extreme base; legs, including coxæ, brownish-yellow; abdomen mostly yellow, the second segment, lateral and apical margin of third and the following segments fuscous or black. Head very wide, more than three times as wide as thick antero-posteriorly; eyes large, rounded, whitish (after death) and pubescent; mandibles pale rufous, the tips black. Antennal club large, fusiform, as long as the pedicel, and funicle united; first funicle joint less than half the length of the pedicel, the other funicle joints transverse. Thorax convex, with two punctate lines in front of the scutellum, the latter semicircular, convex; metanotum very short, striated, bounded by a carina posteriorly, the angles produced into a minute tooth. Wings subhyaline, pubescent, extending beyond tip of abdomen; the venation dark brown; the marginal vein short, stout, very little longer than thick; the stigmal long, slender, ending in a small knob. Abdomen oblong oval, one-third longer than the head and thorax together, microscopically sculptured but lustrous, the first and second segments about equal in length, striated.

Described from 7 ♀ specimens, reared by Mr. J. H. Emerton from the egg cocoon of an unknown spider.

EXTRACTS FROM CORRESPONDENCE.

Another Lead-boring Insect.

* * * I inclose a drawing of a piece of lead pipe which I have that was cut by the larva of *Monohammus confusor*, or from the description I think it was that insect. You will note that the borer ate through the wood and upon coming to the lead did not stop. The lead is 2½mm. thick. A leak in the pipe led to investigation, when the hole was found, and the grub was also discovered. It was a new house, only recently built. The piece of wood and pipe both shown in drawing.—[A. J. Cook, Michigan, November 4, 1891.

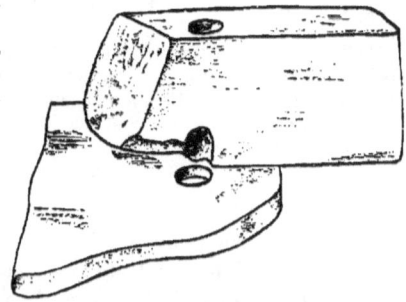

FIG. 23.—Lead pipe bored by an insect larva.

Red Ants in California.

In southern California we were quite troubled by the small red ant, destroying the bark of our young orange trees, doing their work just below the surface of the ground. We tried various things; among others, put bits of marrowbone near the tree, and when the ant had settled upon the bone put the bone into hot water; but this makes a good deal of work in an orchard of any size. At last my hired man thought that perhaps the Horned Toad, so plentiful in that locality, might be an assistant in ridding us of the little pest; so he captured some of the little fellows and put them close to the trees that were being eaten by the ant, and I am informed that the pest has disappeared. My orchard is at North Cucamonga, Cal.—[W. D. Turner, Illinois, March 9, 1891.

Gall on a common Weed.

I inclose a field weed, which I wish you would have examined and report to me what kind of worm or insect it is that occupies those balls; whether it is an insect that damages corn, wheat, and other grain. Is this the kind of worm that damaged corn to such an extent here last spring, which is commonly called Cut-worm?—[T. O. Storla, Aurora County, S. Dak., January 29, 1891.

REPLY.—The common field weed which you send has no popular name, but is known to botanists as *Lygodesmia juncea*. The round galls so common upon this weed are made by a Cynipid gall fly known as *Antistrophus l-pisum* Walsh. As the plant has no economic value, and as the insect is confined exclusively to this one species, its presence in such numbers need not be a cause of anxiety to you. It has no connection whatever with the insects which damage corn, wheat, or other grain. The Antistrophus develops within the gall, and the adult flies issue to lay their eggs upon the same weed and thus produce other similar galls.

A Clerid Beetle found in Plush.

We send inclosed two worms found in a piece of plush. Would you kindly tell me what they are and whether they are liable to injure goods. The darker worm was found in a substance resembling silk, and which adhered pretty firmly to the plush.—[L. Sahm, jr., Indiana.

REPLY.—One of the larvæ forwarded had transformed to pupa in transit, but the other is still active. It is the larva of a beetle of the family Cleridæ and the genus *Necrobia*. This family of beetles is, as a rule, carnivorous or predaceous in the early stages. It is therefore probable that the larvæ were attracted to the goods by the presence of other larvæ, the latter probably of some of the common "Clothes Moths." We hope to rear the imago, and should much like to have other specimens. If it turns out, as seems probable, that this larva will prey upon the various clothes moths that so trouble the housekeeper it is well to know the fact, as possibly it may be encouraged and utilized to advantage. On the other hand, one of the species of the genus, namely, *Necrobia rufipes*, is known to be injurious to preserved meat and has been found particularly bad in hams. An account of its injuries has been published in our Sixth Report on the Insects of Missouri, p. 96. The species sent by your correspondent is smaller, yet all the species of the genus in the larva state, so far as known, feed on dead rather than live animal matter, and the presumption is that in this case the two specimens had left some such matter and got on the plush accidentally, or they may have fed on the exuviæ of the clothes moths. The substance resembling silk may have been the cocoon of the clothes moth larvæ, or else a cocoon made by the *Necrobia* larva itself preparatory to pupation.—[September 16, 1891.]

A Twig-girdler of Fig Trees.

I send you a specimen of twig girdler just received from a correspondent in New Orleans. He says: " " " "It is playing sad havoc with our fig trees. Its mode of attack seems to be confined to girdling the branches, irrespective of size, and no doubt it would undertake to girdle the trunk if chance had placed it there." On referring to your description of *Oncideres cingulatus*, in your Horticultural Report of 1882, I find that it does not seem to fit this case. Please do me the favor to name the specimen and the remedy or preventive for me in answering the inquirer through the columns of the Cultivator.—[R. J. Redding, Georgia, April 21, 1891.

REPLY.—The insect is one of considerable interest, and judging from the pupa alone it is probably the Cerambycid beetle *Ptychodes 3-vittatus*. We would strongly urge that you request your correspondent to send a number of twigs, so that we may breed the adult and make sure of the determination. The best remedy will be to burn the infested twigs.—[April 28, 1891.]

An old Enemy of the Colorado Potato Beetle.

Under another cover I have inclosed a blue bug for inspection. For some days I noticed the remains of young potato bugs, which caused me to suspect there was an enemy at work. After a few days' watching I saw a blue bug by the remains of a potato bug recently killed, but before I had time to see whether it was at work or not it quickly disappeared. On the 18th inst. I saw the inclosed bug by the side of a potato bug, which was standing erect and in lively motion. The bug ran at once, but I succeeded in capturing it and placing it in a glass jar, together with potato vines and potato bugs. This morning I found some of the bugs dead and the blue one engaged upon one of the remains.—[C. H. Taylor, South Dakota, June, 1891.

REPLY.— ` ` ` The specimen proves to be an old friend, *Lebia grandis*, one of the Ground-beetles, which was discovered feeding upon the Colorado Potato Beetle as long ago as 1868. We figured and mentioned this insect in our Third Report of the Insects of Missouri, published in 1871, and it is also figured and described in our small work on Potato Pests, published by the Judd Company. [June 23, 1891.]

Do Ground-beetles destroy Peach-tree Borers?

I send by this mail some black beetles for name and habits. I do this at the request of one of my farm hands, who insists that wherever he finds them around the peach trees he finds the borers dead, and it is his opinion that they are enemies to the Peach-tree Borer. He says he has in quite a number of cases found the beetle in the hole made by the borer and on following it up found it dead. Will you kindly let me know whether the subjects before you have the valuable qualities cited above.—[H. Swineford, Virginia, July 30, 1891.

REPLY.—The insects which you send are *Scarites subterraneus* and *Harpalus pennsylvanicus*, both Ground-beetles of predaceous habit, which, in all stages, feed upon and destroy other insects. It is quite likely that your farm hand is correct in his statements, although we are not aware that either of these beetles has ever been actually found preying upon the Peach-tree Borer.—[August 4, 1891.]

Good Results from Spraying for Codling Moth.

Please allow me to acknowledge my very great obligation to you for bringing to my attention, through your official publications, the use of arsenical poisons for destroying Codling Moth and other noxious insects.

I have a fine young apple orchard of fifty acres, all Newtown Pippins, immediately adjoining which on the north is an older and much neglected orchard belonging to a neighbor.

The old orchard has been badly infested with worms for many years, and until the present season the north half of my orchard has been practically worthless, the trees shedding most of their fruit in May and early part of June, the little which remained being so wormy as to be largely unfit for market, while the south half has borne fair crops, comparatively free from worms.

Soil, drainage, and other conditions being similar throughout, I am constrained to the belief that the near proximity of the old and worm-infested trees to the north side of my orchard is the cause of the difference above noted.

Acting upon information obtained from one of your pamphlets, I bought last spring a full spraying outfit, using the Climax preparation of London purple sold by the Nixon Company.

Soon after the blossoms fell I began spraying on the side nearest the old orchard, the machine working perfectly, the Climax nozzle breaking up the solution into a fine mist which completely enveloped the trees.

After working a day and a half and applying the poison to about one-third of the trees, I suspended operations on account of the weather becoming so windy as to make the work exceedingly disagreeable, one of the men being made sick by having the poison blown into his face.

Influenced to some extent by the skepticism of my neighbors, most of whom regarded the experiment as highly dangerous, and confessing to no small lack of faith myself, I regret to say that I allowed other work on the farm to interfere, and never finished the work of spraying.

With the mental reservation that should the heretofore barren north side where the poison had been applied do as well as the south half, I would spray more thoroughly next year, I waited the outcome with an indifference born of unbelief. Please note the result. From the sprayed trees, not quite one-third the whole number, I gathered 1,000 barrels of A 1 merchantable fruit so entirely free from worms that sorting was almost unnecessary, while the remaining two-thirds of the orchard yielded 883 barrels of good fruit, quite one-fifth of the apples on the unsprayed trees being wormy and unfit for sale. The market price of apples in this section the past season was from 60 to 75 cents per barrel, one or two choice lots of Ben Davis and York Imperial bringing $1 per barrel, while my fruit sold in the orchard nearly a month before picking at $2.55 per barrel.

I estimate the cost of failure to spray the whole orchard at $2,500, but consider the lesson cheap at the price, as I shall never have it to learn again, and feel confident that with ordinary care no harmful results will follow the spraying.—[John S. Lupton, Virginia, November 20, 1891.

The Tin Can Remedy for Cut-worms.

To protect cabbage, tomato, and other small plants, after transplanting them, from the ravages of "Cut-worms" can be accomplished cheaply and effectually by inclosing the plant and fencing out the depredators. Around almost every dwelling are to be found numbers of discarded tin cans that have been used for preserving fruit, oysters, and the like. If these cans be collected and each held for a few minutes over a hot fire the bottoms and tops will drop off and then the rest of the can should be slipped over a round stick of wood and with a chisel cut in the middle and the two halves hammered smooth and round, and it will then make the fence to protect the plants. See that no "Cut-worms" are in the ground near the plants, then place this fence around the plant and push it a little into the earth, and the plant will be protected and beyond the reach of its spoilers. After all danger from "Cut-worms" is past the fencing can be taken away and housed for future use.

There is no better or more profitable use that old cans can be put to than doing the work of protecting our garden plants from one of their greatest enemies.

In place of tin cans a fencing may be manufactured from tin or zinc. They should be about 2½ inches high and 3 inches in diameter. The top should be a little larger than the bottom so that they will nest together to save room when not in use. Their seams should be lapped and hooked together like stove pipe so that they may be easily separated and taken from the plant in place of slipping them over the leaves, as is to be done when the cans are not used.

While this kind of a fence is a protection to small plants it is not so protected by "letters patent," and may be used by all persons who have faith enough to give it a trial, and I hope that they may have reason to feel thankful for having seen this article.—[T. B. Ashton, Kansas, January 27, 1891.

REPLY.—* * * Your idea has been suggested before, but is nevertheless a good one. We have recommended the use of tin cans in just this way for a number years to small gardeners. * * *—[January 31, 1891.]

A Sphinx Larva feeding on Mints.

Last year I found a dozen larvæ of some species of Sphinx feeding on Pennyroyal and wild Mint, color purple-black with minute white spots all over the surface, shiny on each side, a row of oval yellow spots, head having a reddish tinge, anal horn black with purplish-red point. I have never seen them before; from this what were they?—[George W. Berry, Iowa.

REPLY.— * * * The Spinx larvæ which you found upon Pennyroyal and wild Mint were those of *Sphinx eremitus*. You will find this larva figured in the Annual Report U. S. Department of Agriculture for 1870, page 80, while it is described by the Rev. T. W. Fyles in the *Canadian Entomologist*, Vol. xi, 1879. According to Prof. Snow specimens taken in Kansas are light green in color, while Mr. Fyles describes his Canadian specimens as sepia black. It is the only Sphingid whose larva is known to feed upon mints.

The Clover-hay Worm.

I send you herewith specimens of worms found in a mow of two-year old hay just taken out. They eat the inside out of the stems. Cattle refuse to eat this hay. I inclose stems of hay. They have never been known in hay before in this section.—[Ed. V. Bohl, Illinois, April 13, 1891.

REPLY.—* * * The worms you found in your hay mow are samples of the so-called Clover-hay Worm (*Asopia costalis*). This insect is frequently reported from Ohio, Illinois, Missouri, and the more southern states. The eggs are laid by a small moth in stacks of clover hay. These worms hatch from the eggs and feed upon the dry hay, transforming to moths again in June or July. New hay should never be stacked in contact with old, and the worst infested stacks are those which have been placed upon the same sites for successive years. When practicable it is well to build the stack on good rail ventilators with an air passage underneath. It is also well to salt the hay two or three feet from the bottom.—[April 20, 1891.]

A California Twig-borer: Is it Anarsia?

A few days ago I went up to Kern County to investigate the gray Otiorhynchid I sent you as having been received with the statement that it was very destructive to deciduous fruit trees. You pronounced it probably an undescribed species of *Ophryastes*. I saw the owner of the trees where this weevil was found, but neither he nor any other person that I interviewed on the subject had actually seen the beetle engaged in feeding upon the trees; all reported having found them resting motionless in the forks where the branches start out from the trunk of the tree, and I strongly suspect that the weevils were there simply for shelter. The owner informed me that several of the lateral branches on these trees were observed to wither and die, and upon splitting them open he found a larva which had burrowed from the terminal bud toward the base of the branch, and this he pronounced to be the larva of the above-mentioned weevil. I strongly suspect, however, that it was the larva of the Tineid *Anarsia lineatella*, which in the northern part of the State is known to have this habit. He informed me that his trees, which were set out the past spring, were obtained from an Alameda County nurseryman, so it is very probable that the eggs of the *Anarsia* were on the trees when he set them out. He has 50 acres set out to peach, apricot, prune, apple, pear, and walnut trees and grapevines, but the apricots suffered most from the attacks of this twig borer. He estimates that fully 800 of his apricot trees have been attacked by them, and on the greater number of these from four to six of the lateral branches had been destroyed.

When he first sent me the weevils I advised him to spray his trees with Paris green and water, one pound to 180 gallons, and this he did, and informs me that it stopped the work of the twig-borers very effectually. When he saw a branch beginning to wither he at once removed and burned it, but he says that after applying the Paris green he did not find any more withered branches, and I could not find any at the time of my visit.

On my way back I obtained a few of the weevils above referred to, but did not learn what their food-plant is.—[D. W. Coquillett, California, June 7, 1891.

The Red-humped Caterpillar killed by Parasites.

Will you please inform me what parasite it is that kills the caterpiller? I herewith inclose you dead caterpillars found in my orchard by the hundred. You will observe a hole in each worm, and I would like to know its enemy, not that I regret their destruction, but I would like to protect the enemy. * * *—[B. L. Fetherolf, Pennsylvania, September 9, 1891.

REPLY.—The larvæ sent is a common pest of the Apple, known as the Red-humped Caterpillar, the scientific name of which is *Œdemasia concinna* Abbot and Smith. The parasite which has infested all the specimens collected by you is a species that has been bred by the Entomologist from this same insect, and it has recently been described by Ashmead as *Limneria œdemasiæ*. This parasite belongs to the family Ichneumonidæ, and a second parasite which also attacks this insect, but has not up to the present time been described is known to entomologists. The *Limneria* gives promise of being a very efficient aid in keeping *Œdemasia* in check.—[September 18, 1891.]

Treatment of Grain infested with Angoumois Moths.

* * * I am very anxious to get some information relative to *Gelechia cerealella*. I visited a farmer to-day and found his crop of wheat in a sad condition. A large percentage of it is ruined already, and he was fanning it over to try to save it in that way. The pile of thrashed grain was very warm, and this was not caused by moisture, but through the effect of the insect. Upon examination this evening I find mine that was thrashed on the 10th instant is getting warm in the pile. * * * [R. B. Farquhar, Maryland, September 14, 1891.

REPLY.— * * * Nothing has been written or suggested as a means against this insect when infesting grain in shock in the field or in stack, and to reach the pest under such conditions would be a very difficult, if not impossible undertaking. It appears, however, to be feasible to destroy the larva by the same means that is employed against it in granaries, namely, the application of carbon bisulphide. To use this in the field in shocks or even in stacks would necessitate covering the stack or shock with a tent similar to the tent used in fumigating orange trees with hydrocyanic acid gas in California, inserting the bisulphide into the body of the shock or stack by means of a long tin tube. This would be rather an expensive treatment, and no experiments have been made from which any guaranty of success following it could be given. It might, however, be worth a trial, and I should be glad to have you report the results of any experiments you might make in this direction. The tent, to prevent the escape of the fumes of this substance, which is very volatile, should be thoroughly oiled or painted and the connection with the ground should be made as tight as possible by means of earth or boards. It seems that the difficulty arises from allowing the shocks to remain so long in the field after harvesting, but I am not at all sure that the infestation does not sometimes take place, that is, that the eggs are deposited in the heads before the wheat is cut. This is more apt to be the case if the wheat is allowed to become very ripe before harvesting. Would it not be advisable to adopt the plan of the Western farmer before the advent of the self-binder and head the wheat, threshing immediately, so that it can be stored in bins, where it will be comparatively exempt from the attacks of the moth and where treatment with remedies is more easy and satisfactory?

If, however, as appears from your letter, you have just threshed your wheat, it ought to be possible to destroy the insects and prevent further injury. This can be done if the grain is stored in comparatively tight bins. The treatment consists in the use of bisulphide of carbon, which should be added near the top of the pile of grain at the rate of one and a half pounds of bisulphide to each ten bushels of grain. A ball of tow attached to a stick may receive the charge of bisulphide, like a sponge, and be plunged into the top of the grain. When necessary the stick may be withdrawn and a fresh charge inserted. The action of the bisulphide in a comparatively tight bin lasts ordinarily about six weeks, after which a fresh charge is required. The substance does not injure the wheat in the least, provided it is not used too freely nor for too long a period.—[September 17, 1891].

Treatment of the Boll Worm.

I wrote you some months ago in regard to best methods of combating ravages of the Boll Worm and you were kind enough to reply. Now I seek additional information, as I see abundant evidences that we will lose our cotton again by them.

(1) What poison is best, Paris green or London purple?

(2) For small farmers, what method of application is most efficient?

(3) If by spraying, what apparatus is most satisfactory; the same, if dusting the poison on is advised?

(4) If spraying is advised, what is the proper strength of poisoned water? How much poison to gallon?

(5) What is the chemical name of Paris green and London purple, and if either can be made soluble in water and still retain its poisonous properties? * * *
—[H. L. Tate, Smith County, Tex.

REPLY.—The fourth report of the United States Entomological Commission contains in its first part, treating of the Cotton Worm, an elaborate chapter on the application of arsenical poisons to the cotton plant, and upon referring to that portion of the report (pp. 136-153) you will find full particulars regarding the points you ask me in your last letter. We have pointed out that a *timely* application of Paris green or London purple not only protects the plants from the Cotton Worm, but is at the same time the best remedy that can be recommended for the destruction of the *young* Boll Worms before these enter the bolls. The report was published in 1885, and since that time no new discoveries have been made regarding the mode of application of these poisons.

(1) London purple can not be said to be better than Paris green, but is a good substitute and much less expensive (see 4th Report, pp. 143 and 151).

(2) This depends entirely upon circumstances. Water is often not handy, and small planters are liable not to have any spraying apparatus on hand. For these

reasons the dusting method is often resorted to, but it is much more expensive on a large scale than the spraying method. In a general way it may be said that the spraying method is very much preferable, especially in dry or tolerably dry weather, while in very wet weather the dusting method gives most satisfaction.

(3) Any of the improved force pumps which are now in the market, in connection with a good atomizing nozzle, and more especially the "Riley" or "cyclone nozzle" which is described on pp. 211-219 of the 4th Report. For the dusting method several excellent and simple hand dusters can now be obtained, or, if nothing else be at hand, a flour sieve, with a double layer of fine muslin covering the bottom, will answer the purpose.

(5) Neither Paris green nor London purple, being compounded substances, has a chemical name. An analysis of London purple is given on page 149 of the report. Neither is soluble in water, though London purple has a larger proportion of soluble matter.

The chief requirements in successfully coping with either of the worms are: (1) watchfulness for the first appearance on the underside of the leaves and early spraying before the leaves become seriously eaten or ragged; (2) spraying as far as possible on the underside of the leaves and as finely as possible, in order that the poison may adhere and not be washed off.

The Strawberry Leaf-roller.

The object of this note is to ask you what we should do with our berry patches that are troubled with leaf-roller. A bug or fly deposits an egg on the tender leaf; in time it is hatched out, and as the worm grows it rolls up the leaf, and thus absorbs the vitality of the strawberry plant. * * * I have twenty-two acres of strawberries that were somewhat troubled with it last year and I fear it more than all other insects that infest the strawberry. Would spraying kill it? As it is so completely hid beneath the folds of the leaf I hardly think spraying would reach it. [B. F. Smith, Kansas, April 18, 1891.

REPLY. The insect which is damaging your strawberries is probably the common Strawberry Leaf-roller (*Phoxopteris comptana*, Frol.). It is originally a European species and was probably imported into this country in the sixties. In Illinois, as was discovered in 1867, there are two broods during the year. The worms of the first brood, which appear during the month of June, change to the pupa state within the rolled-up leaf and become small reddish brown moths during the month of July. The moths pair and the females lay their eggs upon the plants and the second brood of worms which hatch reach full growth about the end of September and pass the winter in the pupa state. Farther south there is a third brood, but the insect always winters in the pupa state within the leaves.

As with many other strawberry insects, the best remedy consists in burning over the field soon after the fruit is gathered, and you are doubtless aware that this does not injure the plants, which invariably send up new strong leaves and make a dense growth by fall. The repetition of this treatment for two more years will reduce the insect to insignificant numbers. The best plan is to first mow the whole field over as close to the ground as it can be cut with a mower and then leave the cut leaves and foliage to dry for a few days. Then loosen and rake up the straw mulch, sometimes spreading it over the rows, and fire the field in a gentle breeze. If there is no mulch scatter straw lightly over the plants.—[April 22, 1891.]

The Electric-light Bug.

Inclosed please find an insect which is known as the "Electric-light Bug." No one with whom I am acquainted ever saw the insect until the steamers which run Red River put on the electric light. They fly against the lights and are killed thereby, and fall upon the boat's deck. * * * [John L. Kimball, Louisiana, March 8, 1891.]

REPLY.— * * * The insect sent is one of our largest water bugs, and is commonly known as the Giant Water Bug. Its scientific name is *Benacus grisens*, and it is frequently attracted to the electric lights in cities, but except as attracted to light is seldom met with. The name Electric-light Bug is, therefore, not at all inappropriate. This insect lives in the water, both in its early stages and as an adult, and feeds upon other water insects and small fishes.—[March 16, 1891.]

The Woolly Root-louse of the Apple.

* * * I am thankful for your information and advice, and note fully what you offer as a cure and remedy. I put out an orchard of 1,000 trees last February. The weather and season were very favorable to young trees, and they had a good chance to do well, if, in my opinion, they had not received this blight or injury in the nursery before they were set out. Out of 1,000 trees I find over 700 in a sickly and dying condition. I must confess that I was not posted in buying my trees, but I have learned a lesson, and a severe one. I commenced my orchard by cutting out the brush and timber and breaking and cultivating three times. The trees were set out and in about two months I noticed that, while all had put out some leaves and showed some life, the leaves soon commenced to turn yellow and refused to grow. I then examined several that were dead, and found some diseased roots, such as I sent you. Afterwards, the more I took up the more I found to be affected, until I came to the sad conclusion that all my trees were in the same condition. Not wishing to start out in this way with a lot of patients on hand needing doctoring and care, I thought I would try to find out what was the matter, and perhaps I could learn what would cure them; but I fear the remedy will cost more than a new tree. Hot water for 1,000 trees, besides the emulsion and the cost of application, would cost far more here than new trees. Now, what I am coming to is a few questions, and will you be kind enough to answer them?

(1) If new trees will cost $4.50 to $6 per 100, would it not be best to get new trees rather than try to cure the disease by hot water and kerosene emulsion.

(2) As the ravages of this insect are apparent on all my trees, will it be wise or safe to try a cure and let them stand?

(3) Have you any data to show that diseased trees attacked by this louse have been cured and made healthy, strong, and fruitful trees? Would not a doubt still exist, even if a remedy had been administered, that the tree might never amount to anything?

(4) Would I be safe in planting new trees in the same old hole when these had died and been pulled up? Would the disease probably be left in the ground on the removal of the diseased tree?

(5) Had I better pull these up, take them to some convenient and safe place, burn them, and have a man spade or shovel out the place of setting and would there then be any danger in replanting?

(6) Older fruit-raisers claim that I had better remove the trees, plow up the entire ground and let it be exposed to the action of winter weather; and some even go to the extent of saying that I run risk in planting any sooner than another year. What is your opinion?

(7) Some say my ground gave the disease to the trees. If it were in the ground, would the disease be all alike? There is no difference in any part of the orchard and there was never an apple tree near it before. It had been forest or bush land previously, all new, and my opinion was and is that these trees were diseased and affected before I got them. What is yours?

(8) If I take up these trees and burn them, how had I better prepare the ground for the new ones? Can I put on lime or ashes in the same place, and how long before would I be safe in planting?

(9) Does this louse attack other trees besides the Apple?

(10) Is this identical with what is called the Phylloxera or root parasite of the Grape that has killed and ruined so many of the vineyards of France?

(11) Is there danger of leaving the disease in other roots in the ground, such as sprouts of Oak, Hickory, Sumach, or Sassafras, and returning to new trees set out afterward?

(12) I have often seen this white, cloudy appearance on the roots, near the top of the ground, and in and around the young tree stock or trunk, one to three inches above the ground. Does this convey disease or infection to other trees near by?

(13) Suppose a tree, infected, stands twenty feet from one that is entirely free, or, suppose an infected tree stands twenty feet in an orchard from any surrounding tree or trees, is there any way, by wind, air, fog, dampness, or migration, that these other trees could become diseased or infected?

(14) Are ashes (unleached) or lime the best to use in the holes of the displaced trees? * * * [James W. Simpson, Arkansas.

REPLY.—* * * (1) New trees costing from $4.50 to $6 per hundred would probably cost less than the application of the remedy suggested, but the labor of taking up the old trees and planting the new ones is at least an offset to the labor of applying the insecticides; and you will find after all that the remedy is cheaper.

(2) The remedy suggested, if thoroughly applied, will be safe and sure, and it will not be dangerous to let the infested trees stand after they have been treated.

(3) Whether the trees will, after treatment, become as strong, healthy, and fruitful as they would if they had not been attacked, is a question which can only be decided by ocular examination of their present condition. The extent to which they have been injured already can hardly be determined at this distance.

(4) If new trees were planted immediately in the old holes, the probabilities are that some lice will have been left in some of the holes and that the new trees will become infested.

(5) This plan will answer if the old earth is removed and new earth taken from a distance of several feet from the infested trees is filled in.

(6) The plan proposed by your neighbors will be effectual, but that suggested in the answer to No. 5 will answer equally as well.

(7) Your ground did not give the disease to the young trees, as the insect occurs only on the Apple and some few allied trees, such as the wild Haw and other species of *Cratægus*.

(8) Either ashes or lime placed abundantly in the holes will destroy the few lice which will be left. I should say that a month of this treatment would suffice.

(9) This question is answered under No. 7.

(10) No. It is quite different from Phylloxera, agreeing only in having an underground and an aërial form.

(11) No. Only of those mentioned in No. 7.

(12) The insect is spread by the occasional appearance of a winged generation of lice which fly for some distance. These usually, if not invariably, develop above ground on the trunk of the tree or the larger branches.

(13) Answered under No. 12.

(14) Either will do. I have no idea as to their relative merits in such a case.

On the whole, I would certainly recommend you, if your orchard is as badly infested as I infer from your account, not to plant new trees in the same orchard after rooting up and destroying those now in the ground without first grafting upon some resistant variety. This may take a little longer to renew your orchard, but will in the end be the most satisfactory course. The experience in New Zealand and Australia shows very fully that the Northern Spy and Winter Majetin are practically proof against the insect and by grafting upon these and taking care that the new stock does not sucker below ground, you will, in my judgment, most successfully contend against the insect; for, however thoroughly you may now free your orchard, there is nothing to prevent continual introduction in the winged form from other orchards in your neighborhood, even if miles away. I do not, of course, know whether the two varieties which I have indicated will succeed in your locality, but the probabilities are that they will do very well as stocks, even if they should not be desirable to grow for their fruit. I shall be glad to learn the course pursued by you and its success.

The Grape Phylloxera in the United States.

May I venture to ask you to write me briefly your views of Phylloxera in the United States. If, in your opinion, it is on the increase or decrease, and if there is occasion for any serious alarm in any section of this country as to the future of the grape crop. I desire the information for a French correspondent prominent in the agricultural societies of France.—[Burnet Landreth, Pennsylvania, September 19, 1891.

REPLY.—There is in this country, for the most part east of the Rocky Mountains, very little to be feared from the Phylloxera, at least so far as our native vines are concerned. Most of the American varieties of grapes are resistant to the root-form of this insect and hence suffer little injury. The leaf-gall form is not particularly serious in its effect on the vine, except in a few thin-leaved varieties. The damage done by the Phylloxera in France and other parts of Europe where it has obtained a foothold is due to the root-form exclusively. All European vines or varieties derived from the European grape, *Vitis vinifera*, are especially liable to this form of attack and rapidly succumb to the Phylloxera.

The danger in this country then is confined to those localities, chiefly in California, where European varieties are grown, and in the Sonoma Valley region considerable difficulty has already been experienced. The remedy here will be the adoption of the means which long experience has shown to be valuable in France, viz, grafting susceptible European sorts on resistant American varieties, and also the use of such remedial measures as experience has shown to be practically valuable. These remedies are referred to in the publications which I have already mailed to you. In other parts of the United States it will occasionally be necessary to abandon the cultivation of particular varieties, such as the Catawba and Delaware. The Clinton is particularly liable to the attacks of the leaf-gall form, and occasionally the multiplication of the lice upon the leaves is so great as to seriously injure the plant. The Catawba and Delaware and various hybrids with *vinifera* succumb occasionally to the root form. The Clinton stocks, however, are especially valuable on account of their resistant qualities, since the lice are seldom found to any great extent on the roots of this variety and the vine is so vigorous a grower that a slight attack does little injury. As long, therefore, as we continue to grow our native grapes, we need have little fear of Phylloxera. This insect, as you doubtless know, is a native of this country, and our native vines have acquired, by long association with the Phylloxera, certain resistant qualities which are entirely wanting in the European grapes.

With regard to Phylloxera damage to grapes grown under glass I would refer you to a report by myself, published in the Annual Report of the Department of Agriculture for 1884, pp. 408-9, which you will probably find of interest in this connection.—[September 24, 1891.]

Mites on a Maple Aphid.

I mail you to-day slides with mite which attacks *Drepanosiphum acerfolii*, Thomas. Saw a great number of these scarlet mites each fastened at base of wing of this common Maple Aphid, but the Aphid is so active that I secured but three specimens. Have also seen this mite on the Hickory Callixtenus. Can you give me name of mite in case you recognize it, without trouble or especial study?—[J. G. Monell, Missouri, August 5, 1891.

REPLY.—* * * The mites which you send are immature and in bad condition. They evidently belong to the genus *Erythræus*, but it will require better material to enable a correct determination.—[August 4, 1891.]

Scales from Tahiti.

The inclosed samples were taken from trees recently brought in from Tahiti. The large ones resemble the color of the bark, adhere very firmly, and are like *Lecanium oleæ* in resisting disinfectants, even hydrocyanic acid gas. These samples have all been subjected to the gas treatment and appear to be dead excepting the large round species which we are unable to name satisfactorily. On the fruit you will find two other varieties which do not appear on the tree except occasionally on foliage. * * [W. E. Collins, California, July 2, 1891.

REPLY.—Three different scales were found upon the samples of twigs and fruit which were received recently from Tahiti. The large round species is *Chionaspis biclavis* Comstock, described originally from specimens found upon several imported plants in the greenhouse at the Department. It has never been found elsewhere before receipt of this specimen from you and its original habitat has always been in doubt for the reason that in our greenhouses it infests trees from several different localities. The narrow scale on both twigs and fruit belongs to the species known in Florida as the Purple Scale (*Mytilaspis citricola*), a form which is now almost cosmopolitan in its distribution. The round scale on the fruit is the common Red Scale (*Aspidiotus aurantii*). All these scales were dead on receipt except the *Chionaspis*. —[July 10, 1891.]

Plant-louse on Celery.

I send a sprig of celery from a garden near my office having upon it specimens of an Aphis which our hop-growers claim to be identical with the genuine Hop-louse. The patch of celery from which this was taken was nearly ruined by this louse last season, the insect working upon it from early in the autumn. Whether or not this is the Hop-louse, it is certain that the genuine hop pest has been seen from time to time all winter upon the old vines and rubbish in some of the gardens, and our farmers say from the willows along the river banks. * * * [W. W. Corbett, Washington, March 4, 1891.

REPLY.—The insect is not the Hop-louse, but seems to be *Aphis pastinaci*, the common Parsnip Plant-louse. They were all dried or badly damaged, so that it is impossible to accurately determine them. * * * The supposed Hop-louse which you mention as having been seen on willows along the river bank is undoubtedly a distinct insect. The Hop-louse has been studied for years, and is not known to go from the hop plant to plants of other than the genus Prunus. Your informants are also probably in error about the wintering of the Hop-louse on the old vines. * * * [March 16, 1891.]

The Rose Diaspis.

I mail you today box of cuttings from a rose bush badly affected by scale insects, which may possibly be the Icerya described in INSECT LIFE for November, 1890, page 93. I first noticed it on a fine climbing rose which covered the side of my house at Fern Bank, Ohio. This was in the spring of 1889. It spread rapidly, and by last season covered the bush completely, although the shoots reached to the eaves of the house, and last summer the bush died down completely and all the shoots were cut off and burned. The root, however, still lived and threw up new shoots, but I see the scale has begun to appear on them also. What treatment can you suggest for the case?—[Edwin A. Hill, Ohio, January 5, 1891.

REPLY.—The insect is not the *Icerya rosæ*, as you suggest, but the common Rose Scale of this country and Europe—*Diaspis rosæ*. You will find this insect figured and described in the Annual Report of this Department for 1880 (pp. 312-313 Plate 5, Fig. 1). Your best remedy will be to spray your bushes thoroughly with a dilute kerosene-soap emulsion, made according to the formula given in Circular No. 1 of this Division.—[January 3, 1891.]

Scale Insects from Trinidad.

Referring to your letter of the 20th instant, I beg to observe that by the British steamship *Alps*, which leaves Port of Spain for New York this day, I send you some of the insects you mention, "White Cottony Scale."—[W. P. Pierce, U. S. consul, Trinidad, B. W. I., February 7, 1891.

REPLY.—The insect known in Trinidad as the White Cottony Scale is probably new to science, and differs decidedly from the scale insects which have this popular name in other portions of the world. It is a species of the genus Orthezia. The branches and leaves also bore three other species of bark lice, viz: The form known in Florida as the Purple Scale (*Mytilaspis citricola*); the Orange Chionaspis (*Chionaspis citri*), and a new species of the genus *Aspidiotus*. Your sending was, in fact, of much greater interest than I had anticipated, and I am greatly indebted to you for your prompt courtesy.

A Vegetarian Mosquito.

A friend of mine, a physician of St. Louis, who is interested in entomology, made a business trip to New York about the end of last August, and there, while taking supper at a restaurant, had occasion to notice at his table a Mosquito which, after hovering around for some time, alighted on a boiled potato which had been peeled and was still warm. The insect repeatedly plunged its sucker into the tuber, and the act lasted long enough for the proprietor of the place, who had been called by my friend, to also observe it and establish the fact that the Culex was *making a vegetarian repast*. It is admitted that country mosquitoes are sometimes obliged to content themselves with the juices of the plants which grow around their haunts, but have those of Gotham become so sybaritic as to appreciate the nutritive qualities of potatoes stripped of their jackets?

The story was told me by a person whom I have no reason to suspect of telling fairy tales, and I do not think it impossible. If you think the incident will interest your readers you might relate it to them, and perhaps other curious observations of a similar nature will be reported by others.—[Emile J. Longuemars, Missouri, September 21, 1891.

REPLY.—We are obliged to you for the account of the Mosquito which ate boiled potatoes. As you say, the statement that country mosquitoes sometimes feed upon vegetable juices is well understood, but it is always supposed that they prefer animal blood; consequently, that the New York individual should ignore the numerous sanguinary opportunities about him and should partake of such a civilized meal is certainly exceptional. Many insects which annoy man normally feed on vegetable juices.—[September 24, 1891.]

Gregarious "Snake-worms."

About fifteen years ago, while rambling on a farm, I found a peculiar, rope-like something. I first thought it a strange sort of snake; but upon close observation I found it to be composed of leaden-colored worms about one-fourth of an inch long, and about as large in body as a pin. Those in the lead were moving in unison, but so slowly that the motion was not much more than perceptible. None of the worms would go in one division that belonged in either of the other divisions; then those divisions of minor rank would retract and fall in with the main body. I have told my story to different persons, and was laughed at on account of it. One morning several years ago I found a similar sight, and went on to the schoolhouse where I was then teaching, got six or eight of my scholars, took them to the spot, and showed the strange sight to them. My friend Mr. Munger tells me he saw a like sight once. On each occasion the rope of worms was about half as large as a man's little finger, diminishing in size toward the higher extremity, and was about fifteen inches in length. My question may seem quite simple to a specialist, but I have never found an explanation in any text-book, newspaper, or public document.[—Joshua Wood, Missouri, January 17, 1891.

REPLY. * * * The peculiar object which you so well describe was a mass of the little larvæ of the genus Sciara, the adults of which are small midges or gnats with feathery antennæ. These insects have long been known to have this gregarious habit and are often found in dense batches under the bark of trees. When about to transform to the pupa state they congregate in great numbers, forming processions like that which you describe. They have been known in Europe to form masses four or five inches wide and ten or twelve feet long. The name "Army Worm" is applied to them in Europe, but although it is an appropriate title, it is applied to an entirely different insect in this country. Here they are ordinarily called "Snake-worms" and the masses which they form are conversely called "Worm-snakes." * * *—[January 22, 1891.]

Abundance of the Clover Mite in Michigan.

* * * The Clover Mite is fairly swarming in the lower stories of our college building. In the chemical laboratory, which is in the basement, they seem to feed on a mold that gathers on the window sashes. They also breed in great numbers, and we find them in all stages of development.—[Charles A. Davis, Michigan.

Urine recommended for Eel-worms.

We have received from one of our correspondents a communication in which he claims to have used human urine with marked beneficial effects upon peach trees affected with Anguillula. He claims that a few applications of the urine to trees badly diseased effected a permanent cure. What do you think of it? Admitting the truth of the statement, what are the elements of urine that had the beneficial effect? If that element could be determined by analysis and experiment, would it not be possible to incorporate it in a fertilizer, which would act in the dual capacity of manure and insecticide? * * *—[S. Weller Johnston, Florida, June 11, 1891.

REPLY.— * * * I should not accept the statement of your correspondent as to the effect of urine upon peach trees affected with Anguillulidæ without the most careful corroborative tests. So many of these recommendations come to me that it is absolutely impossible to try them all, and it will be well for you to advise with some one on the ground who has facilities to experiment. We should say that the active destructive principle would be the uric acid, in case it turns out that the gentleman is correct.—[June 18, 1891.]

GENERAL NOTES.

VEDALIA AND ICERYA IN NEW ZEALAND.

We have elsewhere in these pages referred to the curious see-saw game which Vedalia and Icerya have been playing for some time in parts of New Zealand, but the following presentation of the case is so interesting that we reprint it from the columns of the *Garden and Field* (Adelaide, South Australia) of last June. It is written by our correspondent, Mr. R. Allan Wight, of Auckland.

SIR: It may interest some of your readers to hear news of your native ladybird, *Vedalia cardinalis*, which has done such good service of late years both in New Zealand and California, against *Icerya purchasi*. It will be remembered that the beetle, although native to Australia, has never been any other than an inconspicuous and rare insect in its own country, and that it was in New Zealand that it first shone out in all the glory of a conqueror of one of the greatest of known pests. So it is now that in New Zealand must be written the last pages of its interesting life. Having been very lately sent by the New Zealand government to Auckland, to collect some of these insects for Icerya-afflicted districts, I had a good opportunity of observing the stages Vedalia and Icerya had passed through. Some two years ago everything seemed white around Auckland with the clustering Icerya, a great many orange and lemon trees (including one entire lemon orchard) were dead, and the prospect was as gloomy as could be, till Vedalia (which had been accidentally imported from Australia) appeared on the scene. Astonishing as it may seem to be, and incredible, within one year hardly any of the scales were left, and the ladybirds had also disappeared. The little beetles are rank cannibals when pressed by hunger, and as no one was able to discover any other food but Icerya upon which they will feed, it was feared that, in the absence of Icerya, they would become extinct. Therefore considerable uneasiness was felt when, some time ago, the scale again began to increase rapidly, and spread everywhere, and, as yet, no Vedalia were to be seen.

On the 8th of April last I arrived in Auckland to see whether it would not be possible to procure a few, when I found that in the meantime they had appeared and cleared off the accumulated Icerya with an incredible celerity, and then vanished for a second time. Even in a district some 30 miles from the city, where only at the end of last December I had seen many thousands of Icerya females, with full ovisacs and larvæ without number, only nine ovisacs of eggs and about 50 scales could be obtained wherewith to feed any Vedalia that might be procured on a voyage. On all the Acacia hedges around Auckland in every direction for miles and miles, where formerly buckets full of ovisacs could have been gathered in a few chains, there was not a scrap of even a torn one to be seen, and in all the nurseries, whose owners had formerly been in despair, not one single specimen of either insect was to be procured. Only after many days of fruitless search an Acacia hedge was come upon where 79 Vedalia were procured and sent to Nelson, an intended shipment to the Cape of Good Hope having been abandoned. From observation, which it is needless to particularize, the following conclusions were arrived at: (1) That Vedalia has unquestionably some other food resources besides Icerya and its cannibal practices, although it could not be determined at the time; (2) that in its first attack upon Icerya it *runs over* the enemy and leaves a few eggs (two or three) in some 5 or 6 per cent of the ovisacs, and it is these and the few larvæ which escape that found the second Icerya invasion; (3) that the beetles keep on the hedges all through the winter months, although so hidden as not to be easily captured, without a net; (4) that Vedalia larvæ soon perish for want of food, but in the imago state they will live for a very long time, probably nearly throughout their natural life, feeding upon their own eggs, which they devour as soon as laid; (5) that this exhausting system of warfare will very soon cause both insects to become exceedingly rare, but that Icerya will always have a great advantage in its food being abundant and always at hand, whereas that of Vedalia is at best uncertain and doubtful.

These conclusions are little other than a fulfillment of Prof. C. V. Riley's predictions written in the pages of INSECT LIFE.

THE CHINESE INSECT-FUNGUS DRUG.

Through the courtesy of Mr. A. C. Jones, United States consul, stationed at Chin Kiang, China, and the commissioner of customs of that port, we have received specimens of the official preparation of the parasitic fungus, *Cordyceps chinensis*. This Cordyceps is parasitic on a native Chinese caterpillar, and is not unlike a congeneric North American species, *Cordyceps (Torrubia) rareneIii* Berkeley, known as the White Grub Fungus. A somewhat full account of these fungi, together with figures of the White Grub parasite and host was published in the *American Entomologist*, Vol. III, pp. 137–140.

The accompanying letter of transmittal, containing interesting notes on two species of insect fungus, is reproduced herewith:

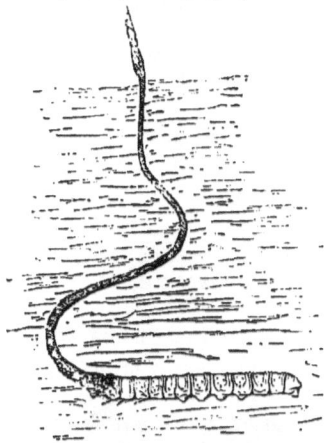

FIG. 24.—*Corydyceps chinensis* growing upon its host larva in its natural underground position. Natural size (redrawn from an unpublished figure by A. C. Jones).

In the catalogue of the Customs Office it is called, Chung-ts'ao, or Tung-chung-hsia-ts'ao, *Corydyceps chinensis.* A kind of fungus.

In winter an insect, in summer a plant. It grows upon the head of a caterpillar, as a disease of the insect. It is sold in small packages, generally tied together with red cotton. Each of the many pieces forming the small bundles consists of two distinct portions, the larger portion belonging to the insect of a yellowish brown color more than an inch long, showing rings, joints, and grub, and the upper fungus portion, consisting of a spurred filament of a grayish brown color, flexible, more or less twisted, and internally of a light color.

In former times it was esteemed even more highly than ginseng, as a medicine. It comes from the provinces of Hupeh, Szechuan, and Thibet.

I find in Frank Leslie's *Popular Monthly* of April, 1891, that a similar plant insect has also been discovered in New Zealand, and is called in the article alluded to the "Aweto," and is described as the oddest insect in existence; so odd that unless it were vouched for and explained scientifically it would be considered a hoax. It is not easy to decide whether it ought to be classed under the fauna or flora, for it is as much vegetable as animal, and in its final stage it is a vegetable and nothing else. At first it is a perfect caterpillar and a fine one, growing to 3¼ inches in length. Until it is full-grown it conducts itself very much like any other insect, except that it is never found anywhere but in the neighborhood of the Rata tree, a large scarlet-flowered Myrtle, and that it habitually buries itself a few inches in the ground. Then, when full-grown, it undergoes a wonderful change. For some inexplicable reason the spore of a vegetable fungus, the *Sphæria robertsii* fixes itself directly on its neck, takes root, and grows, like a diminutive bulrush, from 6 to 10 inches high, without leaves, and with a dark-brown head. This stem penetrates the earth over the caterpillar, and stands up a few inches above the ground. The root grows simultaneously into the body of the caterpillar, which it exactly fills in every part, without altering its form in the slightest degree, but simply substituting a vegetable

FIG. 25.—*Corydyceps chinensis,* the commercial article. Natural size (original).

substance for an animal substance. As soon as this process is completed both the caterpillar and the fungus die, and become dry and hard, but without shriveling at all. The thing is then a wooden caterpillar, so to say, with a wooden bulrush standing up from its neck.

In China the head of the bulrush is gathered, carefully tied in little bundles, and sold at a high price for medical purposes. The native physicians use it in cases of diseases of the throat and lungs.

The accompanying figures illustrate the parasitized grub in the earth (Fig. 24) and a commercial bundle of larvæ and fungi. The first is copied from a drawing sent by Mr. Jones, and the second is drawn from the specimens themselves.

THE DIFFICULTY OF DISINFECTING IMPORTED PLANTS.

On page 441, volume III, we published an account of certain experiments with date palms introduced by the Pomologist of the Department, in which we endeavored to eradicate the scale insects with which the plants were infested. We there showed how great was the difficulty in effecting a complete extermination of the scales by means of the insecticide washes which are so successful in the orchard. We notice that Mr. Alexander Craw, of California, in pursuance of his duties as quarantine officer, has been having the same difficulty with regard to the scales upon orange trees imported from the Sandwich Islands. It is stated in the *California Fruit Grower* of August 1st that after fumigating four times with hydrocyanic gas the scales were not all killed. The writer of the note in the California paper deduces from this fact the conclusion that if this repeated application of the most powerful of our "disinfectants" does not entirely destroy the scale on nursery stock there is little chance of eradicating the same pest in orchards, and that the only panacea for this is to be found in nature's own remedy, the parasites. He seems to have overlooked the point, however, that these scales upon more or less dormant trees during shipment are themselves to a certain extent dormant and much more than normally resistant and that the same application which failed to destroy these would undoubtedly prove more efficacious in the growing orchard.

A very full report of Mr. Craw's experiments and the difficulty which he had in performing his duties on account of strenuous objections from the consignees is given in the *Pacific Rural Press* of September 12. The whole matter was thrown into the courts and a decision was reached that the trees should remain in quarantine until the owners could prove that they were clean. The scale insects infesting these particular trees were determined by Mr. Craw as follows: *Mytilaspis citricola, Lecanium hesperidum, Aspidiotus rapax Aspidiotus limoni, Aspidiotus* sp. near *ficus, Parlatoria* sp., *Dactylopius citri, Chionaspis biclaris*. Of these the *Dactylopius* and *Chionaspis* were found the most difficult to kill, the latter being a mining scale.

FUMIGATING AT NIGHT NOT NECESSARY.

It is now claimed by a careful experimenter at Los Angeles that fumigating orange trees in the daytime with hydrocyanic acid gas is just as efficacious as fumigating at night, if sufficient care is exercised in preparing the chemicals. For this information we are indebted to the *California Fruit Grower* of September 26.

HEMLOCK DAMAGE BY THE LARCH SAW-FLY.

The newspapers during the past summer have contained many items concerning the great damage done to hemlock timber in Elk and Potter counties, Pa., by an insect which causes the tops of the trees to turn brown over large areas. The insect has recently been determined as the Larch Saw-fly (*Nematus erichsonii*), a full account of which is given in our Annual Report for 1883, pp. 138–146. Its appearance upon Hemlock in such destructive numbers in Pennsylvania is entirely new, and considerable damage is to be feared. Nothing satisfactory has been suggested in the way of remedies which are applicable in the forest on a large scale. Spraying with the arsenites is the best that can be done. Such extraordinary multiplication of this species is, however, usually followed by corresponding diminution, and it will be encouraging for the Pennsylvanians who are interested in the lumber and tanning industries to remember that since the great destruction caused by this insect in Maine in 1881–'82 it has not attracted so much attention.

A CLEMATIS ROOT-BORER.

(*Acalthoë cordata*.)

In *Garden and Forest* for October 21 Mr. J. G. Jack has an interesting article on this Sesiid root-borer in the roots of Clematis, accompanying it by a series of handsome figures from the pencil of Mr. C. E. Faxon. The insect was originally described by Harris in the *American Journal of Science* for 1839. Mr. Jack reared it in 1890 from an old plant of *Clematis virginiana* in the shrub collection of the Arnold Arboretum at Cambridge. The moth emerged July 23. The eggs, he states, are deposited soon after the issuing of the moths, and larvæ of various sizes are found the following June. The male moth is remarkable for possessing an orange anal tuft about as long as the abdomen. According to Harris, the insect feeds upon the common wild Black Currant in addition to the Clematis, in the former case living within the stems. Mr. Jack has not, however, found it in this plant.

We have had this curious insect in our collection since 1874, when we received the larvæ from Mr. Thomas Meehan, of Germantown, Pa., feeding in the stems of *Clematis virginiana*. The larva was a dingy white, with short legs, very little darker than the body. The head was

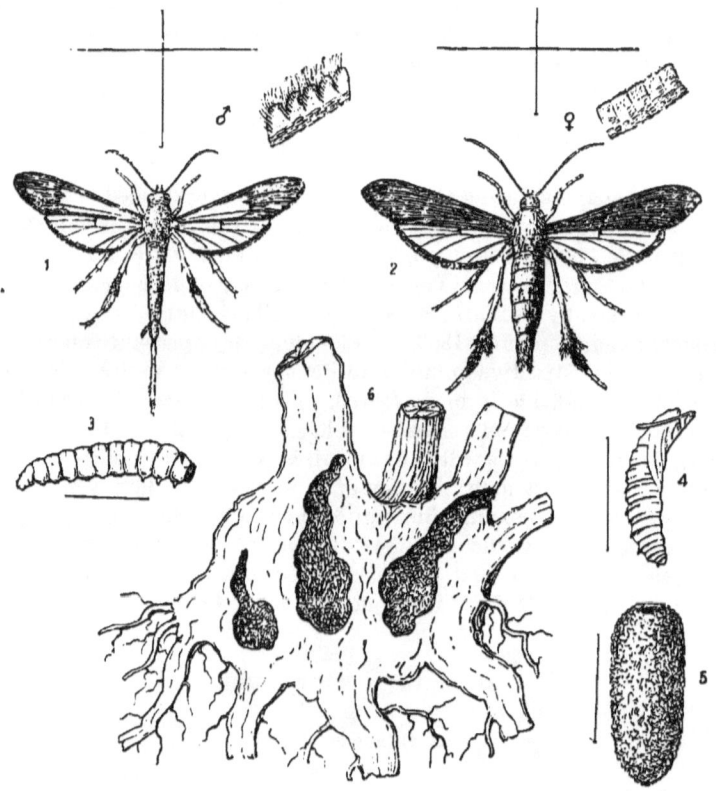

FIG. 26—*Acalthoë cordata* 1, male 2, female 3, lawa 4, pupa 5, cocoon 6, burrow in roots of Clematis (after Faxon).

shiny brown, black at the tip, the mouth-parts also black. The cervical shield was light brown in color, with two darker brown spots just behind it. The spiracles were brown. The moths began to issue June 24. On June 4, 1881, Mr. Meehan sent us another specimen with the information that the insect attacked *Clematis ritalba* as well as *C. virginiana*. Through the kindness of Mr. Stiles, editor of *Garden and Forest*, we are enabled to reproduce Mr. Jack's figures of the insect.

THE SPREAD OF THE GYPSY MOTH.

We observe that the Gypsy Moth has recently been reported as having made its appearance in Maine, several orchards having become infested. It is supposed to have been carried into that State in carriages of tourists from Massachusetts. This report is by no means unexpected but needs verification.

MICROPTERYX: A REMARKABLE LEPIDOPTEROUS LARVA.

At the meeting of the Entomological Society of London, July 1, 1891 (see Proceedings, published in the Transactions Ent. Soc., Lond., Part III, 1891), Dr. Algernon Chapman exhibited the larvæ of *Micropteryx calthella*, stating that they were obtained by placing the moths in a cage with damp moss or leaves and other débris from the surface of the ground. The moths crept into this to the depth of half an inch, laying their eggs in groups of six to twelve in narrow cavities. The larvæ produced from these eggs had a length of about a millimeter, possessing on each segment eight processes of globular form, each raised upon a very slight pedicel. The remarkable fact is that besides the thoracic legs each of the eight abdominal segments is said by Dr. Chapman to possess a pair of minute jointed legs of the same type as the thoracic.

On the supposition that no mistake has been made, this larva is very remarkable in the order Lepidoptera. It is worthy of remark, however, that while the species of Micropteryx, so far as known, are leaf-miners, and nothing remarkable in their structure has hitherto been noted, since they are like some other Tineid miners, apodous, this species *calthella* has been placed by Heinemann in the genus Eriocephala, concerning the larval habits or structure of which nothing appears to be known. We hardly dare suggest the possibility that Dr. Chapman has mistaken the eggs of some other creature for those of this species; but as the larvæ are mentioned as only a millimeter long, there is a possibility that this peculiarity is one of the first larval stages only, and is therefore comparable to other postembryonic abnormalities which are noticed in other Lepidopterous larvæ.

DAMAGE TO APPLE TREES NEAR LONDON.

According to *Bell's Weekly Messenger*, London, July 6, many apple trees in London suburban gardens are in danger from the attacks of myriads of the larvæ of the small Ermine Moth (*Hyponomeuta padella*). Many trees have been killed already. Such a state of affairs as this is inexcusable, for the reason that this insect is not at all a difficult one to fight. The fact that the larvæ spin their cocoons in company renders hand destruction very easy, and where they can not be reached by hand a jet of kerosene emulsion from a bucket pump will penetrate the web and destroy the insects. In our visits to London we have always noticed that this insect, as also the Woolly Aphis and the Codling Moth, were unusually abundant and destructive to the apple trees, which are quite commonly grown in the gardens of the outlying districts; but our English fruit-growers in those days were profoundly ignorant of the simpler means of dealing with these enemies.

AN ENEMY OF THE TUSSOCK MOTH.

Under the above heading the *Pacific Rural Press* of November 7 prints some interesting notes concerning a new coleopterous enemy of *Orgyia leucostigma*. Extracts are given from two letters, both from Watsonville, Cal., bearing on this subject. Mr. W. R. Radcliff says: "They seem to be a 'sure shot' on the eggs of the Tussock Moth, and are plentiful and industrious," and Mr. James Gally reports that there was "scarcely a sound bunch of eggs" to be found in the orchard belonging to his father's estate. Specimens of the insect that has been doing such efficient service were shown to Mr. C. W. Woodworth, of the University of California Agricultural Experiment Station, who pronounced them to be the larvæ of a beetle of the family Dermestidæ. The specimens sent him perished, unfortunately, and he was consequently unable to refer them to the exact species.

THE "BLACK VINE-WEEVIL"—A HOT-HOUSE PEST.

In a letter recently published in the *Entomologist's Monthly Magazine* (Vol. II, No. 19, second series) Mr. Theodore Wood furnishes some notes on the so-called Black Vine-weevil (*Otiorhynchus sulcatus* Fab.), which he finds destroying the fronds of the ferns in his greenhouse. The beetles were observed at night clinging to the fronds and nibbling their edges. Little more than the midribs were left by them in some cases. The insects had hibernated as larvæ in the pots, and the pupæ and freshly developed beetles were found buried in the earth. The writer believes the insect quite partial in its tastes, attacking, in his experience, chiefly the Hart's Tongue (*Scolopendrium vulgare*).

Mr. W. W. Fowler, in an editorial comment, mentions having received the same species from a gardener who had found it destructive to Maiden Hair ferns in one of his houses. The larvæ were found at the roots.

Mr. E. A. Butler, in No. 20 of the same volume, adds that he has found *O. sulcatus* and what appeared to be its larva damaging a species of Saxifrage.

This insect has already been referred to in Vol. III. of INSECT LIFE (pp. 37–38). It is a northern species, common to Europe and North America, and what Mr. Wood regards as its favorite food plant, the fern *Scolopendrium vulgare*, is also common to both hemispheres. Dr. Hagen has recorded the beetle as having damaged the flowers and in some cases the bulbs of Cyclamens in greenhouses in Massachusetts, but it is still comparatively rare in this country. In Europe it has been long known as a pest, attacking the Grape, Strawberry, and Raspberry, and Miss Ormerod records an instance of its having ravaged a field of mangel-wurzels in England. The beetles feed at night and remain under shelter during the day. Its nocturnal habits render it comparatively easy to deal with. The larvæ are not so readily destroyed, but the beetles may be shaken at night from the plants infested by them or may be captured by what is known as the "chip-trap" process, both well-known methods employed against our native Plum Curculio.

HEMP AS A PROTECTION AGAINST WEEVILS.

Mr. J. B. Hellier, of Grahams Town, Cape Colony, writes to the *Agricultural Journal* of Cape Town that the combings of Hemp produced in the manufacture of the fiber are used in India as a defense against weevils in grain. He further states that the leaves of the Hemp, which grows plentifully in the colony, are being extensively used there for the same purpose. When placed among the bags and heaps of grain these leaves, it is reported, are quite an effective protection against the weevil.

CAVE GLOW-WORMS OF TASMANIA.

At a recent meeting of the Royal Society of Tasmania an account of some recently discovered caves was given by Mr. Morton, who had visited them. In the first chamber entered by the visiting party their lights became extinguished and the ceiling and sides of the caves presented a curious sight, seeming to be studded with diamonds, this effect being due to the myriads of glow-worms hanging from the walls and ceilings. Further exploration revealed still grander sights in the other chambers of the cave. The glow-worms were the only living things seen.

THE BEST MOSQUITO REMEDY.

Mr. C. H. Russel, of Bridgeport, Conn., has recently communicated to us the following interesting fact: A very high tide recently broke away the dike and flooded the salt meadows of Stratford, Conn. The receding tide left two lakes nearly side by side, of the same size. In the one lake the tide left a dozen or more small fishes, while the other one was fishless. A recent examination showed that while the fishless lake contained tens of thousands of mosquito larvæ, that containing the fishes had in it no larvæ.

An English gentleman living on the Riviera, according to a correspondent of *Nature*, having been troubled by mosquitoes, discovered that they bred in the large tanks kept for the purpose of storing fresh water, which is rather a rare commodity at this Mediterranean resort. He put a pair of carp in each tank and succeeded in this way in extirpating the insect pest.

The utilization of fish in this way is an old suggestion, and a very practical one under some circumstances. Many people suffer from the mosquito plague when the insect breeds in a circumscribed and easily accessible place, and where it could be destroyed by some such method as that used by the level-headed Englishman.

THE TRUE BUGS OR HETEROPTERA OF TENNESSEE.*

No. 3 of Vol. IV of the Bulletins of the Tennessee Experiment Station is devoted to the Heteroptera of that State, and in it Prof. Summers has given an excellent series of keys to the families and genera of this division of insects. In an introductory note he treats of the general characters of the group, describes the structures mainly depended upon in classification, and presents a figure in which these structures are carefully explained.

The keys for the determination of the genera are models, and it is only to be regretted that such families as the Capsidæ, Lygæidæ, Coreidæ and Pentatomidæ could not have been treated in the same manner, but any one familiar with the Hemiptera can appreciate the difficulty of presenting adequate keys in these families at present.

The bulletin closes with a brief discussion of remedies to be used against the Hemiptera and is naturally devoted to the preparation and use of kerosene emulsion, which is recognized as of most general use in the treatment of these suctorial insects.

With the exception of a few oversights in proof-reading, leaving some misspelled technical names, the typography is excellent, and the figures will add much to the usefulness of the bulletin to the general public.

The description of species would in many cases be insufficient for certain determination, but, for the purpose intended, the treatment of the species mentioned is commendable.—Herbert Osborn.

THE PHYLLOXERA IN FRANCE AND THE AMERICAN VINE.

We have not before noted the encouraging Associated Press dispatch published in our papers of last summer concerning the relief which has come to the vine-growing industry of France through the use of American stock upon which to graft the European vine.

Pasteur says: "I have often heard our wine-growers praise the American vines."

Senator Meinadier says: "My department, the Gard, was the first invaded by the Phylloxera. We had 93,000 hectares of vineyard, of which only one-eighth escaped. To-day we have about 1,000 hectares treated by submersion, about 1,000 by insecticides, and nearly 30,000 planted with American vines."

Dr. Menudier, Vice President of the Department Phylloxera Committee, says: "Since 1889 the territory in the Department of the Lower Charente covered with American vines has nearly doubled."

In the department of which Marseilles is the capital that region planted with American vines equals that planted with French vines. A professor of agriculture

---

*Bulletin of the Agricultural Experiment Station of the University of Tennessee. July 1891. H. E. Summers, Consulting Entomologist.

in the department of the Puy-de-Dôme writes: "French vines grafted on American stocks yield a wine as good as, if not better than, that given by the ungrafted French species."

The report from the famous Burgundy vineyards is most encouraging and shows that the day is rapidly approaching when that region will stand where it did before the Phylloxera invasion. Similar reports have been received from other great wine districts, and it is now the generally accepted opinion that within ten years the vintage of France will be greater than ever before and not inferior in quality.

REMEDIES FOR THE PHYLLOXERA AT THE CAPE OF GOOD HOPE.

We learn from an article by Hon. A. Fischer, Secretary for Agriculture, Cape Colony, in the *Agricultural Journal*, Cape Town, May 7, 1891, that up to the time of publication all discoverers of so-called Phylloxera remedies have been given an opportunity to exhibit their means at the expense of the Government, only the material being furnished by the persons concerned. Mr. Fischer in this article disparages future miscellaneous and uninformed endeavors to find a remedy, on the ground that all substances and means which have been brought to the consideration of the Department by inventors have been already tried by scientists and practical men of almost the whole world during the last twenty-five years, so that there is hardly a chance that any one will "just happen" to find a remedy. The only wise course, he decides, is to concentrate the expenditure of the government on protecting as far as possible the area as yet uninfested and in procuring Phylloxera-proof American vines. The text upon which the article is based is a report by Baron Von Babo, acting inspector of vineyards, upon a remedy submitted by a Mr. Von Schade, which proved not only absolutely ineffectual against the Phylloxera, but detrimental to the vine-roots.

ABUNDANCE OF THE PEAR-TREE PSYLLA IN NEW YORK.

Dr. Lintner has announced in the *Country Gentleman* of August 6 that the Pear-tree Psylla (*Psylla pyricola*) has become exceptionally abundant in several of the Hudson River counties of New York State. The leaves of the young shoots turn yellow and sickly and the twigs themselves become covered with honey-dew and attract smut fungi. They become so abundant as to give the twigs the appearance of having had a coat of black paint. Many leaves drop and frequently the fruit is blighted. Dr. Lintner urges an application of kerosene emulsion, both while the insects are at work and during the winter; at the latter time for the destruction of the eggs.

THE EVOLUTION OF A NEWSPAPER STATEMENT.

The absurd statement which we published upon page 427 of Volume III, to the effect that some one in Arizona had captured a butterfly which he sent to the Smithsonian and received in exchange for it a few days after a check for $1,500, probably had its origin in a statement which we published over a year ago that the expedition to Australia in search of Vedalia cost some $1,500; in other words, that Vedalia might be called a fifteen-hundred-dollar insect. This curious error is equaled by one which we have just noticed in a recent (New York) paper, where the following statement is made: "It is estimated that the cereal crop of Canada has been damaged fully $38,000,000 by insects." This is a plain perversion of a statement made by Mr. James Fletcher in his annual address as president of the Association of Economic Entomologists, delivered at the meeting held in Washington in August last, and which has received wide newspaper comment. Mr. Fletcher, however, said that one-tenth of the agricultural product of the United States, namely, an amount of the value of $380,000,000, is lost through insect ravages. By a very general error in the first newspaper statements concerning this address, the amount was placed at $38,000,000 instead of $380,000,000. Since then the fact that Mr. Fletcher is Dominion Entomologist of Canada seems to have been responsible for the mistake of transferring this loss from the United States to Canada, while in some manner the damage, instead of applying to the total agricultural product, has been restricted to the cereal crop. This is a striking illustration of the worthlessness of many of such uncredited statements in the newspapers and of the **manner** in which newspaper paragraphs are sometimes evolved.

A NOTE ON PHYSIOLOGICAL CHEMISTRY.

Mr. E. B. Poulton and Mr. W. H. Blandford brought out two interesting points at the meeting of the Entomological Society of London, June 3, 1891 (Trans. Ent. Soc. Lond., 1891, part 3, pp. xv–xvi). Mr. Poulton announced that with the assistance of Prof. Meldola he had ascertained that the hardened walls of the cocoons of *Eriogaster lanestris*—the common small Eggar Moth of England—are produced not by tightly woven silk alone, but by a loose and open framework of silk, over which a paste of calcium oxalate is poured from the malpighian tubules and also probably from the anus. Mature larvæ were exhibited, dissected so as to show that the malpighian tubules were injected with a chalky secretion, the oxalate of lime.

Mr. Blandford said that he had himself verified the statement that uric acid can be detected in the malpighian tubules of insects, and Mr. McLachlan agreed that the demonstration that these organs are renal organs is now satisfactory. This discussion seems to us rather remarkable, since, although the malpighian tubules were at first considered as biliary in their function, the chemical determination of uric acid in these organs was demonstrated in the case of *Sericaria mori* as early as 1816 by Brugnatelli and Wurzer.

ANNUAL MEETING OF THE ENTOMOLOGICAL SOCIETY OF ONTARIO.

The annual meeting of the Ontario Entomological Society was held November 25, 1891, in London, Ontario. The annual address was delivered by the President, Rev. J. C. S. Bethune, who gave a review of the work of the society for the year, and mentioned as the principal injurious insects of the season the Eye-spotted Bud-moth (*Tmetocera ocellana*), the Lesser Apple Leaf-roller (*Teras minuta*), the Oblique-banded Leaf-roller (*Cacœcia rosaceana*), in addition to the ordinary species which are abundant every year. He recommended that more attention be paid to forests and insects injurious to forest trees. Mr. Bethune was reëlected president for next year. We notice that Mr. J. Alston Moffatt's collection of Lepidoptera has been purchased by the society.

A JAPANESE PARASITE OF THE GYPSY MOTH.

As stated upon p. 41, vol. III, INSECT LIFE, we learned in the fall of 1890, through the kindness of Rev. Henry Loomis, of Yokohoma, that a species of Apanteles infests the Gypsy Moth in Japan. Mr. Loomis, during a visit to this country, called upon us in November and informed us that he had sent specimens of this Apanteles in the pupa state last summer to the Massachusetts Board of Agriculture. We have been unable to learn what disposition has been made of these specimens, but Mr. Loomis promises to send us others upon his return to Japan. It will be remembered that upon p. 297, vol. III. we also published a communication from Mr. A. G. Butler, of the British Museum, in which he stated that the Japanese have at least four species closely allied to *Ocneria dispar*, but that none of them corresponded exactly with this species. We questioned Mr. Loomis very closely as to the identity of the species occurring in Yokohama and he showed himself very familiar with the characteristics of the insect and was strongly of the opinion that it is identical with the species occurring in this country. He has promised, however, to send us specimens so that this point will be definitely settled.

PROFESSOR SMITH'S EUROPEAN TRIP.

Partly under the auspices of the National Museum, Professor J. B. Smith recently made a brief study trip to Europe, for the purpose of examining the Lepidoptera in the principal museums. During his trip he accumulated a large number of notes which he thinks will result in placing the collections of the National Museum on a footing which will make its material in the Noctuidæ almost equal in value to types. In London he studied the British Museum collections and succeeded in identifying nearly all of Walker's types, as well as most of the species described by Guenée, and made, in addition, critical comparisons between the collections of Grote, Zeller, Guenée and Walker. While in

London he visited Mr. W. Schaus, Jr., who has collected in Mexico and South America, and who possesses many of the types described in the *Biologia Centrali-Americana* and will probably donate his collections to the National Museum. At Paris Prof. Smith found many of the insects studied by Guenée and Boisduval in the museum in the Jardin des Plantes. At Berlin he studied the collections of the Royal Museum and at Dresden the Staudinger collections, having an opportunity to compare a large series from the Siberian, Alaskan, and Icelandic and other arctic faunal regions. He hopes soon to publish the synonymical notes which he has collected, and informs us that these will sadly disarrange the just-published check list of the Noctuidæ. One of the results of his journey, which he mentions to us incidentally, is to the effect that *Zanclognatha minimalis*, which we referred to on p. 111 of the current volume of INSECT LIFE, is the same as *Hermia protumnosalis* Walker and that the latter name must replace Mr. Grote's name.

Prof. Smith's experience in London, Paris, and Berlin corroborates our own in similar investigations, in that the collections in London are by all means the most available, important, and instructive to the student; those of Berlin next, while those of Paris are in a most unsatisfactory condition, and are of comparatively little avail. He reports that he found no collections superior to the National Collection in condition, arrangement, and accessibility of material.

A USEFUL BEETLE MITE.

It seems that the common *Uropoda americana* Riley, found so abundantly upon the Colorado Potato Beetle, has appeared in great numbers on the grounds of the Experiment Station at Columbus, Ohio, and has nearly exterminated the Striped Cucumber-beetle. Our agent, Mr. Webster, has sent numbers of these mites to several different localities with the idea of colonizing them in localities where this beetle is abundant. He announces, in the *Indiana Farmer* of August 8, that he is willing to send a supply of mites to any gardener who may apply.

CHANGE OF LOCATION.

Prof. Charles W. Hargitt, formerly professor of biology in Miami University at Oxford, Ohio, and one of the charter members of the Association of Economic Entomologists, has been appointed to the chair of biology in Syracuse University, to succeed Prof. Lucien M. Underwood, who has gone to De Pauw University.

ENTOMOLOGICAL SOCIETY OF WASHINGTON.

November 5, 1891.—Messrs. Theo. Gill and C. W. Stiles were elected active members of the society, and Rev. C. J. S. Bethune, of Port Hope, Canada, and Prof. H. A. Morgan, of Baton Rouge, La., corresponding members.

Under short notes, etc., Mr. Schwarz exhibited some fine and complete examples of the galleries made by *Hylesinus sericeus* in the bark of *Abies menziesii*, from the Wahsatch Mountains of Utah. These galleries closely resemble those made by the species of *Scolytus*.

Mr. Schwarz also exhibited a species of the family Monommidae collected on Key West and at Biscayne Bay, Florida, and stated that after a careful study he has come to the conclusion that it is identical with *Aspathinus ovatus* Champion, recently described, from Central America, which adds a new genus to our fauna. Discussed by Messrs. Marlatt, Howard, Mann, and Schwarz.

The Secretary read a note by Mr. William D. Richardson, of Fredericksburg, Va., corresponding member of the society, on the life-history of *Lema sayi*. The food-plant of this species is *Commelyna virginica;* the eggs are laid singly on the leaves, and the larvae usually bore in the flower stalks, ejecting their fæces from the entrance hole of the burrow. Discussed by Mr Schwarz.

Dr. Marx exhibited two remarkable spiders occurring in our fauna: (1) a representative of the South American genus *Nops*, characterized by having but two eyes; (2) a puzzling species, the affinities of which he pointed out. It resembles an *Epeira*, but is altogether different in characters.

Mr. Howard read a paper entitled "Unmotherly Aphids" recounting the conjoint observations of Messrs. Howard, Chittenden and Marlatt of the curious fact of the deposition of the winter eggs of *Nectarophora liriodendri* in numbers on the pupal shells of Cicada which were attached to the trunk of a tree near the Agricultural Department building. Various interesting comments were made on this incident and the communication provoked considerable discussion.

Mr. Schwarz read a paper on the time of flight in Scarabæid beetles, in which he related an observation made last June by Mr. H. G. Hubbard and himself concerning an undescribed species of *Lachnosterna* which flies before sunset in the Alpine regions of Utah. He added remarks on the flying habits of other species of *Lachnosterna* and of Scarabæid beetles in general. It appears that in this family the unity in habit regarding the time of flight is generally maintained so far as genera are concerned, and that there are comparatively few exceptions to this rule.

Mr. Howard read a paper on the "Habits of Melittobia," suggested by Mr. Ashmead's communication at the preceding meeting. He gave a comprehensive review of the literature, showing all of the hosts of this genus of parasites, proving that it is both parasitic and hyperparasitic. He added an account of the rearing of *M. pelopœi* Ashm., from dipterous puparia found in Pelopæus cells by Mr. A. N. Caudell. Discussed by Mr. Ashmead.

Mr. Banks read a paper entitled "A New Genus of Phalangiidæ from North America," in which, under the name *Caddo* nov. gen. *agilis* n. sp., he described a peculiar Phalangiid collected in woods near the seashore on Long Island. Figures representing the peculiar features of the insect were exhibited. Discussed by Messrs. Gill, Stiles, Fox and others.

Dr. Marx gave some remarks on the geographical distribution of spiders, and stated that the Drassidæ, formerly supposed to be boreal in habitat, were now found to occur in the tropics in abundance, and that, in fact, we have not a single family that is entirely northern in range. In the Attidæ, however, certain genera may prove to be altogether boreal, but the family is not well worked up.

December 3, 1891.—Under short notes Mr. Howard recorded the capturing on the window sill of his residence, November 16 of an active female of *Mantis (Stagmomantis) carolina* Burm., this giving a record of occurrence later than that previously recorded by Mr. Lugger, viz., November 11.

Dr. Marx read a paper entitled "Life History of *Thelyphonus giganteus* Lucas," in which, after dwelling on the importance of even fragmentary records of the history of little known or rare animals, he gave an account of his having kept in confinement the young of this Arachnid for over a year. The specimen came from Florida to Prof. Riley, and was, when received, in its first stage and newly hatched. It fed readily on roaches but refused flies. A description was given of the first stage, and also after the first skin had been cast, which did not occur for over a year.

Discussed by Messrs. Mann, Marx, Test, Ashmead, Schwarz, Howard, Banks, and Marlatt.

Mr. Pergande presented a note on the "Peculiar Habits of *Ammophila gryphus* Smith." A very interesting description was given of the actions of a female of this insect about the site of a completed and closed burrow, in which later examinations showed that she had deposited the full-grown larva of *Heterocampa manteo* Doub. = *subalbicans* Grt., having first deposited an egg about midway of the body of the host larva. A figure was exhibited showing the larva with the egg *in situ* together with the specimen itself and an example of the *Ammophila*.

Discussed by Messrs. Fox, Ashmead, Schwarz, and Marlatt.

Mr. Linell presented a note on the North American species of *Valgus* in which, after a reference to the bibliography of the three native species of the genus, a table for their separation was given.

Discussed by Mr. Schwarz.

Mr. Banks gave some notes on *Prodidomus rufus* Hentz, a spider which has not been seen since Hentz' time. His remarks comprised a reference to the bibliography of the species, a statement of its relationship and characteristics, together with a careful description based on immature specimens found among loose papers in a drawer last summer.

Discussed by Messrs. Fox, Gill, Marx, Howard, and others.

Mr. Chittenden presented by title a paper on "Food Habits of Chrysomelidæ."

Mr. Schwarz called attention to a statement by Dr. M. Busgen (in his recent work on the honey-dew of Aphids) to the effect that the honey-dew is not, secreted from the nectaries as hitherto supposed, but ejected from the anus. He also referred to an interesting work recently published by C. A. Piepers on the migratory movements of butterflies on the island of Java, and gave a brief résumé of the author's explanation of these phenomena which are comparable to the nuptial flight observed in other insects.

C. L. MARLATT,
Recording Secretary.

SPECIAL NOTES.

A Bulletin on Wireworms.*—Prof. J. H. Comstock and his assistant, Mr. M. V. Slingerland, have just published a very full and careful bulletin on the subject of Wireworms. The bulk of the bulletin is taken up with an account of a careful and extensive series of experiments for preventing the ravages of these insects or for destroying them in their different states. The preventive experiments were conducted entirely in the direction of protecting seed. The following substances were used: Paris green and flour, tar, salt solution, copper solution, chloride of lime and copperas solution, kerosene oil, turpentine, and a strychnine solution. The details of the experiments show that no practical results are likely to be obtained in this direction.

The results of the experiments for the destruction of the larvæ show that it is not worth while to attempt to starve out the worms by leaving land in fallow through the season; that the growing of Buckwheat, Mustard, or Rape upon infested land does not rid it of Wireworms. Kerosene emulsion and pure kerosene as well as crude petroleum, while moderately effective, are not recommended on account of their cost. The killing power of salt, kainit, muriate of potash, lime, chloride of lime, and gas lime upon the larvæ was carefully tested with the result that salt was found to be the only substance from which any practical results were obtained. Used at the rate of eight tons per acre the worms will be destroyed, but there will be no chance for vegetation for some time afterwards, and as a matter of course the remedy will be so expensive as to preclude its use except upon very valuable land. So far in the course of the experimentation against the larvæ, scarcely any practical results have been obtained, but the work against the adult beetles was more satisfactory. Fall plowing is shown to destroy the perfect insects. The early recommendations in regard to trapping the beetles with baits of clover and dough are repeated. Trap lanterns were used without satisfactory result. The closing portions of the bulletin include a consideration of the life-history of *Agriotes mancus*, *Asaphes decoloratus*, *Melanotus communis*, *Drasterius elegans*, and *Crypto-*

---

* Cornell University Agricultural Experiment Station, Bulletin No. 33.

hypnus abbreviatus, careful and extended descriptions of the larvæ being given in each case. The experience with Drasterius would indicate, in connection with our own experience, which is quoted, that the larva combines the carnivorous and phytophagous habit, as in so many other insects.

In Bulletin No. 85, of the New Jersey Experiment Station. Prof. J. B. Smith gives his experience with kainit against wireworms which he found on a large scale to be strikingly successful. Prof. Comstock's experiment was conducted in the laboratory and on a small scale.

Insects Injurious to the Blackberry.*—Prof. John B. Smith has published a little bulletin under this title, in which he indicates the importance of the small fruit industry in portions of New Jersey and considers the following enemies of the Blackberry: The Red-necked Cane-borer (*Agrilus ruficollis*), the Blackberry Crown-borer (*Bembecia marginata*), the Giant Root-borer (*Prionus laticollis*), and the Blackberry Midge (*Lasioptera farinosa*). The life-histories of these insects are presented in a lucid and popular manner and the author's original results are indicated, as compared with those from other sources which are duly credited. We notice that the acting director of the New Jersey Experiment Station has the habit of signing his name at the end of the bulletins, which gives the erroneous impression to one not examining the paper carefully that he is the author. Some other arrangement, like a formal letter of submittal, could be made to advantage.

Farm Practice and Fertilizers to control Insect Injury.†—Under this title Prof. Smith has brought together a number of very useful suggestions to farmers and which involve the application of preventive or remedial measures as a part of the regular farm routine. He discusses in the main the value of fall plowing, the use of different commercial fertilizers, rotation of crops, clean culture, and the effect of different seasons of planting and of harvest. The bulletin is principally suggestive and many of the suggestions are founded upon experiments and upon the published experience of other entomologists. It is written in a clear and practical manner and is calculated to make a favorable impression upon the intelligent farmer. Prof. Smith places entire credence in the popular idea of farmers that where kainit is freely applied as a fertilizer to the roots of orchard trees it will appear upon the surface of the leaves. He even goes so far as to state that where this substance has been thus applied he has seen every leaf covered by a per-

---

*New Jersey Agricultural College Experiment Station, Special Bulletin N. John B. Smith, Entomologist.

†New Jersey Agricultural College Experiment Station. Bulletin No. 85. December 18, 1891.

ceptible glaze which had a distinctly salty taste. We do not dispute the fact, but the inference is startling and we leave it to the plant physiologists to deal with.

Dr. Cooper Curtice on the Cattle Tick.—We have just received from the author reprints of two papers entitled, respectively, "The Biology of the Cattle Tick" and "About Cattle Ticks," from the Journal of Comparative Medicine and Veterinary Archives, July, 1891, and January, 1892. In the first of these papers, which was originally read before the Biological Society of Washington February 3, 1890, Dr. Curtice gives a full account of certain careful observations which he made while connected with the Bureau of Animal Industry of this Department on the life-history of the common Cattle Tick (*Ixodes bovis* Riley) for which he has erected the new genus *Boöphilus*. Dates of egg-laying, hatching, molting, and coupling are given, with careful descriptions of the different stages. In the second paper the life-history of the insect is completed and a careful account of its habits is given. The author shows that cattle should be kept in good condition in order to resist the pest, and as an actual application he recommends the kerosene emulsion, which is reported by Dr. Francis, of Texas, as "working to a charm." The author touches briefly upon the supposed connection between the Cattle Tick and the Texas fever, and states that it has been thoroughly demonstrated that the fever may be spread by these creatures.

Dr. Curtice on the Ox Warble.*—We have also received from Dr. Curtice an author's extra of his valuable paper upon the Ox Warble of the United States, an advance item from which we published in INSECT LIFE, Vol. II, pp. 207–8. In this paper Dr. Curtice announces his conclusion, that the Ox Warble Fly of the United States is *Hypoderma lineata* Villers and not *Hypoderma bovis* Linn., as was formerly supposed. In support of the conclusion he adduces the results of his examination of the material in adults from the United States National Museum collection and of a very large series of larvæ in the collection of the Bureau of Animal Industry of this Department. He has adopted the diagrammatic method of representation of the armature of Hypoderma larvæ, invented by Brauer, and shows by an original diagram the correspondence of the armature of American larvæ with *H. lineata* and not with *H. bovis*. We have already (Vol. III, p. 432,) indicated and confirmed these conclusions in a paper before the Entomological Society of Washington last May, and later before the Society for the Promotion of Agricultural Science. He reiterates his revolutionary

---

*The Oxwarble of the United States, by Cooper Curtice, Veterinarian. Journal of Comparative Medicine and Veterinary Archives, Vol. XII, No. 6, p. 265. June, 1891.

conclusion referred to in INSECT LIFE (II, 207), to the effect that the larvæ do not puncture the skin on hatching from the egg, but are licked by the cattle, swallowed and lodged in the back of the mouth, or œsophagus, from which point they travel through the œsophagus and then through the subcutaneous connective tissue to some convenient point on the back of the animal, where they bore through the skin to the outside and form their characteristic cysts. Dr. Curtice adduces a great deal of evidence in support of this conclusion, and we have already expressed our views on the subject. The paper is well illustrated by figures prepared under Dr. Curtice while he was connected with the Bureau of Animal Industry and which have been loaned to him by the Director of the Bureau, Dr. Salmon. We shall not consider in detail the evidence which Dr. Curtice brings forward, but hope to do it soon at some length in a paper upon certain Œstridæ which has for some time been ready for publication, as we were much interested in the subject and have taken particular pains to verify the fact that our common Ox Warble is *H. lineata*.

A Careful Study of the Hessian Fly.—We have received from our correspondent, Mr. Fred. Enock, a brochure entitled "The Life History of the Hessian Fly," which is extracted from the Transactions of the Entomological Society of London, Part II, 1891. We have been familiar for sometime with Mr. Enock's careful studies of this important pest, and are therefore not surprised at the close research exhibited in this paper. It is the most important contribution to our knowledge of the Hessian Fly which has been published of late years, and the facts which it details can not but prove valuable to the practical side of the investigation. Mr. Enock agrees with us that the Hessian Fly was present in England in barley fields long before it was discovered in 1886 and announced as a new pest. His observations cover particularly studies of the eggs, larvæ, pupæ, and parasites. He has shown by examination, observation, and counting that the number of eggs deposited by a single female varies from 100 to 150, instead of from 80 to less than 100 as stated by Wagner. He has made a series of most careful observations upon the use of the "anchor process" or "breastbone" of the larva in turning about within the puparium. In the course of the investigation of this particular point he has spent many hours watching the living insects under the microscope. He has followed the insect from egg to adult with great care, and found that in one instance it took sixty-three days. He has made careful observations upon the climbing powers of the pupa, and has observed the insect in this stage to cut its way through the leaf sheath by means of the chitinous beak upon its head and work its way out until the leg sheaths were free, the abdomen being held in the orifice. Satisfactory tests were made to see whether the females would reproduce parthenogenetically, but with only negative results. The author also records some interesting facts concerning retardation of development. On April 25, 1889, he received a sack of barley screenings from the 1887 harvest, and out of 100 puparia he found in 15 still living larvæ. These were shriveled, but upon being placed in damp sand they apparently entirely recovered, and on May 9 a perfect male insect issued. Others appeared from June 3 until July 2, some females being among those last appearing. From this observation it appears that the insect may rest two years in the puparium. This is confirmatory of what we have published on the subject and has an important bearing upon the argument advanced by Wagner, Hagen, and others, to the effect that the length of the journey would have precluded the introduction of the insect by the Hessian troops during the Revolutionary War. The paper is illustrated by a handsome plate showing the larva and pupa in different stages of growth and illustrating the manner in which the larva turns beneath the leaf sheath. Mr. Enock concludes his paper with a strong plea for the establishment of a Government Bureau of Entomology, and pays INSECT LIFE, as well as the Division from which it emanates, some very high compliments for which we beg to thank him.

Bacteria normal to digestive Organs of Hemiptera.*—In this article Prof. S. A. Forbes announces the interesting discovery that certain cæcal appendages of the small intestine which are always present in the higher Heteroptera are invariably filled with bacteria which do not occur in other portions of the body. These cæca were first noticed by Léon Dufour, who called them "*cordons valvuleux*," and vary in number, shape, and disposition. They are well furnished with tracheal branches and connect freely with the interior of the intestine. Prof. Forbes has found them in the Lygæidæ, Coreidæ, Pentatomidæ, and Corimelænidæ, but failed to find them in the Capsidæ, Nabidæ, Reduviidæ, and Aradidæ, and generalizes to the effect that they are found in the higher Heteroptera and are absent in the lower, while in those intermediate in the scale they may be present in one genus and absent in another. The bacteria found belong to the species known as *Micrococcus insectorum*. Where they were most abundant (as in the case of dying Chinch Bugs) the epithelium of the cæca was completely disorganized, only the basement membrane remaining. The structure and arrangement of the cæca in several of the genera examined are carefully described in this paper, but the author states that he has no present desire to speculate concerning the meaning of the bacterial contents of the organs, and offers this paper simply as a preliminary account of the several investigations upon which he is now engaged, and

---

* Article I. Bulletin of the Illinois State Laboratory of Natural History, vol. IV., pp. 1 to 6.

which comprehend the distribution of the cæca, their various relations to the bodies of the species possessing them, and the kinds and nature of the bacteria constantly harbored by them. The discovery is one of great interest and may become of importance. We hope that Prof. Forbes will not confine himself to the Hemiptera in his investigations, but will also follow the organs in other orders of insects which have been similarly assumed to have pancreatic functions, such as the ramified appendages of the stomach in Gryllotalpa.

Plutella cruciferarum in England.—The English Board of Agriculture has just published a special report of the Intelligence Department, by Mr. Charles Whitehead, on an attack of the Diamond-back Moth Caterpillar. Mr. Whitehead has given in this report a full account of the damage done by this insect during 1891 in various districts in England, to which we have already referred on page 81 of Vol. IV. The author gives descriptions of the different stages of the insect, an account of previous attacks by the same species in Great Britain, a general review of its distribution, and some account of the presence of the species in foreign countries, in which, curiously enough, he makes no mention of its occurrence in New Zealand or the United States. Under the heading "Extent and nature of the injuries and losses to crops" a most deplorable state of affairs is indicated, in some cases the loss on the Turnip and Swede crop reaching 60 per cent. The season seems to have been a favorable one for the development of Tineina of many species, and in a number of cases the severity of the present season's attack by the Plutella has been directly traced to carelessness in allowing the growth of Wild Mustard, Charlock, Shepherd's Purse, and other Cruciferous weeds in the vicinity of the fields the previous fall.

The damage was mainly done in the vicinity of the seacoast, where wild Cruciferous plants grow in great abundance. The dry weather, so marked in the early part of the season of 1891, also aided in the rapid development of the insect. A number of remedies were tried by farmers, and Mr. Whitehead summarizes these in his general conclusions. A mixture of soot in lime was shown to be the best remedy tried. Paraffin (kerosene), quassia, and carbolic acid solutions are said to have been "efficacious to some extent." Brushing off the caterpillars by means of boughs fastened to horse hoes (cultivators) proved to be a good practice, especially where the hoes were followed by other hoes or "scufflers" to bury or kill the caterpillars. Mr. Whitehead finally advises cutting down the Cruciferous weeds in the spring, as they may serve as breeding places for the first brood of the insect, but he is of the opinion that the unpropitious weather of the latter part of the season and the hosts of parasites which have been developed will have reduced the insect to such a point that next year will show but slight damage. Among natural enemies *Limneria gracilis* and *L. tibialis* were noted. Of these *L. gracilis* greatly predominated.

Bulletin No. 14 of the Oregon Station.—In this bulletin, which is preliminary in its character, Prof. Washburn introduces the subject by a "A Plain Talk About Insects," in which he gives some idea about transformations and classification of insects, tabulates the injurious species of 1891, and treats briefly the Grain Weevil (*Silvanus surinamensis*), a sugar-beet beetle (*Monoxia guttulata*), and the Tent Caterpillar (*Clisiocampa* spp.). He quotes an actual experience in the use of bisulphide of carbon against the Grain Weevil, showing that 2 quarts, when used in each of two bins 20 by 20 feet, gave excellent results, the total cost for treating 3,000 bushels of wheat being $3. The sugar-beet beetle is one of the Leaf-beetles, and has been commonly destructive to Sugar Beets raised in Oregon. They were successfully destroyed by the use of Paris green in the proportion of 1 pound to 100 gallons of water, 6 pounds of whale oil soap being added to this amount of the poison, presumably in order to fix the mixture to the leaves.

Entomology at the Leland Stanford, jr., University.—Prof. J. H. Comstock, of Cornell University, has been engaged by President Jordan to deliver a course of lectures at the Leland Stanford, jr., University, commencing January 4, 1892, and extending over a term of three months. We understand that it is to be an annual arrangement, and that Professor Comstock will spend his winter vacation in California in this work in the future.

New Edition of Bulletin No. 6, Division of Entomology.—Owing to the fact that the first edition of Bulletin No. 6 of this Division, which treats of the Imported Elm Leaf-beetle, was exhausted some years ago, and to the further fact that there is still a constant demand for information concerning this important elm pest, a new edition has been published which will be sent on application. The old bulletin is reprinted and an appendix is added which discusses the question of the number of annual generations, and gives the result of some additional experience in the matter of remedies.

Popular Lectures on Insects.—Beginning December 28, 1891, and continuing twice a week until January 21, 1892, the entomologist delivered a series of popular lectures before the Lowell Institute in Boston, Mass. The following topics were treated: I, Scope and importance of Entomology: II, Means of dealing with our insect foes; insecticides and insecticide appliances: III, Some insect foes to cultivated plants and domestic animals: IV, Little known facts about well known household

---

*Oregon Agricultural Experiment Station. Bulletin No. 14. Entomology. F. L. Washburn, Entomologist. Corvallis, Oregon, 1891.

pests: V, Organized insect societies, ants, bees, and wasps: VI, Galls and gall insects; saw-flies; caprification; parasitism: VII, Some interesting insects of various orders: VIII, Insects vs. flowers; entomophilous and entomophagous plants.

Spraying for Plum Curculio in Ohio.—Mr. J. S. Hine, in the Journal of the Columbus Horticultural Society for September, 1891, records the results of spraying with Bordeaux mixture for different fungous diseases of fruits and of Paris green and London purple for the Curculio. He found that where plum trees were first treated with the Bordeaux mixture the foliage was not damaged by subsequent spraying with Paris green in the proportion 3 ounces to 50 gallons of water. Mr. Hine advises, however, the addition of 3 pounds of lime to the above amount.

Testimony concerning the Value of Entomological Work.—A most interesting pamphlet entitled "Examination of Mr. James Fletcher, Entomologist and Botanist to the Dominion Experimental Farms, before the Select Standing Committee on Agriculture and Colonization," July 4, 1891, has just reached us. It is a parliamentary document and its title well indicates its contents. Mr. Fletcher's testimony was particularly strong and places the value of entomological work upon a very high footing. He spoke very highly of the work done in this direction by the Government of the United States and said that he expected before long to be able to devote the whole of his time to Entomology.

Entomological News.—This interesting periodical, the inception of which we announced some two years ago, is now beginning its third volume. It is peculiarly well adapted to the use of amateur entomologists and contains each month an article upon elementary entomology. Its summaries of current entomological literature are very valuable to the working entomologist. With each number of late there has been published a full-page phototype of some striking insect.

THE POTATO-TUBER MOTH.

(*Lita solanella* Boisd.)

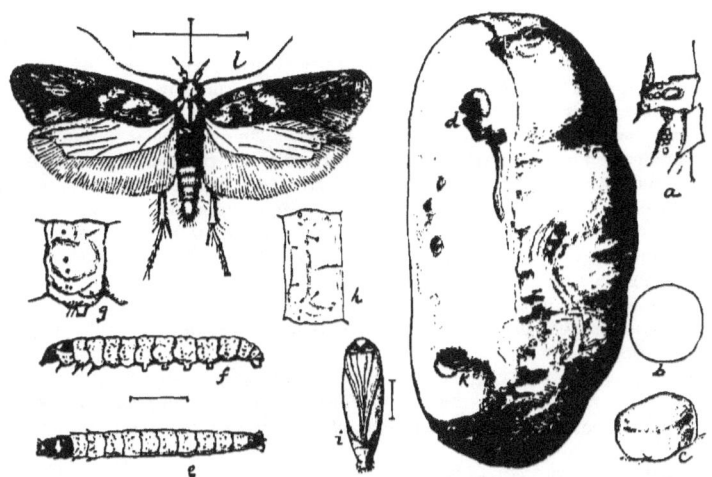

FIG. 27.—*Lita solanella* Boisd.: *a*, section of tuber showing eye and eggs deposited about it—natural size; *b*, egg, dorsal view; *c*, egg, lateral view—greatly enlarged; *d*, *k*, mines of larva in potato; *j*, pupa at end of mine, seen through skin of potato—somewhat reduced; *e*, larva, dorsal view; *f*, larva, lateral view; *g*, larva, third abdominal segment, lateral view; *h*, larva, dorsal view—still more enlarged; *i*, pupa; *l*, moth—enlarged. (Original.)

For many years past potatoes have suffered in New Zealand, Tasmania, and different parts of Australia from the ravages of a small moth of the Tineid family Gelechiidæ, the larvæ of which bore into stored potatoes and those which are still in the ground. The insect has been treated of by a number of Australian authors, but particularly by Mr. J. G. O. Tepper in the Transactions and Proceedings of the Royal Society of South Australia, vol. IV, p. 57, and by Mr. Henry Tryon in his Report on Insect and Fungus Pests [of Queensland], No. 1, 1889, pp. 175-181. It was first referred to, although without name, by Capt. H. Berthon in the Papers and Proceedings of the Royal Society of Van Diemens Land, vol. III (1855), part 1, p. 76, and was first described by Boisduval in 1874, who stated that it was very injurious to potatoes in Algeria. He states that the eggs are laid upon the young plants as soon as they put out from the ground and the newly hatched larvæ bore through the tubers, filling their burrows with black excrement and completely spoiling them. The identity of the Algerian species and that in Australia seems to have been accepted by Tepper, Meyrick, and other competent authorities. The habits of the insect in Australia are well and concisely given by Tryon, whose account we quote:

HABITS OF THE INSECT.

When fully established in a district, both those potatoes which are in the ground and those which have been removed from it and are stored are subject to the attacks of the moth. At Toowoomba, as far as we learn, it is only those tubers which have been dug up which, as yet, suffer.* Mr. G. Searle, in reply to our questions, remarks:

"I am perfectly sure that the insect is not in the potato while this is in the ground. We are almost daily using potatoes which were all dug at one time, immediately picked up, and placed in a dry-goods cask in which straw was placed between each layer of tubers. The cask is covered up by a corn bag, and, with the exception of a few near the top of it, none are affected by the moth." In Tasmania it was "invariably found that the moth attacks the roots. The uppermost potatoes, those which are nearest the surface, are of course most easily reached, nor is it by any means a difficult matter for the insect to penetrate to the depth of three or four inches when the soil is open, uncompressed, or lumpy. Not a single case of an infected stalk has yet been detected, but constant and numberless have been the instances in which, when uncovering the potatoes at the depth just indicated, moths have been dislodged and flown uninjured away."

Of course some of these, however, as must have occurred to the author of these observations, might have hatched from pupæ still in the ground; but in anticipation of this objection he adds:

"The potatoes, whilst lying exposed in rows, were attacked by the insects * * * and it was always noted that the moths, when unengaged in laying eggs, were almost always to be found beneath the clods of earth with which the ground was encumbered."

Otto Tepper remarks:

"My opinion is that the eggs are first deposited by the moths under the stalk near the ground, when the infant grub burrows through the soil till reaching the tubers; or the moth itself burrows, as many are found to do, and deposits the eggs direct upon the tubers. My reason for this is the fact that the longer the tubers are left in the soil the more infected they will prove to be."

Boisduval's observations, too, though somewhat different as to detail, support this view as to the mode in which the moths find access to the tuber, whilst the latter is still beneath the surface of the ground.

What is the nature of the operations which take place beneath the surface of the ground may be concluded from what was noticed in our breeding apparatus. The moths had no partiality for perfectly sound tubers, but would attack those which had previously afforded sustenance to a generation of their kind. In a sound potato the eggs were laid several side by side in contiguity to an "eye" of the tuber; in a diseased one, on the earth-covered surface of a cocoon, within the hole previously excavated by a caterpillar which had emerged for the purpose of pupating, or amongst the "frass" surrounding the entrance to this cavity. As many as twenty-six eggs, laid by a single moth, were in one instance counted in the same location. The eggs hatch in a week or ten days, and often more quickly.

The young caterpillars immediately proceed to burrow into the tuber, at first concealing themselves beneath numerous particles of rejected food material fastened together with web, the number of which particles is being continually increased by similar matter brought to the surface. The channel thus formed is also lined with web, so that when the substance of the tuber is broken down these burrows appear as hollow tubular bodies. The caterpillars arrive at their full size in from two to three weeks† and then find their way to the surface of the potato and burrow out-

---

*We, however, bred a specimen of the insect from a potato *leaf* sent by Mr. G. Searle. This the caterpillar had folded up.

†Tepper makes the minimum to be forty-five days.

wards through the skin. They then spin a cocoon either within the hole thus formed or, more generally, on the surface of the tuber adjacent to it, or, as is often the case, on the sides of the receptacle containing this amongst the other outlets, and then immediately transform into the chrysalis phase. Two or three chrysalids may be placed side by side. They are always completely covered by particles of "frass" or earth. The fully matured insect, the moth, emerges from the chrysalis shortly after two weeks have elapsed. The union of the sexes almost immediately takes place and another generation of potato-destroyers arises. The moth is quite a night-flying insect and only lives a few days.

The number of caterpillars which a single potato may support is very large, and limited only by the amount of food which it yields. Meyrick mentions that one tuber must have contained quite forty larvæ, and we have bred fifty-eight from eight potatoes. "Their voracity, however, is so great and their diligence in their vocation so untiring, that a couple of individuals will thoroughly riddle and destroy a potato of fair size during their brief but mischievous career." (*Berthon*.) They continue to feed in the tuber when even this becomes completely rotten, and in confinement "deposit their eggs on potatoes when these have become not only putrid but externally shrivelled-up lumps, whence fresh larvæ are constantly being hatched." (*Tepper*.)

When potatoes are attacked they soon manifest little heaps of earthy substance on their surface, which conceal the chrysalids of the insects or the entrances to the galleries, which section of the tubers discovers. This penetrating their substance causes potatoes affected to rot and become worthless. We do not know how soon the potatoes are first attacked, but if prior to the culms being dry, as is highly probable, those, too, will no doubt evidence well marked symptoms.

EXTENT OF RAVAGES OF MOTH.

According to Boisduval, as quoted by Meyrick, in certain districts of Algiers during a single season three-fourths of the potato crop was destroyed by this pest. Otto Tepper thus relates his Adelaide experiences:

As far as my continued observation goes the insect causes now (*i. e.*, in 1881), in its immature form of the caterpillar or grub, the destruction of hundreds of tons of potatoes every year by boring them, and thereby inducing putridity. During late years I have scarcely ever been able to get half a dozen pounds without finding a considerable percentage more or less affected in this way.

Again,

That these moths occur in other situations less confined than the entomologist's hatching case was gleaned latterly from the information a farmer gave me when speaking about the subject. He said that he had several bags of potatoes of his own production, and quite healthy when dug, placed in his storeroom, where they were left undisturbed for a considerable time. When he at last came to open a bag for use, lo! quite a swarm of little moths greeted the event, and to his surprise he found the tubers spoiled by the grubs to a great extent.

APPEARANCE OF THE INSECT IN AMERICA.

The first week in November, 1891, we received from Mr. W. A. Webster, of Bakersfield, Kern County, Cal., two potatoes infested by the larvæ of what is without doubt this insect. The larvæ were working just under the skin of the potato, forming long and narrow mines and large irregular blotches, giving the tubers a scabby appearance. The larvæ were white with a very pale pinkish band across the dorsum of the abdominal segments. The head, cervical plate, and thoracic legs were black and the face brownish. The cervical plate possesses a narrow, pale median line, the piliferous warts were minute and black and the anal plate yellowish, dusky, or black. These larvæ spun their cocoons either under the epidermis of the potato or outside, generally in some depression. In the latter case it was covered with particles of the skin of the tuber so that it was difficult to detect. Several other potatoes were received early in December. From these two lots a large series of the moths were bred. They issued almost daily from November 13 well on into December. The different stages of the insect, drawn from life, are show at Fig. 27.

We supposed at first that the insect had been accidentally imported from either New Zealand or Australia upon one or more of the regular steamers in the steward's supplies, as potatoes are not imported commercially to any extent from either of these countries. Mr. W. A. Webster, however, writing under date of November 26, informs us that the potatoes sent were of the first crop and had been out of the ground probably since August: that they were obtained from a Chinese gardener and that he is strongly impressed with the possibility that the insect was imported from China, as goods are constantly being brought over by Chinese merchants and many seeds and bulbs as well. Mr. Webster is positive that this is the first season that the insect has been found near Bakersfield.

REMEDIES.

It is strange that this insect should make its appearance at a comparatively inland point like Bakersfield, and this fact makes it all the more important that strenuous efforts should be made to stamp it out before it obtains a foothold. Wherever the insect is found we urge the immediate destruction of the infested potatoes. No remedy, for the present, will be necessary beyond the careful examination of potatoes and the immediate sequestration and destruction of all found to be infested. Sound potatoes, also, should be more carefully packed or stored in tight rooms.

A GENUS OF MANTIS EGG-PARASITES.

There are, according to Westwood's revision, more than five hundred species of Mantidæ in different parts of the world, and it is safe to say that in almost every instance where any species has been at all carefully studied it has been found that its egg masses are pierced by a species of the peculiar Chalcidid genus Podagrion. Very few of these forms have been described, but a large number exist in the various museums. Westwood mentions the rearing of several tropical species; Walker has described a species from Australia: *P. pachymerus* is a common parasite of the European "Praying Mantis;" the U. S. National Museum contains two species bred from the egg-cases of our common North American Mantis (*Stagmomantis carolina*), as well as a punctured egg-case from Australia, collected by Mr. F. M. Webster, and a species from Japan sent by Mr. Koebele. Mayr mentions incidentally the fact that there are several species in his own collection and that of the Zoölogical Museum in Vienna bred from the eggs of exotic Mantidæ, and Westwood summarized as long ago as 1844 ten species, three of them from gum copal, two from Europe, two from the Isle of France, one from King Georges Sound, one from Brazil, and one from New South Wales.

This genus, which was originally erected by Spinola in 1811, was subsequently described under the name of Palmon by Dalman in 1825, as Priomerus by Walker in 1833, and as Bactyrischion by Costa in 1857. It seems to form in certain features or characters a link between the subfamilies Chalcidinæ and Toryminæ, having the enlarged hind thighs of the former

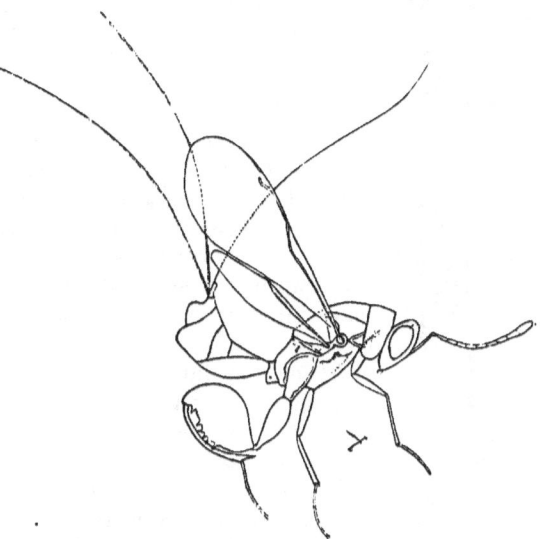

FIG. 28.—*Podagrion mantis*, adult female—greatly enlarged (original).

subfamily and the very long ovipositor of many members of the latter. It has been placed, indeed, in the latter subfamily by Walker and other writers, but recent authors, following Mayr, have concluded that this genus bears a stronger relationship to the Chalcidinæ, and Mr. Howard has so placed it in his generic synopsis of the Chalcididæ. In antennal structure and the character of the pronotum, in addition to its enlarged and dentate posterior femora, it is closely allied to the other genera of this latter subfamily. Its lengthy ovipositor, which is, in fact, almost the only character which it has in common with the Toryminæ, is simply particularly developed for the special needs of the insect, as without it the thick and tough egg-cases of Mantis could not be pierced. Our American species has frequently been reared, and was mentioned as long ago as 1854 by Glover. Professor Riley reared it in 1868 in Missouri, and specimens have since remained undescribed in his collection. It was not, in fact, until 1885 that it received a specific name. In this year Mr. Ashmead described it as *P. mantis* (properly *mantidis*) in the *Canadian Entomologist*.

Our object in publishing this note at this time is mainly to introduce a figure of this remarkable insect in order to enable its ready recognition by those who rear it in the future. The "Rear Horse" or "Camel Cricket" is so common an insect and one which attracts such general attention that its commonest parasite should be known.

We show at Fig. 30 a cross section of the egg-case collected by Mr. Webster in Australia, as it exhibits an interesting variation in the arrangement of the eggs. The tough, horny substance forming the outer layer of the case is much thicker than in our species, and the inner pod contains the eggs in layers and arranged concentrically about a central channel, toward which the head end of each points, enabling each of the young Mantids to issue without interference with its neighbors. The egg-case, however, contains several dead specimens of a species of Podagrion. These in every case hold a reversed position, with the head away from the central channel, and, as evidenced by the round holes through the outer crust of the case, they were enabled by this fact to gnaw directly out through the crust of the inner pod and through the outer casing. With the egg-cases of our common *Stagmomantis carolina* there is no such concentrical arrangement of the eggs, and the outer envelope is comparatively thin. The eggs all stand on end as shown by Fig. 31, which exhibits a cross section of one of these cases. All of the eggs, however, are inclined somewhat toward the two central channels, so that the young, on hatching, possess the same free method of exit. With the parasites, however, the case is somewhat complicated. The holes of exit are seen pierced through the sides of the egg-case just as with the Australian species, but, as none of the eggs have their bases directly toward the sides of the case, but only to the surface of attachment of the egg masses, the parasites are obliged, before gnawing their way out, to twist about within the narrow space to which they have been confined and gnaw their way through the envelope in what must be a cramped and disadvantageous position.

FIG. 29.—Egg-cases of *Stagmomantis carolina*—natural size (after Riley).

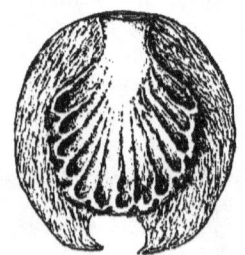

FIG. 30.—Cross section of egg-case of Australian Mantid—slightly enlarged (original).

FIG. 31.—Cross section of egg-case of *Stagmomantis carolina*—slightly enlarged (original).

The time of issuing of the parasites and the time when the young Mantides make their appearance seem to bear a somewhat constant relation, in that the parasites generally issue from one to three weeks before the eggs hatch, or would have hatched. In Missouri, in 1870, parasites issued May 9 and young Mantids May 14. In Washington, D. C., in 1881, parasites issued May 12 and young Mantids May 21. In California, in 1888, parasites issued in March from an egg mass received from Japan, while the young Mantids made their appearance April 16. The present year parasites issued in April from egg masses received from Arizona, from which the young Mantids issued May 18.

NOTES ON THE GRAIN TOXOPTERA.

(*Toxoptera graminum*, Rond.)

By F. M. WEBSTER.

This is a grain-affecting Aphidid which the U. S. Entomologist has been studying for some years. Though of foreign origin, without much doubt, it has probably been a constant inhabitant of our grain fields for a number of years, its numbers being too limited to attract attention, or it may have been confused with other species occurring in much greater numbers. Buckton* states that the species, during the summer, inhabits Triticum, Hordeum, Avena, Sorghum, and Zea; but at that time (1881) it was not known in England, and the literature at my disposal does not indicate that it has since appeared in that country. That the species at times becomes exceedingly abundant is indicated by Rondani's account of its appearance in 1853 "in the streets of Bologna in innumerable swarms, to the annoyance of the inhabitants."†

My own acquaintance with the species began early in July, 1884, while studying the habits of Isosoma, at Oxford, Indiana. Some time after the middle of June growing wheat was transferred from the field to a breeding-cage, and apterous, agamic females of this Toxoptera were observed infesting the leaves of these plants early in July. Since that time it has appeared in wheat fields year after year in increasing abundance. The species winters over in fields of fall-sown wheat, and probably rye also, reproducing rapidly in the fall as long as the weather remains mild, even though during the night the temperature may fall considerably below the freezing point. During the mild winter of 1889-'90 they were observed reproducing during mild weather throughout the entire winter. During midsummer the species will live on the leaves of all kinds of grain, including corn. Orchard grass appears to suit their purpose almost as well as grain, but I did not rear them on Eragrostis, Panicum, Setaria, Agrostis, Poa, or Bromus.

---

*Buckton's British Aphides, vol. 3, pp. 135,136.
†Ann. delle Scien. Nat., de Bologna.

Wishing to determine the rapidity of reproduction among the females, and with this object in view, I placed a pupa on a growing wheat plant on April 8. On the morning of the 9th she developed to a winged adult and reproduced as follows:

April 10, produced 3 young.	April 18, produced 1 young.
April 11, produced 3 young.	April 19, produced 3 young.
April 12, produced 2 young.	April 20, produced 2 young.
April 13, produced 2 young.	April 21, produced none.
April 14, produced 2 young.	April 22, produced 3 young.
April 15, produced 4 young.	April 23, produced 4 young.
April 16, produced 2 young.	April 24, produced 4 young.
April 17, produced 1 young.	April 28, produced 1 young.

This last was produced in my absence from home and between the 25th and 28th, on which date the female was found dead in the cage. The first born young developed to adult females on the 18th, and began reproducing. The progeny of those born on the 18th began reproducing on the 25th, so that although the female with which I began only survived about two weeks, she lived to produce 37 young, and died a great-grandmother. From further studies of the development of other species of Aphides, it seems quite probable that the apterous females are even more productive. The winged female is rather more of a differentiator than a producer. While the wingless mother may usually be observed on a leaf, with her numerous family gathered about her, the winged parent will often wander about, seemingly perfectly regardless of the environment in which she leaves her offspring.

The young invariably molt the second day after birth, and reach the adult stage on the seventh day. By invariably I mean during the ordinary breeding season. In cool weather, and during winter, the development is without doubt very much retarded. While a brood of young is developed every seven days, it will be observed from the foregoing that broods become so intermixed with their progeny that all apparent division lines are obliterated, and if one attempts to keep the run of the broods, he will find himself completely overwhelmed in the maze of enumeration, ere he has made a beginning. The species appears to be essentially leaf-infesting; in no case, so far as I have observed, extending its depredations to the ears of grain or heads of grasses.

Up to 1890, though occurring sometimes in considerable abundance, there had been no indication of serious trouble by reason of the presence of these insects in our grain fields. As early as January 22, Dr. Riley wrote me of the abundance of the species in fields of wheat, especially of East Tennessee, where its numbers were at that time creating some anxiety among wheat growers.* Again, under date of May 2, he wrote that complaints had reached him of the ravages of the grain louse in many of the more southern of the grain-growing States during the winter months, but whenever specimens had accompanied

---

*For report of occurrence of the species in Tennessee and Texas, see INSECT LIFE, vol. III, pp. 73, 126.

these reports they usually proved to be Toxoptera. At Lafayette this was by far the most abundant species wintering over in the wheat fields, and examinations in April showed them to have survived the winter in great numbers. They did not appear to increase rapidly, and I had ceased to anticipate trouble from them, when early in June letters from the southern part of Indiana gave the information that the grain Aphis was appearing in the wheat fields precisely as it had done the previous year, and was also ravaging the oat fields. A visit to Posey County on the 11th day of June revealed the true state of affairs. There were *Siphonophora arenæ* on the wheat in considerable abundance, and many also on the oats, but the number on the latter grain was no comparison to those of the Toxoptera. Not only were the larger leaves covered with them in many cases, but the tender unfolding leaves also, while there were myriads of the brown parasitized females everywhere on the plant. The oat crop was there a total failure, many fields being at that time as brown as though the entire growth of plants had been winter-killed. There was no lack of proof that the damage, so far as due to insect attack at all, had been done by this species.

From notices appearing in Illinois and Missouri papers, I am inclined to the opinion that the Toxoptera was equally abundant in portions of these States. In the extreme southern portions of Indiana the oat crop was a total failure; in many cases I was at a loss to account for this destruction, as its magnitude did not correspond to the numbers of the Toxoptera, notwithstanding its numbers were enormous. A solution of the problem, however, came from an unexpected quarter. Prof. B. T. Galloway, Chief of the Division of Vegetable Pathology, had, during the summer, discovered a bacterial disease in the oats plants, of which I had no knowledge, and his paper on a "New Disease of Oats" read at the Indianapolis meeting of the American Association for the Advancement of Science,[*] relieved me from my dilemma. While the Toxoptera can not be held entirely responsible for the failure of the oats crop during that season, as serious damage occurred where the insects were not sufficiently abundant to be noticeable, yet they certainly aggravated the work of destruction in several States, and in southern Indiana, at least, greatly emphasized the effect of this disease, showing us clearly that the species may in future prove a serious pest to the oats crop.

The young and apterous agamic females may be confused with the true Grain Aphis, *Siphonophora arenæ*, by casual observers, but the winged female has the cubital vein of the wing but once forked, thereby distinguishing it from all others of the subfamily Aphidinæ. These Toxoptera are great favorites of ants, while I have never yet observed an ant in attendance on *Siphonophora arenæ*, Prof. A. J. Cook notwithstanding.

---

[*] Preliminary notes on a new and destructive oat disease, by B. T. Galloway and E. A. Southworth. The Journal of Mycology, vol. vi, no. 2, p. 72, September, 1890.

The males and oviparous females begin to appear late in October. These females differ somewhat in appearance from the others previously observed, they being more elongate and pointed posteriorly. The color does not materially differ, except that the eggs show through the transparent skin, appearing like indistinct, oblique, lighter lines. They may be farther distinguished from the viviparous females by their position upon the leaf, in which, instead of being perfectly natural, the body is often thrown out at right angles to the leaf; in fact, so far as I have observed, this is the rule and not the exception. The eggs are of a glossy green immediately after deposition, but later turn to a jet black color.

THE LARGER DIGGER-WASP.

By C. V. RILEY.

FIG. 32.—Female Sphecius carrying a Cicada to her burrow—natural size (original).

One of the most common of our digger-wasps, as well as one of the largest and most conspicuous, is the *Sphecius speciosus*, a brown-black insect with yellow markings on its abdomen, and commonly known as *the* Hornet. That it feeds in the larva state on our large Dog-day Harvest-fly or Cicada (*Cicada pruinosa*) has long been known to naturalists, but is not known to people generally, though the curious habit of the wasp in seizing and straddling its larger victim and laboriously climbing up some tree, from which it can take a descending flight to its burrow, is frequently observed and rarely fails to elicit inquiry as to what the purpose of the acts may be. In fact, almost every year some one comes to me with a graphic description of the curious acts of this wasp, which he has observed, and wants to know why she drags the Cicada about so ruthlessly, instead of at once devouring it. Much might be said about the intelligence which the female digger-wasp exhibits in thus managing a victim much larger and heavier than herself, and what is true of this particular species is true of other digger-wasps in providing for their young. Some of the hitherto unrecorded facts in reference to this more common and conspicuous species will serve to indicate the general habits and life-history of all.

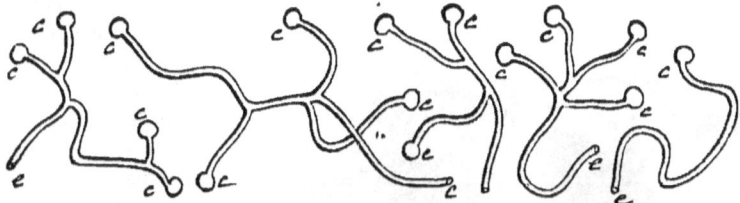

FIG. 33.—Burrows of *Sphecius speciosus*: *e, e, e*, main entrance; *c, c, c, c*, chambers for larvæ and their food—greatly reduced (original).

During the latter half of July and the 1st of August, when the note of the Cicada in question is filling the air with its vibrations, our digger-wasp is not idle, but may be observed in rapid, strong flight about the trees harboring its prey. The sudden cessation of the regular note of the unsuspecting Cicada and in its stead a distressing, discordant cry will catch the ear of the observer and apprise him that something is wrong, if he be in any way acquainted with the subject of the tragedy that is being enacted. A quick thrust of the sting of the wasp into the body of its victim paralyzes the latter and throws it into a comatose condition, from which it never recovers. The vital functions are suspended or greatly reduced, but not entirely stopped, and it becomes the nonresisting, half inanimate prey of the delicate larva of the wasp. The effect produced by the sting of one of these wasps on the insects which they provide for their young has always been a subject for speculation, and a curious fact is that should the egg of the wasp fail from any cause to hatch, the paralyzed victim nevertheless remains in a state of suspended

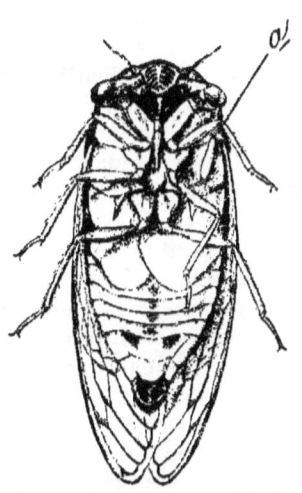

FIG. 34.—Adult Cicada with Sphecius egg attached at *a*—natural size (original).

animation, which will last under favorable conditions for a year and how much longer is not known. In this preliminary struggle with the Cicada both the wasp and its victim often fall to the ground, and the wasp must then carry the latter back into the tree to get a vantage point from which to fly in the direction of her burrow. Frequently it will be necessary to carry the Cicada several times up into a tree, with the expenditure of great labor, before the burrow of the wasp is reached.

The particular species of wasp under consideration chooses for burrows the dryer and more elevated portions of lawns, especially the slight terraces along the sides of roadways. Experience shows that the species requires comparatively dry ground in which to undergo its transformations, excessive moisture inducing mold in the stored Cicadas, many of the specimens unearthed being destroyed by this agent. On the other hand, in dry earth I have found Cicadas in excellent preservation, which had evidently been placed there a year previous, but under which the wasp egg had failed, for some reason, to hatch. The burrows consist of a gently sloping entrance, extending for about 6 inches, when ordinarily a turn is made at right angles and the excavation continued 6 or 8 inches further, terminating in a globular cell about 1½ inches in diameter. Frequently a number of branches leave the main burrow at about the same point, and terminate, after a length of 6 or 8 inches, in cells similar to the one described. More commonly, however, the branches leave the main burrow at irregular intervals. The different types of burrow are shown in the illustration. (Fig. 33) *e* representing the entrance and *c* the cell. The cells, which are remarkably uniform in size and shape, contain one or sometimes two Cicadas, those stored with two being on the whole the more numerous. In the cells containing two Cicadas the larva acquires larger size, and as the female wasp is a good deal larger than the male, this would indicate that one Cicada only is required for the latter and two for the former, though I have no idea that the amount of nourishment influences the sex (a favorite theory with some naturalists) for I believe that sex is predetermined in the egg.

FIG. 35.—Cicada in burrow of Sphecius, with full-grown larva of latter feeding—natural size (original).

The exceedingly delicate, pure white, elongate-ovoid egg of this species is deposited in such a position as to be covered by the median thigh of the Cicada. (See Fig. 34.) In hatching, the larva does not emerge from the skin of the egg, but merely protrudes its head and begins at once to draw nourishment from between the sternal sutures of the Cicada. (See Fig. 35.) The egg requires but two or three days to hatch, and the larval life is very brief, not much exceeding a week. The general form of the mature larva is shown at Fig. 36 *a*. It possesses great extensile and retractile power, which enables it to thoroughly explore and exhaust the body contents of its prey. At full growth it measures from 1¼ to 2 inches in length, and is nearly white in color. The head and mouth parts (Fig. 36 e, f, g) are remarkably well developed for a Hymenopterous larva. The cocoon is constructed very rapidly, not

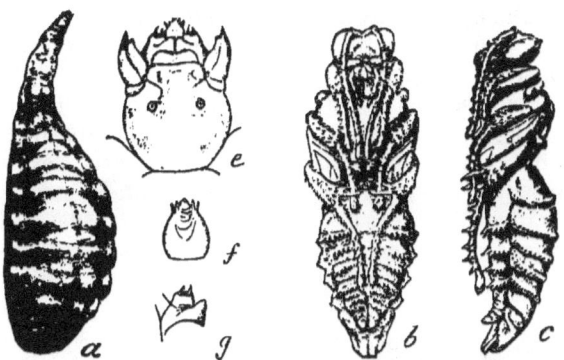

FIG. 36.—*Sphecius speciosus*: a, larva; b, pupa from below; c. same, from side—natural size; e. head of larva; f, labium of same; g, maxilla of same—enlarged (original).

more than two days being required for this purpose. The larva in the act of constructing its cocoon is shown in Fig. 37. The cocoon at first consists of an open cylinder, the ends of which are ultimately closed. It is constructed of earth, with enough silk incorporated to make a rather dense body. About the middle of the cocoon are a number (about a dozen) of very curious pores (Fig. 38) and these have, so far as I know, never before been observed or described in the cocoons of any other fossorial wasps, and their use can only be surmised.

In the completed cocoon they are cap-

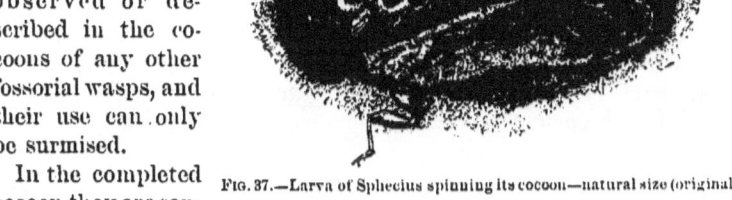

FIG. 37.—Larva of Sphecius spinning its cocoon—natural size (original).

ped on the inside, but during construction they must have been open and afforded a means of entrance for air, for ventilation, and respiration. They are placed in two irregular rows on one side of the cocoon and rise like minute tubercles with a truncate rim somewhat above the general surface exteriorly. They are composed of a glue-like substance and penetrate the wall of the cocoon, broadening to the inside, where they are closed, first, by a lining of silk, then by a thickened layer of the glue, and finally by silk which gives this median portion of the cocoon, inside, a paler coloring than the rest. In the cocoon of *Bembea obsolotus*, which I have received from Mr. Coquillett from southern California, and which is composed of agglutinated sand, these perforations are smaller and in a single row of seven or eight encircling the middle, but they have a similar structure.

The larva remains unchanged in this cocoon over winter, and transforms to the pupa state in the spring, shortly before the appearance of the mature insect. The pupa (Fig. 36 *b, c.*) resembles the mature insect in general appearance, but, as in all such cases, is soft-fleshed and whitish in color. It rapidly hardens and changes to the dark color of the imago, which is ready in a few days to gnaw its way out of the pupal cell, and, passing through the burrow made by the perfect insect the previous year, begins again the cycle of existence which its emergence has just completed.

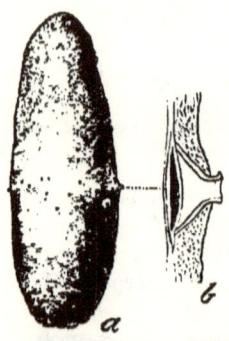

FIG. 38.—*a*, cocoon of Sphecius natural size; *b*, enlarged section of pore (original).

This, as I said before, will serve as a type of the development and life history of the other fossorial wasps, although they differ greatly in the style of burrow and form of cell which they make to protect their future progeny, and in the character of the food with which they provision such cells. A most interesting article could, in fact, be written on the habits of these different species, some of which use spiders of various kinds, including Tarantulas, while others use various soft larvæ, especially those of a Lepidopterous nature. Those who are interested in further details on the subject will find a popular exposition in the first volume of the *American Entomologist*, written mainly by my associate on that journal, the late B. D. Walsh.

If man could do what these wasps have done from time immemorial, viz, preserve for an indefinite period the animals he feeds on by the simple insertion of some toxic fluid in the tissues, he would be able to revolutionize the present methods of shipping cattle and sheep, and to obviate much of the cruelty which now attends the transportation of live stock and much of the expense involved in cold storage.

THE HABITS OF ELASMUS.

By L. O. Howard.

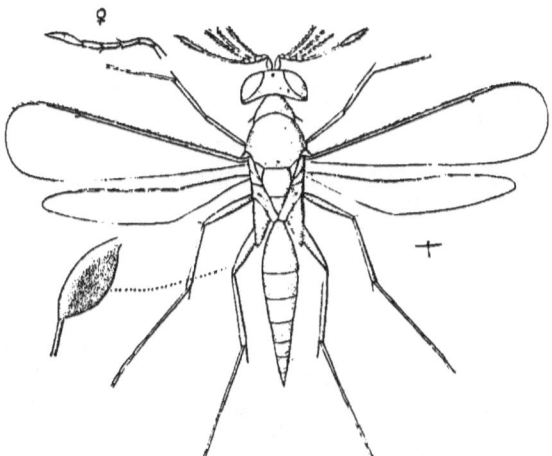

Fig. 39.—*Elasmus rarius*, male—greatly enlarged (original).

The Chalcidid parasites of the genus *Elasmus* Westwood differ so markedly in their structure from all of the other members of the family that they have been placed alone in a separate subfamily Elasminæ. The most striking characters of these minute creatures are their greatly enlarged and flattened hind coxæ, the large meso-postscutellum and the long marginal vein. They have also enlarged hind femora like the Chalcidinæ, except that they are more flattened, and they have flabellate antennæ in the male as in certain Eulophinæ. The species are rather rare in Europe but seem to be more common in this country. Differing from other characteristic and restricted groups these insects vary greatly in their host relations. They attack, generally, two classes of insects: small Lepidopterous larvæ and Microgasters. The European species have been reared from *Psyche graminella*, *Epichnopteryx helix*, *Cecidomyia rosaria*, and a gall on *Populus tremuloides*. Thomson makes the general comment upon the species of this genus that they are parasitic upon Microgasters.

The four species first reared in this country were *E. rarius* How., *E. nigripes* How., *E. pullatus* How., and *E. tischeriæ* How. All of these were indicated in the notes of the Division as having been reared from Tineid leaf-miners, but it is interesting to note that in the cases of *E. rarius* and *E. pullatus* Microgasters were also bred from the host insects. *E. albicoxa* How., was found in the breeding jar with eggs of *Limenitis disippus*, and may come either from a leaf-miner in the Willow leaves upon which these eggs were laid or from the Microgaster which commonly preys upon the young larvæ of this butterfly, *Apanteles limenitidis* Riley.

E. tischeriæ was reared under circumstances, however, which leave no doubt that it is a primary parasite of *Tischeria solidaginifoliella*. I have recorded upon page 29 of Bulletin No. 5 of this Division the fact that not only was no Microgaster observed, but the Elasmus larva was several times found feeding externally, just prior to pupation, upon the larva of the leaf-miner. This observation definitely settles the fact, till then unproven, that Elasmus is sometimes beneficial. Another species as yet undescribed has also been reared from the cocoons of *Aspidisca splendoriforella*, upon which species it is undoubtedly a primary parasite.

The Microgaster feeding habit would rest upon the general statement of Thomson were it not for the fact that we have reared a large series of *Elasmus atratus* How. MS., from the cocoons of *Apanteles hyphantriæ* Riley, and from the cocoons of *Limneria pallipes* Prov., which, as well as the Apanteles, is parasitic upon *Hyphantria cunea* in the District of Columbia. This curious variation in host habit is so interesting that we bring together the facts and illustrate the genus by Fig. 39, which represents the male of *E. rarius*. Entomologists who may be engaged in rearing the Microlepidoptera will probably meet with other species of this genus, and there is every reason to suppose that the group is largely represented in the United States. It is perhaps still more largely represented in the West Indian fauna, since we have found eight species in a small collection made by Mr. H. H. Smith on the island of St. Vincent.

The illustrations upon Plate IX of the Annual Report of the Entomologist, Annual Report of the U. S. Department of Agriculture for 1888, at Fig. 2, represent a new genus of Elasminæ from Australia to which Prof. Riley has given the MS. name *Euryischia lestophoni*. This insect is parasitic upon *Lestophonus iceryæ* Williston, a small Dipterous parasite of the Fluted Scale.

BEES OF GREAT VALUE TO FRUIT AND SEED GROWERS.

By Frank Benton.

At last fruit-growers and bee-keepers are getting into right relations with each other. The numerous discussions which have taken place regarding the value of bees as fertilizers of fruit blossoms and of those blossoms of plants grown for their seeds, and regarding the alleged damage to fruit by bees have led to close observation and careful experimentation, the results of which show that the interests of these two classes of producers conflict in but trifling respects—that, in fact, bee-keepers and fruit-growers are of great help to each other, and even indispensable if each is to obtain the best results in his work.

Bee keepers have never complained but that the growing of fruit in the vicinity of their apiaries was a great benefit to their interests, hence their position has been merely a defensive one, the battle waxing warm only when poisonous substances were set out to kill off the bees, or when fruit-growers sprayed their orchards with poisonous insecticides during the time the trees were in blossom, or again when efforts were made to secure by legislation the removal of bees from a certain locality as nuisances. Fruit-growers first relented when close observation and experiment showed that wasps bit open tender fruits, birds pecked them, they cracked under the action of sun and rains, and hail sometimes cut them, the bees only coming in to save the wasting juices of the injured fruit. The wide publicity given to the results of the experiments made under the direction of the United States entomologist and published in the report of the Commissioner of Agriculture for 1885 have no doubt contributed much to secure this change among fruit-growers.

But now it would appear that the bees have not only been vindicated, but that in the future fruit-growers are likely to be generally regarded as more indebted to bee-keepers than the latter are to the fruit-growers, for the amount of honey the bees secure from fruit blossoms comes far short of equaling in value that part of the fruit crop which many accurate observations and experiments indicate is due to the complete cross-fertilization of the blossoms by bees. The observations and researches of Hildebrand, Müller, Delpino, Darwin, and others, as well as the excellent explanation of the subject in Cheshire's recent work,* have gone far to prove how greatly blossoms depend upon the agency of bees for their fertilization and hence for the production of seeds and fruits

The facts they have brought forward are gradually becoming more widely known among fruit-growers and bee-keepers, and additional evidence accumulates. A case illustrating very clearly the value of bees in an orchard has recently come to the notice of the writer, and its authenticity is confirmed by correspondence with the parties named, who are gentlemen of long and extensive experience in fruit-growing, recognized in their locality as being authorities, particularly in regard to cherry-culture. The facts are these: For several years the cherry crop of Vaca Valley in Solano County, Cal., has not been good, although it was formerly quite sure. The partial or complete failures have been attributed to north winds, chilling rains, and similar climatic conditions, but in the minds of Messrs. Bassford, of Cherry Glen, these causes did not sufficiently account for all the cases of failure.

These gentlemen recollected that formerly when the cherry crops were good wild bees were very plentiful in the valley, and hence thought perhaps the lack of fruit since most of the bees had disappeared, might

---

*"Bees and Bee-keeping, Scientific and Practical," by Frank R. Cheshire, F. L. S., F. R. M. S., vol. I, pp. 279-328.

be due to imperfect distribution of the pollen of the blossoms. To test the matter they placed therefore several hives of bees in their orchard in 1890. The result was striking, for the Bassford orchard bore a good crop of cherries, while other growers in the valley who had no bees found their crops entire or partial failures. This year (1891) Messrs. Bassford had some sixty-five hives of bees in their orchard, and Mr. H. A. Bassford writes to the Entomologist: " Our crop was good this season, and we attribute it to the bees." And he adds further:

Since we have been keeping bees our cherry crop has been much larger than formerly, while those orchards nearest us, five miles from here, where no bees are kept, have produced but light crops.

The *Vacaville Enterprise* said last spring, when referring to the result of the experiment for 1890:

Other orchardists are watching this enterprise with great interest, and may conclude that to succeed in cherry culture a bee-hive and a cherry orchard must be planted side by side.

And now that the result for 1891 is known, "others," so Mr. Bassford writes, "who have cherry orchards in the valley are procuring bees to effect the fertilization of the blossoms."

SOME BRED WEST VIRGINIA BRACONIDÆ.

By A. D. HOPKINS, *Morgantown, W. Va.*

(*West Virginia Agricultural Experiment Station.*)

Subfamily **BRACONINÆ**.

Parasites.	Host.
Bracon belfragei Cress	*Lixus scrobicollis*. Cocoons found in larval mine of host in pith of *Ambrosia artemisiafolia* (Ragweed). April 9. Imago emerged May 12.
Bracon mavoritus Cress	*Lixus scrobicollis*. Cocoons found in pith of *Ambrosia trifida* in larval mines of host, Dec. 24. Imago found emerged Feb. 24. Same in *Ambrosia artemisiafolia*, Apr. 20. Larva (?) taken feeding on pupa of host, Dec. 24. *Tetropium cinnamopterum*. Imago taken in sapwood of *Abies nigra* in pupal chamber of host, July 8.
Bracon simplex Cress	Buprestid and Longicorn larvæ. Taken with ovipositor inserted in bark of *Fagus ferruginea* (Beech) infested by host. *Neoclytus* larva. Taken with ovipositor inserted under bark of *Abies nigra*, Aug. 29. Observed frequent at same time on Spruce logs, and flying in Spruce forests.*

---

* Lumbermen supposed this to be the insect which killed the trees.

| Parasites. | Host. |

Bracon agrili Ashm..................*Neoclytus erythrocephalus.* Cocoons found frequent under bark and in sapwood of *Carya alba* (Hickory) in larval and pupal mines of host, Apr. 25. Imago emerged May 18.

Bracon agrili Ashm......................Two specimens taken with ovipositor inserted in Longicorn larvæ, under apple bark, July 20.

Bracon xanthostigmus Cr.................*Agrilus ruficollis.* Cocoons found in pith of Blackberry cane in larval mines of host, May 20. In same, under bark of Raspberry canes, Mar. 11 and Apr. 25. Imagos emerged Apr. 7 and June 16. Flying Aug. 24. Also bred from Gouty Gall on Blackberry cane, May 2. Imagos emerged Apr. 7.

Bracon lixi Ashm.. MS ....*Lixus scrobicollis* (?) Cocoons found in pith of *Ambrosia trifida*, in larval mines of host, Dec. 24. Imago found, emerged Feb. 24.

Bracon pectinator Say................ ....*Melanophila fulroguttata.* Bred from cocoons found in larval mines of host, Mar. 30.

prestid and Longicorn larvæ. Cocoons found in mines of host under bark of *Abies nigra*, Mar. 31. Imago emerged Apr. 20.

Buprestid larva. *Chrysobothris femorata* (?). Bred from cocoons found under White Oak bark in mines of host, Apr. 9.

Bracon eurygaster Brullé.................Longicorn larva. In mine ot host under bark of dying Elm (*Ulmus rubra*), August.

Subfamily Exothecinæ.

Rhysipolis biformis Ashm., MS...........Buprestid or Longicorn larva. Bred from cocoon found under bark of dead *Abies nigra*, in mines of host. Mar. 31. Sept. 14.

Subfamily Rhyssalinæ.

Rhyssalus pityophthori Ashm., MS.......*Pityophthorus* sp. Bred from Yellow Pine twigs infested by host July 29.

Subfamily Spathiinæ.

Spathius clavipennis Ashm., MS ....*Polygraphus rufipennis.* Bred from cocoons found under bark of dead *Abies nigra*, in mines of host March 26. Imago emerged April 20.

Spathius brunneus Ashm.................*Scolytus muticus* (?) and *Agrilus fallax.* Bred from branches of *Celtis occidentalis*, infested by these two beetles May 2.

| Parasites. | Host. |

Spathius canadensis Ashm ....*Phlaosinus graniger*. Bred from cocoons found plentiful under bark of *Juniperus virginiana* (Red Cedar) in mines of host Apr. 14, 18, 23. Imago emerged May 10.
Tomicus sp. Bred from cocoons in mines of host in White Pine bark, Mar. 31.
Dryocates autographus. Cocoons found under bark of dead *Abies excelsa* in mines of host, Mar. 15. Imago emerged Apr. 6.
Curculionid. Bred from cocoons and larva found under bark of dead *Pinus inops* in cocoons of host. Sept. 23.
Magdalis olyra (?). Bred from branches of *Carya alba* infested by larva, pupa, and beetles, Apr. 29.

Spathius brevicaudus Ashm. MS .... *Dryocates autographus*. Bred from cocoons in mine of host under bark of dead *Abies excelsa*, Nov. 10, 1890, and Mar. 15, 1891.

Spathius simillimus Ashm. MS .... Bred from unknown cocoon found in sapwood of decaying *Abies nigra*, host unknown, Mar. 29.
Buprestid larva. Cocoons taken in mines of host, Mar. 31. Imago emerged May 1.
Agrilus bilineatus. Cocoons found in green bark on White Oak stump in mines of host Apr. 25. May 2, and May 4. Imagos emerged May 18 and 25.

Spathius unifasciatus Ashm. MS .... *Scolytus 4-spinosus*. Bred from cocoons found under bark of *Carya alba* in larval mines of host, Apr. 29.

Subfamily **Hecabolinæ**.

Lysitermus scolyticida Ashm. MS .... *Scolytus 4-spinosus*. Bred from cocoons found under Hickory bark in mines of host, Apr. 30.

Cænophanes languriæ Ashm. MS .... *Languria* (?) larva. Cocoons taken in pith of *Ambrosia trifida* containing larvæ of host, Dec. 24. Imago found emerged Feb. 24. Same in *Ambrosia artemisiæfolia* Nov. 13. Imago found emerged Feb. 24.

Cænophanes pityophthori Ashm. MS...... *Pityophthorus* sp. Bred from cocoon found in mine of host under bark of small dying Spruce (*Abies nigra*), Feb. 24.

Cænophanes anthaxiæ Ashm. MS .... *Anthaxia viridicornis*. Bred from section of Willow infested by host, and from cocoons found in mines of same host, May 4, June 24.
Agrilus larva. Cocoon taken from mines of host under bark and in sapwood of Dogwood (*Cornus florida*), Apr. 14. Imago emerged May 26.

Cænophanes hylotrupidis Ashm. MS ..... Longicorn larvæ. Bred from cocoons found in mines of host in *Juniperus virginiana*, Apr. 4.

Subfamily **Doryctinæ**.
Parasites. *Host.*
Doryctes erythromelas Brullé............Longicorn (?). Bred from cocoon found in mine of host, Apr. 3.

Subfamily **Rhogadinæ**.
Rhogas intermedius Cress...............*Acronycta americana* larva. 76 imagos emerged from host Oct. 5. Flying Sept. 15.

Subfamily **Microgasterinæ**.
Apanteles congregatus Say.............Cocoon found under bark of dead Norway Spruce. Imago emerged Feb. 27.
Apanteles xylina Say ....*Pionea rimosalis*. Bred from cocoons on and with host on Cabbage, July 26.*
Apanteles sp. ....*Orgyia leucostigma*. Bred from host, Oct.
Apanteles flavicoucha Riley............Bred from cocoons found on weed stubble, Apr. 23. Imago emerged Apr. 30.

Subfamily **Agathidinæ**.
Microdus simillimus Cress ....*Lixus scrobicollis* and Lepidopterous larvæ. Bred from cocoons found in Ragweed pith infested by host, Apr. 27. Imagos emerged May 1. Plenty on Gooseberry bushes in bloom and infested by *Nematus ventricosus*, May 2.

Subfamily **Calyptinæ**.
Calyptus tibiator Cress..................Lepidopterous larva. Cocoons taken from pith of *Ambrosia artemisiæfolia* in mines of host, Apr. 27. Emerged May 8. Flying, May 8.

Subfamily **Helconinæ**.
Helcon ligator Say ....*Scolytus muticus* and *Agrilus egenus*. Bred from branches of *Celtis occidentalis* infested by host.
Helcon tetrapodii Ashm. MS.............*Tetropium cinnamopterum*. Cocoon found in pupal chamber of host in sapwood of Spruce log (*Abies nigra*) July 8. Imago emerged July 14.

Subfamily **Aphidiinæ**.
Aphidius avenaphis Fitch................*Aphis mali*. Bred from Aphids on nursery stock, July 20.

The Braconidæ mentioned above were determined by Dr. Riley and Mr. Ashmead; the Buprestidæ and Cerambycidæ imagos by Dr. Horn, and the Scolytidæ by Mr. W. Eichhoff, Germany. Mr. Ashmead has prepared descriptions of the new Braconidæ.

* This species was found plentifully wherever the host was observed. Gardeners generally were destroying the cocoons, supposing they were the eggs of the caterpillars.

NOTES ON THE HABITS OF SOME CALIFORNIA COLEOPTERA.

By D. W. Coquillett, Los Angeles, Cal.

Tritoma californica.—Found several larvæ in lamellæ of fungi on a rotten willow stump February 24. Beetles issued April 29.

Anthaxia æneogaster.—Found this beetle in a burrow beneath the bark of a dead and dry branch of *Juglans californica* February 6. In a similar situation was a nearly grown larva, evidently of this species.

A second beetle was in its burrow in a dead and dry branch of *Juglans californica* March 9; it was in the solid wood, and its burrow was next to and at right angles with the surface.

Hydnocera scabra.—Two larvæ were found beneath loose bark on an apple tree infested with Woolly Aphis January 16. I placed in its cage two Tineid larvæ, which it attacked and extracted their juices. Spun in bottom of box a thin white cocoon, through which the pupa is plainly seen. Pupated May 10; beetle May 30. Found a pupa among dead leaves in crotch of orange tree June 4, and the beetle issued June 13. One in cocoon of *Carpocapsa pomonella*, beneath loose bark on an apple tree, March 24.

Hedobia granosa.—Found a tough gray elliptical cocoon 3 by 5^{mm} long, beneath loosened bark of a dead, dry branch of *Juglans californica* February 7; the beetle issued March 8 through a large irregular hole on one side, just before the end.

Trilleta expansa.—Found many larvæ in dead and dry wood of *Quercus agrifolia* September 22. Two living beetles were found in the breeding can February 21, and twelve more March 26.

Sinoxylon declive.—Two beetles of this species were in the can containing orange wood July 20 (the same wood as that from which *Lyctus striatus* mentioned below were bred); five more July 26, three of them in their burrows in the wood; these burrows usually extend lengthwise with the grain, are cylindrical, and packed firmly with gnawed wood. In these burrows I found larvæ which agree closely with those of *Psoa maculata*.

Mr. Edwin C. Van Dyke informs me that he has bred this species from dead Acacia wood and also from *Umbellularia californica*. The pupa is similar to that of *Psoa maculata*.

Before pupating the larva gnaws a burrow to the surface nearly at right angles to its regular burrow and takes up a position about three-fourths of an inch from its mouth, packing it firmly on either side, and pupating in the cell thus formed. In the burrow the larva presses the hind half of its body against the under side of the front half, pressing the legs forward. I found the pupa in the orange wood July 27. Mr. Compere, of Los Angeles, informs me that these beetles sometimes bore into the pith of rather large sized rose bushes that have been cut off near the top. At Orange a *Sinoxylon declive* was found in its burrow in a piece of orange wood turned into a potato masher and left in the turning lathe over night. The beetle had burrowed into this stick during the night.

Sinoxylon suturale.—Found several pupæ and a few recently transformed beetles in their burrows in dead grape vines October 4. They were mostly at the joints, usually two at each joint. In one of the burrows I found a parasitic pupa not inclosed in a cocoon. The parasite issued October 28.

Amphicerus punctipennis.—On the 4th of October I found two of these beetles in a burrow in a dead and dry branch of a fig tree. March 26 I found three beetles, each in a burrow in a dead and dry grape cane. They had evidently burrowed into the cane while in the beetle state, since their heads were turned in an opposite direction from the mouth of the burrow. Two of the beetles were dead, but the third was still alive.

Psoa maculata.—Found many larvæ in dry apple limbs October 9. Several had entered the tips of the lateral short branches and extended their burrows down the main branches, packing them with a sawdust-like substance. October 11 I found several larvæ and one pupa in dead and dry prunings of grapevines.

On the 1st of January I found four beetles and eleven pupæ in a rotten stem of *Audibertia polystachya;* the beetles had but recently escaped from the pupæ and no larvæ were found. By the 14th of January four beetles had issued. I captured a beetle of this species at Santa Barbara April 11.

Lyctus striatus.—Found several pupæ in a dead grapevine October 4; they were in their burrows between the joints. Two beetles issued October 10, and three others were in their burrows October 22.

October 28, 1888, I obtained several pieces of wood from a trunk of an orange tree that had been cut down about two years previously; at that time there were numerous round holes in it about one-sixteenth of an inch in diameter, and upon splitting it open I found a great many burrows closely packed with the gnawed wood. I inclosed this wood in a tin can, and one beetle was found June 1, 1889; the can was last examined May 15. When next examined, June 19, three beetles were found; twelve were found July 20 and three July 26.

March 21 I obtained several pieces of dead and dry sycamore wood containing the burrows of wood-boring insects, and June 1 two living and two dead beetles of this species were found. This box was last examined May 15.

Phymatodes juglandis.—These beetles were in their burrows in the sapwood just beneath the bark of a branch of *Juglans californica* March 9. Some of them were still soft, having but recently issued from the pupa state. In this same situation I found a pupa and several legless larvæ, evidently of this species.

Xylotrechus nauticus.—Found several larvæ of this species in a dead and dry stump of *Quercus agrifolia* December 9, 1889; they bore oval holes in the wood, the holes extending from the interior of the stump direct to the surface and continuing nearly through the bark. In some of these burrows I found three dead beetles of *X. nauticus*. A living beetle was in this box July 17, 1890.

Ipochus fasciatus.—Found four larvæ October 10 in dead and dry apple twigs. When extended the body is a trifle thicker at each end than in the middle. August 2 one was still a larva, and in one of the burrows I found a dead beetle. Found several adults of this species beneath projecting bark on apple tree June 4.

Cassida texana.—Found many larvæ and five beetles on *Solanum xanti* May 12. Beetles issued May 29.

Phlœodes diabolicus.—Found three larvæ in rotten willow stumps February 28. Found one in rotten sycamore log March 24. September 8 found several of these larvæ in a rotten willow stump, and in the same stump I found a pupa, evidently of this species, and a beetle still in its cell in the rotten wood.

Cœlocnemis californicus.—Three larvæ were taken, May 20, in a rotten sycamore stump. One pupated July 3 and the beetle issued July 18.

EARLY PUBLISHED REFERENCES TO SOME OF OUR INJURIOUS INSECTS.

By F. M. WEBSTER.

It was in the legislature of one of the western States, I believe, that, in a speech opposing a certain measure, a member stated that we had no destructive insects until the advent of entomologists, and, now, the more entomologists the more bugs and the greater the damage. Among the unentomological an insect is new or old according as it has happened to be observed, and while no one would for a moment concur in the opinion of the statesman, as above expressed, nevertheless even the entomologist is sometimes puzzled to determine whether or not he is dealing with a new subject or an old one, and often, too, after he has carefully followed his new depredator through its entire cycle, at the expense of weeks of study, and publishes his results, ere the ink of the printer is dry, in some old dusty volume, where he least expects it, he will find that as much or even more had been learned years before.

Then, too, the early history of some of our best known species is enveloped in obscurity, and it is probable that they were destructive in the fields of the aborigines long before the advent of the white man. John Josselyn, who styled himself "gentleman," and made a voyage to New England in 1638–'39, and again in 1663, remaining until 1671, tells us in a record of his voyages that, in the cornfields of the natives, "there is a bug that lies in the earth and eateth the seed, that is somewhat like a maggot, of a white color with a red head, and about the bigness of one's finger, and an inch or an inch and a half long," which in our day we at once recognize as the white grub. For many years these worms were believed to turn to briers. In 1824 Mr. Jacob Cist figured the fungus parasite of these worms, *Torrubia ravenelii*, and though he disapproved of the brier theory, he accounted for the presence of the growth by considering it to be the sprouts of corn originating from kernels which had been eaten by the worm.*

William Wood, who visited this country in 1629 to 1633, stated that the Indians exceeded the English husbandmen in keeping their fields clean of weeds and "undermining worms." As early as 1736 John Bartram complains of his plums being destroyed by an insect, and, later, states that all stone fruits except the Peach were subject to attack, some kinds of cherries outgrowing it.†

In a paper read before the Agricultural Society of Bucks County, Pa., July 29, 1822,‡ Mr. James Worth calls attention to the following insects affecting wheat: First, a little worm found in the lower part of the stalks of wheat and rye, in spring and fall, and about the joints in June; second, a worm in the straw above the upper joints, which causes the early change of color of the ear, assuming a ripe appearance but producing no grain; third, a species of louse or Aphis which infest grounds and feed upon the roots of wheat, corn, young trees, etc., and do immense damage. Under the head of the first there was doubtless a confusion of *Isosoma hordei* (and possibly *tritici*, also, as the larvæ are described later as being pale yellow with brown spots about the mouth) and *Meromyza americana*, and possibly also a species of *Oscinis*. The second points unerringly to *Meromyza*, the larvæ being clearly described in Memoirs of Penn. Agricultural Society, Vol. 1. p. 165, and antedates the discovery and description of the species by Dr. Fitch about thirty-four years.

According to a notice in the *Prairie Farmer*, p. 216 of volume for 1845, this insect was reported in Michigan. Of this notice the following sentence is very significant: "In one instance nine eggs were found in a single straw, one of which had just hatched." Specimens of infested straw were also forwarded to the *Country Gentleman* from Scipioville, N. Y., in 1879, which the sender stated contained eggs, besides larvæ and pupæ.

Now, the eggs of any of the insects known to affect this portion of the stem of the wheat plant, are by far too minute to be noticed by the unskilled observer. As we have elsewhere shown,§ the larvæ of *Meromyza* are attacked by a species of mite, *Heteropus ventricosus*, the gravid

---

*American Journal of Science, Vol. 8, pp. 269-271, Pl. 4.
† The Cultivator. New Series. Vol. 7, p. 269.
‡ American Farmer, Vol. 4, p. 394.
§ Rep. Comm. Agr., 1884, p. 390.

female of which has the appearance of a globular egg, and it seems at least reasonable that reports of eggs having been found in connection with these larvæ were due to a confusion of the parasites whereby they were taken for eggs. This question is of peculiar interest, as, if this be true the occurrence of *Heteropus* in America in 1845, would by several years antedate its discovery and description in England by Newport. In 1856, Dr. Asa Fitch described under the name of *Aphis maidis* a species of Aphides affecting the stems of roasting ears, in August.* And in 1863 Mr. B. D. Walsh reared what, until quite recently, at least, was supposed to be the root form of this species from roots of corn.† Thirty-four years prior to the appearance of the first of these publications, Mr. Tho. Emory, of Poplar Grove (State not given). in a communication relating to a disease of wheat known as "Sedging," says, "I believe this insect is the same as that known by the name of the root-louse in corn, so frequently found in that plant, growing after clover, when the land is early flushed, and which occasions so stunted and diseased growth that it rarely recovers until late in the summer, and not then if the season is dry."‡

Another corn insect was reported from Buckingham, Va., in 1828, by Mr. Charles Yancey, the depredator being "a little white worm with copper-colored head," which perforated the stalks of young corn just below the surface of the ground, which destroyed the growth.§ This depredator and its method of attack agree so closely with what we know of the larvæ of *Diabrotica 12-punctata*, which has since been observed working similar injury in Virginia,|| that it appears quite probable that this is an early exhibit of its destructive propensities. The injury to Blue Grass, which has since been found to be largely caused by a species of Thrips, was observed in New York as early as 1844, but the depredator was not discovered.¶

The advent of the Striped Cucumber Beetle, *Diabrotica vittata*, is enveloped in obscurity, but the use of covered frames for the protection of the vines dates back to 1823.** The small beetle, *Byturus unicolor*, though studied as a raspberry insect by both Fitch†† and Packard‡‡ in 1870, bobs up serenely in the Rural New Yorker as a new depredator, from Michigan, in 1885.§§

The new inspiration given to the studies of the economic features of entomology by the establishment of experiment stations is very proper,

---

* Second Rep. Ins. N. Y., pp. 318-320, 1856.
† Proc. Ent. Soc. Phil., vol. 1, p. 300, 1863.
‡ American Farmer, vol. 4, p. 71, May 24, 1822.
§ American Farmer, vol. 10, p. 3, 1828.
|| Insect Life, vol. 4, p. 104.
¶ The Cultivator, New Series, vol. 1, p. 206, July, 1844.
** American Farmer, vol. 4, p. 374, 1828.
†† Fourteenth Report, p. 358.
‡‡ Insects, New and Little Known. Pamph., p. 12.
§§ Rural New Yorker, August 22, 1885.

and the feeling of emulation among scientific workers quite commendable, yet in all of this activity it is well before one does the honors of introducing to his fellows a new-found depredator to look well to it that some one has not performed the same office even before the time of either himself or his immediate ancestors. .The earlier agricultural and horticultural publications of the country are full of references to the depredations of insects whose names, if they had any, were unknown to the observer, yet often the most important characteristics are so clearly described as to leave little or no doubt as to the species involved.

THE COLOR OF A HOST AND ITS RELATION TO PARASITISM.

By C. W. STILES, Ph. D., and A. HASSALL, M. R. C. V. S., *Bureau of Animal Industry, U. S. Department of Agriculture.*

In Prof.Wallace's book on Darwinism, it is stated that white cattle are more subject to the attack of flies than dark colored cattle, and that white fowls are more subject to the gape-worm disease than dark fowls. In regard to the former statement, two explanations immediately occurred to us, *i. e.*, (1) the flies would be more easily seen upon a white background than upon a dark background, and the assumed correlation between the host and its parasites would be in this case only apparent, or (2) the white color might attract the flies more than a dark color. It is, in fact, a common household belief that if objects of various colors are suspended from the ceiling of a room, the light-colored objects attract the flies more than the dark colored objects. We can hardly see, though, how the white color of fowls can stand in any relation to their Nematode parasites, since the latter have no organs of sight, and the only explanation which we could imagine was that the white fowls are constitutionally weaker than dark fowls, and would on this account succumb more easily to the ravages of the worms than darker fowls with hardier constitutions. There is, however, serious objection to assuming that white fowls are inferior to dark fowls, since white breeds of fowls exist which are very hardy—the White Leghorn, for instance.

Upon inquiring among our friends we find the most contradictory opinions in regard to the two statements by Wallace mentioned above. Mr. Howard states that there is certainly no connection between the color of cattle and the Horn-fly (*Hæmatobia serrata*); several persons have noticed that white horses are attacked more by flies than dark horses, while other persons are not willing to admit this statement. From two sources we have the statement that on two farms it was very noticeable that the white chickens were considerably weaker than the dark fowls, while from other sources we have the opposite statement.

In hopes of obtaining some decisive evidence for or against Professor

Wallace's statements we cordially invite correspondence upon this subject with veterinarians, stock-raisers, and farmers, and shall be pleased to compile the result of this correspondence for a later issue of this journal.

EXTRACTS FROM CORRESPONDENCE.

The Effects of a Spider Bite on a Child.

On the 5th of last October I returned home with my wife and infant child from a week's visit in Boston, arriving about 7 o'clock p. m., and as soon as the cradle was ready the child was soon asleep, being very tired. We had been home nearly two hours and the child in bed an hour or a little less when we were startled by piercing cries from the bedroom. Taking up a lamp and followed by my wife I hastened into the room, much startled by the unusual severity of the crying. The little one was sitting up in her cradle and seemed to be in great pain and badly frightened; yet we could see no signs of illness nor cause for fright, and it was some time before my wife could quiet her. At last the crying gave place to sobbing, with less frequent spells of convulsive trembling, that at first had been almost constant. So, thinking all was favorable, I returned to my letters, leaving my wife with the infant in her arms. I had been at my desk but a few minutes when I was called again to the side of the child, when my wife drew my attention to the child's left eye, and there I noticed for the first time that the under lid was highly inflamed and somewhat swollen, the swelling extending for nearly an inch along the lid, and with the exception of a slight tinge on the cheek the inflammation was confined at this time to the lid.

Thinking it was the result of the bite of a mosquito, I bathed the swollen part with a solution of Hamamelis, and for a time this seemed to soothe the pain, and my wife soon felt warranted in again placing her in the cradle. Again I was called into the room by my wife, who informed me that a spider was on the pillow. Taking the lamp I examined the cradle, and, sure enough, there was a small and rather handsome colored spider, which I secured and placed in a pill box for future identification. The child was very fretful, and the inflammation and swelling were rapidly increasing, and now (at 10:30 p. m.) it covered the whole under eyelid and extended to the side of the nose and cheek. The child was in a high fever, the skin dry and hot, pulse rapid, but seemed very weak. She no longer cried as before, but the restlessness increased, while there was almost incessant trembling, as if in great fear or very cold. A 5 per cent solution of carbolic acid was used two or three times, but later on was discarded for ammonia. No special benefit could be observed by the use of either, Hamamelis having the most soothing effect. A little past midnight the inflammation had extended to the upper eyelid, and it soon became evident that it was following a rapid course that would include the right eye, and had already worked downward halfway to the lip on the left cheek. Before 2 o'clock it had crossed the nose, and quite a severe swelling began on the eyelids, but before it reached the right eye it had extended on the left side of the forehead nearly to the hair. At 3 o'clock the inflammation remained the same; the left eye could scarcely be opened, and that only with great difficulty, the fever still high, but pulse more normal, nervous twitchings of the muscles less, and quiet sleep took the place of the uneasy naps.

There was no nausea at any time, and after 3 o'clock food was taken. In the morning the fever had subsided, but the inflammation and swelling were as virulent as ever, and it was not until the end of the third day that it had subsided sufficiently to be considered much better, and nearly two weeks before no trace could be seen of it. The place where the spider inflicted the wound was very minute, scarcely noticed until after the inflammation had reached its limit, and looked more like the puncture caused by the sting of some small Hymenopterous insect than anything else; the wound was of a higher color and there was a hard but small lump on the lid for some days.—L. E. Hood, Massachusetts.

[The spider sent by Mr. Hood was *Latrodectus mactans*.]

Insect Pests in Bermuda.

(Extract from a Report by Vice-Consul J. B. Heyl, of Bermuda.)

This island was clear of insect pests until some time in 1858 or 1859, when a vessel was brought here in distress, with a cargo of oranges, which were sold at auction, and the fruit was carried all over the island, and in a few months our flourishing trees were covered with an insect which gave the trees the appearance of being whitewashed. This insect fed on the bark of the tree, extracting the yellow sap therefrom and causing the bark to curl up. Every device thought of was tried, but the island was soon cleaned of nearly every tree. All this came from the distress cargo.

Another insect was afterwards introduced in peaches. The island at that time was stocked with a delicious peach. This insect was a small white maggot, which destroyed all the peaches on the island. As the infested fruit fell to the ground no trouble was taken to destroy it, and the insects increased so that they attacked other fruit, mangoes, loquats, etc. The maggot turned into a very small bug. * * *

REPLY.— * * * The maggot in Peach has been recently studied and reported upon in No. 1 of vol. III, INSECT LIFE. * * * The scale-insect on the bark of Orange is the *Chionaspis citri* of Louisiana, treated in various reports of the Entomologist, which are now unfortunately out of print. The best remedy for this insect is the application of a kerosene-soap emulsion, the formula for which is given on page 3 of Circular, No. 1, new series.

Insect Injury to Cocoanut Palms.

I take the liberty to address you with a view to ascertain if it would be possible to have a remedy for the destruction of an insect called, in the island of St. Domingo, *Catarron*, and in Cuba *Cucarachon*, which attacks young cocoanut trees on the second or third year of their growth.

I own a cocoanut plantation in Samana Bay, St. Domingo, and I have found out that from the month of March to September this insect is very active in destroying young cocoanut trees. It confines, apparently, its work to the night time. I think that the *Catarron* belongs to the family of the nocturnal *Cucujo* of the West Indies or the Firefly of this country. Its size is about 1½ an inch in length, by 1 inch wide, and it is perfectly harmless. As a further illustration of the manner in which this insect accomplishes its destructive work, I will state that the young cocoanut tree, after sprouting on a seedling bed, is planted from four to six inches in the ground, leaving one-half or three-quarters over the soil. The worm attacks the tree on any side and perforates the husk to the nut, continuing its work until the sprout under the husk is reached and the heart of it is destroyed.

I have submitted the idea that perhaps by submerging the tree in coal tar mixed with bitter aloes and Paris green, the bug might be prevented from invading the husk; but they say that the fume of coal tar will kill the plant. The main point is to find some *lasting* matter to cover the surface of the husk, without injuring the tree, that will at the same time protect it against the voracity of the insect. [M. Pomarez, New York, November 10, 1891.

REPLY.—On page 136 of the current volume we have published some information relative to the Palm Weevil, which may or may not be the insect of which you complain. * * * It may be that you will consider the suggestion concerning trap palms of some practical value in your case. As you particularly mention, however, the desirability of a preventive wash, I may state that in some portions of the country the apple-tree borers are prevented from entering the trunks of apple trees by painting the trunks with soft soap reduced to the consistency of a thick paint by the addition of a strong solution of washing soda.—[November 12, 1891.]

Biological Notes on Micracis, Chramesus, and Coscinoptera.

The remarks in INSECT LIFE, vol. IV, p. 94, concerning *Micracis suturalis* and *M. aculeata* Lec., require a little consideration. Whatever may have led Messrs. Eichhoff, Judeich, and Nitsche to express the opinion that the life duration of Scolytidæ is only one year (normally), certain it is that the foregoing species, as well as *Chramesus icoriæ* Lec., are biennial, uninfluenced appreciably by indoor breeding, and even triennial. when the wood in which they breed is kept two years. *Narrative.—*A hickory tree was deadened early in 1888, was cut down about the middle of April, 1889, and a barrel of the limbs placed in the open air in the yard, covered on top with canvas, protected by a cover of boards. A number of *Chramesus icoriæ* appeared five or six weeks afterward, but no *Micracis*, as certainly would have been the case had these species been annual alone, as in this case indoor breeding could scarcely have been a retarding factor. Next season, 1890, from May 15 to July, great numbers of *C. icoriæ* and *M. aculeata* emerged, with *M. suturalis* in less abundance. The same barrel of wood this season, 1891, yielded quite a number of the former two species and a few of the latter: had the tree remained standing. I conclude no *Micracis* would have appeared the first year from the egg, and that all would have emerged the second year, as the condition of the limbs the third year would certainly have been adverse to so prolonged a development. There is a possibility that some of the Scolytidæ may be either annual or biennial. one of the determining factors being the time of oviposition. May or August. (For further observations. see *Can. Ent.*, vol. XXIII, p. 65.)

The article of Mr. Cockerell's cited (ib., p. 148) has not been seen. The reason for suggesting that the chrysomelide larvæ sent by him found in an ants' nest were most probably *Coscinoptera vittigera* was that that species came abundantly from the same region with the larvæ. The article in the *American Naturalist* on the ants' nest habit of *C. dominicana* had not been seen, nor the figures in the *Sixth Missouri Report* and third volume of the *American Entomologist* consulted. *Narrative.—*Five larvæ, probably half grown, were received perhaps in April. Only two of the cases were unbroken. All were placed in a cage, with earth and dead old leaves; all soon died except one in a case. which fed for five or six weeks, doubling the size of its case, finally closing it, not abruptly, but roundly. The larvæ were of a dirty pale color, with a yellow head dashed with brown, and had formidable mandibles. The case externally was entirely smooth, without ribs or inequalities. the ends were nearly of the same diameter and shape, that at the head being smaller; it seemed to be composed of particles of ash-gray earth united by a secretion, and was not readily soluble in cold water. This case did not much or at all resemble the figure of *C. dominicana* given in the *Sixth Missouri Report*, but rather that of *Chlamys plicata*, without its gibbosity. The larva died without pupating. with its head at the entrance. To absolutely determine the species the imago must be bred. The larva of these sac-bearing Chrysomelidæ are possibly carnivorous as well as feeders on old leaves, as suggested by the experiments of W. S. Barnard (*American Entomologist*, vol. III, 227), and from which it is proven that *C. dominicana* can breed without the intervention of an ant's nest. An ant's nest, however, must prove very attractive to such larvæ, as there is found an abundance of good food, plenty of clay prepared from which to construct their cases, and also good shelter from the disintegrating effects of prolonged rains.—[John Hamilton. M. D., Pennsylvania, December 11, 1891.

Remedies for Wireworms.

Please tell me if there is a more economical remedy to kill wireworms than salt? If not, how large a quantity would it require to kill every one and not affect the next crop? Would fall plowing alone help the matter?—[T. E. Martin, New York, October 16, 1891.

REPLY.—Wireworms are the larvæ of Click Beetles, and by destroying the beetles before they have deposited their eggs, from which the wireworms issue in the spring, the crop of worms will be greatly reduced. This affords the best means of limiting the damage resulting from their attacks. The use of salt is rather doubtful on acconut of the large amount necessary to cover a sufficient area to kill the worms, and fall plowing would not be of the slightest benefit. A very effectual and practical remedy consists in attracting the beetles to poisoned bait. Some elaborate experiments in this direction have been made by Prof. Comstock and show that the beetles can be easily attracted to baits of clover which have been poisoned by wetting with one of the arsenicals. These baits consist of small bunches of the freshly cut plant, about one-fourth pound in weight, distributed throughout the field and protected and kept moist by being covered with boards.

As an indication of the efficiency of this method it is stated that a series of twelve traps yielded in three days, 482 beetles or an average or more than 40 per trap. These traps should be put out during the early summer, and the beetles killed within the majority of cases have not deposited their eggs and the consequent depredations of their larvæ, the Wireworms, will be greatly diminished. It frequently happens that the infested areas are rather limited in extent and do not cover the entire field, and where this is the case the labor of distributing bait will be greatly lessened. The bait should be renewed once or twice per week during the early part of summer. In place of the clover, corn-meal dough and sliced potatoes are used, but clover has proven itself the most valuable. Where a field has become extensively infested by the worms there is little which can be done so far as any actual experiment has shown. It has been found that a heavy top dressing of kainit acts fairly well against the Cutworms, and as this is a valuable fertilizer, no harm certainly could be brought about by experimenting with it against Wireworms. If you are in position to try this remedy it would give us pleasure to receive a report upon it from you. The starving-out remedy is efficacious, but this means the total loss of one crop from the infested field, as the land is left in fallow through one entire season. As the worms, however, may remain for three years in the larval state, this method is sometimes used. It has frequently been claimed that by sowing the infested field to buckwheat; the worms will be starved out, as they will not eat of this crop. This, however, has been disputed and we would hardly recommend it without more authoritative information.*—[October 24, 1891.]

Coleopterous Larvæ in a Cistern.

I send you herein larvæ from a neighbor's cistern brought me for identification. They have been pumped up from the same cistern for several years in varying quantities; what are they? * * * —[M. C. Read, Ohio, December 11, 1891.

REPLY.—* * * While we are not able to determine these larvæ definitely they seem without doubt to belong to some beetle of the family Dascyllidæ. Your neighbor should search for beetles in and about his cistern and send them on. In that way we can probably identify the species.* * * —[December 16, 1891.]

A Longicorn Borer in Apple Roots.

I send a worm and some pieces of apple-tree root. * * * This apple tree is five years old, never very thrifty, which I supposed was in the kind of tree, Autumn Straw-

---

* See also special note on p. 231 of the current volume.

berry; this past summer it acted as if it was troubled with leaf blight. I sprayed four times with copper solution and three times with London purple, to no purpose; also looked for borers, but found none, or any signs, except that the bark at the base of the tree had turned black. I have just dug up the tree and found twenty-seven of these worms eating the roots.—[H. H. Gushee, Tennessee, November 7, 1891.

REPLY.—* * * The large grubs which you send are the larvæ of one of the long-horned beetles known as *Orthosoma brunneum*. These insects are not very abundant, and cases of damage to orchard trees are rare, so that you probably have no reason to fear any great injury from them.—[November 12, 1891.]

Was it Diabrotica 12-punctata?

The following extract from a letter written by Mr. Charles Yancey, of Buckingham, Va., dated March 8, 1828, and published in the *American Farmer*, Vol. 10. p. 3, describes a depredator whose method of work seems quite similar to that of this species. The writer was of the opinion that "the fly" deposited its eggs in the fall, upon the stalks of Carrot weed and also on Hogweed.

"SIR: I am much annoyed with a little white worm having a copper-colored head. They perforate the stalks of young corn just below the surface of the ground, which destroys its growth. The corn is not exempt from their depredations until it joints. I have listed my corn lands, leaving the clover in the middle of the rows to supply them with food. This is a palliative but not a remedy."

For my own part I can not call to mind any insect except the larvæ of *Diabrotica 12-punctata*, which answers this description both as to form, color, and method of work.—[F. M. Webster, Ohio, December 28, 1891.

The Clover-leaf Beetle in western Pennsylvania.

Phytonomus punctatus.—If not known from some other source, it may be of interest to state that this beetle has reached this part of Pennsylvania (Allegheny County), though its depredations have not attracted the attention of agriculturists as yet. Three years ago I saw specimens which were taken here and in the adjoining county of Westmoreland; this season, 1891, I took a few specimens in nearly every collecting tour in June to July, and saw on the pavements of the city an occasional individual. From the statements of collectors I learn it is now not uncommon in parts of Westmoreland County.—[John Hamilton, M. D., Pennsylvania, December 11, 1891.

The Rice Weevil in dry Hop Yeast.

I to-day had a sample of dry hop yeast sent me from Ocala, Fla., filled with little black bugs, that bore through the yeast and apparently feed upon it.

I would like to have you identify them for me. What I would like to know is: Are they peculiar to the southern climate, or are they a bug that attacks yeast in the northern latitudes?—[F. B. Thurber, New York, October 19, 1891.

REPLY.—The "little black bugs" in dry hop yeast are specimens of the so-called Rice Weevil, a cosmopolitan insect which feeds upon all stored farinaceous products and upon drugs and many other substances, seeming to prefer those which have a vegetable origin. They are more liable to abound in southern climates, but if they once obtain a foothold in an establishment like yours in New York, they will be liable to do considerable damage. Their occurrence in dry yeast is not remarkable, but so far as I know it has not been reported before.—[October 21, 1891.]

How to kill Tree-borers.

Quite a number of ways for destroying the larvæ of various kinds that live in the bark and sapwood of the apple and other varieties of fruit trees, have been published, but none of them are as good, in my judgment, as the way that I now recommend.

I know of no better way of effectually putting a stop to their depredations than by using unadulterated kerosene quite freely wherever the castings of the larvæ are seen protruding through the bark. As soon as the kerosene comes in contact with these sawdust-like castings it is absorbed and carried by capillary attraction until it permeates the whole burrow and comes in contact with the larvæ, and then, soon, this noted little tenant is lifeless.

In using kerosene there is no use in cutting, digging into, or in any way mutilating the tree to find the larva. The fluid kerosene will find it, and this is enough for practical purposes, and then Nature "steps in" with her "healing art" and mends the damage done to the tree. The amount of kerosene used for this purpose is so small that it endangers in no way the health of the tree. A person can visit and inspect many trees in a single hour, and, if necessary, apply the spout of a can and flow a small amount of kerosene in various places.

The beauties of this way of killing the borers are no mutilation, quick work, sure death, and little expense.—[T. B. Ashton, Kansas, November 13, 1891.

Note on the Carphoxera Herbarium Pest.

Carphoxera ptelearia.—This moth, which is so well described in the November number of INSECT LIFE, I became well acquainted with practically fifteen years ago, while collecting plants in Southern California. Dried plants are nearly all subject to the attacks of this insect in this country, and in two or three weeks they will destroy a nice specimen, as they attack the buds and flowers first.

It is about ten years since I first mounted a dozen of the little moths in my entomological cabinet, and there they have remained to this day, unseen and unstudied by Eastern entomologists except once, about six years ago, when a prominent New York entomologist saw them. He thought them a species of Eupithecia. He took away specimens of the moth, and also of the larva which I got for him from my dried plants, but I never heard from him about them.

This moth lives and breeds largely in barns where loose or unbaled alfalfa hay is kept. Sometimes when I walk on a mow of loose hay a swarm of the moths, hundreds in number, will arise from the hay. In fact the moth is quite at home here.

As of late years I have been more interested in entomology than in botany, I have asked Mr. S. B. Parish, a competent botanist of this place, about his experience with the pest in recent years. His observations indicate that a preference is shown by the larvæ for some plants while others are evidently avoided. Plants preferred are Stillingia, all Lupines, Vicinus, and nearly all the Compositæ; and those avoided noticeably are most of the Euphorbiaceæ, Crotons, all grasses, and particularly all ferns.

Now as to means of defense against the pest. First, it is evident that the moths find their mates or pair while in flight, at night, and any means of preventing their pairing strikes at the root of the evil at once. To this end a tight cabinet of small compartments is the best remedy. Or, wrapping the herbarium specimens in large sheets of paper will help, if tight cabinets can not be had. Second, poisoning, and frequent handling of the plants.—[W. G. Wright, California.

Treatment of the Squash Borer.

Having seen several communications in relation to *Melittia cucurbitæ*, in INSECT LIFE, I would like to state my observations of the insect during the past few years. Living as I do in the market gardening district of Long Island, I have had a good opportunity of doing so. I find that the moths begin to come out by the middle of June and continue to do so until the middle of August or even later. During the past season I caught something over 200 of them and did not begin to take them until after the 12th of July; on the 6th of July, on my return from the Jamesburg convention of entomologists, in conversation with Prof. J. B. Smith he made the observation that they were all gone, when I asserted that I could catch 100 of them if he wished them. He said that I could not do it, so when I got home I began catching them and took the above number and gave over. But a friend of mine, Mr. A. Van Siclen, a market gardener, continued to kill them on his vines, and he told me that as near as he could judge he killed 500 more before they ceased coming out. The female after she issues from the ground, which usually occurs about 10 o'clock a. m., does not have any connection with the male until the evening, as I have never found them paired through the day. After pairing the female does not commence to lay her eggs till the second day.

Prof. Smith says they lay the eggs at the bottom of the vine, even on the leaves. The larva on coming out seeks a suitable place and goes to work; if in case it falls from the vine it crawls about until it finds another, when it immediately goes to work, which accounts, in my opinion, for the greater number being found at the root of the vines. But I have found them in the vine a long distance from the root, six or seven feet in some cases. If every egg was laid in the proper place (and the female lays some 150 or more) there would not be a single vine come to perfection; as it, is a being many of them are lost by falling from the vine and dying of starvation, or by great eaten by the ants. Prof. Smith says that to eradicate them you must crush the eggs by rubbing, which would be a very laborious process, as it would necessitate going over the vines a great number of times. I consider it far preferable to kill the adult insect, which may be done very readily after 5 p. m. or before 7 a. m., as between these hours the insects are quite torpid. They will always be found sitting on the upper side of the leaf (I have never found one under) and generally near the junction of the leaf and the stalk. Any one may know them by their big red hind legs. By placing one hand under the leaf and moth and striking it with the other the moth may readily be killed. I had no trouble in placing the cyanide bottle over them in that manner, and even when I made a miss of it the moth would fall to the ground and I would get it there. As they become quite torpid on the approach of evening and do not become active until the sun shines warm again, it is useless to seek them in the bright sunshine. I have also caught them on cloudy or rainy days.

As the farmers do not plant the Hubbard or Boston squash for winter use until July, I would advise the planting of a couple of rows of white squash early in the spring. One on each side of the ground to be planted later on, and as they would be quite grown by the time the moths began to come out and as they naturally seek the largest vines it would enable the farmer to catch them without having to go over the whole patch, while the other vines were small, but later on he would have to go over the whole patch. One of my farmer friends tried it this summer and found it a great success, having the best crop he ever had, scarcely losing a vine. I would also advise the burning of the vines in the fall after becoming dry, as some of the larvæ, especially the later ones, make their cocoons in the vines, but the earlier ones invariably go into the earth, about one inch deep, and if left undisturbed would come out in June, but the farmer in plowing turns them under so much deeper that it takes them much longer to work their way to the top of the ground, where I have found many of the vacant pupa skins sticking half way out.—[J. V. D. Walker, New York, December 23, 1891.

Where are the Eggs of the Clover Hay-worm laid?

The theory advanced by Prof. Webster in regard to the Clover Hay-worm that "the eggs may be deposited on the plants in the field and the larvæ thus be drawn to the stack or mow," is not corroborated by my experience of the present season. On June 15 and 17 I mowed clover, and on the latter date put one load in a barn. Being interrupted by rain nothing more was done, except to dry out the wet hay, until the 22d when it was put in stacks in the field where it grew. On the 23d the remainder, amounting to several tons was mown, and on the 24th was hauled to another barn. Within the present week I have carefully examined the hay in both barns and find it entirely free from worms, while the stacks are badly eaten, and swarming with worms of all sizes. Evidently, if larvæ or eggs had been upon the growing clover the worms should now be found in all of the hay.—[G. M. Dodge, Missouri, December 27, 1891.

The Box-elder Bug attacking Fruit in Washington State.

FIRST LETTER.—Inclosed I send some bugs for your inspection. They appeared last year, but did no damage till this summer, when they attacked the fruit in great numbers, destroying large quantities of plums, peaches, apples, and some grapes. They suck the juice from the fruit, leaving it dry and fibrous. When about half grown they begin to grow wings and become spotted with black. Before that time they are blood-red. [I. N. Newkirk, Columbia County, Washington, October 22, 1891.

REPLY.—The insect which you sent is a rather common bug known scientifically as *Leptocoris trivittata*. In some parts of the West this bug has in late years become known as the "Box-elder Bug" on account of its seeming preference for the Box-elder (*Negundo aceroides*), a tree which is commonly grown for shade in many of our cities. We have seldom heard of this insect damaging fruit as you describe, but in 1885 received a similar account from Kanab, Kane County, Utah. The Entomologist would be much interested to know whether the Box-elder tree grows in the vicinity of your orchard. In the Utah occurrence insects bred upon the Box-elder and deserted this tree for the ripening fruit. The best remedy which can be recommended is to spray the bugs wherever noticed in any numbers with a dilute kerosene-soap emulsion made according to the formula given upon page 3 of Circular No. 1, second series. The application should be made as early in the season as possible, as the bugs breed rapidly, and every one killed in the spring will be a considerable saving. Search should be made for their breeding places, and they should be destroyed, if possible, before they make their appearance upon the fruit. [October 30, 1891.]

SECOND LETTER.—In reply to your inquiry relative to the growth of Box-elder in the vicinity of those Box-elder Bugs, as you call them, I will make a general statement which I deem pertinent to the inquiry. The bugs have been generally distributed in Columbia and Garfield counties, within the bounds of my knowledge. There are quite a number of timber cultures scattered through these counties in which Box-elder is the principal timber used. I have a grove of these trees standing beside my orchard. These bugs are a tolerable make-shift for bedbugs when young, crawling into beds and biting quite sharply. They have been noticed hanging in bunches like bees, to Box-elder branches.—[I. N. Newkirk, Washington, November 10, 1891.

Notes on the "Blood-sucking Cone-nose."

FIRST LETTER.—Is not the *Conorhinus sanguisugus* a relative of the genus *Reduvius*? They fly at night, alighting in a straight flight near a light, to seek on landing a dark nook to hide. They are more common in fresh, cool, damp weather, becoming scarce towards July. They are very active. I found one disturbing a settlement of bedbugs, another eating what I think was a young Blattid. Their bite is very severe and deep. I believe they have some hooks to cling with while sucking, and have a kind of venom, making the wound sore and itching, with a burning pain lasting two, three, and four days. While at a high temperature the sensation is more acute, the general effects do not last so long. I use volatile alkali against all such stings of insects so far with success; never tried spiders yet, and do not care to. [Emile J. Longuemare, Missouri, September 14, 1891. * * *

REPLY: *Conorhinus sanguisugus* comes very close in classification to the genus *Reduvius*, and both genera occur in the same subfamily. Your having observed *Conorhinus* feeding on a Blattid (?) is very interesting and well worth going on record. Your experience also with the bite of this insect is quite a common one, and many of us have experienced, to our sorrow, the severity of the wounds resulting from the venom of the insect. [September 16, 1891.] * * *

SECOND LETTER.— * * * My experience with *Conorhinus sanguisugus* is rather limited. Along in the summer, about May 20, my attention was drawn to this Hemipteron by being bitten by what I supposed to be bedbugs. A careful search was promptly made, but no bugs could be found. Still we were bitten, and one morning my mother handed me a big bug distended with blood, and for several mornings by looking we were enabled to find from one to two about the bed. The log house which we rent is roughly built, and they hid in the walls during the day and came out at night. There were not many, for after killing a dozen or so we were not bothered any more. This bite was not much more severe than that of a bedbug, and no ill consequences followed like those of which I have read. Those captured on the bed in the morning were gorged with blood, as stated in my letter on page 466 of volume III, INSECT LIFE. I have caught them out in the woods and I do not see what they get to suck blood from out there. I suppose in cases where their bites prove seriously injurious the person must be in ill health. * * * [A. N. Caudell, Indian Territory, October 29, 1891.

The Orange-leaf Aleyrodes.

I send a few leaves from orange trees on my plantation at this place (lat. 27° 30'). From last April to August I had millions of a tiny white-winged insect (pink tint), on some 300 or more of my trees and caused them to disappear by using whale-oil soap, lime, etc. Three hundred trees are now black with the smut, leaves, branches, and all. Is this insect *Aleyrodes citrifolii?* Does this insect or smut hurt the vitality of the tree in any way? The smut is on the fruit also, and some of my oranges have been rendered almost insipid (usually delicious) either by the insect, smut, or the insecticide applied (probably the latter). Any suggestion from you touching this miserable pest and how best to get rid of the winged insect, if it again appears, and the smut, will be very gratefully received.—[Charles H. Foster, Florida, January 8, 1891.

REPLY.— * * * The insect which you send is, as you suppose, *Aleyrodes citrifolii*. The smut fungus is the result of the abundance of these insects. The work of the 'insects undoubtedly reduces the vitality of the tree, and while the fungus mycelium does not penetrate the plant substance, yet, by forming a dense coating, it undoubtedly still further reduces its vitality. The insect is now upon the leaves in its wingless form, and many of the specimens sent by you were still living and about full grown. The tiny white-winged form is the adult insect. The immature insects can be destroyed by the application of a dilute kerosene-soap emulsion made according to the formula on page 3 of Circular No. 1 of this Division and the smut fungus can be removed from the trees by spraying with a strong whale-oil soap solution (7 pounds of the whale-oil soap to 28 gallons of water). This is so strong, however, that it will damage the foliage if allowed to remain on long, and it should, therefore, be allowed to remain on the tree only about two hours, and the tree should then be sprayed with pure water. The strong alkaline solution will cut the fungus, so that it can be easily washed off by the water spray.—[January 14, 1892.]

Orange Chionaspis in Florida.

I inclose section of an orange twig on which is some kind of scale insect that is new here. It is, so far as I know, confined to one locality, but seems to be spreading rapidly. * * * [E. Bean, Florida, October 23, 1891.

REPLY.— * * * The scale which you send is the Orange Chionaspis (*Chionaspis citri* Comst.). This insect occurs in the West Indies and is the commonest orange scale in Louisiana. It is rare in Florida and, in fact, we have only received it once from your State. In Louisiana it does considerable damage to orange trees and if it appears to be spreading with you there is every reason to believe that it will become seriously injurious unless remedial measures are undertaken. You will find the species mentioned upon page 40, of Hubbard's "Insects Affecting the Orange."—[October 26, 1891.]

On the Treatment of Human Patients affected with Screw Worm.

I have delayed answering your kind communication relating to the Texas Screw Worm, *Compsomyia (Lucilia) macellaria*, until hearing from the Louisiana and Texas Experiment Stations, to which you referred me. I am in receipt of their bulletins on the subject, and find them very complete in every detail. Yet the remedies which are described in the bulletins as being efficacious in the destruction of the Screw Worm (chloroform, ether, carbolic acid, bichloride mercury, turpentine, etc.), are scarcely applicable to human patients, owing to the extreme sensitiveness of the parts affected. I have tried all of the enumerated materials for the destruction of the Screw Worm, and my experiments scarcely tally with those of the bulletins. For example, I have found the worm to live for four minutes in pure carbolic acid; in strong turpentine for fifteen minutes. Chloroform has proved most satisfactory, as the maggot was killed by immersion for thirty seconds.

It is, however, unnecessary to add, that it is impossible to apply these medicaments in pure form in so sensitive a locality of the delicate mucous membrane of the nose and pharynx; again, in a diluted form, such remedies would accomplish but little. Therefore, in treatment of my patients medicaments were unsuccessfully tried, and surgical measures had to be instituted. * * *—[M. A. Goldstein, M. D., Missouri, December 13, 1891.

Bot-fly Larvæ burrowing under the Skin of Man.

* * * In reference to the article in INSECT LIFE, vol. II, pp. 238, 239; "A grub supposed to have traveled in the human body," I greatly regret that I have no more separata left of my article in the Swedish "*Entomologisk Tidskrift*," on the occurrence of Dipterous grubs under the skin of man. As pointed out in this article, we have known of such occurrences in some districts of our country for one hundred years past and up to the present time. Many of these grubs I have myself seen and examined, and they were all of them Hypoderma larvæ (*sine dubio—Hyp. bovis*), and as a rule they have undertaken longer ramblings under the skin, always in upward directions, previous to their appearance through an opening in a tumor on the upper part of the body (head, neck, shoulders, etc.). All of them lived in this manner for months, and came out in the course of the winter months (February or so), but were always still much too young to be hatched. However, I have no doubt at all, that they belong to *Hyp. bovis*, as it is especially in those persons who take care of cattle in the summer months that such grubs are to be found during the winter. It is evidently the smell of cattle which attracts the Bot Fly to them. *Hyp. diana* does not occur in our country.

The article may be found in the *Entomologisk Tidskrift*, Stockholm, 1886, pp. 171–187, and contains also a short historic résumé of all accidents of this kind observed up to that time, and which have been published here in Norway and elsewhere.—[W. M. Schoyen, Norway, November 11, 1891.

REPLY.—* * * The facts which you give me concerning this traveling larva of Hypoderma are very interesting, and I will look up the article in the *Entomologisk Tidskrift* for 1886. As you will have noticed probably upon pages 201 and 207, vol. II, INSECT LIFE, Dr. Cooper Curtice, formerly of this Department, claims to have proven that *Hypoderma bovis* frequently hatches from the egg in the œsophagus of cattle, pierces the œsophagal walls and travels through the subcutaneous tissue until it reaches a point under the skin of the back where it becomes more or less encysted. The facts which you give have a strong bearing on this more or less theoretical position of Dr. Curtice.—[November 27, 1891.]

The Horn Fly in Mississippi.

It may be of interest to entomologists to know that this insect has of late been reported in many localities in the eastern portion of this State. Early in October I received a letter from Mr. A. H. Bush, of Macon, requesting information in regard to a "troublesome fly" that had appeared in his herd of cattle early last May. From the habits of the insects as given by Mr. Bush I was quite sure that the insect was the Horn-fly, and a visit to Macon November 2 proved this to be the case. At this time but a few flies were to be seen, but I was informed that before a cold snap of the week preceding the fly had been very numerous.

Desiring to know the extent to which this insect was distributed throughout the State, an inquiry was inserted in the *Southern Live Stock Journal*, and the answers to this inquiry showed the insect to be present in nearly all of the eastern portions of the State. The statements of correspondents and personal observations as to the habits of the insect agree with those of Messrs. Riley & Howard, and Smith, most of the farmers estimating the decrease in the flow of milk at nearly one-half. In localities from which the Horn-fly was reported, it seems to have appeared late in May and was especially numerous during July and August. The fact that it had not been reported from the western portion of the State leads to the conclusion that it has not yet reached this locality, or at least not in numbers sufficient to attract attention.

The spread of this insect may be watched with interest. First attracting attention in New Jersey in 1887, its spread southward and westward has been rapid, this year having appeared in Ohio, Kentucky, and Mississippi. As to its future distribution and abundance, of course none can say, but it seems to me probable that it will eventually become a more serious pest in the Southern than in the Northern states. It is to be hoped however that the parasites reported in the last report of the Entomologist of the Department (p. 248) will greatly lessen the numbers of this insect in the future.—[Howard Evarts Weed, Mississippi, December 6, 1891.

A southern Cricket destructive to the Strawberry.

I send sample of a cricket, together with some of its young. Is it a new species? Its burrow, when plowed out, was some 6 or 8 inches deep and perhaps 2 feet long. This applies to all the species. In an oblong oval chamber at the end of the channel leading to the burrow I found the cricket hovering its young, some thirty in number, like a hen and chickens. During fall and winter this insect is, if numerous, very destructive to young strawberry plants, cutting off the leaves and carrying them into its hole. A pocket or cave near the surface is always found full of the cut leaves. Have never seen one on the surface, unless dug out, except at twilight, when it comes out to feed. Have fed them meal soaked in strychnine, arsenic, and Paris green. Although they would carry it into their holes they were alive when dug up afterward. A little hot water poured in their holes kills them. That is the only remedy we have found, and answers the purpose very well. I am most perplexed about Nature's mistake in this case, and in course of time shall expect to see this insect change its form into something like the Mole Cricket, as its tools to dig with are entirely inadequate to do the digging it does. The piles of dirt are forced up, and it looks as if a sausage stuffer did it. At first I supposed it merely cleaned out the holes of the Mole Cricket, but I found by observation that I was mistaken. It is very strong and active and altogether an interesting insect. It is always the imperfect insect that does the damage, and, as I observe, lives a year before it breeds. I might write much more of its habits, but I expect it is a common species already known and written up. It is called the White or Cotton Cricket here in the South. Out of hundreds dug up this is the only adult or perfect specimen I have seen.—[M. Knickerbocker, Florida, October 11, 1891.

REPLY.—* * * The cricket arrived in good condition, and is new to the collection of the National Museum. It is a species of the typical cricket genus Gryllus and is likely to be new to science.—* * * [October 17, 1891.]

Insanity caused by Mosquito Bites—Hibernation of Mosquitoes.

I was interested in reading a recent number of INSECT LIFE (Vol. IV, p. 85) to the effect that the poison of the Mosquito was provocative of insanity. When I was engaged in exploring in the vicinity of the north shore of Lake Superior about twenty-five years ago, I had more than one proof of this fact. One of my men was badly bitten and seemed to suffer more than any others of the company. He became violently insane and ran off in the woods, and in spite of all efforts he eluded pursuit and was never found again. Another man on a different occasion was affected in a similar manner, and was captured with difficulty after a long chase in which he exhibited the utmost terror, but after a few days' close confinement in the camp he regained his reason. Afterwards he was so seriously affected by the poison that he had to be sent home. I have noticed that the poison affected persons differently, causing severe swelling in some, fever in others, pains in the limbs in others, while some were but slightly annoyed. I was myself very little troubled by these pests or the Black Flies, and found a wash of ammonia to relieve all the injury to the skin. One warm day in March, although the snow was several feet deep and the ice on the lakes was five feet in thickness, the Mosquitoes appeared in swarms, literally blackening the banks of snow in the sheltered places. These were evidently the insects of the previous summer which were wintering over. The Indians told us that the Mosquitoes lived over the winter, and the old ones were the most annoying to them.—[H. Stewart, North Carolina, November 3, 1891.

REPLY.—This statement concerning the biting of the hibernating Mosquitoes in the northwest is paralleled by the experience of Dr. E. Sterling, published in INSECT LIFE, p. 403, Vol. III.—[November 5, 1891.]

Death of an Infant from a Spider Bite.

The inclosed clipping is from the *Cincinnati Enquirer* of October 11, 1891, and being on the subject of spider bites, concerning which there has been some insertions in INSECT LIFE, may be of interest to you.—[Edwin A. Hill, Ohio, October 23, 1891.

MADISON, IND., *October 10.*

Several days ago the infant daughter of Thomas Davison, the stove merchant, was bitten upon the finger by a spider. The mother brushed the insect away, and no evil effects were noticed for several hours, when the hand began to swell and a physician was called. The member continued to swell and blood poisoning set in, from the effects of which the child died to-day.

REPLY.— * * * Thank you very much for your clipping regarding spider bites. It is a pity that all of these indefinite stories can not be thoroughly investigated.—[October 26, 1891.]

On the poisonous Bite of the Spider, *Latrodectus mactans*.

I send you by today's mail a black spider that has the reputation of being very poisonous, in fact, several people have died from the effects of the bite and others have been very sick. Would you please name it for me? * * * [Alvah A. Eaton, California, November 14, 1891.

REPLY.— * * * The spider which you send as possessing the reputation of being very poisonous, is *Latrodectus mactans*, a near relative of the well-known "Katipo" of New Zealand. There is no doubt that the spiders of this genus Latrodectus are very poisonous and that their bite has been followed by severe illness and in some cases by death. The actual records of fatal cases are, however, few, and if you can give me names and dates of any fatal cases concerning which you make the general statement, you will place me under obligations. If you can in any of these cases refer me to the medical attendant, I shall be glad to open up correspondence with him. On pages 204-211 of vol. I, INSECT LIFE, you will find an article on this spider, with illustrations of the different forms and an account of a fatal case in North Carolina.— * * * [November 28, 1891.]

Death due to the Whip Scorpion and Tarantula.

* * * While I was in El Paso sometime since, some workmen were excavating for a smelting furnace. One of them dug out of the ground a Whip Scorpion (we called it *Thelephonus excubitor*) and was stung by it, and died a few hours afterward. Whether the man was in good health or not I am not able to say. I have known of two healthy men bitten by a Tarantula, that made only an ugly sore; a girl of twelve years of age was bitten by one and died from the effects of the bite, but I am again unable to say whether she was in good health or not. It seems that a very trifling thing will sometimes cause death when a person is not healthy.

The Mexicans call the Telephonus *vinagron*—smelling of vinegar.—[G. W. Dunn, California, November 2. 1891.

Tame Birds as Insect Destroyers in Greenhouses.

A glass roof on the back building of our dwelling gives us a garden 20 by 28 feet in the third story which is warmed at night by waste heat from kitchen, dining, and other rooms below. This attic garden we use as a laboratory for testing soils, plant foods, and insecticides. We also winter our more tender and valued plants in it, and this bring the insects and eggs along, so that all we have been able to do, with smoking twice a week with tobacco stems and using other insecticides, was to keep the Aphis in check, and get crops of lettuce and radishes far below what they might be under other circumstances. We were obliged to exercise great care, or the smoke would kill the more tender flowering plants. We experienced much more trouble with insects in this garden than in our larger plant houses outside. Being anxious to find some means of managing the insect pests, less injurious to the plants, we directed our studies to birds and placed in an Indigo Bird—*Fringilla cyanea*—soon after planting, and we are now marketing better radishes than at any time during the five years we have been using the place. When we placed the bird in, the room was swarming with wasps and various kinds of flies, which in a few days disappeared. During this time the bird ate none of his seed. It is yet too wild to hunt or eat during our presence.

We do not claim to have discovered a complete remedy from a single or so short a trial; but the testimony so far is favorable, and my object in this letter is to encourage others to make experiments. We placed a wire screen over the ventilating door to prevent the bird's escape. We believe that these birds, and perhaps any of the *Fringilla* family, might be domesticated so as to occupy our gardens during summer, and remain in our plant houses during winter if fed and protected. *Sylvia sialis*, our Blue Bird, *Sylvia domestica*, the House Wren, and others of that family, we have no doubt, would clear plants of the Red Spider, which is often troublesome. We once placed a wounded Crow Blackbird in a conservatory, and when he recovered he would turn up the leaves with his great bill and look under them for insects. In that case the conservatory adjoined our dining room, and a Robin and a Mocking Bird would come to my shoulders, one on each, while at dinner. I learned of their power of wing from strokes on my neck when they were fighting each other. As to the work of putting in wire doors and wires over the ventilators, the beautiful plumage and melodious songs doubly repay all that. The beauty of the richest collection of plants is heightened by the lively flitting of birds, and birds never seem so pretty as when perching on plants. We were glad to notice your statement that the Quail, Cardinal Grossbeak, and other birds ate the Potato Beetle, and presume you will join us in our effort to cultivate public opinion to such a degree as will insure a better protection for and a more friendly relation with our birds.—[R. Bingham, New Jersey, December 1, 1891.

GENERAL NOTES.

MORE INTERNATIONAL EXCHANGES OF VEDALIA.

We are pleased to record another successful shipment of Vedalia from one country to another. On November 10 at our direction Mr. Coquillett started a shipment of live Vedalia to New Zealand. The former sending consigned to Dr. B. Locking, of Nelson, had failed owing to the opening of the package by the customs and post-office authorities in New Zealand, who repacked it in such a careless manner that the insects escaped. With this last sending, therefore, great care was taken. Mr. Coquillett accompanied the package to San Francisco and placed it in charge of a responsible person on board the steamer, who transmitted it with great care, and the result is that we have just learned from Dr. Locking that the package arrived intact and that the insects were alive. There were about 20 living beetles besides larvæ in different stages of growth which reached New Zealand in good condition. Icerya has been increasing recently, as we have elsewhere stated, and has again become a pest in certain portions of New Zealand. Vedalia has been found living, having carried itself over successfully from its previous abundance in 1888, but of this fact we were apprised after our shipment had been started. There is no doubt, however, but that these specimens consigned to Dr. Locking will aid greatly in the extermination of the Icerya.

Another attempt has also been made to send Vedalia to Egypt. On December 13 Mr. Coquillett sent a package containing an abundant supply of both Vedalia and Icerya, by express, to Washington, D. C. Owing probably to the great rush of Christmas business the express company did not deliver it until December 25. The box was opened and the Vedalia were found to be in a most admirable condition, while there was still a plentiful supply of Icerya alive for them to feed upon. The orange twigs, from which the Iceryas had begun to migrate on account of withering, were renewed from the Department conservatories, the box was repacked, and Mr. Howard took it the same afternoon to New York, where it was placed in charge of the butcher on board the steamship *Etruria*, with instructions to keep it cold on the transatlantic journey and to deliver it to the agents of Pitt & Scott, the European forwarding agents in Liverpool. It was calculated that this journey from Washington will occupy sixteen days, so that there is every reason to anticipate an arrival in Alexandria in good condition.

HARMLESS SPIDER BITES.

In refreshing contrast to the usual indefinite and often exaggerated accounts of spider bites and their effects, there has come to us the following from Mr. Th. Pergande, of this Division:

On the morning of October 25, 1891, Mr. Pergande found a fine specimen of a large brown spider, *Lycosa viridicola* Emerton, in the kitchen of his residence in this city. He raised it up and was bitten on the terminal joint of his thumb. The sensation was like the prick of a fine needle, and a minute red spot was produced. A mild lancinating pain was felt in the thumb and in all of the fingers of the same hand for the rest of the day and passed away at night. The bite occasioned no further inconvenience, although the red spot could be observed for several days.

In this case, then, we have the spider caught in the act of biting and scientifically determined and the effects of the bite carefully noted. Similar cases are very rare, but it is only upon such that we ever have any positive and scientific statement as to the effects of spider bites.

Mr. Edwin A. Hill, of Cincinnati, Ohio, was kind enough to send us in November a clipping from a Cincinnati paper with the sensational heading: *Spider stung*. "*Mrs. Medora Estes dying in great agony. She was bitten on the hand by one of the household pests. The poison has extended to every part of her system. Sad plight of the well-known teacher of elocution.*" The article went on to give an account of the case, and the statement was made that "* * * last evening it was not thought that Mrs. Estes could survive the night. The poison has worked its way to every part of the body and in several places broken out in fearful ulcers, causing the lady untold agony." Mr. Hill was kind enough to send us also the address of the attending physician, Dr. F. H. Schell, and we immediately wrote to him for the details of this striking case. Under date of November 30 he wrote us as follows:

There was nothing in the case of so-called spider bite! The newspaper account was a case of extraordinary exaggeration and misinformation. A spider, however, did bite or sting my little daughter upon the eyelid last summer, the only result of which was a slight tumefaction, which subsided in a couple of days.

INSECT EMBRYOLOGY.

Under the title "*Lehrbuch der vergleichenden Entwicklungsgeschichte der wirbellosen Thiere*," Drs. Korshelt and Heider are issuing a comprehensive work, of which the second part, just published, contains the embryology of the Arthropoda. The portion containing the embryology of insects, profusely illustrated (pp. 759–890), is well deserving of a careful perusal by even the best-read entomologists, since we find in this portion a long-felt need, *i. e.*, an impartial review and comparison of all the works on insect embryology up to date. Heretofore we have been obliged to rely on Balfour or hunt up the original articles, but Balfour's text-book is now far behind the times, and the articles published since then are very scattered. In the new text-book, however, we find everything in a nutshell. It is impossible to give a complete review of the work in this place. Suffice it to say that the work of Heider, Graber, Heymons, Metschnikoff, Wheeler, and many other embryologists finds in this text-book a logical arrangement which renders the treatise the best thing of its kind in existence.—C. W. STILES.

A EUROPEAN WHITE GRUB FUNGUS.

In the *Comptes Rendus* of the 3d of August, 1891, M. Alfred Giard has given a summary of our information upon this interesting fungous disease of the larvæ of the European Cockchafer. He states that this disease was first observed in epidemic form in Normandy in 1866, and was again discovered in Germany in 1869. Since the latter year it has been found more or less commonly all through northern France. It should be known scientifically as *Isaria densa* Link, this name having priority over *Botrytis tenella* Saccardo. The disease communicates itself readily from one White Grub to another, and can be transmitted equally well by inoculation or by aspersion to insects of different orders, but the infested insects produce the spores spontaneously only when they live underground or in a humid condition. Under contrary conditions the hyphas and the spores can be obtained by placing the mummified insects in a moist chamber. The fungus can be easily cultivated, not only upon meat, as the old observers have stated, but also, as M. Giard was the first to show, upon the most variable solid or liquid media. These cultures can be made at all seasons, and the dried spores will retain their germinating capacity for more than a year. The fungus can be experimentally communicated to the Silk-worm, but there are few chances for this disease to occasion epidemic in the magnaneries, for instead of easily producing efflorescences and spores, as in worms infested with muscardine, the worms mummified by *Isaria densa* remain in the sclerotic condition until they are placed in a moist chamber.

The author has indicated how, with liquid cultures properly diluted or with a mixture of spores and dried earth, the grub can be readily reached and infested at the moment when it rises to the surface of the ground. He considers this method of utilizing the fungus much more practical than those suggested by MM. Prillieux and Delacroix, and less complicated that those suggested for the use of other cryptogamic diseases by MM. Brefeld, Cienkowsky, Metschnikoff, and others. He has great confidence in the employment of this fungus to reduce the damage caused by the White Grub to the minimum, and believes that agriculturists will be able to arrive at this important result without great expense. He claims the priority for this suggestion, and he accepts the responsibility of all that he has said both in this paper and in a former one relative to the destruction of the White Grub by Isaria, but he reserves his opinion upon the possible employment of this fungus against other injurious insects, and particularly against those which live in the open air or in dry places.

We have already mentioned in these pages (Vol. IV, p. 152) the fact that a French firm has commercially adopted the use of this cryptogam, and it will be noticed by comparison that the method recommended differs from the one suggested by M. Giard.

Some discredit is cast upon the practical utility of this method by

M. Jean Dufour in the *Chronique Agricole, Viticole et Forestier du Canton de Vaux.* November 10. 1891. pp. 376–84, where he gives the life-history of this parasite and records a series of experiments conducted in the laboratory in pots, together with corresponding experiments in the field. These experiments showed that the disease can be disseminated to a certain extent by infesting the soil with artificial cultures or with fragments or entire specimens of diseased larvæ, but they also indicated to M. Dufour's satisfaction that the method is not entirely effective as a remedy, even in the laboratory experiments where the conditions could be accurately governed. A large percentage of the treated larvæ resisted the disease, and in the field experiments the percentage of affected larvæ was considerably less.

In view of the differing opinions among actual experimenters we may safely render a verdict of not yet proven. This idea of destroying injurious insects by contagious diseases is such a fascinating one that only the most careful investigators will escape the danger of drawing ill-founded deductions from their experiments.

PARIS GREEN AND THE HONEY BEE.

Prof. J. A. Lintner, of New York, was present at one of the sessions of the late convention of the North American Beekeepers' Association, held at Albany, and "asked to be allowed to say a few words" in regard to the practice of spraying fruit trees with arsenical poisons. He thought experiments were necessary to *prove* that bees were ever killed by the spraying of fruit trees. He doubted if they ever were killed in this way, and desired that samples of bees apparently killed in this manner be sent him for analysis, which would be satisfactory proof.

A committee of three was appointed to look after a series of experiments to prove this and to act with Professor Lintner.

To those familiar with the literature of bee culture I need not say that there is little room for doubt as to the injury done by spraying during fruit bloom. Instances and complaints are heard on every side during the spring. One speaker on the subject said, " Beekeepers never have good, strong, healthy colonies die during apple bloom. It is a thing unheard of except where trees have been sprayed in the neighborhood during bloom." But the convention evidently saw wherein present proof was defective and hence appointed the committee. It is hoped that positive proof will be forthcoming that if necessary proper laws may be made regulating the spraying so that the rights of the little busy bee may not be interfered with.—J. H. LARRABEE.

EAST INDIA BEETLES.

We have received through the Trustees of the Indian Museum the continuation of the Catalogue of the Coleoptera of the Oriental Regions, by the late E. T. Atkinson. This installment is published as a supplement to Part 2, No. 2, Vol. LIX, of the Journal of the Asiatic Society of Bengal, and includes catalogues of the families Dytiscidæ, Gyrinidæ, Paussidæ, Hydrophilidæ, Silphidæ, Corylophidæ, Scydmaenidæ, Pselaphidæ, and Staphylinidæ. The catalogue is synonymical, bibliographical, and geographical, and has every appearance of a complete and painstaking work. It is the fourth of the catalogues prepared by Mr. Atkinson, who, as he wrote us before his death, intended to publish in this form as far as he should be permitted, catalogues of the entire class Insecta. We earnestly hope that workers in the field of oriental entomology will take up the task which Mr. Atkinson projected and will carry it to completion on the lines which he marked out.

THE COLORADO POTATO BEETLE IN NOVA SCOTIA.

The Provincial Government Crop Report of Nova Scotia for August (Halifax, N. S., August 15, 1891), publishes condensed abstracts of correspondence relating to the Colorado Potato Beetle. Correspondents were requested to mention date of first oviposition, extent of damage, remedies applied and method of application, and results. Reports were received from all but five of the eighteen counties of the Province. In a few instances only did the insects occur in sufficient abundance to do serious damage, but the report shows that the species has become distributed throughout a large section of the Province. The following abstract from correspondents' reports will serve to show the popular sentiment:

Upper Kennetcook, Hants County: Eggs began to be deposited as soon as there was a stalk to deposit on. Can not tell what the damage will be yet. Hand-picking, and Paris green applied with a sprinkler. I think life is too short to hand-pick potato bugs, and that every man who has a potato patch should be compelled by law to use Paris green.

Lower Horton, King's County: * * * *Law* should be passed compelling everyone to destroy pests, and fine for neglect. *Inspector* should be appointed in every district with power to act if owner will not, and charge him for the work.

A REMARKABLE BUTTERFLY ENEMY.

At a meeting of the Entomological Society of London, held September 2, 1891, Mr. W. L. Distant exhibited specimens of an Orthopterous insect—*Hemisaga hastata* Sauss., one of the Locustidæ—which he had observed in the Transvaal to attack and feed on *Danais chrysippus*, a butterfly previously supposed, from its protective character and distasteful qualities, to have complete immunity from the predaceous enemies of butterflies. The Hemisaga is said to lurk among the tops of tall flowering grasses and to sieze the butterfly as it settles on the bloom. After close watching and observation. Mr. Distant could find no other enemy of this butterfly.

A NOTE ON THE ANGOUMOIS GRAIN MOTH.

Rev. James P. De Pass, director of the Florida Experiment Station, in Bulletin No. 16 of the station, devotes some two pages to the subject of "The Weevil," meaning, presumably, the "Fly Weevil," or Angoumois Grain Moth (*Gelechia cerealella*.) The author falls into the common error of considering that it is necessary for the moth to puncture the grain to oviposit, and that consequently this must be done when the corn is " in the milk," considering it to be unproven that the insect will propagate in hard corn. Nevertheless, his experience is interesting as showing that the common practice of pulling fodder in July results in preventing the shuck from adhering naturally to and covering the ear, thus affording the moths a sure entrance to the grain for oviposition. In the same way he believes that the final working of the crop in common practice in Florida is apt to produce a similar effect. His remarks are based upon three years' experience, and the suggestions are certainly worthy of test.

INJURY TO FOLIAGE BY ARSENITES. A CHEAP ARSENITE. COMBINATION OF ARSENITES AND FUNGICIDES.

In Technical Bulletin No. 77*b*, of the North Carolina Experiment Station,* Mr. B. W. Kilgore, assistant chemist of the station, gives the results of his investigations of the cause and prevention of injury to foliage by arsenites, and of experiments in combining arsenites with fungicides. In this work Mr. Kilgore has gone over much the same ground covered by Mr. Gillette in Bulletin No. 10 of the Iowa Station, and by Mr. Woodworth in Bulletin No. 14 of the Arkansas Station. Some of the conclusions reached are as follows:

That soluble arsenic compounds cause "burning" or " scorching" to foliage, the injury being in direct proportion to the quantity of these compounds present.

That the addition of lime to Paris green or London purple mixtures, used to prevent this injury may be applied with as great safety ten days after as one hour after mixing, because all soluble arsenites in London purple and Paris green are changed almost immediately by lime into insoluble arsenite of lime.

That white arsenic mixture should be permitted to stand for some time before application to foliage, for the reason that several days are required to completely change it to insoluble arsenite. This change may be facilitated by treating the mixture with boiling water, which fact he has utilized in the preparation of a cheap arsenite described below.

That Bordeaux mixture prevents the solubility of the arsenites by virtue of its lime, hence this fungicide may be safely applied in combination with London purple and Paris green.

The arsenites combined with Eau Celeste are not safe to use on foliage, because of their solubility in this fluid.

---

*On the Cause and Prevention of the Injury to Foliage by Arsenites, together with a new and cheap Arsenite, and Experiments on Combining Arsenites with Fungicides. By B. W. Kilgore, North Carolina Agricultural Experiment Station, Bulletin No. 77*b*; Technical Bulletin No. 2: July 1. 1891.

The cheap arsenite referred to is a mixture of 1 pound of the commercial white arsenic to 2 pounds of lime, made by boiling them together for half an hour in 2 to 5 gallons of water, and then diluting to the required volume, say 100 gallons.

THE CORN ROOT APHIS.

As Article XII, Vol. III, of the Bulletin of the Illinois State Laboratory of Natural History, Dr. Clarence M. Weed publishes his "Sixth contribution to a knowledge of the life history of certain little-known Aphididæ," giving in this seven-page instalment a partial account of the biology of the Corn Root Aphis (*Aphis maidis* Fitch). He estimates that there is no connection between the root and aërial forms of *Aphis maidis* and gives a summary of the life-history of the former, describing for the first time the wingless male (taken *in copula* with an oviparous female) and the egg. To consult this series of six contributions which Dr. Weed has now published the student will have to examine two numbers of "Psyche," two bulletins of the Ohio Agricultural Experiment Station, one number of INSECT LIFE and one number of the Bulletin of the Illinois State Laboratory, a fact which is to be regretted.

MOSQUITO LARVÆ AS SUPPOSED INTERNAL PARASITES.

The idea that the larvæ of the mosquito may occasionally become true internal parasites of man has been brought forward by an Italian author, E. Tosatto, and has been adopted by Prof. R. Blanchard in the second volume of his "Traité de Zoologie Médicale" (Paris, 1890). The matter would hardly deserve mention were it not stated in a general work of the high character of Blanchard's, but the fear lest it should become adopted by other authors of books of reference has induced Dr. Eugenio Ficalbi to carefully review the evidence brought together by Tosatto in a recent number of the Bullettino della Società Entomologica Italiana.* Dr. Ficalbi was not contented with showing the weakness of the evidence upon which Tosatto founded his claim, but tested the matter by himself swallowing at different times eggs, larvæ in all stages, and pupæ of the mosquito. He adds: "It is useless to say that I have digested them all completely without being in the least disturbed and without inducing any parasitism." ("Inutile dire che ho digerito completamente tutto ciò, senza provare mai il minimo disturbo e senza andare incontro a parassitismo.") The author does not deny that Tosatto found the mosquito larvæ in the fæces of his patient, but explains this on the ground that the fæces had been diluted with water which contained larvæ or else the receptacle had been rinsed with water infested with larvæ.

---

* Bullettino della Società Entomologica Italiana. Anno 22. (Firenze 1891) pp. 227–230.

THE HENRY EDWARDS COLLECTION.

We notice from *Science* of March 18, 1892, that the friends of the late Henry Edwards have subscribed $10,000 and the American Museum of Natural History $5,000 for the purchase of the Edwards entomological collection, which will be placed in the American Museum. This enterprise has been carried through by Mr. A. M. Palmer, manager of the Madison Square Theater. It is gratifying to know that this collection will be kept intact and that it will remain in this country.

LOCUSTS IN EGYPT.

We have several times referred to the great damage which was done in Algiers during 1891 by the migratory locusts of the East. It seems, from a report just published by the Ministry of Public Instruction at Cairo that a great deal of damage was done in Lower Egypt as well, by swarms of the locusts flying eastward from the higher regions of Tripoli. This report, which is submitted by Prof. Williamson Wallace, of the Tewfikieh College of Agriculture at Gheezeh, contains a summarized account of the life-history of *Pachytilus migratorius*, which differs in no way from its life round in India and Algeria. The first swarms, although attracting considerable attention, did not rouse the people to the necessity of attempting any remedial work. When they began to breed, however, a most energetic effort was made to rid the country of the plague. Orders were issued from the Ministry of the Interior pointing out the gravity of the situation and instructing the moodeers, or governors of districts, to use every means in their power for the destruction of the locusts. By the 15th of May the locusts had spread to every province of Lower Egypt except Dakahlieh. It was found that the eggs had been principally deposited on the sand islands in the course of the western branch of the Nile in cotton fields.

In the fields occupied by the winter crops, such as wheat, barley, beans, and clover, scarcely any eggs were found, as the ground at that time was too hard to be pierced by the ovipositor of the insect. This restriction of the infested area was a great advantage, as the young cotton plants gave but little cover to the locusts, and the proprietor of the field, as a matter of course, immediately reported the presence of the locusts, since instant action could alone save his crop. The old simple methods of destruction were found to be the most effectual. Long, dry trenches were dug, into which the locusts were driven by bands of men and children often numbering several hundreds, each armed with a palm branch. They were then covered with earth or burned with straw or cornstalks. In the course of six weeks the insects were practically exterminated. Few of the young ones ever reached full growth, and these few were speedily destroyed by birds, among which the common Crow was particularly active. The Cypriote screen-and-trap system was tried, but is not recommended by Prof.

Wallace in cultivated lands. He states that it is only useful where locusts are known to exist in waste lands and where several miles of screens are erected to arrest the natural march of the insects. Some attempt was made at gathering the locusts by hand, and the Government offered 2 piasters per oke (8.8 cents per 2¾ pounds), but the people did not seem to realize that they would be paid until most of the eggs were deposited!

Prof. Wallace states that small flights of locusts are frequently heard of in some parts of Egypt, and that forty years ago they bred in the country in great numbers and were exterminated by the people in much the same manner as this year. Comparatively little damage was done to crops the present year.

LEPIDOPTERA WHOSE FEMALES ARE WINGLESS.

M. G. A. Poujade, in *La Nature* for December 26, 1891, gives an admirable summary of the natural history of the European species of Lepidoptera without wings, in the course of a series of articles upon the influence of artificial light upon insects. He calls attention to a most interesting observation by Giraud, made as far back as 1865, and which has seldom been repeated, to the effect that the wingless females of Hibernia and Cheimatobia were found around the lanterns in the Bois de Boulogne where they were supposed to have been either attracted by the light or the abundance of male insects which had been so attracted, and had climbed up the lamp-posts and had taken their position upon the glass sides of the lamp. The more natural explanation seems to us that these females had been carried by light-attracted males while in the act of copulation and had been deserted on the glass side of the lamps. It would be very interesting to know whether similar observations have ever been made in this country in districts where the Canker Worm is abundant.

TOBACCO INSECTS IN FLORIDA.

In Bulletin No. 15 of the Florida Experiment Station, entitled "Tobacco and its Cultivation," mention is made of the damage done to the crop by Cut Worms, the Bud Worm (probably *Heliothis armigera*) and the Horn Worm (*Protoparce carolina*). Paris green and flour, in the proportion of one pound of the poison to four or five pounds of flour, is the mixture recommended as a remedy for these pests. It is supposed by the author of the bulletin that the poison may injure the texture of the leaf and also the flavor of the tobacco. Experiments on this point are promised for the coming season.

INSECT DISEASES OF THE MEDITERRANEAN ORANGE.

In the *Mediterranean Naturalist*, a monthly journal of natural science published at Malta, we find an article by the editor, John H. Cooke, entitled "Diseases of the Mediterranean Orange," in which the Rust Mite (*Typhlodromus oleivorus*), two species of Dactylopius, the Flat Scale (*Lecanium hesperidum*) and the Fruit Fly (*Ceratitis citriperda*) are specifically mentioned. Nothing new in the way of remedies, however, is suggested.

SPRAYING FOR THE CODLING MOTH.

The effectiveness of spraying against the Codling Moth is shown by the interesting results of a comparative test made by Mr. Waldo F. Brown and quoted from the *New York Tribune* in the *American Cultivator* for January 2, 1892. Mr. Brown carefully examined two trays of unassorted apples, each containing 100, the fruit in one tray being taken from a tree which had been sprayed, and in the other from an unsprayed tree adjoining. The apples were divided into three grades, first, second, and third, No. 1 being perfect apples, No. 2 having one or two blemishes, and No. 3 being almost worthless. In the tray containing fruit from the unsprayed tree there were 4 perfect apples, 58 second-class, and 38 culls, while the tray filled from the sprayed tree contained 84 first-class, 9 second-class, and 7 culls.

A NEW LOCALITY FOR ICERYA PURCHASI.

Mr. J. W. Douglas announces in the *Entomologist's Monthly Magazine* for December, 1891, that Mr. D. Morris, assistant director of the Royal Gardens at Kew, has sent specimens of *Icerya purchasi* received from St. Helena. They were found upon rose bushes which had been imported from the Cape of Good Hope. Mr. Douglas positively recognizes the species and recommends that the most strenuous exertions be made to exterminate it at once.

THE USE OF VASELINE WITH CARBON BISULPHIDE.

Practice has shown that the bisulphide of carbon does not give so satisfactory results in very siliceous earth as in others.

Dr. Albin Meunier has been endeavoring to render this action uniform by assisting the diffusion of this substance in heavy soils and preventing too rapid evaporation in those that are too light.

The bisulphide was mixed with vaseline boiling at 350°, which is quite harmless to plants, even in large quantity. This diminished the evaporation. Though the bisulphide can be separated from vaseline by fractional distillation, on account of the great difference between the boiling points, yet its evaporation at ordinary temperatures is considerably diminished by the addition of vaseline, which retains considerable quantities for days in spite of a considerable surface of evaporation.

Five thousand seven hundred kilos of carbon bisulphide mixed with vaseline were employed in the Department of the Rhone in 1888 with such results that in 1889 89,585 kilos were employed, and in 1890 242,392 kilos in the following departments: Rhône, Isère, Ain, Saone-et-Loire, Côte-d'Or, Loire, Ardèche, and Drôme, and it is estimated that 500,000 kilos will be required in 1891.

The mixture is employed as the pure sulphide. Its efficiency is increased by inserting one portion at a distance of 10 or 12 cm. from the stock and spreading the rest over a hectare. About 2000–2500 hectares are under treatment in this way.

For four years this mixture has been employed on 15 to 20 hectares at St. Étienne-la-Vauenne (Rhône) This property was kept at its average rate of production by pure sulphide, but its production has been increased threefold by the new treatment. Phylloxera is no longer found on the root, the vegetation is luxuriant, and numerous rootlets have appeared—a sure sign of increased vitality.—*Journal of Chemical Industry* for November, 1891.

The foregoing is taken from an article by one of the champions of the new insecticide, and would seem to indicate that in the mixture of vaseline and bisulphide of carbon we have at length obtained the long-sought complete remedy for the Grape Phylloxera.

The fact remains, however, that various careful experimenters in France, such as MM. Gastine, Marion, Vermorel, and others, have given the vaseline mixture thorough trial and have published their conclusions at length in various scientific and practical journals, notably *Le Progrès Agricole et Viticole*, to the effect that the vaseline, so far from improving and completing the action of the bisulphide of carbon, actually hinders it, and this disadvantage increases in proportion to the amount of vaseline employed. The claim is admitted that the vaseline prevents the rapid vaporization of the bisulphide, but it is affirmed that the action becomes so slow or is so much checked that little benefit results, and the general diffusion of the vapor through the soil in sufficient quantity to be insecticidal is prevented.

MR. KOEBELE'S RECENT SENDINGS.

On pages 163, 164 of the current volume we recorded Mr. Koebele's efforts down to November 1, 1891. The December steamer brought over a number of additional specimens of the two species of Orcus—viz, *Orcus chalybeus* and *O. australasiæ*—which he had found preying upon the Red Scale, and upon species of Chionaspis, as well as upon *Aspidiotus rossii*. He also sent a number of Scymnids, which prey upon the Red Scale as well as upon the Black and Flat Scales. Perhaps the most interesting species sent, however, was a new species of Vedalia, which he found feeding in small numbers upon *Icerya purchasi*. According to Mr. Koebele, Mr. Olliff has one specimen of the new species in his collection, and will soon describe it. Mr. Tryon, of Brisbane, Queensland, has two specimens. The insect was met with quite often near Paramatta and eleven larvæ were found upon one Icerya.

Another interesting find was the Coccinellid known as *Cryptolæmus montrousiæ*, the larvæ of which feed upon a species of Dactylopius infesting Aurocaria. This insect was found everywhere, and always upon some Dactylopius. A large number of specimens were sent.

A further letter dated January 25, and an accompanying sending, have also been received, and another lot of Coccinellids was sent over, consisting chiefly of the two species of Orcus, and numerous specimens of a small Scymnus preying upon the Red Scale. A number of the larvæ and chrysalids of *Thalpochares cocciphaga*, the Lepidopterous insect which preys upon large scales like *Lecanium* and *Monophlœbus*, were also sent. More specimens of the new species of Vedalia were found, and a most interesting Blastobasis, which is very destructive to a Chionaspis upon Orange, has also been discovered. Mr. Koebele writes that whole branches are spun over with a fine web interwoven with the remains of scale insects, and under this web hundreds of the Blastobasis larvæ can be found upon each tree. Should it be possible to import this insect in good condition, it will undoubtedly prove of great value in orange orchards infested not only by *Chionaspis citri* but also by the species of Mytilaspis and Parlatoria. For some reason this last sending did not reach Los Angeles in good condition. Only a very few of the Coccinellids were alive and still fewer of the Thalpochares. The boxes containing the Blastobasis were sent direct to Washington, and careful examination shows only two living larvæ and a few pupæ, which appear to be unhealthy, and from which we may not succeed in rearing the moths. Mr. Coquillett is taking every pains to thoroughly acclimatize the specimens sent to him at Los Angeles, and on the whole it seems probable that some good may be accomplished, particularly if he is able to acclimatize the two species of Orcus.

A LEAF-MINER IN WHEAT.

Early in November, in a small plat of wheat sown on the grounds of the Experiment Station, at Columbus, Ohio, on July 20, a single larva was observed mining in one of the larger leaves of one of the plants, near the upper extremity. The infested plant was transferred to the insectary, where the larva continued to feed, working its way downward near the edge of the leaf toward the base. November 16 it abandoned the plant and was placed in a small glass tube. The length of the larva at this time was about 10 mm., the color yellowish, with dorsal transverse dark bands. After spinning a very thin white cocoon, through which its every movement could be clearly observed, it passed into the chrysalis stage on the 18th. The chrysalis was 4 mm. in length, and from it the imago emerged December 1. The adult proved to be *Elachista præmaturella* Clem., kindly determined for me by Miss Murtfeldt.

In the Tineina of North America (edited by Stainton), p. 133, Dr. Clemens simply states that "the imago may be taken on the wing in

April," while Mr. V. T. Chambers, *Can. Ent.*, vol. VI, p. 76, says that a species, which he doubtfully refers to this, was found by him in the pupal stage in Blue Grass pastures, and expresses the opinion that the larvæ were probably miners in the leaves of that grass.

My rearing was, of course, untimely, and it is altogether probable that, under a natural environment, the imago would not have emerged until early spring. Therefore it seems probable that in central Ohio the species is two-brooded, eggs being deposited in April or early in May, and again in September of October.—F. M. WEBSTER.

ENTOMOLOGICAL SOCIETY OF WASHINGTON.

January 7, 1892.—Election of officers for 1892 resulted as follows: President, C. V. Riley; first vice-president, C. L. Marlatt; second vice-president, William H. Ashmead; treasurer, E. A. Schwarz; recording secretary, Nathan Banks; corresponding secretary, L. O. Howard; additional members of the executive committee, William H. Fox, George Marx, and B. E. Fernow.

In the report of the Recording Secretary it was shown that during the year 1891 17 new members had been added to the rolls of the society, raising the total number to 53 persons, of which number 27 are active and 26 corresponding members.

The retiring President, Dr. Marx, delivered his annual address on "An Introduction to a Monograph of the American Ticks (Ixodidæ)." In an introductory chapter the author drew attention to the absence of monographic works which would attract and facilitate the work of the beginners in arachnological studies, and also the inherent difficulties in the obscurity of many of the classificatory characters. He pointed out the nature and extent of the work already done in the various groups of Arachnida, and followed with a reference to the bibliography of the writings, both foreign and American, on the Ticks of this country.

A full chapter on the morphology of the Ticks followed, and also extended notes on the biology of these parasites, in which personal observations were recounted, showing that Ticks are not necessarily parasitic on warm-blooded animals, but may reach full growth and in fact complete the cycle of their existence on a strictly vegetable diet; and also that Ticks after being gorged with blood may revert to vegetable food. The address was discussed by various members.

C. L. MARLATT,
Recording Secretary.

February 4, 1892.—Messrs. D. G. Fairchild and M. B. Waite were elected active members of the Society.

Under the head of short notes Mr. Ashmead made some interesting remarks on Eunotus, a peculiar Chalcidid genus, new to the United States. It was his opinion that it belonged to the subfamily Aphelininæ.

Mr. Banks exhibited a specimen of Loxosceles, which had but six developed legs.

Dr. Marx exhibited a peculiar Theridiid spider with extremely long mandibles.

Dr. Stiles made some instructive remarks on the liver-fluke story that was circulated in certain papers. According to this story the young stages of the liver-fluke were passed in the House Fly, whereas they are passed in snails.

Mr. Mally read a paper on "An Insectivorous Primrose." He drew attention to the fact that *Œnothera speciosa* captures small Dipterous insects upon its gummy style and stigma. But one species was seen trapped. As the insect could not be eaten by the plant, the author thought that the insect must in some way aid the fertilization of the ovules. Discussed by Messrs. Ashmead, Test, Schwarz, Marx, Howard, Stiles, and Marlatt.

Mr. Howard contributed an important paper on "Hymenopterous Parasites of Spiders," being a complete revision of our knowledge of these interesting insects, both European and American. Lists and breeding notes were given and specimens exhibited. He also called attention to the habits of Mantispa and some Acroceridæ, which in Europe are known to be parasitic on spiders. Discussed by Messrs. Ashmead, Marlatt, Test, Schwarz, Fox, and Marx.

Dr. Stiles made a few remarks on various Nematode genera parasitic on spiders.

Dr. Marx read a few additions to his paper on ticks.

Prof. H. E. Summers was invited to speak, and he made some instructive remarks on collecting and labelling.

NATHAN BANKS,
Recording Secretary.

SPECIAL NOTES.

Prof. Forbes' Sixth Report.—The Seventeenth Report of the State Entomologist of Illinois has just been issued from the press of the State Printer at Springfield. It covers the years 1889 and 1890. Although long delayed, this report is welcome to entomologists, and contains the usual array of excellent and well illustrated articles. The topics treated are the Fruit Bark-beetle (*Scolytus rugulosus*); the use of arsenical poisons on Plum and Peach for the Curculio; the American Plum-borer (*Euzophera semifuneralis*); the common White Grubs; additional notes on the Hessian Fly; summary history of the Corn Root-aphis; a bacteriological disease of the large Corn Root-worm (*Diabrotica 12-punctata*), and the diseases of the Chinch Bug. Most of these topics have been treated by Prof. Forbes in more or less ephemeral publications during the past three years, and are now for the first time put into permanent shape. The report is prefaced by three excellent colored plates by the Art Publishing Company of Boston, illustrating *Aphis maidis*, *Aphis maidi-radicis*, and *Siphonophora avenæ*, and concludes with four plates in black and white, illustrating some of the other insects treated. As an appendix to the report an analytical list of the entomological writings of the late Dr. William LeBaron, second State Entomologist of Illinois, is published, together with a half-tint portrait of Dr. LeBaron, which we find very good and natural.

Insects injurious to stored Grain.—Mr. H. E. Weed, Entomologist of the Mississippi Experiment Station, has just published a little 16-page bulletin devoted to the subject of stored-grain insects. He finds that the principal insect pests which affect stored grain in Mississippi are the Angoumois Grain-moth (*Gelechia cerealella*), the Black Weevil (*Calandra oryzæ*), and the Red Grain Weevil (*Silvanus cassiæ*). He mentions several other wide-spread species, and recommends the ordinary bisulphide of carbon treatment in quarantine bins. The popular idea of the efficacy of China berries has received a careful test with the same negative results obtained by us in 1878–'80. Original figures are given of *Pteromalus gelechiæ* Webster, *Carpophilus pallipennis*, *Calandra oryzæ* (larva, pupa, and adult), *Silvanus cassiæ* (larva, pupa, and adult), *S. surinamensis*, and *Tribolium ferrugineum*.

A West Virginia Bulletin.—Bulletin No. 21, of the West Virginia Agricultural Experiment Station, Morgantown, W. Va., is a joint production of Messrs. A. D. Hopkins, entomologist, and C. F. Millspaugh, botanist, and treats of injurious insects and plant diseases. It is a compilation of general methods recommended by the best authorities in this country for use against noxious insects and plant diseases, and contains brief directions for the preparation and use of all the better known insecticides and fungicides.

Entomological Notes from Australia.—Number 11, Volume II, of the *Agricultural Gazette*, of New South Wales, contains two entomological articles, the first entitled "A new scale-insect destroying Saltbush," and the other "Notes on current Work," both by Mr. A. Sidney Olliff, the recently appointed Government entomologist. The new scale-insect is a Pulvinaria which Mr. Olliff has named *P. maskelli*. The saltbushes are fodder plants of several genera, the species most affected being *Rhagodia hastata* and *Atriplex nummularia*. Several natural enemies of the scale-insect have been found, and as a remedy it is advised to cut down and burn infested plants before the eggs have hatched. After the hatching of the eggs, spraying with dilute kerosene emulsion is recommended.

Under the head of "Notes on Current Work" the damage done by *Lecanium hesperidum* to the Pepper Tree, particularly from the subsequent smut fungi, is mentioned and a bark-boring beetle (*Bostrychus jesuita*) is recorded as boring in pepper and white cedar trees. The Orange Rust Mite is also said to occur in numbers at Kurrajong.

Miss Ormerod's Fifteenth Report.[*]—We have just received from Miss Eleanor A. Ormerod, honorary consulting entomologist of the Royal Agricultural Society of England, her fifteenth report upon observations of injurious insects and common farm pests. This report fully sustains the reputation of the series. It comprises 168 pages and is illustrated by numerous text figures. A number of British crop pests are treated, very few of which occur in this country. One of the most interesting articles is that upon the Apple Saw-fly (*Hoplocampa testudinea ?*). The larvæ of this insect work in a particularly destructive way, boring into the very young fruit. In the orchards attacked the quantity of fruit destroyed was very great, and Miss Ormerod is of the opinion that this insect does considerable damage, for which the Codling Moth is

---

[*] Report of Observations of Injurious Insects and Common Farm Pests, with Special Report on Attack of Caterpillars of the Diamond-back Moth, during the year 1891, with Methods of Prevention and Remedy. Fifteenth Report. By Eleanor A. Ormerod, F. R. Met. Soc., etc. London: Simpkin, Marshall, Hamilton, Kent & Co. Limited. 1892. 18 pence.

held responsible. The remedies proposed are gathering windfalls and removing the surface earth under the infested trees. Another interesting article treats of the occurrence of one of the common mites (*Tyroglyphus longior*) in great numbers in hay in stacks and when stored in lofts. Considerable attention is given to the use of Paris green against leaf-eating orchard caterpillars, and the advisability of mixing softsoap with Paris green is considered at some length. The conclusion reached is that whatever arsenic is set free in the soap solution is neutralized by the free alkali of the soap, but the mixture as a whole is a tenacious, sticky mass, which it is difficult to properly dissolve in water. The bulk of the report is occupied with a consideration of the Diamond-back Moth (*Plutella cruciferarum*) which, as we have already stated, occurred in enormous numbers in certain parts of England last summer. The article includes a great deal of interesting correspondence with a number of Miss Ormerod's intelligent co-workers. Last year's occurrence of this species was a very exceptional one, and according to Miss Ormerod seems to have been due rather to the fact that moths were borne in on easterly winds in the spring rather than that they bred where first noticed. The remedies are those mentioned by Mr. Whitehead, whose paper we reviewed in the last number of INSECT LIFE.

Bulletin No. 5 of the New Mexico Station.[*]—Mr. C. H. Tyler Townsend is the author of a brief bulletin just received which treats of the Vine Leaf-hopper, the Codling Moth, the Green June-beetle (*Allorhina sobrina*), and Root-borers (Larvæ of *Prionus* spp.). He finds that the kerosene emulsion is the only practical remedy for the Vine Leaf-hopper, and that it should be applied early in the season and directed against the under sides of the leaves. After the insects have acquired wings it is too late to do effective work. The Codling Moth, it seems, has just been found for the first time in the Mesilla Valley, although it has occurred abundantly in other portions of New Mexico for some time. The Allorhina here mentioned has previously been referred to by the author in the current volume of INSECT LIFE (p. 25) as *A. nitida*.

A Bulletin on Spraying.—The Department has just published, as "Farmers' Bulletin No. 7," a short consideration of spraying fruits for insect pests and fungous diseases, with a special consideration of the subject in relation to the public health. This bulletin puts the reasons for spraying and the best formulæ in condensed shape for the use of the practical fruit-grower.

[*] New Mexico College of Agriculture. Agricultural Experiment Station. Bulletin No. 5, March, 1892. Notices of importance concerning Fruit Insects. Las Cruces, N. Mex., 1892.

Entomological Notes from the Indian Museum.—Volume II of the interesting Indian Museum Notes, to which we have occasionally referred in these pages, has just reached us through the courtesy of Mr. E. C. Cotes and the Indian Museum trustees. It consists of four parts: Part 1, devoted to Miscellaneous Notes; part 2, to the Wild Silk Insects of India; part 3, to the White Insect Wax of India; and part 4, to the Locusts of Bengal, Madras, Assam, and Bombay. The volume, as a whole, is so important that it deserves a more extended notice than we can give it. The illustrations are handsome lithographic plates, part 2 carrying no less than fifteen of these plates, figuring twenty-nine species of the large silk moths. Part 1, upon Miscellaneous Notes, contains more matter of interest to entomologists in this country, a number of cosmopolitan pests being mentioned. Among them are the Angoumois Grain Moth (*Gelechia cerealella,*) the Sugar-cane Borer (*Diatræa saccharalis*), the Corn Worm or Boll Worm (*Heliothis armigera*)—here recorded as feeding upon the fruit of the Cape Gooseberry—and the so-called American Blight (*Schizoneura lanigera*). Several new species of scale-insects are described by Mr. Maskell, and a new Tineid (*Gracilaria theivora*), which mines the leaves of the Tea Tree, is described by Lord Walsingham. Part 3 is interesting as giving some definite information upon some white wax producers. *Ceroplastes ceriferus* is reported as rare in India, while the Fulgorid which produces an abundant supply of white sugary wax, is determined as *Phromnia marginella.* The trustees of the museum deserve every credit for their enterprise in publishing these valuable notes, which are of great interest to us and to entomologists all over the world, aside from their great value to the country from which they emanate.

Since the above was written we have received Part 5 of Vol. II, in which the principal article is by Mr. W. L. Sclater on "The Economic Importance of Birds in India." There are short articles on the methods of destroying locusts in Tunis, on the gas treatment for scale-insects (reprinted from Mr. Coquillett's report in Bulletin 23 of the Division of Entomology), on Paris green as an insecticide (from Miss Ormerod's leaflet of February, 1891), and on insecticide washes against Date Palm Scale, reprinted from INSECT LIFE (Vol. III, p. 441).

Two new Bulletins of the Division of Entomology.—Since the publication of the last number of INSECT LIFE, Bulletins No. 26 and 27 of the division have been issued from the press. No. 26 contains reports of observations and experiments in the practical work of the division for the season of 1891, and is comparable to Bulletins Nos. 21 and 23, which cover, respectively, the seasons of 1889 and 1890. Bulletin No. 27 contains reports of the damage by destructive locusts during the season of 1891, giving full accounts of a trip through the Northwest by Mr. Bruner, a journey through California by Mr. Coquillett, and a trip to Kansas by Prof. Osborn.

THE PEA AND BEAN WEEVILS.

The life-histories of these two insects have been comparatively well known to economic entomologists for many years, but even in recently published accounts some misstatements are to be found, and there is little wonder that with practical people the question should still be raised as to whether either or both will continue to breed in stored seeds. The text for this résumé of the main facts in the life-histories of these insects will be found in the following communication from Peter Henderson & Co., the large seed dealers in New York City:

> We send some beans infested with what we suppose is the Bean Weevil (*Bruchus fabæ*). The ravages of this insect are enormous and we think are increasing. We are led to believe that the eggs are laid on the pod when growing, and that it is in the larval stage that all the feeding and consequent damage is done; further, that after the larval and feeding stage it passes into the chrysalis, and there remains dormant until spring or artificial warmth leads it to emerge from the place prepared by the larva. We also are of the opinion that the adult insect is perfectly harmless to any seed beans, notwithstanding the opinion of one of our large growers, who claims that "the bugs travel from bag to bag and bin to bin and eat the holes," similar to the ones in sample sent. Our limited knowledge of entomology leads us to suppose his theory is totally impossible, but, seeing that such an important issue is involved, we take the liberty to ask the benefit of your knowledge. * * *

Comparatively full accounts of both the Pea Weevil and the Bean Weevil were published in the Third Report on the Insects of Missouri (pp. 44 to 50 and 52 to 56), and from these accounts and our subsequent notes we have prepared the following summary:

THE PEA WEEVIL (*Bruchus pisi* Linn).

The adult Pea Weevil is shown at Fig. 40*b*, with the natural size indicated at the small outline below. It is about 5 mm. long and its general color is rusty black, with more or less white on the wing-covers, and a distinct white spot on the hinder part of the thorax, near the scutellum. The beetles begin to appear about the time the peas are in blossom, and when the young pods form the females lay their eggs upon the surface without attempting to insert them. These eggs, as shown at Fig. 41, are deep yellow in color, 1.5 mm. long, three times as long as wide, fusiform, pointed in front, blunt behind, but larger anteriorly than posteriorly. They are fastened in front by some viscid fluid which turns white in drying. It is probable that the

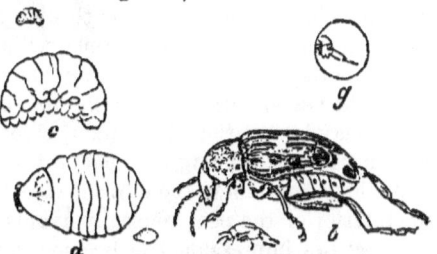

FIG. 40.—PEA WEEVIL: *b*, adult; *c*, full-grown larva; *d*, pupa; *g*, pea, showing exit hole enlarged, nat. size indicated by smaller figures below (after Curtis).

egg-laying occurs generally at night. Where the insects are abundant a single pod will often be found to carry as many as 15 or 20 eggs, which is an evidence of faulty instinct, since only one larva can develop in a single pea. The newly hatched larva is deep yellow in color, with a black head, and bores directly through the pod into the nearest pea, the hole in the pod soon growing over, while a mere speck upon the side of the pod is the only indication of its entrance. The statement has been generally made that, in feeding, the larva seems in the majority of cases to avoid the germ of the future sprout so that most of the "buggy" peas will germinate as readily as those which have been untouched. This must, however, now be qualified, as we shall show in a later paragraph. The full-grown larva is indicated at Fig. 40c. Before transforming to pupa, it cuts a circular hole quite to the thin outer membrane of the pea, thus providing for the future exit of the beetle. It then lines the interior of its excavation with a thin smooth layer of paste, excluding all excrement, and then transforms to the pupa state. The adult beetle in issuing has only to eat through the thin membrane left by the larva. It has been proved that the beetle would die if the larva had not prepared this passage way, and has been asserted that it will perish if the hole is pasted over with a piece of paper thinner than the hull itself.

FIG. 41.—Egg of Pea Weevil—enlarged (after Riley).

Sometimes many of the beetles will issue in the fall of the year, but as a general rule they remain in the peas through the following winter, and many are planted with seed peas. As far as is known the insects on issuing will not oviposit upon the dry peas, and a sure remedy will, therefore, be found in keeping seed peas in a close receptacle over two seasons before planting. The beetles will all issue at the customary time, but will soon die. When it is necessary to plant the first season the entire lot of seed should be thrown into water, when the "buggy" ones will float, and should be removed and destroyed, sound ones only being planted. Infested peas may also be disinfected by placing them in a tight vessel with one of a number of different insecticides, among which may be mentioned camphor, chloroform, ether, and bisulphide of carbon, the latter being the cheapest and most efficacious.

We have just noted the current idea that the larva, while working in the interior of the pea, generally avoids the germ or plumule and from this fact the impression has become more or less prevalent that peas which have been eaten by weevils are none the less available for seed. There has been many a discussion on this subject in the columns of the agricultural press, and while the weight of evidence has always been contrary to the use of damaged seed peas, still the question can not be said to have been definitely set at rest before the publication of the results of Prof. E. A. Popenoe's careful experiments, in Bulletin No. 19 of the Kansas State Experiment Station. This investigator conducted a germination test of 500 peas of ten sorts with the result that but one-fourth germinated, and the partial destruction of the cotyledons rendered the further growth of these doubtful. A check lot of the same number of sound peas gave a germination of 97 per cent. An examination of 275 injured peas showed but 69 in which the germ was not wholly or partially destroyed. Moreover, Prof. Popenoe further states:

In a field test of the growth of sound as compared with weeviled peas, the results were more decisive from a practical standpoint. In this test 23 varieties were represented, each by 100 sound and 100 weeviled peas, taken as they came, without further selection. The seeds were planted in the garden in parallel rows, the sound and weeviled peas of each sort side by side, the rows 18 inches apart. The planting was done on the 5th of June, and the dryness of the season hindered the perfect germination and growth to a noticeable degree. Of the sound peas 68 per cent came up, and 64 per cent made strong plants. In 10 varieties of the weeviled peas no seeds germinated; the remaining 13 varieties were represented in all by 58 plants, or 4.4 per cent, in germination, of which but 49, or 3.8 per cent, grew to average size and strength.

This evidence practically settles the long mooted question, and it is safe to say definitely that weeviled or "buggy" peas should not be planted.

THE BEAN WEEVIL (*Bruchus fabæ* Riley).

This congeneric insect resembles the species we have just treated, in general appearance. It appears to be a native American insect, and probably fed originally upon some wild bean. It is said to have been first noticed upon cultivated beans about 1860 in Rhode Island, is now generally distributed throughout the United States, and has been carried by commerce to different parts of the world. The adult beetle is shown at Fig. 42, and it will be noticed that the main points of difference are the absence of the white markings. The general color is tawny gray with more or less dull yellowish, and it is somewhat smaller than the Pea Weevil.

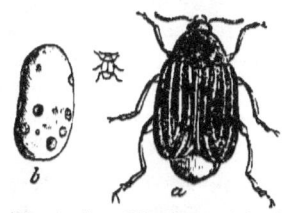

Fig. 42.—Bean Weevil: *a*, adult; *b*, damaged bean—enlarged (after Riley).

In its life-history this species differs from *Bruchus pisi* in two important points. Largely on account of its smaller size and the greater size of the seed which it infests, a number of individuals will develop in a single bean. As many as 28 have thus been found feeding at once. A second point of difference, and one of great economic importance, is that the insects will continue breeding indefinitely in stored beans. We showed this to be the case in 1882, but recent writers have, for the most part, ignored this interesting fact. The eggs are primarily laid upon the bean pod in the field, and the larva enters the seed in the same manner as does the Pea Weevil. The rate of growth is similar, and some individuals, as with the other species, may issue the same fall, others hibernating within the beans and issuing in the spring. If easy means of exit are not present, the females will soon begin to lay their eggs upon the stored and damaged beans, and another generation will soon develop. This may go on indefinitely, or until the food supply is exhausted, although in closed receptacles the beetles always appear anxious to escape.

The first published record of this continuous breeding in stored beans was probably our note in 1882, above alluded to, where, in reply to a question from a correspondent in Bremen, Ohio, we wrote: "Unlike the Pea Weevil, the Bean Weevil continues to multiply in the stored beans. These, when infested, are usually reduced at last to nothing but powder, and have no value as seed."

In 1878–'79 we made a number of observations upon this species, from which some interesting points have been determined. On December 31, 1878, we received from Indian Territory a lot of badly infested beans, from which many beetles had already issued. Close examination showed that larvæ in all stages of growth and pupæ were still contained in the beans. January 21, 1879, a dozen beetles, just issued, were placed in a vessel with sound black beans for observation. Two days later quite a number of eggs had been deposited. They were simply glued to the outside of the beans, no cavity having been provided for them by the beetles. A few were found loose in the jar. These eggs were 0.7 mm. long and 0.3 mm. in diameter at the stoutest part. They were white, and closely granulated. February 8, or sixteen days after oviposition, two of the eggs hatched. The young larvæ moved about quite briskly, and when in motion curved the body at each step. This it is enabled to do by the possession of temporary legs, while its other characters, as compared with those it assumes within the bean, fit it for moving over and penetrating the smooth but rather thin skin of our ordinary beans.

BRUCHUS FAB.E—*First larva.*—The larva at this stage presents a very curious appearance and differs widely in important characters from the second stage. The body is hardly so stout in proportion to its length; the prothoracic plate bears two pairs of projecting spurs, the hinder pair having each a serrate edge of four teeth, and the anal plate also bears four horny, pointed tubercles. On the head there are two very evident eye spots; the antennæ are four-jointed, and bear side pieces arising from the basal joint. The mandibles have two blunt teeth and the labium is large and fleshy, and is differentiated into two viscid, papillose paraglossæ and a central ligular prominence with two papillæ. The insect at this stage differs, however, most notably from the more mature larvæ in possessing six postembryonic legs, as shown at Fig. 43. Each of these legs is composed of three apparent sclerites, the basal one stout, coxa-like, and scarcely differentiated from the body. The second is long and slender and may correspond to the fused femur and tibia. This joint bears several hairs at its tip and gives rise to the third joint, which we may call the tarsus, and which is much more slender than the second joint and is broadened at its tip into a flat pulvillus, bearing at the heel a single delicate spur, as shown at Fig. 43*g*. Nine spiracles are plainly seen, eight being abdominal and one mesothoracic. There is a row of very long, subdorsal hairs, a shorter row between this and the median line, and another lateral row intermediate in length between the two just mentioned.

We are not aware that similar structural peculiarities in the first larval stages of Bruchus have been pointed out before. They seem to indicate, perhaps, affinities with the Chrysomelidæ, and are evidently of advantage in aiding the young creature in the work it has to do. This stage is very evanescent, as the necessity for locomotive organs is transitory. Immediately after finding the proper spot for entering the bean, the larva gnaws its way in and molts.

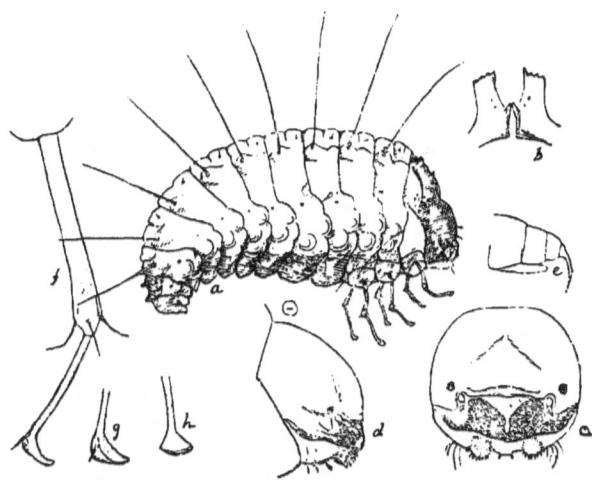

Fig. 43.—*a*, First larva of *Bruchus fabæ* greatly enlarged; *b*, thoracic processes; *c*, head from front; *d*, same from side; *e*, antenna; *f*, thoracic leg; *g*, rear view of tarsus; *h*, same, front view, still more enlarged (original).

Other eggs hatched on February 10, and February 17, and on February 21 a small discolored spot was discovered on one of the beans, and underneath the skin was found one of the young larvæ. After entering the bean it had cast a skin, which was found in the burrow. After this molt the larva had lost its legs and become stout, acquiring the normal characters of its later stages. One bean which was carefully examined contained 17 larvæ, 8 of which were nearly full-grown, while 9, which had entered the bean later, were in different stages of development. On January 28 a single impregnated female was confined with several beans in order to ascertain the number of eggs laid by a single individual. From January 31 to February 25, 68 were deposited, when the female died. Careful experiments with isolated individuals were conducted in order to ascertain the exact length of a single generation, with the result that sixty-six days was found to be the average time from the deposition of the eggs to the issuing of the adults.

The larva before transforming frequently makes two possible points of future exit, one at each end of its burrow, and occasionally the whole outer surface of the burrow remains covered simply by the thin outside skin of the bean.

The remark which we have just made regarding the germination of weeviled peas, will apply equally well to beans damaged by Bruchus.

Mr. Popenoe has experimented with beans as well as with peas, with the following result:

Fifty per cent starred: of these, three-fifths might have grown into plants, as the injury was restricted to the seed leaves. But the remaining two-fifths were variously mutilated by the loss of a part or the whole of the germ or plumule, so that under no circumstances could they have made plants. Here, then, but 30 per cent could have passed the germinating stage, and these, owing to more or less considerable injury to the seed leaves, would probably have made plants of low vigor. In a check lot of perfect beans of the same varieties and in the same numbers, planted alongside, 95 per cent germinated.

The remedies for this insect are the same as for the Pea Weevil, except that keeping the imported seed over two years in tight vessels will be of no avail for the Bean Weevil. Careful experiments with bisulphide of carbon show that in this substance we have an almost perfect remedy for both species.*

THE OX BOT IN THE UNITED STATES.

HABITS AND NATURAL HISTORY OF HYPODERMA LINEATA.

By C. V. RILEY.

A good deal has been written recently about this insect, both in this country and Europe, and, as has been intimated in previous numbers of INSECT LIFE, some interesting discoveries have been made, which have materially modified the old conceptions of the life-history and habits of the species. Of first importance is the fact which has been recently developed, namely, that the older Ox Bot-fly, *Hypoderma bovis*, hitherto supposed to be the common species of both America and Europe, is in reality either a very rare insect in this country or possibly does not occur here at all.

THE AMERICAN SPECIES IS HYPODERMA LINEATA.

The Ox Warble of this country is referable to a distinct species, *Hypoderma lineata* Villers. It was first described in 1789 as *Œstrus lineatus* (Ent. Linn. III. p. 249). It was subsequently described by Dr.

---

* Since this article was prepared, and just as it was being sent to the printer, we received Dr. J. A. Lintner's Seventh Report on the Injurious and other Insects of the State of New York, and find an elaborate article upon the Bean Weevil, covering pages 255 to 279. Dr. Lintner gives an admirable summary of the previous knowledge concerning this insect, overlooking, however, our note of 1882, to which we have referred, and adding observations of his own proving successive broods in stored beans and showing the duration of a single generation to be about two months. The article also discusses at length the question of synonymy, into which we have purposely not entered in this paper, and although he uses the name *Bruchus obsoletus* Say at the head of the article, he finally concludes that *Bruchus fabæ* of Fitch should in reality hold unless an earlier European synonymy should be established, as seems probable. This question, however, we will discuss in our next issue.

Fr. Brauer as *Hypoderma bonassi* in 1875 (Verhandl. der K. K. Zool. Bot. Gesellsch. in Wien, 1875, p. 75, pl. IV, Figs 2, 2ᵃ) from the larva only, specimens of which had been received from Dr. H. A. Hagen, of Cambridge, obtained in Colorado by Mr. J. A. Allen, from the American Bison or Buffalo. Mr. Allen found it comparatively rare on the Buffalo, his specimens having been obtained from one individual of many examined. Clark in his "Essay," etc., 1815 (pp. 37 and 72), considered it a variety of *bovis*, and later, 1843, as the male of *bovis*. Dr. Brauer has shown it to be a distinct species, but its host relations were not established until 1890. On the authority of the observations of Winnertz, Brauer, in his monograph mentioned as the probable hosts the cow and sheep. All doubts on this point were, however, dispelled by the observations of the late Dr. Adam Handlirsch independent of, and later in connection with, Dr. Brauer, and detailed in Dr. Brauer's recent communication.*

In 1888 Dr. Handlirsch took adults of this insect in a field in which cattle were pastured, and in 1889 Handlirsch, while in company with Dr. Brauer, found a puparium in a cow pasture, which was smaller than the puparium of *bovis*, resembling somewhat that of *H. diana*, and he also took adults of *lineata* in the same pasture. This puparium, however, upon comparison, was found to agree entirely with the larvæ obtained from the American bison referred to above.

Again, in 1890, Brauer, in company with a brother of Dr. Handlirsch, visited the same region and obtained some larvæ from the backs of cattle, one of which belonged to *bovis* and three to *lineata*. The larvæ referred to *lineata*, obtained from cattle by Brauer, differ in no wise from the larvæ obtained from the American bison, and the puparium mentioned also presents a full agreement with the characters of this larva. The adults of *lineata* taken in Europe also agree in every particular with those received from the United States. Both these species of Hypoderma occur, on the authority of Brauer, throughout Europe, having been found in Switzerland, Norway, Crimea, the Balkans, the Caucasus, England, Lower and Upper Austria, etc. In Styria and Hungary, however, he found only *Hypoderma bovis*. These species not only occur very commonly throughout the regions named, but frequently on the same animal.

Whether *lineata* is of European or American origin remains to be determined. In North America Brauer quotes it from Texas and on Williston's authority as ranging to Arizona and Northern California, while in 1853 Walker described it from Nova Scotia as *Œstrus supplens*. It is possible that it was originally the bot of our native buffalo. Its comparative rarity on the bison, however, and its great abundance on do-

---

* Verhandlungen der Kaiserlich-koeniglichen Zoologisch-Botanischen Gesellschaft in Wien. Wien, 1890, p. 509. "Ueber die Feststellung des Wohnthieres der *Hypoderma lineata* Villers durch Dr. Adam Handlirsch und andere Untersuchungen und Beobachtungen an Oestriden."

mestic cattle, both in this country and Europe, throw considerable doubt on this supposition, and also leave the question of its original habitat in doubt. Two flies referable to this species, a male and a female, were bred by Dr. Cooper Curtice, April 16, 1891, from larvæ extracted from the back of an animal. I have also a specimen from Prof. Herbert Osborn, reared from a bot collected in Illinois. Careful examination of these specimens, together with the balance of the material in the National Collection, comprising in all some 33 specimens, shows that they all belong to *lineata*. Of this material 16 specimens were received from correspondents as the Heel Fly from various points in Texas; two by the same name from New Jersey. one of which was reported to have been ovipositing just above the hoof of a cow; five specimens were collected in Colorado, of which one differs from the normal type in having a scantier pubescence on the face; one specimen is from southern Georgia and three are without any locality label. In addition to the bred specimen from Prof. Osborn, he sent for comparison three collected specimens taken at Ames, Iowa, and one in Colorado. An examination of the larvæ in the National Collection also shows a full agreement with the larvæ of *lineata*. These are from Arkansas, Texas, Illinois, Nebraska (three of which were taken from a buffalo bull by Mr. L. Bruner), and others without date or locality. Dr. Salmon also has a large series of larvæ numbering above 500 specimens, all of which were examined by Dr. Curtice and by myself and Mr. C. L. Marlatt, and prove to belong to *lineata*. These were taken for the most part at the Washington abattoir and from cattle from Virginia, West Virginia, Ohio, and Maryland. A large number of them were, however, taken in Texas, and others came from various localities. I have corresponded also with Dr. Williston and a number of others who either have private collections or are in charge of public collections, and have been unable to secure from any source whatever either a larva or adult referable to *boris* and collected in this country. My examination of this material has been greatly facilitated and the results made more conclusive by the kindness of Dr. Brauer in sending, at my request, authentic specimens of the larva, puparium and adult of *H. boris*.

LIFE-HISTORY OF HYPODERMA LINEATA.

Chiefly through the investigations of Dr. Cooper Curtice, late of the Bureau of Animal Industry of this Department, some curious and anomalous facts have been discovered, which have thrown a good deal of light on the actual life-history of this bot-fly, and have shown the previously accepted views to be erroneous. A preliminary notice of these facts was given by Dr. Curtice in INSECT LIFE. Vol. II (pp. 207, 208), and a full account has since appeared in the *Journal of Comparative Medicine and Veterinary Archives*. Vol. XII. pp. 265–274. June, 1891. Dr. Curtice had not witnessed the actual mode of oviposition or the position of the eggs in a state of nature, nor has anyone recorded the facts up to the present time. It will be remembered that in the summary of the life-history of the better known Ox Warble, viz, *Hypoderma bovis* (INSECT LIFE, Vol. II, pp. 172-177), the actual mode of oviposition was shown to be not absolutely known, and that between the two opposing views that were held, viz, insertion of the egg in the skin, or its attachment to the skin or to the hair, a number of reasons based on recollection, on the structure of the ovipositor and on the structure of the egg, were urged in favor of attachment rather than of insertion. From the structure of the egg Dr. Curtice also drew the conclusion that the egg is attached to the hair of the animal, but from the other facts observed by him he also concluded that the young larvæ are licked off by the cattle, swallowed or lodged in the back of the mouth or esophagus, and penetrate the esophageal walls. These conclusions were deduced from the presence of the young grubs in the esophageal walls in November, and long before they are found in the backs of the cattle. Later, about Christmas time, they appear suddenly in full force under the skin of the back. The earliest larvæ occurring beneath the skin differ in no wise from those found in the esophagus. By the latter part of January or the beginning of February all have disappeared from the esophagus, together with all traces of the inflammatory action in that organ so noticeable in January. The larvæ at this stage are able to pierce through the esophagus and wander through the tissues to the back. The wandering of the larvæ is further shown, according to Dr. Curtice, by the fact that they have been found near the eleventh rib on the thoracic side, also in the spinal column, in the subcutaneous muscles, and connective tissue. Dr. Curtice has also found in the esophageal muscular coats wounds which he believes to have been caused by the larvæ in penetrating them. He has also found on the inside of freshly removed hides, which carried larvæ in the first or cutaneous stage, small gnawed spots which he believes to have been made by these larvæ. He says also:

> The earliest grub holes that I have been able to find are very uniform in size, corresponding with the caliber of the grubs contained in them, and had no appearance of the sac which forms later. The walls were rough, as if gnawed, and the hole was cylindrical to near the epidermis, when it suddenly contracted. Now the freshness of the wound and the absence of inflammatory action is a very good index of the lateness of the wound, for, when a wound is exposed to the air, germs are sure to enter, a sac grows and secretes pus. Were the wound of a more remote date it would be quite of another character, as every pathologist will admit.

Upon this theory Dr. Curtice explains the "lick" as nothing more than an effusion of serum into the connective tissue caused by the inflammation induced by the wandering of the young grubs, and it appears also in the walls of the esophagus just before the disappearance of the grubs therefrom. These licks disappear from beneath the hide when the grubs become stationary and the "sacs" are well formed. On reaching a suitable point in the back the warbles are supposed to bore through the skin, caudal end first; this end being provided in this stage with numerous rows of short stout spines (Figs. 48*d* and 49*c*).

In further evidence of this view he cites the difference in the anal spiracles of the esophageal or subcutaneous stage and the second stage of the larva. In the former, as shown at Figs. 48*d* and 49*c*, these are small, indicating a limited respiration, and in the latter (Fig. 49*f*) they are much more prominent, indicating that as soon as the grub reaches the air a larger respiratory apparatus becomes necessary. He argues further from the nature of the food in the alimentary canal of the larvæ of the first and second stages as follows:

The differences in the food between the subcutaneous stage and the first cutaneous stage, or certainly the second stage, is quite marked. Before the tunnel is made or completed the contents of the alimentary canal are yellow, like the inflammatory effusion it (the larva) excited, but after the sac forms, after it (the larva) loses the mouth hooks in the second stage, the contents become much darker, like the pus secreted from the lining membrane of the sac.

The different stages of the larvæ in the skin cysts can, he says, be easily connected by dissecting out the whole cyst, and obtaining the molted skin of the earlier stages. On reaching full growth the warble forces its way out through the breathing hole, works into the ground, and transforms to a perfect fly in from three to six weeks. Curtice's specimens appeared after six weeks, Osborn's after four weeks, and one bred by Mr. G. W. Holstein, of Albany, Texas, after about three weeks.

As will be gathered from what has already been said in INSECT LIFE, I have heretofore taken Dr. Curtice's views with some caution, feeling, however, that his facts justified his conclusions, and showed clearly enough that at least a portion of the young bots are thus licked into the mouth and pass to the back through the esophagus and other tissues, and the only question in my mind was whether this mode of development was not exceptional and whether direct penetration into the skin did not also occur. The first point, viz, that our Ox Bot is *H. lineata*, having been confirmed and settled as indicated in the preliminary portion of this article, I have been for some time very anxious to learn the actual facts in reference to oviposition, and have delayed publishing the present article, for which most of the illustrations have long since been made, in order to obtain these additional facts. I am glad to be able through the efforts of a reliable agent in Texas, who prefers to remain anonymous, to present the facts of oviposition, and, as will be seen, they fully confirm Dr. Curtice's views. They are also confirmatory of the fragmentary and in most cases unsubstantiated accounts of various observers, which I shall refer to later, and, it seems to me, put at rest all question as to the habit of Hypoderma in this regard.

A careful watch was maintained for the Heel Fly on the ranches along the Pedernales River, and on January 29 of the present year a single specimen of the fly was captured on the muddy banks of this stream about 2 o'clock, at which time many head of cattle were standing in the middle of the shallow crossing. Further search for the flies in the first days of February resulted in the discovery along the banks of the stream, and in similar situations, of about one hundred, none of which seemed to cross the river or to go to cattle standing in the middle of the stream. The cattle on clear days came to the river about 9 o'clock in the morning, and remained standing in the middle of the river until 5 o'clock in the afternoon, when they went to grazing, to return at 9 o'clock the following morning. Most of the cattle stood on flat rocks protruding out of the water, so that no part of their body or legs were submerged; but in spite of this fact, while they were standing in the river they were unmolested. The actual oviposition of these insects, which are found to occur in such extraordinary numbers, was witnessed on March 1 and the two or three following days. An old and feeble animal, which had laid down and had not strength to rise, was observed to be attacked during this time by about 50 flies, of which upward of a dozen were captured. The flies were observed to approach

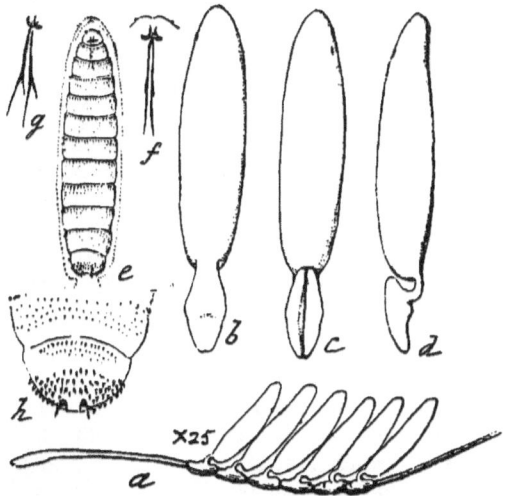

FIG. 44.—HYPODERMA LINEATA: *a*, eggs attached to hair; *b, c, d*, dorsal, ventral, and lateral view of egg; *e*, embryonic or first larva, as seen in egg; *f, g*, mouth-parts of same enlarged; *h*, anal segments of same still more enlarged (original).

very swiftly and deposit their eggs anywhere on the sides, belly, or tail, near the anus, and on the front legs. The flies were left unmolested in many cases until, after remaining on or about the animal from five to ten minutes, they flew off. The eggs were then found without difficulty, usually placed four to six together, and fastened to the hair. Flies were also captured and eggs were deposited in confinement. A large number of the flies and eggs, both dried and in alcohol, were sent to me. The structure of the lower portion of the egg, which has been more or less correctly shown in some of the earlier illustrations, is well adapted for clasping a hair. It consists of two lobes, forming a bulbous enlargement, which is attached to the egg by a broad but rather thin neck, so that when the latter is viewed sidewise it appears as a slender pedicel. (See Fig. 44 *a, d*.)

The eggs, so far as the observations of my correspondent go, have failed to hatch when removed from the animal and placed in moist situations, but an examination of some received, which were placed in alcohol as soon as collected, shows that the larvæ in them were already fully developed. In fact, there is every reason to believe that, as in the case of so many other Diptera, the embryon is already fully developed when the egg is laid—which confirms the view that the larva is licked up by the tongue of the animal either directly out of the egg, as in the case of that of *Gastrophilus equi*, the Horse Bot, or, as must more often happen, is taken with the egg still attached to the hair, as the egg-laying season is coincident with the shedding season, and cattle have a great habit of licking themselves at this particular time, thus taking a great deal of hair not only into the mouth, but, as we know, frequently into the stomach as well, where it forms the well-known hair-balls. In either event the larvæ would seem to need the heat and moisture of the animal's saliva for their well being. That the larva is easily released from the eggshell is shown by the fact that the shell splits open very readily at its anterior end.

When we come to look more closely into the matter, the old idea that the larvæ enter directly from the egg into the animal through the skin, seems otherwise quite untenable, for the delicate larva which would hatch on the flanks, legs, and tail of the animal would scarcely be able to wander to the back and penetrate the skin in the locations where the warbles are always found, all of which lends confirmation to the views here presented, viz. that the larva is licked into the mouth and wanders as described, through the esophagus into the subcutaneous tissue, finally reaching the dorsal region.

The observations here recorded render significant the fact that this insect is known by stockmen, particularly throughout the South and West, as the Heel Fly, a name which has originated from the fly having been noticed in some instances to oviposit on or near the heel of the animal. Thus of ten reports received from stockmen in Texas, seven say that the fly oviposits on the heel or just above the hoof, two on the belly and sides, and one did not know.*

It would thus seem that the normal place of oviposition, when the animals are on their feet and moving, is somewhere near the heel, from which the popular designation comes, and judging from the habits of other bot-flies, in which the method of oviposition is characteristically distinct, we may safely conclude that the method here described is the

* Mr. Conrad L. Fuchs, Tiger Mill, Burnet County, Texas, writes, in substance, as follows: "When I was using a half-broke ox team some fifteen years ago I could not work them (on account of this fly) without keeping their heels smeared with kerosene. This I applied by means of a rag tied to a long stick. The steers soon learned the benefit and would allow me to apply the oil without kicking. The fly would hesitate to oviposit ('take a hold or sit to the heels'), thus giving a chance to see it. Except for this hesitation it could not be seen because of its quick flight.

normal one for our species, and it gives a significance to the habit which cattle have, when attacked, of running to and standing in water. The strongest objections hitherto, in my own mind, to considering the habit of entering the animal as here described, the normal one, have been the following: First, the fact that the young larva found in the esophagus or muscular tissue has been a very smooth larva, a characteristic which seems inconsistent with the power of clinging to the tongue or penetrating the lining of the esophagus; secondly, the long period from the time the egg is taken into the mouth, *i. e.*, in the spring, to the time of the presence of the larva as observed by Dr. Curtice in the passages, as described, this being during the months of December and January. The figures of the embryonic larva, or first larva from the egg (see Fig. 44e), will show at once, however, that this newly-hatched larva is provided with a number of spinous points which admirably fit it for clinging to the tongue or to the roof of the mouth, while the peculiar arrangement of the stronger anal hooks is admirably adapted to penetrating the walls of the esophageal passages. Now such a spiny creature would undoubtedly cause an undue amount of inflammation in penetrating and wandering through the animal's tissues; and we find, therefore, that upon the very first molt it loses these spines and becomes almost entirely smooth, with the exception of some minute spines around the anal portion. The movement of this young larva in the body of the animal must be extremely slow, and its development still slower, or perhaps for a time entirely retarded. The most cursory examination of this larva in this smooth second stage, however, shows that the skin is underlaid with numerous and extremely well-developed muscular bands, which must materially help it to push its way through the tissues, however slowly.

In reference to the second point, while it seems at first sight strange that there should be this slow development during the nine or ten months of its wandering life, we have positive evidence that such is the fact in the case already recorded in INSECT LIFE, Vol. II, pp. 238-9. Here the extensive wandering in a child of a grub which was doubtfully referred to *Hypoderma diana* is given by Dr. Elizabeth R. Kane, of Kane, McKean County, Pa. The case occurred in the practice of Dr. Sylvanus D. Freeman, of Smethport, McKean County, Pa., who, on the 22d of February, 1889, had been called to attend a child which was supposed to be suffering from erysipelas. The child was a boy 3 or 4 years old, and suffered sufficient pain to prevent his sleeping at night, the cause being attributed to something working under the skin. This worm, or what the mother called a "pollywog," had been first noticed five months before, being then under the skin near the sternal end of the right clavicle, and it had, in the five months, traveled up and down the chest in front, down one arm to the elbow and over one side of the back. It was only toward the time at which Dr. Freeman had been called in that the serious annoyance had been caused. I was not sufficiently acquainted with the distinguishing characters between the young larvæ of *Hypoderma lineata* and the other species at the time when the doubtful determination was made, and am now inclined to believe that the specimen was a partly developed larva (third stage) of *Hypoderma lineata*, as the egg or larva of this species is much more likely to have been swallowed in milk than that of *H. diana*, which infests deer.*

An interesting letter called forth from the above experience has already been published on p. 275 of this volume of Insect Life from Prof. W. M. Schoyen, Government Entomologist, Christiania, Norway, referring to a communication of his own on the occurrence of Dipterous bots under the skin of man, from which I reproduce the following:

As pointed out in this article, we know of cases of traveling grubs under the human skin in some districts of our country from over one hundred years ago up to the present time. Many of these grubs I have myself seen and examined, and they were all of the Hypoderma larvæ (*sine dubio—Hyp. boris*), and, as a rule, they have accomplished longer ramblings under the skin, always in an upward direction, previously to their appearance, through an opening in a tumor on the upper part of the body (head, neck, shoulders, etc.). All of them have lived in this manner for months, and came out in course of the winter months (February, etc.), but were always still much too young to go through their transformations. However, I have no doubt at all that they belong to *Hypoderma boris*, as it is especially with persons who look after or take care of cattle in the summer months that such grubs are to be found during the winter. It is evidently the smell of cattle which attracts the bot-fly to them. *Hypoderma diana* does not occur in our country.

The article may be found in the *Entomologisk Tidskrift*, Stockholm, vol. VII (1886), pp. 171-187, and contains also a short historic résumé of all accidents of this kind observed up to that time, which have been published here in Norway and elsewhere.

DIFFERENCES BETWEEN THE LARVÆ OF H. BOVIS AND H. LINEATA.

Dr. Brauer has devised a very convenient and original method of showing diagrammatically the spiny armature of the larvæ of *Hypoderma* by means of which the dorsal and ventral surfaces as well as the three rows of lateral protuberances are shown together, so that different species may be readily compared.

I reproduce his diagrams (Figs. 45 and 46) of the larvæ of *boris* and *lineata* (*bonassi*), together with his table for distinguishing the larvæ of the two species.

In the diagrams and table the first two joints are considered as cephalic and marked 1, since, as Brauer observes, this is necessary for comparison with described larvæ which as a rule have been considered to have but eleven segments. The wide spaces represent the dor-

---

* Reëxamination of the specimens which I have been able to make through the kindness of Dr. Freeman, since the above was written, shows that this supposition is correct, and that the larva is undoubtedly that of *lineata*, and is of the second subcutaneous or third larval stage—the spiny areas and other characteristics agreeing exactly with this stage.

The known habits of this larva render this determination doubly sure, and indicate that the penetration to the surface may, under unfavorable or unnatural conditions, be delayed until the second subcutaneous stage is assumed.

sal (the left) and the ventral (the right) surface and the narrow spaces the three rows of lateral protuberances. The spines on the upper and lower border of the segments are represented by dots.

TABLE.

HYPODERMA LINEATA.	HYPODERMA BOVIS.
Last segment only, bearing anal spiracles. entirely naked.	The two terminal segments entirely naked.
Dorsal surface.	*Dorsal surface.*
Penultimate segment (10) spined as the preceding ones on posterior margin.	Penultimate (10) and 9, together with lateral protuberances, naked.

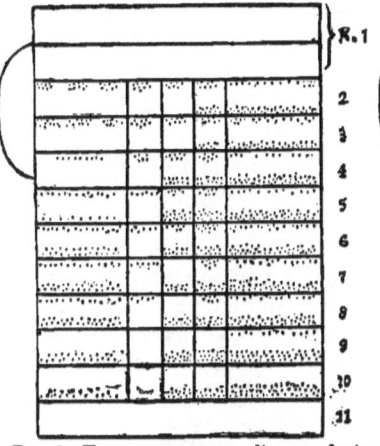

FIG. 45.—HYPODERMA LINEATA—diagram of spiny armature (after Brauer).

FIG. 46.—HYPODERMA BOVIS—diagram of spiny armature (after Brauer).

Segments 2 and 3 and often 4 spinose only anteriorly; 5, 6, 7 and 8 spinose on both anterior and posterior margins. Segments 2-8 with the upper lateral protuberance spinose on the anterior margin; 2 and 3 with the middle protuberances on the anterior margin; 4, 5, 6, on both anterior and posterior margins; 7, 8, 9 and 10 only on the posterior. and 2-10 of lower series spinose on both anterior and posterior margins.	2, 3, 4 and 5 spinose on both anterior and posterior margins; 6, 7, and 8 only on the posterior margin; 9, 10 and 11 naked. 2, 3, 4 and 5 upper and middle protuberances. and 2-8 of lower, spinose on anterior margin.
Ventral surface.	*Ventral surface.*
Segments 2-9 spinose on both the anterior and posterior margins, especially and in greater amount the latter. 10 only on posterior margin; 11 naked. Stigmal plates flat hardly excavated towards the pseudo-stigmatic orifice, or else with radiating furrows as in *H. diana.* Body slender and more rugose: the escaped larva grayish brown striped with whitish gray.	Segments 2-9 spinose on both anterior and posterior margins. more copiously on the posterior margin and on the anterior margin of the 9th segment also. Stigmal plates, convex, punctured and with radiating furrows, each deeply excavated, funnel-form, or auriform, towards the pseudo-stigmal orifice. Body thick, rounded scarcely rugose; the escaped larva deep brown.

I find from an examination of a large series of specimens of *lineata* that the armature particularly of the lateral protuberances is subject to some variation, and have shown in the accompanying diagram (Fig. 47) the maximum armature; but the chief characters distinguishing the larvæ, namely, the stigmata and particularly the armature of segments 9, 10 and 11, are constant in *lineata* at least, and also in the few larvæ of *bovis* which I have had opportunity of examining.

DESCRIPTIVE DETAILS.

THE EGG.—The egg, including the pedicel or clasping base, is 1 mm. long and 0.02 mm. wide at the greatest diameter. In color it is dull yellowish white, and the surface is smooth and shining. As may be seen by the illustrations (Fig. 44 *a*, *d*), the egg consists of two distinct parts, viz, the egg proper and the clasping base which firmly secures it to the hair and connects with the egg proper by a thin but rather wide pedicel. This base is made up of two lips or valves, which close over the hair and thus give a very secure attachment. The egg is narrow, ovoid, broadest at its middle and larger at the base than at the tip, which is more or less abruptly and obliquely truncate. (Fig. 44.)

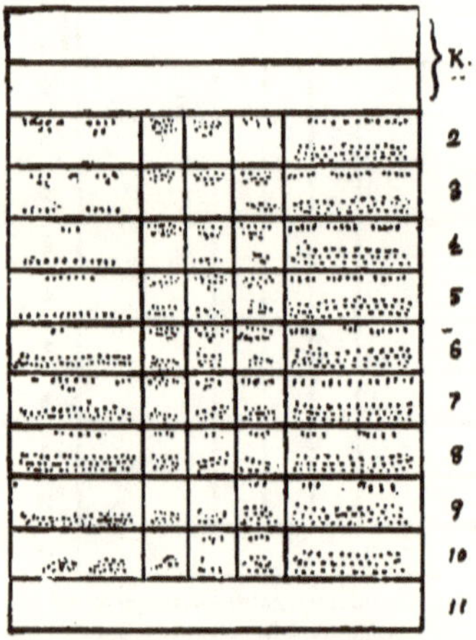

FIG. 47.—HYPODERMA LINEATA—diagram of maximum armature (original).

THE LARVA: *First stage.*—This stage (Fig. 44 *e*), when ready to leave the egg, or when first hatched, is 0.08 mm. long by 0.02 mm. in width, tapering above. Within the egg it just fills the cavity, and may be seen through the shell and quite readily removed. It is dull white in color, with the surface from the second to the twelfth joints distinctly and densely spinous. The armed area occupies the entire surface of these joints, except a narrow lateral free space. The arrangement of the spines on these joints, except the last, is uniform, with perhaps a slight increase in the size of the spines from the second to the eleventh joint. The armature of these joints and of the anterior half of the twelfth consists of a rather prominent and posteriorly directed row on the anterior margin of each joint, followed by numerous smaller prickles which decrease in size and abundance towards the posterior margin of the joint. The posterior half of the terminal joint is armed with very much larger and slightly curved prickles or spines, which point posteriorly on one side and anteriorly on the other. (See Fig. 44 *h*.) The anal spiracles are represented by dark circular spots, and terminate in two prominent spines. The anterior spiracles appear as two minute elevations, and the mouth-parts consist of two dark-brown crescent-shaped hooks, the upper extremity of which projects, and two long supporting rods which furcate basally, and on the tips of which the hooks articulate. (Fig. 44 f, g.)

Second stage.—In the absence of any knowledge of an intermediate form, the larva found in the esophagus may be considered as the second stage (Fig. 48 a). The individuals vary in length from 11 to 14 mm. and are quite smooth and devoid of prickles, except some minute ones, which appear like black specks partly surrounding the anal spiracles (Fig. 48 d) and a few extremely minute ones just above the mouth-parts (Fig. 48 c). The former, or those around the anal spiracles, are of peculiar structure, and consist of a circular, brownish-black, slightly elevated base, in the center of which arises a short, stout, posteriorly curved and very minute spine, less than one-half the diameter of the base in length. The mouth-parts are more prominent than in the first stage and the apical portion is broadened and furcate near the base (Fig. 49 b, c). This larva does not differ in any essential way from the stage first found under the skin in the back before the perforation to the surface is made. (See Fig. 49 a, b, c.)

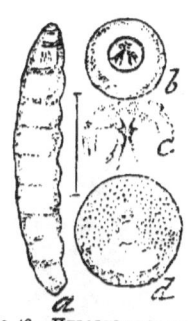

FIG. 48.—HYPODERMA LINEATA. Second stage of larva from esophagus. a, larva; b, enlargement of cephalic segments, end view; c, mouth-parts; d, enlarged end view of anal segment, showing spiracles and spines (original).

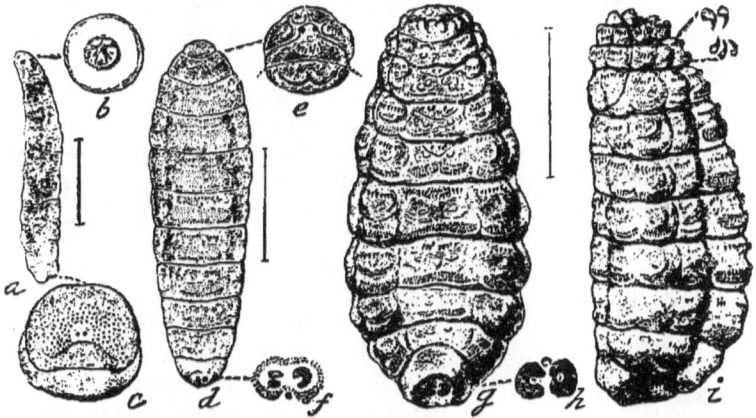

FIG. 49.—HYPODERMA LINEATA: a, second stage of larva from back; b and c, enlargement of extremities; d, ventral view of third stage with details of extremities at e and f; g, dorsal view of mature larva with enlargement of anal spiracles at h; i, ditto, lateral view—natural size indicated by side lines (original).

Third stage.—In this stage, which is the second form of the larva found in the back (Fig. 49 d, e, f), the larva again diverges markedly from the second or preceding stage and acquires many of the characteristics of the mature larva. It tapers, however, considerably toward the posterior extremity rather than the reverse, and the spinous armature varies considerably in different specimens, but ventrally is similar to that of the adult, the spines being, however, more numerous and less prominent. The lateral armature is sometimes almost wanting, but occasionally occurs to the amount shown in the figure (Fig. 49 *d*). The dorsal armature is much more scanty, and is either limited to the first and second joints or frequently entirely wanting.

Fourth stage.—The fourth and last larval stage is shown with characteristic armature at Fig. 49 *g, i*, dorsal and lateral views. Its chief difference from the larva of *boris*, as already shown in the tabular statement, is that the penultimate segment ventrally and also dorsally is spinose, as the preceding ones on the posterior margin while in *boris* it is distinctly unarmed. The full-grown larva when escaping from the back is of a grayish-white color and ranges in length from 22 to 25 mm.

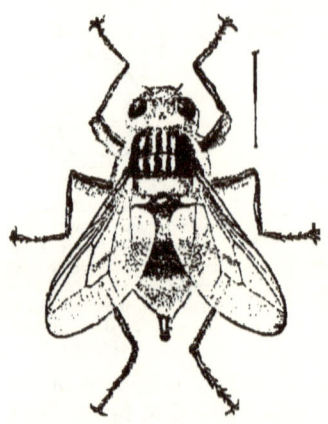

Fig. 50.—HYPODERMA LINEATA—female, natural size indicated by side line (original).

PUPARIUM.—Once out of the back the larva rapidly darkens and contracts, and the puparium, which is merely the contracted and hardened larva, becomes dark brown, almost black, but otherwise possesses all the superficial characteristics of the larva.

IMAGO.—Length ½ inch (⅝ with ovipositor extended); general color, black; body more or less densely clothed with yellowish-white, reddish, and brownish-black hairs. The front, sides, and back of the head, the sides of the thorax, a band across the base of the scutellum and the basal segments of the abdomen, are covered with long, yellowish-white almost white, hairs. The head above, central thoracic region, including prothorax and mesothorax, middle segments of the abdomen above, and legs, clothed with brownish-black hairs, which on the head and thorax are more or less intermixed with whitish hairs. The covering of hairs is shorter and scantier on the head and thorax and the tip of the scutellum and following parts of the thorax, together with four prominent raised lines on the thorax, indicated in the drawing by high light, are smooth and highly polished. The hairs of the terminal segments of the abdomen are reddish-orange, which color also predominates on the hind tibiæ. (See Fig. 50.)

Fig. 51.—HYPODERMA LINEATA—ovipositor of female; *a*, from side; *b*, tip, from below—enlarged (original).

The ovipositor of the female is black and shining and armed at tip of segments with a few scattering reddish hairs (see Fig. 51 a, b). The wings are slightly and uniformly dusky, with the veins dark brown. The surface is finely striate or wrinkled.

COMPARISONS WITH HYPODERMA BOVIS.

In connection with this account of *Hypoderma lineata*, I have thought it well to reproduce the figures of *H. bovis*, published in Vol. II of INSECT LIFE, with some few descriptive notes as to the mature fly, especially as there are some errors in the descriptions of these figures in the previous article.*

The differences between the larvæ have already been pointed out, and the egg of *bovis*, which I have not seen, but the figure of which (Fig. 52 a) is copied from Brauer, is evidently of very much the same nature as that of *lineata*. The perfect fly in *bovis* is a much larger, stouter insect than in *lineata*, being fully twice the size in bulk. Exclusive of the ovipositor, it measures five-eighths of an inch, and the general distribution in color of the hairs cloth-ing the body is similar to that of *lineata*, except that the light hairs of

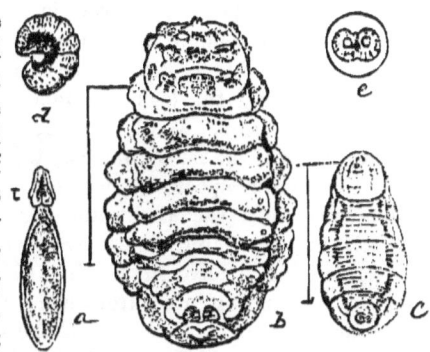

FIG. 52.—*Hypoderma bovis: a*, egg; *b*, full-grown larva, dorsal view; *c*, puparium, dorsal view; *e, d*, anal stigmata of larva; one of same still more enlarged—all enlarged (after Brauer).

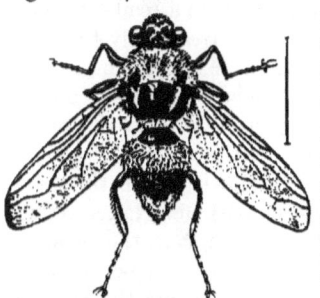

FIG. 53.—*Hypoderma bovis*—enlarged (after Brauer).

the head, thorax, and basal segments of the abdomen are of a darker lemon yellow. These yellow hairs cover definitely the anterior half of the thorax, not intermixed with black, while the central thoracic region is smooth, more shining, and is without the light-colored hairs, as indicated in the figure copied from Brauer (Fig. 53). The legs are comparatively stouter, and the hair covering the basal joints, including the femora, is comparatively shorter and less dense than in *lineata*. The wings also are somewhat lighter colored, with the veins reddish or reddish brown.

---

*By oversight, Fig. 33*d*, INSECT LIFE, Vol. II. was described as the newly-hatched larva, whereas it is the enlarged spiracle of the mature larva. So also the ovipositor, shown at Fig. 35, p. 173, *ibid.*, was that of *Hypoderma lineata*, and not of *bovis*, as stated.

SUMMARY AND CONCLUSIONS.

The facts here recorded, in the light of the hitherto universally accepted views in reference to the life-history of the Ox Bot, are extremely interesting. They may be summarized as follows:

FIG. 54.—*Hypoderma bovis*; head of female fly from the front — enlarged (after Brauer).

In North America, so far as we yet know, *Hypoderma bovis* does not occur. Considering the frequency with which cattle have been imported into this country from abroad this fact seems almost incredible, yet until the species is observed and recorded we must consider its presence in America as merely conjectural. The American Ox Warble, in every case so far observed, is the larva of *Hypoderma lineata*. This species has come to be known, especially through the South and Southwest, as the Heel Fly, on account of the habit which the female has of frequenting the legs of animals for purposes of oviposition. While the eggs are laid on other parts of the body that may be reached by the tongue, the species shows quite a strong tendency to select the flanks and legs around the heels, and the habit, almost everywhere observed, that cattle have of seeking to protect their legs by running into water during the botfly season finds its explanation in these facts. The eggs are attached firmly, by a strong cleft, in rows of from five to ten or more, to the hairs.

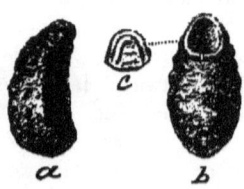

FIG. 55.—*Hypoderma bovis*: a, puparium, from side; b, same, from above, showing exit hole of adult; c, cap which splits off to allow the adult to issue—natural size (after Clark).

When the cattle lick themselves, the young larvæ are taken into the mouth, as, under pressure and moisture, the egg readily splits at its anterior end and releases the young larva, which is already well developed when the egg is laid. Doubtless quite frequently the eggs with the contained larvæ are taken with the hair in this licking, but in either event the larva in leaving the egg is armed with many minute spines, which permit it to adhere to and to penetrate the walls of the esophagus. Here it soon molts and takes on the second of smooth stage, which for eight or nine months wanders slowly in the tissues of its host. The slow movement and the little nourishment taken reduce the inflammation and irritation to a minimum; in fact, the most remarkable thing in the life-history of this larva is the long period of latency and the slight development that takes place during the summer and autumn months. During the late winter the larva reaches a point beneath the skin in the region of the back and penetrates the skin, anal end first as Dr. Curtice believes, and as seems most probable. Here it molts a second time and reassumes its spinous character, producing more or less inflammation and developing rapidly with its enlarged spiracles fitted for more perfect breathing. The third molt soon follows, and we get the more strongly spined grub, with its still larger spiracles, which lives in the swellings or sacs so well known to stockmen. It finally works its way out, drops to the ground, which it enters, and where it contracts, hardens, and darkens in color. In a few weeks afterward the perfect fly issues.

That such is the normal and invariable life-history of *Hypoderma lineata*, I think there can no longer be a doubt, and the burden of proof of any departure from it will rest hereafter with those who contend otherwise. That the remarkable life-history of such a well known insect, and one which does so much injury to our cattle interests, should have remained so many years unknown, is only another illustration of the fact that we have yet much to learn of our commonest species.

That this life-history of *Hypoderma lineata* will be fruitful in bringing to light the actual facts in reference to the European *Hypoderma bovis* there can be little doubt. The unity of habit in the same genus, the structure of the egg, as already known, of *Hypoderma bovis*, and the fact that nothing definite is yet known of the earlier larval stages or the mode of oviposition, all convince me that this species will be found in Europe to have a precisely similar life-history. I would call upon those who read INSECT LIFE and who have occasion to make observations to endeavor, in the light of what is here recorded and of what Dr. Curtice has already written, to obtain the facts in reference to *Hypoderma bovis*.

THE RAVAGES OF THE LEOPARD MOTH IN BROOKLYN.

By NICOLAS PIKE, *Brooklyn, N. Y.*

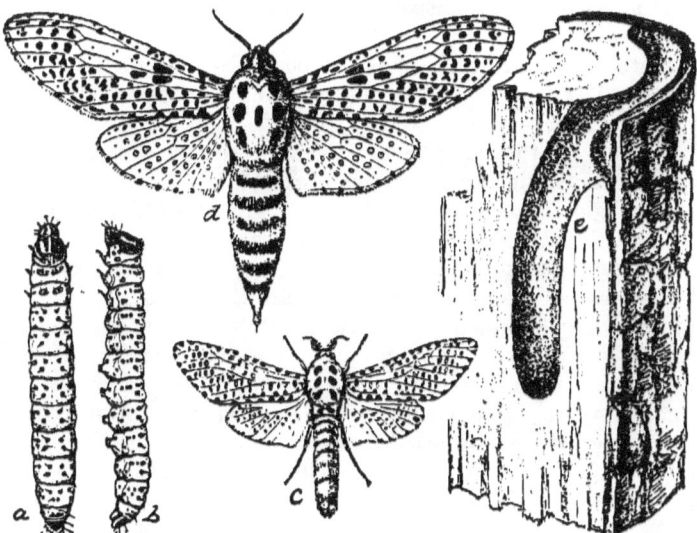

FIG. 56.—The Leopard Moth: *a*, larva, dorsal view; *b*, larva, side view; *c*, male moth; *d*, female moth; *e*, larval burrow—natural size (original).

The appearance of the *Zeuzera pyrina* or Leopard Moth was first observed by me about five years ago. A number of Maple trees near my house were somewhat injured, as I then supposed, by boys, who in their mischief had broken numerous branches, particularly on some young trees not long planted. The following year I noticed branches broken near the top of some old trees quite out of reach of the boys. I had some cut off, and after careful examination I found it to be the work of an insect; what, I did not know. The larvæ I procured failed to mature, so that I was still in the dark as to the moth.

On looking over a work on entomology, I found it must be the *Zeuzera pyrina* or Leopard Moth therein described. In 1889 I found it had affected nearly all the trees, mostly Maples, from Carlton Avenue to the entrance of the park. In 1890 it had spread to many trees in Prospect Park and also on the Eastern Boulevard. It showed its ravages the whole length of this fine roadway, which is shaded by Elms and many varieties of Maples. In 1891 it had begun its ravages all over the city of Brooklyn, not an avenue or street but had abundant proof of its presence, and I have proof that it has already spread to Astoria, New Rochelle, Jamaica, New Lots, and Flatbush.

This Leopard Moth is quite a large one, and from its peculiar markings is easily recognized, being white with black markings; the larvæ are also white with black dottings, brown head and posterior segments. The eggs are deposited in or near the crotch of a tree, and not long after they are hatched they enter the crotch (but not always), boring, either upwards or downwards, into the heart of the tree. The hatching takes place early in June and the young at this time cluster together for some hours before they separate and begin the battle of life each on its own account.

This is the time when trees known to be affected should be carefully examined. The eggs are laid in a group and are covered with a loose fluffy covering. They could be very easily destroyed at this time, and perhaps some of the insecticides recommended by the Department of Agriculture might be advantageously used.

Electric lights should be placed in all public parks and in every street planted with trees. Numbers of moths are found in the bowls of the electric lights near the Plaza and elsewhere in the season, and hundreds are seen dead on the ground under the lamps. It would also be a good plan to build fires in the vicinity of trees that are affected in the month of May before the eggs are deposited, as the flames would attract the moths, and probably very many would be destroyed.

Everyone who has shade trees and ornamental shrubs near his dwelling, or is interested in arboriculture and their protection, should use his influence in the coming spring to help in saving them.

The following is a list of the trees affected by this terrible pest that I have personally observed in my studies of its ravages, and doubtless there are many more shrubs I have not inserted. Elms and Maples appear to be the favorite trees, for certainly there is hardly one of them in Brooklyn or its vicinity not affected by this insect. Unfortunately the presence of the pest is not discovered till much damage is done. All broken limbs should be cut off at least a foot below the fracture and burned, and this would help to check the insect.

It is a very serious subject and should interest everyone, for it is quite certain that the Leopard Moth has come to stay, and will, I fear, be more difficult to eradicate than the Gypsy Moth, as it is a general feeder.* Formerly it was a comparatively easy matter to grow fruits for market, but now, with tenfold demands for them, and the terrible increase of imported pests, it is difficult for a farmer to realize a fair remuneration. Success can only be obtained by eternal vigilance and unremitting care, and withal how many failures occur. It is most sincerely to be hoped that everyone who has the real welfare of our country at heart will see the importance of using every means to check the ravages of the moth before it spreads destruction to all our shade and fruit trees and those of our forests.

Trees and Shrubs affected by Zeuzera pyrina.

Acer campestris—English Maple.
Acer dasycarpum—White or Silver Maple.
Acer lobelii—Lobel's Maple.
Acer macrophyllum—Large-leaved Maple.
Acer platanoides—Norway Maple.
Acer polymorpha—Japanese Maple.
Acer rubrum—Red or Swamp Maple.
Acer saccharinum—Sugar Maple.
Broussonetia papyrifera—Paper Mulberry.
Celtis occidentalis—Hackberry.
Carya porcina—Pignut.
Cratægus sp.—Hawthorn.
Liquidambar styraciflua—Sweet Gum.
Liriodendron tulipifera—Tulip Tree.
Quercus alba—White Oak.
Tilia europa—European Linden.
Tilia americana—American Linden.
Ulmus campestris—English Elm.
Ulmus montana—Scotch Elm.
Ulmus tuberosa—European Cork Elm.
Pyrus aucuparia—Mountain Ash.
Apples.
Pears.
Currants.

HOW FAR DO BEES FLY?

By FRANK BENTON.

Items under the above heading have been going the rounds of the papers, and the opinions expressed differ greatly, some claiming "that bees will not go farther than two or three miles," while others think the distance is greater, one even naming 12 miles as the limit. After mentioning the fact that the bee makes 190 wing-strokes in a second, one of the items widely copied says that "scientists claim that 190 strokes per second would propel the bee forward at the rate of a mile per minute," and then that "conservative writers admit the bee's velocity to be at the rate of at least 30 miles per hour." The same writer then goes on to say: "Basing our calculations on the latter

---

*The Gypsy Moth is also a very general feeder, but, being a leaf-feeder, is easy to reach with insecticides.—EDS.

figures and supposing that they can keep up for twenty minutes, no matter how heavily laden on the return trip, the rate of speed on the outgoing would take them 10 or 12 miles from the home line."

It is quite difficult to determine the rate of speed attained in flight by bees. Therefore any computation of the distance they go after honey which is based upon their supposed speed is liable to great error. The number of wing-strokes per second, 190, as recorded above, was obtained by Prof. Marey* by what is known as the "graphic method." A bee was held so that when its wings were in motion one of them would strike very lightly the surface of a revolving cylinder covered with smooth paper slightly smoked, and at the same time a style fixed in the end of a tuning-fork was arranged to record on the paper the vibrations of the fork. The tone of the latter being known, and hence also the number of vibrations it makes per second, it was easy to compare the number of these actually recorded with the record of the bee's wing for the same time, and thus arrive at the number of strokes the bee makes in a second. It is evident, however, that the friction of the bee's wings against the paper must lessen somewhat the number of strokes, and indeed Prof. Marey observed that as he lessened this friction the velocity increased considerably. If the note made by the bee's wings when she is in vigorous flight could be accurately determined, the corresponding number of vibrations required per second to produce that pitch would represent the wing-strokes made by the bee causing the sound. Dr. H. Landois* thinks the note of a bee in full flight ranges from A to C of the first and second leger of the treble clef. This gives over 400 vibrations per second. If, then, "190 strokes per second would propel the bee forward at the rate of a mile per minute" (a claim by no means to be accepted as proven, and if Landois has determined the note correctly, over 2 miles per minute would be the speed attained.

Conservative authorities are disposed to place the rate of speed attained by bees much below 30 miles per hour, even no more than 18 to 20 miles, and nothing is better recognized than that bees when fatigued, when flying from flower to flower, or when returning heavily laden to their hives, proceed far more slowly than when outward bound. Thus the calculation that they go 10 or 12 miles from home is plainly erroneous.

However difficult it is to determine their rate of speed, and hence however erroneous any calculations based upon such determinations may be, it is not at all difficult to tell practically how far bees actually do go after honey. *Apis mellifica* has been introduced into regions where the species did not exist before, and careful observations have been made regarding the range of its flight, and also the yellow varieties have been taken to countries or localities where only brown or

---

*Animal Mechanism: A Treatise on Terrestrial and Aërial Locomotion. By E. J. Marey. International Science Series). 1883.

*Die Ton-und Stimmaparate der Insekten. Von Dr. H. Landois. Zeitschrift für wissenschaftliche Zoologie, 1867, p. 105.

black bees were found, and the dark varieties have been experimented with in regions where only yellow bees were natives. In this manner it has been readily and accurately determined that they generally work within a distance of 2 miles from their hives, although they will in rare instances go as far as 4 or 5 miles, and a resident of an island off the coast of Texas reported, several years ago, having followed his bees in a boat, and found them working on the mainland, a distance of 7 miles from their hives. But no practical bee-keeper would expect favorable results from pasturage located over 3 miles from his apiary, and marked advantage can only be awaited when the honey sources are located within 2 miles in a direct line from the apiary.

NOTE ON THE WATER-BUG, FOUND BY REV. J. L. ZABRISKIE.

By E. BERGROTH, M. D., *Tammerfors, Finland*.

In INSECT LIFE (vol. IV, pp. 198–200) the editors have given a good description, with figures, of a very remarkable aquatic bug, found on Long Island by the Rev. J. L. Zabriskie. From the figures given it is evident that the insect is an adult form and belongs to the male sex. There can be no doubt as to these points. The presence of two ocelli and the remarkable structure of the antennæ and of the hind femora are good generic characters of this insect. As it was found on running water I presume the singular antennæ are of good service to fasten the animal on moist and slippery stones and piles. A microscopic examination of the pale hyaline cushion of the third antennal joint would be of great interest; I think it will prove to be a sucking disk.

The insect undoubtedly belongs to a new genus and species, which I propose to name *Rheumatobates* rileyi*. It is, with the recently described genera *Hermatobates* Carp. and *Hemidiptera* Léon, one of the most curious and interesting Hydrometridæ hitherto discovered.

THE LOCUST OR GRASSHOPPER OUTLOOK.

There has recently gone out from Washington a popular article on insects used as food for man, with some of our writings of many years ago palmed off as current, and with a sensational introduction to the effect that grasshopper injury is predicted by the Department of Agriculture for this season. As the announcement is entirely unjustified and without authority, we have concluded to reproduce here a summary of the situation as given by the Entomologist last August

---

* 'Ρεῦμά=stream; Βάτης=one who treads.

before section I of the American Association for the Advancement of Science.

During the present summer (1891), and especially during the past six weeks, the papers have contained numerous reports concerning serious grasshopper ravages in various parts of the country, in some cases the reports being quite sensational and well calculated to create apprehension as to the safety of our crops and as to the possibility of serious locust devastation this fall or next year. I have felt that perhaps a few words indicating the exact state of the case and summarizing the investigations made, whether by agents of the Department or others, will be of service in giving our farmers the true condition of things. While, from the investigations made a year ago and the reports of locust injury it did not seem probable that there could be very much foundation for the reports of the present year, I deemed it quite desirable to endeavor to ascertain the facts as closely as possible. Accordingly Prof. Lawrence Bruner was instructed to examine fully the regions in the northwestern States where the injuries were reported, and he has been over eastern Colorado, eastern and North Dakota, western Minnesota, and portions of Montana and Wyoming. Prof. Herbert Osborn was instructed to visit the western parts of Kansas and investigate the southwestern portion of the State, examining all localities from which any reports of injury could be obtained. Prof. F. H. Snow and Prof. E. A. Popenoe, on behalf of the State authorities in Kansas, thoroughly examined the section of country in southeast Colorado, passing over the country embraced in northern Kansas, and thus connecting the territory covered by Professors Bruner and Osborn, so that it may be stated that the plains region from northern Minnesota west to Montana and south to the Arkansas River, has been pretty thoroughly examined. Mr. Nathan Banks was instructed to visit south Texas and New Mexico to inquire into the reports of injury in those sections.

It may be stated in brief that the depredations in eastern and southeastern Colorado have been due to the exceptional multiplication of the Long-winged Locust (*Dissosteira longipennis*). This species always occurs in that section, and some of the first insects which I collected in Colorado on my first visit in 1867, were of this species, and are now in the National Collection. It has never yet been reported in such immense and injurious numbers, and its work the present year furnishes another illustration of the fact that we never know when a species that has hitherto been looked upon as harmless may become seriously injurious to agriculture. During the latter part of July millions of pupæ and full-grown larvæ of this species were found ranging over large areas of eastern and southeastern Colorado, moving in vast bodies all the way from Akron to the Arkansas River to the south. The insects moved in a body in various directions, choosing, as Prof. Bruner reports, the roads for their line of march rather than the prairies. Normally this species frequents partially bare hill slopes and plains where the grasses are scant, and Prof. Bruner's view of the matter is that the past few years have been favorable to its excessive multiplication, but that during the present year the exceptionally heavy rains which have occurred in that region have caused an unusually abundant growth of grasses and other vegetation, and the locusts have been compelled to move in search of more open country and have frequented the roads, upon which they congregated and which they followed in vast bodies. He found, in going some distance away from the roadways, where the vegetation was at all rank, that but few insects were found. This species, in size and length of wing, much more closely resembles the migratory and destructive species of Europe and some other countries than does the Rocky Mountain Locust (*Caloptenus spretus*), and there seems to be no particular reason why, at times, it should not become destructive and fly in vast swarms from one locality to another. So far as past experience justifies calculation, however, it will not do so, and I think there is little reason to fear any continued and widespread injury from this species.

The locusts found further north have consisted of several species, most of which are known as sedentary; that is, not ordinarily migratory. But one of them, namely, the Pellucid Locust (*Camnula pellucida*), is the species that has already done much damage, and is one of the Pacific migratory forms. Commencing in Idaho it has been gradually working eastward, and is now found in portions of Montana, North Dakota, Wyoming, and western Nebraska. The gradual eastward spread and increase of this species deserves attention, but so far as the reports go it has nowhere been sufficiently numerous to justify alarm.

The true Rocky Mountain Locust, the species which we most have to fear (*Caloptenus spretus*), was found in considerable numbers in North Dakota and Minnesota, in some counties proving quite destructive, but owing to vigorous measures which have been adopted, especially in Minnesota by the State authorities, chiefly under the direction of Prof. Otto Lugger, of the Minnesota Experiment Station, they have been very largely destroyed, and there is little probability that they will spread extensively from the localities in which they now occur. The destructive species most commonly found in southwest Kansas was the Differential Locust (*Caloptenus differentialis*). It has devastated the alfalfa fields in the irrigated territory along the Arkansas River for a distance of some 50 miles. This is a widespread species east of the Rocky Mountains, occurring all over the country, and it is one of the species which acquires the power of extended flight only in very dry seasons and under certain favorable conditions. Ordinarily the female is too heavy-bodied and short-winged to become migratory. There is no fear of widespread injury from this species. The accounts from southwest Texas have been very greatly exaggerated, and little injury could be found by the agent sent there. The species were also those indigenous to the region and not of a migratory form that had come from other parts. The reports from Ohio and from some of the other Eastern States, though not investigated particularly, need not concern us, because they are known to be based upon the undue multiplication of some of the indigenous Eastern species, which never acquire the destructive powers of the Western migratory forms.

On the whole, therefore, it is safe to conclude that while there are several localities where locusts have been more or less destructive and required attention, there is no cause for widespread alarm and no reason to believe that any general injury will result in 1892. * * *

EARLY PUBLISHED REFERENCES TO SOME OF OUR INJURIOUS INSECTS. II.

By F. M. WEBSTER, *Columbus, Ohio.*

Of the present known insect pests of the wheat field, indigenous to this country, there are very few that were not known as such during the first three decades of the present century. The Joint Worm, *Isosoma hordei*, was observed in its destructive work long before mentioned by either Harris or Fitch. Mr. James Worth, of Sharon, Bucks County, Pa., observed the larvæ in 1821,* and not only these but other wheat stem-burrowing larvæ, one of which infested volunteer wheat. The adult of one species, probably the Joint Worm, was reared as early as 1823 by Mr. Joseph E. Muse, of Cambridge, E. S., Maryland, who supposed it to belong to the genus Tenthredo.† Mr. Worth says one of the

---

* American Farmer, Vol. 4, p. 394.
† Loc. cit., Vol. 5. p. 113.

broods of larvæ found by him was "in the culm near the root," where they "cause an enlargement of the stem," and Mr. Muse states that the larvæ producing his species of Tenthredo "burrow in the stems and feed upon them." Still, as long ago at least as 1843 and 1844 there was what, in the light of a recently published article on "Wheat and Grass Saw-flies,"* might have been a serious attack of Saw-fly larvæ on wheat. A correspondent, "P. C.," Penn's Manor, Bucks County, Pa., in the Cultivator,† calls attention to the ravages of a worm about an inch long, its head brownish green, with two brown spots, which ascended the straws and cut off the heads, soon after the latter had been put forth. In some fields one-fifth of the heads had been eaten off, the Mediterranean variety being the most injured. So far as known the ravages had been confined to within a few miles of correspondent's locality.

A short time ago the writer reared a leaf-miner in wheat, the larva attacking the tip of the larger leaf, the species involved being *Elachista præmaturella* Clem. And now, through fear of temptations, which might in future influence him to pose as the original discoverer of the first wheat leaf-miner, he proposes to put such an aspiration forever beyond his reach by placing again on record the following letter, first published in 1822:‡

CULPEPER COUNTY, WOODVILLE, VA.,
May 28, 1822.

To the Editor of the American Farmer:

DEAR SIR: Inclosed you will receive a few blades of wheat, and by examination you will find that a deposit of eggs has been made by the fly in a mode not heretofore mentioned by anyone.

The germs are now in the maggot state and occupy an apparently comfortable position in the substance of the blade, and most generally the top blade. You will find them between the surfaces, which are membraneous, a fact which I never before observed. As they progress, feeding on the green pulp, they enlarge the cavity or bag and the leaf then exhibits the appearance called "fired," which must proceed either from an absorption or change of the color of the pulp. Whether the season or some adventitious circumstance has produced this aberration, or whether its consequences will be more or less injurious to the farmer, must be left for time to disclose. The injury is most prevalent in rank wheat.

Yours respectfully,

PHILIP THORNTON.

Just what Mr. Thornton's leaf-miner was we may never know, but it must certainly have been a leaf-miner and not, as he supposed, the Hessian Fly.

Speaking of the Hessian Fly, *Cecidomyia destructor*, reminds me that the modern entomologist is liable to make a considerable number of old discoveries. When we figured and described the effect of the fly on young wheat in the fall, in 1887,§ we fully believed we were the first to

---

* Insect Life, Vol. 4, pp. 168, 179.
† The Cultivator, Albany, N. Y., N. S., Vol. 2, p. 148, 1845.
‡ American Farmer, Vol. 4, p. 183.
§ Circular No. 2, Purdue University, Agricultural Dept., Nov. 21, 1887.

do so. Since that time, however, we have found that the same difference was fully illustrated as early as 1820,* and though the figures were possibly less artistic than our own, they conveyed the idea equally as well. Three years later, in the same publication, Mr. Thomas Beesley, of Cape May, wrote, advising those who wished to find the fly in fall wheat to "look for the spears that are darkest and stand most upright."† And, as if this were not enough to punish us for our rash aspirations, we find that in 1840 "J. G.," a correspondent of the *Farmers' Cabinet*, place of residence not stated, reports that he had (October 23) just finished plowing up a field of wheat which "was the best field to appearance in the neighborhood," but not one plant or shoot could the owner find in the whole field "but what had from two to a dozen, or more, nits or eggs at the root."‡ This communication appeared to "move" another correspondent of the same publication, who signs himself "Thirty years a farmer, Delaware County," no State given, but whose "thees" betoken a Quaker, states that he also finds one of his fields, until lately "growing handsomely," now dying, "a mass of corruption, and a greater portion rotted off at the ground."§

In the Third Report of the U. S. Entomological Commission (p. 210), considerable space is given to the development of this insect during the summer months. It does not seem, however, that Michigan flies, as there cited, differ materially from those of other localities, nor had they improved much upon the habits of their ancient brethren, for, in 1820, Mr. James Worth observed the adult April 19; eggs, April 24; pupæ, May 15; adults early in June, and on the 12th of same month all stages were observed. Adults were noticed from the 15th of the following August until October, and again November 25, and he reared them indoors December 25 and February 20. In summing up the matter he says: "It may then be said that during the past year (1820) there have been three complete broods and partially a fourth."‖

The Stalk-borer, *Gortyna nitela*, seems to have formed a taste for wheat at an early day, although little is said of the habits of the larvæ prior to 1840. Dr. Harris found a larva in potato stalks in 1848, which seems to have prompted his description.¶ Mr. Thomas Beesley, of Cape May, as early as 1823, mentions a worm which ate into the straw about the second or third joint,** while Mr. Jabez Jenkins, of West Whiteland, Chester County (Pa.?), stated in 1840 that a new enemy of wheat had made its appearance in his and an adjoining county, the same being "a worm about three-quarters of an inch long, of a brown

---

* American Farmer, Vol. II, p. 174, 1820.
† Loc. cit., Vol. V, p. 165, 1823.
‡ Farmers' Cabinet, Vol. V, p. 138, 1840.
§ Loc. cit., p. 172.
‖ American Farmer, Vol. III, p. 188, also loc. cit., p. 213.
¶ Entomological Correspondence, p. 315.
** American Farmer, Vol. V, p. 165, 1823.

color, striped at both ends, with a reddish head." It bored into the stalk, injuring the fields "in some degree."*

The Boll Worm, *Heliothis armigera*, seems to have stolen in upon us at an early day, in an obscure manner also. In 1820 a correspondent of the *American Farmer*, writing under date of September 20, stated that about two weeks previous the pods of his cotton had been attacked by a large green worm, from 1 to 1½ inches long, which ate its way into the pod, and did not leave it until it had completed the destruction. Some of the worms were smaller, and some were brown, and some brown and red. The injury seemed to be severe, with a prospect of one-fourth of the crop being destroyed.† In 1842 "J. A. P.," Brinkville, Ill., wrote the *Cultivator*, asking for information in regard to what was there known as "the corn worm." About the time the corn began to form on the cob a dark, slate-colored worm, from one-fourth to seven-eighths of an inch in length, appeared on the ear, under the husk, "having ground a hole in them to pass through," and continued to eat until frost killed them. Sometimes six or eight worms were found in a single ear, late planted corn being most injured. The editors replied that they had received similar complaints the previous year from the South and West, but could give no further information.‡

While the agriculturists of the early part of the present century were of necessity, much hampered by a lack of knowledge in regard to these pests, and must have been often seriously disappointed in casting about for information, yet they do not appear to have ceased to contrive ways for destroying them. The trapping and killing of cutworms by poisoned clover or other fresh herbage is now coming quite rapidly into use, but, except in the use of poison, does not differ from the method advocated in 1838 by "a subscriber" in the *Cultivator*, who saved his corn by "placing compact handfuls of elder sprouts, milk-weed, clover, mullein, and almost any green vegetable that happened to be at hand, in every fifth row and sixth hill, pressing the mass down with the foot." These traps were placed in the field just before the corn came up, and examined for the worms which were beneath them, and these were killed with a sharp instrument, as many as 200 having been thus destroyed under a single handful of herbage, one man being able to collect the material and apply it to 5 acres in a day.§ I find this communication marked, presumably by Dr. Fitch, as I have his copy of the volume, but do not know that he ever further noticed the matter in print.

---

* Farmers' Cabinet, Vol. v, p. 68, 1840.
† American Farmer, Vol. ii, p. 236, 1820.
‡ The Cultivator, Vol. ix, p. 86, 1842.
§ The Cultivator, Vol. vi, p 63, 1838.

STRANGE DEVELOPMENTS OF STOMATA ON CARYA ALBA CAUSED BY PHYLLOXERA.*

By D. A. OWEN, *Franklin, Ind.*

The stomata or breathing pores of *Carya alba* are naturally all developed upon the lower epidermis of the leaf. But, owing to the ovipositing of the Phylloxera in the leaf through the lower epidermis, there is developed upon the upper side a hemispherical gall. This gall, like all other galls, is the nest of the insects, and in due time the young of the Phylloxera may be seen issuing from a slit upon the lower side of the leaf.

Upon the lower epidermis, beneath the gall, may be seen a changed form of cell structure in which there are to be found in almost every case no stomata. But upon the upper side of the gall there are stomata invariably found, but not in as great abundance as are found upon the lower epidermis of a normal leaf.

In and around the opening of the gall there are to be found numerous single-celled hairs, all of which point outwards, as if guarding the ovum and young from the ravages of an enemy.

That which remains yet to be solved is: For what purpose are these stomata developed upon the upper side of the gall? Does the plant develop these trichomes for its own use, or for the protection of the insect? Is the insect injurious or beneficial to the plant?

It is hoped future investigations will solve some of these problems.

EXTRACTS FROM CORRESPONDENCE.

Destruction of Plant-lice in the Egg State.

Do you think it practicable to destroy the eggs of the Aphis by spraying any substance on the tree or shrub during the latter part of the winter? I have tried kerosene in various strengths up to 30 per cent, and it does not do the work. I have been experimenting in the hope of finding something that will dissolve the shell of the egg, but find it extremely resistant, scarcely yielding to the strongest acids and alkalies. I have been advised to try some of the fixatives that entomologists use for staining chitine, but nothing that I have tried appears to penetrate the shell at all, so far as I can determine with the microscope. Please tell me if any experiments have been made in this line, and if you would advise me to continue my investigations.—[E. S. Goff, Wisconsin, March 10, 1892.

REPLY.—I do not think that you will find any substance that will destroy the egg of plant-lice as effectually as will the kerosene emulsion. I think it more than probable that you will find that the eggs which you have treated, though they may show signs of life, will not hatch. My past experience would indicate that the eggs of plant-lice when thoroughly sprayed with kerosene-soap emulsion did not hatch, and

---

* Read before the Indiana Academy of Sciences, December 30, 1891.

it is upon this that I base my conclusion. I fear it will be difficult to use any other substance that will destroy the eggshell and not injure the plant. I would by all means advise you to continue your investigations, as I consider it a very important matter.—[March 15. 1892.]

Remedies for Leaf-cutting Ants.

Would you be kind enough to give me a remedy against cutting-ants? We are troubled a great deal by them; they get into our gardens, vineyards, and orchards, and strip all plants of their leaves. There are a great many of them here, and we want to know the best way to get rid of them. * * * —[Jno. G. Kenedy, Nueces County, Tex., February 29, 1892.

REPLY.— * * * The most important point in the warfare against the Leaf-cutting Ant (*Œcodoma ferrens*) is to discover their nests; these are large subterraneous structures extending in powerful colonies, from 10 to 15 feet below the surface of the ground and having several entrance holes. From the latter the ants move after dark along well-defined pathways to the orchard or garden they intend to raid. If the country be open it is not a difficult matter to follow up the moving columns of ants with the aid of a lantern and thus to discover the nest, although the latter is not rarely several hundred feet distant from the tree or vine which the ants defoliate. If, however, it is in dense shrubbery it is usually extremely difficult to locate it. The nest once discovered its inhabitants can be exterminated by pouring bisulphide of carbon into the entrance holes, say at least one pint in each hole if the colony is large. Should there be no bisulphide of carbon at hand the application of cyanide of potassium dissolved in water may be tried. Pouring kerosene or boiling water into the holes or building large fires over the nest are probably less efficacious remedies, but will no doubt help to lessen the number of the ants or at least to discourage them for a time from further raids.

During my stay in Texas in 1879 I witnessed a successful method of protecting a vineyard from the attack of the Leaf-cutting Ant. The vineyard of Mr. Kessler, near Columbus, is surrounded by extensive and very dense shrubbery which was full of the ants. At first these did great injury, but, owing to the nature of the grounds, their nests could not be discovered. Mr. Kessler finally fought them in the following way: Armed with a lantern and a large bottle containing a solution of cyanide in water he made, every evening, the circuit of his vineyard. The columns of ants moving from the woods toward the vines could thus readily be found, and across each of their pathways a strip of about 3 inches in width and 5 inches in length was moistened with the cyanide solution. The ants never went around the poisoned spot, but always attempted to cross it, when they were at once killed by the poisonous fumes. This performance was repeated night after night. except in very rainy weather, and the vineyard was effectually protected.

A new Fumigator for Scale-insects.

I have just returned from Riverside. where I went in company with Mr. John Scott, our county horticultural commissioner, for the purpose of investigating a new kind of fumigator that was reported to be much simpler and cheaper than those heretofore in use. At Riverside we were met by Dr. N. H. Claflin, the horticultural commissioner for that district, accompanied by Mr. C. W. Finch, who has charge of the fumigation under Dr. Claflin's direction, and by whom the fumigator in question was devised.

This fumigator is indeed an extremely simple affair, and, at the same time, it appears to serve all the purposes of the more elaborate and expensive ones. Instead of tents, sheets of 8-ounce drill are used; these are octagonal in outline, as it was found to be easier to construct them of this form than to make them circular. The sheet used to show us the working of the fumigator measured 63 feet in its greatest diameter, and was large enough to inclose a tree at least 24 feet high. It had been oiled with boiled linseed oil, to each gallon of which 1 pound of melted beeswax had been added for the purpose of rendering the cloth more durable. The sheet, when completed, cost about $75.

The apparatus for placing this sheet over the tree consists of two upright poles, to the top of which are attached the pulleys through which pass the ropes used for hoisting the sheet. The uprights consist each of a pine scantling, 3 by 4 inches in diameter and 24 feet long. A crosspiece 5 feet long is bolted to one end of this scantling, with a brace extending from each end of the crosspiece to a point on the scantling a few feet from its base; this crosspiece is for the purpose of preventing the scantling from falling over to one side when it is raised to a perpendicular position. These uprights are very light affairs, and one man can carry them about with ease.

When the sheet is to be placed upon a tree, it is brought close to one side of the tree and thrown upon the ground. The two uprights are next elevated on opposite sides of the tree from each other, and leaned until their upper ends are nearly above the sheet as it rests upon the ground; a stay rope attached to the upper end of each upright and held by men stationed several yards from the base of the uprights, and in an opposite direction from the sheet, prevents the uprights from falling over in one direction, while the crosspiece at the base of each upright prevents it from falling over sidewise. The hook at the end of the rope which passes through the pulley at the upper end of each upright is then hooked into an iron ring fastened to a rope that is sewed across the tent about 6 feet from its edge; the opposite ends of the ropes passing through the pulleys are then drawn downward until the sheet is drawn to the upper ends of the uprights, after which these ropes are fastened to the braces on the uprights, and the men holding the stay-ropes draw the tops of the uprights toward them, thus drawing the sheet over the tree, and after it has been drawn far enough, the lower ends of the ropes passing through the pulleys are unfastened and the sheet allowed to fall down over the tree, the uprights at the same time being allowed to fall flat upon the ground.

When the sheet is to be removed from the tree this can be done either by hand or by the use of the uprights, and if each tree in the row is to be treated the sheet can be drawn off of one tree and placed over the next without the necessity of lowering the uprights, since one man can carry the foot of the upright several feet forward with ease at the same time that the sheet is attached to the top of it.

Five men can operate this apparatus with less labor than is required to manipulate the fumigators now in use, and by the one pair of uprights and ropes at least half a dozen sheets could be operated by the one set of men, without any loss of time. I am informed that the cost of this apparatus, including half a dozen sheets large enough to cover trees 24 feet high, will not exceed $450, this being only about one-third of the cost of fumigators for operating six tents as at present used.

This sheet-fumigator can be used in places where the ordinary kind could not be used; for instance, on steep hillsides, or among trees planted so closely together that an ordinary fumigator could not be driven between them. The sheet, in being pulled off of the tree, does not catch beneath the branches, as the ordinary tent is very liable to do.

As this new fumigator can be easily constructed by almost any fruit-grower, we may reasonably expect that this method of destroying scale-insects will come into more general use.—[D. W. Coquillett, California, March 18, 1892.

Life-history of and Remedies against the Mosquito—The House Fly.

Will you be so kind as to give me the life-history of the Mosquito—hibernation, duration of life of individual, and best means of preventing their propagation? I desire to impress upon our citizens the importance of destroying the first brood of injurious insects that appear in spring.

Does the domestic fly pass through the winter in the adult state only? " " "—[W. L. Jones, Georgia, March 1, 1892.

REPLY.— " " " The main facts in the life history of the Mosquito are as follows: The eggs are laid in boat-shaped masses upon the surface of usually more or less stagnant water, and the larvæ, commonly known as "wigglers," are aquatic. Their development is rapid, and with one species at least it has been ascertained that the entire life-round from egg to adult is undergone in less than two weeks. There are, therefore, several annual generations. The insects hibernate as adults, and possibly in some one of the other stages. It must be remembered that in speaking of the Mosquito we are using a comprehensive term which includes many distinct species, the natural history of which undoubtedly varies to some extent. The most important work to be done in the way of prevention consists in the draining of the swamps and stagnant ponds where possible, the treatment by kerosene of restricted bodies of stagnant water which can not be drained, and the introduction of fish into fishless ponds where these insects are breeding. These are methods which will tend to the reduction of the number of mosquitoes in many restricted localities, but there are many other localities in which these means are not practicable. In such cases we must attack the adult insects. The best thing to do in the house, after screening the windows thoroughly, is to burn pyrethrum powder and sweep up the stupefied insects as they fall to the floor.

In answer to your question as to the hibernation of the domestic fly, I may state that it hibernates exceptionally in both the larva and pupa, but chiefly in the adult state.—[March 3, 1892.]

Is the Ground-beetle, *Scarites subterraneus*, herbivorous?

Will you kindly inform me if the ground-beetle, *Scarites subterraneus* Fab., has ever been considered a vegetable-eater? I have always supposed it to be carnivorous in habit, and was greatly surprised to find a specimen deeply imbedded in a potato one day last fall. About 300 hills of potatoes were planted as an experiment on low, wet land, and while the crop was as large as expected, but few potatoes were obtained, owing to the ravages of wire worm. It may be that the Scarites was after one of the wire-worms.—[Lewis E. Hood, Massachusetts, February 17, 1892.

REPLY.— " " " Your experience with *Scarites subterraneus* is very interesting. So far as I know, this species has never been recorded as having the vegetable-feeding habit. Several Carabids feed exceptionally upon vegetable material, and it would not be surprising if this species should occasionally be found to have this habit. I think, however, that your supposition that the specimen which you found was searching for wire-worms is more plausible than to suppose that it was making a meal of the potato.—[February 19, 1892.]

The so-called California "Wine Bee."

Will you kindly furnish me with anything you may have in the way of information in regard to a bee called the "California wine bee?"—[H. W. Bausch, Ohio, March 10, 1892.

REPLY.—You probably refer to a ferment which, when introduced into the proper liquid, produces a weak alcoholic liquor variously styled as "wine," "beer," etc. This same subject was brought to my attention a short time since, and the liquor was said to be due to the action of certain animals (?) called "California bees," and probably your wine bee is the same thing. In the case just mentioned the liquor was made by taking cold water, sweetened with either brown sugar or molasses, and adding to it some of the ferment or "mother." This latter assumes various globular shapes, and these bodies, during the action of the ferment, move about in the liquid and are the so-called bees. After about forty-eight hours the liquor becomes what is styled beer or wine, and can be drawn off and a new supply of sweetened water added.—[March 14, 1892.]

Grasshopper Outlook in California for 1892.

We were visited by grasshoppers in this vicinity last year and much damage was done by them. We should very much like to know whether there is a probability of their being with us another year or not.—[C. M. Silva & Son, California, February 16, 1892.

Reply.— * * * The subject of grasshopper damage in your State was investigated last year by an agent of this Division, under instructions. The probabilities favor a decided decrease over the damage of last season. The natural enemies of the locust were reported as being present in considerable numbers, and the probabilities are that we will have a season comparable to that of 1886, when, after the very severe locust year of 1885, almost no damage was done.—[February 23, 1892.]

Loss from Grain Weevils in Texas—The Bisulphide of Carbon Remedy.

For many years in succession I had my corn in the bin more or less ruined by weevils. From my own experience in this line, and what I know from other sources, I should judge that there is *an annual loss of over a million of dollars from weevils in Texas alone.*

Last fall, in putting up my corn, I placed two open bottles containing bisulphide of carbon about 4 feet apart on the floor of the bin. The mouths of these bottles were covered with a single layer of cheese-cloth, and each bottle covered with an old broken box. The corn was thrown on these boxes and the bin filled to its utmost capacity.

The result of this experiment was highly successful. What live weevils were admitted from the field were destroyed, and none further appeared. Thus at a cost of 50 cents, with very little trouble, I effectually protected about 500 bushels of corn against the weevils. Another feature about this experiment is that I have noticed neither mouse nor rat in the bin, nor any traces of them, which was not the case before, for in previous years they too had done great damage to the corn.—[G. P. Hackenberg, M. D., Texas, January 28, 1892.

Addition of Lime to the Arsenical Spray.

* * * The first application to my apples was made when the apples were about the size of cherries, with blossom end erect, using London purple in the proportion of 4 ounces to 50 gallons of water, to which was added about 6 or 8 pounds of slaked lime. The second was made about two weeks later and the third in three weeks, just before harvest, the last solution containing one-half pound London purple to 50 gallons of water and about 10 pounds lime. As to results, our apples were practically free from worms, and in the many bushels which we have used in the past winter but one wormy apple has been found. Before picking time an examination of the trees showed that on the unsprayed trees fully 50 per cent were wormy, while on the sprayed those which were wormy were very few, and these all fell off in the fall. The trees retained their leaves late in the fall and the fruit was very free from the green fungous growth which affects the apple in this section. The two last results I attribute to the large quantity of lime used, the leaves looking as if whitewashed after drying. No such perfect and fair fruit was raised in our immediate section as my own.—[E. P. Carroll, jr., Pennsylvania, February 22, 1892.

Physianthus vs. the Codling Moth.—A Disclaimer.

* * * I note your reference on page 98 of your Annual Report for 1887 to Physianthus. My connection with the matter was, however, misunderstood by most of the newspaper people who wrote on the matter. A friend of mine residing at Wauganui sent me some seeds of the Physianthus, stating that he believed that it would be useful by catching the Codling Moth, and asked me to distribute the seeds among

Aukland orchardists. I published his views on the matter in an Auckland newspaper, offering to give seeds to any applicant who cared to give the plant a trial. Somehow, perhaps through want of clearness in my language, it was assumed that I recommended the cultivation of the plant for the purpose of destroying the Codling Moth, and the matter was referred to in newspapers all through the colony, and I believe elsewhere as well. Personally, I never entertained much hope of the plant being of real use, and I see that you express a similar opinion in your pamphlet.

The Codling Moth has done very serious injury in many apple orchards here. But orchardists are beginning to recognize that if the trees are carefully sprayed with Paris green, and bandaged, the injury is reduced to a small percentage. It is, in fact, the old story of attention and careful culture *versus* neglect.—[T. F. Cheeseman, Auckland, New Zealand, December 31, 1891.

A Sesiid Pest of the Persimmon.

I send a small piece of the stem of the native Persimmon (*Diospyros virginiana*) in which you will find a living specimen of a borer which is giving us a great deal of trouble in this district. The center of the stem is quite hollow from the ground line to a depth of 22 inches. The piece sent was at a depth of from 17 to 22 inches below the surface and was growing in a perfectly perpendicular manner.

What is the specific name of the borer and what can we do to destroy it? Many fine trees of *Diospyros kaki* on the native roots have died in this vicinity from this cause.—[J. W. Lever, Florida, February 20, 1892.

REPLY.— * * * The insect which you send is an interesting species of the same group to which the common Peach-Tree Borer belongs. It is known as *Phemonoë 5-caudata*. This insect, although previously known to bore into the Persimmon, has never been sent to us as a pest of economic importance. The surest way to get rid of it would be to dig up and burn every infested tree. If this be done the number will be so reduced that future damage will be slight for a time, but to protect other trees it may be well to remove the earth from around the roots, fill in with ashes, and mound up for some distance. The lower portion of the trunk may be still further protected by a sheathing of straw set upon end and tied with cord. The exact time of egg laying is not known with this species, but if it can be ascertained a still further protection will be found in washing the trunks of the young trees with Paris green and water in the proportion of one-fourth pound to 40 gallons of water during the egg-laying season.—[February 24, 1892.]

A Cayenne Pepper Feeder.

I mail you herewith larvæ of a moth and of an Anthrenus, together with the Cayenne pepper in which they were found living. A specimen of the moth is also sent. These moth larvæ are quite injurious to Cayenne pepper in one of the drug houses of this place. They spin a sort of web, thus fastening many grains of coarse pepper together. The Anthrenus larvæ may be here simply to feed on the cast-off skins of the larvæ and the dead moths, but it looks as if this was at least a proof of the ineffectiveness of the old plan of sprinkling pepper on the floor under carpets to prevent the ravages of the carpet beetle.—[H. F. Wickham, Iowa, February 28, 1892.

REPLY.— * * * The Anthrenus larvæ are those of *A. varius* while the Lepidopterous larvæ belong evidently to the genus Ephestia. The moth, however, was so badly damaged that specific determination is impossible. Lasioderma, Sitodrepa, and a few other beetles have been found in Cayenne pepper, so that your observation is not unprecedented.—[March 9, 1892.]

An early Use of Kerosene.

Much has been written lately in regard to the use of kerosene emulsion; do you think that the mixture referred to could possibly have been one? I quote verbatim from the *Zoölogist* (Newman's), August, 1868, p. 1339:

"The Secretary mentioned that petroleum oil, especially in the crude state, had in France been found of great use in destroying insects; the petroleum was mixed with water, in the proportion of an ounce to half an ounce to a pint of water, but when applied to fruit trees or delicate plants the quantity of oil was still less; a very weak solution with a watering pot was said to be very efficacious against the larvæ of Cockchafer, and a strong solution poured into the holes and down walks infested by insects were said to kill them rapidly. Another application of the solution was said to rid dogs and other animals of parasites; but the parts must be rubbed with soap a few minutes after the solution was applied." * * * —[H. F. Wickham, Iowa, March 3, 1892.

REPLY.— * * * The mixture mentioned in the passage which you quote is by no means an emulsion, but I am always glad to meet with early references to the use of kerosene.—[March 17, 1892.]

List of Coccidæ observed in Jamaica.*

(1) *Aspidiotus ficus* (Riley MS., Ashm.) Comst. Kingston.
(2) *Aspidiotus minutus* Ckll. MS. On Cocoanut Palm, near Montego Bay. Collected by Dr. Sinclair. Not yet studied sufficiently; seems not to be mature. Occurs with *A. rapax* var., but the young of that species, when of the size of *minutus*, are black with a slight, pale rim.
(3) *Aspidiotus personatus* Comst. Kingston. (Also Barbadoes.)
(4) *Aspidiotus rapax* var. *palmæ* v. nov. Ckll. MS. On Cocoanut Palm, near Montego Bay (Dr. Sinclair).
(5) *Aspidiotus rufescens* Ckll. MS. *A. rufescens* Ckll. *Jamaica Post*, December 14, 1891, p. 5. Very near to *A. articulatus* Morgan (1889). On many trees. Kingston. Abundant. (Also Barbadoes.)
(6) *Aspidiotus uvæ* Comst.? A species on Grape, doubtfully referred to this; not yet studied.
(7) *Ceroplastes cirripediformis* Comst. Kingston.
(8) *Ceroplastes floridensis* Comst. Kingston.
(9) *Ceroplastes jamaicensis* Ad. white. Basin Spring. (Gosse.) Not seen by me.
(10) *Chionaspis vandalicus* Ckll. MS. =? *Diaspis vandalicus*. Galver. Abundant on Cocoanut, near Montego Bay. (Dr. Sinclair.) Probably the same as the *D. vandalicus* of Cuba, of which, however, I know no proper description.
(11) *Chionaspis* sp. Kingston. ♀ scale white. Not studied.
(12) *Chionaspis* sp. Kingston. ♀ scale dark. Not studied.
(13) *Dactylopius* sp. on *Acalypha*. Kingston. Not yet enough studied.
(14) *Diaspis* sp. on *Capsicum*. Kingston. Not yet enough studied.
(15) *Diaspis pelargonii* Ckll. MS. On *Pelargonium*. Cinchona plantation. (Coll. W. Harris.) Near to *D. rosæ*, but seems to differ somewhat.
(16) *Fiorinia camelliæ* Comst. On Cocoanut, near Montego Bay. (Coll. by Dr. Sinclair.) On the same leaves I find a curious yellow creature, with a fringe all round, and some pink filaments at each end, so it is possibly the young form of Fiorinia?
(17) *Lecanium* (?) *dendrophthoræ* Ckll. MS. On *Dendrophthora*. Cinchona plantation. (Coll. W. Fawcett.) This I have already discussed in previous letters. I keep it provisionally as a Lecanium, but quite expect it is (as I supposed) a Pulvinaria or Lichtensia.
(18) *Lecanium* sp. Very near the last. On *Plumieria rubra*. Kingston. *Neobernardia* n. nom. (gen. or subg.) Ckll. MS. = Bernardia Ashm. (Nom. *P. Br.* in Euphorbiaceæ.) †

---

* I have examined all of the above except *Ceroplastes jamaicensis*. —T. D. A. C.

† It is not considered as a rule that preoccupation in botany prevents the use of a name in zoölogy, though I am myself of opinion that it ought to. But in the present case we might get a *Bernardia* (Ashm.) living on a *Bernardia* (*P. Br.*), which would be rather confusing. T. D. A. C.

(19) *Lecanium* (*Neobernardia*) *oleæ* Bernard. Kingston.
(20) *Lecanium* (*Neobernardia*) *hemisphæricum* Targ. Kingston. Cockerell and Bath (Mrs. Swainson.)
(21) *Mytilaspis citricola* (Pack.) on oranges, etc.
(22) *Orthesia prælonga* Douglas. Kingston.
(23) *Parlatoria* sp. On *Acalypha*. Kingston. Not studied.
(24) *Parlatoria pergandei* var. *crotonis* Ckll. MS. v. nov. Extremely close to *pergandei*, but seems to differ slightly in the arrangement of the plates. On Variegated Croton. Kingston.
(25) *Planchonia fimbriata* Westw. On Akee. Kingston. Last segment of ♀ reminds one of Diaspis.
(26) *Pseudococcus ruber* Ckll. MS. n. sp. Nearest *P. ulicis* Dougl. I have no Pseudococcus to compare this with, but I suppose it to belong to that genus. The legs are dark brown. On *Euphorbia*. Kingston.
(27) *Pulvinaria* sp. On Akee. Kingston. Not studied.
(28) *Vinsonia stellifera* (Westw.) Dougl. On Mango. Cumberland Pen. There are also about half a dozen other species, not yet examined, belonging to various genera.—[T. D. A. Cockerell, Jamaica, Dec. 23, 1891.

The Broken-tail Snail in Bermuda.

* * * I now send you specimens of the "Broken-tail Snail" which is literally eating up the island and is very destructive to the gardens and the fields of potatoes. We destroy them with salt, lime, and such things, but the surest way is to catch and destroy. My gardener spends nearly two hours each morning catching them, in a garden of about 10 rods, getting half a bucketful each day. Where they can all come from is a question to me, as I have all around my garden a border 10 feet wide which is kept perfectly clean and very few snails we can find crawling on this spot.

Is there any known disease to which these snails are subject and is there any way of causing an epidemical scourge among them? At the rate they are increasing they will soon have complete possession. Some people have already abandoned their gardens and given up this struggle for vegetables. * * *—[Gen. Russell Hastings, Hamilton, Bermuda Island, March 9, 1892.

REPLY.— * * * The animal which you call the "Broken-tail Snail" has never been known as a pest within the limits of the United States, although it occurs in small numbers near Charleston, S. C. It is a European species, and has been introduced into your island. I can make no suggestions regarding remedies which have not already been published in Bermuda. * * * I assume that you must have seen the little pamphlet recently published by the Board of Agriculture, in response to an advertisement offering prizes for descriptions of the history of the Spiral Snails, and the most efficacious, expeditious, and economical methods to effect their extermination. The species has been named for me from your specimen by Mr. Wm. H. Dall, our best authority on Mollusks, as *Rumina decollata* L. With regard to the practical use of some disease or some parasite, I may state that I know of no disease, and while certain snails are secondary hosts of some Entozoa, unfortunately these creatures find their primary hosts in domestic animals, so that they can not be utilized.—[March 17, 1892.]

Bumble-bees and the Production of Clover Seed.

Do Bumble-bees have anything to do with the production of clover seed? * * * [Mrs. C. H. Pike, Michigan, March 4, 1892.

REPLY.— * * * Numerous experiments have placed the matter beyond doubt, and it is safe to say, with all positiveness, that Bumble-bees are very important agents in bringing about the fertilization of clover blossoms, which, as is well known, must take place before seed will form, and also to say that these bees are especially serviceable in bringing about cross-fertilization.

Darwin's experiments in this direction are especially valuable. He protected 100 heads of Red Clover (*Trifolium pratense*) with netting in such a way as to prevent the visits of insects and found that not a single seed was produced, although 100 heads visited by bees at the same time produced 2,720 seeds. Striking results were also obtained with other clovers. Five or six times as many seeds of Scarlet Italian Clover (*Trifolium incarnatum*) were produced when bees were allowed to visit the blossoms as were obtained from the same number of blossoms covered with netting. Cross-fertilized plants of common White Clover (*Trifolium repens*) yielded, in Darwin's experiments, ten times as many seeds as plants fertilized with their own pollen. In another experiment 20 unprotected heads of White Clover gave 2,290 seeds, while 20 heads from which insects were excluded gave but a single seed and that imperfect.

As Bumble-bees visit flowers of Red Clover more than do other bees, and the size and weight of their bodies is such as to render them capable of effecting the fertilization of the flowers, it is safe to say that they are the chief agents. In attempting to secure the honey located in the nectary at the base of the stamens, the Bumblebee presses the keel or carina and the alœ (wings) of the flower downward, and the style being curved, with the terminal stigma rising above the surrounding anthers, the stigma strikes the underside of the bee's head and receives the pollen brought from another clover blossom, and the stamens, which are shorter than the pistil, only touch the bee after fertilization has been accomplished and yield their pollen for the next fertilization.

The common Bumble-bee was imported by the British Government into Australia and New Zealand about the year 1884 for the express purpose of effecting the fertilization of Red Clover in those colonies. After various trials the experiment was successful. The hibernating queens, for which one shilling (24 cents) each was paid, were packed in moss, placed in the refrigerator of the steamer, and were gradually revived upon approaching their destination and then set free. Official reports concerning the results of the experiment are not at hand, but numerous reports in the press have shown that the experiment was successful; that the bees have multiplied with wonderful rapidity and spread over the whole of the cultivated portion of the country in these comparatively few years, and that abundance of seed is produced as a result, where before Australia and New Zealand had to import their Red Clover seed.

Chapter XVI in volume I of Cheshire's "Bees and Bee-keeping," entitled "Bees as Fertilizers," would doubtless give you information which you could use in handling this question.—[March 12, 1892.]

GENERAL NOTES.

INSECTS ON THE SURFACE OF SNOW.

We have seen during the winter a number of newspaper items stating that in different parts of the country insects of one sort or another had been observed in great numbers upon the surface of snow. In no case in the newspaper accounts were the particular species determined scientifically.

On February 11 Mr. John Burroughs, of West Park, N. Y., sent us a number of half-grown larvæ of *Leucania phragmatidicola*, which were found on snow in the fields and along the roads, usually not far from trees. This was immediately after a snowstorm. A week later, on

February 18, another snowstorm occurred and the worms were found again.

On the 2d of March, Mr. Samuel Auxer, of Lancaster, Pa., reported a similar occurrence of worms upon the surface of snow, and the specimens which he sent proved to be the larvæ of some Dipterous insect of the family Bibionidæ. With the Bibionid larvæ were specimens of a Noctuid larva differing from any with which we are familiar. Later advices from Lancaster, this time from Mr. J. R. Henkel, stated that these insects were found upon the umbrellas of "some of our citizens," indicating that they had come down with the snow.

On February 27 Prof. S. F. Clark, of Williams College, Williamstown, Mass., sent in specimens of a larva of a Cecidomyia which had appeared in the vicinity of Blackinton, Mass., on the top of the snow just after a heavy snowstorm. Prof. Clark wrote that the insects were present in great numbers and covered many acres and were on and about a path over which a man walked for a mile.

Almost every winter we have received accounts similar to those which we have mentioned, although they have seldom been accompanied with specimens, and never, to our knowledge, have the reports been as general as during the past winter. The insects received before have been the larvæ of Chauliognathus and the Bronzy Cut-worm (*Nephelodes violans*). Occurrences of the latter on snow have been recorded by Dr. Lintner in his Fourth Report, pp. 54 to 57, and we have mentioned them in our Annual Report for 1890, p. 244.

All of these insects hibernate in the larva state. Our explanation of this interesting phenomenon is, in the majority of cases, that the larvæ, hibernating near the surface of the ground, have been tempted from their winter quarters by a warm, sunshiny day. While out a very sudden freeze ensues, the ground becomes solid, and the larvæ are unable to return to their former position. Then a snowstorm follows and the insects struggle to the surface of the snow, warmed by the sun, where they are plainly seen from their contrasting color. This explanation, however, will not suffice for all cases, and we believe that in some instances the smaller larvæ actually snow down. In such cases they have been lifted from the earth by some severe storm in milder regions to the south and carried in upper air currents to great distances, being precipitated again with the snow.

VEDALIA IN SOUTH AFRICA.

The *Agricultural Journal*, published by the Department of Agriculture of Cape Colony, of February 11, 1892, contains a formal account of the result of Mr. Louw's trip to this country and a definite statement of the success of the importation of Vedalia into the Colony. Mr. Louw gives a full report of his trip, one of the objects of which was to obtain a supply of this beneficial insect. He took with him two boxes of Vedalia given to him by Mr. Coquillett, in Los Angeles, Cal., one of which he kept in his cabin and the other he placed in the ice box. The Secretary of the State Board of Horticulture of California also, by arrangement, forwarded one box of Vedalia and another box of food by express to New York, meeting Mr. Louw at that point. On December 23, 1891, Mr. Louw left New York, feeding both boxes of ladybirds from time to time, and on the 29th of January, 1892, he handed them over to the Secretary of the Agricultural Department of the Cape Colony in perfect condition. In the same number of the same journal the editorial statement is made that almost all of the insects in the box which was placed in the cool chamber survived the journey as well as the others, which were constantly tended. The insects were disposed as follows: A small number were placed in the open air on an infested tree in the Cape Town Botanic Gardens, and the larger portion was divided into two parts, one of which was placed on an infested orange tree at Stellenbosch and kept under wire, while the other was taken to an estate called "Fernwood," owned by a Mr. Rudd, where a glass house similar to that used in California has been erected around an orange tree. A similar glass house is already stocked with the Rodolia mentioned elsewhere in this number. If this experiment should prove a success, which it now bids fair to do, we will have repaid to one English colony the favor which another one has done us.

Since this note was prepared the Secretary of Agriculture has received from Mr. Louw a personal letter acknowledging his indebtedness to this Department, and particularly to the Entomologist, for assistance rendered in the importation of this insect.

A later number of the *Agricultural Journal* (10th March) announces the receipt of a sending of Vedalia from Mr. Koebele, whom we had instructed to attempt to send a consignment from Australia. According to the published note, four specimens only survived the journey, but it is possible that even this small number may do some good if properly cared for.

LEGISLATION AGAINST INSECTS IN CALIFORNIA.

The *California Fruit Grower* of January 9, 1892, publishes an account of a recent meeting of the San Diego County Horticultural Association, an organization comprising twenty-eight horticultural societies. "The Red Spider," "Silk Culture," and "Fig Caprification" were among the subjects discussed.

Resolutions requesting the board of supervisors of the county to take action for the protection of its citizens in the use of hydrocyanic acid gas for fumigation of fruit trees infested with scale-insects and other pernicious pests were adopted, as follows:

Whereas the process of spraying fruit trees for the destruction of scale and other noxious insects with the various compounds and washes is not a success, the result seldom being adequate to the labor and money expended; and

Whereas certain scale-insects have been brought into this county which have thus far resisted the best efforts made to eradicate them; and

Whereas they are now a standing menace to the Citrus fruit industry and their extermination must be accomplished; and

Whereas the hydrocyanic acid gas process has been thoroughly tested and found to be a safe and perfect remedy for exterminating all kinds of scale, if used in season: Therefore,

Resolved by the county horticulturists here assembled, That the board of supervisors of this county be, and are hereby, requested to take such action as will protect any citizen of this county in the use of said hydrocyanic acid gas.

A subsequent edition of the same journal publishes in detail a stringent ordinance issued January 12 by the board of supervisors of Santa Clara County.

Section 1 of this ordinance decrees that no "trees, vines, shrubs, scions, cuttings, buds, grafts, or fruit pits" shall be brought into the county without notice being given to the horticultural commissioners within twenty-four hours after the arrival of such articles, that they may be carefully inspected and, if necessary, disinfected.

Section 2 further decrees that if any such be found to be diseased or infested with injurious insects that they be removed from the county limits or be destroyed.

Section 3 provides that the commission may hold in quarantine any articles that fall within the provisions set forth in section 1 for such time as may be deemed necessary for the safety of the horticultural interests of the county.

Section 4 provides specifically against the introduction of peach yellows, peach rosette, or black knot.

Section 5, bearing more particularly against the introduction of noxious insects, reads as follows:

Whenever any trees, vines, or other articles mentioned in section 1 of this ordinance, brought into Santa Clara County from any district, State, Territory, or foreign country, shall, upon examination or inspection by the horticultural commissioner, be found infested with any scale, insect, bug, moth, pupæ, larvæ, or eggs, curculio or other insect or fungus injurious to fruit, trees, shrubs, or vegetable growth, the said articles shall be ordered disinfected by said horticultural commissioner, or by him declared a nuisance and summarily abated, and whether it be so disinfected or declared a nuisance and destroyed being wholly within the province and judgment of said horticultural commissioner or commissioners.

Section 6 provides that all plants brought into the county shall be properly labeled with the name of the owner, agent, or shipper, of the grower, and such further evidence as the commission may require to determine the locality where grown.

For violation of any of the provisions of this ordinance the offender is liable to imprisonment for not less than ten days nor more than one hundred or to a fine of not less than $10 nor more than $100, or both.

The *Pacific Rural Press* publishes in full an ordinance to regulate the horticultural interests of San Bernardino County, Cal. It is issued by the county board of supervisors under date of October 1, 1891, and does not differ materially from the ordinance just mentioned.

Section 5 is directed particularly against scale-insects. It reads as follows:

Every owner or owners, person or persons, in charge or possession of any orchard, nursery, or other premises in San Bernardino County on which are growing any trees, vines, shrubs, plants, flowers, or vegetables infested with red, cottony cushion, or any other apparently dangerous scale, or the eggs, larvæ, or pupæ thereof, shall when required by the county board of horticultural commissioners, as in their discretion may seem necessary, cut back, disinfect, fumigate, or burn said infested trees, vines, shrubs, plants, flowers, or vegetables, as well as other articles that may be in the vicinity of such infested articles.

RAPHIDIA IN NEW ZEALAND.

We have already mentioned our attempts to introduce the California Raphidia, which feeds upon the Codling Moth larva, into New Zealand, and the failure of the first attempt by mail. We learn from the *New Zealand Farmer*, of October, 1891, that the specimens carried over by Mr. Koebele, on his way to Australia, arrived in good condition. They were nearly all in the pupal condition upon arrival. Dreading the severity of the New Zealand winter, our correspondent, Mr. R. Allan Wight, sent a few of them to Mr. C. French, in Melbourne, to be acclimatized there. The American ladybirds, carried over at the same time, also arrived in good condition. Mr. Wight states that *Cycloneda sanguinea* and *Hippodamia convergens* began at once to feed upon the "Woolly Aphis" (*Schizoneura lanigera*).

THE STRAWBERRY LEAF-ROLLER IN KENTUCKY.

In *Agricultural Science*, Vol. V (pp. 211-212), Mr. H. Garman has an article on the Strawberry Leaf-roller (*Phoxopteris comptana*), in which he adds to our knowledge of the life-history of this insect and describes and figures the egg. The author's observations prove conclusively the existence of three, and only three, broods of the insect in his locality, a fact which was partially proven for southern Illinois by Forbes in his thirteenth report as entomologist of Illinois. The life-history, according to Mr. Garman, is for Kentucky, in brief, about as follows:

Oviposition for the first brood takes place the last week in April, the larvæ hatching the last week in May, and attaining full growth by the first week of June. Pupation takes place soon afterward and the moths appear from June 11-26. The second brood appears the first week in July, the larvæ becoming full grown the last week of that month, and during the first week of August the moths emerge. The larvæ of the third brood begin work about September 1, remain on the plants until cold weather, when they seek shelter for pupation. The adults emerge at the appearance of warm weather, but most of them do not appear until the middle of April.

ICERYA ROSÆ IN JAMAICA.

Mr. T. D. A. Cockerell has sent us specimens of *Icerya rosæ*, R. and H., which were found by Dr. Strachan, of Kingston, upon the leaf of Amherstia. Other specimens were found upon rose in the same garden. For the reason that this species is known in this country only at Key West, we have anticipated that it would prove to be a West Indian form, and this sending by our friend Mr. Cockerell is confirmatory. Mr. Cockerell, by the way, is making a careful study of the Coccidæ of Jamaica, and has already obtained many interesting forms.

THE PHYLLOXERA AT THE CAPE OF GOOD HOPE.

According to recent advices *Phylloxera vastatrix* is still spreading into new territory in Cape Colony. The *Agricultural Journal* of the Department of Agriculture at Cape Town, for January 28, 1892, states that the only safe plan as yet known is to find out which of the Phylloxera-proof American varieties suits the particular soil, then to make a nursery with such cuttings and graft the susceptible European vines on them. Experience shows that this process is much easier in the South African climate than in the older grape-growing countries. The frequently recommended plan of growing the European vines from seed is once more shown to be useless. Such vines are not resistant to the Phylloxera.

A NEW TREE BAND.

The *Philadelphia Record* of March 3 describes a device which is said to have been invented by Carl Hering the well-known electrician, for the destruction of caterpillars which may be attempting to climb trees. Mr. Hering's scheme is simply to run alternate wires of copper and zinc around the trees at a distance of one-half inch apart. The supposition is that the body of the caterpillar will form a circuit between the two wires and that the insect will be destroyed, or at least deterred from climbing higher.

A TRUE BUG DAMAGING PEANUTS IN CHINA.

M. A. Giard, in the *Comptes Rendus* of the Biological Society of France, has published a short paper in which he reviews the damage done by *Halticus minutus* to the peanut crop in Cochin China. He reviews the general subject of injuries by different Pentatomidæ, particularly by congeneric forms, and states that the enormous peanut crop of French Cochin China is threatened with absolute destruction by this insect. Kerosene is recommended as a remedy and the artificial cultivation of *Micrococcus insectorum* is suggested.

SARCOPHAGA IN THE HUMAN EAR.

Under the title "Abnormal Living Entozoa in the Human Ear," Dr. Walter B. Johnson, of Paterson, N. J., has published in a recent number of the *Ophthalmic Record* an account of the occurrence of a maggot in the ear of one of his patients. The latter was a strong, well nourished man, who was suffering from an old suppurated Otitis Media in the left ear, which had been under observation for some time. When admitted to Dr. Johnson's infirmary an examination showed the external auditory canal to be filled with a muco-purulent discharge of considerable thickness, yellow in color and excessively odorous. After removing this the tympanum was found to contain a large perforation, in which was noticed a white substance, which was at first thought to be white, exfoliated skin. Later the white material was observed to move, and it was then concluded that some living organism was present. After an ineffectual effort to remove it by syringing, the ear-forceps were used, and the object was seized and instantly removed. It held to the mucous membrane with sufficient force to cause some hæmorrhage. It was found to be an "ordinary maggot," half an inch long, "very fat and quite lively." The specimen was sent to the Rev. Samuel Lockwood, of Freehold, N. J., who reported that it was the larva of the Flesh Fly or Meat Fly—*Sarcophaga carnaria*. The larva was full grown and just on the point of transforming. In Dr. Lockwood's opinion it was about ten days old.

On the supposition that the rupture in the ear drum was an old one, the parent fly was probably attracted to the external ear by the purulent discharge, which undoubtedly preëxisted. If, however, the maggot itself made the perforation, Dr. Lockwood suggests that it might have entered when very young through the Eustachian tube. Supposing the patient to have eaten cold tainted meat, and, when a morsel was in his mouth, to have coughed from some cause or other, or in some way to have dislodged a very young larva, so that it was thrown upon or near to the opening of the Eustachian tube, its occurrence in the ear would be accounted for. These alternatives were placed before Prof. Johnson by Dr. Lockwood, and the information elicited from the patient seems to prove the correctness of the former hypothesis. This case, although by no means unprecedented, is an interesting contribution to Myasis records.

THE JAPANESE PEACH MOTH.

Through the kindness of Prof. C. Sasaki, of the Royal Agricultural and Dendrological College of Tokio, we have received specimens of the peach moth which was referred to at some length on pages 24 to 66 of Volume II of INSECT LIFE. It will be remembered that Prof. Sasaki judged the insect to be a species of Carpocapsa closely allied to our Codling Moth. An examination of the specimens received shows, in spite of their injured condition, that the insect is a Tineid rather than a Tortricid, agreeing almost exactly in venation with the genus Carposina, varying from it only in two minute points in the hind wings. We have sent for additional material which, if it arrives in good condition, will enable a more accurate verdict.

A NEW WEST INDIAN SUGAR-CANE ENEMY.

We have received from gentlemen in Trinidad and Barbados specimens of a Scolytid beetle—*Xyleborus piceus* Zimm.=*X. perforans* Woll.= *X. affinis* Eich.—which is said to do great damage to the growing crop of sugar-cane upon these islands. We have received but few particulars as to the method of work of this insect, although canes which have been sent in have been badly riddled by its minute burrows and Mr. F. Carmody, Government Chemist at Port of Spain, informs us that the healthy growing canes are attacked. Through Dr. W. A. Culpeper, of Bridgetown, Barbados, we learn that the specimens have been referred to Miss Ormerod, who accurately determined them and suggested the possibility of applying a soft-soap wash and kerosene emulsion to the canes. This method it seems to us will be hardly practicable, although it would undoubtedly be efficacious if it could be applied economically. This insect occurs in this country, boring into many different trees and always perferring diseased or dying wood. In the absence of definite information it seems to us that in the West Indies the sugar-cane feeding habit has been acquired through the oviposition of the beetles upon the more or less moribund cut ends of the canes sometime after harvest, the larvæ subsequently perhaps working into the young sprouts. We look for the best remedy in the line of trapping the insects in cane trash which should be displayed at the proper time and subsequently burned. Fuller information, however, is expected later and we promise a more definite article in the near future. The subject is one of considerable interest on account of the great value of the sugar industry in some of our southern States.

THE HOP LOUSE IN THE EXTREME NORTHWEST.

We have had considerable to say in these pages concerning the presence of *Phorodon humuli* in the hop fields of Oregon and Washington during the past season. As a general thing our recommendations have been followed, and wherever the kerosene emulsion has been properly made and carefully applied it has been successful. The Entomologist of the Oregon Experiment Station, Mr. F. L. Washburn, has used it with success, and his correspondents, with very few exceptions, are pleased with the treatment. Some discredit has been cast upon the mixture by certain growers, and one firm interested in the sale of quassia chips has naturally given the preference to the quassia mixture, the only advantage of which is in use late in the season, when the burrs are formed. The kerosene emulsion should be used earlier, as it is apt to induce moldiness of the burr.

Early the present spring specimens of the wingless plant-louse were found in the ground of hop fields and sent to the secretary of the State board of horticulture of Washington, who forwarded them to us under the supposition that they might prove to be some form of the Hop Louse.

An examination at this office showed them to be wingless agamic females of a species of the genus Tychea, and to have no connection whatever with Phorodon. But our determination reached Washington after the matter got into print, and the *Post-Intelligencer* of Seattle published a long account, under some startling headlines, claiming that the Entomologist of this Department had made a mistake in the life-history of the Hop Louse, and that the insects found in the soil were the stem-mothers of *Phorodon humuli*. Mr. S. A. Tonneson, the Secretary of the State Board of Horticulture of Washington, in an interview reported in this article, is more guarded in his statements than the headlines of the article would indicate, and acknowledges the possibility of a mistake. Sooner or later the hop growers of Washington and Oregon will realize all we have said on this subject is true, and that one of the best ways to fight the Hop Plant-louse is to destroy the first generation on plum trees early in the spring with the kerosene emulsion.

MORE CALIFORNIA NOTES.

The State inspectors have been actively enforcing the quarantine laws, and, as we learn from the *Pacific Rural Press* of January 9, during the preceding week large numbers of diseased fruit trees imported from the East were seized and condemned. Peach Yellows and the Plum Curculio were the principal pests found. Trees to the value of $5,000 were condemned. Protests by eastern nurserymen were sent in and claims made that neither the Peach Yellows nor the Plum Curculio would flourish in California. The same point was raised, it will be remembered, a year or so ago with regard to the Florida species of Mytilaspis upon Orange, viz, the Purple Scale and the Long Scale, but we notice from the *California Fruit Grower* of January 23 that John Scott, Horticultural Commissioner of Los Angeles County, has proven "beyond a doubt" that the Purple Scale will thrive in California and that trees brought into the State three or four years ago are now covered with the pests. The *Anaheim Gazette* is responsible for the statement that the cold snap in December or January killed off many Red Scales in the Anaheim region. Seedlings, which had been badly infested, were found after the cold snap without a sign of scale upon them. The frost was supposed to have killed them and the subsequent rains to have washed them off.

A HONEY BEE ENEMY IN CALIFORNIA.

Our agent, Mr. D. W. Coquillett, of Los Angeles, Cal., has sent us specimens of the Heteropteron *Apiomeris flaviventris* which he has seen feeding upon honey bees. Both the adults and the nymphs were engaged in this destructive occupation.

THE ANGOUMOIS GRAIN MOTH IN PENNSYLVANIA.

This well-known pest to stored grain is found commonly through the Southern States laying its eggs in corn before harvest, but has heretofore been known only in granaries in the North. Recent communications, however, from Pennsylvania and New Jersey, near Philadelphia, indicate that where wheat is stacked in the field and left until fall and winter before threshing, the moths oviposit in it abundantly and in some places have done serious damage. The probabilities are that this habit originated in some wheat field in the vicinity of a large granary, the moths flying out from the building in late summer to the wheat stacks in the field, which afforded exceedingly appropriate places for egg-laying. Our correspondents inform us that when the wheat is threshed soon after harvest it does not become infested, so that by following this course and occasionally spraying the storage places in the spring with kerosene or kerosene emulsion all danger may be averted.

THE SOUTH AFRICAN LADYBIRD ENEMY OF ICERYA.

We mentioned in our 1886 report the fact of the occurrence in Cape Colony of a native ladybird which feeds extensively upon the Fluted Scale, and which was named by the late E. W. Jansen *Rodolia iceryæ*. This insect has done much effective work in the eastern provinces and has been recently carried to the western provinces and colonized under glass in the hope that it will be acclimatized there. The experiment from latest accounts seems to be a success.

ON THE DATE OF THE INTRODUCTION OF THE EUROPEAN WHEAT SAW-FLY.

In Bulletin No. XI of the Cornell University Agricultural Experiment Station, Prof. J. H. Comstock reports the Wheat Saw-fly (*Cephus pygmæus* L.) as having first been observed at Ithaca, N. Y., in 1887, this being the first published record of the occurrence of the insect in this country. Further records are published in INSECT LIFE, Vol. II, p. 286, viz, its occurrence in Canada in 1887, and at Buffalo, N. Y., in 1888.

Other imported pests that might be mentioned are known to have been present in limited numbers and restricted localities for twenty years and more before attaining economic importance, and, since at the time of the publication of this bulletin (November, 1889) the insect had become rather abundant, it might be assumed that it was introduced quite a number of years earlier. A single specimen was taken by me at Ithaca, but unfortunately the exact date of capture was not noted. I am inclined to believe, however, that this specimen was found about 1881 or 1882, and am positive that it was not taken later than 1884, and possibly as early as 1878 or 1879.—F. H. CHITTENDEN.

AN IMPORTANT PUBLICATION ON SPIDERS.

Mr. Nathan Banks has just published in the Proceedings of the Academy of Natural Sciences, Philadelphia, a paper entitled "The Spider Fauna of the Upper Cayuga Lake Basin," in which he considers three hundred and sixty-three species and describes many new forms. The paper is illustrated by five plates of structural details. Judging from the comparative table of local lists of spiders the upper Cayuga Lake basin seems to be a particularly favorable region of country for these arthropods.

AN ALEYRODES ON THE STRAWBERRY.

Mr. H. Garman gives an account in *Agricultural Science* (Vol. v. pp. 264–5 of *Aleyrodes vaporarium?* Westw., a nearly cosmopolitan greenhouse pest, which he finds on the Strawberry on the grounds of the State College at Lexington, Ky. Toward fall the young scales are present in abundance on the under side of the leaves. The winged adults of the brood appear late in the fall, and, after leaving eggs for another generation, disappear. Young scales, which the writer believes hatched from the eggs deposited by the fall brood, are to be found on strawberry leaves in March of the next season. This scale is not confined to the Strawberry but attacks also the Tomato, and the same or a closely related species is found on the leaves of *Abutilon avicenne*.

ABUNDANCE OF ATTAGENUS PICEUS IN ILLINOIS.

One of our Illinois correspondents, Mrs. Horace French, of Elgin, Kane County, writes us under date of February 19, 1892, of the destructive Carpet Beetle, *Attagenus piceus* Ol. (*megatoma* Fab.), specimens of which she has sent us, in that locality. This beetle, for which there is no common name, is a member of the family Dermestidæ and a near relative of the so-called Buffalo Moth, or Buffalo Carpet Beetle. Previous mention has been made of this species in INSECT LIFE, Vol. III (pp. 65, 66, and 170). According to our correspondent, many houses in Elgin are infested with the Buffalo Carpet Beetle, but little damage is done except during the warmer months, while the Attagenus seems to work constantly throughout the year, unmindful of change of temperature.

A Peoria housekeeper has had a similar annoying experience, being compelled to keep all articles of woolen, silk, or fur wearing apparel, not in constant use, tied up in strong paper bags. Mrs. French mentions a dozen or more remedies which she had employed, but all with indifferent success. Her house was so completely overrun with the pests that after taking up carpets and discovering the full extent of their ravages, it was deemed unsafe to replace them.

Benzine, in the form of a spray, if carefully and persistently applied to the walls and crevices of the floor, will eventually rid infested houses of these insects. It is advisable at the same time, for greater thoroughness, to fill the floor cracks with plaster paris in fluid form. After this has "set" it will greatly reduce the number of possible lurking places. The free use of benzine has accomplished immunity from the pest in cases fully as bad as those recounted.

QUASSIA VS. PETROLEUM FOR THE HOP LOUSE.

We have received information of late from several correspondents in Oregon and Washington State to the effect that the quassia wash, used by English hop-growers, has proved more effective than kerosene emulsion against the Hop Louse. A company has recently issued a circular extolling the excellence of quassia as a specific against the Hop Louse, and its superiority over the kerosene emulsion.

We must again reiterate the statement made on page 84 of the current volume that quassia was carefully tried in our experiments made in 1887 against the Hop Louse, and the result recorded in our Annual Report for 1888. When applied pure it kills the lice with which it is brought into direct contact, but owing to the fact that it will not spread, like the kerosene emulsion, it can not be considered as efficient if used alone.

The reported dissatisfaction with the kerosene treatment is undoubtedly due to failure to produce a proper emulsion, according to formulæ and directions given in Circulars Nos. 1 and 2 of this Division, and moreover, to the fact, probably, that the application was made too late to be of service.

A WESTERN ENEMY OF THE WHITE-MARKED TUSSOCK MOTH.

Through the help of Mr. C. W. Woodworth, of the University of California, we hope to make some attempt to bring *Perimegatoma variegatum* to the east this season. This Dermestid beetle is a very effective destroyer of the eggs of the White-marked Tussock moth, and if it can be successfully acclimatized will prove a very valuable insect in many of our Eastern States.

A NEW COTTON-STAINER IN JAMAICA.

We have received from Mr. T. D. A. Cockerell specimens of *Dysdercus andreæ*, with the information that it attacks the bolls of cotton and in the same manner as does *D. suturellus* in this country, Cuba, and the Bahamas. It is curious that *D. andreæ* should replace *D. suturellus* in Jamaica. According to Mr. Cockerell, it is very abundant and probably occurs throughout the island. Remarks were made upon the damage done by this species to the cotton crop by Dr. Phillipo, at the meeting of the Institute of Jamaica, held December 14, 1891.

ADDITIONS TO THE INSECT COLLECTION OF THE AMERICAN MUSEUM.

We learn from recent New York papers that the American Museum of Natural History, Central Park, New York, has recently been enriched in its entomological department by the donation of the collection of Mr. James Angus, of West Farms, N. Y., containing, it is said, 10,000 specimens of 1,700 species of Lepidoptera and a number of insects of other orders. The excellent collection of the late Mr. S. Lowell Elliot has also been donated to this museum by his widow. Mr. Elliot's collection is particularly valuable, for the reason that the specimens (mainly Lepidoptera) were nearly all reared and are in prime condition. The addition of these collections, together with that of the late Henry Edwards, mentioned in our last number, will place the American Museum on an excellent footing in the order Lepidoptera. It is to be hoped that the trustees will see that the material receives competent care.

THE USE OF ELECTRICITY AGAINST MIGRATORY LOCUSTS.

Mr. Andreas Schmidt, of Bucharest, Roumania, has forwarded to the Secretary of the Interior a description and photographs of a device for the destruction of migratory locusts by electricity. One method of applying the invention consists in the erection of a rampart of earth 35 centimeters high, surrounding the infested area, a ditch being left by the removal of the earth to form the said rampart. Along the top of this earthen wall and inclining over the ditch, run two conductors, positive and negative, insulated and separated from each other by a thin strip of rubber, which is necessary to prevent the current from leaping across. The idea is that, the current being "on," the grasshoppers will crawl up the wall, complete the circuit by their own bodies, and instantly drop dead into the ditch. Flags are placed at intervals along the top of the wall to give warning of its presence. In another application of the same idea, the grasshoppers crawl up the inclined plane formed by a sheet of cloth sloping to the ground.. If the positive and negative conductors can be brought so close together that the grasshopper's body will form a bridge from one to the other every time, death is certain. The inventor claims that the expense of such an installation as he proposes is extremely small, and that the method, for rapidity and certainty, throws all others into the shade, as applied to grasshoppers.

ANOTHER IMPORTED SCALE-INSECT.

The Olive in Europe suffers from the attacks of several destructive scale-insects. Two of these, *Lecanium oleæ* and *Aspidiotus nerii*, have already made their appearance in this country and are also known in other localities where the Olive is cultivated, as in Australia. A third, *Pollinia costæ*, a curious form, the female of which is a degraded, almost amorphous creature, covered with a dirty waxen test, has recently made its appearance in California upon certain Olive trees which were imported direct from Italy five years ago. Specimens of this insect were sent to us from Los Angeles recently by Mr. Coquillett, and at once specifically recognized. If, as we believe, the insect is not elsewhere found in this country, every effort should be made to stamp it out upon the few trees which it infests at present.

A NEW PLANT-LOUSE ENEMY.

Mr. Webster sent us early in April specimens of a small slug which which he had found feeding upon plant-lice upon the leaves of Dock. We sent the slugs to Mr. W. G. Binney, Burlington, N. J., who determined the species as *Limax campestris* Binney, and stated that he had never known the species to feed in this way before.

"Still," he remarks, "slugs will eat almost anything that presents itself—vegetable matter usually, but in captivity they prey upon one another—will take sponge cake, strawberries, flour, lettuce, etc. The marginal teeth of their lingual membrane are aculeate. In the true carnivorous slugs all the teeth are such." From this it appears that the instance observed by Mr. Webster was exceptional, and probably does not promise any particular benefit.

THE TWIN-SCREW MOSQUITO.

One of the best of recent newspaper hoaxes was that which appeared in the New York *Sun* early in March, concerning a new product of the New Jersey marshes, which it is proposed to dub the Twin-screw Mosquito. Some hundreds of specimens of this creature were "shot" by a party of hunters on the Hackensack Meadows. They are described as resembling two mosquitoes with the bodies united behind, thus giving a piercing apparatus to each end. A long, pseudo-technical description, reputed to come from Prof. George Hume, of Jersey City, accompanied the article, and a very good illustration of a male and female mosquito in copulation pictures the new terror.

ECONOMIC ENTOMOLOGY IN NEW SOUTH WALES.

The *Agricultural Gazette* of New South Wales for December, 1891, contains an excellent article upon the Plague Locust, by Mr. A. S. Olliff, and some entomological notes by the same author. Mr. Olliff attacks the locust problem from the standpoint of American writers, and gives a careful review of the work which has been done by the Entomological Commission of this country, adopting the recommendations of the commission, and urging thorough study of the permanent breeding grounds of the Australian species. This plan would be quite in accordance with our own ideas, and the locust problem in Australia can receive no intelligent treatment without a preliminary survey of this nature. The entomological notes include some consideration of the Spinning Mite or Red Spider of Australia, which is a species of Tetranychus allied to *T. telarius*, and an announcement of the fact that the Entomologist is about to begin the study of the Australian ticks.

LIVING VEDALIAS AT LAST REACH EGYPT.

It will be remembered that we have been endeavoring for some time to send living Vedalias to Alexandria, Egypt, in order to ascertain whether this species will destroy *Icerya ægyptiacum*, which is doing considerable damage to the Fig and Orange trees in the gardens of that city. Several sendings having failed we have at last been informed by our esteemed correspondent, Rear Admiral R. N. Blomfield, R. N., that of a lot shipped by Mr. Coquillett from Los Angeles, Cal., and repacked in Washington, D. C., about March 6, six adult beetles and several larvæ reached Alexandria alive. They have been liberated upon an infested orange tree, but we have not yet been informed as to whether they have begun to breed and feed upon the Egyptian Fluted Scale. The Vedalia is so uniform in its tastes and we have failed so signally to induce it to feed upon anything but *Icerya purchasi* that there is some little doubt as to the success of this experiment. We have never, however, tried it upon a congeneric species before, and it may be on account of the very close relationship of the Egyptian to the California and Australian insect that the Vedalia will find in it appropriate food.

SELF-MUTILATION IN ORTHOPTERA.

It has often been observed that many animals, when kept in captivity, develop certain unnatural traits. One of these is a tendency to self-mutilation—an instinct on the part of the animal which impels it to devour the extremities of its own body.

Dr. Franz Werner, of Vienna, Austria, has recently published[*] some interesting observations in this direction on European Orthoptera. From a number of species kept under observation Dr. Werner concludes that a tendency to self-mutilation does not prevail in the truly phytophagous families, such as the Acridiidæ and Gryllidæ, but that it seems to be confined to the raptatorial species and that it is most strongly developed in certain predaceous Locustidæ with poorly developed wings. In all observations ample nourishment was provided, but this did not prevent the specimens from eating first their tarsi, especially those of the anterior pairs of legs, then the tibiæ, and finally the females commenced to eat their own ovipositors. Among the species observed the rare *Saga serrata* excelled all others in its avidity to devour its entire legs, while *Mantis religiosa* was contented with chewing up its tarsal joints. Of *Barbitistes serricauda* Dr. Werner was not able to collect perfect examples, for as soon as a captured specimen is held between the fingers it bites off its own front legs with great rapidity. In most instances the chewing is deliberate and evidently without sensation of pain.

---

[*] Zoöl. Anzeiger, xv, No. 384, Feb. 15, 1892, pp. 58-60.

NORTH AMERICAN TACHINIDÆ.

There are few families of Diptera of greater importance to the economic entomologist than the Tachinidæ, comprising as it does the chief parasitic Diptera which help to check many of our most injurious insects. Our former assistant, Prof. C. H. Tyler Townsend, now of the New Mexico Agricultural College, has recently taken up the study of these little flies which have been sadly in need of systematic study. He is publishing a series of papers in different entomological serials giving descriptions of new species and new genera. These fragmentary formal communications are doubtless looked upon by Prof. Townsend as merely preliminary and with a view of securing priority, and it is greatly to be hoped that they will all be brought together in some future monographic work by the same author. It is to be regretted that these descriptions are being published at the very time that the renowned Dipterologist, Dr. F. Brauer, is monographing the family, as we fear that synonyms which otherwise might be avoided will necessarily result. It may not be out of place to repeat here the warning of our friend Baron Osten Sacken, who is a master in systematic entomology and to whom North American Dipterology is more indebted than to anyone else. He says in his last important contribution:

If I am asked now what the *desiderata* for the future of this branch of science in America are, I would answer:
 1. Continue the publications of North American Diptera in monographs.
 2. Avoid as much as possible the publication of detached species either singly, or in numbers.

The cases where the publication of detached species of Diptera can be really useful in the present state of American Dipterology are rare, and will easily suggest themselves to the good sense of the unprejudiced.

Conscientious monographs are always useful.

NEW SPECIES OF COLEOPTERA.[*]

We have received from Captain Casey a copy of his third paper of "Coleopterological Notices," which is a continuation of a series begun in 1889 in Vol. V of the Annals of the New York Academy of Sciences. In this paper the author furnishes a revision of the Cistelidæ of the United States, defines ten new genera, and describes as new upwards of 100 species, principally of the Heteromera and Cerambycidæ, many of them founded on unique specimens. The following genera are proposed: Chrotoma, Thesalia, Valenus, Idiobates, Palembus, Rues, Tedinus, Negalius, Adrimus, Dinocleus, all, except the last two mentioned, being established on single species. Synoptic tables are furnished of the following genera: Lyctus (including Trogoxylon), Polyphylla (*P. 10-lineata* group), Tetropium, Rhopalophora, Crossidius, Sphænothecus, Ipochus, Psenocerus, Hyperplatys, Spalacopsis, Epitragus, Epitrag-

---

[*] Coleopterological Notices, III. By Thos. L. Casey. Extr. from Annals N. Y. Academy Sciences, Vol. VI, November, 1891.

odes, Anepsius, Eulabis, Pyrota, Dinocleus, Cleonus, Lixus, and the different genera of Cistelidæ.

Some changes are noticeable, e. g., the genus Trogoxylon is merged in Lyctus and the latter removed from the Ptinidæ and placed in the Clavicorn family Cucujidæ, a change which is scarcely warranted when the biological affinities of this genus with the Ptinidæ and the wide divergence of its earlier stages from those of the Cucujidæ are taken into consideration.—F. H. C.

FOURTH ANNUAL MEETING OF THE ASSOCIATION OF ECONOMIC ENTOMOLOGISTS.

COLUMBUS, OHIO, *May 10, 1892.*

In accordance with an action of the Association, taken at the Washington meeting, the fourth annual meeting will be held at Rochester, N. Y., two days prior to the meeting of the American Association for the advancement of science.

All members intending to present papers are requested to forward titles to the undersigned before August 1, in order that the program may be prepared in proper season.

The proceedings of our meetings are attracting the attention of working entomologists of other countries, and it is to be hoped that members will spare no efforts to make the coming meeting even better than those which have preceded it. Owing to the continued ill health of President Lintner, and in order to relieve him of as much labor as possible, all correspondence, unless of a nature necessitating his attention, may be addressed to the Secretary.

F. M. WEBSTER,
Secretary, Association of Economic Entomologists.

ENTOMOLOGICAL SOCIETY OF WASHINGTON.

March 3, 1892.—Nineteen persons present. Mr. William Ross Harris, of Tyler, Tex., was elected a corresponding member of the society. Dr. Stiles gave a talk on the "Histology of Ticks." He made some blackboard sketches and exhibited a number of slides illustrating the subject. He dwelt especially on the cuticular tissue, alimentary canal, stigmata, excretory organs, and glands of the head. Discussed by Dr. Marx.

Dr. Theo. Gill presented a paper on "The Larva of Insects as an Intercalated Stage." He quoted and criticised certain statements in Agassiz's "Classification of Animals from Embryological Data." From these criticisms he argued to show that the larva of insects was an added or intercalated stage. He had prepared a table giving the distribution of fossil insects. This showed that the Orthopteroid, Neuropteroid, Hemipteroid, and Coleopteroid insects were not only the insects of the Palæozoic, but also the prevailing insect types of the Mesozoic age. The Diptera, Lepidoptera, and Hymenoptera, which have a larva or caterpillar stage, were later developments. Discussed by Messrs. Ashmead, Banks, and Gill.

Thursday, April 7, 1892.—Twenty-one persons present. Mr. George D. Bradford, of New York was elected a corresponding member. The discussion of Dr. Gill's paper entitled "The Larva of Insects as an Intercalated Stage," postponed from the preceding meeting of the Society, was taken up and participated in by Messrs. Stiles, Riley, Gill, and Banks. Dr. Riley presented two papers, one "On certain peculiar Structures of Lepidoptera" and the other, "Descriptions of new Prodoxidæ." He spoke of various interesting structures of the Prodoxidæ, calling attention more particularly to the saw-like ovipositors, the maxillary tentacles the cenchri-like spots on the thorax and certain radiate and chitinous bodies in the *receptaculum seminis*. The remarks were illustrated by large figures. He also spoke of the resemblance of *Pronuba synthetica* to certain saw-flies. Specimens of the insects described were exhibited. Professor Riley's second paper was read by title only and was presented for publication. The discussion of these papers was participated in by Messrs. Howard, Marlatt, and Stiles. Professor Riley also presented a paper on "Coleopterous Larvæ with Dorsal Appendages," in which he described the larva of various species of Mordellistena which have rows of tubercles on the back which facilitate moving in the hollows of plants and the larger burrows of other insects. He also described similar tubercles in certain Cerambycid larvæ. Discussed by Messrs. Smith and Schwarz. Mr. Doran read a paper entitled "On the Heat Produced by *Sylvanus cassiæ*," in which he recorded some observations which he had made on the amount of heat produced by these beetles in meal, but offered no definite explanation of the phenomenon. Discussed by Messrs. Marlatt, Riley, Austin, and Schwarz.

NATHAN BANKS,
Recording Secretary.

Thursday, May 4, 1892.—Nineteen persons present. Prof. H. E. Summers, of Champaign, Ill., was elected a corresponding member of the society.

Mr. W. H. Ashmead presented some "Notes on the genus Enicocephalus, Westw." Bibliographical and critical notes were given and the announcement was made of the discovery also of a new species in Utah by Mr. E. A. Schwarz. The genus can not be included in any of the present subfamilies in the Reduviidæ, to which it belongs, and the new subfamily Enicocephalinæ was erected for it. The new species was named *Enicocephalus schwarzii*. Discussed by Messrs. Schwarz, Riley, Ashmead, Hubbard, and Heidemann.

Mr. Mally read a paper on *Micromus insipidus*, pointing out some observations on the food and life-habits of this Neuropteron made in the South, where he found it feeding on Aphides. Discussed by Messrs. Ashmead and Riley.

Mr. Howard presented a note on "The Hibernation of Carpenter Bees," showing that males as well as females winter over. Discussed by Messrs. Riley, Ashmead, Hubbard, Marlatt, and Howard.

A paper by Dr. Bergroth, of Tammerfors, Finland, entitled "Notes on Nearctic Aradidæ" was read by the Corresponding Secretary, to whom it had been sent for publication in the Proceedings of the Society.

Mr. F. M. Webster had forwarded a paper for presentation at this meeting of the Society on "The Food-plants of the Lixi." The communication gave a review of the knowledge of the habits in this respect of this genus of beetles, both of foreign and American species. Discussed by Mr. Schwarz.

Mr. Hubbard presented a note on the larva of Amphizoa, and gave a résumé of the disposition of this anomalous insect in systematic classification by various authors, together with the arguments adduced in support of the diverging views. He presented drawings of the larva and described its habits. The communication was discussed at some length by Mr. Schwarz and also briefly by Messrs. Ashmead, Gill, Riley, and others.

Mr. Masius gave his recent experience with the poisonous bite of *Benacus griseus*. In handling specimens of this insect he had received a severe sting on the hand which proved to be very painful. The pain and swelling increased for two or three days, and became so troublesome that a physician was consulted. In five days the trouble had about entirely disappeared, although at the time of the meeting the injured part was still sore. Discussed by Messrs. Howard, Ashmead, Riley, and others.

C. L. MARLATT,
Rec. Secretary, pro tem.

SPECIAL NOTES.

Close of Volume IV.—With this number we close Volume IV of INSECT LIFE, and regret to have to announce that the current demand for the bulletin has exhausted the earlier numbers of this volume, so that in future no regular sets can be obtained. The reader will have noticed that the numbers have been issued bimonthly rather than monthly. In fact for reasons over which the editors have no control the issue of INSECT LIFE as a regular monthly periodical has been practically abandoned, though the numbers issued throughout the year will continue as heretofore to constitute one volume, and each volume will be so paged and indexed. The present number includes the title-page and index to the volume, so as to facilitate the binding of the same.

Seventh Report of the New York State Entomologist.*—Dr. Lintner's seventh report is the largest and in some respects the most important of the series which he has published since he assumed the office of State Entomologist of New York in 1880. The care with which Dr. Lintner treats every insect which comes to his attention, the almost invariable accuracy of his statements and conclusions, and the admirable manner in which he presents his subjects, render most welcome the appearance of a new report from him. In the present volume, which covers something over 400 pages, he has treated at greater or less length some thirty species, and adds, in an Appendix, reprints of addresses before the New York State Agricultural Society and the Western New York Horticultural Society, with his usual long list of publications during the year, which the report represents, adding thereto a bibliography of his own writings during the years 1878 and 1879, immediately before he assumed the office which he now holds. The report is illustrated with forty text figures, and the index and table of contents are, as usual, models of care. The most important articles in the report, from an economic standpoint, are those upon the Bean Weevil and the Chrysanthemum Leaf-miner.

---

* Seventh Report on the Injurious and other Insects of the State of New York. (From the forty-fourth report of the New York State Museum.) Albany, 1891.

Bulletin No. 19 of the Massachusetts Station.*—In this bulletin the leading article, upon the Gypsy Moth, is by Prof. Fernald, he having been appointed entomological adviser to the Gypsy Moth committee of the State Board of Agriculture. The article is a full descriptive account of the insect in its different states, with a summary of its present distribution and its food-plants, also an interesting paragraph on the parasites of the species, in which are mentioned as feeding upon the eggs *Trombidium bulbipes* Pack., *Nothrus* sp. near *ovivorus* Pack., and a species of Phlœothrips. As issuing from the pupa *Theronia melanocephala* Br. and *Pimpla pedalis* Cr.—both Ichneumonids—are mentioned, also an undescribed Chalcidid of the genus Meraporus. In addition to these, several undetermined species of Diptera were reared, and a Soldier Bug (*Podisus spinosus* Dall.), black ants and spiders were found destroying the larvæ, while ten different species of birds were also observed to feed upon them. In Bulletin 26 of this Division, Mr. Henshaw has recorded, upon page 81, a few additional facts upon the natural enemies of Ocneria; no other true parasites, however, being mentioned. The article is illustrated with the five excellent plates and the map which were used in the Report of the State Board of Agriculture. The bulletin also contains a summarized account of "Barnard's insect trap," experiments with Paris green on apple trees, especially against the Tent Caterpillar, and closes with an account of cranberry insects, studied from the Massachusetts standpoint, the accounts of the insects so far treated agreeing in general with those by Prof. John B. Smith, whose bulletin on cranberry insects we reviewed in Vol. II, upon page 337.

Contagious Diseases of the Chinch Bug.†—Prof. F. H. Snow, in his first annual report as Director of the Experiment Station, University of Kansas, gives a complete summary of his work upon the contagious diseases of the Chinch Bug, preliminary accounts of which have appeared in INSECT LIFE (Vol. III, pp. 279–284, and Vol. IV, pp. 69–71). The report includes about 140 pages in brevier type, devoted to the reports of farmers and others who have experimented with Prof. Snow's diseased bugs, and the reports as a whole are favorable to the conclusion that the disease can be successfully disseminated. To these reports is added a consideration of the meteorological conditions governing the increase of the Chinch Bug, and a history of the literature on microphytous diseases of the Chinch Bug in the United States. We can see no reason for changing the opinions which we have already advanced upon the practical aspect of this subject and in spite of the great length of its present treatment the all-important point of the possible coincident origin of the disease without artificial infection is by no means settled.

---

* Hatch Experiment Station of the Massachusetts Agricultural College, Bulletin No. 19, Report on Insects, May, 1892. Amherst, Mass., 1892.

† University of Kansas. Experiment Station. First Annual Report of the Director for the year 1891. Topeka, April, 1892.

Injurious Insects of 1891 in Colorado.*—Prof. C. P. Gillette, in Bulletin No. 19 of the Colorado Agricultural Experiment Station, has published a careful and well-illustrated series of articles upon a number of injurious insects which have appeared during the past season in the State to which his labors have been transferred. A number of the insects treated are more or less novel, which renders the bulletin more interesting to the economic entomologist than are the generality of such papers. The species treated are the Fruit-tree Leaf-roller (*Cacœcia argyrospila* Walk.), a Tortricid moth which has done serious injury to the buds of Apple, Cherry, Rose, Currant, Raspberry, and Gooseberry; the Box-elder Leaf-roller (*Cacœcia semiferana* Walk.); the Grape-vine Leaf-hopper (*Typhlocyba vitifex* ? Fitch); the Gooseberry Fruit-fly (*Trypeta canadensis* Loew); the Imported Currant Borer (*Sesia tipuliformis* Linn.); the Western Currant and Gooseberry Span-worm (*Thamnonoma 4-linearia* Pack., and *T. flavicaria* Pack.); the Spotted Bean-beetle (*Epilachna corrupta* Muls.); the Squash Root-maggot (*Cyrtoneura stabulans*), and the Pea-weevil (*Bruchus pisi*). The illustrations are twelve in number and are all original. The most interesting article, perhaps, is that upon *Epilachna corrupta*, which we have frequently mentioned in these pages as doing considerable damage to beans in New Mexico, from which locality it has been reported by our old-time friend and correspondent Judge J. F. Wielandy. According to Prof. Gillette it is a most important enemy of the Bean in Colorado. No experiments have been made with remedies against this species, but the gathering of the eggs and the use of the arsenites and kerosene emulsion are recommended.

A Bulletin of the Oregon Station.†—Bulletin 18, of the Oregon Experiment Station, by Mr. F. L. Washburn, has appeared. It is somewhat of an emergency publication and designed particularly to meet the wants of fruit-growers. The subtitles are as follows: Insects injurious to young Fruit Trees, the Codling Moth, Kerosene Emulsion, Wireworms, and Flea-beetles. Many of the species here considered were discussed somewhat more at length in Bulletin No. 5 of the same station, and a detailed list need not be given here.

We quote the following notes concerning the comparative value of the kerosene emulsion and extract of quassia for the Hop Louse:

Prof. C. V. Riley, United States Entomologist, recommends this emulsion for the Hop Louse, 1 part emulsion to 25 parts of water, and it has proved of great benefit in this direction.

In Bulletin No. 10, from this Station, kerosene emulsion, 1 part to 30 parts water, was recommended as a good spray for the hops, and for plum trees in the spring, before the louse had migrated to the hops.

---

* State Agricultural College. Agricultural Experiment Station. Bulletin No. 19. Observations upon Injurious Insects, Season of 1891. Fort Collins, Colo., May, 1892.

† Oregon Agricultural Experiment Station Bulletin No. 18. Entomology. F. L. Washburn, Entomologist. Corvallis, March, 1892. [pp. 16, figs. 14.]

From answers to many inquiries sent to hop-growers of this State we learn that it was tried the past season in many cases, and generally with success, though several reports came in of its failure. Such failures must be ascribed to the fact that it was not, in those cases, properly made or properly used. Under the right conditions it is a perfect success.

We are prompted here to mention the fact that a prominent hop. nrm in Washington State is issuing a circular to the effect that an extract of quassia chips is the only remedy for this pest, and denouncing kerosene emulsion as of no value against the Hop Louse. This is both unjust and untrue, as repeated experiments have proven.

The writer reports success against flea-beetles on radishes from the use of a tobacco wash prepared by boiling 1 pound of waste stems in 2 gallons of water. The success of this treatment is ascribed largely to the fertilizing qualities of the tobacco.

The Mouth-parts of Copris carolina.*—The importance of this little paper by Prof. Smith is derived from the fact that he here names the parts of the compound mandible of this Scarabaeid in which these sclerites are particularly well differentiated. and homologizes these parts with those of the maxillæ. This is. curiously enough, an important bit of work which seems not to have been done before. Comstock. in his "Introduction to Entomology," called attention to the want which Prof. Smith's paper has thus promptly filled. The sclerite which homologizes with the *cardo* of the maxilla he names *sub-basalis;* that which is the homologue of the *stipes* he calls the *basalis*. The homologue of the *galea* he names the *terebra*. while the maxillar *lacinia* is homologized with the mandibular *prostheca* of Kirby and Spence. the latter being the only part which had previously received a name. Two other sclerites which he calls the *molar* and *conjunctivus* he does not attempt to homologize. For the rest, the paper describes briefly the remaining mouth-parts. showing a remarkable development of the epipharynx, indicating that in other Scarabaeids this organ is more or less paired. Prof. Smith is of opinion that further studies of this sclerite will disclose species in which it is completely divided.

This paper again suggests strongly to us the necessity for a uniform nomenclature of the insect exoskeleton. The thoracic nomenclature of MacLeay is a well-grounded philosophical system and should be generally adopted. We need. however. an extension of the principles used in this system to other parts of the body. and particularly to the mouth-parts. Having once satisfied ourselves of the homologic relationship of the sclerites of the maxilla. labium. and mandible, uniformity in the nomenclature of these parts becomes almost a necessity. The objection urged against such a nomenclature will be naturally the repetition of the qualifying term, but the advantage to be gained by a clear and thorough understanding at once conveyed by such a term will

---

*The Mouth Parts of Copris carolina. with notes on the homologies of the mandibles. By John B. Smith. Trans. Amer. Ent. Soc., XIX, pp. 83-87. Plates II and III.

much more than compensate for the disadvantage mentioned. For instance, the homologies once accepted, how much better it would be to call the sclerite named *terebra* by Prof. Smith, at once plainly, the *mandibular galea*, especially since the use of the word terebra alone is confusing and necessitates the use of the same qualifying adjective. With the parts of the labium there is naturally less reason for uniformity of nomenclature from the fact that the halves of this organ are so frequently consolidated. Yet even here the nomenclature should convey the homologic idea. Just as we say "maxillary palpus" and "labial palpus" why should we not say "maxillary galea" and "labial galea" instead of "galea" and "paraglossa"?

Bulletins on Spraying with Insecticides and Fungicides.—Following the lead of Massachusetts, New York, New Jersey, and other experiment stations and the U. S. Department of Agriculture, the Michigan and Pennsylvania stations have fallen into line and issued each a bulletin on spraying against insects and fungous diseases.

The Michigan station publishes, under the title "Insecticides and Fungicides,"* a bulletin of 26 pages by Mr. L. R. Taft, horticulturist of the station, devoted principally, however, to fungicides. The combined use of fungicides and insecticides is reported as satisfactory under the proper conditions.

The Pennsylvania station bulletin † is by Mr. George C. Butz and bears the title "Information on Spraying Fruits."

These bulletins are of the practical order, furnishing directions for the preparation and application of the principal chemicals used against insects and plant diseases, without entering, to any extent, into the details of experiments.

Insects which burrow in the Stems of Wheat.‡—Under this caption our agent, Mr. F. M. Webster, summarizes the history and development of, and remedies for, the Joint Worm, the Wheat Straw-worm, the Wheat-stem Saw-fly, the Grain Bill-bug, the Stalk Borer, the Wheat-stem Maggot, and the Companion Wheat-fly. All the articles are well illustrated, and the bulletin as a whole is well calculated to interest grain growers.

* Insecticides and Fungicides. By L. R. Taft, Michigan Agricultural Experiment Station, Agricultural College. Horticultural Department. Bulletin 83. April, 1892. [pp. 26, figs. 11.]

† Information on Spraying Fruits. By George C. Butz. Pennsylvania State College Agricultural Experiment Station, Bulletin No. 19. April, 1892. [pp. 13, figs. 6.]

‡ Bulletin of the Ohio Agricultural Experiment Station. Second Series. Vol. v, No. 4. April, 1892.

Mr. Lawrence Bruner's Report as Entomologist to the State Board of Agriculture in Nebraska.—Mr. Bruner's reprint of his report from the Annual Report of the State Board of Agriculture for 1891 has been received. He devotes the seventy pages allotted to him to a consideration of the insects which affect Corn. He shows that the corn crop is the most important of the staples of Nebraska and that probably one-seventh of the crop is annually destroyed by insects. He lists something over one hundred species, and describes their habits and the remedies to be used against them in a clear, popular, and condensed manner, illustrating the paper with 88 figures, none of which are original.

Annual Report of the New Jersey Entomologist.—Pages 343 to 426 of the Annual Report of the New Jersey Agricultural Experiment Station, 1891, is occupied by the Report of the Entomologist. In the general review of the season it is noted that much damage was done by the Melon Plant-louse, the Corn Bill-bug, and the Pear Midge. The bulk of the report is taken up with articles which have already appeared in bulletins and which have been duly noticed in these pages.

SOME INTERRELATIONS OF PLANTS AND INSECTS.*

By C. V. Riley, Ph. D.

It is my purpose tonight to present some phases of the curious interrelations between plants and insects. In doing this I shall not have time to deal with the remarkable series of results that have followed the more careful and accurate investigations of the so-called insectivorous or carnivorous plants, and which have shown that these plants are not only possessed of the power of movement depending upon nerve stimuli, that may be likened in almost every respect to the automatic movements of animals, but that they actually possess digestive powers and properties which, chemically and functionally, are the same as those by which animals digest their food. It is my desire rather to call your attention to certain phases of plant fertilization by insects. I need not tell the members of this society that the old idea that flowers are endowed with beauty and fragrance for our particular pleasure has been effectually set aside and that these attributes have come to be looked upon in their true light, as essential to the plant's existence and perpetuation; that, in other words, color, form, odor, secretions, and the general structure of flowers all have reference to insects. Nor need I dilate on the need of cross-fertilization in plants generally or the modification which insect pollenizers have undergone as a consequence

---

* Read before the Biological Society of Washington, April 2, 1892.

of this need. Some of the more interesting facts are particularly well exemplified in our orchids, to the philosophic study of which Darwin's important work "On the Fertilization of Orchids" gave a distinct impulse. But here we have adaptation of the plant only, and with scarcely an exception most flowers, including those of our orchids, may be fertilized by different insects. There are, in fact, few which are dependent on a single species for pollination, and, so far as I know, our yuccas furnish the only instance of this kind. It is to the fertilization of these plants that I would first draw your attention.

The Yuccas (Fig. 57) are a characteristic American group of liliaceous

FIG. 57.—Flower of *Yucca aloifolia* fully opened.

plants, finding their home more particularly in the southern United States and Mexico. There are many species which have been divided even into subgenera by Dr. Engelmann, as Sarcoyucca, Clistoyucca, Chenoyucca, and Hesperoyucca; but for our present purpose they may all be included under the one genus Yucca, as they all possess certain characteristics in common, viz, a thick, submucilaginous root, which is in reality a subterranean stem; lance-shaped, evergreen leaves, narrow or broad, rigid or flaccid, and with the edge either filamentose, smooth, or more or less distinctly serrate. The leaves produce a coarse fiber, valuable for certain kinds of fabrics, while the trunks of the tree Yuccas have been used to make the toughest kind of paper. The fruit of some species, as of *aloifolia* and *baccata*, is fleshy and edible. It is, however, the flowers to which I would draw more especial attention. They are produced in large panicles, and are characterized, as a rule, by the anthers not reaching anywhere near the stigma, so that fertilization unaided can take place only by the merest accident. The Yuccas show great variation in detail, both in leaf, general habitus, flower-stalk, flower and fruit, from the common sessile *Yucca filamentosa* of our gardens to the arboreal forms, like *brevifolia* of the Mojave Desert and *filifera* of Mexico. My remarks will be based chiefly on *Yucca filamentosa*, which is indigenous to the Southeastern States and is cultivated beyond its natural range, under a number of horticultural variety names, in our gardens.

An examination of the flower will show at once the peculiarities which I have alluded to as characteristic of the genus. The stamens or filaments are bent away from the stigma and do not reach more than two-thirds the length of the pistil, the stigmal opening being at the tip of the prolonged style and nowhere within reach of the stamens, while the pollen either remains attached to the open and withered anthers or falls in different sized lumps on the underside of the perianth. It can not be introduced into the stigmatic tube without artificial aid, and the plant depends absolutely on the little white moth belonging to the Tineina and known as *Pronuba yuccasella* Riley (Fig. 58).

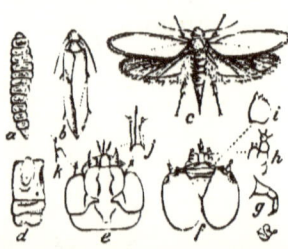

FIG. 58.—PRONUBA YUCCASELLA: *a*, larva; *b*, ♀ moth with closed wing; *c*, do. with wings expanded, natural size; *d*, side view of larval joint; *e*, head of larva, beneath; *f*, do. above; *g*, thoracic leg of same; *h*, maxilla; *i*, mandible; *j*, spinneret and labial palpi; *k*, antenna, enlarged.

STRUCTURAL CHARACTERISTICS OF PRONUBA.

Upon a superficial view, this little moth shows nothing very peculiar. The general coloration is white, the primaries being purely white on the upper surface, so that when at rest in the half-open flowers of

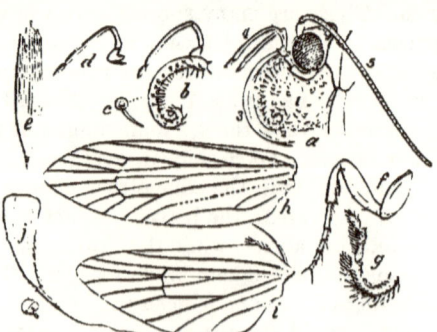

FIG. 59.—PRONUBA YUCCASELLA: Generic characters—*a*, side view of head and neck of female denuded, showing how the collected load of pollen (1) is held by the tentacles (2); *b*, maxillary tentacle and palpus; *c*, an enlarged spine; *d*, palpus separated; *e*, scale from front wing; *f*, front leg; *g*, palpus; *h*, *i*, front and hind wings denuded; *j*, anal joint of female with ovipositor.

the Yucca it is not easily detected. The under surfaces, however, are dusky, and offset in flight the whiteness of the rest of the body, so as to render the species somewhat difficult of detection while flitting from plant to plant. The male shows no very marked peculiarities to distinguish him from the other members of the family, the most noticeable being, perhaps, the prominence of the exposed parts of the genitalia. The female, however, shows some remarkable structural peculiarities (Fig. 59), which admirably adapt her for the functions she has to perform, for she must fertilize the plant, since her larvæ feed upon the seeds.

Now, if I should ask any well-informed entomologist what are the characteristics of the Lepidopterous moth in the imago state, he would unhesitatingly answer: The lack of all prehensile organs, and a coiled tongue capable of sucking liquids. If, again, I should ask what distinguishes the Lepidoptera from, say, the Hymenoptera, in the methods of oviposition, he would answer that the Lepidoptera lay eggs possessing, it is true, an infinite diversity of form, but usually attached externally to some part of the food-plant of the species, while the Hymenoptera, as a rule, secrete theirs, and are furnished with either a puncturing, boring, or sawing instrument for that purpose. The generalization would be entirely justified, though there are many curious exceptions to it, especially in the very group Tineina to which our Yucca Moth belongs. It is, however, necessary to state these general truths in order to convey a just idea of the exceptional nature of the two organs to which I wish to draw your attention. The first is a pair of maxillary tentacles which are prehensile and spinous on their under surface. They are peculiar to the genus Pronuba and exist in no other genus of the many thousands of butterflies and moths.* The other organ is the ovipositor, which, instead of being a simple opening, as typically found in Lepidoptera, is here modified into a complex combination of lance and saw. Ordinarily it is withdrawn and hidden, but when in action is projected far beyond the tip of the abdomen, and is then seen to consist of two principal parts, the basal part being imbricato-granulate, *i. e.*, having a delicate, file-like structure, the terminal part being smooth, but having near the end a dorsal serrate chitinous wing and a still more strongly toothed corneous tip. The internal structure is seen to consist of two stout rods extending along the thin walls to the very tip, and of a ventral canal or passage-way for the delicate oviduct, which is silk-like and elastic and may be extruded for a great length from an outlet near the end of the ovipositor. This oviduct is smooth basally, but armed along its terminal third with retrorse hairs, increasing somewhat in numbers and strength toward the tip, around which they are almost spinous. At first sight these would seem to be out of place and to im

---

* There are over 12,000 described species of Lepidoptera from Europe and America, and those from other parts of the world will double this number. Nearly as many more remain, perhaps, to be described.

pede rather than aid the insertion of such a delicate filament; but, as we shall presently see, the act of oviposition is a most intricate and difficult one and these hairs are doubtless sensitive and tactile, and serve the double purpose of enabling the moth to feel her way in the ovarian cell and of temporarily anchoring in the soft wall thereof while the egg is being passed to its destination. It will be seen that this ovipositor is admirably adapted for cleaving through the young fruit, and then running the egg into the ovarian cavity, as will be presently described. The manner in which this ovipositor is worked by the four rods attached to strong muscles is indicated at Fig. 60. C, the two inner rods forming.

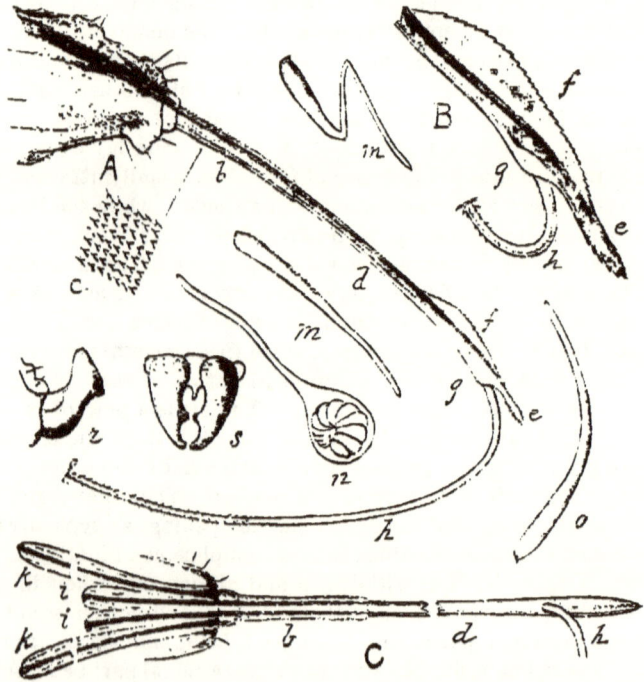

FIG. 60.—A. tip of anal joint and vaginal projection of ♀ *Pronuba yuccasella* from side, showing ovipositor with parts extended; b. basal joint; c. its file-like surface; d. terminal joint with its dorsal serrate wing (f), its dentate tip (e), its ventral membranous outlet (g), and the extended oviduct (h); B. the same parts further enlarged; C. ventral view of tip of abdomen, showing the two pair of rods i, i and k, k, with their muscular attachments, the parts of the ovipositor similarly lettered as in A; m, m. eggs taken from Yucca pistil; n, egg, showing development of embryon; o, mature egg from ovary of ♀; r, s, genital claspers of ♂, lateral and dorsal view—all enlarged, the eggs with the pedicels rather too thick.

as already indicated, the rigid portion of the ovipositor proper and the imbricate basal portion of the covering facilitating the invagination of the basal part when the ovipositor is withdrawn. The two outer rods are attached to strong, muscular tissue in the walls of the vagina, and when the ovipositor is extended to its utmost limit this vaginal portion is partially extruded so as to appear like a basal subjoint. More detailed characterization of these parts is unnecessary in this connection.

THE ACTS OF POLLINATION AND OVIPOSITION.

Having thus drawn attention to the most characteristic structures of Pronuba, we shall better understand the following account of the acts of pollination and oviposition which I quote from an article recently prepared for the Annual Report of the Missouri Botanic Garden:

Though all the acts of the female are nocturnal, it is not at all difficult to follow them with a lantern, for, albeit ordinarily shy, she may be closely approached when about to oviposit. Her activity begins soon after dark, but consists, at first, in assiduously collecting a load of pollen. She may be seen running up to the top of one of the stamens and bending her head down over the anther, stretching the maxillary tentacles, so wonderfully modified for the purpose, to their fullest extent, the tongue uncoiled and reaching to the opposite side of the stamen (Fig. 61). In this manner she is able to obtain a firm hold of the stamen, while the head is kept close to the anther and moved peculiarly back and forth, something as in the motion of a caterpillar when feeding. The maxillary palpi are used in this act very much as the ordinary mandibles are used in other insects, removing or scraping the pollen from the anthers toward the tentacles. After thus gathering the pollen she raises her head and commences to shape it into a little mass or pellet by using her front legs, very much as a cat does when cleansing her mouth, sometimes using only one leg, at another time both, smoothing and pressing the gathered pollen, the tentacles meanwhile stretching and curving. After collecting all the pollen from one anther she proceeds to another and repeats the operation, then to a third and fourth, after which, with her relatively large load—often thrice as large as the head—held firmly against the neck and front trochanters, she usually runs about or flies to another plant; for I have often noticed that oviposition, as a rule, is accomplished in some other flower than that from which the pollen was gathered, and that cross fertilization is thus secured.*

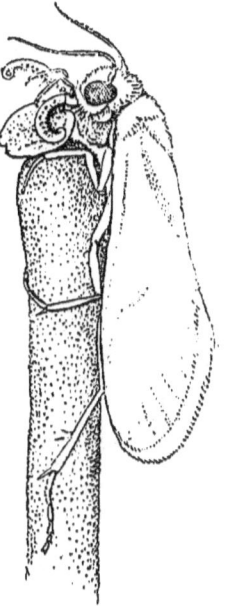

FIG. 61.—Female *Pronuba yuccasella* gathering pollen, — × 5.

Once fully equipped with this important commodity, she may be seen either crawling over or resting within the flower, generally with the head toward the base. From time to time she makes a sudden dart and deftly runs around the stamens, and anon takes a position with the body between and the legs straddling two of them, her head being usually turned toward the stigma. As the terminal portion of the stamens is always more or less recurved, she generally has to retreat between two of them until the tip of her abdomen can reach the pistil. As soon as a favorable point is reached, generally just below the middle, she rests motionless for a short time, when the abdomen is slightly raised and the lance-like ovipositor is thrust into the soft tissue, held the best part of a minute, while the egg is conducted to its destination, and then withdrawn by a series of up-and-down motions.

---

* The actions here described are sometimes quite deliberate, but often they are too rapid to be analyzed, and the running to the top of the stamen and the motion of head in gathering the pollen are in time and manner much the same as in thrusting the pollen into the stigma.

In non-technical language, the pistil or the young fruit, below the stigmatic tube, shows externally at this time six quite distinct longitudinal divisions, each having a median ridge, there being six corresponding depressions or concavities in which the six stamens fit, especially at the base. Technically the pistil is a three-celled

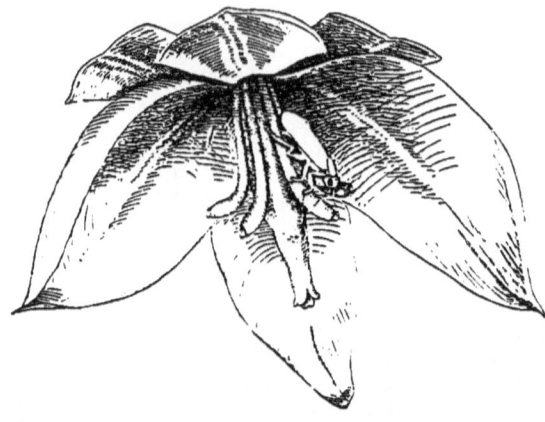

FIG. 62.—Flower of *Yucca filamentosa* with near petals removed, showing Pronuba in act of ovipositing.

ovary, the style bifid at the tip and united so as to form the stigmatic tube. A transverse section anywhere about the middle will show that each of the six longitudinal sections contains a row of ovules within an ovarian cell. More strictly, the ovules are in pairs, as there are but three primary sections or carpels, divided by three

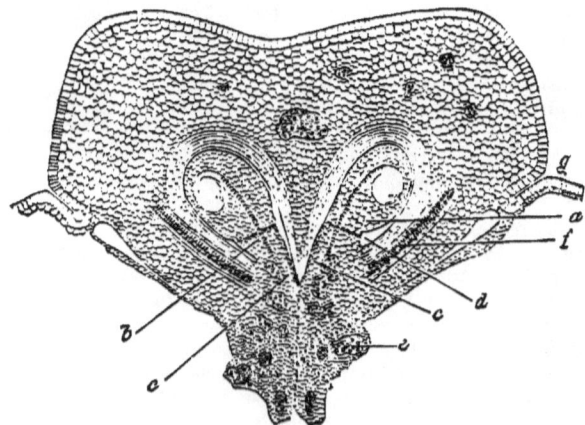

FIG. 63.—Transverse section of one of the carpels of Yucca pistil: *a*. ovule; *b*. funiculus; *c*. placenta; *d*. ovarian cell; *e*. fibro-vascular bundles; *f*. fibro-vascular tissue; *g*. primary dissepiment—× 9.

primary divisions or dissepiments. Fig. 63 shows a transverse section of one of these primary divisions or carpels, which well indicates the position of the ovule (*a*), the funiculus (*b*), the placenta (*c*), and the ovarian cell (*d*). As the fruit enlarges, the three secondary dissepiments narrow and coalesce, while the other three widen, so that the pod becomes practically three-lobed, and the seeds are more distinctly in pairs, the inner sides straight and the external quite convex. In oviposition the young fruit is pierced just within the ridge in the depression occupied by the stamens, and almost always on the side of one of the primary or deeper divisions where the walls are thinnest, so that the ovipositor enters the ovarian cell at the external or rounded side of an ovule and does not ordinarily touch the ovule itself. Rarely, however, the ovipositor penetrates the ridge and passes between two of the ovules, or sometimes even penetrates one, this last case being, however, quite exceptional.

The egg is an extremely delicate, thread-like structure, averaging 1.5 mm. in length and less than 0.1 mm. (Fig. 60, *m*, *n*, *o*) in diameter, tapering at the base and enlarging slightly toward the capitate end, which has also a slightly indurated point. It is impossible to follow it with the unaided eye, or in fact with an ordinary

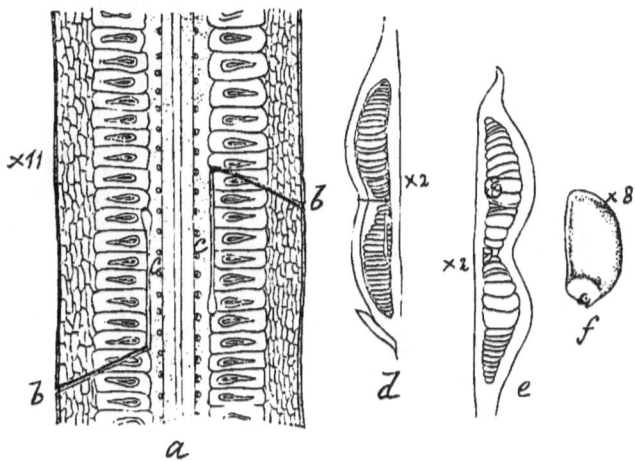

FIG. 64.—*a*, longitudinal section of pistil of *Yucca filamentosa*, showing (*b*, *b*) punctures of Pronuba, and (*c*, *c*) the normal position of her eggs in the ovarian cell; *d*, section of a punctured carpel 7 days after oviposition, showing the egg yet unhatched and the manner in which the ovules in the neighborhood of puncture have been arrested in development so as to cause the constriction; *e*, section of an older carpel, showing the larva above the original puncture; *f*, a seed 13 days from oviposition, showing young larva at funicular base—enlargements indicated.

lens, even if the pistil be at once plucked and dissected; but by means of careful microscopic sections we may trace its course. From the position assumed by the moth, the ovipositor punctures the pistil somewhat obliquely, but as the egg is much longer than the diameter of the ovarian cell, the delicate oviduct of the moth bends and then runs vertically along the inner part of the cell next the placenta, and leaves the egg extending in this longitudinal direction along some seven or eight ovules, as shown in the illustrations (Fig. 64 *c*, *c*). The apical end of the egg soon enlarges (Fig. 60, *n*), and the embryo may be seen developing in it very much as in the case of the similarly elongate egg of gall-flies (Cynipidæ), though the pedicel does not shorten, as observed in these last. Segmentation is noticeable on the second day, and the Yucca ovule at once begins to swell and enlarge, the irritation (doubtless mechanical) influencing the plant tissue much as in the case of the punctures of the gall-flies just mentioned. Sometimes two or more adjacent ovules are thus affected.

It may be well right here to look a little more closely into the minuter characteristics of the Yucca flower at this stage of its development, that we may understand more fully the action and influence of the moth. In my first article, published some twenty years ago, announcing the discovery of Pronuba and its action on Yucca pollination, I was strongly inclined to the idea that the act of pollination had some compensating inducement to the moth, aside from the impelling instinct of perpetuation of the species. At that time it was supposed that the stigmatic liquor was nectarian, and the conclusion was justifiable that the moth,

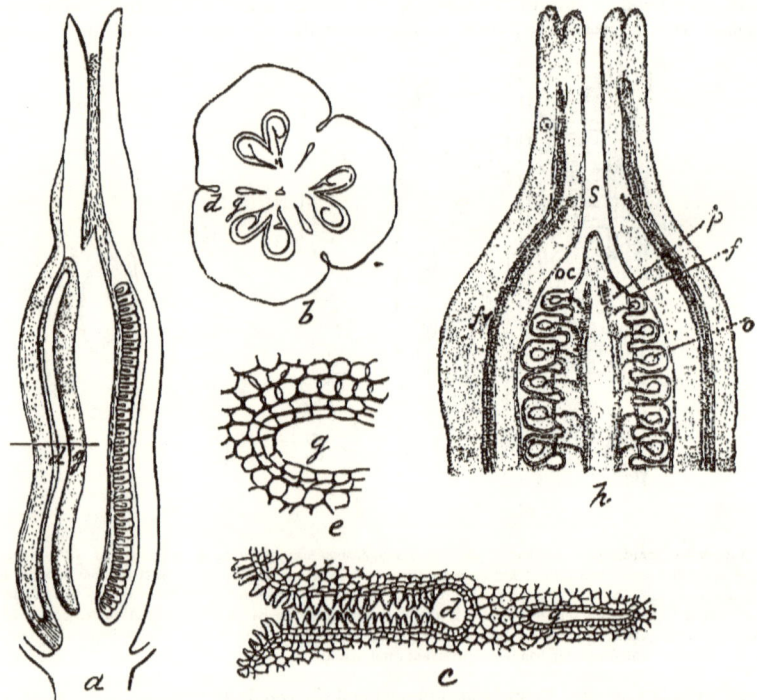

FIG. 65.—Nectar apparatus of Yucca: *a*, longitudinal section of pistil, with duct (*d*) and gland (*g*); *b*, cross section about middle, showing same parts; *c*, still more enlarged cross section of nectar apparatus; *e*, structure of septal gland—after Trelease; *h*, longitudinal section of top of pistil, showing stigmatic tube (*s*) ovarian cell (*o c*), ovule (*o*), funiculus (*f*), placenta (*p*), and fibro-vascular tissue (*f r*).

attracted to it for feeding purposes, would incidentally induce pollination. On this view of the matter it did not require a great stretch of the imagination to conceive that the pollen might also incidentally accumulate in the spines, and that the vigorous action of the head that had been noticed might even be considered as an effort to get rid of the incumbrance while feeding. In those days I was more imbued with the common notion that lower creatures are impelled for the most part unconsciously to their acts. Twenty years of study and experience have only served to prove the acts of Pronuba the more unselfish and without food inducement. A longitudinal section of the upper portion of the pistil will show the style with the stigmatic tube, which at this time communicates with the ovarian cells. Now, Trelease has shown that the stigmatic liquor is not nectarian, but that the slight amount of nectar associated with the flower is secreted in pockets formed by the partitions that separate the three cells of the pistil, and which open externally near the style by a contracted pore from which the nectar is poured through a capillary tube to the base of the pistil. The accompanying illustration (Fig. 65) renders this more intelligible, *a* being a longitudinal section through the center of a pistil, showing the septal gland (*g*), the duct (*d*), and the outlet at the base; *b* a cross section of the pistil about the middle, also showing the duct (*d*), and gland (*g*); *c*, a more enlarged cross section of the nectar apparatus; *e* showing more fully the structure of the septal gland, while *h* is a longitudinal section of the top of the pistil, through the lobes, showing how the stigmatic tube (*s*) connects with the ovarian cell (*o c*), *o* being the ovary, *f* the funiculus, *p* the placenta, and *f v* fibro-vascular tissue.

These interesting facts, which I have fully verified, show that nectar-feeding insects seek it not about the stigma, but at the base of the stamens or of the petals, whether within or without. In short, the nectar in these Yucca flowers has no value in pollination, and Pronuba, in collecting the pollen and transferring it to the stigma, finds no food compensation, a conclusion which is confirmed by a study of the minute structure and internal anatomy of the moth, which indicate that the tongue proper, though strongly developed, has to a great extent, if not entirely, lost its function as a sucking organ, and that the alimentary canal is practically functionless, being aborted before reaching the anus. This defunctionization, if I may use the term, of important structures has not proceeded so far in *Pronuba yuccasella* as in *P. maculata*, which pollinizes *Yucca whipplei*. Those not familiar with the structure of Lepidoptera will hardly appreciate the modifications to which I shall allude, however, without the preliminary statement that the tongue in Lepidoptera consists of two distinct parts (maxillæ) which are more or less concave on their inner side and united at the borders of the concave portion by certain locking arrangements to form between them the sucking tube. Now, while in most cases the two parts may be relaxed and separated by force, in nature they are never so separated, while the tip of the tongue is more or less acuminate and the two parts here very firmly united.

In *Pronuba yuccasella* I had often noticed that the two parts became separated, and in fact were almost always separated toward the tip, thus suggesting the loss of function as a sucking organ, but otherwise the tongue is strongly developed, and, with the exception of the weakness of the locking arrangement, not particularly abnormal. In *Pronuba maculata*, however (Fig. 66), the two parts of the tongue are but very feebly united, and often more or less disconnected, and are actually thickly covered with minute hairs and more sparsely with longer spinous hairs, intermixed; they are also swollen and enlarged toward the base. The import of this fact can be best conveyed to you by the statement that in all other Lepidoptera that I know of the tongue is a smooth organ and in no way armed, except near the tip. In short, the tongue in *Pronuba maculata* has become an accessory tentacle, serving

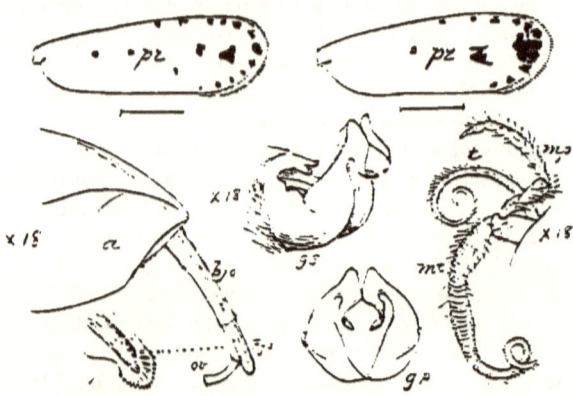

FIG. 66.—PRONUBA MACULATA: *a* tip of female abdomen; *b f o.* basal joint of ovipositor; *t f o.* terminal joint of ovipositor; *o v.* oviduct; *m p. max.* palpus; *m t.* maxillary tentacle; *t.* tongue; *g s.* claspers of male from side; *g r.* claspers of male from behind—enlargement indicated; *p r.* front wings, showing arrangement of spots in two of the more common forms, hair lines showing natural size.

and helping in pollination, but probably incapable of use for feeding purposes. These structural peculiarities justify the conclusion which observation confirms, that Pronuba does not feed in the imago state. In other words, she has no incentive to go to the stigma with her load of pollen, other than that of pollinizing, and the slight amount of nectar which the plant secretes is well calculated to lead other insects which seek it away from the stigma and thus not to interfere with Pronuba's mission.

DEVELOPMENT AND TRANSFORMATIONS OF PRONUBA.

On this subject I need only remark that the action of oviposition causes a disorganization of the plant tissues in the immediate neighborhood of the apical portion of the egg and the swelling of the adjacent ovules; that the embryo develops in the capitate end of the egg, and while the larva is white at first, or of the exact color of the young ovule, it becomes slightly greenish or roseate when full grown, which is in about a month, or coincident with the ripening of the seed. It perforates the capsule and drops to the ground, having six thoracic legs, which doubtless aid it at this period of its life. It remains through the fall, winter, and early spring months in a tough cocoon, transforms to the chrysalis

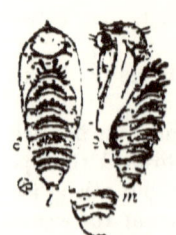

FIG. 67.—PRONUBA YUCCASELLA: *l*, male; *m*, female chrysalis.

state about a week before the Yuccas bloom again, and finally issues as a moth to continue the annual cycle of its career. The chrysalis (Fig. 67) has a capitate spine and a series of dorsal spines, some of which are spatulate and admirably fitted for helping it to work through the ground.

The effect of the puncture of the female moth on the fruit is at once noticeable by a darker green discoloration externally. In time this becomes a depression, causing a constriction of the pod, and the irregularities of the pod (Fig. 68, *b*, *c*), which have been supposed to be characteristic of the genus Yucca, are really due to these punctures, which ordinarily occur just below the middle. The absolute need of

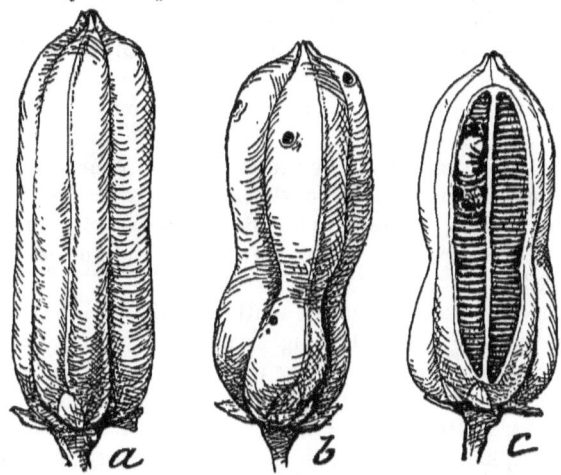

FIG. 68.—Mature pods of *Yucca angustifolia:* *a*, artificially pollinized and protected from Pronuba; *b*, normal pod, showing constrictions resulting from Pronuba puncture and exit holes of larva; *c*, one of the lobes cut open, showing larva within.

Pronuba in the pollination of our dehiscent Yuccas I have proved over and over again in many ways. The plant never produces seed where Pronuba does not exist; it never produces seed when she is excluded artificially, and experiments which I have made with artificial or brush pollination all show that it is much more difficult to insure complete fructification than would at first appear, and that the act of pollination is rarely performed with a brush or by using the flower's own filaments as successfully as it is done by Pronuba. It is *Pronuba yuccasella* which pollinizes all our Yuccas east of the Rocky Mountains, so far as known, and the species is remarkably uniform in character, its appearance being coetaneous with the flowering of *Yucca filamentosa*. On the western plains its appearance has become adapted to the flowering of *Yucca angustifolia*, but in the east, where these two species of Yucca are frequently grown side by side, *Y. angustifolia* flowers two or three weeks earlier than *Y. filamentosa*, and generally too early to receive the visits of Pronuba, so that it produces seed only on very rare occasions.

Yucca brevifolia is pollinized by *Pronuba synthetica* Riley, the most remarkable species of the genus, having very stout maxillary tentacles, a very stout ovipositor, shorter than that of *yuccasella*, but characterized chiefly by having fuliginous and unscaled wings, and a polished, naked, and flattened body—structures all well adapted for crawling between and about the compact and crowded flowers, with their thick and leathery petals, but very abnormal in the Lepidoptera. In fact, this species strongly recalls in its general aspect some of the saw-flies belonging to the genus Dolerus, the resemblance being heightened by the rather conspicuous, cenchri-like spots, and by the conspicuous division between the thorax and abdomen. It also strikingly recalls some of the Neuroptera, as *Sialis infumata*.

Now, these resemblances to insects of different Orders, and to families which are generally considered to be of low type within their Order, can not possibly be mimetic, as there can be no conceivable cause, purpose, or advantage in the mimicry. It is also impossible to account for these resemblances upon any present genetic connection. Yet we are hardly justified in disposing of them as merely accidental and without meaning. They suggest a possible synthesism in the past, when types were less specialized and present Orders had not become so well differentiated.

Yucca whipplei, which occurs in southern California, has flowers distinguished by their relatively long and stout stamens, the pollen of which is copious and glutinous, not to say mucilaginous, and a short, contracted style, with the stigma, however, expanded and covered with sticky threads. It is pollinized by *Pronuba maculata* Riley, which, as already shown, has a tongue modified into an accessory pollen-gathering organ. If any species of Yucca would seem not to need a special insect for pollination, *Yucca whipplei* is that species; for the long stamens, the sticky and abundant pollen, and the peltate, hairy stigma would all seem to facilitate ordinary pollination. Nevertheless, the very restricted style would seem to be purposely developed to counteract these other facilities, and we find a Pronuba associated with it, with a remarkably modified tongue, and with the maxillary tentacles very long and attenuated at the tip—structures which doubtless enable the moth to perform the act of pollination. I have never been able to observe the act, nor has anyone yet recorded either the acts of pollination or oviposition. There will be nothing peculiar about the latter, but I shall be very glad to get actual experience in reference to the former, as I am satisfied that the observed facts will show, still more fully than in the case of *Pronuba yuccasella*, that the special modifications of both flowers and insects have gone on until the mutual interdependence has become absolute.*

---

* Since this was written Mr. D. W. Coquillet has, at my solicitation, carefully watched the acts of pollination and oviposition in this species, and his accounts as communicated show that the actions of *Pronuba maculata* are substantially similar to those of *P. yuccasella*.

There is much yet to learn of the pollination of other species of Yucca, and I am particularly anxious to obtain the insects which will doubtless be found associated with them. The Regal Tree Yucca, *Yucca filifera*, of northeastern Mexico, reaching a height of 50 feet, with its pendulous panicles 5 or 6 feet long, has a very elongate pistil and comparatively short stamens. The few pods which I have been able to examine indicate the presence of a Pronuba and doubtless of a distinct species which will prove very interesting. *Yucca baccata*, *Y. treculiana*, and all the species which are sufficiently distinctive in character and in range may be expected to have special Pronubas associated with them.

THE BOGUS YUCCA MOTH.

An interesting fact connected with Pronuba and Yucca pollination is that there is always associated with *Pronuba yuccasella* another moth, which bears such a remarkable superficial resemblance to it, though possessing no power of pollination, that it has caused much confusion in the past on the part of careless observers and led to a good deal of misstatement and error. This is what I have called the Bogus Yucca Moth, *Prodoxus decipiens* (Fig. 69). In size it is somewhat smaller, on the average, than Pronuba, and, while found associated with it, appears rather earlier.

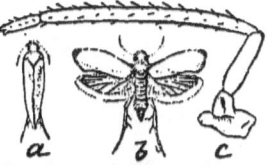

FIG. 69.—PRODOXUS DECIPIENS: *a*, imago, wings closed; *b*, female imago, wings expanded—natural size; *c*, enlarged maxillary palpus with its basal tubercle.

The female has no maxillary tentacle, but otherwise the genus has all the characteristics which would place it in the same family as Pronuba. The ovipositor is a stronger instrument (Fig. 70), but structurally homologous. The eggs are thrust into the stem while yet tender; they are elongate in form, but short and rounded at both ends, resembling the undeveloped ova in the ovaries of Pronuba. The larva is absolutely apodous (Fig. 71*a*), forms its cocoons within the stem, and transforms the ensuing year to a chrysalis, which has a much stronger capitate spine, but the barest trace of dorsal spines on the abdominal joints. It issues partly from the stem in giving out the moth. As I have elsewhere remarked:

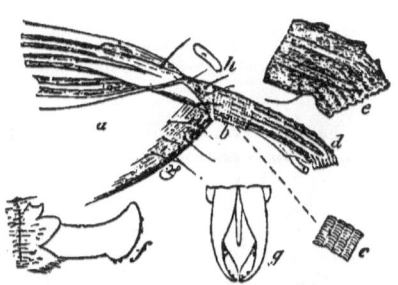

FIG. 70.—GENITAL CHARACTERS OF PRODOXUS DECIPIENS: *a*, tip of ♀ abdomen rendered somewhat transparent; *b*, basal joint of ovipositor; *c*, its sculpture; *d*, terminal joint of same, its tip more enlarged; *f*, genitalia of ♂ from side; *g*, do. from above; *h*, egg.

Who, studying these two species in all their characters and bearing, can fail to conclude that, notwithstanding the essential differences which distinguish them not only specifically but generically, they are derived from one and the same ancestral form? Pronuba, depending for its existence upon the pollination of the flower, is profoundly modified in the female sex in adaptation to the peculiar function of pollination. Prodoxus, dwelling in the flesh of the fruit or in the flower stem, and only indirectly depending upon the fructification of the plant, is not so modified, but has the ordinary characters of the family in both sexes. In the former the larva quits the capsules and burrows in the ground; it has legs to aid in its work, while the chrysalis is likewise beautifully modified to adapt it to prying through the ground

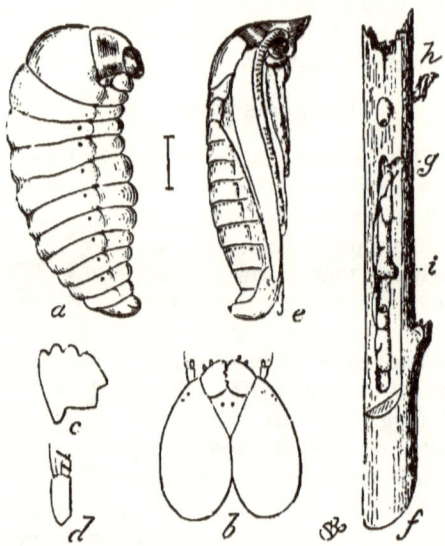

Fig. 71.—PRODOXUS DECIPIENS: *a*, larva; *b*, head from above; *c*, *d*, left jaw and antenna; *e*, pupa; *f*, infested stem cut open to show the burrows, castings, cocoons, and pupa shell (*h*); all enlarged but *f*, the hair line between *a* and *e* showing natural length.

and mounting to the surface. The latter, on the contrary, never quitting the stem, has no legs in the larva state, and in the chrysalis state is more particularly adapted, by the prominence of the capital projection, to piercing the slight covering of the stem left ungnawed by the larva. The former is very regular in its appearance as a moth at the time of the flowering of the Yuccas in their native range. The latter appears earlier, as the food of its larva is earlier ready, and the female could not oviposit in the riper stem.

OTHER SPECIES OF PRODOXUS.

Some ten species of this genus Prodoxus have been described, all of them having the very same structural characteristics and in the adolescent states being scarcely distinguishable. *Prodoxus decipiens* is associated with *Pronuba yuccasella* east of the Rocky Mountains, and *Prodoxus sordidus* is similarly associated with *Pronuba synthetica*, breeding in the flower-stems of *Yucca brevifolia*. All the other species are associated with *Pronuba maculata*, breeding either in the base of the capsules or in the flower-stem or the main stem of *Yucca whipplei*. I have found Prodoxus larvæ in the stems of all other Yuccas which I have been able to examine, and doubtless a number of other species are yet to be discovered and characterized. The species so far known are interesting in that they illustrate in a remarkable manner what I have called fortuitous variation, or superficial colorational characters; also a great tendency to graduate into each other by variations among themselves, not only in the structure of the ovipositor and the male genitalia, but in the wing markings. The time to which these remarks are limited will prevent going into descriptive details, and I content myself with illustrating, in this connection, a few of the more distinctly marked species (Figs. 72, 73, 74, and 75).

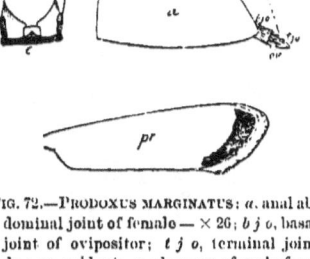

FIG. 72.—PRODOXUS MARGINATUS: *a*, anal abdominal joint of female — × 26; *b j o*, basal joint of ovipositor; *t j o*, terminal joint do.; *ov*, oviduct; *c*, claspers of male from above — × 18; *pr*, front wing—hair line showing natural size.

The genus interests us most, however, in indicating how Pronuba, with all her abnormal peculiarities, has been evolved; for though we have striking differences in habit and mode of development of larva, pupa, and imago, between Pronuba and Prodoxus, yet the affinities are equally striking, and the two genera exemplify, in an exceptional degree, the power of natural selection to intensify habits and structures in opposing directions according to the requirements of the species. Prodoxus is practically dependent upon Pronuba, for if the latter did not fructify the plant the former would in time have no flower-stems to breed in, and while Prodoxus has gone on generation after generation, with comparatively little change, Pronuba has become profoundly specialized to fit it for a more specific purpose.

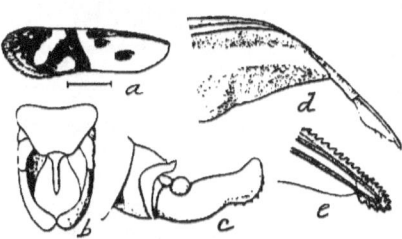

FIG. 73.—PRODOXUS Y-INVERSUS: *a*, left front wing, hair-line underneath showing natural size; *b*, genitalia of male, dorsal view — × 14; *c*, do., lateral view — × 18; *d*, anal joint of female with ovipositor exserted, lateral view — × 20; *e*, tip of ovipositor still further enlarged.

CAPRIFICATION OF THE FIG.

It was my purpose here to explain to you some interesting facts as to the caprification of the fig, and the remarkable structural peculiarities and influence of the caprifig insects. It is, however, a somewhat complicated subject, and I could not, within the time allotted to me, do justice both to it and the matter of Yucca pollination. As an indication, however, of how profoundly modified in this particular case the plant and the insect have become in their mutual adaptation. I may state that the perfect Smyrna fig, the most esteemed of the edible varieties, can be produced only by the intervention of the *Blastophaga psenes*, and that Dr. D. D. Cunningham has recently shown, in the Annals of the Royal Botanical Gardens of Calcutta (Vol. I. Appendix I. 1889 , by repeated examinations of the fruit of *Ficus roxburghii*, that pollination, in the ordinary meaning of the term, is, in that particular case, out of the question, and that the development of the seed in this species is exclusively due to the stimulation of the tissues caused by the puncturing of the Blastophagas; in other words, that these insects actually represent the male element in the fertilization. This certainly is the most extraordinary phenomenon in the history of fertilization, and if confirmed—and Dr. Cunningham has been most careful and circumspect in his work—it will give a more striking instance than any we have hitherto obtained of the mutual interdependence which plants and insects may attain and the surprising manner in which they may modify each other.

FIG. 74.—PRODOXUS COLORADENSIS: *a*, left front wing, hair-line underneath showing natural size; *b*, male genitalia, dorsal view — × 15; *c*, do., lateral view — × 15.

FIG. 75.—PRODOXUS RETICULATUS: Female with wings expanded—hair-line showing natural size.

GENERALIZATIONS.

The peculiarities which I have endeavored to present to you are full of suggestion, particularly for those who are in the habit of looking beyond the mere facts of observation in endeavors to find some rational explanation of them; who, in other words, see in everything they observe significances and harmonies not generally understood. The facts indicate clearly, it seems to me, how the peculiar structures of the female Pronuba have been evolved by gradual adaptation to the particular functions which we now find her performing. With the growing adaptation to Pronuba's help, the Yucca flower has lost, to a great extent, the activity of its septal glands; yet coincident with this loss we find an increase in the secreting power of the stigma. This increase of the stigmatic fluid doubtless had much to do originally with attracting the moth thereto, while the pollenizing instinct doubtless became more and more fixed in proportion as the insect lost the power or desire of feeding.

With the mind's eye I can look back into the past and picture the gradual steps by which the Prodoxids to which I have alluded have differentiated along lines which have resulted in their present characteristics. On the one side I see variations which have become sufficiently fixed to be considered specific; yet which can have no especial bearing on the life necessities of the species, but are a consequence rather of that universal tendency to variation with which every student of nature becomes profoundly impressed. Thus the wing markings vary from a darker general coloring, as in *Prodoxus cenescens*, to a more uniform intermixture of the black scales among the white, as in *cinereus*, or a sparser intermixture thereof, as in *pulverulentus*. The disposition of the black scales is in spots or bands, whether transverse or longitudinal, as in *marginatus*, *reticulatus*, *y-inversus*, etc. These are fortuitous variations, for I can not believe that the disposition of these marks, where, as in these cases, they take every form that is conceivable, can be of any benefit to the species, any more than the mere variation in the number of lobes in the leaves of different oaks growing under like conditions can be of any particular benefit to the species, however useful to us in classification.

ON FORTUITOUS VARIATIONS.

In my address before the Section of Biology of the American Association for the Advancement of Science, at Cleveland, in 1888, I have discussed the various forms and causes of variation, and especially the limitations of natural selection, stating expressly that this last "deals only with variations useful to the organism in its struggle for existence and can exert no power in fixing the endless number of what, from present knowledge, we are obliged to consider fortuitous characters," and I have long recognized, from my studies of insect life, the existence of these fortuitous variations. The subject has since been very well elaborated by Prof. Ward in his communication to the Society (December 15, 1888) on "Fortuitous Variation as Illustrated by the Genus Eupatorium," and in his Annual Address (January 24, 1891) on "Neo-Darwinism and Neo-Lamarckism," and the Prodoxidæ furnish an excellent illustration of this fortuitous variation. Yet at the same time that we note this chance variation, as exemplified in a number of the species of Prodoxus, which are mere ravagers or despoilers and have not been brought into any special or mutual relations with the plant, we have, on the other hand, in *Pronuba yuccasella*, correlated with the other striking structural modifications which have brought it into such special relations with the plant, an elimination of all maculation or markings upon the primaries, and a purely white coloring so fixed that it shows absolutely no variation over half the continent. The structural variation has been necessary, a consequence of effort, environment, and natural selection. The color variation, on the contrary, has not been absolutely necessary, yet has nevertheless gone on in lines which, tending to give greater protective resemblance to the flower, have in the long run proved to be perhaps the most advantageous. I thus recognize three distinct lines of variation as exemplified in these Prodoxidæ, and what is true of them is, I believe, true of all alliances of organisms. The first and most important is structural and generic; it is absolutely essential and is preserved in its perfection by the elimination, through natural selection, of all forms departing from it. The second is merely coincident, not essential, but nevertheless along lines that are of secondary advantage. The third is purely fortuitous, affects superficial features in the main, is unessential (a consequence of the inherent tendency of all things to vary), and takes place along all lines and in all directions where there is no counteracting resistance.

TRANSMISSION OF CHARACTERS THROUGH HEREDITY.

Now, when it comes to the bearing which the history of these little moths has upon some of the larger questions that are now concerning naturalists (for instance, the transmission of acquired characters, or the origin, development, and nature of the intelligence displayed by the lower animals), broad fields of interesting opinion and conclusion open up before us—fields that can not possibly be explored without trenching too much upon your time. I will close, therefore, with a few summary expressions of individual opinion, without attempting to elaborate the reasons in detail, and with the object of eliciting further discussion, which is one of the objects of this paper. My first conviction is that insect life and development give no countenance to the Weissmann school, which denies the transmission of functionally acquired characters, but that, on the contrary, they furnish the strongest refutation of the views urged by Weissmann and his followers. The little moths of which I have been speaking, and indeed the great majority of insects, all, in fact, except the truly social species, perform their humble parts in the economy of nature without teaching or example, for they are, for the most part, born orphans, and without relatives having experience to communicate. The progeny of each year begins its independent cycle anew. Yet every individual performs more or less perfectly its allotted part, as did its ancestors for generation after generation. The correct view of the matter, and one which completely refutes the old teleological idea of the fixity of instinct, is that a certain number of individuals are, in point of fact, constantly departing from the lines of action and variation most useful to the species, and that these are the individuals which fail to perpetuate their kind and become eliminated through the general law of natural selection.

Whether these actions be purely unconscious and automatic or more or less intelligent and conscious does not alter the fact that they are necessarily inherited. The habits and qualities that have been acquired by the individuals of each generation could have become fixed in no other way than through heredity. Many of these acts, which older naturalists explained by that evasive word "instinctive," may be the mere unconscious outcome of organization, comparable to vegetative growth; but insects exhibit all degrees of intelligence in their habits and actions, and they perform acts which, however voluntary, and, as I believe, conscious, in many cases, as in that of our Yucca moth, could not be performed were the tendency not inherited. Every larva which spins or constructs a hibernaculum or a cocoon, in which to undergo its transformations, exemplifies the potent power of heredity in transmitting acquired peculiarities. A hundred species of parasitic larvæ, e. g., of the family Braconidæ, which in themselves are almost or quite indistinguishable from one another structurally, will nevertheless construct a hundred distinctive cocoons—differing in form, in texture, in color, and in marking—each characteristic of its own species and in many instances showing remarkable architectural peculiarities. These are purely mechanical structures, and can have little or nothing to do with the mere organization or form or structure of the larva, but they illustrate in the most convincing manner the fact that the tendency to construct and the power to construct the cocoon after some definite plan must be fixed by heredity, since there is no other way of accounting for it. This fact alone, which no one seems to have thought of in the discussion, should be sufficient to confound the advocates of the non-transmissibility of acquired characteristics.

Thus to my view modification has gone on in the past, as it is going on at the present time, primarily through heredity, in the insect world. I recognize the physical influence of environment; I recognize the effect of the interrelation of organisms; I recognize, even to a degree that few others do, the psychic influence, especially in higher organisms—the power of mind, will, effort, or the action of the individual as contradistinguished from the action of the environment; I recognize the influence of natural selection properly limited; but above all, as making effective and as fixing and accumulating the various modifications due to these or whatever other influences, I recognize the power of heredity, without which only the first of the influences mentioned can be permanently operative.

Let us stop for a moment to ponder what the intricate adjustments between plants and animals, and especially between plants and insects, mean when they have become so profoundly modified by each other that their present existence actually depends the one on the other. As paleontology shows, and as Prof. Ward has more particularly so well explained, there was for ages no vegetation but the flowerless plants. The first were the low cellular cryptogams, consisting chiefly of marine algæ, and these, the lowest and first organisms upon the planet, have endured through all geologic time and obtain to-day. Next, beginning in the upper Silurian, and reaching their maximum in the Carboniferous, came the vascular cryptogams, of which the ferns constituted the bulk. Arborescent and gigantic, as compared with present forms, they mingled with the now extinct Lycopodineæ to form the bulk of the forests of the coal period. Then came the Phænogams, or flowering plants, and in this great division the Cycadaceæ and Coniferæ (pines, firs, etc.) were the chief forms during Mesozoic times. So far the seed has been exposed. Now come the Angiosperms, in which the seed is protected in the ovary or pericarp, and the Monocotyledons (palms, sedges, etc.) precede the Dicotyledons, while of these last the Apetalæ, Polypetalæ, and Gamopetalæ succeed each other in the order of their naming.

In brief, to use his own words, the development has been from the simple to the complex; from the flowerless to the flowering; from the endogenous to the exogenous; from the apetalous to the gamopetalous; and this succession corresponds to the best systems of classification of existing forms.

Both Cryptogams and Phænogams began existence during the Silurian, and there has been a race for supremacy ever since, with our present flora as the result. It is also a fact of the greatest significance that the same paleontological evidence which gives us this record also tells us that there has been a corresponding development of insect life, from the lower Neuroptera and Orthoptera, which prevailed in the days when Anemophilous plants reigned, to the higher Hymenoptera and Lepidoptera which appeared only as the higher flowering plants developed in the Jurassic and Cretaceous.

I do not hesitate in this connection to refer to another of Prof. Ward's conclusions set forth in one of his interesting articles, namely, that most of the higher flowering plants would speedily perish were insect aid withdrawn, and that but for such aid in the past we should now be without most of our gorgeous flora, and that insects have actually paved the way for man's existence by the part they have played in the development of fruit and nut bearing plants.

A NEW ICERYA PARASITE.

By L. O. Howard.

In the last number of INSECT LIFE we announced the finding of *Icerya rosæ* Riley & Howard (previously found only at Key West, Fla.), upon the island of Jamaica, by Mr. T. D. A. Cockerell. Since the publication of this note Mr. Cockerell has reared a parasite from this species, which, in case it appears to be abundant, may well be expected to feed upon allied species of this destructive genus. He writes us under date of March 6, 1892:

> Some weeks ago I put a few of the Icerya (females and larvæ) into a glass-topped box in the Museum for exhibition, without any of the plant or anything else. . The other day, on looking at them, I saw a dead winged insect at the bottom of the box, and thought it must be a male Icerya, but on examination it proved to be a Chalcid parasite.

The specimen was sent to the Entomologist by Mr. Cockerell for name, and its apparent economic importance seems to justify this isolated description.

The insect belongs to the subfamily Encyrtinae and the genus Cerchysius. This genus was erected by Westwood in 1832 (London and Edinburg Philosophical Magazine and Journal of Science, Vol. I, July to December, 1832, p. 127), with very brief characters, for *Encyrtus urocerus* Dalman. The genus, however, is rejected by Mayr, who retains *urocerus* in the genus *Encyrtus*. Thomson makes use of Cerchysius, with a somewhat indefinite diagnosis. In certain material collected on the island of St. Vincent by Mr. Herbert H. Smith, and sent to Prof. Riley, I have found three species which possess in part the characters of Dalman's *E. urocerus*, and I have deemed it best to use the generic name Cerchysius, especially as the terebral characters alone separate the forms from all other members of the true genus Encyrtus. The characters which may be deemed of generic value, and in which the St. Vincent species as well as that from Jamaica agree, are as follows:

Genus CERCHYSIUS Westwood.

Female.—Head subsemiglobose; eyes rather widely separated; ocelli forming a right angled triangle; antennae inserted below middle of face; scape somewhat widened below and reaching nearly or quite to vertex; flagellum long, slender, and cylindrical; club very slightly enlarged. Mesoscutum and scutellum somewhat flattened, either plane or together somewhat tectiform, the scuto-scutellar furrow forming the ridge in the tectiform species; scapulae meeting at apex. Abdomen triangular or subtriangular; terebra exserted for at least half the length of the abdomen proper. Legs rather longer than normal, resembling in this respect those of Leptomastix; middle tibial spur nearly or quite as long as first tarsal joint. Wings with short marginal and rather short postmarginal and stigmal veins, the latter subequal in length; a narrow, oblique, hairless streak extending from costal margin at stigmal vein to near base of wing on anal margin.

Male.—Differs from female mainly in the funicle joints of the antennae which are plano-convex dorsally and slightly concave ventrally, subequal in length, each about three times as long as broad, and each furnished with two whorls of long hair. The spur of the middle tibia is rather longer than the corresponding first tarsal joint.

CERCHYSIUS ICERYÆ, sp. nov.

Female.—Length (to tip of terebra) 1.3 mm; expanse 2.7 mm.; antennal scape nearly cylindrical; flagellum unfortunately broken off in both antennae of the only specimen reared. Head and mesonotum very finely shagreened, the head with additional sparse fine punctures; lateral ocelli close to border of eyes, mesonotum glistening, with a few delicate sparse punctures particularly observable upon the scutellum; mesoscutellum with a delicate longitudinal impressed furrow from anterior apex to near middle; mesopleura finely shagreened, glistening; abdomen smooth, subtriangular; terebra as long as abdomen. Wing veins dark brown, marginal very short; fore-wings hyaline with a roundish dusky spot below stigma. General color honey-yellow, legs lighter than the body; especially front coxae and middle tibiae and tarsi; eyes black, ocelli dark, reddish brown; pronotum dusky near center; mesoscutum dusky at central anterior margin, metanotum fuscous; third joint of abdomen above black; apical half of mesopleura black; hind tibiae black except at tip.

Described from one female specimen reared by Mr. T. D. A. Cockerell, at Kingston, Jamaica, from *Icerya rosæ*.

THE WEST INDIAN RUFOUS SCALE.

(*Aspidiotus articulatus*, Morgan.)

By T. D. A. COCKERELL, *Kingston, Jamaica*.

In August, 1889 (*Ent. Mo. Mag.*, Vol. XXV, p. 352), Mr. A. C. F. Morgan published a description of *Aspidiotus articulatus*, a new species from Demerara, as follows:

Early in July, 1891, I found the same species at Barbados, and on arriving at Jamaica found it again abundantly on various plants in Kingston. The scale is circular and quite flat, whitish in color, but always appearing reddish or orange in the center, owing to the body of the animal showing through. It is an extremely easy species to identify, because the scale on being pushed or lifted by a knife blade at once comes off, leaving the very flat female Coccid beneath, which is recognized by its orange color and its strong segmentation, which latter character is easily seen with an ordinary pocket lens.

The figures given (l. c. Pl. V, Figs. 3, 5) by Morgan show the characters of the terminal plate, but otherwise are not very characteristic. In Fig. 5 the proportions of the parts are not good, and the general shape, so different from that observed by me, that I at first regarded the Jamaican form as a new species, allied to but distinct from *articulatus*. However, I sent specimens of my species to Mr. Morgan, who identified them as *articulatus*, and wrote suggesting that his ♀ might have been gravid. This could hardly be, as I took a ♀ full of eggs off a rose bush in Kingston, and it was quite of the usual shape; but Mr. Morgan very kindly sent me one of his Demerara specimens, and on comparing it with mine I found them identical in all essential particulars.

The normal (and, according to my experience, invariable) shape of the thorax is in outline that of a hemisphere, sometimes more or less compressed. The abdomen forms a triangle, of which the base is about one-fifth longer than either side. The terminal segment is large and well marked off from the rest. The eggs are oval, and many may at times be counted within the body of the ♀. I have examined very many specimens of the ♀, and all have been flat, none even rounded and plump, like some of the other species.

The peculiar characters of this species are so marked that it ought surely to be placed in a new genus or subgenus, but pending a revision of *Aspidiotus* it may be convenient to regard it as the type of a section, *Articulati*.

FOOD-PLANTS.

A. articulatus abounds on a great variety of plants. In Kingston I have found it on Olive, Lignum Vitæ, Oleander, Rose, Orange, *Ficus*, Cocoanut, and other palms, and various plants not identified. It normally infests the upper surface of the leaves, but also occurs on the fruit of the Orange. Morgan, as quoted above, records it from *Dictyospermum*.

HABITS AND HABITAT.

The Rufous Scale is extremely abundant at Kingston; but at Moneague I found it more rarely; and at Mandeville, nearly 2,000 feet above sea level, it was not to be seen, and the oranges and cocoanuts, so far as observed, were free from scales. This immunity in the mountain regions has been attributed,* no doubt correctly, to the damp and comparative coolness, a hot and relatively dry climate being necessary for their favorable existence.

It is also to be observed that while some palms, on which there are no other *Diaspinæ*, are so badly infested that the surfaces of the leaves are in places absolutely covered by scales; others, which support *Ischnaspis*, *Aspidiotus palmæ* (n. sp., Ckll. MS.), *A. ficus*, *Diaspis*, or *Chionaspis*, are less preyed upon by *A. articulatus*. It is not always a question of want of room, as some of these species do not cover the leaves in the manner of the Rufous Scale, but there seems to be a form of natural selection at work, so that when one species has obtained a footing on any given tree, another has difficulty is establishing itself. This may serve to account for the fact that although *A. articulatus* is common in Barbados, and Cocoanut is one of its known food-plants, some badly infested leaves of Cocoanut from there show no *A. articulatus*, but quite different species. In Kingston, some palms are, one might say, smothered in *A. articulatus;* while others, which support different kinds in addition, are on the whole less severely attacked, notwithstanding the greater number of *species* infesting them. In this way, it seems possible that a species of Coccidæ might be indirectly beneficial by keeping off another species more destructive than itself.

REMEDIES.

The remedies usually employed for other species of *Diaspinæ* will be appropriate for *A. articulatus;* but as it infests so great a variety of plants it will be more difficult to control than others, which, like *A. palmæ*,† are apparently confined to one. I learn from Prof. Riley that it has never yet been detected in the United States, and as it is a very undesirable insect, due measures should be taken in order that it may not be accidently imported. Whether it exists throughout the West Indies remains to be ascertained. From its occurrence both in Barbados and Jamaica, this might be expected, but it must be remembered

---

* See *Journ. Inst. Jamaica*, Vol. 1, p. 48, (1892).

† The difference of taste between some closely allied species of insects is very remarkable. *A. palmæ* seems confined to Cocoanut, but *A. rapax*, a very close ally, lives on many different plants. In Lepidoptera *Deilephila lineata* is almost omnivorous, whereas *D. euphorbiæ* eats one species of Euphorbia only, I believe.

that the Royal Mail steamers ply between those two points, so that a scale would be much more likely to be carried from Barbados to Jamaica than from Cuba. there being no regular communication with the latter island.

LIFE-HISTORY OF CALOTHYSANIS AMATURARIA WALK., A GEO-METRID MOTH.

By A. S. PACKARD, M. D., *Providence, R. I.*

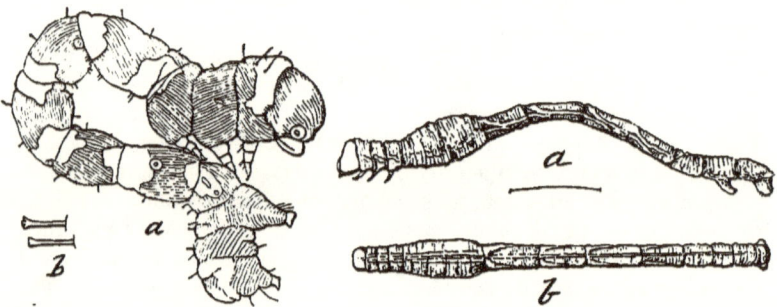

FIG. 76.—*Calothysanis amaturaria:* a, young larva; b glandular hairs—enlarged (original).

FIG. 77.—*Calothysanis amaturaria*, full grown larva: a, from side; b, from above—enlarged (original).

In August, 1890, I received from Mr. Frederick B. Simpson, of New York City, the larvæ of this geometer, which, after rearing, I identified, and as the transformations of this genus have hitherto been unknown, and the appearance and markings are very singular, I asked Mr. Simpson to send me the eggs, which he kindly did, also at my request preparing for me the following account of its habits:

The moths emerge usually between 12 m. and 4 p. m. Coition takes place very soon after emergence; it does not last long. I have not yet noted the length of time. The female commences to lay on the same day that she emerges. The eggs are laid promiscuously, some on the food-plant and some on adjoining plants; when deposited on the food-plant they are usually placed upon and underneath the edges of the leaf near the tip, but sometimes upon the stem and rarely in the middle of the leaf. I measured one egg. It was 0.023 inch long and 0.012 in width. When first laid the eggs are of a very light yellow (almost white), but within twenty-four hours they turn red. I found, however, one moth that laid a few eggs which did not turn red (I send them in piece of paper in box with others), but, strange to say, all other eggs laid by the same female turned red. The light ones were the first laid.

The food-plant is the Wild Buckwheat.

Mr. Simpson sent me about 73 eggs laid in New York "August 14 and 15 by ♀ taken August 14." By this statement we infer that the whole lot were laid by a single moth. He afterwards wrote me that some eggs " which were laid August 16–18 and hatched August 22–23 molted yesterday, August 31. I send you by this mail some of the larvæ; their length immediately after molting was 0.27 inch."

Eggs.—Length scarcely ⅔ mm. Regularly oval cylindrical, being rather long. The surface coarsely pitted, and under a half-inch objective seem to be marked with deep, well marked, close-set pits which are rounded at the bottom with distinct five-sided edges or rims. They are laid either scattered or in rows of three or four, not placed exactly end to end, but with one end directed a little to one side of the line.

Freshly hatched larva.—Length, 3-4 mm. Body of the usual Geometrid shape, not being swollen on the thoracic segments. The head is of moderate size, slightly wider than the body, and of the same reddish-brown color as the body; it is spotted with white in front, with two white spots above transversely arranged, and two large ones on the clypeus longitudinally arranged. The body is long and slender, dark reddish brown, marked with bright white irregular patches. Prothoracic segment with a large white oval spot next to the head, and a white dot on each side, the two succeeding segments reddish-brown with no marks. The first six abdominal segments each with a large white triangular showy spot on each side and meeting above. Each spot is composed of several large flat warts. The side of the suranal plate is lined with white, and the sides of the anal legs bear several flattened white warts. All the legs are dark. The abdominal segments each bear a few scattered short glandular hairs which are swollen at the end and divided into three lobes. The larvæ were not carried on to the second stage. One freshly hatched larva was observed September 6 which only measured 2 mm. in lengh.

Stage III?—Length 10 mm. The larva now resembles in shape and markings the full grown insect. The head is dark brown, with four longitudinal whitish stripes. The body is dark brown with indefinite, fine, longitudinal, blackish lines. Behind the thoracic segments the two basal abdominal segments are swollen forming a barrel-shaped enlargement with no white markings on this portion. Behind, in the middle of the body, are four sets of whitish yellow or tawny marks arranged at nearly equal distances apart, two slashes on each side, with a third oblique line passing over the back and nearly meeting the one from the other side; the ends on the back being sienna-brown; and between their points the faint yellowish white or tawny linear dorsal line is more distinct than elsewhere, the line not reaching the swollen anterior part or the posterior end of the body. Described September 2.

Full-grown larva.—Length, 20 mm. The head is a little flattened in front, slightly wider than the prothoracic segment. The body is much swollen on the first and second abdominal segments, so as to be twice as thick as in the middle or as the rest of the body. The thoracic segments increase in size towards the swollen portion behind, but the third abdominal segment is of the same thickness as those behind it. The body is of a rich velvety brown-black, with a broken light dorsal line, which is most distinct over the sutures. On each side of abdominal segments 3 to 6 are three oblique white slashes, forming very conspicuous marks; two of the slashe. nearly meet above, near the sutures. The head is dark, with two lateral white stripes continued back upon the first and second thoracic segments. The body elsewhere is faintly striped. The swollen portion behind the thoracic legs, and the dark-brown body with the four sets of three conspicuous white slashes, render it a very curious and conspicuous object. It may resemble a twisted dead or blackened portion of a leaf, or leaf-stalk, and it may have acquired the swollen appearance as a terrifying or deterrent feature. The young larva when 10 mm. long holds itself up much looped, supported by its anal legs, and sways itself to and fro sideways, and if one touches another it will strike at the other, simulating the actions of snakes when striking at an assailant.

Pupa.—Length, 12-13 mm. The head in front projecting forward, with two low conical piliferous tubercles. Two small dark tubercles at the base of the antennæ, and two larger ones in the middle of the head between them. Towards these tubercles the back of the thorax slopes evenly down, so that an angle or ridge is formed extending across the thorax between the insertion of the fore wings. The body is pale ash-gray, with a greenish tinge on the thorax. The abdomen is slender, conical, ending in a flattened conical cremaster, bearing three pairs of hooks, the distal pair of which are very much the largest and the innermost pair the smallest. The body is mottled and speckled, with a diffuse lateral dark line along the side of the abdomen. The five pairs of spiracles visible are black. The wings are slightly striped with dark specks. A median dark ventral longitudinal abdominal band, and a dorsal irregular dark band.

STEPS TOWARDS A REVISION OF CHAMBERS'S INDEX, WITH NOTES AND DESCRIPTION OF NEW SPECIES.

By LORD WALSINGHAM.

[Continued from p. 389, Vol. III.]

HELIODININÆ.

Heliodines Stn.
Heliodines Stn., Ins. Brit. I.p., 243 (1854): Type *Tinea roesella*, L.
= *Etole* Chamb., Can. Ent., VII, 73 (1875): Type *Etole bella* Chamb.
(= *Etole* Wlsm.; = *Elote* Chamb.; = *Elola* (Frey) Hgn.)

1. Heliodines bella Chamb.

Etole bella, Chamb. Can. Ent., VII, 73–4 (1875): IX. 72 (1877).
Bull. U. S. GG. Surv., III, 144 (1877): Jr. Cin. Soc., N. H., II, 199, 204, Fig. 54 (1880).
Elote bella, Chamb. Bull. U. S. GG. Surv, IV, 128 (1878).
Etole bella, Wlsm. Pr. Zoöl. Soc., Lond., 1881, 324, Fig. 1.
Etola bella (Frey) Hgn. Pap., IV, 154 (1884).
Imago: August (Chamb.).
Hab: Texas (Chamb.); *Colorado*, Denver (Chamb.); *California*, Los Angeles Co. (Wlsm).
A specimen of this species from Los Angeles was submitted to me for examination by Dr. Riley in 1877.

2. Heliodines tripunctella, sp. n.

Antennæ, gray.
Palpi, shining gray, slightly paler than the head.
Head and *face*, shining gray.
Thorax, gray; beneath, bright orange on the sides.
Fore wings, bright orange, with a small gray spot at the extreme base of the costal margin, followed by two costal spots, one before, the other at about the middle; the first of these is preceded by a similar spot on the dorsal margin; these three spots are all shining metallic steel-gray and from the outer costal spot proceeds a shining gray band which follows the costal margin to the apex, and passing around it at the base of the gray cilia, reaches along the dorsal margin to a point opposite the middle space between the two costal spots. Underside bronzy brown.
Hind wings, bronzy brown; cilia brownish gray. Underside bronzy brown.
Abdomen, orange tipped with gray at the extreme apex. Underside gray.
Legs, brownish fuscous with obscure pale bands on the hind tibiæ.
Exp. al: 9 mm.
Hab: Texas. (Belfrage, three specimens, two of which are from the Zeller collection.)
Type ♀ *Mus. Wlsm.*

3. Heliodines sexpunctella, sp. n.

Antennæ, grayish fuscous.
Palpi, subocherous.
Head and *face*, shining gray.
Thorax, shining gray; grayish fuscous beneath.
Fore wings, bright orange, the costal and dorsal margins tinged with fuscous on the basal half; with 6 shining, metallic, grayish-bronze spots, 3 costal and 3 dorsal, the former preceding the latter in each case; a little beyond the outer costal spot a shining, grayish-bronze metallic band, internally dark-margined, passes along the costa and around the apex, reaching to the outer dorsal spot at the anal angle; cilia gray. The metallic spots are internally dark-margined, but this is only visible in certain lights. Under side grayish fuscous.
Hind wings, bronzy-brownish; cilia gray.
Abdomen, grayish fuscous.
Legs, pale grayish fuscous, obscurely banded with subocherous at the spurs.
Exp. al.: 10 mm.
Hab: Arizona. (Morrison.)
Type ♀ *Mus. Wlsm.*
This species differs from *bella*, Chamb., in the absence of a basal spot or streak, in the number of spots and in the color of the under side of the thorax.

4. Heliodines extraneella, Wlsm.

Heliodines extraneella, Wlsm. Pr. Zoöl. Soc. Lond., 1881. 323–4. Pl. xxxvi, 15.
Imago. July 23. (Wlsm.)
Hab: California—Pitt River (Shasta Co. Wlsm).
Type Mus. Wlsm.

5. Heliodines unipunctella, sp. n.

Antennæ, palpi, head and *face* gray.
Thorax, gray (slightly darker than the fore wings). Underside gray.
Fore wings, shining gray, with a single bright orange quadrate spot before the middle of the costa. This is margined by a few fuscous scales at the base are some scattered orange scales above and below the fold, indicating the possible presence of a more ornate basal patch in finer specimens. Under side, grayish fuscous.
Hind wings, shining gray, with gray cilia. Under side, grayish fuscous.
Abdomen shining gray, with a broad orange band occupying several segments below the middle. Under side, gray.
Legs, gray.
Exp. al.: 12 mm.
Hab: California—Los Angeles (Osten Sacken 1878).
Type ♂ *Mus. Wlsm.*
This species is described from a single specimen in the Zeller collection.

SUGAR-CANE INSECTS IN NEW SOUTH WALES.

By Albert Koebele, *Special Agent.*

During the month of January, 1891, I had the pleasure of traveling with Mr. Rudolph Helms, chemist to the Colonial Sugar Company, through their sugar-cane fields from the Clarence to the Tweed River, and have had, through the generosity of this company, which kindly placed at my disposal steamers and other conveniences, a good opportunity of looking into the diseases of this plant.

The following insects were observed as being injurious to sugar cane: (1) The larva of a Noctuid, (2) Scarabæid larvæ, (3) wire-worms or Diabrotica larvæ.

THE NOCTUID LARVA.

This ranks first in injuring or destroying many of the plants in all parts visited, and seems to be evenly distributed from the Clarence to the Tweed River, being somewhat more numerous in the first locality mentioned. This larva is most numerous on the outer rows, so much so that in some places, as on the Clarence River, the entire plants were often destroyed, not bearing a single healthy or even living cane, while many fields, especially on the Richmond and Tweed, rarely showed any traces of the insect.

The abundance of the larvæ on the outskirts of the fields and places exposed to the winds may be readily explained. The moths which are on the wing at night and nearly always fly against the wind will often settle on the first plants reached, and there deposit their eggs. A second reason may be the usual strong winds during daytime not so readily allowing the minute flying enemies mentioned below to hunt up their hosts on the outer exposed parts of fields.

The eggs are, without doubt, deposited on the tops of plants and rarely in numbers, quite likely behind the young leaves, for very often but a single larva or the work of such could be found upon a plant. The moth has a casual resemblance to our Arzama which lays its eggs in clusters intermixed with the hairs of the bushy anal segments of the female. Although I have looked, I have never found a trace of such eggs. In this species the last segment is not provided with tufts, and the habits no doubt also differ. As the traces of young larvæ always indicated, they enter the tips of plants and work their way downward to the heart, which they destroy. If not forced to leave on account of decay they will begin irregular tunnels several inches deeper, and, if full grown, pupate in one of them, providing first an opening lightly spun over for the moth to issue. The dry and dead top leaves always afford a favorable place in which to pupate. If the larvæ are compelled to leave the boring on top they come lower down and begin their destructive work behind the leaves, often girdling the entire plant, and, if the entrance is found, usually on one of the eyes. The tunnels run very irregularly up and down, and sometimes the plant is nearly cut off, and this may be the case as low down as on the ground. It is uncertain where the larvæ will again enter a plant after leaving a burrow, but, in the first place, no doubt they look for shelter from their enemies, and perhaps sometimes enter the plant at or below the surface of the ground. Often plants six feet high were found uninjured down to the base and here entirely cut up. Young shoots seem to be eagerly sought and entirely destroyed down to the roots, and one larva is able to destroy several such before becoming mature. In instances where several larvæ had been at work upon one plant, this was often destroyed completely; not a single healthy cane was left, and frequently four or five parallel tunnels could be found within one stalk. In rare cases the whole inside of the cane is a complete mass of fibers.

During the time of my visit the most of the larvæ were nearly full grown, although some were found measuring not more than one-half inch in length. The chrysalids were not so numerous, and some of these had already hatched. From these meager observations alone it can not be said with any certainty how many broods there are annually, yet it is almost safe to say not more than two, allowing for irregularities in this warm climate. All the large larvæ found were no doubt of the first brood or from larvæ that had hibernated and pupated, say, about October and November. The duration of the pupa state, judging from specimens bred in confinement, is extremely short, only from ten to twelve days, varying, however, with the temperature. During spring it may even take twice this length.

Two species of parasites were observed to prey upon this insect. The first is a species of Microgaster, which destroys fully one-half of the larvæ, and from 50 to 80 specimens were bred from single individual larvæ. No doubt these little parasites are in constant search for their hosts, and not only deposit their eggs within such larvæ as have left their tunnels and are searching for new places, but also enter the open holes in the plant in search of them. All of the bred specimens were from grown or nearly grown larvæ. The larvæ of the parasites, as is well known, leave their host when full grown and spin a white silken cocoon on the outside and together, generally in the place prepared by the larvæ for pupation, and in four or five days, as repeatedly observed during January, the active little insects emerge to begin their useful work anew. This is certainly the most beneficial agent in keeping this serious pest to cane-growers in check, and without which it would not be possible to grow this crop successfully. I might also prove its usefulness upon other and closely-related species in distant countries if an opportunity were given.

We may safely say that the whole life cycle of this parasite, from egg to imago, will not take more than fifteen to eighteen days during the warm months, and that about twelve broods may be expected during the year to two of the moth. Thus it will be seen of what infinite value such minute insects are.

The second species is a Chalcidid and parasitic upon the chrysalis of the moth. This also is a very interesting little insect. The chrysalis of the moth is stung by the parent parasite, and as many eggs are laid within as will entirely fill the shell with the larvæ as these become full grown. They then pupate, both within and without, making similar cocoons of the foregoing, and in due time the mature insects, which are half as large as the Microgaster, make their appearance. Very few holes for egress are made, and often all issue from a single one. A few hundred may be bred from the chrysalis of the cane-borer moth, and as the life history, as far as is known, is of brief duration, this parasite is nearly if not wholly as valuable as the first in keeping the borers down. As may be inferred from analogy, this Chalcidid will not only be found preying upon this particular chrysalis, but on a great variety of Lepidopterous chrysalids, as is the case with related American forms.

In addition to those parasites numerous small ants of two species, were observed to form colonies in and around the burrows, and wherever these were present it was but very rarely that either larvæ or chrysalids could be found, and often dead larvæ or chrysalids and remains of such were found that were destroyed by them.

Numerous Carabid beetles were also present on the ground at the base of the plants and no doubt assist materially in reducing this pest.

SCARABÆID LARVÆ.

Varies species of Scarabæid beetles are always present in cane fields and especially so in recently cleared ground. Of these a species of Anaplognathus, commonly called "Christmas Beetle," was most numerous and is often plowed up both in the larva and imago state. Two other species of large Scarabæid larvæ were found behind the plow, as well as a species of Heteronyx, together with larvæ and pupæ, no doubt of the same species.

The larvæ of the beetles are injurious by eating the roots of various plants, and as their transformation is very slow they remain a long time in the ground, and in the absence of any other roots they naturally attack those of the sugar cane. If numerous they will become a serious pest, as insects of this sort often devastate whole fields.

As a remedy it is suggested in the first place that diligent search be instituted for the larvæ and beetles while plowing and harrowing. This could be done by children. The mature insects, which come out chiefly at night, may also be found in the daytime feeding on the leaves of Eucalyptus trees, which are often defoliated by them. By shaking the trees in the early morning the beetles will drop to the ground and remain motionless for some time, when they can be gathered and destroyed. They are also readily attracted by lights and may be collected with traps consisting of a bright light placed over a tin or other vessel about a foot deep by two feet wide with perpendicular sides and with about two inches of water in the bottom. Many such simple traps could be placed over the fields in December and January, when the beetles are on the wing. Dark nights are best for attracting insects. Without doubt the presence of toads, if these were introduced, would have a remarkable effect in diminishing the numbers of these as well as many other injurious insects.

WIRE WORMS, OR DIABROTICA LARVÆ.

About Coudong on the Tweed River in the early part of spring a large number of the young plants were destroyed to such an extent that in some of the fields in a distance of 40 or 50 yards all had to be replanted, often the second time. This had been done, it was claimed, by wire-worms (Elaterid larvæ). During my visit these larvæ had disappeared, and only in one instance, while digging up one of the plants, one of these or a similar larva was found at the roots of a healthy plant adjoining one which had been destroyed. The burrow within the dead plant had been made, to all appearances, some months before.

The plant on which this larva was found did not show any traces of having been injured in the slightest degree. This particular larva was, however, completely crushed in taking out the plant and could not be recognized as an Elaterid. It had more resemblance to a Chrysomelid, probably Diabrotica, beetles of which, in fact, had appeared for the first time, it was said, in very large numbers in this locality, feeding upon tassels of cane.

Two of the larvæ found during spring within the narrow burrows below ground were promised to be forwarded to Sydney for a more careful examination.

Should these prove to be the larvæ of Diabrotica, as I am inclined to believe is the case, since hardly any Elaterid beetles were met with, it would be highly advisable to destroy the beetle with an arsenical poison by spraying the tassels of corn. Paris green would act admirably, about one pound of this to two hundred gallons of water.

The larvæ of Diabrotica are destructive to corn and no doubt to cane as well in America, and as maize is planted extensively in this locality these beetles will probably increase greatly from year to year if proper steps are not taken to destroy them. In the same district, during a certain time of the year, it is claimed that the "blight" is destroying the corn. I should not hesitate in saying that the real agent of this is not fungoid, as is claimed, but the larvæ of this Diabrotica boring in the the plants below the surface. In this conclusion I may be wrong, but investigation at the proper time would reveal the facts.

NOTES ON LACHNOSTERNA.

By G. H. PERKINS, *Burlington, Vt.*

The following notes, taken from a more extended series of observations upon Lachnosterna made at the Vermont Experiment Station, may be of some interest to entomologists.

On January 28, 1891, a considerable number of larvæ of Lachnosterna were dug from sandy grassland. There being a foot or more of snow over the sod the soil beneath was not frozen. Larvæ were abundant at depths varying from not more than three or four inches below the sod to over a foot below. All were active and most were found in their usual feeding position. They were for the most part fully grown. Other lots of the grubs were obtained from the same locality in March and April. Some of those found in March were in frozen soil, but they did not seem affected by it, but were as lively and vigorous as in summer; others were black and dead. Several of those found at this time were infested by from half a dozen to a dozen mites of the genus Tyroglyphus or Rhizoglyphus, I think. A lot set aside for identification was unfortunately lost; hence I can not with certainty give even the genus. Although the mites appeared to be parasitic on the larvæ, the latter were not apparently injured by them. On larvæ dug early in April *Cordyceps rarenellii* Ber. was growing. From each lot of larvæ, from twenty-five to fifty were taken and placed in large boxes of soil and supplied with turf. While most of these larvæ were of full size, *i. e.*, from 1.4 inch to 1.6 inch long, two other smaller sizes also occurred, one of them about 1 inch long, and the smallest 0.5 inch to 0.6 inch long. The color is more nearly pure white in the smaller larvæ and these are more active than the larger ones. The confined larvæ were hatched during the spring and summer, in order that any tendency to pupation might be noted, but most of them were unchanged until September, when they pupated, and the last of September and early in October all left the earth as perfect beetles. About 4 per cent of the several hundred kept changed to imagos in early summer.

Only larvæ were found January 28, but at each subsequent digging a few beetles were found with the larvæ. They did not voluntarily come from the ground till about the 1st of May, from which time they grew more and more abundant, until early in June, when they began to decrease, and by the last of June all had disappeared. It should be said that the spring was cold and that the beetles were far less numerous during the season than usual. Dr. Horn's paper in Trans. Am. Ent. Soc., Vol. XIV, and especially Prof. Smith's article in Proc. Nat. Mus., 1888, p. 481, enable students of the genus to identify species in a manner hitherto impossible. Using the above papers as guides it was found that all of the beetles appearing at first were *L. dubia* Smith, and the same is true this present year, for up to this time, May 10, I have found only this species. Later *L. fusca* Frohl. appears and soon is as numerous as *L. dubia*, and throughout the season these two species, found in about equal numbers, are the principal forms, but now and then a stray specimen of several other species occurs. These are *L. grandis* Smith, *L. arcuata* Smith, *L. insperata* Smith, *L. rugosa* Mels., but only a few specimens of any of these were taken.

After the disappearance of the beetles, toward the last of June, none are found until the last of September, or early in October, when a few individuals of a new brood come from the ground. So far as observed these are about equally *L. dubia* and *L. fusca*.

Many experiments were made to ascertain, if possible, what substances could be economically introduced into the soil infested with white grubs which should destroy them, while not injuriously affecting the crops. Although the results reached were less definite and satisfactory than were desired, it may be worth while to state some of them as briefly as possible. Several of the larvæ infested with Cordyceps were placed in a box of sandy soil and such conditions preserved as were thought favorable to the development of the fungus. Healthy larvæ were also placed in this box. The fungus did not develop spores and the uninfested larvæ were not attacked during the time of the experiment, but this may not have been sufficient for the production of the desired result. The accounts of Prillieux and Delacroix in *Compte Rendus*, May 11, 1891, show that the European Melolontha can be successfully attacked by a fungus, and culture tubes are offered for sale.

Freezing the earth even when the degree of cold was not below zero F. destroyed all contained larvæ. This is remarkable because, as has been noticed, active and apparently healthy grubs were found in frozen earth in the field. In the boxes, however, they did not withstand cold very much below freezing. Experiments were made to ascertain the possibility, or feasibility, of starvation, with the result that very few larvæ were affected even when kept for months in soil more free from organic matter than that of any cultivated field would be, and it does not seem at all probable that this method, which has been recommended by some of our best entomologists, is of any value. A dry soil is very unfavorable to the larvæ, and if very dry they speedily perish. On the other hand, they are not unfavorably affected by a moist or even very wet soil, at least for some time.

Several of the potash salts were used in the form of strong solution, 1 ounce in 1 pint of water and poured over soil containing larvæ. The results were not such as to recommend the use of these salts, although they are far from valueless. The sulphate of potash on the whole proved most useful, but to destroy any considerable portion of the grubs an amount larger than would generally be economical was necessary. Common salt and wood ashes were each tested both in solution and as lye and mixed with the soil dry, but the grubs were not seriously injured by them. Bisulphide of carbon was more effective and without doubt could be used to advantage in many cases. Kerosene emulsion, however, is better in its results as well as cheaper and seems on the whole decidedly preferable to any substance tried. Poured over grass in dilution such that the grass was uninjured, it yet destroyed most of the larvæ. Red ants are a great aid in destroying the grubs, and very likely other species than that noticed, the common red ant, are equally valuable. A box in which a number of the larvæ were living having been discovered by the ants they at once took possession and promptly destroyed every one of them, and this leads to the conclusion that perhaps we are more deeply indebted than we have been aware to ants for destroying those larvæ which inhabit the ground.

It will be noticed that the above observations in respect to the pupation of the white grub agree with the very interesting account given by Prof. S. A. Forbes in his last report, and as the localities are quite widely separated it is of interest to note the entire agreement of the results. In Vermont, as in Illinois, the species of Lachnosterna pupate and come out as beetles in the early fall, a few to emerge at once from the earth, and to remain not dormant, but apparently as active as usual, in the ground until, in this region, about the 1st of May, when they begin to come from their hiding place.

THE FIRST LARVAL STAGE OF THE PEA WEEVIL.

In our last number we published a short popular article upon the Bean and Pea Weevils, calling attention for the first time to a most interesting post-embryonic larval stage of the Bean Weevil, in which the larva is possessed of false legs which serve its locomotive needs until it has entered the bean, when, with a cast of the skin, they are lost and the larva assumes the ordinary weevil form. At that time material was not at hand to enable us to verify our suspicion that a similar stage would be found in the larva of the Pea Weevil, but we have recently received fresh pea-pods from the West which bore eggs of *Bruchus pisi*, and we have found them in our own garden.

The fact that the Pea Weevil deposits its egg on the outside of the pod, fastening it thereto, has long been known, and we have found, as we surmised would be the case, that the newly-hatched larva of this species has the same characteristics as those we have described in the case of the Bean Weevil. The only difference is that the temporary legs are much shorter and stouter, though similarly constructed, the tarsus proper being a mere spatulate pad. A further difference exists in that the spurs on the prothoracic segments are more elaborate and conspicuous, consisting of six strong, retrorse spines, anteriorly preceded by two more prominent plates also pointing posteriorly and strongly toothed along their exterior border. There are no anal spurs or spines. An interesting fact connected with this larva is, that while ordinarily entering the pea direct from the amber-colored egg, as previously recorded, it sometimes enters the pod in the neighborhood of the egg and then mines along the inside of the pod for some distance, being quite active and moving rapidly and with ease. This doubtless occurs wherever the egg hatches before the peas are sufficiently developed, the larva living as a miner until the pea is nearly full grown, and the entrance of the larva into a pea in such case would seem to be rather by chance than by design. As in the case of the Bean Weevil, however, the larva molts and loses its legs and other post-embryonic characters as soon as it has entered the pea.

EXTRACTS FROM CORRESPONDENCE.

On some of the Insects described by Walsh.

According to the Bibliography of Economic Entomology, pp. 373, 374, the types of *Heptagenia maculipennis* Walsh, *Conotrachelus crataegi* Walsh, and *Anthonomus prunicida* Walsh, were destroyed. If you know of any collection in which there are specimens of these species determined by Walsh, please give me the number of specimens. Any information concerning the following insects will be very thankfully received:

Caloptenus differentialis Uhler MS.
Xiphidium longicaudum Walsh MS. ♀ ♂.
Orchelimum arboreum Walsh MS. ♂ =*glaberrimum*? Burm.
(Ecanthus bipunctatus ♂ ♀ (♀ only described).
Platamodes illinoiensis Walsh MS.

These names are copied from the labels of some specimens in a collection of insects presented to the Illinois Wesleyan University in about 1863 by Dr. Walsh. Some of them are now in very bad condition. * * * [Charles C. Adams, Illinois, March 27, 1892.

REPLY.—* * * Typical specimens of Walsh's *Heptagenia maculipennis* are apparently not preserved. Walsh described the species from fifteen specimens (Proc. Ent. Soc. Phila. II, 1863, p. 206), and I can not understand why it is that he never sent specimens either to Dr. Hagen or to myself. Dr. Hagen apparently never referred to this species, and it remained also unknown to Mr. Eaton in his Monograph of the Ephemeridæ.

Typical specimens of *Conotrachelus crataegi* and *Anthonomus prunicida*, compared with Walsh's types, and some of them from him, are in my own cabinet. Moreover, there are in the Le Conte collection, now at Cambridge, Mass., specimens of both sexes, which were sent by Walsh to Dr. Le Conte. These are, in all probability, typical specimens, but so far as I remember they are not labeled as such.

Caloptenus differentialis Uhler MS. is no doubt the species subsequently described by Thomas and now known as *Melanoplus differentialis* Thos.

Xiphidium longicaudum and *Orchelimum arboreum* have never been described or even mentioned by Walsh in his writings; therefore of no particular value. The former is possibly the species referred to by Walsh in Proc. Ent. Soc. Phil., Vol. III, 1884, p. 581, but it can not be identified in the absence of Walsh's original specimens. *Orchelimum arboreum* Walsh MS. has likewise never been described, and appears to be the "*Orchelimum*, perhaps *glaberrimum* Burm.," mentioned by Walsh, *l. c.*, p. 232.

Œcanthus bipunctatus. If Walsh did not make a mistake in the determination, this may be *Œc. bipunctatus* De Geer, but from McNeill's "List of the Orthoptera of Illinois," I see that it is very rare in Illinois, and thus the probability is that Walsh's specimens must be referred to some other species.

Platamodes illinoiensis Walsh MS. I fail to find any reference to this name in Walsh's writings, and the species can not be identified. It is possibly *Ischnoptera pennsylvanica* De Geer or *I. unicolor* Scudd., since it must be assumed that Walsh was familiar with the cosmopolitan species of Blattidæ occurring in Illinois.—[March 30, 1892.]

A Chalcid Fly in a new Role ; Is it parasitic on the Clothes Moth?

I send specimens of an insect that has been troubling a patient of mine, Mrs. Sumner Bull. Some three years ago she first noticed them and since they first made their appearance they have continued to infest the house, and by their buzzing and biting have kept her and her guests awake nights. They bite very quickly and fly away; the bite is not as troublesome as that of a mosquito, but is very much like that. Their buzzing is very similar to a mosquito. I hope that you may be able to classify the specimens sent and tell us what to do to get rid of them. They have become so annoying to the household and especially to Mrs. Bull herself that her health has really suffered by reason of them.—[J. M. Granniss, M. D., Connecticut, March 9, 1892.

Reply.—Examination of the specimens shows that they are Chalcidids of the genus Necremnus, the species being undescribed. If your patient is not mistaken in attributing her discomfort to these particular insects they are probably parasitic upon Clothes Moths in her house, as all other species of the genus so far as known are parasitic upon Tineina. Further details, however, are much desired, as well as other specimens, and also information as to why the lady considers these to be the insects which are troubling her. Has she caught them in the act of biting?—[April 25, 1892.]

On Figs grown without Caprification.

I learn from my friend, Mr. S. H. Scudder, of Cambridge, Mass., that last fall you presented to the Library Association a case of figs which were pronounced equal to any Smyrna figs the members ever tasted. The impression has got out that these were true Smyrna figs that had been caprified by the Blastophagas introduced by Mr. Shinn, but Mr. Eisen writes me that this can not be true. May I beg you to let me know whether the figs were anything other than fine specimens, well preserved, of some particular Adriatic fig. * * *—[C. V. Riley, Washington, D. C., February 17, 1892.

Reply.—* * * The figs presented to the Library Association were grown on my orchard farm at Loomis, Placer County. They were the so-called White Adriatic. They, no doubt, were the best fig grown in California, but I do not think they were superior to the Smyrna. Their excellence was due to having been grown in a foothill country, elevation 400 feet, and also because they had not been irrigated. I shall send you a box of this year's growth when the crop matures, i. e., September.

I am engaged in solving the question whether a good fig can be produced from the seed of the Smyrna fig. In 1885 and 1886 I sowed the seed, fixing 1895 as the date when figs would be produced. I neither believe nor disbelieve in the theory of caprification. The writings of Meyer, Lombush, etc., all indicate that the authors were never on the spot to carry on practical experiments. But I may say that the experiment of Prof. Eisen and myself was startling to a mere agnostic.

I have had some correspondence with Mr. Van Deman who sent Eisen a collection of "Smyrna cuttings," but they were nearly all Italian fig cuttings. Mine died owing to the neglect of my foreman.

The experiment of caprification will be continued this summer at Mr. Shinn's, Niles, Alameda County.—[E. W. Maslin, San Francisco, Cal., May 31, 1892.]

On the Beaver Parasite.

A friend of mine is preparing a work on the Beaver, and asked me if I could procure a copy of your interesting article on *Platypsyllus castoris* published in Vol. I of Insect Life. Is there any chance of finding specimens of the parasite, either living or dead, on the dried skins of the Beaver, and if so, are they confined to a certain part of the skin or on all parts of the body? I looked over a few skins this morning but could find nothing resembling a parasite of any kind or stage except the curious white cocoon-like object, of which I inclose a small lot, which were very abundant among the hairs, especially around the ears. Can you tell me what they are? * * *—[Albert F. Winn, Province Quebec, Canada, May 28, 1892.

Reply.—" * * The finding of Platypsyllus material on beaver skins is not at all improbable, and careful combing should produce some specimens at least of the larvæ and also perhaps of the adult. The former, however, will be very much shriveled and will hardly be recognized except by some one familiar with their appearance, as they are quite small. They would be found on almost any part of the beaver, but perhaps most frequently on the upper and anterior portions. The specimens which you send, and which you state occurred abundantly among the hairs around the ears look surprisingly like a cluster of dried and flattened eggs, and it was at first suspected that they might be those of Platypsyllus, for which we have been looking for many years, but upon examination they proved to be much too large, and are undoubtedly epithelial cells which have been cast off. Their resemblance to eggs or minute cocoons is, however, very striking and deceptive —[May 31, 1892.]

Blister Beetles in Texas.

FIRST LETTER.—Inclosed find some insects which the natives call the Spanish Fly. They prove very destructive to Irish potatoes, and when those are not to be had, tomatoes, beets, etc., are not despised. They do not seem to breed here. A patch of potatoes at night might not have an insect in it, but in the morning they are covered. They feed together in swarms and seldom fly in the daytime. They will commence to feed on one row and follow it clear across and do not often jump across to adjoining rows till the end of the patch is reached. We kill them mostly with hot water and burn them with coal-oil fires on a long stick with a swab saturated. I am now trying Paris green. They are feeding on potatoes where applied, but appear as lively as ever.—[William Pocock, Texas, May 22, 1892.

REPLY.—* * * The insect which is damaging your potatoes is one of the Blister Beetles known as *Epicauta lemniscata*, previously referred to in the current volume on page 77. Your neighbors are nearly right in calling them the "Spanish Fly," as they belong to the same family and possess in some degree the same vesicating properties. This, and several allied species, frequently do considerable damage throughout the Western States to the potato crop, as well as to beans and many garden vegetables. The Paris green treatment which you have begun is comparatively successful, and although at first you may be unable to see any markedly beneficial results a little persistence on your part will eventually rid your vines of the insect. In some parts of the West the plan has been followed of driving the insects with the wind into a windrow of hay or straw or other dried vegetation, which is then burned. The beetles do not breed upon the potato, but in their early stages are parasitic upon the eggs of locusts and other insects.—[May 28, 1892.]

SECOND LETTER.—I send specimens of an insect which reached here last night in considerable numbers, and which immediately began an attack on various plants, and the name of which I would like to know.—[J. O. Skinner, Surgeon U. S. Army, Texas, May 13, 1892.

REPLY.— * * * The insect is one of our large Blister Beetles knows as *Macrobasis atrivittata* Lec. This and other species are frequently abundant in the Western States, and when occurring in numbers often do great damage to cultivated crops. They are most interesting from a biologic standpoint, from the fact that they are hypermetamorphotic, the larvæ undergoing several distinct metamorphoses. They are, in the main, parasitic in their early stages on the eggs of locust.—[May 18, 1892.]

The Twelve-spotted Asparagus Beetle.

I send some insects which are on the asparagus plants on a farm adjoining mine. I have examined five other beds on neighboring farms and do not find them on any of the other beds. The Asparagus Beetle was very thick on this bed, so the owner, Mr. Veach, cut down every stalk save about four, which he left for experiments. He cuts now as fast as it is fit. This red beetle appears in considerable numbers on the stalks that are left, but does not seem to eat either the asparagus or the larvæ of the Asparagus Beetle. What are they and what do they feed on? Are they injurious or not?—[A. P. Gordon-Cumming, Carroll County, Md., June 6, 1892.

REPLY.—The insect is congeneric with the Asparagus Beetle and is known scientifically as *Crioceris 12-punctatus*. Like the Asparagus Beetle it is a comparatively recent importation from Europe, and was first noticed near Baltimore. It spreads slowly and still occupies only a limited region in Maryland and the District of Columbia. It feeds upon asparagus in all of its stages, and is not known to have another food-plant. It is not, however, as destructive as its congener. We have no specimens of the larva of *C. 12-punctatus*, but these will doubtless be found upon asparagus at this time or a little later. Can you not ask your neighbor, Mr. Veach, to look out for them and send specimens to us?—[June 7, 1892.]

A Wood-borer mistaken for a Household Pest.

A number of our good people have brought me specimens of the Clytus, and in awe have complained of their houses being overrun with the beetle. In every case I have found on inquiry that the family was in the habit of having open wood fires, usually Hickory, and that the beetle was usually more abundant in the room in which the fireplace was located. This I think explains the occurrence of the "borers."—[Chas. C. Beach, M. D., Connecticut, April 22, 1892.

REPLY.—Your note relative to the issuing of "Clytus" (*Cyllene picta*) from the Hickory pile is interesting, but the same thing is frequently called to my attention by correspondents. The appearance of these insects in the house is frequently considered a great mystery.—[April 25, 1892.]

A new Fruit Pest—*Syneta albida* Lec.

We inclose under separate cover some specimens of an insect that is very numerous here this season, though they have been here for several years. They attack the foliage and blossoms of nearly all the fruit trees, though they are not so bad on peach trees as on cherries and apples. They are on hand as soon as the buds open and continue to work, cutting the stems of the fruit about half through, as the inclosed specimens show. We think of spraying for them with Paris green if they do not soon disappear. Will you kindly examine the inclosed specimens and advise us of the best course to pursue and the treatment which will probably be most effective. A sudden jar of an infested tree causes a shower of them to fall to the ground with wings spread, where they immediately begin to fold their wings under the cases and crawl to shelter, in a short time finding their way on the trees again, though they do not readily take flight.—[Seth Lewelling & Co., Oregon, April 29, 1892.

REPLY.—The insect which you send is one of the leaf-beetles (Chrysomelidæ) known as *Syneta albida*, concerning the habits of which we have previously known almost nothing. It has never been brought to the attention of economic entomologists before as a specially injurious species, and your letter, therefore, is of great interest. The early stages of the insect are not known. As the beetles fall so readily a great many could be destroyed by jarring them from the trees upon sheets saturated with kerosene, or if you spray your trees with Paris green or London purple in the proportion of 1 pound of the poison to 250 gallons of water (300 for peach) you will be able to destroy them with less trouble. I shall be glad to hear from you as to whether this damage is at all common in your State or vicinity, or is it confined locally to your orchards?—[May 7, 1892.]

On the Date of Introduction of the Potato Tuber-moth.

I found the larva of the Potato Tuber-moth, which is described in the current volume of INSECT LIFE (pp. 239-242), in potatoes purchased in the market at Los Gatos, Cal., the last week in June in 1888. I was a stranger to the country and as the larva was strange to me I did not know how common it might be in California. Not a large number were found, but a few were discovered while preparing the potatoes for food. They were doubtless the same as those described, for I observed them closely at the time and my recollection agrees exactly with both the illustration and description given.—[William L. Drew, Iowa, April 21, 1892.

The East Indian Sugar-cane Borer.

In a recent number of INSECT LIFE (Vol. IV, pp. 95-103) I find a most interesting review by Mr. Howard of what is known about the Sugar-cane Borer, *Diatræa saccharalis*, with a valuable foot-note describing the results of your examination of moths reared from Maize and Sugar Cane.

The question of the specific identity of the borers which attack Sugar Cane, *Sorghum vulgare*, and Maize is a very important one, especially in India, where they do a great deal of damage to all three crops, and where therefore it is specially desirable to settle definitely to what extent the refuse of a crop of Sorghum (for instance) is liable to be detrimental to a crop of Sugar Cane or Maize growing in the neighborhood.

We have reared a number of moths from Sugar Cane in Calcutta, and though they differ from each other a good deal in size and coloration I am strongly inclined to look upon them as representing merely the varieties likely to be found in one species. We have also reared moths from Maize and I think there can be no doubt as to their identity with the moths we have reared from Sugar Cane. In the case of the *Sorghum vulgare* borer we have not yet been successful in rearing the moth, owing to the numerous Chalcidid parasites (described by Mr. Peter Cameron as *Cotesia flaripes* n. sp.) with which the caterpillars that were sent to this Museum were afflicted.

I am sending you a moth reared from Sugar Cane in Calcutta inclosed in this letter, and should be very much obliged if you would be so kind as to compare it with your collection and let me know what you think of its identity. I have picked it out as one that represents an average amongst the moths we have reared.

It may interest you to hear that owing to the fact that it is much easier to get sugar-cane stalks than either maize stalks or sorghum stalks in Calcutta, we have used Sugar Cane for rearing the borers sent to the Museum, both from Maize and Sorghum. Maize borers were reared in Sugar Cane from the time they were comparatively small caterpillars until they emerged as moths, and a sorghum borer (the only one of my set that escaped the Chalcidid) was reared in Sugar Cane from the time it was a half-grown caterpillar until it became chrysalid, when it was accidentally damaged in transferring it to fresh Sugar Cane, and thus prevented from emerging as a moth. I have not been able to notice that the caterpillars were any the worse for their change of diet, and this, I think, itself is a very strong indication that the same species attacks the three plants indiscriminately.

It would strengthen the evidence, however, if it should prove that the American species is identical with the Indian one.—[E. C. Cotes, Calcutta, India, February 19, 1892.

REPLY.—Your sugar-cane borer is not the same as ours. It is a Chilo and not a Diatræa and comes near *C. plejadellus* Winck., which bores in Rice in our Southern States, but differs in the very clear-cut terminal dark line between the black spots and fringe. The specimen is badly rubbed, and its exact specific position can not be determined with certainty. It is possible it may be identical with *Chilo infuscatellus* Snell., which infests Sugar Cane in Java. Better specimens are greatly desired for further study and also specimens of the larva.

Without doubt you are perfectly right in assuming that the borers in Sugar Cane, Sorghum, and Maize are all the same, and it is interesting to know that at least one other Crambid agrees with *D. saccharalis* in this particular.—[March 28, 1892.]

Florida Wax Scale on LeConte Pear.

I cut the inclosed twigs and leaves from a LeConte Pear tree. Kindly inform me as to what kind of disease the tree has and what treatment is required for it.—[Herbert J. Pratt, Florida, May 30, 1892.

REPLY.—" * * The Bark-louse, which you found upon your LeConte pears, is the so-called Florida Wax Scale (*Ceroplastes floridensis*). This insect has never before been recorded upon Pear. It has occasionally been found upon Orange. but it has been. up to the present time, only a temporary visitor upon cultivated plants. Its native wild food seems to be the Gall-berry (*Ilex glabra*). Your best remedy will be to spray with a dilute kerosene-soap emulsion, made according to the formula given upon page 3, circular No. 1. of this Division at the time when the young lice are hatching. If the Gall-berry occurs in any abundance near your orchard you are also advised to exterminate it if possible, as it is doubtless responsible for the occurrence of the insects upon your pear trees.—[June 2. 1892.]

The Horn Fly in the South.

Inclosed you will find flies which from habit and appearance are considered by this Department to be the Horn Fly. Before treating the matter in the publication of the department we desire the opinion of the entomologist. The flies annoy cattle very much, and made their appearance in southern Georgia last season and again this season.—[R. T. Nesbit, Commissioner of Agriculture. Department of Agriculture, Georgia, May 25, 1892.

REPLY.—* * * You are correct in determining the species to be the Horn Fly (*Hæmatobia serrata*). The spread of the species during the past two or three years has been remarkable, and it now occurs from New Jersey to Florida and west to Louisiana.—[May 28. 1892.]

The Horn Fly in Florida.

The Horn Fly (*Hæmatobia serrata*), arrived here some time last year, as Dr. Neal says it was not here in 1890. It was quite annoying last fall. From the present outlook it will probably be severe on cattle this year. The first specimens were taken during the first week of April. It is known by some as the "dog fly."—[P. H. Rolfs. Florida, April 22. 1892.

A new Owl Parasite.

I inclose herewith two flies. I took them from the body of a large Horned Owl, killed on Caranchua Bay, Jackson County, Tex.

These specimens could not fly and seemed to be laden with eggs fastened to the hairs on their bodies; they clung tenaciously to the feathers. Would you kindly tell me the name of this fly? I never saw one like it before.—[J. D. Mitchell. Victoria County, Tex., April 17, 1892.

REPLY.—The insect which you send is one of the curious degraded parasitic flies of the family Hippoboscidæ, to which the so-called Sheep Tick belongs. It belongs to the genus Olfersia and, as far as can be determined by comparison with the National Museum collection. it is a new species.—[April 26. 1892.]

Notes on Spiders.

* * * A number of years ago. as I was dressing in the morning. I felt a very sharp pain on the outside of my leg a little way below the hip joint. I thought there was a hornet in my clothes and began to look for it on the double quick, but to my surprise I found a dark-brown spider, such as are common around houses at that time of the year. I am not versed in entomology, so I can not give its name. It was of the kind that weave funnel-shaped webs to catch flies. The pain was very severe for a few minutes. The flesh over a space about the size of a dime turned very white and raised up like a little flat lump, and was quite hard. Several little indentations. as if made by pressing the surface with some sharp-pointed thing. as a pin, were seen. The indentations were so marked I could not fail to notice them. After an hour or so the pain largely subsided. and by next day the mark was mostly gone. My verdict is that some spiders inflict severe pain by their bite.

We have a large black spider here that burrows in the ground, making a burrow almost straight down and sometimes 12 to 15 inches deep and over half an inch wide. They apparently deposit their eggs in them, as I have seen them near their burrows, their bodies completely covered with little spiders that seemed in some way to subsist on the parent. This spider is a powerful fellow, with vicious eye and powerful jaws. I have pinned their bodies with the tine of a pitchfork and they would bite so hard that I could hear their teeth grit on the fork.

I do not know whether they are poisonous or not, but I know I do not want one of them to bite me. They are very quick and active when they want to be so. They have powerful limbs and very large bodies, almost as large as some mounted specimens that I have seen of the Tarantula.—[John March, Wisconsin, April 21, 1892.

Grasshopper Depredations in Ohio in 1891.

I beg leave to call your attention to the depredations of grasshoppers which have been going on in this vicinity for several years past, and especially for the last two years. So great has been their destruction that my Timothy and Clover, as well as permanent pasture, have been destroyed root and branch on several hundred acres of land. The summer of 1890 all of my spring sowing of clover and timothy, about 200 acres, was destroyed by them, and the summer of 1891 all spring sowings and other grasses, amounting to 500 or 600 acres, as I have stated. It is difficult to estimate damages, but they will run up in the thousands. I am carrying on dairying and stock-raising, and it is discouraging indeed to find one's land bare and made so by the ravages of the grasshoppers. My experience is the experience of many others, except probably not on so large a scale. I bought last season of the Nixon Nozzle Company, of Dayton, Ohio, a hand spraying-pump for the purpose of experimenting with the different preparations recommended for the destruction of insects, but to no purpose. I used a preparation made by the Nixon Nozzle Company; I also used Paris green, and applied on grass where the insects were plenty and where stock was not allowed to run. It has no perceivable effect on the hoppers. * * *—[John Ferris, Ohio, April 4, 1892, to F. M. Webster.

Tin-can Remedy and Paper Wrappers for Cut-worms.

I notice in a recent issue of INSECT LIFE you recommend the use of old tin cans for preventing the work of cut-worms upon tomatoes, cabbages, and other plants. I have tried that plan and found that in a hot sunshine it would draw the heat so as to kill tomato plants unless covered during the heat of the day. I then tried wrapping the plants from the roots to top of plant when setting with common newspaper, wrapping it around three or four times and then setting deep, so as to have the bottom of the paper two or three inches below the surface of the ground. I found that this was a perfect protection against cut-worms and that the heat did not hurt the plants. The paper lasts as long as needed in this rainy climate and needs no tying, nor does it ever have to be removed, one operation being sufficient for the whole season, and you are sure there are no cut-worms inside of it, which is not the case when using the cans. I have only used it one year and had such good success I shall try it again.—[James B. Smith, North Carolina, April 9, 1892.]

NOTES FROM CORRESPONDENCE.

The new Herbarium Pest.—Mr. W. H. Evans, of Crawfordsville, Ind., wrote us March 7 that he found recently three larvæ of our new herbarium pest, *Carphoxera ptelearia*, on some Arizona plants of last season's collecting. The plants attacked were Pentstemon and Castillia, and they were badly riddled.

A new Peach Pest.—Through the kindness of Mr. J. L. Hardy, of Harris County, Tex., we have received specimens of a new Aspidiotus upon peach twigs, which we have already received from the same State, and which is undoubtedly abundant and destructive. It is as yet undescribed.

Myriopods injuring Lettuce.—Mr. G. E. Keplinger, of Ohio, complains that his lettuce crop is being destroyed by a Myriopod, which we have determined for him as *Julus virgatus* Wood. They attack the outside leaves near the main stalk. The leaves turn yellow and fall to the ground, and when they are partially decomposed the "Thousand Legs" consume them entirely.

Hibernation of Conocephalus.—Mr. J. Thompson, of Hampton, Va., sent us, under date of February 2, a specimen of *Conocephalus ensiger*, which was active and in the best of condition at this wintry season.

What is the Stink-bush?—We have had some correspondence of late with Mr. S. B. Mullen, of Mississippi, regarding a plant which is known in that part of the country as the "stink-bush." We have been unable to determine it scientifically from the poor specimens which Mr. Mullen has sent in. Insecticide properties are claimed for it in Mississippi. It is an evergreen and is quite abundant in creeks. It has a sickening odor in the summer. Can some of our correspondents identify this plant for us?

A Mistake about Canthon.—A correspondent in Iowa has been misled by a curious coincidence and states that the "tumble-bug" is very injurious to vegetation. A field had been divided by a temporary fence, on one side of which cattle and horses had pastured in the autumn, while on the other side no stock had been feeding. On the side which had been pastured the corn crop was completely destroyed, while on the other side not a hill suffered. Tumble-bug larvæ were found in abundance on the injured side, from which our correspondent arrived at the conclusion previously mentioned. The truth of the matter probably is that the damage was done by cutworms, and it is interesting to note that the uninjured side was fall-plowed while the injured side was not turned under until spring.

A Quarantine Decision in California.—We have already noticed the importation of *Chionaspis biclavis* from the Sandwich Islands into California upon orange trees and also the fact that, failing to rid the trees of the scale, the quarantine officers directed that the entire shipment should be destroyed. The owners commenced legal proceedings, as 60,000 trees were involved, and we learn from Mr. Coquillett that a decision has recently been rendered in favor of the quarantine officers, Judge McKinley directing that the trees should be destroyed immediately.

A Clothes Moth as a Museum Pest.—Mr. F. M. Webster, our Ohio agent, has sent us specimens of *Tineola biselliella*, which he has found eating into a collection of moths. The bodies of the larger moths were badly riddled. We had previously reared this moth from grain with *Gelechia cerealella*, on dead specimens of which it had evidently been feeding, and Dr. Hagen has recorded it as feeding upon insect collections. It attacks principally large-bodied Lepidoptera while upon the spreading boards, but has been carried through several generations on dried specimens.

The Box-elder Bug a Household Pest.—The Box-elder Bug becomes a household pest in winter time. Mr. J. W. Sommers, Wilson, Kans. wrote us under date of March 10 that his house contains large numbers of the bugs, which come out by the hundreds during the day and shelter themselves in the walls of the building at night. An Oregon correspondent had previously reported the same fact, adding the information that they bite like bedbugs.

Importation of Scale-insect Parasites.—Mr. T. D. A. Cockerell writes from Kingston, Jamaica, that in his studies upon bark-lice he finds that specific parasites are rare, although his rearing experiments have not been extensive. He explains this fact theoretically on the ground that there is good reason to suppose that most of the Jamaica Coccids, especially those upon cultivated plants, reached the island within comparatively recent times and many of them probably by human agencies. The parasites would very likely have failed to be introduced at the same time as their host and the probability of the occurrence of native parasites ready to attack scales would be less than in the case of a continent like North America.

The Bite of the Katipo.—Another instance of the bite of the New Zealand Katipo comes to us from Mr. R. Allen Wight under date of February 3. An intelligent man from the seacoast, and to whose statement Mr. Wight gives great weight, induced a yellow-spotted Katipo to bite one of his dogs upon the nose. The dog died in four hours.

Hop Aphis Remedies.—With regard to the comparative value of the quassia solution and the kerosene emulsion for the Hop Plant-louse mentioned elsewhere in this number, Mr. Springer Goes, of Richfield Springs, N. Y., has just written us that although he has not had occasion to use either of these mixtures since 1887, on account of the fact that the lice have done little damage in central New York, he is convinced from his own experience in that year that the kerosene emulsion is superior to the quassia wash when properly prepared and sufficiently diluted. As Mr. Goes is a practical hop-grower, and with his father works the largest hop yards in central New York, his evidence must carry great weight.

Early Appearance of Haltica carinata.—Mr. C. H. Rowe writes us from Malden, Mass., that on March 25, while the weather was quite cold and snow to the depth of six inches was on the ground, Mr. C. J. Tyler, of Georgetown, Mass., found *Haltica carinata* swarming upon his elm trees. It was evidently a case of mistaken instinct that tempted these little flea-beetles from their hibernating quarters at so early a date.

Oniscus damaging Plants.—The sow-bugs of the Isopod Crustacean genus Oniscus are occasionally reported as damaging living vegetation and we have previously recorded such damage to violets in the Southern States. Mr. A. R. Shattuck has recently sent us specimens which he found seriously damaging the roots of young rose bushes. The trapping system by means of slices of potato wet with Paris green or a thorough drenching of the soil with a dilute kerosene emulsion will be the best remedies against these creatures.

The Clover Leaf Weevil in Connecticut.—Mrs. R. H. Russell, of Stratford, Conn., informs us, under date of May 18, that the Clover Leaf Weevil (*Phytonomus punctatus*) is abundant in her vicinity. All of the species which she found, however, were affected by a fungous disease which has been very prevalent in regions infested by this insect. The locality, we believe, is new.

A deserved Honor.—We are greatly pleased to learn that the University of Heidelberg has conferred the degree of Doctor Philosophiæ Naturalis Honoris Causa upon our friend and correspondent, Baron Osten Sacken, who is well known for his studies of Diptera and particularly of the American fauna.

Cut-worms and Wire-worms.—From Mr. C. F. Barlow, of Canastota, N. Y., we received, in the early part of June, a number of specimens of cut-worms damaging onion fields, which proved to be *Agrotis messoria*. Similar damage by this same species we have treated in our Annual Report for 1885. Mr. Barlow also sent a number of wire-worms damaging his celery crop. These proved to be *Melanotus communis* and *Agriotes mancus*.

The Asparagus Beetle in New Hampshire.—Mr. C. E. Jaquith, of Nashua, N. H., has sent us specimens of the Asparagus Beetle (*Crioceris asparagi*). This is the first record of the occurrence so far north as far as we know.

Destructive Locusts Reported.—We learn from Garden City, Kans., the locality of the principal Kansas damage of last season, that the young hoppers are appearing in considerable numbers. We also hear from our correspondent, Mr. F. A. Swinden, Brownwood, Tex., and from one or two other correspondents in Texas, that local species are hatching out in considerable numbers in parts of that State. The species which seems to be most abundant is *Caloptenus differentialis*.

A new Peach Pest.—A correspondent in Goodison, Mich., reports that the Otiorhynchid species, *Anametis grisea*, is doing considerable damage to young peach trees in his orchard. The beetles, according to his statement, hide near the surface of the ground during the daytime and eat the bark and also the buds in places during the night. The same species was received in 1882 from Pewaukee, Wis., and was reported as doing similar damage to apple trees.

GENERAL NOTES.

ADDITIONAL NOTE ON THE SUGAR-CANE PIN-BORER.

We have considerable additional correspondence relative to the damage now being done by *Xyleborus pubescens* to the sugar-cane crop in Barbados, Trinidad, and St. Vincent, as mentioned in our last number. It seems that the insect was investigated to a certain extent by Mr. Herbert H. Smith in the Island of St. Vincent, and that Mr. T. D. A. Cockerell, of Jamaica, has also given some attention to the matter. Both of these gentlemen agree with us that the Xyleborus can not be the prime author of the damage to cane, the former considering that it only follows the attacks of the Larger Sugar-cane Borer (*Diatræa saccharalis*), while the latter thinks that it usually follows the work of a weevil (*Sphenophorus* sp.). This further correspondence has developed the interesting fact that the insect is by no means confined to the sugar cane, Mr. F. Carmody, the Government chemist at Port au Spain, writing us that it breeds in Mahogany, while Mr. H. Caracciolo, also of Port au Spain, has ascertained that the alarming increase of the insect is coincident with the recent and general change in the method of disposing of the crushed cane—magass or bagasse. Formerly, he writes us, it was the custom of planters owning sugar mills to burn this refuse, whereas recently they have begun to use it as manure. The scattering of quantities of this dead vegetable matter through the fields must afford a most appropriate nidus for the beetles, which doubtless oviposit upon it very extensively. Their very numerous offspring, developing at the time when the bagasse has become too decomposed for further oviposition, will naturally take to such canes as are weakened by the attacks of the other insects mentioned, or even to healthy canes. The resumption of the old practice of burning this refuse will undoubtedly cause a decrease in the number of the insects.

THE BLOOD TISSUE OF INSECTS.

Dr. William Morton Wheeler, of Clark University, Worcester, Mass., has just completed a series of three articles entitled "Concerning the 'Blood tissue' of the Insecta," in *Psyche*. The first article appeared in February, 1892, the second in March, and the third in April. The subject is one which has been comparatively little studied, and Dr. Wheeler has had a practically new field. Under the head of blood tissue he includes the following structures: (1) the blood corpuscles; (2) the fatty body proper; (3) the pericardial fatty body; (4) the œnocytes; (these four structures have already been classified as blood tissues by Wielowiejski, and to them Dr. Wheeler adds the following:) (5) the garland-shaped cord of Muscid larvæ, and (6) a peculiar organ found in the embryos and young larvæ of Blatta and Xiphidium, called by Dr. Wheeler the subœsophageal body. The conclusions which he derives from his careful considerations of these six structures are as follows:

(1) The fat body of the Insecta is derived from the mesoderm—being a differentiation of portions of the cœlomic walls and therefore metameric in origin.

(2) The œnocytes are derived by delamination or immigration from the ectoderm, just caudad to the tracheal involutions. They are also metameric organs.

(3) They are limited to the eight trachigerous abdominal segments.

(4) They appear to be restricted to the Pterygota, in all the members of which group they probably occur.

(5) They give rise neither to the fat body nor to the blood, but represent organs *sui generis*.

(6) After their differentiation from the primitive ectoderm they never divide, but gradually increase in size.

(7) The blood corpuscles of these Insecta appear to arise early in embryonic life and perhaps also in post-embryonic life from undifferentiated mesoderm cells. The evidence of the derivation of the blood corpuscles from the fat body as such is unsatisfactory.

(8) The subœsophageal body arises in the trito-cerebral segment apparently from the mesoderm. Though it resembles the fat body, it must be regarded as a distinct organ. It disappears during larval life.

DAMAGE TO BOOTS AND SHOES BY SITODREPA PANICEA.

Two interesting cases of damage to boots and shoes have come to our knowledge almost simultaneously from two widely separated quarters of the world. Mr. Walter W. Froggatt, in Technological Education Series Bulletin No. 8, of the Technological Museum, Sydney, N. S. W., has given an account of the damage done in Sydney by the larvæ and adults of *Sitodrepa panicea* in trunks of imported boots. It seems that on the 7th of last October he examined five infested trunks and found that men's leather boots, ladies' kids, and carpet slippers were all attacked in the same manner. The method of work of the beetles seemed to be to riddle the soles with small transverse and vertical burrows; they also attacked the tips of the uppers and occasionally damaged the sides. So far as known all of the damaged goods were of English manufacture, and none of those from continental houses showed any signs of the pest. A Chalcidid parasite was also found, which, from the figure given, seems to belong to the subfamily Pteromalinæ. Treatment with bisulphide of carbon was recommended by Mr. Froggatt, who also urges that immediate measures be taken to stamp the insect out, on the supposition that it is a new importation.

Only a day or two after this little paper reached us we received specimens of the same insect from Mr. John P. Campbell, of Athens, Ga., with an account of almost precisely similar damage to boots in a boot and shoe establishment in that city. We recommended substantially the same measures which we had already proposed in a case of similar damage by *Dermestes vulpinus*, described in our Annual Report for 1885, and requested particulars as to the locality from which the boots were received. We have not yet been informed as to this point, and so far as we know this habit of the beetles is new to the United States.

Sitodrepa panicea is now a cosmopolitan species. It is something of a museum pest and breeds also in stored farinaceous products, becoming also somewhat of a pest in stored drugs of different kinds. It feeds, therefore, upon both animal and vegetable substances.

THE WEEVILS OF THE TERTIARY.

Mr. Samuel H. Scudder has published in the Proceedings of the Boston Society of Natural History (Vol. xxv, pp. 370–386) a preliminary notice of the tertiary Rhynchophora of North America. In his work upon fossil insects, he has discovered an unexpectedly large number of tertiary Rhynchophora, about 880 specimens having passed through his hands. More than half of them are from Florissant, Colo. Mr. Scudder has monographed the group, and his paper is now printing. The present paper is published by permission of the Director of the U. S. Geological Survey and contains the generalizations and summaries of the work minus the dry descriptive details.

NEW APPLICATION OF THE TERM "WIRE-WORM."

In this country the term "wire-worm" is almost universally applied to the larvæ of beetles of the family Elateridæ, on account of their lengthened cylindrical shape and hard, chitinous covering. Occasionally also it is applied to certain of the cylindrical Myriopods of the family Julidæ. In South Africa and the Australian colonies, however, we notice from recent colonial papers that the Liver Fluke (*Strongylus contortulus*) is known to stock-raisers by this same popular name of wire-worm. The matter of popular names is one of considerable importance to the economic entomologist, and all new names, however local, should be placed on record, with the proper identification, in some entomological journal. We invite correspondence in this direction.

FEATHER FELTING.

There is occasionally sent in to the National Museum or the Department of Agriculture a sample of the felting of bits of feathers into the substance of bed ticking or pillow casing which is said to have been done by some insect. This felting is frequently very beautifully done, and the inside of the cloth next to the feathers appears like a velvet tissue. Ordinarily the breaking up of the feathers which results in this felting is done by *Attagenus piceus*, a Dermestid beetle which is particularly fond of feathers. We have just received a very fine specimen from Lucy C. Eaton, of Truro, Nova Scotia, in which the work was done by *Tinea pellionella*, one of the commonest of the northern clothes moths. It must be remembered in these cases that the felting is not done by the insects, but by the mechanical action of the feather barbules themselves. When the feathers have once become broken up into small bits by the action of the insects, then through the constant pressing together of the pillow they gradually work themselves into the cloth covering in which they are held by their microscopic retrorse serrations. To one who looks at a fine specimen of this accidental felting there can not fail to come the suggestion that feathers could be commercially used in this way. The matter has been occasionally referred to in print, notably in the *American Naturalist* for December, 1882, and in INSECT LIFE, Vol. II, pp. 317-318.

DAMAGE TO CARNATIONS BY THE VARIEGATED CUT-WORM.

According to the *American Florist* of February 25, Mr. Edwin Lonsdale read a paper before the then recent meeting of the American Carnation Society, in which he described an interesting case of damage in a hothouse to the buds of carnations. The damage was done by the half-grown larvæ of *Argrotis saucia*. Four or five hundred buds were destroyed in one house in less than a month. By spraying with Paris green and by persistent search for the larvæ at night further damage was averted.

This is evidently another case of an introduction of cut-worms into a hothouse with new soil in the fall. It is a matter of great importance that new soil brought into hothouses should either be sterilized or that it should be procured in spring and left in heaps from which all vegetation should be carefully removed throughout the entire summer. By fall all cut-worms will have deserted the heaps and the earth can then be safely used. An instance of an almost precisely similar character has been brought to our knowledge near Washington and the source of infestation was clearly traced to earth taken in the fall from beneath sod in a pasture field which was badly infested with cut-worms.

A LARCH ENEMY.

In one of Mr. John G. Jack's interesting series of articles, entitled "Notes of a Summer Journey in Europe" (*Garden and Forest*, February 24, 1892, p. 87), he writes from Berlin that the European Larch is sometimes seriously injured and often killed by the larva of a little moth (*Coleophora laricella*), which eats out all the interior of the leaves, leaving only the dry, hard, shriveled epidermis. The introduced Japanese Larch, however, is not affected by the pest. According to Mr. Jack this same insect has been introduced into Massachusetts for a number of years, and its ravages have been sometimes quite noticeable in the Arnold arboretum. The Japanese Larch is also immune in this country.

HESSIAN FLY IN NEW ZEALAND

As we reported in Vol. I of INSECT LIFE, the Hessian Fly was first authentically determined as occurring in New Zealand in 1888. The locality in which it occurred was at that time somewhat restricted, but we now learn from the *New Zealand Farmer* of February last that the insect has spread, and occurs in a number of districts. Two annual crops of wheat are grown in New Zealand, and the article referred to anticipates that there will be three or perhaps four generations of the Hessian Fly in that colony. The remedies recommended in the third report of the U. S. Entomological Commission are summed up, and the Ministry of Agriculture is urged to print in concise form matter upon the life-history and remedies, and distribute it throughout the wheat-growing regions of the colony. This same journal in 1887 was strenuous in its warnings to the Department of Agriculture concerning the introduction of this insect in packing straw from Europe and America, but no precautions were taken. The source of the infestation is not known.

INCREASE OF THE WHEAT STRAW-WORM.

Recent reports from Lincoln and McPherson counties, Kansas, indicate that the Wheat Straw-worm (*Isosoma tritici*) has been on the increase for several years past. Many wheat fields in central Kansas were seriously damaged during the season of 1891 by this insect. As we have frequently pointed out, wheat growers are always able, by the sacrifice of one crop of straw, to effectually control this pest, as the great majority of the larvæ feed in the stalk above the point of cutting.

GREAT DAMAGE BY BUFFALO GNATS.

We notice in the *Iowa State Register* for May 15 a statement coming as a telegraphic dispatch from Louisville, Ky., dated May 8, to the effect that a report from western Kentucky estimates that 1,000 horses have been killed by Buffalo Gnats this year. It is likely that this report is exaggerated, but there is little doubt that the gnats are more abundant than usual this year. It will be noted again that this is a year of floods, and the old relations between the gnats and the overflow of the Mississippi River are sustained.

THE HOP LOUSE IN OREGON.

A strong defense of true scientific work has recently been made by Mr. F. L. Washburn, in the columns of the *Morning Oregonian* of Wednesday, June 1. In this article Mr. Washburn reviews the life-history of the Hop Plant-louse (*Phorodon humuli*) and handles without gloves the statements of certain hop growers who claim to have proved that the life-history of this insect as published by the senior editor is incorrect. An intelligent hop grower, Mr. T. D. Linton, of Eugene, Oregon, one of Mr. Washburn's correspondents, has followed the early generations on Plum with extreme care, and fully substantiates our published records. The publication of premature and unwise statements regarding supposed discoveries of other food-plants and other modes of hibernation than those which are normal to the species has done much harm in Oregon and Washington by inducing hop-growers to neglect the surest remedy and preventive, viz, the use of a few plum trees as a trap crop upon which the lice can be killed by spraying with kerosene emulsion in the spring before the damage to Hop has begun. Such published statements have done their harmful work for this season, but we hope that Prof. Washburn's able efforts and the corroborative testimony which he is bringing forward will do much towards clearing away these misconceptions and inducing proper remedial work another spring.

FOOD-PLANT AND NEW HABITAT OF THE MONTSERRAT ICERYA.

We recently received through Mr. H. Caracciolo, of Trinidad, specimens of *Icerya montserratensis*, which we described in INSECT LIFE, Vol. II, No. 3, from specimens received from Montserrat in the Leeward Islands. The type specimens, it will be remembered, occurred upon a species of Chrysophyllum and upon the Cocoa Palm and the Banana. The specimens just received from Trinidad, Mr. Caracciolo informs us, occur upon the *Clusia alba*, which they destroy.

A DISEASE CAUSED BY PARASITES IN THE EARS OF CARNIVORA.

We have received from the authors, MM. Railliet and Cadiot, a pamphlet extracted from the *Comptes Rendus des Séances de la Société de Biologie*, February, 1892, which contains an interesting account of their observations and experiments upon a parasitic disease of the ears in dogs, cats, and ferrets. It is known that certain Acarids—e. g., *Symbiotes auricularum*—dwell in the auricular shell and external auditory canal of animals, and cause the infested individuals to scratch violently; in one case, which came under their observation, the authors attributed to this cause the death, in violent convulsions, of a female cat. They conducted certain experiments with a view of ascertaining the possibilities of transmission of the disease from animal to animal, and found that "otacariasis," as the disease has been named by Neumann, is easily transmitted from diseased to healthy animals of the same species, but with more difficulty between the cat and the dog, and that it does not take place at all between the dog and the ferret. The insects were found in great numbers in the cerumen or waxy secretion of the ear, and in the experiments were transferred with the wax directly from the ear of the diseased individual to that of a healthy one. The treatment, where any is used, should consist in cleansing the ear with warm soapy water, followed by injections of potassium sulphate one-twentieth strong.

THE ITCH CAUSED AMONG CATS AND RABBITS BY SARCOPTES MINOR.

The question of the transmissibility of this disease of cats and rabbits has lately been investigated by M. A. Railliet, who gives the result of his researches in the *Comptes Rendus de la Société de Biologie*, April, 1892. The disease manifests itself by patches of a whitish eruption, mainly upon the lips, forehead, around the eyes and ears, and upon the neck of the animal, the mite causing the disease (*Sarcoptes minor* Furst) being found in vast numbers beneath the crusts of this eruption. The author's experiments upon the transmissibility of the disease were made by removing these crusts, with the insects beneath, from a diseased to a healthy subject. M. Railliet thinks it would be premature to draw from his experiments any fixed conclusions, and gives the following as the results of his investigations:

(1) That it was impossible for him to transmit the itch caused by *Sarcoptes minor* from the rabbit to other rabbits, or to cats, to rats, or dogs;

(2) That it is easily transmitted from cat to cat;

(3) That it is transmitted only with great difficulty from the cat to the rabbit; and

(4) That rabbits which have contracted the disease from a cat can transmit it to other rabbits.

FUNGUS DISEASE OF THE MIGRATORY LOCUST.

Apropos to the note on page 151 of the current volume, upon this subject, we have received from M. Brongniart, of the Museum d'Histoire Naturelle at Paris, a note in which he says:

It is a pity to let erroneous ideas persist on this subject. My researches—M. Giard to the contrary notwithstanding—show that the Migratory Locust (*Schistocerca peregrina*) offers several parasites. 1) Two forms of Botrytis, which kill the insects rapidly; (2) certain forms of Fasarium (= *Lachnidium acridiorum* Giard) which do not kill the insect; (3) the form Polyrhizium (Giard), which does not kill the insect, etc.

M. Giard and my colleague Künckel have not studied the forms Botrytis, and therefore conclude that they do not exist, yet Dr. Delacroix and I have clearly shown these destructive forms of Botrytis to whomsoever would look.

THE SALTBUSH SCALE OF AUSTRALIA.

We noticed, upon page 294 of the last number, Mr. A. Sidney Olliff's preliminary notice of a new species of Pulvinaria destroying the fodder-plant known as the saltbush, in New South Wales. In No. 3, Vol. III, *Agricultural Gazette*, of New South Wales, he devotes a full-page plate to this interesting insect, which he has named *Pulvinaria maskelli*, and gives a full account of its habits, with extended description of the species and descriptions of two of its natural enemies, viz. *Thalpochares pulvinariæ* and *Chrysopa ramburi* Sch.

A PROPOSED INSECTICIDE FOR TEA-BUSHES.

Mr. G. F. Strawson, in a letter to *Bell's Weekly Messenger* of October 26, proposes the use of a combination of benzine and naphthaline in the proportion of one part of the naphthalin to eight of benzine, for use against the insects which attack tea-bushes. The problem of an efficient insecticide for use upon this crop is a difficult one, since it must be nonpoisonous, inodorous, and tasteless, and must not injure the tender foliage. The experiments which Mr. Strawson has made with this compound show that it is efficacious against various forms of insect life, and that it evaporates so rapidly and so throughly as to leave the tenderest foliage unharmed, after a few hours leaving no trace of the application, either by taste or smell.

ANOTHER INSTANCE OF THE VALUE OF SPRAYING FRUIT TREES.

The good that may be accomplished by spraying fruit trees at the proper time, for the Codling Moth and Plum Curculio, is becoming very well understood, but we deem it advisable to occasionally mention instances in which the use of the remedy seems to have brought about exceptionally good results. Thus in previous numbers of the current volume we have given the experiences of Mr. J. S. Lupton, of Virginia, and Mr. W. F. Brown, of New York. The following note we take from the *Indiana Farmer* of February 13, 1892.

I sprayed all my fruit trees twice, and the result is that they are all loaded down with fruit and free from the Apple Worm. *There is not one in a hundred apples that is wormy.* I have forty apple trees and some pears, and I have to prop the trees up to keep them from breaking down. Most of my neighbors that did not spray their trees have no fruit but what is wormy. This is the first year I have ever had a good crop of apples.

A NEW INSECTICIDE.

We have seen a somewhat indefinite item in a recent number of the *Scientific American* concerning the use of monosulphide of potassium, which, it is stated, has been discovered by Mr. Dubois to be a cheap and effective insecticide. Experiments show that the hatching of locust eggs is prevented by a light sprinkling with a solution of this substance, while adult insects of several kinds have been quickly killed in the same manner. The substance, it is stated, acts as an excellent fertilizer for such plants as require potash. We publish this note simply as a suggestion to experimenters.

THE IBIS AS A LOCUST DESTROYER.

The Australian correspondence of the *Mark Lane Express* of March 7 has a paragraph relating to the value of the Ibis to farmers in the recent locust incursions of last year and the present. In the Glen Thompson district several large flocks, one said to number fully 500 birds, have been seen eating up the young locusts in a wholesale manner. Other insectivorous birds are flourishing upon the same diet. Recently near Ballarat Victoria, a swarm of locusts was noted in a paddock, and "just as it was feared that all the sheep would have to be sold for want of grass, flocks of starlings, spoonbills, and cranes made their appearance, and in a few days made so complete a clearance of the locusts that only about 40 acres of grass were lost."

A SCALE-EATING MOUSE.

The following is taken from a recent exchange. The scale-insect mentioned is probably *Lecanium persicæ*, and we see no reason to doubt the statements made:

The mouse has never been regarded with an eye of favor by the gardener, and certainly the mischief which it does is more apparent than any benefit it confers as a general rule. But it would seem that the mouse is distinctly useful on occasion, as the following, addressed to an English contemporary, clearly proves: "I was much surprised to see a mouse yesterday clearing the scale from a peach-tree trained against a wall under glass. It was very active, and during the ten minutes I watched it must have eaten 200 of these pests. It was too busy to notice me, though I stood opposite it and within a few feet. It would run over and under the smallest twigs, and fixing its hind feet for support would run its nose along the midrib of the underside of every leaf, and race up and down the stem searching for and devouring its prey without a second's pause. I left it as busy as I found it.

SPIDERS OF THE DISTRICT OF COLUMBIA.

Dr. George Marx has just issued author's extras of his presidential address, read before the Entomological Society of Washington, January, 1891, covering pages 148-161 of volume II of the Proceedings of that Society. His address is prefaced with a plea for the publication of local fauna lists on account of their great value in the study of the important subject of geographical distribution, and concludes with a careful seasonal and locality list of the spider fauna of the District of Columbia, tabling 160 genera, represented by 306 species.

ANNUAL MEETING OF THE ENTOMOLOGICAL CLUB OF THE AMERICAN ASSOCIATION FOR THE ADVANCEMENT OF SCIENCE FOR 1892.

WASHINGTON, D. C., *June 15, 1892.*

The Annual Meeting of the Entomological Club of the American Association for the Advancement of Science will be held during the meeting of that body at Rochester, N. Y., August 17 to 20, 1892, at such times as will least conflict with other features of interest to the members. The meeting of the Association of Economic Entomologists, which will be held at the same time and place, will add to the attractions for all interested in the Science, and it is hoped that members will make it a point to be present and assist in making the Rochester meeting a successful reunion of all the working entomologists of America. It is urged, also, that every member prepare a paper or papers for presentation before the club, furnishing the Secretary with the titles in advance, so that a preliminary program may be drawn up. As most of the members of the club are also members of the Association of Economic Entomologists, it is suggested that subjects relating to applied entomology be presented before the latter society, reserving for the Club matters of a more purely scientific interest. Systematic, biologic, or anatomical studies, together with collecting notes, are especially desired and appropriate.

C. L. MARLATT,
Secretary Entomological Club A. A. A. S.

ENTOMOLOGICAL SOCIETY OF WASHINGTON.

June 2, 1892.—The following names were presented for corresponding membership:
Proposed by Mr. Marlatt: Dr. S. W. Williston, Prof. F. H. Snow, Mr. V. L. Kellogg, Mr. Warren Knaus, Mr. W. J. Fox, Dr. Henry Skinner, Mr. F. A. Marlatt.
Proposed by Mr. Chittenden: Mr. Berthold Neumoegen, Mr. Edw. L. Graef, Mr. Ottomar Dietz.
Proposed by Mr. Mally: Mr. T. Wayland Vaughan.
Proposed by Mr. Howard: Prof. A. J. Cook, Prof. J. H. Comstock, Mr. M. V. Slingerland, Mr. S. H. Scudder, Mr. G. C. Davis, Miss Mary E. Murtfeldt, Dr. William M. Wheeler, Prof. C. H. Fernald, Prof. C. P. Gillette, Mr. C. F. Baker, Rev. W. J. Holland, Mr. Samuel Henshaw, Prof. P. H. Rolfs, Dr. J. A. Lintner, Mr. H. A. Gossard, Prof. G. F. Atkinson, Dr. C. M. Weed, Prof. F. L. Harvey, Prof. F. L. Washburn.

The persons named were duly elected corresponding members.

A new publication committee, consisting of Messrs. Marlatt, Banks, Howard, Schwarz, and Linell, was appointed by the President to take up the publication of the proceedings of the first six months of the current year.

Dr. George Marx presented the first paper of the evening, entitled "Remarks on two new publications on the Spiders of the United States, by N. Banks and Eugene Simon." After some preliminary remarks he contrasted the two papers, which cover practically the same ground, and one of which—that of Mr. Banks—was based on literature now out of date and written without the aid of type specimens, while the other was based on fuller knowledge, better command of the literature, and an acquaintance with the types. He gave an account of the writings on this group of Arachnids and deplored the conditions which led to the publication of necessarily incomplete and inaccurate work. Discussed by Messrs. Gill and Riley.

Mr. Otto Heidemann exhibited drawings of certain rare Capsids and pointed out some of the characters used by European authors to distinguish the species and genera in Capsidæ and showed their applicability to American species, illustrating his remarks with some very careful and artistic drawings of rare Capsidæ. He described also his method of making these drawings. Discussed by Messrs. Riley, Gill, and Heideman.

Mr. Howard presented a brief note upon Chalcidid parasites of Bark-lice, basing his remarks upon a paper published in the Swedish language by Christopher Aurivillius in the *Entomologisk Tidskrift* for 1888. Aurivillius concludes that these parasites do not interfere seriously with the economy of the Coccidæ, claiming that the females are pierced so late in life that the egg-laying is not hindered, while the males, when parasitised, are destroyed. Mr. Howard said that this state of affairs was the exception, as bark-lice are attacked by Chalcidid parasites at all stages of growth, and when once infested development is immediately arrested. A glance through the collection of Coccidæ in the U. S. National Museum easily proves this and shows that Aurivillius's generalization must have been made upon a very insufficient number of instances. Discussed by Prof. Riley and Mr. Ashmead, who fully indorsed Mr. Howard's position.

The society then adjourned to meet the first Thursday in October, 1892.

C. L. MARLATT,
Recording Secretary pro tem.

INDEX TO ILLUSTRATIONS.

Acalthoë cordata, Fig. 26, p. 220.
Bean Weevil, Fig. 42, p. 299.
Bruchus fabæ, Fig. 43, p. 301.
Carphoxera ptelearia, Figs. 6, 7, 11, pp. 109, 110, 112.
Cephus occidentalis, Fig. 15, p. 177.
Cordyceps chinensis, Figs. 24, 25, p. 217.
Corn stalk-borer, larger, work of, Fig. 3, p. 99.
Cratotechus sp., Fig. 19, p. 195.
Diabrotica 12-punctata, Fig. 5, p. 104.
Diatræa saccharalis, Figs. 2, 4, pp. 95, 101.
Dolerus arvensis, Fig. 13, p. 172.
Elachistus apilosomatis, Fig. 20, p. 196.
Elasmus varius, Fig. 39, p. 253.
Helia æmula, Fig. 8, p. 110.
Helia americalis, Fig. 10, p. 111.
Homalotylus obscurus, infesting Coccinellid larva, Fig. 17, p. 193.
Hypoderma bovis, Figs. 45, 52, 53, 54, 55, pp. 311, 315, 316.
Hypoderma lineata, Figs. 44, 48, 49, 50, 51, pp. 307, 313, 314, 315, 316.
Hypoderma lineata, diagram of spiny armature, Figs. 46, 47, pp. 311, 312.
Lead pipe bored by larva, Fig. 23, p. 202.
Leopard moth, Fig. 56, p. 317.
Lita solanella, Fig. 27, p. 239.
Lithocolletis, Figs. 16, 18, pp. 193, 194.
Mantid, Australian, cross section of egg case of Fig. 30, p. 244.

Minie ball gnawed by wood-boring larva, Fig. 1, p. 81.
Nematus marylandicus, Fig. 14, p. 175.
Panchlora viridis, Fig. 12, p. 120.
Pea Weevil, Figs. 40, 41, pp. 297, 298.
Podagrion mantis, Fig. 28, p. 242.
Praon, cocoon of, Fig. 21, p. 196.
Prodoxus coloradensis, Fig. 74, p. 374.
Prodoxus decipiens, Figs. 69, 70, 71, pp. 371, 372.
Prodoxus marginatus, Fig. 72, p. 373.
Prodoxus reticulatus, Fig. 75, p. 374.
Prodoxus y-inversus, Fig. 73, p. 373.
Pronuba maculata, Fig. 66, p. 368.
Pronuba yuccasella, Fig. 58, 59, 60, 61, 67, pp. 360, 362, 363, 365, 368.
Sphecius (speciosus), Figs. 32, 33, 34, 35, 36, 37, 38, pp. 248, 249, 250, 251, 252.
Stagmomantis carolina, Figs. 29, 31, p. 244.
Water-bug, Hydrobatid, undetermined, Fig. 22, p. 199.
Yucca aloifolia, flower fully opened, Fig. 57, p. 359.
Yucca angustifolia, mature pods, Fig. 68, p. 369.
Yucca filamentosa, Figs. 62, 64, p. 364.
Yucca, nectar apparatus, Fig. 65, p. 366.
Yucca pistil, section of carpel, Fig. 63, p. 364.
Zauclognatha minimalis, Fig. 9, p. 111.
Calothysanis amaturasia, Figs. 76, 77, p. 382.

ERRATA.

Page 94. under *Spermophagus robiniæ*, third line, the remainder of this paragraph, beginning "Eichhoff asserts," etc., belongs to the paragraph on *Micracis*.
Page 111, Fig. 9, and first line under the figure, for "*miniralis*" read *minimalis*.
Page 123. under "subfamily Ceraphroninæ," third line, for "*rawayana*" read *rerayana*.
Page 125, line 14, for "*Aleurodes.*" read *Aleyrodes*.
Page 130, below middle of page. for "*xanthhomelaena*" read *xanthomelæna*.
Page 162, lines 11 and 13. for "*Melitobia*" read *Melittobia*.
Page 162. line 17, for "*cementaria*" read *cementarius*.
Page 163. last line, for "*consor*" read *consors*.
Page 206. reply to second letter, for "*Spinx*" read *Sphinx*.
Page 207. line 4, for "*Arnarsia*" read *Anarsia*.
Page 214. signature of second article. for "Longuemars" read Longuemare.
Page 221. third line under second heading. for "*Hypomomeuta*" read *Hyponomeuta*.
Page 244, first line, *delete* "properly *mantidis.*"
Page 352. line 11. for "*Sylvanus*" read *Silvanus*.

AUTHORS' INDEX.

A.

Adams. Chas. C., letter. 393.
Aldrich, J. M., article, 67.
Allen, Harold E., letter, 270.
Allison. Henry, letter, 142.
Alwood. William B., articles, 58. 68.
Ashton. T. B., article, 206; letter, 271.
Atkinson. G. F., abs. arts., 31.

B.

Bagster, C. B., letter, 77.
Bausch. H. W., letter, 330.
Beach, Chas. C., M. D., letter, 396.
Bean. E., letter, 274.
Beckwith, M. H., abs. art., 42.
Benton. Frank, articles, 254, 319.
Bergroth, E., M. D., letter, 80; note, 321.
Berry, George W., letter, 206.
Bickford, L. F., letter, 146.
Bingham, R., letter, 278.
Bohl, Ed. V., letter, 206.
Bonelli, Daniel, letter, 145.
Boyle, Arthur, letter, 137.
Brown, E. Scott, letter, 146.
Bruner, Lawrence, article, 18; letters, 146.

C.

Caudell, A. N., letters, 133, 274.
Carroll. E. P., letter, 331.
Cheeseman, T. F., letter, 331.
Chittenden, F. H., notes, 344, 350.
Clark, Thomas R., letter, 77.
Cockerell, T. D. A., article, 380; letter, 333.
Collins, W. E., letter, 213.
Cook. A. J., articles, 62, 67; letters 139. 202.
Coquillett, D. W., articles. 260; letters, 76, 79, 206, 328.
Corbett, W. W., letter, 213.
Cotes. E. C., letter, 397.
Crawford, R. M., letter, 140.
Culver, Frederic F., letter, 78.

D.

Davis. Chas. A., letter, 215.
Davis, G. C., article, 64.
Dimmock, George, letter, 76.
Dodge, G. M., letter, 272.
Drew, Wm. L., letter, 396.
Dunn, G. W., letter, 278.

Dury, Charles, letter, 137.
Eaton, Alvah A., letter, 277.
Eisen, Gustav, article, 128.
Erkel, F. C., letter, 139.

F.

Farquhar, R. B., letter, 207.
Ferris, John, letter, 399.
Fetherolf, B. L., article, 207.
Fletcher, James, address, 4–16.
Forbes, S. A., article, 170.
Foster, Charles H., letter, 275.
Frierson, G. A., letter, 143.

G.

Garman, H., article, 182.
Gillett, B. B., letter, 147.
Goff. E. S., letter, 327.
Goldstein, M. A., M. D., letter, 275.
Gordon-Cumming, A. P., letter, 395.
Gossard, H. A. (and H. Osborn), article, 56.
Granniss, J. M., M. D., letter, 393.
Gushee, H. H., letter, 269.

H.

Hackenberg, G. P., letter, 331.
Hamilton, John, M. D., article, 129; letters, 268, 270.
Hassall, A. (with C. W. Stiles), article. 265.
Hastings, Gen. Russell, letter, 334.
Henry, W. A., letter, 141.
Henshaw, P. T., letter, 144.
Heyl, J. B., letter, 267.
Hickey, John B., letter, 136.
Hill, Edwin A., letters, 213, 277.
Hood, L. E., article, 266; letter, 330.
Hopkins, A. D., article, 256.
Horn, George H., letter, 137.
Howard, L. O., articles, 48, 95, 193, 253, 378.
Howard, L. O. (and C. V. Riley), editorial articles (unsigned), 122, 127, 198, 239, 242, 297, 321. 392.
Hunter, William N., letters, 132, 133.

I.

Irwin, W. N., letter. 140.

J.

Jamison, I. J., letter, 140.
Johnston, S. Welber, letter, 215.
Jones, A. C., letter, 217.
Jones, W. L., letter. 329.

415

K.

Kellicott. D. S., article, 35.
Kenedy, John G., letter, 328.
Kimball, John L., letter, 209.
Knaus, Warren, letters. 75, 142.
Knickerbocker, M., letter, 276.
Koebele, Albert, article, 385.

L.

Lamb, H. J., letter, 77.
Landreth, Burnet, letter, 212.
Larrabee, J. H., letter, 282.
Leeson, J. J., letter, 135.
Lever, J. W., letter, 332.
Lewelling & Co., Seth, letter. 396.
Longnemare, Emile J., letters. 273.
Lupton. John S., letter. 204.

M.

March, John, letter, 399.
Marlatt. C. L., note. 153.
Marlatt. C. L. (and C. V. Riley), article, 168.
Martin, T. E., letter, 269.
Maslin, E. W., letter, 394.
Mik, Joseph, article, 113.
Mitchell, J. D., letter, 398.
Monell. J. G., letter, 212.
Morse, L. D., M. D., letter. 134.
Motte, Luke Smith, letter, 141.
Murtfeldt, Mary E., articles, 192, 200.

N.

Nesbitt, R. T., letter. 398.
Newkirk, I. N., letters, 273.
Noble, George, letter. 135.

O.

Ormerod, Eleanor A., article, 36.
Osborn, Herbert, articles, 49, 63, 187, 197; note, 224.
Osborn, H. (and H. A. Gossard), article, 56.
Owen, D. A., article, 327.

P.

Packard, A. S., M. D., article. 382.
Park, J. T., letter, 147.
Pearson, James, letter. 142.
Peirce, J. Dexter, letter, 80.
Perkins, G. H., article, 389.
Pierce, W. P., letter, 214.
Peyton, Mrs. R. E., letter, 139.
Pike, Mrs. C. H., letter, 334.
Pike, Nicolas, article, 317.
Pocock, Wm., letter, 395.
Pomarez, M., letter, 267.
Popenoe, E. A., abs. art., 41.
Pratt, Herbert J., letter, 397.

R.

Read, M. C., letter, 269.
Redding, R. J., letter, 204.

Richman, E. S., letters, 135.
Riley, C. V., articles. 32, 43, 104, 108, 119, 248, 302, 358; letter.
Riley, C. V. (and C. L. Marlatt), article, 168.
Riley, C. V. (and L. O. Howard), editorial articles (unsigned), 122, 127, 239, 242, 297, 321, 392.
Rolfs. P. H., letter. 398.

S.

Sahm, L., jr., letter, 203.
Schoyen. W. M., letter, 275, 310.
Schwarz, E. A., letter, 75.
Silva & Son, C. M., letter, 331.
Simpson, James W., letter, 210.
Skinner, J. O., letter, 395.
Smith, B. F., letter, 209.
Smith, James B., letter. 399.
Smith, John B., articles. 27, 30, 43.
Smiths and Powell, letter, 135.
Snow, F. H., article, 69.
Snow, T. N., letter, 80.
Southwick, E. B., article, 59.
Stewart, H., letter, 277.
Stiles, C. W. (and A. Hassall), article, 265.
Stiles, C. W., note, 280.
Stockley, George W., letter, 74.
Storla, T. O., letter, 203.
Strayer, J. S., letter, 79.
Sturge, Joseph, letter, 143.
Swineford, H., letter, 204.

T.

Taty, H. L., letter, 208.
Taylor, C. H., letter, 204.
Taylor, John, letter, 76.
Tepper, J. G. O., letter, 74.
Thurber, F. B., letter, 270.
Townsend, C. H. T., articles, 24, 25, 26.
Triplett, Frank, letter, 75.
Turner, W. D., letter, 203.

V.

Van Eps, George W., letter, 138.

W.

Walker, J. V. D., letter, 272.
Wallace, Paul, abs. art., 64.
Walsingham, Lord, article, 384.
Waters, George F., letter, 138.
Webster, F. M., articles, 121, 245, 262, 323; letters, 270; note, 291.
Weed, H. E., abs. art., 34; letter, 270.
Weir, J. Jenner, letter, 138.
Wickham, H. F., letters, 332, 333.
Wight, R. Allan, letter, 215.
Winch Bros., letter, 77.
Winn, Albert F., letter, 394.
Wood, Joshua, letter, 214.
Wright, W. G., letter, 271.
Wynkoop, E. H., letter 76.

GENERAL INDEX.

ABBREVIATIONS USED: Abs., abstract; art., article; descr., description; extr., extract; m. or men., mention; mm., mere mention; n. g. or gen. nov., new genus; n. sp., new species; ref., reference; rem., remarks; rept., report; rev., review; sp., species of; syn., synonym, synopsis.

Reviews and notices of agricultural experiment station publications are entered under the general heading "Experiment Stations," and not under authors or States.

A.

Acanthia, affinities of, 188, 189.
Acanthoderes decipiens, reared from maple, 65.
Acarids, in ears of Carnivora, 407.
Acarina, origin and development, 182.
Acid, uric, excreted by insects, 226.
Acoloides emertonii, n. sp., descr., 202.
 saitidis, reared from spider eggs, ref., 124, 202.
Acorn worm, a misnomer, 130.
Acridiidæ, not self-mutilating, 349.
Acridium americanum, habits and occurrence, 20.
 frontalis, on sorghum, 51.
 shoshone, in Nevada, 145.
Acroceridæ, parasitic on spiders, mm., 292.
Acronycta, smeared = Acronycta oblinita.
 oblinita, on smartweed, 132.
Adimonia cavicollis, syn. note, 94.
Adoxus vitis, in California, ref., 167.
Adrinus, nov. gen., ref., 350.
Ædilis nodosus = Acanthocinus nodosus, 132.
 obsoletus = Acanthocinus obsoletus, 132.
Ægeria pyri, on apple trees in Mississippi, mm., 34.
Agallia sanguinolenta, on grass, m., 198.
Agrilus, material in National Museum, 137.
 ruficollis, in New Jersey, 28, 29; ref., 232.
 torpidus, on willow, 66.
Agriotes mancus, damaging celery, 401.
 life-history, ref., 231.
Agrotis annexa, on Amarantus and cotton, abs., 31.
 messoria, damaging onions, 401.
 saucia, damaging carnations, 405.
 ypsilon, attacked by Hister, 76.
Agrypnus murinus, larvæ infesting a child, 158.
Alaus oculatus, on oak and aspen, 65.
Alcathoë caudata, 219, 220.
Aleochara, habits, remarks on, 27.
Aletia, see Cotton worm.
Aleyrodes, orange leaf, see A. citrifolii.
 citrifolii, smut fungus resulting from, 274.
 vaporarium, on strawberry in Kentucky, 345.
Allorhina nitida, also referred to as A. sobrina.
 dipterous parasite bred from, mm., 26.
 in New Mexico, ref., 92.
 on oak, 75.
 white grub of, 25.
Allorhina sobrina, in New Mexico, ref., 295.

Allygus irroratus, on grass, m., 197.
Alypia 8-maculata, in New York City, 61.
Amblyaspis minutus, bred from Cecidomyia, 124.
American blight, in India, ref., 296.
 plum borer, in Ills., report, ref., 293.
Amitus aleurodinis, bred from Aleyrodes, 125.
Ammophila gryphus, peculiar habits of, rem., 230.
Amphicerus punctipennis, habits of, 261.
Amphicosmus, n. g., ref., 158.
 elegans, n. sp., ref., 158.
Amphizoa, notes on, rem., 352.
Anabrus simplex, in Idaho, 146.
Anametis grisea, damaging peach, 401.
Anaplognathus sp., in cane field, m., 388.
Anarsia lineatella, suspected of injuring fruit trees, 206.
Anepsius, synopsis, 351.
Anguillulidæ, urine recommended for, 215.
Augoumois grain-moth. See Grain-moth.
Angus, James, collection of, 347.
Anisopteryx autumnata = pometaria.
 pometaria, occurrence in Cal. doubtful, 167.
Anomala pinicola = A. lucicola, 132.
Anopedias error, bred from Diplosis, 125.
Anomis erosa, in Jamaica, mm., 157.
Anthaxia æneogaster, on Juglans californica, 260.
Anthonomus musculus, so-called, on blackberry, 76.
 prunicida, types of, 358.
Anthomyia, Aleochara larva feeding on, mm., 27.
Anthomyia ceparum, in Sweden, ref., 2.
Anthrenus varius, injuring Cayenne pepper, 332.
Antiopa (butterfly), voice of, 166.
Antispila nyssæfoliella, on sour gum, 138.
Antistrophus 1-pisum, galls on Lygodesmia, 203.
Ants, black, enemies of gypsy moth, ref., 354.
 Chrysomelid larvæ in nests of, 148.
 leaf-cutting, remedies for, 328.
 red, carrying off Termes, mm., 146.
 destroying white grubs, 391.
 in California, 203.
 white, flight of, 146.
Ants' nests, bark-louse in, 158.
Apanteles, bred species, 259.
 congregatus, probably bred from Sphinx, 134.
 hyphantriæ, Elasmus atratus bred from, 254.
 limenitidis, parasite possibly bred from, 254.
 sp., infesting Gypsy Moth, 227.

417

Apate basilaris = Sinoxylon basilare.
Aphanogmus floridensis, host of, 123.
Aphelenchus sp., on Chrysanthemum, etc., 31.
Aphid, mites on, 212.
Aphides, in grass, mn., 198.
　Micromus insipidus attacking, rem., 352.
　on apple, etc., 44.
Aphididæ, host plants of, rev., 83.
　in Dr. Bos's compendium, ref., 149.
　life-history of, ref., 285.
Aphidius avenaphis, bred from Aphis mali, 259.
Aphids, honey dew of, rem., 230.
　unmotherly, 229.
Aphis, black, of peach, in Cal., ref., 167.
　corn-root, notice of article on, 285.
　early account of, 263.
　eggs destroyed by kerosene emulsion, 327.
　grain, confused with grain Toxoptera. m., 247.
　hop, in California, ref., 167.
　　quassia vs. petroleum for, 84, 342, 346, 355, 401.
　　trap remedy against, 406.
　remedies used against, m., 278.
　-lion, habits, m., 147.
　maidis-radicis, in Ills. report, ref., 293.
　maidis, early accounts of, 264.
　　in Ills. report, ref., 293.
　　on corn, 285.
　pastinaci?, on celery, 213.
　peach, in New Mexico, ref., 92.
　rosæ, Capsus capillaris feeding on. 160.
　woolly, in Australia, ref., 2.
　　in New Mexico, ref., 91.
　see also Plant-louse.
Apiomeris flaviventris, feeding on honey bee in California. 343.
Apion nigrum, on locust, 94, 131.
　rostrum, not on locust, 94, 131.
Apis mellifica, introduction of, 320.
Aporia cratægi, social, ref., 84.
Apple saw-fly. See Saw-fly.
Arachnida, not mentioned as beneficial in Dr. Bos's work. mm., 149.
　remarks on, 291.
Aradidæ, nearctic, paper on, rem., 352.
Army worm, in Jamaica. m., 157.
　wheat head, in Kansas, mm., 71.
　and saw-flies confounded, 173.
Arsenical poisons for Curculio, ref., 293.
Arsenical spray, addition of lime to, 331.
Arsenicals, against codling moth, good results from use of, 167, 204, 288, 409.
Arsenites, chemical tests of, rev., 88.
　experiments with, ref., 2, 284.
　historic notes on, 62.
　relative susceptibility of plum and apple to, 40.
Asaphes decoloratus, life-history of, ref., 231.
Ash borer, see Trochilium fraxini, 68.
Ashmead, W. H., rev. of generic synopsis of Coccidæ of, 150.
Asopia costalis, in ants' nests, mm., 112.
　notes on, 206.
　some studies of, art., 121–122.
Asparagus beetle, in New Hampshire, 401.
　twelve-spotted, in Maryland, 395.
Aspathinus ovatus, reported from Florida, 229.

Aspidiotus articulatus, article, 380–382.
　habits and habitat, 381.
　remedies against, 382.
　aurantii, from Tahiti, 213.
　ficus, in Jamaica, mm., 157.
　limoni, from Sandwich Ids., mm., 218.
　nerii, mm., 347.
　n. sp., mm., 214.
　palmæ, seems confined to cocoanut, m., 382.
　perniciosus, remedy, note on, 83.
　rapax, a general feeder, mm., 382.
　　from Sandwich Ids., mm., 218.
　　on peach, 399.
　rossii, Orcus spp. on, 289.
　sp., near ficus, from Sandwich Ids., mm., 218.
　species observed in Jamaica, 333.
Aspidisca splendoriferella, Elasmus bred from, 254.
Association Economic Entomologists, address of president, 4–16.
　attendance of, 1, 4.
　election of officers, 47.
　new members elected, 17.
　report of third annual meeting of, 4.
　revised list of members, 73.
Athysanus exitiosa, in grass, mm., 197.
　? sp., in grass, m., 197.
Atkinson, E. T., notice of article by, 282.
Atropos, affinities of, 188, 189.
Attagenus megatoma = A. piceus.
　piceus, abundant in Ills., 345.
　felting done by, 404.
Attidæ, distribution of, mm., 229.
Aulacizes irrorata, possibly feeding on grass, 197.
Australia, Koebele's trip to, 163.

B.

Bacveria, normal to digestive organs of Hemiptera, rev., 235.
Bacterial disease, of chinch bug, extr., 88.
　of corn root worm, ref., 293.
Bag worm, in New York City, 60.
Balaninus, popular names proposed for species, 130.
　caryæ, habits of, 93.
　caryatrypes = proboscideus.
　nasicus, habits of, 93, 130.
　obtusus, on hazelnuts, m., 130, 131.
　proboscideus, habits of, 93, 131.
　quercus, habits of, 93, mm., 130.
　rectus, habits of, 93, 130.
　　in "Can. Ent." v. III, pp. 137-8 = B. uniformis, 93.
　uniformis, habits of, 93, mm., 130.
Barbitistes serricauda, self-mutilating, 349.
Bark-lice, Chalcidid parasites of, 411.
Bark-louse, from ants' nests, 158.
　on LeConte pear, 397.
　oyster-shell, in Australia, ref., 2, 89.
　scurfy, in New Mexico, ref., 91.
Barnard's insect trap, account of, ref., 354.
Baryconus œcanthi, bred from Œcanthus, 124.
Bassus scutellatus, parasite of Diptera, nm., 48.
Bean beetle, spotted, in Colorado, ref., 355.
　Epilachna, in New Mexico, m., 26.
　weevil, see Weevil.
Beaver, parasite of, 394.
Bee, honey, death from sting of, 159.

Bees, at South Dakota station, 68.
  carpenter, hibernation of, rem., 352.
  how far do they fly? art., 319.
  valuable to fruit and seed growers, art., 254–6.
Bee flies, new genera and species, rev., 158.
Beetle larvæ, in intestines of child. 158.
Beetles, East India, catalogue of, notice. 282.
Bembecia marginata. supposed larva. on blackberry, 29.
Benacus griseus, at electric lights, 210.
  bite of. rem., 352.
Benzine, insecticide for tea-bushes, 408.
Bibionid larvæ found on snow, 336.
Bill-bug, corn. in New Jersey, 44, ref., 358.
  grain, in wheat, ref., 357.
Birds, destroying gypsy moth, ref., 354.
  destroying insects, 286.
  in India, ref., 296.
  tame, as insect destroyers, 278.
Bird lice, affinities of, 188.
Black ants, see Ants.
Blackberry borers, and gall makers. art., 27–30.
  crown borer = Bembecia marginata.
  midge = Lasioptera farinosa.
Blackbird. crow, as insect destroyers, 278.
Blastobasis sp., preying upon Chionaspis, m., 290.
Blastophaga psenes, first introduction of, into Cal., 94, art. 128–129.
  relation to Smyrna fig, 374.
Blissus leucopterus, in Nebraska, 133.
Blister beetles, in Texas. 395.
  on cabbage, 77.
"Blood-sucking cone-nose," 273.
Blue bird, suggested remedy for red spider, 278.
Bogus Yucca moth = Prodoxus decipiens.
Boll-worm, early reference to, art., 326.
  in corn, in New Mexico, m., 26.
  in India, ref., 296.
  injury attributed to. due to other insects, m., 17.
  in Mississippi, m., 34.
  in Nebraska. 133.
  treatment of. 208.
Bombi, introduced into New Zealand, 157.
Bombyliidæ, new species of, rev., 158.
Boöphilus, genus erected for Ixodes bovis, 233.
Boots. Sitodrepa panicea damaging, 403.
Bordeaux mixture, as an adjunct in spraying with arsenicals, 238.
  experiments with, ref., 2.
  in combination with insecticides, 284.
Borers, notes on a few, art., 64, 67.
  on blackberry, art., 27.
  squash, habits and remedies, art., 30.
Bos, J. Ritzema. rev. of work of, 149.
Bostrychus jesuita, in Australia, ref., 294.
Bots under the skin of man, 275, 309, 310.
  See also Ox bot.
Box-elder bug, a household pest, 400.
  attacking fruit in Washington State, 273.
  leaf-roller, in Colorado, ref., 355.
Bracon. bred species of, 256, 257.
  sp., bred from Saperda concolor galls, 66.
  sp., Hylesinus aculeatus reared from, 66.
Braconidæ, characteristic cocoons of, 377.
  list of bred species, art., 256–259.
Bronzy cutworm, on snow, ref., 336.

Bruchus fabæ, art., 299.
  description of larva, 300.
  pisi, arts., 297, 392.
  in Colorado. ref., 355.
  rufimanus, injurious in Sweden, ref., 2.
  scutellaris, parasite, mm., 49.
  temperature of peas infested by. 160.
Bruner, Lawrence, notice of report by, 358.
Bryobia pratensis, on clover in Iowa, ref., 87.
Bud-moth, eye-spotted, injurious in Canada, 227.
Bud worm, injuring tobacco, ref., 287.
Buffalo gnats, damage by, 406.
  notes on, 143.
  moth. see Carpet beetle.
Bug, an interesting aquatic, art., 198–200.
Bugs, true, of Tennessee, rev., 224.
Bumble bee, in New Zealand, 157.
  and the production of clover seed, 334.
Butterflies, migratory movements of. rem., 230.
Butterfly, erroneously reported as having sold for $1,500, ref., 226.
  remarkable enemy of, 283.
Byturus tomentosus, on raspberry in England, m., 38.

C.

Cabbage caterpillar, remedy for, mm., 13.
  maggot, Aleochara larvæ said to breed in, mm., 27.
  Plusia, see Plusia.
  Plutella = Plutella cruciferarum.
  root maggot, late planting a remedy for, 13.
  worm, imported in Ohio, ref., 2.
Cacœcia argyrospila, in Colorado, ref., 355.
  rosaceana, parasite of, mm., 195.
  injurious in Canada. m., 227.
  semiferana, in Colorado, ref., 355.
Cacus œcanthi, bred from Œcanthus, 124.
Caddo, n. g., ref. to paper on, 229.
  agilis, n. sp., on Long Island, 229.
Cadiot, M., rev. of article by, 407.
Cænophanes, bred species of, 258.
Calandra oryzæ, in Miss. bull., ref., 293.
Calcium oxalate, produced by an insect, 226.
California notes, more, 343.
Callixenus damnalis, hickory, mites on, mm., 212.
Caloptenus bivittatus = Melanoplus differentialis.
  differentialis, ref., 323, 401.
  spretus, ref., 322, see also Melanoplus spretus.
  See also Melanoplus.
Calothysanis amaturaria, life-history, art., 382–384.
Calyptus tibiator, hosts of, 259.
Camnula pellucida, habits and occurrence, 19, 20, 22, mm., 23, 146, 323.
Camponotus mellens, Coscinoptera dominicana larvae in nests of, 148.
Canker-worm, fall, occurrence'in California doubtful. m., 167.
Canker-worms, in California, ref., 167.
Cantharides, mites among, 185.
Canthon, mistake about, 400.
Caprification of fig., 373, 394.
Capsidæ, new species, exhibited, 161.
  remarks on, 411.
Capsus capillaris, feeding upon Aphis rosæ, 160.

Carbon bisulphide, against Angoumois grain-moth, 207.
   use of, with vaseline, 228.
Carp, a remedy for mosquitoes, 223.
Carpet beetles, in Illinois, 345.
Carphoxera, n. g., described, 112.
   ptelearia, note on. 271, 399.
      n. sp. art., 108–113.
      plants infested by, list, 109.
Carpocapsa pomonella, Hydnocera scabra in cocoon of, 260.
Carpophilus pallipennis, in Mississippi, ref., 293.
Casey, Capt. T. L., rev. of article by. 350.
Cassida texana, on Solanum xanti, 262.
Catalpa Sphinx or hawk-moth=Sphinx catalpæ.
Cattle ticks, see Tick.
Case-moth, pine=Oiketicus huebneri.
Cecidomyia, larva of, found on snow. 336.
   destructor, early reference to, art., 324.
   rosaria, Elasmus reared from, 253.
Cecidomyiid, gall-maker on blackberry, 30.
   on Vicia sativa. 39.
Cecropia (moth), in New York City, mm., 61.
Centipede, poisonous qualities of, 147.
Cephus occidentalis. n. sp., notes on, 177–178.
   pygmæus, date of introduction, 344.
      in America, ref., 168, 344.
   sp. in California, ref., 169.
Cerambycid larvae, dorsal appendages of, 352.
Cerambycidæ, new species and genera in, ref., 350.
Ceratitis citriperda, on Mediterranean orange, ref., 288.
Cerchysius, characters of genus, 379.
   iceryæ, bred from Icerya rosæ, 378.
Cerocephala pityophthori, host of. 123.
   scolytivora, host of, 122.
Ceroplastes, observed in Jamaica, 333.
   floridensis on LeConte pear, 397.
   ceriferus, in India, ref., 296.
Ceroplatymerus caryæ, bred from Cecidomyiid gall, 125.
Chætocnema pulicaria, in grass, mm., 198.
Chaitophorus viminalis in Wyoming, ref., 90.
Chalcidid, bred from gypsy moth, ref., 354.
   notes on. 49.
Chalcididæ, effort to introduce, m., 163.
   methods of pupation, art., 193–196.
Chalcidids, parasitic on bark-lice, rem., 411.
Chalcid fly, as a household pest, 393.
Chalcids, on Phytoptus ribis, m., 38.
Chalybion cœruleum, Melittobia reared from cells of, mm., 162.
Chambers's Index, steps towards a revision of, art., 384–385.
Chauliognathus, larvæ of, found on snow, 336.
Cheimatobia, female at light, 287.
   brumata, injurious in Sweden, ref., 2.
Chemistry of insects, 226.
Chermes, on pine in New South Wales, ref., 89.
Cheyletus, habits and affinities. 185.
Chilo infuscatellus, on sugar-cane, ref., 96, 102.
   possibly in India, 397.
   saccharalis, article on. 95–103.
      distribution, remarks, 25.
      in New Mexico, art., 24, 103.
      in Mississippi and Louisiana, 103.

Chilocorus bivulnerus, attempt to introduce, in Honolulu, mm., 163.
China berries, against grain moths, ref., 293.
Chinch bug, bacterial diseases of, art., 69–71, 88, 235, ref., 292, rev. 354.
   estimates of damage done by, 12.
   falsæ. in Wyoming, 140.
   in Nebraska. 133.
   kerosene emulsion against, 141.
   on corn in Mississippi, mm., 34.
Chionaspis. found in Jamaica, 333.
   biclavis, from Sandwich Ids., 218, 400.
      from Tahiti, 213.
   citri, Blastobasis, a remedy for, 290.
      from Trinidad, mm., 214.
      in Florida, 274.
   orange, see C. citri.
   spp., Orcus preying on, m., 289.
Chlorops tæniopus, in Sweden, ref., 2.
Chramesus icoriæ, biological notes on, 268.
Christmas beetle, in cane fields, m., 388.
Chrotoma, nov. gen., 350.
Chrysanthemum leaf miner, in New York, ref., 353.
Chrysobothris chlorocephala = scitula, 130.
   scitula, syn., 130.
Chrysocharis singularis, pupa of, 194.
Chrysomela pallida, subsequently described as Gonioctena pallida, 93, 94, 131.
Chrysomelid larvæ in ants' nests, 148.
Chrysomelidæ, food-habits of, ref., 230.
Chrysopa, habits of, 147.
   offensive odor of, 146.
   ramburi, enemy of Pulvinaria, 408.
Chrysophanus dispar, disappearance of, 138.
   hippothoë, C. dispar a local form of, 138.
Cicada pruinosa, fed on by Sphecius speciosus, 248.
   septendecim, old broods of, 141.
Cicadula nigrifrons, on grass, 197.
   4-lineata, in grass, 197.
Cigarette beetle, remedy, 165.
Cimbex americana, on willow, 132.
   parasites of, mm., 67.
Circular No. 1, criticism on, 83.
Cistelidæ, ref. to revision of, 350.
   ref. to synopsis of genera of, 351.
Citheronia regalis, injuring cotton, m., 160.
Cleonus, synopsis, ref., 351.
Clerid beetle, found in plush, 203.
Click beetles, remedies for, 269.
Clisiocampa americana, in New York City, 60.
   californica, C. sylvatica probably mistaken for, mm., 167.
   sylvatica, occurrence in California doubtful, m., 167.
Clothes-moths, as museum pests, 400.
   omitted in Dr. Bos's compendium, 149
   possible parasite of, 394.
Clothilla, affinities of, 188, 189.
Clover-hay worm in Ohio, ref., 2.
   notes on. 206.
   on the place of oviposition, 272.
   some studies of, art., 121–122.
Clover-leaf weevil, in Connecticut, 401.
   in western Pennsylvania, 270.
Clover root borer, in Ohio, ref., 2.

Clover seed caterpillar, art., 56-58.
Clover-seed midge, in Ohio, ref., 2.
  remedy for, 13.
Clover stem borer, misapplication of name, m., 92.
Clythra, in ants' nests in Europe, ref., 148.
Clythrini, myrmecophilous, 148.
Coccidæ, a generic synopsis of, rev., 150.
  Chalcidid parasites of, rem., 411.
  in Dr. Ros's work, ref., 149.
  observed in Jamaica, list of, 333.
  some species possibly beneficial, 381.
Coccophagus citrinus=Encarsia.
Cockchafer, fungous disease of, 281.
Codling moth, good results from spraying for, 167, 204, 288, 409.
  hair-worm parasite of, 140.
  in Australia, ref., 2.
  in England, ref., 294.
  in Mississippi bull., 90.
  in New Mexico, ref., 91, 295.
  Physianthus vs., 331.
  treatment of, 288, ref., 355
  varieties of apple affected by, 133.
Cœlinius sp. on Meromyza, 87.
Cœlocnemis californicus, on sycamore, 262.
Colaspis pallida=Metachroma pallidum, 94, 131.
Coleophora laricella, on larch, 405.
Coleoptera, aquatic, exhibited, 162.
  California, notes on habits of, art., 260-2.
  in National Museum, 137.
  new species of, 350-351.
  occurring in grass, 198.
Coleopterous larvæ, dorsal appendages of, 352,
  in cistern, 269.
  injuring corn in New Mexico, m., 25.
Colias philodice, destroyed by tiger beetle larvæ, 155.
Color of a host and its relation to parasitism, art., 265.
Compsomyia macellaria, treatment for, 275.
Comys fusca, parasite of Pulvinaria, 142.
Conocephalus ensiger, in February, 460.
Conorhinus sanguisuga, notes on, 273.
Conotrachelus cratægi, types of, 393.
Copidosoma, method of pupation, 193.
Copper carbonate, experiments with. ref., 2.
Copris carolina, mouth-parts of, rev., 356.
Coriscus ferus, in grass, m., 198.
Corn Crambid, notes on, abs., 42.
  root Aphis, in Ills. report, ref., 293.
  root plant-louse, see Plant-louse.
  root-worm, bacteriological disease of, ref., 293.
  estimated damage by, and amount saved from, 14, 15.
  rotation of crops a remedy for, 14, 15.
  stalk-borer, larger = Diatræa saccharalis.
  worm. in India, ref., 296.
Coruna clavata = Coryna.
Coryna, identical with Pachycrepis, mm., 196.
  clavata, pupation of, 195.
Coscinoptera dominicana, biological notes on, 268.
  myrmecophilous habits of, 148.
Coscinoptera vittigera, biological notes on, 268.
  probable larvæ of, in ants' nests, 148.
Cotesia flavipes, parasite of sugar-cane moth, 397.
Cotton Aletia, see Cotton worm.

Cotton, leaf-worm, in Miss., m., 34.
  stainer, new, in Jamaica, 346.
  worm, estimated damage done by, mm., 12.
  methods of controlling, 13, 14, 35.
  treatment of, 208.
Cottonwood leaf-beetle, in South Dakota, 67.
Cottony maple scale, see Scale.
Crambus caliginosellus, notes and remedies suggested, 42.
  on corn, 78.
Crane, as a locust destroyer, 409.
Cratotechus, pupation of, 194.
Craw, Alexander, rev. of pamphlets on California insects by, 167.
Cricket, camel = Stagmomantis carolina.
  cotton or white, on strawberry, corr., 276.
  southern, on strawberry, 276.
  western = Anabrus simplex.
Crioceris asparagi, in New Hampshire, 401.
  12-punctata, in Maryland, 395.
Crossidius, synopsis, ref., 350.
Crossocosmia, n. g., descr., 116.
  synonymy of, 116.
Crow, destroying locusts in Egypt, mm., 286.
Cryptohypnus abbreviatus, life-history, ref., 231.
Cryptohænus montrousiæ, feeding on Dactylopius sp., 290.
  importation of, 290.
Crypturgus atomus, = C. pusillus, 132.
Cucujidæ, Lyctus placed in, ref., 351.
Cucumber beetle, striped, expts. against, ref., 2.
  in Miss., ref., 90.
  successfully treated, 138.
Curculio. plum. arsenical poisons for, ref., 293.
  chip-trap process against, mm., 223.
  experiments against, ref., 2.
  in Mississippi, mm., 34; ref., 90.
  in Nebraska, mm., 133.
  in New Jersey. 45.
  spraying for, 238, 409.
Currant borer, imported, in Colo., ref., 355.
Curtice, Cooper, notices of articles by, 233.
Cut-worm, variegated, damaging carnations, 405.
Cut-worms, cabbage, in Ohio, ref., 2.
  damage by Lachnosterna attributed to, 132.
  damaging onions, 401.
  injuring tobacco, ref., 287.
  kainit against, m., 45. 269.
  on cotton, abs., 31.
  remedies for, m., 42, 399.
  tin can remedy for, 205.
Cycloneda sanguinea, successfully carried to New Zealand, 339.
Cyllene picta, mistaken for household pest, 396.
Cyrtoneura stabulans, in Colorado, ref., 355.

D.

Dactylopius citri, from Sandwich Ids., m., 218.
  herbicola, on grass, ref., 90.
  sp., on Acalypha, found in Jamaica, 333.
  sp., preyed on by Coccinellid. m., 290.
  spp., on orange. ref., 288.
Danais chrysippus, Hemisuga hastata feeding on, 283.

Dascyllidæ, supposed larvæ in cistern. 269.
Datana angusii. on walnut. 133.
   ministra. on apple, 133.
   (moths) in New York City, m., 60.
Date palm scale, insecticide washes for. ref., 296.
Deilephila euphorbiæ, apparently restricted to one species of Euphorbia, mm., 382.
   lineata, almost omnivorous, mm., 382.
Delphax ornata. in grass. 198.
Deltocephalus inimicus. in grass. m., 197.
   retrorsus. in grass. m., 197.
   sayi. in grass. m., 197.
Demodex. affinities of, 186.
Dendroides canadensis = bicolor, 130.
Dendrotettix longipennis. habits and occurrence, 20.
Dermestes vulpinus, damaging leather. ref., 403.
Dermestidæ, supposed larva destroying tussock-moth eggs, 222.
Dermestes. pupation under bark, mm., 48.
   vulpinus. and tobacco, article read at meeting Assn. Econ. Entom., mm., 48.
Diabrotica. Uropoda americana on. mm., 27.
   12-punctata. bacterial disease of. ref., 293.
      correspondence supposed to relate to. 270.
      habits and life-history of, art., 104–108.
      probable early account of, 264.
   longicornis, compared with D. 12-punctata. 105–107.
      estimated damage by and amount saved from, 14, 15.
      rotation of crops a remedy for, 14, 15.
   supposed larvæ, in Australia, 389.
   vittata. correction, 107.
      in New Jersey, 44.
Diamond-back moth in England. m., 39, rev., 236; ref., 294, 295.
Diapria. bred species, 126.
Diaspis pelargonii. found in Jamaica. 333.
Diaspis rosæ. notes on, 213.
   sp. on Capsicum, found in Jamaica, 333.
Diatræa crambidoides = D. saccharalis, 102.
   obliteratellus = D. saccharalis. 102.
   saccharalis, art., 95–103, ref., 397. note, 402.
      in India, ref., 296.
   sacchari, probable synonym of saccharalis. 103.
   striatalis, on sugar cane in Java, etc., 96. 102.
Dibolia ærea, occurrence in grass, mm., 198.
Diedrocephalus mollipes. in grass, m., 197.
Differential locust = Melanoplus differentialis.
Digger-wasp, larger, art., 248–252.
Dinocleus, nov. gen., ref., 350.
   synopsis. ref., 351.
Diplosis pyrivora. in New York State, 161.
   in New Jersey, 44.
   tritici, see also Wheat midge.
Diptera. captured by primrose. 291.
   reared from gypsy moth, ref., 354.
Dipterous grubs, under skin of man. 275.
Disinfecting imported plants, difficulty of, 218.
Dissosteira carolina. remark on, 42.
   longipennis, damage attributed to, due to Colorado potato beetle, m., 17.
      habits and occurrence. 18. 19. mm., 23, 52. 55, 72, 322.
      notes on recent outbreak of. abs., 41.

Dissosteira carolina, obliterata, occurrence, 19.
   spurcata, a form of D. obliterata. mm., 19.
Dolerus arvensis, larvæ of, 170, 171, 172.
   collaris, notes on, 170. 172. 173.
   fulviventris, on Equisetum ? mm., 169.
   gonagra on meadow grass, mm., 169.
   habits of British species. 169.
   hæmatodes, on Juncus. mm., 169.
      in Europe, mm., 169.
   larvæ of. 170.
   niger, on Festuca ? mm., 169.
   notes on genus. 169.
   palustris, on Equisetum palustre, mm., 169.
   parasites of, 178.
   resemblance of Pronuba to, 370.
   sericeus, notes on, 172, 173.
   unicolor = arvensis ♂, 172.
Dorcaschema nigrum. habits of. 130.
Doryctes erythromelas, breeding note, 259.
Doryphora 10-lineata, rare in New Mexico. 26.
Dragon-flies, correction to a note on, 80.
Drassidæ, distribution of, mm., 229.
Drasterius elegans, life-history of. 231.
   on corn, mm., 107.
Drepanosiphum acerifolii, mites on. 212.
Drugs, Sitodrepa panicea infesting, 404.
Ducks vs. potato beetles, corr., 76.
Dysdercus andreæ. damaging cotton in Jamaica, 346.
   suturellus, mm., 346.
Dytiscus marginalis. in gas-impregnated water, 160.

E.

Eacles (moth) in New York City, mm., 61.
Ear-worm, corn, see Boll worm.
Early references to injurious insects, art., 323.
Eau celeste, not safe to use in combination with arsenites, ref., 284.
Economic entomologists, fourth annual meeting of the association of, 351, 352.
Economic entomology, see Entomology.
Edema albifrons, injury by, in Michigan, 139.
Edwards, Henry, collection of, 286, 347.
Eel-worms, urine recommended for, 215.
Eggar moth, calcium oxalate secreted by, 226.
Elachista præmaturella, leaf-miner in wheat, 290.
   early reference to. 324.
Elachistus, pupation of, 195.
   cacœciæ, pupation of. m., 195.
   spilosomatis, pupation of. 195.
Elasmus, habits of, art., 253.
   albicoxa, habits of. 253.
   atratus, a secondary parasite, 134, 254.
   nigripes, habits of, 253.
   pullatus, habits of, 253.
   sp., primary parasite on Aspidisca splendoriferella, 254.
   tischeriæ, habits of, 253.
   varius, habits of, 253.
Elaterid larvae, in intestine of child. 158.
   said to injure sugar cane in N. S. W., 389.
Electric-light bug, 209.
Electric lights against insects. 318. 340.
Electricity against migratory locusts. 347.

Elliot, S. Lowell, collection of, 347.
Elm borer, see Zeuzera.
Elm leaf-beetle, bulletin on, notice, 237.
　in New York City, 61.
Emphylus americanus, in ants' nests, m., 162.
Encarsia citrinus, synom. of, m., 168.
Enchodes sericea, on aspen, 65-'66.
Encyrtus urocerus, characters of, 379.
Enicocephalinæ, a new sub-family, 352.
Enicocephalus, notes on, rem., 352.
　schwarzii, n. sp., rem., 352.
Enock, Fred., review of paper by, 234.
Entomological Club A. A. A. S., meeting, notice, 410.
Entomological commission, comments and corrections on 5th report of, 92-94, 129-132.
　classification, a curious bit of, 82.
"Entomological News," note on, 238.
Entomological Society of Ontario, annual meeting of, 227.
　of Washington, abstracts of proceedings. 161, 228, 229, 291, 351, 352, 411.
　work in Central Park, abs., 59-62.
　work, testimony concerning value of, 238.
Entomologist, Government, appointment of, 82.
Entomologists, economic, association of, see Association.
Entomology, at Leland Stanford, jr., Univ., 237.
　economic, benefit derived by public from researches in, 14.
　in England, notes on, art., 36-39.
　notes on, from South Dakota, 67.
　Mr. Fletcher's address on, 4-16.
　notes and index in, rem., 15, 16.
　experiment station publications on. see Experiment stations.
　outlines of (text book), rev., 1.
　popular, rev. of book on, 166.
　publications of National Museum on, 155.
　work in Mississippi, abs., 34.
Entozoa, Sarcophaga mistaken for, 340.
Ephestia sp., found in Cayenne pepper, 332.
Epicærus imbricatus, on apple, 77.
Epicauta lemniscata, on cabbage, 77.
　in Texas, 395.
Epichnopteryx helix, Elasmus reared from. 253.
Epilachna borealis, in New Jersey, 44.
　bean, in New Mexico, m., 26.
　corrupta, in Colorado, 355.
Episcopus ornatus, in grass, m., 198.
Epitragodes, synopsis of, ref., 350.
Epitragus, synopsis, ref., 350.
Epitrix subcrinita, on beans and tomato in Utah, 135.
Epizeuxis æmula, on dead leaves, 111.
Eriogaster lanestris, calcium oxalate a secretion of, 226.
Ermine moth on apple, 221.
Erythræus? mite on Aphid, 212.
Eucheira socialis, silk nests of, 84.
Euderces pini, correction, 132.
Eudioptis hyalinata, in Jamaica, mm.. 157.
Eufitchea ribearia, on gooseberry. 67.
Eulabis, synopsis, ref., 351.
Eulophine genera, pupation of, 194.
Eumenes fraterna, nest of. ref., 166.

Eunotus, remarks on, 291.
Euplectrus, Comstock's, mm., 195.
　? parasite on Dolerus, 178.
　pupation of, 195.
Eupogonius pinivora, apparently valid, 131.
　tomentosus, injuring apple, 43.
Euryischia lestophoni, parasite on Lestophonus ieeryæ, m., 254.
Euzophera semifuneralis, in Ills. report, ref., 293.
Experiment stations:
　Colorado bulletin 19, rev., 355.
　Cornell Univ. bulletin 33; rev., 231.
　Iowa, bulletin 14, rev., 87.
　Kansas, University of, report, rev., 354.
　Massachusetts, bulletin 19, rev., 354.
　Michigan, bulletin 38, notice, 357.
　Mississippi, bulletin, rev., 293.
　　bulletin 14, rev., 90.
　New Jersey, Agricultural College, special bulletin N, rev., 232.
　　bulletin 82, rose-chafer, rev., 2, 3.
　　bulletin 85, rev., 232.
　　repts. of entom. of, rev., 88, 352.
　New Mexico, bulletin 3, 91.
　　bulletin 5, ref., 295.
　Ohio, bulletin 2, Vol. I, second series, rev., 2.
　　bulletin 4, Vol. V, second series, notice, 357.
　　bulletin on wheat midge, rev., 91.
　Oregon, bulletin 14, notice. 237.
　　bulletin 18, rev., 355.
　Pennsylvania, bulletin 19, rev., 357.
　Tennessee, bulletin IV, No. 3, rev., 224.
　West Virginia, bulletin 21, rev., 294.
　Wyoming, bulletin 2, rev., 90.
Experiments in controlling insects, ref., 2.

F.

Fall web-worm=Hyphantria cunea.
False chinch-bug=Nysius angustatus.
Farmer's Bulletin No. 7, rev., 295.
Farm practice to control insect injury, rev.. 232.
Feather felting, note on, 404.
Fertilization of plants, art., 358-378.
Fertilizers to control insect injury, rev., 232.
Fig-leaf beetle=Galerucella semipullata.
Fiorinia camelliæ, found on Cocoanut in Jamaica, 333.
Fire-flies, swarming of, 85.
Fish, a remedy for mosquitoes, 223.
Flea-beetle, grape, in New Jersey, m., 44.
　grape-vine, in New Mexico, ref., 91.
　injurious, in Utah, 135.
　turnip, sowing between broods a remedy for, mm.. 13.
　wavy-striped. in Ohio, ref., 2.
Flea-beetles, in Oregon bulletin. ref., 355.
Flesh-fly, in human ear, 341.
Fletcher, James, testimony of, in regard to value of entomological work, 238.
Flies, destroyed by indigo bird, 278.
　disease of, 152.
Flight of bees, art., 319.
Fly, house, liver fluke not parasitic on, 291.
"Fly weevil," in Florida, 284.

Forbes. S. A., reviews of articles by, 88, 235.
 Sixth Report, rev.. 293.
Forest and shade-tree insects, comments and corrections, 92–94, 129–132.
Formica fusca?, Coscinoptera larvæ in nests of, 148.
 integra (rufa). Helia americalis in nests of, 111.
 obscuripes, Coscinoptera dominicana larvæ in nests of, 148.
 sanguinea. Emphylus americanus in nests of, m.. 162.
Fox. Wm. J., paper on digger wasps. rev., 83.
French. C.. "Handbook of destructive insects of Victoria " * " rev.. 1.
Fringilla cyanea, as an insect destroyer, 278.
Frit-fly, in Sweden. ref.. 2.
Foggatt, W. W., rev. of article by, 403.
Fruit bark-beetle, in Illinois. ref.. 293.
 fly, gooseberry, in Colorado. ref., 355.
 insects. bulletins on, rev.. 295, 355.
 on Mediterranean orange. ref.. 288.
 Syneta albida, a new pest of. 396.
 tree leaf-roller, in Colorado. ref., 355.
Fulgoridæ. on grass, 198.
Fumigating at night not necessary, 219.
Fungicides. combination with arsenites, 284.

G.

Galeruca gelatinariæ, mm.. 130.
 sanguinea = Adimonia cavicollis. 94.
 a European insect, 131.
 vittata = Diabrotica vittata.
Galerucella semipullata, on fig in Australia. 89.
Gall, Cynipid. on Lygodesmia, 203.
Gall makers, on blackberry. art.. 27.
Garman, H., rev. of article by, 339.
Gas treatment for scale insects. ref.. 296.
Gastrophilus equi, horse bot. ref.. 308.
Gelechia cerealella, in India, ref., 296.
 Tineola biselliella bred from. 400.
 in Florida, 284.
 in Mississippi bulletin. ref.. 293.
 treatment of, 207.
Geocoris sp., in grass, m.. 198.
Geophilidæ, notice of paper on. 155.
Germination of weevil-infested beans. art.. 301.
 peas. 298.
Giant root borer, see Prionus laticollis.
Giard, Alfred. review of article by. 281.
Gibson, W. H., review of book by, 166.
Glow-worms in caves in Tasmania. 223.
Glyciphagus cursor, among Cantharides. feathers, etc., nm., 185.
 prunorum. habits, 185.
 spinipes. among Cantharides. mm.. 185.
Gonioctena pallida, on poplar. mm., 94.
Goniozus cellaris, host of. 122.
 foveolatus, host of. 122.
Gortyna nitela, early reference to. art., 325.
Government work and the Patent Office. abs. art.. 46, 47.
Gracilaria theivora. in India. ref., 296.
Grain moth. Angoumois, in India. ref.. 296.
 in Mississippi. ref.. 293.
 in Pennsylvania, 344.

Grain moth in Florida. ref.. 283.
Grain weevil, red. in Miss. bull., ref.. 293.
 weevils, in Texas. loss from. 331.
 bisulphide carbon for, ref., 91. 207, 331.
Grape bags, use of. by wasps, art., 192–193.
Grapholitha interstinctana, art.. 56–58.
 on clover in Iowa, ref.. 87.
 destroyed by stacking hay. m.. 13.
Grapholitha schistaceana. on sugar cane in Java, mm.. 102.
Grapta sp.. in New York city. mm., 61.
Grasshopper, outlook, art.. 321.
 in California for 1892, 331.
 plague in Mich., 145.
 See also Locust.
Grasshoppers, destructive. losses by, and amounts saved from, 12.
 in Idaho, 140.
 in Iowa Bull., ref.. 87.
 in Ohio, 399.
Grossbeak, cardinal, eating potato beetle, 278.
Ground beetle, is it herbivorons? 330.
 as destroyer of peach-tree borers, 204.
Gryllidæ, not self-mutilating, 349.
Gryllus sp., destructive to strawberry, 276.
Grypotes unicolor, doubtfully a grass feeder. 198.
Gypsy moth, disappearance of in England, 138.
 in Massachusetts bulletin. rev., 354.
 Japanese parasite of. 227.
 men., 319.
 reported from Maine, 220.
Gyropus. affinities of, 190.

H.

Hadena basilinea, in Sweden. ref.. 2.
 revision of subgenera of. notice. 155.
Hadronotus, bred species, 124.
Hæmatobia alcis, moose fly, 156.
 serrata, in South, 398.
Hæmatopinus, affinities of, 188.
 antennatus, peculiar structure of. 190.
 suis. peculiar structure of. 191.
Hair worm. parasite of codling moth, 140.
Haltica alni = H. bimarginata, 131.
 carinata. early appearance of. 401.
 foliacea, on grape, 135, 136.
Halticus minutus, ref. to article on. 340.
Hargitt, Charles W., change of location. 228.
 kerosene and pyrethrum against, rem.. 33.
Harlequin bug. in Mississippi, mm.. 34.
Harpalus pennsylvanicus, said to destroy Colorado potato beetle. 204.
Harvest fly. dogday. fed upon by Sphecius speciosus. 248.
Heel fly, see Ox bot and Hypoderma lineata.
Heider, and Korshelt. rev. of work. 280.
Helcon. bred species, 259.
Helia æmula, on dead leaves. 111.
 (Epizeuxis) americalis. in Formica nests. 111.
Heliodines bella, notes on. 384.
 extraneella, notes on, 385.
 notes on species of art., 384–385.
 sexpunctella, sp. n.. description, 385.
 tripunctella, sp. n., description, 384.
 unipunctella. sp. n.. description. 385.

Heliothis armigera, early reference to, art., 326.
 in corn in New Mexico, m., 26.
 in India, ref., 296.
 mm., 287.
Hemidiptera, mm., 321.
Hemiptera, bacteria normal to digestive organs of, rev., 235.
 development of wings in apterous forms, 154.
Hemisuga hastata, feeding on Danais chrysippus. 283.
Heptagenia maculipennis, types of, 393.
Herbarium, new pest of, art., 108–113.
 pest, ref., 162. note, 309.
Hermatobates, mm., 321.
Hermia protumnosalis, syn., 228.
Hessian fly, early reference to, art., 324.
 importation of parasite from Europe, art., 179.
 in Illinois, report, ref., 293.
 in Kansas, mm., 71.
 in New Zealand, 405.
 late sowing a remedy for, mm., 13.
 life-history of, rev., 234.
Heterocampa manteo, Ammophila ovipositing in, m., 230.
 subalbicans = H. manteo.
Heteromera, new genera and species in, ref., 350.
Heteronyx sp., in cane fields, m., 388.
Heteroptera, of Tennessee, bull. on, rev., 224.
Heteropus ventricosus, probably mistaken for insect eggs, 263.
Hibernia, female at light, 287.
Hickory horned devil = Citheronia regalis.
 injuring cotton, m., 160.
Hippodamia, feeding on rust spores, mm., 35.
 convergens, identified, 135.
Hippodamia convergens, said to be an injurious insect, 34, 35.
 successfully carried to New Zealand, 339.
Hister 6-striatus, attacking Agrotis larva, 76.
Historic notes, some, art., 62.
Homalotylus, method of pupation, 193.
 obscurus, appearance of Coccinellid larva infested by, 193.
Homohadena, revision of, notice, 155.
Honey bee, effect of Paris green on, 282.
 enemy in California, 343.
Honey dew, of Aphides, rem., 230.
Hoplocampa testudinea, in England, 38; (?) ref., 294.
Hop louse, erroneously reported on celery and willow, 213.
 in the extreme Northwest, 342, 343.
 See also Aphis and Plant-louse.
Hopper dozers, experiments with, for grass leaf-hoppers, rev., 87.
Horn fly in Kentucky, 144.
 in Southern States, 276, 398.
 in Ohio, 35.
 in various States, treatment, rem., 35, 36.
 remedies for, art., 68, 69, 79.
Horn worm, on tobacco, ref., 287.
Horse bot, Gastrophilus equi, ref., 308.
House fly, Empusa disease of, 153.
 life-history of and remedies, 329.
Household pest, box-elder bug as, 400.
 Chalcidid as, 393.
 wood-borer mistaken for, 396.

How far do bees fly? art., 319–321.
Hydnocera scabra, habits of, 260.
Hydrazine sulphate, possibly a new insecticide, 161.
Hydrobatid, undetermined, art., 198–200.
Hydrometridæ, note, 321.
Hylastes glabratus, syn., 132.
Hylecœtus americanus = H. lugubris, 130.
Hylesinus aculeatus, Bracon sp. reared from, 66.
 sericeus, on Abies menziesii, 228.
Hylobius stupidus = Pachylobius picivorus, 132.
Hylurgops pinifex = Hylastes glabratus, 132.
Hymenoptera, parasitic, in National Collection, art., 122.
Hymenopterous parasites of spiders, rem., 292.
Hyperplatys, synopsis, ref., 350.
Hyphantria cunea, in Nebraska, mm., 133.
 in New York City, 60.
 parasites of, 133; m., 254.
Hypoderma bonassi, synonym of H. lineata, 303.
 bovis, compared with H. lineata, 315.
 in England, 39.
 infesting man, 275, ref., 310.
 not known in North America, 233, 316.
 diana, erroneously reported as infesting a child, ref., 309.
 infesting deer, mm., 310.
 not in Norway, mm., 275, 310.
 lineata and H. bovis, table of differences, 311.
 compared with H. bovis, 315.
 descriptive details, 312–315.
 ox warble of United States, 233.
 under child's skin, 310.
Hypomolyx pinicola = H. piceus, 132.
Hyponomeuta padella, damaging apple, 221.
 sp. on trefoil, 66.
Hypothenemus? on apple, 43.

I.

Ibis, as a locust destroyer, 409.
Icerya, killed off by Vedalia, 134.
 ægyptiacum, 349.
 montserratensis, food-plant and habitat of, 407.
 new parasite of, art., 378.
 purchasi, from St. Helena, 288.
 in New Zealand, 215.
 on Hymenoplea salsola, 160.
 reappearance of, in California, 161.
 Vedalia apparently confined to, for food, 154, 349.
 Vedalia n. sp., preying on, 289.
 rosæ, in Jamaica, 340, ref., 378.
Ichneumonid parasite on Dolerus, mm., 178.
Ichneumonids, bred from gypsy moth, ref., 354.
Idiobates, nov. gen., ref., 350.
Imbricated snout-beetle = Epicærus imbricatus.
Indian Museum notes, rev., 296.
Indigo bird, an insect destroyer, 278.
Injurious insects in England, art., 36–39.
Inostemma, bred species, 124.
Insecta, in Dr. Bos's compendium, ref., 140.
Insect, bacterial disease of, extr., 88.
Insect collections, of the American Museum, additions to, 346–347.
 damage, statistics, committee appointed to compile, 17.

Insect damage. unreliability of testimony of farmers, 17.
  diseases. mode of using. 152.
Insect diseases. of flies, 152.
  of Mediterranean orange. 287.
Insect embryology. notice of work on. 280.
  fungus drug, Chinese. 216-218.
  injury. farm practice and fertilizers to control. 232.
    to cocoanut palms. 267.
  larva. an intercalated stage. rem.. 351.
  larvæ in human ear. 159.
  lead-boring, 202.
  legislation in California. 337.
  -lime, against Psilura monacha. 162.
  parasites. ref.. 167.
  pests, in Bermuda. 267.
  trap. Barnard's. ref., 354.
  wax of India. ref., 296.
Insects, a plain talk about. 237.
  Australian. handbook of, rev., 1.
  beneficial. expeditions to import and export. 163. 289.
    in California. ref., 167.
  blood tissue of, 402.
  California. notes on, 134.
  chemistry of. 226.
  described by Walsh. 393.
  destructive. of California. rev., 167.
  disease of, 151.
  estimated damage in Canada. a correction. 226.
  estimates of damage done by. 11-15.
  forest, corrections to Packard's report on, 92.
  fortuitous variations of, 375.
  injuring tobacco, monograph of. rev., 165.
  injurious, early published references to. arts., 262-265. 323-326.
    electric lights against. 318.
    estimates of amounts saved from. 12-15. 23.
    estimates of damage by. m.. 358.
    in Colorado. rev., 355.
    in Queensland, bull. on. rev., 91.
    of fruit trees. in Oregon. ref.. 355.
    of Nebraska. 132, 133.
    of New South Wales. rev.. 89.
    of Sweden. rev., 2.
    of Utah. 74. 75.
    remedies for. ref., 167.
  interrelations with plants. art., 358-378.
  lead-boring. 81.
  losses caused by. relative, 17.
  of New York State, report on. rev., 353.
  on the surface of snow. 335.
  on tobacco in Florida. 287.
  popular lectures on, 237.
  popular work on. ref., 166.
  remedies consisting of modifications of agricultural methods, 13.
  United States species in Jamaica. 333.
  which burrow in stems of wheat. rev., 357.
"Insect Life." close of volume iv. 353.
Insecticide, a possible new. 161.
  apparatus. ref.. 167.
  machinery, art.. 58, 59.
    see also spraying machinery.
  mechanisms, etc.. patents on. abs. art.. 46, 47.

Insecticide. monosulphide of potassium as. 409.
Insecticides. against rose-chafer, 3.
  and apparatus. ref., 2.
  and remedies against Plutella cruciferarum, 236.
  in Mississippi. rei.. 90.
  used against wire-worms, 231.
Interrelations of plants and insects. art., 358-378.
Ipochus, synopsis. ref., 350.
  fasciatus, on apple. 262.
Ischnoptera pennsylvanica. or unicolor, possibly identical with Platamodes illinoiensis Walsh MS., 393.
Isorhombus arizonensis. bred from Cecidomyiid gall. 125.
Isosoma hordei, early reference to, 263. 323.
  tritici. in Kansas. 71. 75 m., 263, 406.
Itch, caused by Sarcoptes minor. 407.
Ixodes bovis. genus Boöphilus erected for. 233.
  remedies. rem., 35.
Ixodidæ, introduction to monograph of. 291.
  paper on. rem.. 162.

J.

Jack, John G., rev. of article by, 405.
Jassidæ, injuries caused by. 15.
Jassus 4-punctatus. Cicadula nigrifrons allied to, mm.. 197.
  6-punctatus. Cicadula nigrifrons allied to. 197.
Johnson. Walter B.. rev. of article by, 340.
Joint-worm, early reference to. art.. 323.
  in Ohio. ref., 357.
Julidæ, called wire-worms. 404.
Julus virgatus, injuring lettuce, 400.
June beetle. green. in New Mexico bull.. ref.. 295.
  See also Allorhina.

K.

Kainit. against underground insects, ref.. 91, 269.
  against wire-worms. ref., 232; mm.. 269.
  as insecticide, discussed. 42.
  successful against cut-worms and wire-worms, 43, 269.
Katipo, bite of, 161, 401.
Kerosene, an early use of. 332.
  emulsion, against chinch-bug. 141.
    against rose-chafer, 76.
    and pyrethrum, art., 32.
    an experiment with. art.. 63.
    Cook's history of. art.. 62.
    for plant-lice, ref., 87.
    for vine leaf-hopper, ref., 295.
    vs. quassia for hop plant-louse. 84. 342. 346. 355. 401.
Koebele, beneficial insects received from. 289.
  second trip to Australia, 163.
Korshelt and Heider. rev. of work by, 280.
Künckel. bulletin on locust by, rev.. 151.
Künckel d'Herculais. reported death of. 156.

L.

Labeo typhlocybæ. bred from Typhlocyba sp., 122.
Lace-wing, attempt to introduce in New Zealand, m., 163.
  malodorous, 146.

Lachnidium acridiorum, disease of African locust, rev., 151.
Lachnosterna arcuata, in Vermont, 390.
 dubia, in Vermont, 390.
 fusca, in Vermont, 390.
 grandis. in Vermont, 390.
 insperata, in Vermont, 390.
 notes on, art., 389–392.
 rugosa, in Vermont, 390.
 spp., injuring corn, 132.
 on apple, ref., 107.
 time of flight in, rem., 229.
Ladybird, South African, enemy of Icerya, 344.
Ladybirds, for California, from Honolulu, 163.
Lady bugs, see Ladybirds.
Lælius trogodermatis, bred from Trogoderma, mm., 122.
Læmobothrium, special structures of, m., 191.
Lampa, Sven, report of, rev., 2.
Lampronia rubiella, on raspberry in England, 38.
Lampronota frigida, reared from Nematus, 177.
Langlois, and Künckel, on locust disease, 151.
Lasioderma serricorne, remedy discussed, 165.
Lasioptera farinosa, on blackberry, ref., 232.
Latrodectus mactans, poisonous bite of. 267, 277.
Lead, bored by insect, 1., 202.
 -boring insects, 81.
Leaf-beetle, grape, in California, ref., 167.
 -cutting ants, remedies for, 328.
 -hopper, grape, in New Mexico, m., 27, ref., 91.
 in Colorado, ref., 355.
 note on, 142.
Leaf-hoppers, estimate of losses by and amount saved from, 15.
 grass, experiments against, ref., 87.
Leaf-miner, infesting sour gum, 137.
 in wheat, 290.
 on grape, m., 26.
 on Populus fremontii, 27.
Leaf-roller box-elder, in Colorado, ref., 355.
 lesser apple, in Canada, m., 227.
 oblique-banded, in Canada, m., 227.
Leather, damaged by Sitodrepa panicea, 403.
LeBaron, William, entomological writings of, 293.
Lebia grandis, an old enemy of Colorado potato beetle, 204.
Lecanium (?) dendrophthoræ in Jamaica, 333.
 hemisphæricum, in Jamaica, 157, 334.
 hesperidum, Australian ladybird feeding on, mm., 164.
 from Sandwich Islands, 218.
 on Mediterranean orange, 288.
 on pepper tree, 294.
 oleæ, found in Jamaica, 334.
 persicæ, probably eaten by mice, 410.
 in California, 347.
  Australian ladybird feeding on, m., 164.
  Honolulu ladybirds to be tried against, 163.
  type of Bernardia, m., 150.
 preyed on by Thalpochares cocciphaga, 290.
 sp., Comys fusca bred from, 142.
 sp., on Plumieria rubra, in Jamaica, 333.
Legislation against insects in California, 337–339.
Leis conformis, attempted introduction of, 164.
 commonest enemy of woolly root-louse of apple, ref., 164.

Leland Stanford, jr., Univ., entomology at, 237.
Lema sayi, on Commelyna virginica, rem., 229.
Leopard moth, European, ravages in Brooklyn, art, 317.
 trees affected by, 319.
 See also Zenzera pyrina.
Lepidoptera, collection of J. Alston Moffat. m., 227.
 in Dr. Ros's compendium, ref., 149.
 number of described species, 361.
 peculiar structures of, rem., 351.
 whose females are wingless. 287.
Leptocoris trivittata, attacking fruit, 273.
Leptoglossum phyllopus, on currants, 79.
Leptoterna amœna, in grass, 198.
Leptura nitens, synonymical note, 130.
 proxima, reared from maple, 65.
 zebra = L. nitens. 130.
Lestophonus iceryæ, Euryischia lestophoni a parasite of, m., 254.
Leucania albilinea, in Kansas, mm., 71.
 phragmatidicola, larvæ of, found on snow, 335.
 unipuncta, form asticta, occurrence in Jamaica, m., 157.
Liburnia sp. in grass, 198.
Lights, electric, against insects, 318.
Limax campestris, feeding on plant-lice, 348.
Lime, against Diabrotica vittata, 44.
Limenitis disippus, parasites possibly bred from, 253.
Limneria gracilis, enemy of Plutella cruciferarum, m., 236.
 œdemasiæ, parasite of (Edemasia, 207.
 pallipes, Elasmus atratus bred from, 25+.
 pallipes, in webs of Hyphantria, 134.
 tibialis, enemy of Plutella cruciferarum, 236.
Lintner, Dr. J. A., seventh report. rev., 353.
Liopus facetus = Lepturges facetus, 132.
Liotheidæ, affinities of, 190.
Lipeurus, affinities of, 188, 190.
Lita solanella, potato-tuber moth, art., 239–242.
Lithocolletis, appearance of larva infested by Copidosoma, 193.
 hamadryadella, ref., 194.
Liver-fluke, called wire-worm, 404.
 remarks on, 291.
Lixi, paper on food-plants, rem., 352.
Lixus, synopsis, ref., 351.
Locust, differential, ref., 323.
 fungus disease of, rev., 151.
 long-winged, habits and occurrence in 1891, 18, 19, 55, 322.
 migratory, occurrence, 20, 21, 23.
  fungus disease of, rev., 151, 408.
 non-migratory, in Nevada, 144.
 or grasshopper outlook. art., 321–323.
 pellucid, ref., 323.
 plague, Masicera pachytitis a parasite of, 89.
 ponderous, note on, 22.
 post oak, habits and occurrence, 20.
 red-thighed, notes on, 22.
 Rocky Mountain, ref., 322.
  occurrence, 20, 21.
 17-year = Cicada septendecim.
 two-striped, notes on, 21.
 See also Grasshopper.
Locusts, destructive, amount saved from, 23.
 birds destroying, 409.
 crops affected, 52.

Locusts, damage by, in 1892. 401
   estimated injury of. 53.
   in Kansas. 72.
   measures recommended. 54. 55.
   of North America, with notes on occurrences
     in 1891. art.. 18-24.
   parasites and diseases. 55.
   remedies against. 23.
   territory in Kansas affected. 52.
   in Egypt in 1891. 296.
   in Syria. 82.
   in Tunis. ref.. 296.
   migratory, electricity against. 347.
   native. note on. 23.
   of India, ref.. 296.
Locustidæ. disposed toward self-mutilation. 349.
London purple. injury to foliage by. 284.
   used against Fusicladium. mm., 45.
Longicorn borer in apple roots. 269.
Lonsdale. Edwin. rev. of paper by. 405.
Lophyrus rufus. in Sweden. ref.. 2.
Lordotus. synoptic table. ref.. 158.
Loxosceles, with only six developed legs. mm., 291.
Lucilia cæsar, Empusa disease of. 153.
   macellaria, treatment for. 275.
Luperina, revision of. notice. 155.
Lycosa viridicola. bite of. 280.
Lyctus, removed from Ptinidæ. ref.. 351.
   striatus on red oak. 65.
     habits of. 260, 261.
     synopsis. ref.. 350.
   Trogoxylon merged into. ref.. 351.
Lysitermus scolyticida. parasitic on Scolytus
   4-spinosus. 258.
Lygocerus. hosts of. 123.

M.

Macrobasis atrivittata. in Texas. 395.
Macrodactylus sp., on grapes in New Mexico, 26.
   subspinosus, in New Jersey, m.. 44.
Macroteleia floridana. breeding note. 124.
Magdalis olyra. misapplication of popular name
   of. 92. 130.
Mallophaga, in Dr. Ros's work. ref., 149.
   origin and development of parasitic habit in.
     art., 187-191.
Mantis carolina. in November. m.. 229.
   egg-parasites, a genus of. art.. 242-245.
   European praying. parasite of. 242.
   religiosa. self-mutilating. 349.
Mantispa. habits of. 60. 292.
Maple worm. green-striped. mm., 133.
Masicera pachytili. parasite on plague locust.
   ref.. 89.
May beetles. in Nebraska. 132.
Mealy bugs. parasitized by Leptomastix. 162.
Meat fly, in human ear. 341.
Megachile centuncularis. Melittobia reared from.
   mm.. 162.
Melandryidæ, note on habits of. 60.
Melanoplus atlanis. distribution. 21.
   in Idaho. mm.. 146.
   variation in. 21.
   bivittatus. in Idaho. mm.. 146.
     in Nevada. 145.
     notes on. 21. mm.. 23. 50. 55.
   devastator. notes on 21; mm. 22.

Melanoplus devastator, differentalis. in Nevada
   145.
   notes on. 22; mm.. 23. 50. 51, 52. 53. 393.
   femoratus. a form of M. bivittatus 22.
   femur-rubrum. notes on. 22; mm.. 23. 24.
   fœdus. in Idaho, mm.. 146.
   ponderosus. note on. 22.
   spretus, occurrence. etc., 20. 21. 23. 79. 80.
Melanotus communis, damaging celery. 401.
   life-nistory. ref., 231.
Melittia cucurbitæ. habits and remedies. art. 30.
   treatment of, 271.
Melittobia chalybii. bred from cells of Chalybion
   cœruleum. mm., 162.
Megachile centuncularis. mm., 162
   pelopæi. bred from dipterous imparia in mud
     dauber's nest, 134. 162. 229.
   habits of. mm., 229.
   synopsis of paper on. 162.
Melon worm. in Jamaica, mm.. 137.
Menopon. affinities of. 188.
Menopodon pallidum. habits. m.. 188.
Meraporus sp., bred from gypsy moth. ref., 354.
Mermis acuminata, parasite of codling moth. 140.
Meromyza americana, in Iowa. ref.. 87; early
   published references to. 263.
   occurrence in grass. 198.
   mites on, mistaken for eggs. 263.
Messa? marylandicus. see Nematus.
Metachroma. larvæ probably roof-feeders. m., 94.
   6-notata=Paria canella. 132.
   pallidum. syn. note. 94.
Metacosmus exilis, n. sp., ref., 158.
   n. g., ref.. 158.
Meteorus hyphantriæ, on Hyphantria. 133. 134.
Micracis aculeata, biological notes on. m., 131. 263.
   suturalis. biological notes on. 94. 131. 268.
Micrococcus insectorum. a remedy against Halticus minutus. 340.
   disease of chinch bug. ref., 68.
   expts. with, on chinch bug. 71.
   normal to digestive organs of Hemiptera. rev.,
     235.
Microdus simillimus. hosts of. 250.
Microgaster. cocoon clusters of. ref.. 166.
   spp., bred with Elasmus. 253.
Micromus insipidus. paper on, rem., 352.
Micropteryx calthella. remarkable larva of. 221
Minie ball. bored by insect. extr., 81.
Miotropis platynotæ. pupation of. 195.
Mite, clover. in Iowa bull.. ref.. 87.
   in Michigan. 1, 215.
   gall. of black currant. remedy. 38.
   orange rust. in Australia. ref., 294.
   pear-leaf blister-, in Australia. ref.. 2.
   rust. on orange. ref.. 288.
   spinning in Australia. ref., 348.
   useful. on beetles. 228.
Mites. mistaken for insect eggs. 263.
   on cats and dogs. 407. 408.
   on Lachnosterna larvæ. 390.
   on a maple Aphid. 1. 212.
   on Scarites subterraneus. mm., 27.
Monohammus confusor, injuring shoes. 77.
   lead supposed to have been bored by. 202.
Monophlœbus. preyed on by Thalpochares. 290.

Monosulphide of potassium, as insecticide, 409.
Monoxia guttulata, on sugar beet. ref., 237.
Moose fly, new Hæmatobia, 156.
Mordellistena, dorsal appendages of, rem., 342.
Mosquito, a vegetarian. 214.
   bites, insanity caused by, 86, 277.
   fishes a remedy for, 223.
   hibernation of, 277.
   larvæ as supposed internal parasites, 285.
   life-history of and remedies against, 329.
   twin-screw, 348.
Motheral, N. W., note on article by, 83.
Mouse, scale-eating, 410.
Mud-dauber's nest, Melittobia from, 134.
   wasp, Pteromalus puparum reared from cells of, 48.
Murgantia munda, on radish, m., 83.
Murtfeldt, Mary E., "Outlines of Entomology," rev., 1.
Myobia, characters of, m., 185.
Myriopoda, notice of paper on, 155.
Myriopods, called wire-worms, 400.
   injuring lettuce, 404.
Myrmica, bark-louse in nests of, note, 158.
Myrmicocela ochracella, in ants' nests, mm., 112.
Mytilaspis, Blastobasis a remedy for, 290.
   citricola, from Sandwich Islands, mm., 218.
      from Tahiti, 213.
      from Trinidad, mm. 214.
   in Jamaica, mm., 157, 334.
   no efficient enemy known, 143.
   doubtful if certain Florida species will thrive in California, 343.

N.

Nabis, occasional development of wings in, 154.
Naphthaline, insecticide proposed for tea-bushes, 408.
National Museum, entomological publications of, 155.
Nebraska, State board of Agriculture, report, notice, 358.
   University of, department of entomology, Bull. No. 1, rev., 83.
Necremnus sp., possibly parasitic on clothes moth, 394.
Necrobia rufipes, found in plush, 203.
Nectarophora liriodendri, paper on, 229.
Negalius, nov. gen., ref., 350.
Nematode leaf disease, 31.
Nematodes, parasitic on a spider, mm., 292.
Nematus aureopectus, = marylandicus.
   erichsonii, on hemlock, 219.
   marylandicus, notes on, 169, 174–177.
   sp., Ophion parasitic on, 179.
Neobernardia, n. nom. suggested for genus Bernardin, 333.
Nooclytus capræa, habits of, 131.
Nephelodes violans, larvæ of, found on snow, 336.
Neuroptera, resemblance of Pronuba to, 370.
New York State entomologist, seventh report, rev., 353.
Newspaper statement, evolution of a, 225.
Nezara hilaris, both carnivorous and herbivorous, mm., 158.
Noctuidæ, paper on, 155.

Noctuid larvæ, found on snow, 336.
   on sugar cane, 386–388.
Nops, remarkable spider genus, 229.
Nothrus sp., enemy of gypsy moth, ref., 354.
Nysius angustatus, in Wyoming, 140–141.

O.

Oak-bark weevil, misnamed, 130.
Ocneria dispar, disappearance of, in England, 138.
   enemies of, ref., 354.
   reported from Yokohama, 227.
Œbalus pugnax, enemy of grasses, 158.
Œcanthus bipunctatus, rare in Illinois, 393.
Œcodoma fervens, remedy for, 328.
Œdemasia concinna, parasitised by Limneria, 207.
Œdipoda obliterata Stoll., not Dissosteira obliterata, mm., 19.
Œstrus lineatus, = Hypoderma lineata.
   supplens, =Hypoderma lineata, 303.
Oiketicus huebneri, in New South Wales, ref., 89.
Olliff, A. S., articles by, rev., 89, 294.
Oncideres cingulatus, mm., 204.
Onion fly in Sweden, rev., 2.
Oniscus, damaging plants, 401.
Ophion sp., parasitic on Nematus, 179.
Ophryastes sp., said to injure fruit trees, 206.
Orange Chionaspis, see Chionaspis citri.
Orange, insect disease of, 287.
   new means against pests of, 155.
Orchard caterpillar, Paris green for, in England, 36, 37.
Orchelimum arboreum, not described, 393.
Orcus australasiæ, importation of, 164, 289.
   chalybeus, importation of, m., 164, 289.
Orgyia leucostigma, in New York parks, treatment of, 60.
Ormenis pruinosa, in Texas, 142.
Ormerod, E. A., fifteenth report, rev., 294.
   resignation of, as consulting entomologist Royal Agricultural Society, England, 156.
Orthesia occidentalis, n. sp., in ants' nests, 158.
   prælonga, found in Jamaica, 334.
Orthoptera, self-mutilation in, 349.
Oscinis sp., m., 263.
Otiorhynchus sulcatus, a hot-house pest, 222.
Owl, horned, Olfersia sp. on, 398.
Ox bot. in the United States, art., 302–317.
   rev. of article on, 233.
Ox warble, see Ox bot, Warble and Hypoderma.
Oyster-shell bark-louse, see Bark-louse.

P.

Pachycrepis, identical with Coryna, mm., 196.
Pachylobius picivorus, syn., note, 132.
Pachytilus migratorius, in Egypt, 286.
Palembus, nov. gen., ref., 350.
Palm weevil, see Weevil.
Palthis asopialis, on dead leaves, 111.
Panchlora (viridis), art., 119–120; ref., 102.
Paper wrappers, for cut-worms, 399.
Paracosmus insoleus, n. sp., 158.
Parasites, relation of, with host. art., 48–49.
Parasitic Hymenoptera, see Hymenoptera.
Paria canella, syn. note, 132.

Paris green. against orchard caterpillars. ref., 295.
   as insecticide. ref.. 296.
   effect of. on honey bee. 282.
   experiments with. refs., 2. 354.
   historic notes on. art.. 62.
   injury to foliage by, 284.
   methods of applying for cotton worm. 14. 35.
   use of. in England, 36, 37.
Parlatoria. Blastobasis a remedy for. 290.
   pergandei. var. crotonis. in Jamaica. 334.
   sp.. from Sandwich Islands, mm.. 216.
   sp.. on Acalypha. in Jamaica. 334.
Patent Office and Government work, abs. art.. 46.
Pea and bean weevils, art.. 297–302.
Pea weevil. first larval stage, art.. 392.
   in Colorado. ref., 355.
   remedies for, art.. 298.
Peach moth. Japanese, 341.
Peach-tree borer, in Miss., ref., 90.
   in New Mexico., ref., 92.
Pear midge, in New Jersey. ref., 358.
   in New York State. 161.
   slug. in Australia, ref., 2.
Pediculi, in Dr. Bos's work, ref., 149.
Pediculidæ, origin and development of parasitic habit in. art., 187-191.
Pelicot. P.. rev. of paper by, 153.
Pelopæus cementarius, Melittobia reared from cells of, mm., 162, 229.
Pemphigus populi-monilis, in Wyoming. ref., 90.
Pentastomum, origin and development in. 183.
Perimegatoma variegatum. proposed introduction in Eastern States, 346.
Periodical Cicada=Cicada septendecim.
Perisemus prolongatus, bred from Crambus caliginosellus, m., 122.
Petroleum rs. quassia for hop louse. 84. 346.
Phænopria hæmatobiæ. bred from Hæmatobia serrata, 126.
Phalæna saccharalis=Diatræa saccharalis. 95.
Phalangiides, ref. to paper on. 229.
Phanurus ovivorus, host of. 123.
Phemonoë 5-caudata, boring in persimmon. 332.
   remedies for. 332.
Phengodes laticollis, larviform female, m., 162.
Philopterides. affinities of. 190, 191.
Phlepsius irroratus. in grass. m.. 197.
Phlœodes diabolicus. habits of. 262.
Phlœothrips sp., enemy of gypsy moth. ref., 354.
Phorocera pumicata. ref., 115.
Phorodon humuli, in Northwest. 342–343. 406.
Phoxopteris comptana. notes on. 209.
   ref. to article on, by H. Garman. 339.
Phromnia marginella, in India. ref.. 296
Phycitid moth. attacking pecan. 78.
Phyllodecta vittellinæ, probably P. vulgatissima. 131.
   vulgatissima, on Salix longifolia. mm., 131.
Phylloxera. at Cape of Good Hope. remedies. 225.
   grape, in United States. 212.
      remedy suggested for. 269.
   in France. 224.
   vastatrix. at the Cape of Good Hope. 340.
Phymatodes dimidiatus, on oak. 65.
   juglandis. habits of. 261.
   varius, on oak. 65.
Physianthus rs. the Codling moth, 331.

Phytonomus punctatus. in Connecticut. 401.
   in New Jersey. 43.
   in western Pennsylvania. 270.
   killed by fungoid disease. 43.
Phytoptus, affinities of, 183.
   ribis, remedy for. 38.
Pieris destroyed by tiger beetle larvæ. 155.
Pimpla pedalis. bred from galls of Saperda concolor. 66.
   enemy of gypsy moth. 354.
Pithanus. occasional development of wings in. 154.
Pityophthorus sparsus, syn. note, 132.
Planchonia fimbriata, on Akee, in Jamaica, 334.
Plant bug. leaf-footed=Leptoglossus phyllopus.
   fertilization by insects. 157. art.. 254–256. 334.
   art.. 358–378.
   lice. destruction of. in egg state, 327.
   kerosene emulsion for, 87.
   Wyoming bulletin on, rev.. 90.
   louse, corn root, in Neoraska. 142.
      hop. remedies for. 84. 342. 346. 355. 401. 406.
      enemy. a new, 348.
   melon. injury attributed to. due to bacterial disease. mm.. 17.
      in New Jersey, ref.. 358.
   on celery. 213.
   parsnip. m., 213.
Plants and insects. interrelations of. art., 358–378.
Platamodes illinoiensis Walsh MS., possibly Ischnoptera. 393.
Platygaster, bred species. 125.
Platynota rostrana. parasite of. 195.
Platypsyllus castoris, on beaver skins, 394.
Plum borer. American. in Illinois. ref., 293.
   saw fly. see Saw fly.
Plums, dried, Glyciphagus prunorum among. 185.
Plum Curculio, see Curculio.
Plutella cruciferarum, damaging turnip and swede crops in Eastern Britain. 81.
   in England, m., 39; rev., 236.
   in Miss Ormerod's report.-ref., 295.
Pocota grandis. true male of. 86.
Podacanthus wilkinsoni. on Eucalyptus in New South Wales. ref., 90.
Podagrion mantis. parasite of Stagmomantis. 244.
   pachymerus. parasite of European Mantis. 242.
Podisus spinosus. enemy of gypsy moth, ref.. 354.
Pœcilonota cyanipes. on aspen and willow, 66.
Poison traps for cutworms. early use of, art.., 326.
Polistes rubiginosus. using paper bag for nest-building. art. 192–293.
Pollenia rudis, Empusa attacking. 153.
Pollinia costæ. appearing in California, 347.
Polygnotus, bred species. 125, 166.
Polymecus, bred species, 125.
Polyphenus (moth), ref., 166.
Polyphylla 10-lineata. mm., 350.
   synopsis of. ref., 350.
Potato beetle. Colorado. damage done by, attributed to Dissosteira. m.. 17.
   eaten by birds. m., 278.
   eaten by ducks, 76.
   in Georgia, 135.
   in Nova Scotia. 283.
   Lebia grandis an old enemy of. 204.
   rare in New Mexico, 26.
   -tuber moth. art.. 239–242.

Potato beetle, date of introduction of, 396.
  remedies for, 242.
Praon, pupation of, 196.
Prionus laticollis, supposed larva on blackberry,
  29, ref., 232.
Prionus spp. in New Mexico, ref., 295.
Proceras sacchariphagus = Diatraea saccharalis,95.
Proctotrypes obsoletus, bred from Stelidota, 126.
Proctotrypidæ, list of bred species of, 122.
Prodidomus rufus. rem., 230.
Prodoxidæ, descriptions of new species, rem., 351.
Prodoxus ænescens, markings of, m., 375.
  cinereus, markings of, m., 375.
  decipiens, account of, 371-372.
    associated with Pronuba synthetica, 372.
  larvæ, in all Yucca stems, 375.
  marginatus, markings of. 375.
  pulverulentus, markings of, m., 375.
  reticulatus, markings of, 375.
  sordidus, associated with Pronuba synthetica, 372.
  y-inversus, markings of, 375.
Pronuba, development and transformations, 368.
  correspondence on, 74.
  maculata, on Yucca whipplei, 367, 370.
  tongue of, 368.
Prodoxus spp. associated with, 372.
  maxillary tentacles of, 361.
  on special Yuccas, 371.
  ovipositor of, 361.
  pollination and oviposition, 363.
  structural characteristics of. 360.
  synthetica, associated with Prodoxus sordidus, m., 372.
    on Yucca brevifolia, 370.
    resemblance to saw-flies, rem., 352.
    yuccasella, associated with Prodoxus decipiens, 372.
  tongue of, 367.
Yucca dependent on, for fertilization, 360.
Prosacantha caraborum, bred from eggs of Scarites, 124.
Protoparce carolina, on tobacco, ref., 287.
Pseuocerus, synopsis, ref., 350.
Pseudococcus ruber, on Euphorbia in Jamaica, 334.
Psilura monacha, insect lime against, 162.
Psoa maculata, habits of, 260-261.
Psocidæ, affinities of, 188.
Psyche graminella, Elasmus reared from. 253.
Psylla, pear tree = P. pyricola.
  pyricola, habits and characters. 127.
    in New York, 225.
  pyri, habits and characters, 127.
  pyrisuga, habits and characters, 127.
  simulans, characters, 128.
Psyllas, three pear-tree, art., 127.
Pteromalus gelechiæ, in Miss. bull., ref., 203.
  puparum. not parasitic on mud wasp, 48.
  sp., secondary parasite of Hyphantria, 134.
Ptychodes. probably on fig., 204.
Pulvinaria innumerabilis, in Utah, mm., 75.
  maskelli. on salt bush, ref., 294, 408.
  sp., Comys fusca bred from, 142.
  sp., on Akee in Jamaica, 334.
Pyrethrum, kerosene emulsion and, art., 32.
  price of. rem., 33.

Pyrota. synopsis. ref., 351.
Pyrrhocoris. occasional development of wings in 154.

Q.

Quail, eating potato beetle. mm., 278.
Quassia. for hop louse, 84, 342, 346, 355, 401.

R.

Raillict, M. A.. rev. of article by, 407.
Raphidia in New Zealand. 339.
Raspberry beetle, in England, m., 38.
  bud caterpillar, in England. 38.
Rear horse, parasite of. 244.
Red-humped caterpillar, killed by parasites, 207.
  -necked cane borer—Agrilus ruficollis.
  scale, see Scale.
  spider, see Spider.
Reduviidæ, not including Enicocephalus, 352.
Rheumatobates rileyi. 321.
Rhizoglyphus, strictly vegetarian, mm., 185.
  supposed parasite on Lachnosterna, 390.
Rhodobænus 13-punctatus, food-plants of, 159.
Rhogas intermedius, bred from Acronycta americana. 259.
Rhopalophora, synopsis, ref., 350.
Rhynchites bicolor, injuring cultivated roses, 137.
Rhynchophora, tertiary, notice of article on, 404.
Rhynchophorus cruentatus=zimmermanni.
  palmarum, habits of, 136.
  zimmermanni on cabbage palmetto, mm., 136.
Rhyssalus pityophthori, bred from Pityophthorus, 257.
Rhysipolis biformis, breeding habits, 257.
Robinia pseudacacia, not a food-plant of Spermophagus robiniæ, 94, 131.
Rocky Mountain locust, see Locust.
Rodolia iceryæ, feeding on fluted scale in South Africa, 344.
Root-borers (Prionus spp.) in New Mex., ref., 295.
Root louse, woolly, of apple, 210-212.
  Leis conformis most important enemy of, 164
Root maggots, in New Jersey, m., 44.
  worm, corn = Diabrotica longicornis.
Rose bug, see Rose-chafer.
  -chafer, biological notes on. m., 3.
  in New Jersey, rev., 2, 3, m., 44.
  remedies for, 2, 3, 76, 84.
  species of, in New Mexico. m., 26.
Rose Diaspis, notes on, 213.
Rues, nov. gen., ref., 350.
Rumina decollata, destroying gardens in Bermuda, 334.
Rust mite of orange, in N. S. Wales. ref., 89.

S.

Saga serrata. self-mutilating, 349.
Saitis pulex, Acoloides reared from, ref., 202.
San José scale, see Scale.
Saunina exitiosa, remedies for, 43.
Saperda candida, parts of trees attacked, 43.
  concolor, on willow, 66.
Sarcophaga carnaria, in human ear, 341.

Sarcoptes minor, itch caused by, 407.
Sarcoptidæ, origin and development of parasitism in, art., 182.
Saturnia cynthia. ref., 115.
Saw-fly, apple, in England, ref., 294.
   European corn, in N. A., 168.
   European wheat, date of introduction, 344.
   larch, hemlock damage by, 219.
   on gooseberry, mm., 67.
   on sweet potatoes, 74.
   plum, in England, 38.
   wheat-stem, ref., 357.
   willow, injury by, 132.
   parasite reared from, mm., 67.
Saw-flies, remedies for, 179.
   resemblance of Pronuba to, 370.
   wheat and grass, art., 168-79.
Scale, black, exotic ladybird enemies of, m., 163, 164, 289.
   type of Bernardia, m., 150.
   cottony maple, in Utah, mm., 75.
   parasite of, 142.
   flat, Australian ladybird feeding on, mm., 164.
   on Mediterranean orange, ref., 288.
   Scymnids preying on, m., 289.
   Florida wax, on LeConte pear, 397.
   fluted, primary and secondary parasites of, m., 254.
   reappearance of, in Colorado, 161.
   on Hymenoplea salsola, 160.
   -insect, another imported, 347, 348.
   destroying saltbush, ref., 294.
   eaten by a mouse, 410.
   -insects, a new fumigator for, 328.
   argument against spraying for, 154.
   attempt to introduce enemies of, 163-164, 289.
   California, ref., 167.
   fumigator for, 328.
   from Tahiti, 213.
   from Trinidad, 213.
   gas treatment for, ref., 296.
   importation of parasites of, 400.
   infesting orange trees imported from Sandwich Ids., list, 218.
   long, doubt as to its thriving in California, 343.
   purple, from Tahiti, 213.
   from Trinidad, mm., 214.
   in Jamaica, mm., 157.
   no efficient enemy known, 143.
   thrives in California, 343.
   red, Australian enemies of, 164, 289.
   from Tahiti, 213.
   in California, ref., 167.
   killed by cold, 343.
   of Florida = Aspidiotus ficus.
   rose, notes on, 213.
   round, in Jamaica, mm., 157.
   saltbush, of Australia, 408.
   San José, in California, ref., 167.
   remedy, 83.
   West Indian rufous, art., 380.
   white, in Nebraska, mm., 133.
   white cottony, in Trinidad, m., 214.
   yellow, parasite of = Encarsia, m., 168.

Scarabæid beetles, time of flight in, rem., 229
   larvæ, on sugar-cane, 388.
Scarites subterraneus, is it herbivorous? 330.
   mites on, mm., 27.
   said to destroy peach-tree borers, 204.
Scelio, bred species, 124.
Schistocerca peregrina, fungus disease of, 151, 408
Schizocerus privatus, on sweet potatoes, 74.
Schizoneura lanigera, in India, ref., 296.
   in Utah, mm., 75.
   ladybirds feeding on, mm., 339.
Sciapteron tricincta, on willow, 66.
Sciara, gregarious larvæ of, 214.
Scirpophaga intacta, on sugar-cane in Java, 102.
Scolopendra woodii, poisonous qualities of, 147.
Scolytidæ, in Dr. Bos's compendium, 149.
Scolytid in apple twigs, 43.
Scolytus rugulosus, in Illinois report, ref., 293.
   4-spinosus, credited with work of Magdalis olyra, mm., 130.
Scorpion, whip, death due to, 278.
Screw worm, hominivorous habits of, art., 200-201.
   in Mississippi, mm., 34, ref., 90.
   treatment for, corr., 275.
Scudder, S. H., notice of article by, 404.
Scymnids, importation of, 289.
Scymnus collaris, identified, 135.
   New Zealand species sent to California, 163.
Semiotellus destructor, mm., 181.
   nigripes, importation of, 179.
Sericaria mori, uric acid excreted by, 226.
Sesia tipuliformis, in Colorado, ref., 355.
Sesiid pest of the persimmon, 332.
"Sharp Eyes" rev., 166.
Shelton, E. M., notice of paper by, 91.
Shoes, injured by Monohammus confusor, 77.
   injured by Sitodrepa panicea, 403.
Sialis infumata, resembling Pronuba, mm., 370.
Silk culture, note on, abs., 64.
   in California, mm., 337.
   insects of India, ref., 296.
   nests of social larvæ, 84.
   worm, Japanese parasite of, art., 113.
Silvanus cassiæ, in Miss. bull., ref., 293.
   producing heat, 352.
   surinamensis, in Mississippi, ref., 293.
   in Oregon bull. ref., 237.
Sinoxylon basilare, syn. note, 130.
   declive, habits of, 260.
   suturale, on grape, 261.
Siphonophora avenæ, in Illinois report, ref., 293.
   compared with Toxoptera, 247.
   sp. on hop in California, ref., 167.
Sitodrepa panicea, damaging leather, 403.
Sitones flavescens, in Iowa bull., 87.
Skunks, enemies of grasshoppers, m., 51.
Smith, Prof. J. B., European trip of, 227.
   rev. of article by, 356.
Snail, broken-tail, in Bermuda, 334.
Snow, insects found on, 335.
"Snake-worms," gregarious, 214.
Soldier bug, destroying gypsy moth, 354.
Sow bugs, damaging violets, 401.
Spalacopsis, synopsis, ref., 350.
Spalangia, hosts of, 123.

Span-worm, gooseberry and currant, ref., 355.
Sparrow, English, favorable view of, 153.
Spathius, bred species, 257.
Spermophagus robiniæ, not on locust, 94, 131.
Spermophilus 13-lineatus, parasite of, 147.
Sphænothecus, synopsis, ref., 350.
Sphecius speciosus, article on, 248.
Sphenophorus sculptilis, in New Jersey, 44.
   sp., Xyleborus pubescens associated with, 402.
Sphinx eremitus, on mints, 206.
   5-maculata ?, Apanteles bred from, 134.
Spider bite, death of infant from, 277.
   effects on child, 266.
   harmless, 279.
   poisonous quality of. 277, 398.
Spider, egg parasites, art., 202.
   red, birds a remedy for, 278.
      in Australia, ref., 2, 348.
      in California, mm., 337.
   resembling Epeira, m., 229.
Spiders, American, rev. of work on, 168.
   destroying gypsy moth larvæ, ref., 354.
   distribution of, rem., 229.
   Mantispa parasitic in egg-sacs of, mm., 80.
   Nematodes parasitic on, mm., 292.
   recent publications on, rev., 345, 410, rem., 411.
Spilosoma virginica, parasite of, 195.
Spoonbill, as locust destroyer, 409.
Spraying apparatus, see Insecticides, etc.
   Farmer's Bulletin No. 7, rev., 295.
   good results from, 167, 204, 205, 288, 409.
   machinery, in Miss. bull., ref., 90.
      standard fittings for, 58, 59.
   machine used in Central Park, 61.
   see also Arsenicals, etc.
Squash borer, life-habits and remedies, art., 30.
   remedies for, 138, 271.
   root-maggot, in Colorado, ref., 355.
Squirrel, ground, parasite of, 147.
Stagmomantis carolina, eggs of, 244.
   in November, m., 229.
   parasites of, 243.
Stalk-borer=Gortyna nitela.
   in wheat, early reference to, art., 325, ref., 357.
   larger corn, art., 95–103.
   see also Sugar-cane borer.
Standard fittings for spray machinery, abs., 58, 59.
Starling, as locust destroyer, 409.
State entomological report of Ills., 17th, rev., 293.
Stauronotus maroccanus, treatment of, m., 151.
Stenosphenus notatus, habits of, 130.
Stomata on Carya alba caused by Phylloxera, art., 327.
Strawberry leaf-roller, in Kentucky, 339.
   weevil, on blackberry, 76.
Straw-worm, wheat, increase of, 406.
Strongylus contortulus, called wire-worm, 404.
Sturmia (Crossocosmia) sericariæ, 116.
Sugar-cane borer, in India, ref., 296, 397.
   enemy, new West Indian, 342.
   insects in New South Wales, art., 385.
   larger, ref., 402.
   pin-borer, 402.
Sylvia domestica and sialis, suggested remedy for red spider, 278.
Symbiotes auricularum, in ears of Carnivora, 407.

Sympiezus, pupation of, 194.
Synchlora rubivorana, apparent occurrence in Jamaica, rem., 157.
Syneta albida, a new fruit pest, 396.
Synopeas, bred species, 125.
Syrphus flies, attempt to introduce in New Zealand, num., 163.
Systena tæniata, in grass, mm., 198.

T.

Tachina castellanii, 115, 116.
   oudji,=Ugimyia sericariæ, 115, 116.
   on grasshoppers, 51.
Tachinidæ, North American, ref., 350.
Tarantula. death due to, 278.
Tedinus, nov. gen., ref., 350.
Telenomus, hosts of, 123–4.
Tent-caterpillar, apple-tree, ref., 91, mm., 133.
   of forest, in California, ref., 167.
   of Utah, 74.
Tent-caterpillars, affecting honey yield, 139.
   treatment of, 139, ref., 354.
Tenthredinidæ, in Dr. Bos's compendium, ref., 149.
Tenthredo, joint-worm formerly supposed to belong, to, 323.
Tenthredo testudinea=Hoplocampa testudinea.
Teras minuta, injurious in Canada, m., 227.
Termes flavipes, in Washington, mm., 146.
   swarm of, ref., 146.
   morio, a flight of, 146.
Termitidæ, affinities of, 188.
Tetranychus near telarius, in Australia, 348.
Tetropium, synopsis of, ref., 350.
Thalessa, ovipositing, ref., 106.
Thalpochares coccipbaga, importation of, 290.
   pulvinariæ, enemy of Pulvinaria maskelli, 408.
Thamnonoma flavicaria, in Colorado, ref., 355.
   4-linearia, in Colorado, ref., 355.
Thelyphonus excubitor, death due to, 278.
   giganteus, life-history of, rem., 229.
Theronia melanocephala, parasite of gypsy moth, ref., 354.
Thesalia, nov. gen., ref., 350.
"Thousand legs," injuring lettuce, 400.
Thrips sp., on potato, in California, 79.
Thyridopteryx ephemeræformis, in New York City, 60.
Thysanoës fimbricornis, correction, 130.
Tick, cattle, remedies, 34.
   rev. of article on, 233.
Ticks, additions to paper on, mm., 292.
   American, introduction to a monograph of, rem., 291.
   histology of, rem., 351.
Tiger-beetle larvæ vs. Colias philodice, 155.
Tin-can remedy for cut-worms, 399.
Tinea pellionella, feather felting, 404.
Tineid larvæ fed upon by Hydnocera, 260.
Tineina, article on, 384.
Tinæola bisielliella, a museum pest, 400.
Tischeria solidaginifoliella, Elasmus tischeriæ a primary parasite of, 254.
Tmetocera ocellana, in Canada, m., 227.
Toad, horned, as a remedy for red ants, 203.
Tobacco against flea-beetles, 356.
   as insecticide, ref., 2.

Townsend, C. H. T., rev. of article by, 350.
Toxophora vastæ, n. sp., ref., 158.
Toxoptera graminum, reproduction of, 246; art., 245-8.
    grain,=T. graminum.
Tozzetti, A. T., monograph of tobacco insects, rev., 165.
Tree band, a new, 340.
    -borers, how to kill, 270.
Tribolium ferrugineum, in Miss. bull., ref., 293.
Trichacis, bred species, 125.
Trisholcus, bred species of, 124.
Tritoma californica, habits of, 260.
Trogoxylon, merged into Lyctus, ref., 351.
Trombidium bulbipes, parasite of gypsy moth, ref., 354.
Trypeta canadensis, on gooseberry, ref., 355.
Trypoxylon, N. A. spp. of, 83.
Tumble-bug, not injurious, 400.
Tussock moth, white-marked, enemy of, 346.
Twig-girdler, of fig trees, 204.
Tylenchus scandens, or tritici, on grass in Colorado, mm., 32.
Tylonotus bimaculatus, on hickory, 131.
Typhlocyba vitifex?, in Colorado, ref., 355.
Typhlodromus oleivorus, on orange, ref., 288.
Tyroglyphidæ, habits, affinities, etc., 185.
    probable origin of Sarcoptidæ, 183.
Tyroglyphus longior, in Miss Ormerod's report, ref., 235.
    sp., supposed parasite of Lachnosterna, 390.

U.

Ugimyia sericariæ, parasite of Japanese silkworm art., 113-119.
Uji=Ugimyia sericariæ, 114.
Underwood, Lucien M., change of location, 228.
Uric acid in Malpighian tubules of insects, 226.
Urine as a remedy for eel worms, 215.
Uropoda americana, on Diabrotica et al., mm., 27.

V.

Valenus, nov. gen., ref., 350.
Valgus, remarks on genus, m., 230.
Vanessa atalanta, appearance of parasitic pupa on, quotation, ref., 194.
    (butterfly) in New York City, mm., 61.
Vaseline, use of, with carbon bisulphide, 288.
Vedalia (cardinalis), apparently confined to Icerya purchasi for food, mm., 154.
    cost of expedition for importation of, ref., 226.
    exterminating Icerya in California, 134.
    in demand at Cape of Good Hope, 164.
    in New Zealand, 215.
    in South Africa, 336.
    international exchange of, 279.
    sent to Egypt, 349.
    n. sp., on Icerya purchasi, 289.
Veratrin, error corrected, 33.
Vine, see Grape.
    leaf-hopper in New Mexico, m., 27, ref., 295.
    -weevil, a hot-house pest, 222.
Vinsonia stellifera on Mango in Jamaica, 334.
Vrilleta expansa, on Quercus agrifolia, 260.

W.

Walking-stick, in New South Wales, ref., 90.
Wallace, Williamson, notice of, report by, 286.
Warble-fly, in England, 39.
    in Mississippi, ref., 90.
    remedies discussed, 40.
Wasp, caprifig, art., 128.
    paper-making, use of grape bags by, art., 192-193.
Wasps, destroyed by indigo bird, 278.
    digger, article on, 248.
    notice of paper on, 83.
Water-beetles in old gasometer, 160.
    -bug, found by Dr. Zabriskie, art., 198-200, 321.
    giant, 210.
Wax, insects producing, ref., 296.
Weed, Clarence M., notice of article by, 285.
Weevil, bean, art., 297.
    in New York report, ref., 353.
    remedy for, 90, 302.
    black, in Mississippi bull., ref., 293.
    flavescent clover=Sitones flavescens.
    grain (Silvanus surinamensis), ref., 237.
    -infested peas, temperature of, 160.
    palm, notes on, 136-137.
    pea, remedy, 90.
    pea and bean, art., 297.
    red-footed bean, in Sweden, ref., 2.
    rice, in dry hop yeast, 270.
Weevils, of the Tertiary, notice, 404.
Werner, Dr. Franz, rev. of article by, 349.
Wheat bulb-worm=Meromyza americana.
    fly, in Sweden, ref., 2.
    companion, ref., 357.
    midge, bulletin on, rev., 91.
    in Sweden, ref., 2.
    -stem maggot, ref., 357.
    straw worm in Ohio bulletin, ref., 357.
    See also Isosoma tritici.
Wheeler, W. M., rev. of articles by, 402.
White ants, see Ants, also Termes.
    grub, disease of, 152.
    fungus, European, 281-282.
    fungus of, ref., 217.
    of Allorhina, art., 35.
    grubs in Illinois report, ref., 293.
Whitehead, Charles, rev. of article by, 236.
"Wine bee," so-called Californian, 330.
Winter moth, injurious in Sweden, ref., 2.
Wire-worm, new application of term, 404.
Wire-worms, damaging celery, 401.
    N. Y. bulletin on, rev., 231.
    in Sweden, ref., 2.
    (or Diabrotica) on sugar cane, 389.
    remedies for, m. 45, ref., 269, 355.
Wood-borer, mistaken for household pest, 396.
Woolly Aphis or root Aphis=Schizoneura lanigera. See also Aphis.

X.

Xyphidium longicaudum, not described, 393.
Xyleborus piceus, on sugar cane in West Indies, 342.

Xyleborus pubescens, on sugar cane, 402.
    sparsus = Pityophthorus sparsus, 132.
Xylophasia, revision of, notice, 155.
Xylotrechus nauticus, on Quercus agrifolia, 262.

Y.

Yama-mai, 115.
Yellow-jackets, injury caused by sting of, 159.
Yucca moth. See Pronuba and Prodoxus.

Z.

Zabriskie, J. L., note on water bug found by, 321.
Zanclognatha minimalis = Hermia protumnosalis, 228.
    on dead leaves, 111.
Zebra caterpillar, in Ohio, ref., 2.
Zeuzera pyrina, injuring maple, 77-8.
    in New York city, 61.
    ravages of, in Brooklyn, art., 317.
    See also leopard moth.
Zoölogy, economic, compendium of, rev., 149.

PLANT INDEX.

A.

Abies menziesii, Hylesinus sericeus on, 228.
Abutilon avicennæ, scale found on, 345.
Acacia, Sinoxylon declive on, 260.
Akee, Planchonia fimbriata on, 334.
  Pulvinaria sp. on, 334.
Alder, food-plant of Zeuzera pyrina, 77.
Alfalfa, grasshoppers injuring, 50, 51, 52, 144.
Almond, locusts injuring, 144.
Amarantus, Agrotis annexa on, 31.
Ampelopsis, Alypia 8-maculata on, 61.
Apple, Ægeria pyri on, 34.
  Aphides on, 44.
  Cacœcia argyrospila on, 395.
  coleopterous enemies of, 43.
  Diabrotica 12-punctata on, 107.
  Epicærus imbricatus on, 77.
  ermine moth on, 221.
  food-plant of Zeuzera pyrina, 77.
  good results from spraying, 167, 205, 288, 409.
  Hydnocera scabra on, 260.
  insects of, in Victoria, 2.
  Ipochus fasciatus on, 262.
  Leptocoris trivittata on, 273.
  Œdemasia concinna on, 207.
  Paris green experiments on, 334.
  Psylla spp. on, 128.
  spraying trees for orchard caterpillars, 37.
  Syneta albida on, 396.
  Utah Clisiocampa on, 75.
  varieties affected by, 133.
  woolly root-louse of, 210.
Apricot, injured by twig-borers, 207.
  insects affecting, in Victoria, 2.
Arbutus sp. ?, Eucheira socialis on, 84.
Ash, insects on, in South Dakota, 68.
  Neoclytus capræa on, 131.
Asparagus, Crioceris asparagi on, 401.
  Crioceris 12-punctata on, 395.
Aspen, Alaus oculatus on, 65.
  Pœcilonota cyanipes on, 66.
Atriplex nummularia, attacked by Pulvinaria maskelli, 294.
Audibertia polystachya, Psoa maculata on, 261.
Aurocaria, Dactyolopius on, 290.
Avena, Toxoptera graminum on, 245.
Aweto, or insect-fungus, 217.

B.

Banana, Icerya montserratensis on, 407.
Barley, Hessian fly in, 235.
Basswood, tent-caterpillars on, 139.

Bean, Diabrotica 12-punctata on, 107.
  Epilachna (corrupta) on, 26, 355.
  Epitrix suberinita on, 135.
  weevil of, 297, 353.
Beet, Epicauta lemniscata on, 395.
  sugar, Monoxia guttulata on, 237.
Bernardia, also a genus of scale-insects, 333.
Birch, food-plant of Zeuzera pyrina, 77.
Blackberry, borers and gall-makers of, 27–30.
  insects injurious to, 332.
  strawberry weevil on, 76.
Botrytis, disease of Schistocerca peregrina, 408.
  tenella, white grub parasite, 152.
Bouteloua grasses, injured by Dissosteira longipennis, 19.
Box-elder, Cacœcia semiferana on, 355.
  Pulvinaria innumerabilis on, 75.
Buchloë dactyloides, injured by long-winged locust, 19.
Buckwheat, wild, food-plant of Calothysanis amaturaria, 382.
Buffalo grass, Dissosteira longipennis on, 72.
  injured by long-winged locust, 19.

C.

Cabbage, Diabrotica 12-punctata on, 107.
  eaten by Hippodamia convergens, 33.
  Epicauta lemniscata on, 77.
  food of Nysius angustatus, 141.
  insects affecting, in Ohio, 2.
Caprifig, fertilization of, 128.
  insects, remarks on, 373.
Carnations, cut-worm damaging, 405.
Carya alba, stomata caused by Phylloxera on, 327.
Catalpa, injured by Sphinx catalpæ, 139–140.
Cauliflower, Diabrotica 12-punctata on, 107.
Cayenne pepper, moth damaging, 332.
Cedar, red, Capsidæ on, 161.
  white, Bostrychus jesuita on, 294.
Celery, plant-louse on, 213.
  wire-worm damaging, 401.
Charlock, Plutella cruciferarum on, 236.
Chenoyucca, subgenus of Yucca, 359.
Cherry, crop increased by bees, 256.
  Cacœcia argyrospila on, 355.
  insects affecting, in Victoria, 2.
  Syneta albida on, 396.
Chestnut, Balaninus bred from, 93, 130.
  Zeuzera pyrina on, 77.
China berries, against grain insects, 293.
Chinquapin, Balaninus bred from, 93, 130.

Chrysanthemum, Nematodes on, 31.
  leaf-miner of, 353.
Chrysophyllum, Icerya montserratensis on, 407.
Clematis virginiana, Alcathoë caudata on, 219.
  vitalba, food-plant of Alcathoë caudata, 220.
Clistoyucca, subgenus of Yucca, 359.
Clover, Darwin's experiments with, 335.
  destruction of insects affecting, 13.
  imported insects of, in Ohio, 2.
  seed caterpillar of, 56–8.
  seed produced by bumble-bees, 334.
  Sitones flavescens on, 87.
Clusia alba, Icerya montserratensis on, 407.
Cockle-burr, Rhodobænus 13-punctatus on, 159.
Coconnut, Rhynchophorus on, 136.
  scale-insects on, 333, 381.
Cohoon, Rhynchophorus on, 136.
Coleus, Nematode on, 31.
Commelyna virginica, Lema sayi, on. 229.
Cordyceps chinensis, 217.
  ravenelii, 217, 390, 391.
Corn, Aphis maidis on. 264.
  Chilo saccharalis on, 24.
  bill-bug on, in New Jersey, 44, 358.
  boll-worm on, 133.
  coleopterous larvæ injuring, 26.
  Crambus caliginosellus on, 78.
  Diabrotica longicornis on, 133.
  Diabrotica 12-punctata on, 104.
  early account of Aphis infesting, 263.
  food-plant of Gortyna nitela, 140.
  food-plant of Toxoptera graminum, 245.
  injured by boll-worm in New Mex., 26.
  insects affecting in Nebraska, ref., 358.
  Lachnosterna larvæ injuring, 132.
  larva in, 270.
  root Aphis or plant-louse of, 142, 285.
  tumble-bugs not injurious to, 400.
Cotton, Agrotis annexa on, 31.
  Citheronia regalis injuring, 160.
  cut-worm on, 31.
  injury to, erroneously attributed to boll-worm, 17.
Cottonwood, leaf-miner on, 27.
  plant-lice on, 90.
Coulterella, Carphoxera ptelearia on, 108.
Cranberry, Dolerus on, 173.
  insects of, in Mass., 354.
Cratægus, tent-caterpillar on, 75.
Cupweed, new food-plant of Rhodobænus 13-punctatus, 159.
Currant, black, Phytoptus ribis on, 38.
  Cacœcia argyrospila on, 355.
  Clisiocampa sp. on, 75.
  Leptoglossus phyllopus on, 79.
  wild black, Alcathoë caudata on, 219.
Cyclamen, Otiorhynchus sulcatus on. 222.

D.

Dendrophthora, scale on, 333.
Dictyospermum, Aspidiotus articulatus on, 381.
Diospyros kaki, killed by borers, 382.
  virginiana, Phemonoë 5-caudata found on, 332.

E.

Elm, Edema albifrons injuring, 139.
  Haltica carinata on, 401.
  leaf-beetle of, 61, 237.
  tent-caterpillars on, 139.
  Zeuzera pyrina on, 61, 77, 318.
Empusa americana, on flies, 153.
  muscæ, of house fly, 153.
Equisetum palustre, Dolerus palustris on, 169.
Equisetum l, Dolerus fulviventris on. 169.
Eucalyptus, Podacanthus wilkinsoni on, 90.
Euphorbia, Pseudococcus ruber on, 333.
  sp., Deilephila euphorbiæ on, 382.

F.

Fasarium, disease of Schistocerca peregrina, 408.
Fern, maiden hair, Otiorhynchus sulcatus on, 222.
Festuca, food-plant of Dolerus, 169.
  pratensis, Dolerus gonagra on, 169.
Ficus, food-plant of Aspidiotus articulatus, 381.
  roxburghii, development of seed dependent on Blastophaga, 374.
Fig, Amphicerus punctipennis on, 261.
  caprification of, 373.
  Galerucella semipullata on, 89.
  locusts injuring, 144.
  Smyrna, introduction of Blastophaga for, 94.
  dependent on Blastophaga psenes, 374.
  trees injured by Longicorn, 204.
  See also Caprifig.
Figs, grown without caprification, 394.
Fungus, Tritoma californica on, 260.
  disease of locust, 151, 408.
  of European cockchafer, 281.
  smut, caused by Aleyrodes, 274.
Fusicladium, London purple against, 45.

G.

Gall-berry, wild food of Ceroplastes floridensis, 398.
Gama grass, Diatræa saccharalis on, 103.
Gooseberry, Cape, boll-worm on, 296.
  Cacœcia argyrospila on, 355.
  Clisiocampa sp. on, 75.
  Span worm and saw-fly on, 67.
Grain infested with Angoumois moths, treatment of, 207.
  insects injuring in Miss., 293.
  Silvanus surinamensis on, 237.
Gramma grass, Dissosteira longipennis on. 19, 72.
Grape, Adoxus vitis on, 157.
  American, in France, 224.
  Coleoptera on, 261.
  Flea-beetle of, 135.
  leaf-hopper of, in New Mexico, 27.
  Leptocoris trivittata on, 273.
  locusts injuring, 144.
  Macrodactylus sp on, in New Mexico, 26.
  Otiorhynchus sulcatus on, 223.
  Phylloxera on, 212.
Grasses, Oebalus pugnax on, 158.
Grass, blue, Thrips on, 264.
  Dactylopius herbicola on, 90.

Grass, insects affecting. notes on. 197,
   orchard, Toxoptera graminum on, 245.
   saw-flies of. 168–179.
   sesame, Diatræa saccharalis on, 103.
Grease-wood, Nysius angustatus on. 140.

H.

Hart's tongue, Otiorhynchus sulcatus on, 222.
Hedge plant. California, leaf-hopper on, 142.
Helianthus. Rhodobænus 13-punctatus on, 159.
Hemlock, damaged by Nematus erichsonii, 219.
Hemp, as a protection against weevils, 223.
Hesperoyucca. subgenus of Yucca, 359.
Hickory, Balaninus caryæ bred from, 93.
   dead leaves eaten by Epizeuxis æmula. 111.
   Dorcaschema nigrum on. 130.
   Magdalis olyra on, 130.
   Micracis on, 131.
   Stenosphenus notatus on. 130.
   Tylonotus bimaculatus on, 131.
Hop, Aphis of, in California, 167.
Hordeum, food-plant of Toxoptera graminum, 245.
Hymenoplea salsola, new food-plant of Icerya purchasi, 160.

I.

Ilex glabra, native food of Ceroplastes floridensis, 398.
Isaria densa, fungus on cockchafer. 281.

J.

Juglans californica. Coleoptera on. 260. 261.
Juncus canadensis ?, Dolerus on. 173.
   food-plant of Dolerus. 169.

K.

Kale, harlequin bugs stray from. to cabbage, 34.

L.

Lachnidium acridiorum. disease of locust, 406.
Larch, European. Coleophora laricella on, 405.
   Japanese, Coleophora laricella on. 405.
   saw-fly of, 219.
Laurel. California, ladybirds on, 134.
Lecanium hesperidum, from Sandwich Ids., 218.
Lemon, Orcus chalybeus beneficial to. 164.
Lettuce, Myriopods injuring. 400.
Lignum vitæ. Aspidiotus articulatus on, 381.
Linden, Capsidæ on. 161.
   food-plant of Zeuzera pyrina, 77.
Locust, Apion nigrum on. 94. 131.
Lucerne. locusts injuring. 144.
Lupine. Carphoxera on. 271.
Lygodesmia juncea, Cynipid gall on, 203.

M.

Madrono, Eucheira socialis on. 84.
Maize, borers in, 397.
Mangel-wurzels, Otiorhynchus sulcatus damaging. 223.
Mango. Vinconia stellifera on. 334.

Maple, Acanthoderes decipiens reared from. 65.
   Edema albifrons on. 139.
   Leptura proxima reared from, 65.
   Zeuzera pyrina on, 77. 317.
Melon. Aphides on, 44.
   injury to, erroneously attributed to melon plant-louse. 17, 358.
Mint, Sphinx eremitus on. 206.
Mountain ash, food-plant of Zeuzera pyrina. 77.
Mustard. harlequin bugs caught on. 33.
   wild, Plutella cruciferarum on, 236.

N.

Negundo aceroides, Pulvinaria innumerabilis on, 75.
Nyssa, Antispila nyssæfoliella on. 138.

O.

Oak, Alaus oculatus on. 65.
   Allorhina nitida on. 75.
   Balaninus bred from. 93, 136.
   Edema albifrons injuring, 139.
   Lyctus striatus on, 65.
   Palthis and Zancloguathas on dead leaves. 111.
   Phymatodes spp. on. 65.
   tent-caterpillars on. 139.
Oats, Cicadula 4-lineata on, 197.
   Diabrotica 12-punctata on, 107.
Œnothera speciosa, insects captured by, 291.
Oleander, Aspidiotus articulatus, on. 381.
Olive. food-plant of Aspidiotus articulatus. 381.
Onions, root maggots in, 44.
Orange, Blastobasis sp. beneficial to, 290.
   Ceroplastes floridensis on. 398.
   Chionaspis biclavis on. 400.
   Coleoptera found on. 260, 261.
   difficulty of disinfecting imported trees, 218.
   food-plant of Aspidiotus articulatus, 381.
   Orchids, fertilization of. 359.
   Orcus chalybeus beneficial to. 164.
   purple scale of, 143.
   scale-insects on, 274.
   tree injured by ants, 203.
Orgyia leucostigma, new enemy of, 222.
Otiorhynchus sulcatus, hot-house pest. 222.

P.

Palm, cocoa, Icerya montserratensis on, 407.
   Rhynchophorus palmarum on, 136.
Palmetto, cabbage, Rhynchophorus zimmermanni on, 136.
Palms, food-plants of Aspidiotus articulatus, 381.
Panicum. Œbalus pugnax on. 158.
Pea, weevil of, 297.
Peach, Anametis grisea on, 401.
   arsenical poisons for. 290.
   Aspidiotus on, 339.
   borer of, treatment, 43.
   injured by Gortyna nitela, 140.
   Japanese moth of. 341.
   Leptocoris trivittata on, 273.
   plum Curculio on. 34.
   Syneta albida on, 396.
   tree borers of, do ground-beetles destroy? 204.

Peanuts, bug damaging, in China, 340.
Pear, Diplosis pyrivora on, 44.
    Dolerus arvensis on, 172.
    food-plant of Zeuzera pyrina, 77.
    insects of, in Victoria, 2.
    LeConte, Florida wax scale on, 397.
    locusts injuring, 144.
    midge of, 358.
    Psylla pyricola on, 225.
    Saperda candida on, 43.
    Systena frontalis on, 135.
    three Psyllas of, 127.
Peas, weevil-infested, temperature of, 160.
Pecan, Phycitid moth on, 78.
Pelargonium, Diaspis pelargonii on, 333.
Pennyroyal, Sphinx eremitus on, 206.
Pepper tree, Bostrychus jesuita on, 294.
    Lecanium hesperidum on, 294.
Persimmon, Diospyros virginiana on, 332.
Physianthus, against codling moth, 331.
Pine, Chermes on, 89.
    Oiketicus huebneri on, 89.
Plum, arsenical poisons for, 293.
    curculio of, in New Jersey, 45.
    early account of insects attacking, 263.
    Leptocoris trivittata on, 273.
    Phorodon humuli on, 406.
    saw-fly of, in England, 38.
    spraying, against orchard caterpillars, 36, 37.
    susceptibility to arsenites, 40.
    trees sprayed, 238.
Plumieria rubra, Lecanium sp. on, 333.
Polyrhizium, disease of Schistocerca peregrina, 408.
Pomegranate, locusts injuring, 144.
Poplar, Gonioctena pallida on, 67.
    Russian, preferred by cottonwood leaf-beetle, 67.
Populus tremuloides, Elasmus bred from gall on, 253.
Potato, broken-tail snail destroying, 334.
    Epicauta lemniscata on, 395.
    injury to, erroneously attributed to Dissosteira, 17.
    food-plant of Gortyna nitela, 140.
    food-plant of Nysius angustatus, 141.
    Thrips sp. on, 79.
    tuber-moth of, 239, 396.
Populus fremontii, leaf-miner on, 27.
    tremuloides, Enchodes sericea on, 65, 66.
    Gonioctena pallida on, 94.
Primrose, insectivorous, remarks on, 291.
Prunus. hop-louse on, 213.
Ptelea trifoliata, Hyponomeuta sp. on, 66.
Pyrus communis, three Psyllas of, 127.

Q.

Quercus agrifolia, Vrilleta expansa on, 260.
    Xylotrechus nauticus on, 262.
    grisea, Balaninus nasicus bred from, 93.
Quince, Saperda candida on, 43.

R.

Radish, Murgantia munda on, 83.
    remedy for flea-beetles on, 355.
Ragweed, food-plant of Gortyna nitela, 140.
Raspberry, Byturus tomentosus on, in Europe, 38.
    Cacoecia argyrospila on, 355.
    food-plant of Otiorhynchus sulcatus, 223.
Rhagodia hastata, Pulvinaria maskelli on, 294.
Rhus toxicodendron, Carphoxera ptelearia on, 109.
Rose, cultivated, injured by Rhynchites, 137.
    Cacoecia argyrospila on, 355.
    Diabrotica 12-punctata on, 107.
    Diaspis rosae on, 213.
    food-plant of Aspidiotus articulatus, 381
    Icerya purchasi on, 288.
    Oniscus injuring, 401.
Rudbeckia, Diabrotica 12-punctata breeding in, 105.
Rye, early account of insects on, 263.
    wheat midge on, 91.

S.

Salix discolor, Agrilus torpidus on, 66.
    longifolia, Phyllodecta vulgatissima on, 131.
Saltbush, scale-insect on, in Australia, 294, 408.
Sarcoyucca, subgenus of Yucca, 359.
Saxifrage, Otiorhynchus sulcatus on, 222.
Scolopendrium vulgare, Otiorhynchus sulcatus on, 222.
Sesame grass, see Grass.
Setaria, Œbalus pugnax on, 158.
Shepherd's purse, Plutella cruciferarum on, 236.
Silphium perfoliatum, food-plant of Rhodobaenus 13-punctatus, 159.
Smartweed, Acronycta oblinita on, 132.
Soap tree, food-plant of Zeuzera pyrina, 77.
Solanum carolinense, Diabrotica 12-punctata on, 107.
    xanti, Cassida texana on, 262.
Sorghum, Diatraea saccharalis injuring, 98, 103.
    food-plant of Toxoptera graminum, 245.
    grasshoppers injuring, 51.
    vulgare, Chilo sp. on, 397.
Sour gum, Antispila nyssaefoliella on, 138.
Sphaeria robertsii, parasitic on caterpillar, 217.
Sporotrichum, expts. with, on Chinch bug, 71.
Spruce, Helia aemula on, 111.
Squash, Melittia cucurbitae on, 30, 138.
    treatment of borers of, 271.
Stillingia, Carphoxera on, 271.
Stink-bush, correspondence on, 400.
Strawberry, Aleyrodes on, 345.
    food of Nysius angustatus, 141.
    food-plant of Otiorhynchus sulcatus, 223.
    Gryllus sp. destructive to, 276.
    Phoxopteris comptana on, 209.
Sugar-cane, Diatraea saccharalis on, 95.
    borers of, 101-103.
    in India, 397.
    insects of, in N. S. W. art., 385-389
    Xyleborus pubescens on, 402.

Sunflower, Diabrotica longicornis on, 133.
Swede crops, damage to, in Eastern Britain, 81.
Sweet potato. saw-fly on, 74.
Sycamore, Cœlocnemis californicus on, 262.
  Lyctus striatus on, 261.
  Phlœodes diabolicus on, 262.

T.

Tares = Vicia sativa.
Tea bushes, insecticide proposed for, 408.
  tree, Gracilaria theivora, 296.
Timothy, Dolerus on, 173.
Tobacco insects, in Florida, 288.
  monograph of insects on, 165.
  said to be attacked by Balaninus, 93.
Tomato, Epicauta lemniscata on, 395.
  Epitrix subcrinita on, 135.
  food-plant of Gortyna nitela, 140.
Torrubia ravenelii, mistaken for corn sprouts, 263.
  on white grub, 217.
Trefoil, Hyponomeuta sp. on, 66.
Trifolium Darwin's expts, in fertilization of, 335.
Tripsacum dactyloides, Diatræa saccharalis on, 103.
Triticum, food-plant of Toxoptera graminum, 245.
Turnip, damage to, in EastBritain, 81.
  Nysius angustatus on, 141.

U.

Umbellularia californica, ladybirds on, 134.
  Sinoxylon declive on, 260.

V.

Vicia sativa. Cecidomyiid on, 39.
Vine, see Grape.
Violets, Oniscus injuring, 401.
Vitis vinifera, Phylloxera on, 212.

W.

Walnut, food-plant of Zeuzera pyrina, 77.
  injured by Datana angusii, 133.

Wheat, Diabrotica 12-punctata on, 107.
  early accounts of insects on, 263.
  insects affecting, 357.
  saw-flies of, 168-179.
  Toxoptera graminum on, 245.
Willow, Capsidae on. 161.
  Coleoptera on, 66.
  damaged by Cimbex americana, 132.
  Dolerus on, 169, 172.
  parasites possibly bred from leaf-miner on, 253.
  Phlœodes diabolicus on, 262.
  plant-louse on, 213.
  Sciapteron tricincta on, 66.

X.

Xanthium strumarium, Rhodobænus 13-punctatus on, 159.

Y.

Yucca aloifolia, fruit edible, 359.
  angustifolia, pollinized by Pronuba yuccasella, 369.
  baccata, edible, 359.
    Pronuba on, 371.
  brevifolia, arboreal form, 360.
    pollinized by Pronuba synthetica, 370.
  filamentosa, Pronuba yuccasella on, 369.
    structure of, 359.
  filifera, arboreal, 360.
    Pronuba on, 371.
    nectar apparatus of, 366.
  Prodoxus larvæ in all species, 372.
  regal tree = Y. filifera.
    special Pronubas on, 371.
  treculiana, special Pronuba on, 371.
  whipplei, pollinized by Pronuba maculata, 367, 370.
Yuccas, fertilization of, 74, 359.

Z.

Zea. food-plant of Toxoptera graminum, 245.
  mays, food-plant of Diatræa saccharalis, 103.

LIST OF THE PERSONS ENGAGED IN GOVERNMENT ENTOMOLOGICAL WORK.

The following list embraces those now engaged in Government entomological work. The force of the Division of Entomology is more or less inconstant, as it consists of both permanent and temporary employés. Illustrations to this Bulletin, where not otherwise stated, are drawn by Miss Lillie Sullivan, under supervision.

DIVISION OF ENTOMOLOGY, U. S. DEPARTMENT OF AGRICULTURE.

Entomologist: C. V. Riley.
Office staff: L. O. Howard, first assistant; E. A. Schwarz, Th. Pergande, C. L. Marlatt, F. H. Chittenden, W. H. Ashmead, A. B. Cordley, F. W. Mally, Nathan Banks, assistants.
Field agents: Samuel Henshaw, Boston, Mass.; F. M. Webster, Wooster, Ohio; Herbert Osborn, Ames, Iowa; Mary E. Murtfeldt, Kirkwood, Mo.; Lawrence Bruner, Lincoln, Nebr.; D. W. Coquillett, Los Angeles, Cal., Albert Koebele, Alameda, Cal.; J. H. Larrabee, Larrabee's Point, Vt.; Frank Benton, Detroit, Mich.

DEPARTMENT OF INSECTS, U. S. NATIONAL MUSEUM.

Honorary Curator: C. V. Riley.
Aid: Martin L. Linell.

DATES OF ISSUANCE OF THE NUMBERS OF INSECT LIFE, VOLUME IV.

Nos. 1 and 2, issued October 28, 1891.
Nos. 3 and 4, issued December 2, 1891.
Nos. 5 and 6, issued January 15, 1892.
Nos. 7 and 8, issued April 11, 1892.
Nos. 9 and 10, issued June 27, 1892.
Nos. 11 and 12, issued August, 1892.

www.ingramcontent.com/pod-product-compliance
Lightning Source LLC
Chambersburg PA
CBHW032008300426
44117CB00008B/942